Contents

4. MapReduce, Hive and Pig 144

List of Acronyms

3V	Volume, Velocity and/or Variety
4V	Volume, Velocity, Variety and Veracity
ACID	Atomicity, Consistency, Isolation and Durability
ACPAMS	Automotive Components and Predictive Automotive Maintenance Service
ACVM	Automatic Chocolate Vending Machine
ADT	Abstract Data Type
AI	Artificial Intelligence
AM	Application Master
AMP	Algorithms, Machines and Peoples Laboratory at University of Berkeley
ANN	Artificial Neural Network
ANOVA	Analysis of Variance
API	Application Programming Interface
BASE	Basically Available Soft State Eventual Consistency
BFS	Breadth-First Search
BI	Business Intelligence
BIRT	Business Intelligence and Reporting Tools
BLOB	Binary Large Object
BN	Bayesian Network
BNG	Bayesian Network Graph
BP	Business Process
BSON	Binary encoded JSON objects
CAC	Customer Acquisition Cost
CAP	Consistence Availability and Partitioning
CGPA	Cumulative Grade-Point Average
CF	Collaborative Filtering
CBF	Content Based Filtering
CLI	Command Line interface
CLTV	Customer Lifetime Value

CQL	Cassandra Query Language
CRM	Customer Relationship Management
CSV	Comma-Separated Values
CURD	Create, Update, Read and Delete
CV	Customer Value
CVA	Customer Value Analytics
DALS	Distributed regularized Alternating Least Squares
DAS	Direct Attached Storage
DFG	Data Flow Graph
DAG	Directed Acylic Graph
DB	Database
DBA	Database Administrator
DBMS	Database Management System
DDL	Data Definition Language
DFS	Distributed File System
DL	Deep Learning
DF	Data Flow
DFG	Data Flow Graph
DML	Data Manipulation Language
DRM	Distributed Row Matrix
DSMS	Data Stream Management System
DSPCA	Distributed Stochastic Principal Component Analysis
EDP	Electronic Data Processing
ELT	Extract, Load and Transform
ERP	Enterprise Resource Planning
ETL	Extract, Transform and Load
FIM	Frequent Item-set Mining
FL	Flavour (for example of chocolate, candy, ice-cream)
FP	Frequent Pattern
GP	Grade Point
GVUDF	Grouped Vectorized User Defined Function
IDF	Inverse Document Frequency
IIS	IBM InfoSphere Information Server
IR	Information Retrieval
IS	Information Server or Service or System
JDBC	Java Database Connectivity
JN	Journal Node
JSON	JavaScript Object Notation
HITS	Hypertext-Induced Topic Selection
HDFS	Hadoop Distributed File System
HPQS	High Performance Query Structure
IDE	Integrated Development Environment
IO	Input and Output

IOs	Input and Output operations
IPC	Inter Processing nodes Communication, also Inter Process Communication
JDBC	Java Database Connectivity
JTAl	Junction Tree Algorithm
JTG	Junction Trees Graph
JVM	Java Virtual Machine
KBF	Knowledge-Based filtering
KNN	K-Nearest Neighbourhood (most similar items or objects)
LDA	Latent-Dirichlet-Allocation, also Linear Discriminate Analysis
LSI	Latent Semantic Indexing
MIS	Management Information Services or Systems
ML	Machine Learning
MLIB	Machine Learning Library
MN	Master Node
MPP	Massive Parallel Processing
NLP	Natural Language Processing
NM	Node Manager
NN	Neural Network
NNS	Nearest Neighbour Search
NoSQL	No SQL or Not Only SQL
ODBC	Object Database Connectivity
OLAP	On-line Analytical Processing
OLTP	On-line Transaction Processing
ODBC	Object Database Connectivity
ODS	Operational Data Store
ORC	Optimized Row Columnar
OS	Operating System
PCA	Principal Component Analysis
PDF	Probability Distribution Function
POS	Part of Speech
POT	Potential Tables
QL	Query Language
RC	Record Columnar
RDBMS	Relational Database Management System
RDF	Resource Description Framework
RDD	Resilient Distributed Dataset
RFID	Radio Frequency Identification
RTAP	Real Time Analytics Platform
S3	Simple Storage Service at Amazon cloud
sc	SparkContext
SGD	Stochastic Gradient Descent
SGP	Subject Grade-Point (awarded to a student)
SGPA	Semester Grade Point Average

SerDe	Serialization and Deserialization
SN	Shared Nothing
SOA	Service Oriented Architecture
SPARQL	Spark Query Language for RDF
SPCA	Stochastic Principal Component Analysis (SPCA, DSPCA)
SSD	Sum of Squared Distance
SSE	Sum of Squared Error
SSIS	Microsoft SQL Server Integration Services (SSIS)
SSVD	Stochastic Singular Value Decomposition
SVC	Support Vector Classifier
SVD	Singular Value Decomposition
SVM	Support Vector Machine
TF	Term Frequency (in a text document)
UDF	User Defined Function
URI	Universal Resource Identifier
URL	Universal Resource Locator at the web
VUDF	Vectorised User Defined Function
W3C	World Wide Consortium
WRMP	Weather Recording, Monitoring and Prediction
XML	eXtensible Markup Language

Chapter 1

Introduction to Big Data Analytics

LEARNING OBJECTIVES

After studying this chapter, you will be able to:

LO 1.1 Get conceptual understanding of data and web data; classification of data as structured, semi-, multi- and unstructured data; Big Data characteristics, types, classifications and handling techniques

LO 1.2 Get conceptual understanding of scalability, Massively Parallel Processing (MPP), distributed, cloud and grid computing

LO 1.3 Know the design layers in data-processing architecture for the data management and analytics

LO 1.4 Get introduced to data sources, data quality, data pre-processing, and the export of data store (such as tables, objects and files) to the cloud

LO 1.5 Get conceptual understanding of data storage and analysis; comparison between traditional systems such as Relational Database Management System (RDBMS), enterprise servers, data warehouse and approaches for Big Data storage and analytics

LO 1.6 Get knowledge of use cases and applications of Big Data in various fields.

1.1 INTRODUCTION

Two Grand Masters, Magnus Carlsen and Sergey Karjakin, played the final in World Chess Championship held on December 1, 2016. Magnus Carlsen won this final and the title of Grand Master. Sergey Karjakin, in order to win, would have to design a new strategy to defeat Carlsen and other players next year. A Grand Master typically studies the moves made in earlier matches played by Grand Masters, analyzes them and then designs his strategies. Evolving strategy to defeat an opponent could even make good use of the data of Gary Kasparov's matches from 1984. Study and analysis of a large number of matches helps in evolving a winning strategy. Similarly, analytics of Big Data could enable discovery of new facts, knowledge and strategy in a number of fields, such as manufacturing, business, finance, healthcare, medicine and education.

1.1.1 Need of Big Data

The rise in technology has led to the production and storage of voluminous amounts of data. Earlier megabytes (10^6 B) were used but nowadays petabytes (10^{15} B) are used for processing, analysis, discovering new facts and generating new knowledge. Conventional systems for storage, processing and analysis pose challenges in large growth in volume of data, variety of data, various forms and formats, increasing complexity, faster generation of data and need of quickly processing, analyzing and usage.

Figure 1.1 shows data usage and growth. As size and complexity increase, the proportion of unstructured data types also increase.

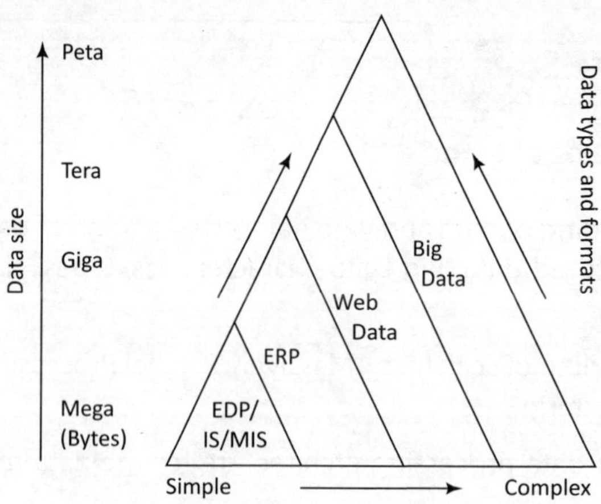

Figure 1.1 Evolution of Big Data and their characteristics

An example of a traditional tool for structured data storage and querying is RDBMS. Volume, velocity and variety (3Vs) of data need the usage of number of programs and tools for analyzing and processing at a very high speed. When integrated with the Internet of Things, sensors and machines data, the veracity of data is an additional V. (Section 1.2.3)

Big Data requires new tools for processing and analysis of a large volume of data. For example, unstructured, NoSQL (not only SQL) data or Hadoop compatible system data.

Following are selected key terms and their meanings, which are essential to understand the topics discussed in this chapter:

Application means application software or a collection of software components. For example, software for acquiring, storing, visualizing and analyzing data. An *application* performs a group of coordinated activities, functions and tasks.

Application Programming Interface (API) refers to a software component which enables a user to access an application, service or software that runs on a local or remote computing platform. An API initiates running of the application on receiving the message(s) from the user-end. An API sends the user-end messages to the other-end software. The other-end software sends responses or messages to the API and the user.

Data Model refers to a map or schema, which represents the inherent properties of the data. The map shows groupings of the data elements, such as records or tables, and their associations. A model does not depend on software using that data.

Data Repository refers to a collection of data. A data-seeking program relies upon the data repository for reporting. The examples of repositories are database, flat file and spreadsheet. [Repository in *English* means a group which can be relied upon to look for required things, such as special information or knowledge. For example, a repository of paintings by various artists.]

Data Store refers to a data repository of a set of objects. Data store is a general concept for data repositories, such as database, relational database, flat file, spreadsheet, mail server, web server and directory services. The objects in data store model are instances of the classes which the *database schemas* define. A data store may consist of multiple schemas or may consist of data in only one schema. Example of only one scheme for a data store is a relational database.

Distributed Data Store refers to a data store distributed over multiple nodes. Apache Cassandra is one example of a distributed data store. (Section 3.7)

Database (DB) refers to a grouping of tables for the collection of data. A table ensures a systematic way for accessing, updating and managing data. A database pertains to the applications, which access them. A *database* is a repository for querying the required information for analytics, processes, intelligence and knowledge discovery. The databases can be distributed across a network consisting of servers and data warehouses.

Table refers to a presentation which consists of row fields and column fields. The values at the fields can be number, date, hyperlink, image, object or text of a document.

Flat File means a file in which data cannot be picked from in between and must be read from the beginning to be interpreted. A file consisting of a single-table file is called a flat file. An example of a flat file is a csv (comma-separated value) file. A flat file is also a data repository.

Flat File Database refers to a database in which each record is in a separate row unrelated to each other.

CSV File refers to a file with comma-separated values. For example, CS101, "Theory of Computations", 7.8 when a student's grade is 7.8 in subject code CS101 and subject "Theory of Computations".

Name-Value Pair refers to constructs used in which a field consists of name and the corresponding value after that. For example, a name value pair is *date, ""Oct. 20, 2018"", chocolates_sold, 178*;

Key-Value Pair refers to a construct used in which a field is the key, which pairs with the corresponding value or values after the key. For example, consider a tabular record, ""Oct. 20, 2018""; ""chocolates_sold"", 178. The *date* is the primary key for finding the date of the record and chocolates_sold is the secondary key for finding the number of chocolates sold.

Hash Key-Value Pair refers to the construct in which a hash function computes a key for indexing and search, and distributing the entries (key/value pairs) across an array of slots (also called buckets). (Section 3.3.1)

Spreadsheet refers to the recording of data in fields within rows and columns. A field means a specific column of a row used for recording information. The values in fields associates a program, such as Microsoft Excel 2013. An example of a spreadsheet application is *accounting*. The application manages, analyzes and enables new values either directly or using formulae which contain the relationships of a field with cells and rows. Examples of functions are SUMIF and COUNTIF, delete duplicate entries, sort using multiple keys, filter single or multiple columns, create a filter using filtering criteria or rules for multi-fields, and create top-n lists for values or percentages.

Stream Analytics refers to a method of computing continuously, i.e. even while events take place data flows through the system.

Database Maintenance (DBM) refers to a set of tasks which improves a database. DBM uses functions for improving performance (such as by query planning and optimization), freeing-up storage space, updating internal statistics, checking data errors and hardware faults.

Database Administration (DBA) refers to the function of managing and maintaining Database Management System (DBMS) software regularly. A database administering personnel has many responsibilities, such as installation, configuration, database design, implementation upgrading, evaluation of database features, reliable backup and recovery methods for the database.

Database Management System (DBMS) refers to a software system, which contains a set of programs specially designed for *creation* and *management* of data stored in a database. Transactions can be performed with database/relational database.

Relational Database is a collection of data into multiple tables, which relate to each other through special fields, called keys (primary key, foreign key and unique key). Relational databases provide flexibility.

Relational Database Management System (RDBMS) refers to a software system used for creation of relational databases and management of data which are stored in a relational database. RDBMS functions perform the *transactions* on the relational database. Examples of RDBMS are MySQL, PostGreSQL (Oracle database created using PL/SQL) and Microsoft SQL server using T-SQL.

Transaction (trans + action) means two interrelated sets of operations, actions or instructions. A transaction is a set of actions which accesses, changes, updates, appends or deletes various data. A command 'connect' enables transfers between DBMS software and a database. The database in return connects the DBMS. An example of this is query transfer from a system to a database. The database in return transfers the answer of the query.

SQL stands for Structured Query Language. It is a language used for schema creation and schema modifications, data-access control, creating an SQL client and creating an SQL server for a database. It is a language for managing relational databases, and viewing, querying and changing (update, insert, append or delete) databases.

Database Connection refers a function DB_connect open () which an application calls to connect to enable the access to the DBMS. The application calls the function DB_connect close () to disable the access.

Database Connectivity (DBC) refers to a standard application programming interface (API), which provides connectivity for accessing the DBMSs. A DBC design is independent of the DB system and OS used. An application written using a DBC can therefore perform operations or actions at both the client and the DB server end. Little changes in code suffice for accessing the data. Two examples of DBCs are Open Database Connectivity (ODBC) and Java Database Connectivity (JDBC).

Database Connectivity Driver refers to a translation layer which resides between an application using the application and the DBMS. The application uses DBC functions through a DBC driver manager with which it is linked. A DBC driver manager manages the drivers associated with the DBMSs. The DBC driver sends the queries to a DBMS. Drivers exist for many data sources and all major DBMSs.

DB2 is IBM RDBMS. DB2 has many features. For example, triggers, stored procedures and dynamic bitmapped indexing for number of application types, such as traditional host-based applications, client/server-based applications and business intelligence applications.

Data Warehouse refers to sharable data, data stores and databases in an enterprise. It consists of integrated, subject oriented (such as finance, human resources and business) and non-volatile data stores, which update regularly.

Data Mart is a subset of data warehouse. Data mart corresponds to specific business entity on a single subject (or functional area), such as sales or finance data mart is also known as High Performance Query Structures (HPQS).

Process means a composition of group of structured activities, tasks or services that lead to a particular goal. For example, purchase process for airline tickets. A *process* specifies activities with relevance rules based on data in the process.

Process Matrix refers to a multi-element entity, each element of which relates a set of data or inputs to an activity (or subset of activities).

Business Process is an activity, series of activities or a collection of inter-related structured activities, tasks or processes. A business process serves a particular goal, specific result, service or product. The business process is a representation, process *matrix* or flowchart of a sequence of activities with interleaving decision points.

Business Intelligence is a process which enables a business service to extract new facts and knowledge that enable intelligent decisions. The new facts and knowledge follow from the previous results of business-data processing, aggregation and analysis.

Batch Processing is processing of transactions in batches with no interactions. When one set of transactions finish, the results are stored and the next batch starts processing. Credit card transactions is a good example of the same. The results aggregate at the end of the month for all usages of the card. Batch processing involves the collection of inputs for a specified period and then running them in a scheduled manner.

Batch Transaction Processing refers to the execution of a series of transactions without user interactions. Transaction jobs are set up so they can be run to completion. Scripts, command-line arguments, control files or job-control language *predefine* the input parameters for the transactions.

Streaming Transaction Processing refers to processing for log streams, event streams, twitter streams and queries. The processing of streaming data needs a specialized software framework. Storm from Twitter, S4 from Yahoo, SPARK streaming, HStreaming and Flume are examples of frameworks for real-time streaming computations.

In-memory means operations using CPU memory, such as RAM or caches. Data in-memory is from a disk or external data source. The operations are fast on in-memory accesses of data, table or data sets, columns or rows compared to disk-accesses.

Interactive Transaction Processing means processing the transactions which involve continual exchange of information between the computer and user; for example, user interactions during e-shopping or e-banking. The processing here is just the opposite of batch processing. Decision on historical data is fast. Interactive query processing has low latency. Low latencies are obtained by the various approaches: massively parallel processing (MPP), in-memory databases and columnar databases.

Real-Time Processing refers to processing for obtaining results for making decisions in real time, processing as and when the data acquires or generates in live data (streaming) with low latency.

Real-Time Transaction Processing means that transactions process at the same time as the data arrives from the data sources. An example of such processing is transaction processing at an ATM machine.

Extract, Transform and Load (ETL) refers to the process, which enables data retrieval, integration, transformation and storage (load). *Extract* means obtaining data from homogeneous or heterogeneous data sources. *Transform* means transforming or optimizing data for the application, and storing the data in an appropriate structure or format. *Load* means the structured data is loaded in the final target database, i.e. data store or data warehouse.

Machine is a computing node or platform for processing, computing and storing. Here, sets of data, programs, applications, DBs or DBMSs reside. When other remote machines access the resources from the machine, it is identified by a name within a network.

Server is a processing, computing and storing node. A server generates responses, sends replies and messages, and renders the data sought. *Server* refers to sets of data, programs, applications, data-stores, DBs or DBMSs which the clients access.

Service means a mechanism which enables the provisioning of access to one or more capabilities. An interface provides the access capabilities. The access to a capability is consistent with various constraints and policies. A *service description* specifies these constraints and policies. Examples of services are web service, cloud service and BigQuery service.

Service-Oriented Architecture (SOA) is a software architecture model which consists of services, messages, operations and processes. SOA components distribute over a network or the Internet in a high-level business entity. New business applications and an application-integration architecture can be developed using an SOA in an enterprise.

Descriptive Analytics refers to deriving additional value from visualizations and reports.

Predictive Analytics refers to advanced analytics which enables extraction of new facts and knowledge to predict or forecast.

Prescriptive Analytics refers to derivation of additional value and undertaking better decisions for new option(s); for example, maximizing profit.

Cognitive Analytics refer to analysis of sentiments, emotions, gestures, facial expressions, and actions similar to ones the humans do. The analytics follow the process of learning, understanding and representing. [Cognitive in English means relating to the process of learning, understanding and representing knowledge. (Collins Dictionary)]

This chapter introduces the readers to the concepts of Big Data, scaling-up and scaling-out of data processing and scalability for storage and analytics. It introduces the concepts of data processing architecture, data sources, data quality and the new technological developments in data management for analysis. These are supported by examples and cases on Big Data analytics. This chapter aims to build a foundation before the in-depth study of Big Data and analytics tools facilitated by the subsequent chapters of the book.

Section 1.2 introduces Big Data and its characteristics, types and classification methods. Section 1.3 describes scalability, scaling up, scaling out of processing and analytics, massively parallel processors, and cloud, grid and distributed computing. Section 1.4 introduces data architecture design and data management. Section 1.5 describes data sources, data quality, data pre-processing and export of data stores to the cloud. Section 1.6 describes traditional systems, such as SQL, Relational Database Management System (RDBMS), enterprise servers and data warehouse for data storage and analysis, as well as the approaches for Big Data storage, processing and analytics. Section 1.7 describes Big Data analytics case studies and applications.

1.2 BIG DATA

LO 1.1

Conceptual understanding of data, web data, Big Data, characteristics, types, classifications and handling techniques

Following subsections describe the definitions of data, web data, Big Data, Big Data characteristics, types, classifications and handling techniques:

Definitions of Data

Data has several definitions. Usages can be singular or plural. "Data is information, usually in the form of facts or statistics that one can analyze or use for further calculations."

[Collins English Dictionary] "Data is information that can be stored and used by a computer program.". [Computing] "Data is information presented in numbers, letters, or other form". [Electrical Engineering, Circuits, Computing and Control] "Data is information from series of observations, measurements or facts". [Science] "Data is information from series of behavioural observations, measurements or facts". [Social Sciences]

Definition of Web Data

Web is large scale integration and presence of data on web servers. Web is a part of the Internet that stores web data in the form of documents and other web resources. URLs enable the access to web data resources.

Web data is the data present on web servers (or enterprise servers) in the form of text, images, videos, audios and multimedia files for web users. A user (client software) interacts with this data. A client can access (pull) data of responses from a server. The data can also publish (push) or post (after registering subscription) from a server. Internet applications including web sites, web services, web portals, online business applications, emails, chats, tweets and social networks provide and consume the web data.

Some examples of web data are Wikipedia, Google Maps, McGraw-Hill Connect, Oxford Bookstore and YouTube.

1. Wikipedia is a web-based, free-content encyclopaedia project supported by the Wikimedia Foundation.
2. Google Maps is a provider of real-time navigation, traffic, public transport and nearby places by Google Inc.
3. McGraw-Hill Connect is a targeted digital teaching and learning environment that saves students' and instructors' time by improving student performance for a variety of critical outcomes.
4. Oxford Bookstore is an online book store where people can find any book that they wish to buy from millions of titles. They can order their books online at www.oxfordbookstore.com
5. YouTube allows billions of people to discover, watch and share originally-created videos by Google Inc.

1.2.1 Classification of Data—Structured, Semi-structured and Unstructured

Data can be classified as structured, semi-structured, multi-structured and unstructured.

Structured data conform and associate with data schemas and data models. Structured data are found in tables (rows and columns). Nearly 15–20% data are in structured or semi-structured form. Unstructured data do not conform and associate with any data models.

Applications produce continuously increasing volumes of both *unstructured* and *structured* data. Data sources generate data in three forms, viz. structured, semi-structured and unstructured. (Refer online contents associated with the Practice Exercise 1.1 for four forms, viz. structured, semi-structured, multi-structured and unstructured sources.)

Using Structured Data

Structured data enables the following:

- *data insert, delete, update and append*
- *Indexing* to enable faster data retrieval

- *Scalability* which enables increasing or decreasing capacities and data processing operations such as, storing, processing and analytics
- *Transactions processing* which follows ACID rules (Atomicity, Consistency, Isolation and Durability)
- *encryption and decryption* for data security.

Using Semi-Structured Data

Examples of semi-*structured data* are XML and JSON documents. Semi-structured data contain tags or other markers, which separate semantic elements and enforce hierarchies of records and fields within the data. Semi-structured form of data does not conform and associate with formal data model structures. Data do not associate data models, such as the relational database and table models.

Using Multi-Structured Data

Multi-structured data refers to data consisting of multiple formats of data, viz. structured, semi-structured and/or unstructured data. Multi-structured data sets can have many formats. They are found in non-transactional systems. For example, streaming data on customer interactions, data of multiple sensors, data at web or enterprise server or the data- warehouse data in multiple formats.

Large-scale interconnected systems are thus required to aggregate the data and use the widely distributed resources efficiently.

Multi- or semi-structured data has some semantic meanings and data is in both structured and unstructured formats. But as structured data, semi-structured data nowadays represent a few parts of data (5-10%). Semi-structured data type has a greater presence compared to structured data.

Following is an example of multi-structured data.

EXAMPLE 1.1

Give examples of multi-structured data.

SOLUTION

Structured component of data: Each chess moves is recorded in a table in each match that players refer in future. The records consist of serial numbers (row numbers, which mean move numbers) in the first column and the moves of White and Black in two subsequent vertical columns. Volume of data, i.e. data used for analyzing erroneous or best moves in the matches, keeps growing with more and more tables, and may eventually become 'voluminous data'.

Unstructured component of data: Social media generates data after each international match. The media publishes the analysis of classical matches played between Grand Masters. The data for analyzing chess moves of these matches are thus in a variety of formats.

Multi-structured data: The voluminous data of these matches can be in a structured format (i.e. tables) as well as in unstructured formats (i.e. text documents, news columns, blogs, Facebook etc.). Tools of multi-structured data analytics assist the players in designing better strategies for winning chess championships.

Using Unstructured Data

Unstructured data does not possess data features such as a table or a database. Unstructured data are found in file types such as .TXT, .CSV. Data may be as key-value pairs, such as hash key-value pairs. Data may have internal structures, such as in e-mails. The data do not reveal relationships, hierarchy relationships or object-oriented features, such as extendibility. The relationships, schema and features need to be separately established. Growth in data today can be characterised as mostly unstructured data. Following are some examples of unstructured data.

EXAMPLE 1.2

Give examples of unstructured data.

SOLUTION

Examples of unstructured data are:

- Mobile data: Text messages, chat messages, tweets, blogs and comments
- Website content data: YouTube videos, browsing data, e-payments, web store data, user-generated maps
- Social media data: For exchanging data in various forms
- Texts and documents
- Personal documents and e-mails
- Text internal to an organization: Text within documents, logs, survey results
- Satellite images, atmospheric data, surveillance, traffic videos, images from Instagram, Flickr (upload, access, organize, edit and share photos from any device from anywhere in the world).

1.2.2 Big Data Definitions

Meanings and various definitions of the word 'Big Data'

Big Data is high-*volume*, high-*velocity* and/or high-*variety* information asset that requires new forms of processing for enhanced *decision making*, *insight discovery* and *process optimization* (Gartner[1] 2012). Other definitions can be found in existing literature.

Industry analyst Doug Laney described the '3Vs', i.e. volume, variety and/or velocity as the key "data management challenges" for enterprises. Analytics also describe the '4Vs', i.e. volume, velocity, variety and veracity. A number of other definitions are available for Big Data, some of which are given below.

> "A collection of data sets so large or complex that traditional data processing applications are inadequate." – *Wikipedia*

> "Data of a very large size, typically to the extent that its manipulation and management present significant logistical challenges." [Oxford English Dictionary (traditional database of authoritative definitions)]

> "Big Data refers to data sets whose size is beyond the ability of typical database software tool to capture, store, manage and analyze." [The McKinsey Global Institute, 2011]

[1] http:// www.gartner.com/it-glossary/big-data

1.2.3 Big Data Characteristics

Characteristics of Big Data, called 3Vs (and 4Vs also used) are:

Volume The phrase 'Big Data' contains the term *big*, which is related to size of the data and hence the characteristic. Size defines the amount or quantity of data, which is generated from an application(s). The size determines the processing considerations needed for handling that data.

Velocity The term velocity refers to the speed of generation of data. Velocity is a measure of how fast the data generates and processes. To meet the demands and the challenges of processing Big Data, the velocity of generation of data plays a crucial role.

Variety Big Data comprises of a variety of data. Data is generated from multiple sources in a system. This introduces variety in data and therefore introduces '*complexity*'. Data consists of various forms and formats. The variety is due to the availability of a large number of heterogeneous platforms in the industry. This means that the type to which Big Data belongs to is also an important characteristic that needs to be known for proper processing of data. This characteristic helps in effective use of data according to their formats, thus maintaining the importance of Big Data.

Veracity is also considered an important characteristic to take into account the quality of data captured, which can vary greatly, affecting its accurate analysis.

The 4Vs (i.e. volume, velocity, variety and veracity) data need tools for mining, discovering patterns, business intelligence, artificial intelligence (AI), machine learning (ML), text analytics, descriptive and predictive analytics, and the data visualization tools.

1.2.4 Big Data Types

A task team on Big Data classified the types of Big Data (June 2013)[2]. Another team from IBM developed a different classification for Big Data types.[3]

Following are the suggested types:

1. *Social networks and web data,* such as Facebook, Twitter, e-mails, blogs and YouTube.
2. *Transactions data and Business Processes (BPs) data*, such as credit card transactions, flight bookings, etc. and public agencies data such as medical records, insurance business data etc.
3. *Customer master data,* such as data for facial recognition and for the name, date of birth, marriage anniversary, gender, location and income category,
4. *Machine-generated data*, such as machine-to-machine or Internet of Things data, and the data from sensors, trackers, web logs and computer systems log. Computer generated data is also considered as machine generated data from data store. Usage of programs for processing of data using data repositories, such as database or file, generates data and also machine generated data.
5. *Human-generated data* such as biometrics data, human–machine interaction data, e-mail records with a mail server and MySQL database of student grades. Humans also records their experiences in ways such as writing these in notebooks or diaries, taking photographs or audio and video clips. Human-sourced information is now almost entirely digitized and stored everywhere from personal computers to social networks. Such data are loosely structured and often ungoverned.

[2] https://statswiki.unece.org/display/bigdata/Classification+of+Types+of+Big+Data
[3] https://www.ibm.com/developerworks/library/bd-archpatterns1/

The following examples illustrate machine-generated data.

EXAMPLE 1.3

Give three examples of the machine-generated data.

SOLUTION

Examples of machine-generated data are:

1. Data from computer systems: Logs, web logs, security/surveillance systems, videos/images etc.
2. Data from fixed sensors: Home automation, weather sensors, pollution sensors, traffic sensors etc.
3. Mobile sensors (tracking) and location data.

Section 1.7 describes Big Data Analytics use cases, case studies and applications in detail. The following example illustrates the usages of Big Data generated from multiple types of data sources for optimizing the services offered, products, schedules and predictive tasks.

EXAMPLE 1.4

Think of a manufacturing and retail marketing company, such as LEGO toys.
How does such a toy company optimize the services offered, products and schedules, devise ways and use Big Data processing and storing for predictions using analytics?

SOLUTION

Assume that a retail and marketing company of toys uses several Big Data sources, such as (i) *machine-generated data* from sensors (RFID readers) at the toy packaging, (ii) *transactions data* of the sales stored as web data for automated reordering by the retail stores and (iii) tweets, Facebook posts, e-mails, messages, and web data for messages and reports.

The company uses Big Data for understanding the toys and themes in present days that are popularly demanded by children, predicting the future types and demands. The company using such predictive analytics, optimizes the product mix and manufacturing processes of toys. The company optimizes the services to retailers by maintaining toy supply schedules. The company sends messages to retailers and children using social media on the arrival of new and popular toys.

The following example illustrates the Big Data features of 3Vs and their applications.

EXAMPLE 1.5

Give an example of features of 3Vs in Big Data and application.

SOLUTION

Consider satellite images of the Earth's atmosphere and its regions. The *Volume* of data from the satellites is large. A number of Indian satellites, such as KALPANA, INSAT-1A and INSAT-3D generate this data. Foreign satellites also generate voluminous data continuously. Satellites record the images of full disk and sectors, such as east and west Asia sectors and regions.

Velocity is also large. A number of satellites collect this data round the clock. Big Data analytics helps in drawing of maps of wind velocities, temperatures and other whether parameters.

Variety of images can be in visible range, such as IR-1 (infrared range -1), IR-2(infrared range -2), shortwave infrared (SWIR), MIR (medium range IR) and colour composite.

Data *Veracity*, uncertain or imprecise data, is as important as Volume, Velocity and Variety. Uncertainty arises due to poor resolutions used for recording or noise in images due to signal impairments.

Data processing needs increased speed of computations due to higher volumes. Need of data management, storage and increased analytics requires new innovative non-traditional methods.

Big Data of satellites helps in predicting weather, and mapping of different crops and from that estimating the expected crop yield.

The following examples explain the uses of Big Data generated from multiple types of data sources.

EXAMPLE 1.6

How are Big Data used in the following companies and services using analytics?

(i) Chocolate Marketing Company with large number of installed Automatic Chocolate Vending Machines (ACVMs)

(ii) Automotive Components and Predictive Automotive Maintenance Services (ACPAMS) rendering customer services for maintenance and servicing of (Internet) connected cars and its components

(iii) Weather data Recording, Monitoring and Prediction (WRMP) Organization.

SOLUTION

(i) Assume ACVM company. Each ACVM sells five flavours (FL1, FL2, FL3, FL4 and FL5) KitKat, Milk, Fruit and Nuts, Nougat and Oreo. The company uses Big Data types as: *Machine-generated data* on the sale of chocolates, reports of unfilled or filled machine *transaction data. Human-generated data* of buyer-machine interactions at the ACVMs. *Social networks and web data* on feedback and personalized messages based on interactions and human-generated data on facial recognition of the buyers. The company uses Big Data for efficient and optimum planning of fill service for chocolates, sentiment analysis of buyers for specific flavours, ACVMs location and periods of higher-sales analysis, assessing needs of predictive maintenances of machines, additions and relocations of machines, and predictions, strategies and planning for festival sales.

(ii) ACPAMS uses Big Data types as: *machine-generated data* from sensors at automotive components, such as brakes, steering and engine from each car; *transactions data* stored at the service website; social networks and web data in the form of messages, feedback and reports from customers. The service provides messages for scheduled and predictive maintenances. The service generates reports on *social networks and updates the web data* for the manufacturing plant. The service generates reports about components qualities and needed areas for improvement in products of the company.

(iii) WRMP Organization uses Big Data types as: machine-generated data from sensors at weather stations and satellites, social networks and web data and the reports and alerts issued by many centers around the world. The organization stores and processes the weather records generated by its stations, social networks and web data collected from other centers. The organization issues maps and weather warnings, predicts weather, rainfall in various regions, expected dates of arrival of monsoon in different regions, issues forecasts on social networks and web pages, generates social network and web data for areal maps of cloud and wind.

1.2.5 Big Data Classification

Big Data can be classified on the basis of its characteristics that are used for designing data architecture for processing and analytics. Table 1.1 gives various classification methods for data and Big Data.

Table 1.1 Various classification methods for data and Big Data

Basis of Classification	Examples
Data sources (traditional)	Data storage such as records, RDBMs, distributed databases, row-oriented In-memory data tables, column-oriented In-memory data tables, data warehouse, server, machine-generated data, human-sourced data, Business Process (BP) data, Business Intelligence (BI) data
Data formats (traditional)	Structured and semi-structured
Big Data sources	Data storage, distributed file system, Operational Data Store (ODS), data marts, data warehouse, NoSQL database (MongoDB, Cassandra), sensors data, audit trail of financial transactions, external data such as web, social media, weather data, health records
Big Data formats	Unstructured, semi-structured and multi-structured data
Data Stores structure	Web, enterprise or cloud servers, data warehouse, row-oriented data for OLTP, column-oriented for OLAP, records, graph database, hashed entries for key/value pairs
Processing data rates	Batch, near-time, real-time, streaming
Processing Big Data rates	High volume, velocity, variety and veracity, batch, near real-time and streaming data processing,
Analysis types	Batch, scheduled, near real-time datasets analytics
Big Data processing methods	Batch processing (for example, using MapReduce, Hive or Pig), real-time processing (for example, using SparkStreaming, SparkSQL, Apache Drill)
Data analysis methods	Statistical analysis, predictive analysis, regression analysis, Mahout, machine learning algorithms, clustering algorithms, classifiers, text analysis, social network analysis, location-based analysis, diagnostic analysis, cognitive analysis
Data usages	Human, business process, knowledge discovery, enterprise applications, Data Stores

1.2.6 Big Data Handling Techniques

Following are the techniques deployed for Big Data storage, applications, data management and mining and analytics:

- Huge data volumes storage, data distribution, high-speed networks and high-performance computing
- Applications scheduling using open source, reliable, scalable, distributed file system, distributed database, parallel and distributed computing systems, such as Hadoop (Chapter 2) or Spark (Chapters 5–10)
- Open source tools which are scalable, elastic and provide virtualized environment, clusters of data nodes, task and thread management
- Data management using NoSQL, document database, column-oriented database, graph database and other form of databases used as per needs of the applications and in-memory data management using columnar or Parquet formats during program execution

- Data mining and analytics, data retrieval, data reporting, data visualization and machine-learning Big Data tools.

Self-Assessment Exercise linked to LO 1.1

1. How do you define data, web data and Big Data? ○○●
2. How do you classify data as structured, semi-structured, multi-structured and unstructured? ○○●
3. Give data example of student records at a University and explain structured data, hierarchical relationships between them. ○●●
4. Recall three examples in Example 1.6. How would you classify data which you shall be using for analytics in these examples? ○●●
5. Consider the usage examples of Big Data for a car company. Assume that company manufactures five models of cars, and each model is available in five colours and five shades. The company collects inputs from customers and sales centres, and inputs of component malfunctions from service centres for different models. The company also uses social media inputs. Explain 3Vs characteristics in this company's data. ●●●

1.3 SCALABILITY AND PARALLEL PROCESSING

LO 1.2

Scalability, scaling up, scaling out in distributed computing, Massively Parallel Processing (MPP), cloud, grid, volunteering computing systems

Big Data needs processing of large data volume, and therefore needs intensive computations. Processing complex applications with large datasets (terabyte to petabyte datasets) need hundreds of computing nodes. Processing of this much distributed data within a short time and at minimum cost is problematic.

Convergence of Data Environments and Analytics

Big Data can co-exist with traditional data store. Traditional data stores use RDBMS tables or data warehouse. Big Data processing and analytics requires scaling up and scaling out, both vertical and horizontal computing resources. Computing and storage systems when run in parallel, enable scaling out and increase system capacity.

Scalability enables increase or decrease in the capacity of data storage, processing and analytics. *Scalability* is the capability of a system to handle the workload as per the magnitude of the work. System capability needs increment with the increased workloads. When the workload and complexity exceed the system capacity, scale it up and scale it out.

The following subsection describes the concept of analytics scalability.

1.3.1 Analytics Scalability to Big Data

Vertical scalability means scaling up the given system's resources and increasing the system's analytics, reporting and visualization capabilities. This is an additional way to solve problems of greater complexities.

Note: ○○● Level 1 & Level 2 category
○●● Level 3 & Level 4 category
●●● Level 5 & Level 6 category

Scaling up means designing the algorithm according to the architecture that uses resources efficiently. For example, *x* terabyte of data take time *t* for processing, code size with increasing complexity increase by factor *n*, then scaling up means that processing takes equal, less or much less than ($n \times$ t).

Horizontal scalability means increasing the number of systems working in coherence and scaling out the workload. Processing different datasets of a large dataset deploys horizontal scalability. *Scaling out* means using more resources and distributing the processing and storage tasks in parallel. If *r* resources in a system process *x* terabyte of data in time *t*, then the (p $\times$ *x*) terabytes process on *p* parallel distributed nodes such that the time taken up remains *t* or is slightly more than *t* (due to the additional time required for Inter Processing nodes Communication (IPC).

The easiest way to scale up and scale out execution of analytics software is to implement it on a bigger machine with more CPUs for greater volume, velocity, variety and complexity of data. The software will definitely perform better on a bigger machine. However, buying faster CPUs, bigger and faster RAM modules and hard disks, faster and bigger motherboards will be expensive compared to the extra performance achieved by efficient design of algorithms. Also, if more CPUs add in a computer, but the software does not exploit the advantage of them, then that will not get any increased performance out of the additional CPUs.

Alternative ways for scaling up and out processing of analytics software and Big Data analytics deploy the Massively Parallel Processing Platforms (MPPs), cloud, grid, clusters, and distributed computing software.

The following subsections describe computing methods for high availability and scalable computations and analysis.

1.3.2 Massively Parallel Processing Platforms

> A solution for Big data processing is to perform parallel and distributed computing in a cloud-computing environment.

Scaling uses parallel processing systems. Many programs are so large and/or complex that it is impractical or impossible to execute them on a single computer system, especially in limited computer memory. Here, it is required to enhance (scale) up the computer system or use massive parallel processing (MPPs) platforms. Parallelization of tasks can be done at several levels: (i) distributing separate tasks onto separate threads on the same CPU, (ii) distributing separate tasks onto separate CPUs on the same computer and (iii) distributing separate tasks onto separate computers.

When making software, draw the advantage of multiple computers (or even multiple CPUs within the same computer) and software which need to be able to parallelize tasks. Multiple compute resources are used in parallel processing systems. The computational problem is broken into discrete pieces of sub-tasks that can be processed simultaneously. The system executes multiple program instructions or sub-tasks at any moment in time. Total time taken will be much less than with a single compute resource.

1.3.2.1 Distributed Computing Model

A distributed computing model uses cloud, grid or clusters, which process and analyze big and large datasets on distributed computing nodes connected by high-speed networks. Table 1.2 gives the requirements of processing and analyzing big, large and small to medium datasets on distributed computing nodes. Big Data processing uses a parallel, scalable and no-sharing program model, such as MapReduce, for computations on it. (Chapter 2)

Table 1.2 Distributed computing paradigms

Distributed computing on multiple processing nodes/clusters	Big Data > 10 M	Large datasets below 10 M	Small to medium datasets up to 1 M
Distributed computing	Yes	Yes	No
Parallel computing	Yes	Yes	No
Scalable computing	Yes	Yes	No
Shared nothing (No in-between data sharing and inter-processor communication)	Yes	Limited sharing	No
Shared in-between between the distributed nodes/clusters	No	Limited sharing	Yes

1.3.3 Cloud Computing

Wikipedia defines cloud computing as, "Cloud computing is a type of Internet-based computing that provides shared processing resources and data to the computers and other devices on demand."

One of the best approach for data processing is to perform parallel and distributed computing in a cloud-computing environment. Cloud usages circumvent the single point failure due to failing of one node. Cloud design performs as a whole. Its multiple nodes perform automatically and interchangeably. It offers high data security compared to other distributed technologies.

Cloud resources can be Amazon Web Service (AWS) Elastic Compute Cloud (EC2), Microsoft Azure or Apache CloudStack. Amazon Simple Storage Service (S3) provides simple web services interface to store and retrieve any amount of data, at any time, from anywhere on the web. [Amazon EC2 name possibly drives from the feature that EC2 has a simple web service interface, which provides and configures the storage and computing capacity with minimal friction].

Cloud computing features are: (i) on-demand service (ii) resource pooling, (iii) scalability, (iv) accountability, and (v) broad network access. Cloud services can be accessed from anywhere and at any time through the Internet. A local private cloud can also be set up on a local cluster of computers.

Cloud computing allows availability of computer infrastructure and services "on-demand" basis. The computing infrastructure includes data storage device, development platform, database, computing power or software applications.

Cloud services can be classified into three fundamental types:

1. Infrastructure as a Service (IaaS): Providing access to resources, such as hard disks, network connections, databases storage, data center and virtual server spaces is Infrastructure as a Service (IaaS). Some examples are Tata Communications, Amazon data centers and virtual servers. Apache CloudStack is an open source software for deploying and managing a large network of virtual machines, and offers public cloud services which provide highly scalable Infrastructure as a Service (IaaS).

> Cloud services offer IaaS, SaaS and PaaS as service models for processing and analyzing the large datasets on computing nodes.

2. Platform as a Service (PaaS): It implies providing the runtime environment to allow developers to build applications and services, which means cloud Platform as a Service. Software at the clouds support and manage the services, storage, networking, deploying, testing, collaborating, hosting and maintaining applications. Examples are Hadoop Cloud Service (IBM BigInsight, Microsoft Azure HD Insights, Oracle Big Data Cloud Services).

3. Software as a Service (SaaS): Providing software applications as a service to end-users is known as Software as a Service. Software applications are hosted by a service provider and made available to customers over the Internet. Some examples are SQL GoogleSQL, IBM BigSQL, HPE Vertica, Microsoft Polybase and Oracle Big Data SQL.

1.3.4 Grid and Cluster Computing

Grid Computing

Grid Computing refers to distributed computing, in which a group of computers from several locations are connected with each other to achieve a common task. The computer resources are heterogeneously and geographically disperse. A group of computers that might spread over remotely comprise a grid. A grid is used for a variety of purposes. A single grid of course, dedicates at an instance to a particular application only. Grid computing provides large-scale resource sharing which is flexible, coordinated and secure among its users. The users consist of individuals, organizations and resources.

Grid computing suits data-intensive storage better than storage of small objects of few millions of bytes. To achieve the maximum benefit from data grids, they should be used for a large amount of data which can distribute over grid nodes. Besides data grid, the other variation of grid, i.e., computational grid focuses on computationally intensive operations.

Features of Grid Computing Grid computing, similar to cloud computing, is scalable. Cloud computing depends on sharing of resources (for example, networks, servers, storage, applications and services) to attain coordination and coherence among resources similar to grid computing. Similarly, grid also forms a distributed network for resource integration.

Drawbacks of Grid Computing Grid computing is the single point, which leads to failure in case of underperformance or failure of any of the participating nodes. A system's storage capacity varies with the number of users, instances and the amount of data transferred at a given time. Sharing resources among a large number of users helps in reducing infrastructure costs and raising load capacities.

Cluster Computing

A cluster is a group of computers connected by a network. The group works together to accomplish the same task. Clusters are used mainly for load balancing. They shift processes between nodes to keep an even load on the group of connected computers. Hadoop architecture uses the similar methods (Chapter 2).

Table 1.3 gives a comparison of grid computing with the distributed and cluster computing.

Table 1.3 Grid computing and related paradigms

Distributed computing	Cluster computing	Grid computing
• Loosely coupled • Heterogeneous • Single administration	• Tightly coupled • Homogeneous • Cooperative working	• Large scale • Cross organizational • Geographical distribution • Distributed management

1.3.5 Volunteer Computing

Volunteers provide computing resources to projects of importance that use resources to do distributed computing and/or storage. **Volunteer computing** is a distributed computing paradigm which uses computing resources of the volunteers. Volunteers are organizations or members who own personal computers. **Projects** examples are science-related projects executed by universities or academia in general.

Some issues with volunteer computing systems are:

1. Volunteered computers heterogeneity
2. Drop outs from the network over time
3. Their sporadic availability
4. Incorrect results at volunteers are unaccountable as they are essentially from anonymous volunteers.

Self-Assessment Exercise linked to LO 1.2

1. Define analytics scalability, horizontal scalability and vertical scalability. ○○●
2. How does platform differ from software? When will a program use SaaS and when PaaS? ○○●
3. List the features of grid computing. How does it differ from cluster and cloud computing? ○●●
4. Why do we use distributed computing for analytics of large datasets? ●●●

1.4 DESIGNING DATA ARCHITECTURE

LO 1.3

Design of data architecture layers and their functions, and data management functions for the analytics

The following subsections describe how to design Big Data architecture layers and how to manage data for analytics.

1.4.1 Data Architecture Design

Techopedia defines *Big Data architecture* as follows: "Big Data architecture is the logical and/or physical layout/structure of how Big Data will be stored, accessed and managed within a Big Data or IT environment. Architecture logically defines how Big Data solution will work, the core components (hardware, database, software, storage) used, flow of information, security and more."

Characteristics of Big Data make designing Big Data architecture a complex process. Further, faster additions of new technological innovations increase the complexity in design. The requirements for offering competing products at lower costs in the market make the designing task more challenging for a Big Data architect.

Data analytics need the number of sequential steps. Big Data architecture design task simplifies when using the logical layers approach. Figure 1.2 shows the logical layers and the functions which are considered in Big Data architecture.

Five vertically aligned textboxes on the left of Figure 1.2 show the layers. Horizontal textboxes show the functions in each layer.

Data processing architecture consists of five layers: (i) identification of data sources, (ii) acquisition, ingestion, extraction, pre-processing, transformation of data, (iii) data storage at files, servers, cluster or cloud, (iv) data-processing, and (v) data consumption in the number of programs and tools.

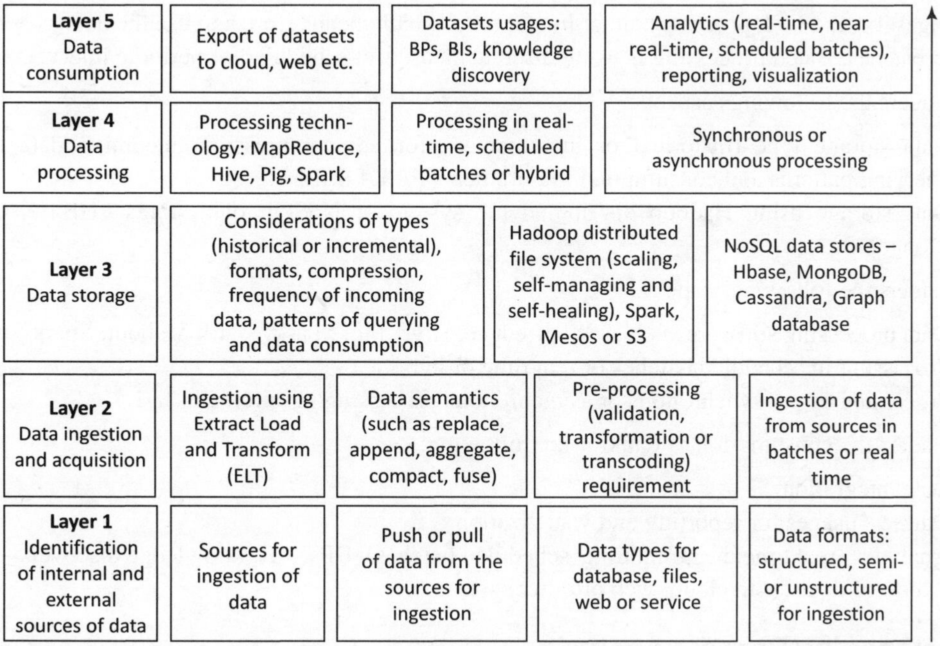

Figure 1.2 Design of logical layers in a data processing architecture, and functions in the layers

Data consumed for applications, such as business intelligence, data mining, discovering patterns/clusters, artificial intelligence (AI), machine learning (ML), text analytics, descriptive and predictive analytics, and data visualization.

Data ingestion, pre-processing, storage and analytics require special tools and technologies.

Logical layer 1 (L1) is for identifying data sources, which are external, internal or both. The layer 2 (L2) is for data-ingestion.

Data ingestion means a process of absorbing information, just like the process of absorbing nutrients and medications into the body by eating or drinking them (Cambridge English Dictionary). Ingestion is the process of obtaining and importing data for immediate use or transfer. Ingestion may be in batches or in real time using pre-processing or semantics.

The L3 layer is for storage of data from the L2 layer. The L4 is for data processing using software, such as MapReduce, Hive, Pig or Spark. The top layer L5 is for data consumption. Data is used in analytics, visualizations, reporting, export to cloud or web servers.

L1 considers the following aspects in a design:

- Amount of data needed at ingestion layer 2 (L2)
- Push from L1 or pull by L2 as per the mechanism for the usages
- Source data-types: Database, files, web or service
- Source formats, i.e., semi-structured, unstructured or structured.

L2 considers the following aspects:

- Ingestion and ETL processes either in real time, which means store and use the data as generated, or in batches. Batch processing is using discrete datasets at scheduled or periodic intervals of time.

L3 considers the followings aspects:

- Data storage type (historical or incremental), format, compression, incoming data frequency, querying patterns and consumption requirements for L4 or L5
- Data storage using Hadoop distributed file system or NoSQL data stores—HBase, Cassandra, MongoDB.

L4 considers the followings aspects:

- Data processing software such as MapReduce, Hive, Pig, Spark, Spark Mahout, Spark Streaming
- Processing in scheduled batches or real time or hybrid
- Processing as per synchronous or asynchronous processing requirements at L5.

L5 considers the consumption of data for the following:

- Data integration
- Datasets usages for reporting and visualization
- Analytics (real time, near real time, scheduled batches), BPs, BIs, knowledge discovery
- Export of datasets to cloud, web or other systems

1.4.2 Managing Data for Analysis

Data managing means enabling, controlling, protecting, delivering and enhancing the value of data and information asset. Reports, analysis and visualizations need well-defined data. Data management also enables data usage in applications. The process for managing needs to be well defined for fulfilling requirements of the applications.

Data management functions include:

1. Data assets creation, maintenance and protection
2. Data governance, which includes establishing the processes for ensuring the availability, usability, integrity, security and high-quality of data. The processes enable trustworthy data availability for analytics, followed by the decision making at the enterprise.
3. Data architecture creation, modelling and analysis
4. Database maintenance, administration and management system. For example, RDBMS (relational database management system), NoSQL
5. Managing data security, data access control, deletion, privacy and security
6. Managing the data quality
7. Data collection using the ETL process
8. Managing documents, records and contents
9. Creation of reference and master data, and data control and supervision
10. Data and application integration
11. Integrated data management, enterprise-ready data creation, fast access and analysis, automation and simplification of operations on the data,
12. Data warehouse management
13. Maintenance of business intelligence
14. Data mining and analytics algorithms.

Self-Assessment Exercise linked to LO 1.3

1. How are data architecture layers used for analytics? ○○●
2. Explain the function of each of the five layers in Big Data architecture design (Figure 1.2). ○●●
3. List the functions of the ELT at data ingestion layer and at data storage layer. ●●●
4. List the functions in data management. ○○●

1.5 DATA SOURCES, QUALITY, PRE-PROCESSING AND STORING

LO 1.4

Data sources, data quality, data pre-processing, and data store export to the cloud

The following subsections describe data sources, data quality, data pre-processing and data store export to the cloud.

1.5.1 Data Sources

Applications, programs and tools use data. Sources can be *external*, such as sensors, trackers, web logs, computer systems logs and feeds. Sources can be machines, which source data from data-creating programs.

Data sources can be structured, semi-structured, multi-structured or unstructured. Data sources can be social media (L1 in Figure 1.2). A source can be *internal*. Sources can be data repositories, such as database, relational database, flat file, spreadsheet, mail server, web server, directory services, even text or files such as comma-separated values (CSV) files. Source may be a data store for applications (L4 in Figure 1.2).

1.5.1.1 Structured Data Sources

Data source for ingestion, storage and processing can be a file, database or streaming data. The source may be on the same computer running a program or a networked computer. Examples of structured data sources are SQL Server, MySQL, Microsoft Access database, Oracle DBMS, IBM DB2, Informix, Amazon SimpleDB or a file-collection directory at a server.

A data source name implies a defined name, which a process uses to identify the source. The name needs to be a meaningful name. For example, a name which identifies the stored data in student grades during processing. The data source name could be *StudentName_Data_Grades*.

A *data dictionary* enables references for accesses to data. The dictionary consists of a set of master lookup tables. The dictionary stores at a central location. The central location enables easier access as well as administration of changes in sources. The name of the dictionary can be *UniversityStudents_DataPlusGrades*. A master-directory server can also be called *NameNode*.

Machine data sources and file data sources in Microsoft applications

Microsoft applications consider two types of sources for processing: (i) machine sources and (ii) file sources.[4]

(i) Machine sources are present on computing nodes, such as servers. A machine identifies a source by the user-defined name, driver-manager name and source-driver name.

[4] https://docs.microsoft.com/en-us/sql/odbc/reference/data-sources

(ii) File sources are stored files. An application executing the data, first *connects* to a driver manager of the source. A user, client or application *does not register* with the source, but *connects* to the manager when required. The process of connection is simple when using a file data source in case the file contains a connection string that would otherwise have to be built using a call to a connect-function driver.

Database data sources and logic-machine data sources in Oracle applications

Oracle applications consider two types of data sources: (i) *database*, which identifies the database information that the software needs to connect to database, and (ii) *logic-machine*, which identifies the machine which runs batches of applications and master business functions.[5] Source definition identifies the machine. The source can be on a network. The definition in that case also includes network information, such as the name of the server, which hosts the machine functions.

The applications consider data sources as the ones where the database tables reside and where the software runs logic objects for an enterprise. Data sources can point to:

1. A database in a specific location or in a data library of OS
2. A specific machine in the enterprise that processes logic
3. A data source master table which stores data source definitions. The table may be at a centralized source (enterprise server) or at server-map for the source.

Specific database instance or file as data sources in IBM i system

A database can be in an IBM **i** data library[6] [IBM i is a computer operating system in which IBM **i** considers everything as an object, each possessing persistence. The system IBM **i** offers Unix-like file directories using an integrated file system.].

IBM applications consider data sources for applications and tools as one which identifies either (i) a specific database instance or (ii) file on a remote system that stores data.[6] Data sources can be shared. The access to source is restricted according to the roles assigned to both the source and the application that use it.

EXAMPLE 1.7

(i) How would you name the data sources of the student grade-sheets?

(ii) How does an analytics application (Analysis_APP) access student grade-sheet data source, using the Data Dictionary or data-source master-table for the grade-sheets of students?

(iii) How does the application connect and access the data source of students' grade-sheets?

Assume each student can have a grade-sheet for each of the six semesters in UG Computer Science programme.

SOLUTION

(i) Assume SemID is distinct key for a semester. StudID is a key assigned to a student, whether in CS or another subject, and whether in UG or PG. A StudID is unique. Data source can be file data source named 'UG_CS_Sem_StudID_Grades' for all UG CS student grades. UG_CS_Sem_StudID_Grades database consists of maximum six grade sheets UG_CS_SemID_StudID_Grades, i.e., one for each semester. Assume that Analysis_APP does not connect or directly links to the

[5] https://docs.oracle.com/cd/E17984_01/doc.898/e14695/undrstnd_datasources.htm

[6] https://www.ibm.com/support/knowledgecenter/en/SSMPHH_9.5.0/com.ibm.guardium95.doc/ common_tools/topics/datasources.html

data source UG_CS_Sem_StudID_Grades database. Then, the Analysis_APP links to a Data Dictionary or data source master table, which is data repository for the pointers of all six semesters of UG Computer Science program and other subject programs.

(ii) Assume that Analysis_APP associates to Oracle data-source master-table. The table stores the data-source definitions for all UG and PG, and all subjects and semester grades of the students. The data-source master-table stores the pointers of all semester grades. The table thus points to UG_CS_Sem_StudID_Grades DB for the student identified by StudID.

(iii) Assume that application deploys Microsoft DB. Then, first Analysis_APP links to a Driver Manager. The Driver Manager then calls the ODBC functions in the Driver Manager. The application identifies the target driver for the UG_CS_Sem_StudID_Grades data source with a connection handle. When the Driver Manager loads the driver, the Driver Manager builds a table of pointers to the functions in that driver. It uses the connection handle passed by the application to find the address of the function in the target driver and calls that function by address.

1.5.1.2 Unstructured Data Sources

Unstructured data sources are distributed over high-speed networks. The data need high velocity processing. Sources are from distributed file systems. The sources are of file types, such as .txt (text file), .csv (comma separated values file). Data may be as key-value pairs, such as hash key-values pairs. Data may have internal structures, such as in e-mail, Facebook pages, twitter messages etc. The data do not model, reveal relationships, hierarchy relationships or object-oriented features, such as extensibility.

1.5.1.3 Data Sources – Sensors, Signals and GPS

The data sources can be sensors, sensor networks, signals from machines, devices, controllers and intelligent edge nodes of different types in the industry M2M communication and the GPS systems.

Sensors are electronic devices that sense the physical environment. Sensors are devices which are used for measuring temperature, pressure, humidity, light intensity, traffic in proximity, acceleration, locations, object(s) proximity, orientations and magnetic intensity, and other physical states and parameters. Sensors play an active role in the automotive industry.

RFIDs and their sensors play an active role in RFID based supply chain management, and tracking parcels, goods and delivery.

Sensors embedded in processors, which include machine-learning instructions, and wireless communication capabilities are innovations. They are sources in IoT applications.

1.5.2 Data Quality

Data quality is high when it represents the real-world construct to which references are taken. High quality means data, which enables all the required operations, analysis, decisions, planning and knowledge discovery correctly. A definition for high quality data, especially for artificial intelligence applications, can be data with five R's as follows: Relevancy, recency, range, robustness and reliability. Relevancy is of utmost importance.

Data quality definitions; Data relevancy, recency, range, robustness and reliability

A uniform definition of data quality is difficult. A reference can be made to a set of values of quantitative or qualitative conditions, which must be specified to say that data quality is high or low.

1.5.2.1 Data Integrity

Data integrity refers to the maintenance of consistency and accuracy in data over its usable life. Software, which store, process, or retrieve the data, should maintain the integrity of data. Data should be incorruptible. For example, in Example 1.7 the grades of students should remain unaffected upon processing.

1.5.2.2 Data Noise, Outliers, Missing and Duplicate Values

Noise One of the factors effecting data quality is noise. Noise in data refers to data giving additional meaningless information besides true (actual/required) information. Noise refers to difference in the value measured from true value due to additional influences. Noisy data means data having large additional information. Result of data analysis is adversely affected due to noisy data.

Noise is random in character, which means frequency with which it occurs is variable over time. The values show nearly equal positive and negative deviations. A statistical analysis of deviation can select the noise in data and true values can be retrieved.

Outliers A factor which effects quality is an outlier. An *outlier* in data refers to data, which appears to not belong to the dataset. For example, data that is outside an expected range. Actual outliers need to be removed from the dataset, else the result will be effected by a small or large amount. Alternatively, if valid data is identified as outlier, then also the results will be affected. The outliers are a result of human data-entry errors, programming bugs, some transition effect or phase lag in stabilizing the data value to the true value.

Missing Values Another factor effecting data quality is missing values. *Missing value* implies data *not appearing in the data set.*

Duplicate Values Another factor effecting data quality is duplicate values. *Duplicate value* implies the same data appearing two or more times in a dataset.

The following example explains noise, outliers, missing values and duplicate data.

EXAMPLE 1.8

Consider use cases of noise, outliers, missing values and duplicate data. Write the effect on the analysis in each case.

SOLUTION

Following are the examples of machine-generated data.

1. *Noise*: Recall WRMP organization for weather recording. Consider noise in wind velocity and direction readings due to external turbulences. The velocity at certain instances will appear too high and sometimes too low. The directions at certain instances will appear inclined more towards the north and sometimes more towards the south.
2. *Outlier*: Consider an outlier in the students' grade-sheets in one subject out of five in the fourth-semester result of a student. A result in a semester shows 9.0 out of 10 points in place of 3.0 out of 10. Data 9.0 is an outlier. The student semester grade point average (SGPA) will be erroneously declared and the student may even be declared to have failed in that semester.
3. *Missing values*: Consider missing values in the sales figures of chocolates. The values not sent for certain dates from an ACVM. This may be due to the failure of power supply at the machine or network problems on specific days in a month. The chocolate sales not added for a day can

be added in the next day's sales data. The effect over a month on the average sales per day is not significant. However, if the failure occurred on last day of a month, then the analysis will be erroneous.

4. ***Duplicate values***: Consider duplicate values in the sales figures of chocolates from an ACVM. This may be due to some problem in the system. The number of duplicates for sales when sent and added, then sales result analysis will get affected. It can even result in false alarms to a service, which maintains the supply chain to the ACVMs.

   Assume network problems on certain instances. The ACVM may not get an acknowledgement of the sales figures from the server, leading to sending an incorrect sales record once again. If this happens then sales figures of chocolates get recorded twice at that instance. For example, if the chocolate sales data gets added twice in a specific day's sales data, the calculation of monthly sales data is adversely affected.

1.5.3 Data Pre-processing

Data pre-processing is an important step at the ingestion layer (Figure 1.2). For example, consider grade point data in Example 1.8. The outlier needs to be removed. Pre-processing is a must before data mining and analytics. Pre-processing is also a must before running a Machine Learning (ML) algorithm. Analytics needs prior screening of data quality also. Data when being exported to a cloud service or data store needs pre-processing.

> Need of data pre-processing for data store portability and usability in applications and services

Pre-processing needs are:

(i) Dropping out of range, inconsistent and outlier values
(ii) Filtering unreliable, irrelevant and redundant information
(iii) Data cleaning, editing, reduction and/or wrangling
(iv) Data validation, transformation or transcoding
(v) ELT processing.

Data Cleaning

Data cleaning refers to the process of removing or correcting incomplete, incorrect, inaccurate or irrelevant parts of the data after detecting them. For example, in Example 1.8 correcting the grade outliers or mistakenly entered values means cleaning and correcting the data.

> Needs of data pre-processing using cleaning, enrichment, editing, reduction and wrangling methods

Data Cleaning Tools Data cleaning is done before mining of data. Incomplete or irrelevant data may result into misleading decisions. It is not always possible to create well-structured data. Data can generate in a system in many formats when it is obtained from the web. Data cleaning tools help in refining and structuring data into usable data. Examples of such tools are OpenRefine and DataCleaner.

Data Enrichment

Techopedia definition is as follows: "*Data enrichment* refers to operations or processes which refine, enhance or improve the raw data."

Data Editing

Data editing refers to the process of reviewing and adjusting the acquired datasets. The editing controls the data quality. Editing methods are (i) interactive, (ii) selective, (iii) automatic, (iv) aggregating and (v) distribution.

Data Reduction

Data reduction enables the transformation of acquired information into an ordered, correct and simplified form. The reductions enable ingestion of meaningful data in the datasets. The basic concept is the reduction of multitudinous amount of data, and use of the meaningful parts. The reduction uses editing, scaling, coding, sorting, collating, smoothening, interpolating and preparing tabular summaries.

Data Wrangling

Data wrangling refers to the process of transforming and mapping the data. Results from analytics are then appropriate and valuable. For example, mapping enables data into another format, which makes it valuable for analytics and data visualizations.

Data Format used during Pre-Processing

Need of data format conversion of data CSV, JSON, key-value pairs or other data from Data Store; for example, in the form of tables

Examples of formats for data transfer from (a) data storage, (b) analytics application, (b) service or (d) cloud can be:

(i) Comma-separated values CSV (Example 1.9)
(ii) Java Script Object Notation (JSON) as batches of object arrays or resource arrays (Example 3.3)
(iii) Tag Length Value (TLV)
(iv) Key-value pairs (Section 3.3.1)
(v) Hash-key-value pairs (Example 3.2).

CSV Format

An example is a table or Microsoft Excel file which needs conversion to CSV format. A student_record.xlsx converts to student_record.csv file. Comma-separated values (CSV) file refers to a plain text file which stores the table data of numbers and text. When processing for data visualization of Excel format file, the data conversion will be done from csv to xlsx format.

Each CSV file line is a data record. Each record consists of one or more fields, separated from each other by commas. RFC 4180 standard specifies the various specifications. A CSV file may also use space, tab or delimiter tab-separated formats for the values in the fields. This is a loose terminology. The following example explains the conversion process.

EXAMPLE 1.9

Consider the example of a table in a grade sheet. A CSV file is easily understandable when the table's first row specifies the column heads. Three columns of the first row are Subject Code, Subject Name and Grade and three columns of the second row are CS101, "Theory of Computations" and 7.8, as shown below:

Subject Code	Subject Name	Grade
CS101	"Theory of Computations"	7.8
CS102	"Computer Architecture"	7.2
-	-	-

SOLUTION

The first and second lines in the CSV file are:

Subject Code, Subject Name, Grade
CS101, ""Theory of Computations"", 7.8.
CS102, ""Computer Architecture"", 7.8.

The two consecutive double-quotes mean that one of the double quotes is retained in the text "Theory of Computations". That one specifies that characters are inside the double quotes and represent a string.

Data Format Conversions

Transferring the data may need pre-processing for data-format conversions. Data sources store need portability and usability. A number of different applications, services and tools need a specific format of data only. Pre-processing before their usages or storage on cloud services is a must.

1.5.4 Data Store Export to Cloud

Export of data from data sources to IBM, Microsoft, Oracle, Amazon, Rackspace or Hadoop cloud services

Figure 1.3 shows resulting data pre-processing, data mining, analysis, visualization and data store. The data exports to cloud services. The results integrate at the enterprise server or data warehouse.

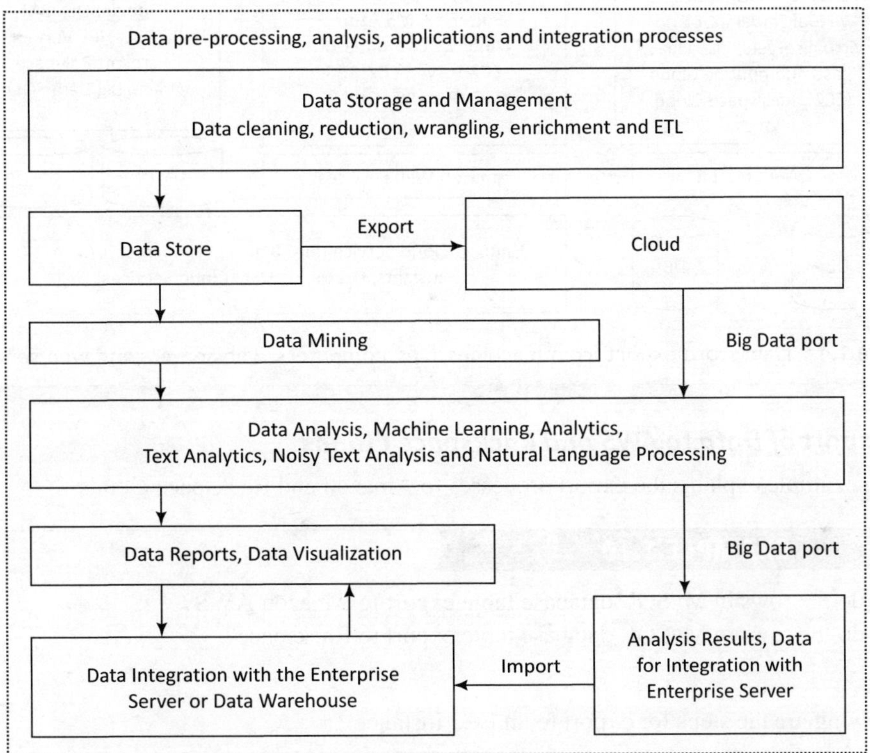

Figure 1.3 Data pre-processing, analysis, visualization, data store export

1.5.4.1 *Cloud Services*

Cloud offers various services. (Section 1.3.3) These services can be accessed through a cloud client (client application), such as a web browser, SQL or other client. Figure 1.4 shows data-store export from machines, files, computers, web servers and web services. The data exports to clouds, such as IBM, Microsoft, Oracle, Amazon, Rackspace, TCS, Tata Communications or Hadoop cloud services.

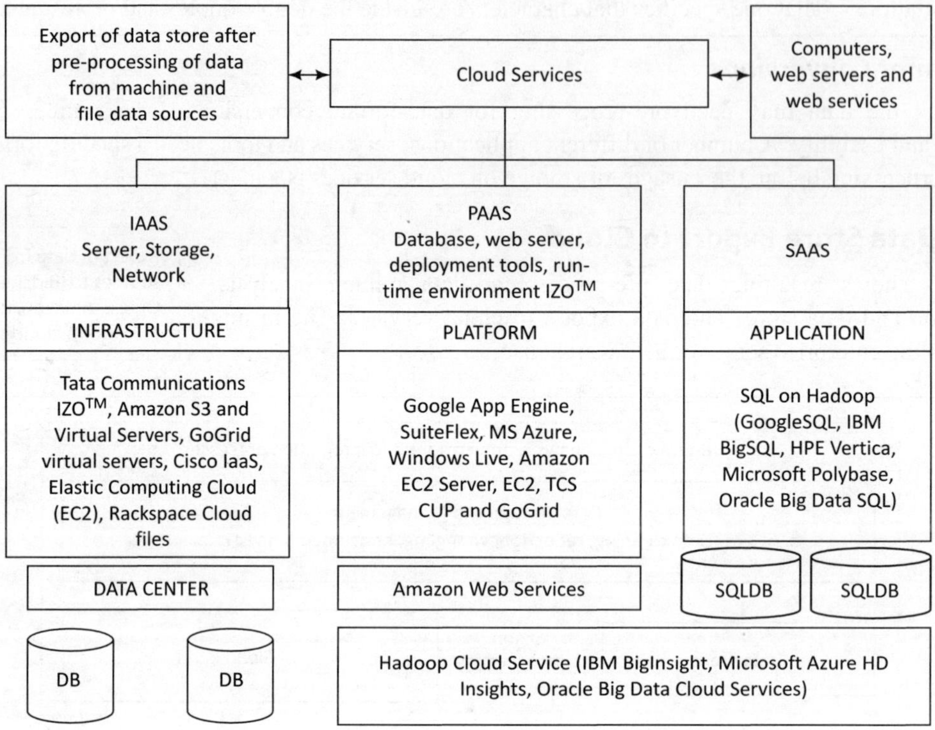

Figure 1.4 Data store export from machines, files, computers, web servers and web services

1.5.4.2 *Export of Data to AWS and Rackspace Clouds*

The following example explains the export processes to Amazon and Rackspace clouds.

EXAMPLE 1.10

(a) How do the rows in MySQL database table export to Amazon AWS?
(b) How do the rows in MySQL database table export to Rackspace?

SOLUTION

(a) Following are the steps for export to an EC2 instance:
   (i) A process pre-processes the data from data-rows at table in MySQL database and creates a CSV file.
   (ii) An EC2 instance provides an AWS data pipeline.

(iii) The CSV file exports to Amazon S3 using pipeline. The CSV file then copies into an S3 bucket.[7] Coping action deploys an EC2 instance.

(iv) AWS notification service (SNS) sends notification on completion.[8]

(b) Following are the steps for export to Rackspace[9]:

(i) An instance name has maximum 255 characters. One or more databases create a database instance. The process of creation can be configured to create an instance now or later. Each database can have a number of users.

(i) Default port number for binding of MySQL is port 3306.

(ii) A command *mysqldump – u root – p database_name > database_name.sql* exports to Rackspace cloud.

(iii) When a database is at a remote host then a command *mysqldump – h host_name -u user_name – p database_name > database_name.sql* exports to the cloud database.

Google cloud platform provides a cloud service called BigQuery.[10] Figure 1.5 shows BigQuery cloud service at Google cloud platform. The data exports from a table or partition schema, JSON, CSV or AVRO files from data sources after the pre-processing.

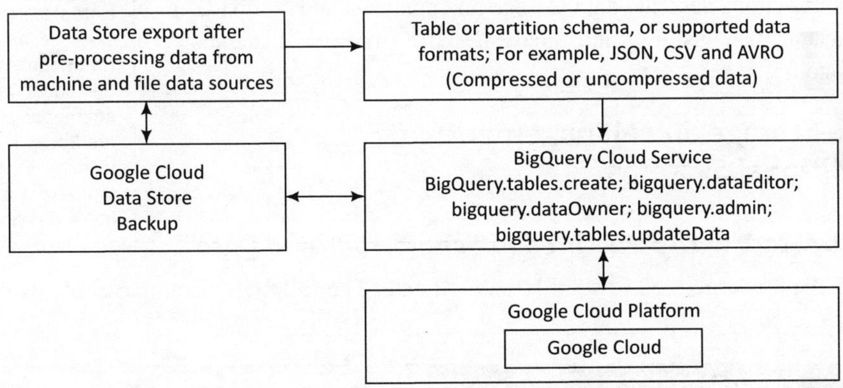

Figure 1.5 BigQuery cloud service at Google cloud platform

Data Store first pre-processes from machine and file data sources. Pre-processing transforms the data in table or partition schema or supported data formats. For example, JSON, CSV and AVRO. Data then exports in compressed or uncompressed data formats. (Avro is a data serialization system in Hadoop related tools for Big Data.)

Cloud service BigQuery consists of bigquery.tables.create; bigquery.dataEditor; bigquery.dataOwner; bigquery.admin; bigquery.tables.updateData and other service functions. Analytics uses Google Analytics 360. BigQuery cloud exports data to a Google cloud or cloud backup only.

[7] http://docs.aws.amazon.com/datapipeline/latest/DeveloperGuide/dp-object-copyactivity.html

[8] http://docs.aws.amazon.com/datapipeline/latest/DeveloperGuide/dp-object-snsalarm.html

[9] https://support.rackspace.com/how-to/cloud-database-instance-parameters/

[10] https://cloud.google.com/bigquery/docs/loading-data

Self-Assessment Exercise linked to LO 1.4

1. Why is data quality important in discovering new knowledge and decision making? ○●●
2. List the examples of cloud services for exporting data stores. ○○●
3. How is conversion to CSV file before data store beneficial? How is conversion to tables from CSV files from data store beneficial? ○○●
4. List the usages of three types of services that clouds offer. List Big Data cloud services, to data sources export from data store, and perform cloud during analytics, visualizations and intelligence discovery. ○●●
5. Consider databases storing the daily sales figures of chocolates, such as KitKat, Milk, Fruit and Nuts, Nougat and Oreo, each at every machine in Example 1.6(i). How will you name the data sources in ACVMs analytics? How will the ACVMs sales be analyzed for each type of chocolate using the data-source master-tables? ●●●

1.6 DATA STORAGE AND ANALYSIS

LO 1.5

Data storage, analysis, Comparison between traditional systems, such as Relational Database Management System (RDBMS), enterprise servers and data warehouse, Approaches for Big Data storage, processing and analytics

The following subsections describe data storage and analysis, and comparison between Big Data management and analysis with traditional database management systems.

1.6.1 Data Storage and Management: Traditional Systems

1.6.1.1 Data Store with Structured or Semi-Structured Data

Traditional systems use structured or semi-structured data. The following example explains the sources and data store of structured data.

EXAMPLE 1.11

What are the sources of structured data store?

SOLUTION

The sources of structured data store are:

- Traditional relational database-management system (RDBMS) data, such as MySQL DB2, enterprise server and data warehouse
- Business process data which stores business events, such as registering a customer, taking an order, generating an invoice, and managing products in pre-defined formats. The data falls in the category of highly structured data. The data consists of transaction records, tables, relationships and metadata that build the information about the business data.
- Commercial transactions
- Banking/stock records
- E-commerce transactions data.

The following example explains the sources and data store of semi-structured data.

EXAMPLE 1.12

Give examples of sources of data store of semi-structured data.

SOLUTION

Examples of semi-structured data are:

- XML and JSON semi-structured documents[7,8]
- A comma-separated values (CSV) file. The CSV stores tabular data in plain text. Each line is a data record. A record can have several fields, each filed separated by a comma. Structured data, such as database include multiple relations but CSV does not consider the relations in a single CSV file. CSV cannot represent object-oriented databases or hierarchical data records. A CSV file is as follows:

```
Preeti,1995,MCA,Object Oriented Programming,8.75
Kirti,2010, M.Tech., Mobile Operating System, 8.5
```

Data represent the data records for columns and rows of a table. Each row has names, year of passing, degree name, course name and grade point out of 10. Rows are separated by a new line and the columns by a comma.

JSON Object Data Formats: CSV does not represent object-oriented records, databases or hierarchical data records. JSON and XML represent semi-structured data and represent object-oriented and hierarchical data records. Example 3.5 explains CSV and JSON objects and the hierarchical data records in the JSON file format.

1.6.1.2 SQL

An RDBMS uses SQL (Structured Query Language). SQL is a language for viewing or changing (update, insert or append or delete) databases. It is a language for data access control, schema creation and data modifications.

> SQL is language for data querying, updating, inserting, appending and deleting the databases.

SQL was originally based on the tuple relational calculus and relational algebra. SQL can embed within other languages using SQL modules, libraries and pre-compilers. SQL does the following:

1. *Create schema*, which is a structure which contains description of objects (base tables, views, constraints) created by a user. The user can describe the data and define the data in the database.
2. *Create catalog*, which consists of a set of schemas which describe the database.
3. *Data Definition Language* (DDL) for the commands which depicts a database, that include creating, altering and dropping of tables and establishing the constraints. A user can create and drop databases and tables, establish foreign keys, create view, stored procedure, functions in the database etc.
4. *Data Manipulation Language* (DML) for commands that maintain and query the database. A user can manipulate (INSERT/UPDATE) and access (SELECT) the data.
5. *Data Control Language* (DCL) for commands that control a database, and include administering of privileges and committing. A user can set (grant, add or revoke) permissions on tables, procedures and views.

SQL is a language for managing the RDBMS. A relational DB is a collection of data in multiple tables, which relate to each other through special fields, called keys (primary key, foreign key and unique key). Relational databases provide flexibilities. Relational database examples are MySQL PostGreSQL Oracle database, Informix, IBM DB2 and Microsoft SQL server.

1.6.1.3 Large Data Storage using RDBMS

> Traditional systems Relational database is collection of data into multiple tables which relates to each other through special fields, called keys

RDBMS tables store data in a structured form. The tables have rows and columns. Data management of Data Store includes the provisions for privacy and security, data integration, compaction and fusion. The systems use machine-generated data, human-sourced data, and data from business processes (BP) and business intelligence (BI).

A set of keys and relational keys access the fields at tables, and retrieve data using queries (insert, modify, append, join or delete). RDBMSs use software for data administration also.

Online content associated with Practice Exercise 1.12 describes the use of tables in relational databases in detail.

1.6.1.4 Distributed Database Management System

> Distributed DB is a collection of logically interrelated databases at multiple systems over a computer network.

A distributed DBMS (DDBMS) is a collection of logically interrelated databases at multiple system over a computer network. The features of a distributed database system are:

1. A collection of logically related databases.
2. Cooperation between databases in a transparent manner. Transparent means that each user within the system may access all of the data within all of the databases as if they were a single database.
3. Should be 'location independent' which means the user is unaware of where the data is located, and it is possible to move the data from one physical location to another without affecting the user.

1.6.1.5 In-Memory Column Formats Data

A columnar format in-memory allows faster data retrieval when only a few columns in a table need to be selected during query processing or aggregation. Data in a column are kept together in-memory in columnar format. A single memory access, therefore, loads many values at the column. An address increment to a next memory address for the next value is fast when compared to first computing the address of the next value, which is not the immediate next address. The following example explains the in-memory columnar format.

EXAMPLE 1.13

Consider analysis of monthly sales of chocolates on ACVMs (Example 1.6) in company's annual profit reports.

(i) How does sales analysis become easy in-memory columnar format?
(ii) How does during an analysis the access is made to few columns in place of from entire datasets?

SOLUTION

All the column 1 values for several days' record is physically together in-memory at consecutive addresses. All the column 2 values are then physically together at the next successive addresses. Then, the column 3 and other columns store at the columnar database in-memory.

The data stores for each record order in successive columns, so that the 100th entry at column 1 and the 100th entry for column 2 belong to the same record and same input accessible from a single row-key. Column vector refers to a vector whose elements are values at column fields.

Analytics, therefore, can be executed faster when data is in the column format, and more rows and few columns need to be selected during analysis. Successive days' sales of each flavour of chocolate stores in successive values in one column from row r to (r + 30) in a month, thirty row-keys for 30 days, and 365 row keys in a year.

Aggregation functions and other analysis functions are easy to run due to successive memory addresses for sales for each day for each flavour. Examples of aggregation functions are sum, count, maximum, minimum, average, minimum and maximum deviation from a specified value.

Online Analytical Processing (OLAP) in real-time transaction processing is fast when using in-memory column format tables. OLAP enables real-time analytics. The CPU accesses all columns in a single instance of access to the memory in columnar format in-memory data-storage.

Online Analytical Processing (OLAP) enables online viewing of analyzed data and visualization up to the desired granularity (fineness or coarseness) enables view by rolling up (finer granulates to coarse granulates data) or drilling down (coarser granulates data to finer granulates). OLAP enables obtaining online summarized information and automated reports for a large database.

Metadata describes the data. Pre-storing of calculated values provide consistently fast response. Result formats from the queries are based on Metadata.

1.6.1.6 In-Memory Row Format Databases

A row format in-memory allows much faster data processing during OLTP (online transaction processing). Refer Example 1.13. Each row record has corresponding values in multiple columns and the on-line values store at the consecutive memory addresses in row format. A specific day's sale of five different chocolate flavours is stored in consecutive columns c to c+5 at memory. A single instance of memory accesses loads values of all five flavours at successive columns during online processing. For example, the total number of chocolates sold computes online. Data is in-memory row-formats in stream and event analytics. The stream analytics method does continuous computation that happens as data is flowing through the system. Event analytics does computation on event and use event data for tracking and reporting events.

1.6.1.7 Enterprise Data-Store Server and Data Warehouse

Enterprise data, after *data cleaning* process, integrate with the server data at warehouse. Enterprise data server use data from several distributed sources which store data using various technologies. All data *merge* using an integration tool. Integration enables collective viewing of the datasets at the data warehouse (Figure 1.3).

Enterprise data integration may also include integration with application(s), such as analytics, visualization, reporting, business intelligence and knowledge discovery. Heterogeneous systems execute complex integration processes when integrating at an enterprise server or data warehouse. Complex application-integration means the integration of heterogeneous application architectures and processes with the databases at the enterprise. Enterprise data warehouse store the databases, and data stores after integration, using tools from number of sources.

Online contents associated with Practice Exercises 1.9 and 1.10 give details of commercial solutions for complex application-integration of processes.

Following are some standardised business processes, as defined in the Oracle application-integration architecture:

1. Integrating and enhancing the existing systems and processes
2. Business intelligence
3. Data security and integrity
4. New business services/products (Web services)
5. Collaboration/knowledge management
6. Enterprise architecture/SOA
7. e-commerce
8. External customer services
9. Supply chain automation/visualization
10. Data centre optimization

Figure 1.6 shows Steps 1 to 5 in enterprise data integration and management with Big Data for high performance computing using local and cloud resources for analytics, applications and services.

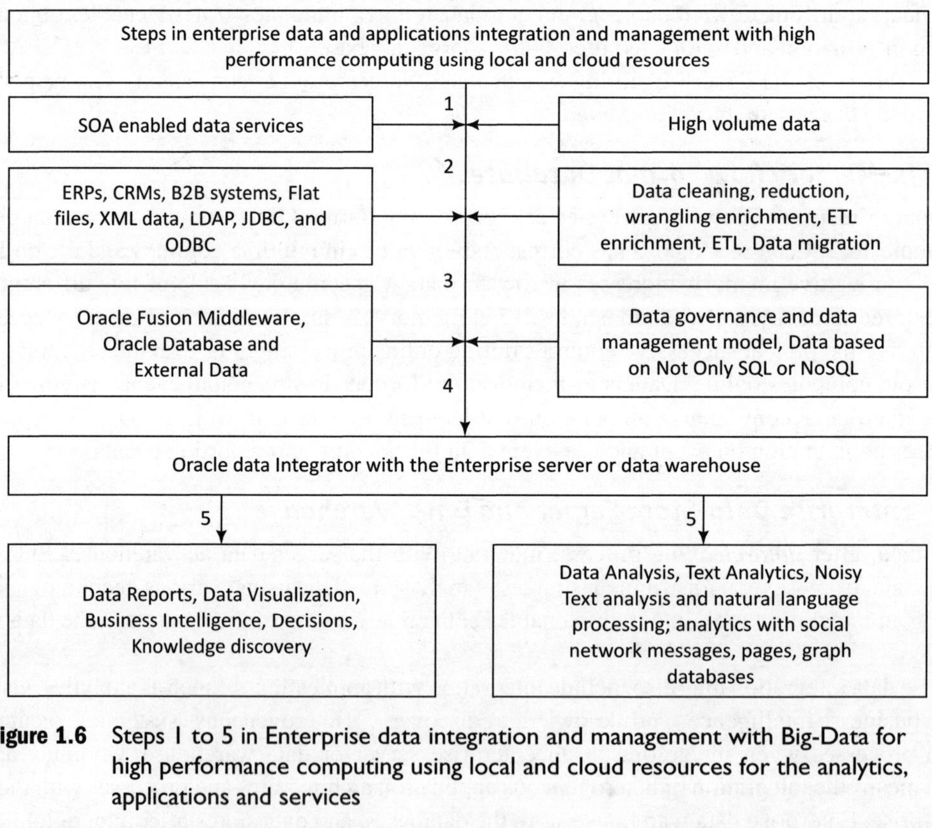

Figure 1.6 Steps 1 to 5 in Enterprise data integration and management with Big-Data for high performance computing using local and cloud resources for the analytics, applications and services

1.6.2 Big Data Storage

Following subsections describe Big Data storage concepts:

1.6.2.1 *Big Data NoSQL or Not Only SQL*

NoSQL databases are considered as semi-structured data. Big Data Store uses NoSQL. NOSQL stands for No SQL or Not Only SQL. The stores do not integrate with applications using SQL. NoSQL is also used in cloud data store. Features of NoSQL are as follows:

NOSQL or Not Only SQL class of non-relational data storage systems, flexible data models and multiple schemas

1. It is a class of non-relational data storage systems, and the flexible data models and multiple schema:
   (i) Class consisting of uninterrupted key/value or big hash table [Dynamo (Amazon S3)]
   (ii) Class consisting of unordered keys and using JSON (PNUTS)
   (iii) Class consisting of ordered keys and semi-structured data storage systems [BigTable, Cassandra (used in Facebook/Apache) and HBase]
   (iv) Class consisting of JSON (MongoDB)
   (v) Class consisting of name/value in the text (CouchDB)
   (vi) May not use fixed table schema
   (vii) Do not use the JOINS
   (viii) Data written at one node can replicate at multiple nodes, therefore Data storage is fault-tolerant,
   (ix) May relax the ACID rules during the Data Store transactions.
   (x) Data Store can be partitioned and follows CAP theorem (out of three properties, consistency, availability and partitions, at least two must be there during the transactions)

Consistency means all copies have the same value like in traditional DBs. *Availability* means at least one copy is available in case a partition becomes inactive or fails. For example in web applications, the other copy in other partition is available. *Partition* means parts which are active but may not cooperate as in the distributed DBs.

1.6.2.2 *Coexistence of Big Data, NoSQL and Traditional Data Stores*

Figure 1.7 shows co-existence of data at server, SQL, RDBMS with NoSQL and Big Data at Hadoop, Spark, Mesos, S3 or compatible Clusters.

Table 1.4 gives various data sources for Big Data along with its examples of usages and the tools used.

Table 1.4 Various data sources and examples of usages and tools

Data Source	Examples of Usages	Example of Tools
Relational databases	Managing business applications involving structured data	Microsoft Access, Oracle, IBM DB2, SQL Server, MySQL, PostgreSQL Composite, SQL on Hadoop [HPE (Hewlett Packard Enterprise) Vertica, IBM BigSQL, Microsoft Polybase, Oracle Big Data SQL]

(Contd.)

Data Source	Examples of Usages	Example of Tools
Analysis databases (MPP, columnar, In-memory)	High performance queries and analytics	Sybase IQ, Kognitio, Terradata, Netezza, Vertica, ParAccel, ParStream, Infobright, Vectorwise,
NoSQL databases (Key-value pairs, Columnar format, documents, Objects, graph)	Key-value pairs, fast read/write using collections of name-value pairs for storing any type of data; Columnar format, documents, objects, graph DBs and DSs	Key-value pair databases: Riak DS (Data Store), OrientDB, Column format databases (HBase, Cassandra), Document oriented databases: CouchDB, MongoDB; Graph databases (Neo4j, Tetan)
Hadoop clusters	Ability to process large data sets across a distributed computing environment	Cloudera, Apache HDFS
Web applications	Access to data generated from web applications	Google Analytics, Twitter
Cloud data	Elastic scalable outsourced databases, and data administration services	Amazon Web Services, Rackspace, GoogleSQL
Individual data	Individual productivity	MS Excel, CSV, TLV, JSON, MIME type
Multidimensional	Well-defined bounded exploration especially popular for financial applications	Microsoft SQL Server Analysis Services
Social media data	Text data, images, videos	Twitter, LinkedIn

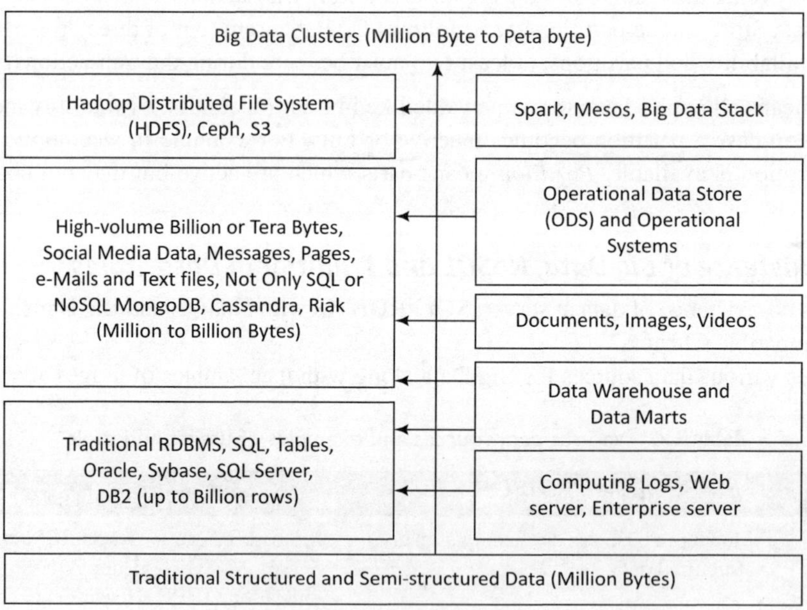

Figure 1.7 Coexistence of RDBMS for traditional server data, NoSQL and Hadoop, Spark and compatible Big Data Clusters

1.6.3 Big Data Platform

A Big Data platform supports large datasets and volume of data. The data generate at a higher velocity, in more varieties or in higher veracity. Managing Big Data requires large resources of MPPs, cloud, parallel processing and specialized tools. Bigdata platform should provision tools and services for:

1. storage, processing and analytics,
2. developing, deploying, operating and managing Big Data environment,
3. reducing the complexity of multiple data sources and integration of applications into one cohesive solution,
4. custom development, querying and integration with other systems, and
5. the traditional as well as Big Data techniques.

Data management, storage and analytics of Big data captured at the companies and services require the following:

1. New innovative non-traditional methods of storage, processing and analytics
2. Distributed Data Stores
3. Creating scalable as well as elastic virtualized platform (cloud computing)
4. Huge volume of Data Stores
5. Massive parallelism
6. High speed networks
7. High performance processing, optimization and tuning
8. Data management model based on Not Only SQL or NoSQL
9. In-memory data column-formats transactions processing or *dual in-memory data* columns as well as row formats for OLAP and OLTP
10. Data retrieval, mining, reporting, visualization and analytics
11. Graph databases to enable analytics with social network messages, pages and data analytics
12. Machine learning or other approaches
13. Big data sources: Data storages, data warehouse, Oracle Big Data, MongoDB NoSQL, Cassandra NoSQL
14. Data sources: Sensors, Audit trail of Financial transactions data, external data such as Web, Social Media, weather data, health records data.

1.6.3.1 Hadoop

Big Data platform consists of Big Data storage(s), server(s) and data management and business intelligence software. Storage can deploy Hadoop Distributed File System (HDFS), NoSQL data stores, such as HBase, MongoDB, Cassandra. HDFS system is an open source storage system. HDFS is a scaling, self-managing and self-healing file system.

The Hadoop system packages application-programming model. Hadoop is a scalable and reliable parallel computing platform. Hadoop manages Big Data distributed databases. Figure 1.8 shows Hadoop based Big Data environment. Small height cylinders represent MapReduce and big ones represent the Hadoop.

1.6.3.2 Mesos

Mesos v0.9 is a resources management platform which enables sharing of cluster of nodes by multiple frameworks and which has compatibility with an open analytics stack [data processing (Hive, Hadoop, HBase, Storm), data management (HDFS)].

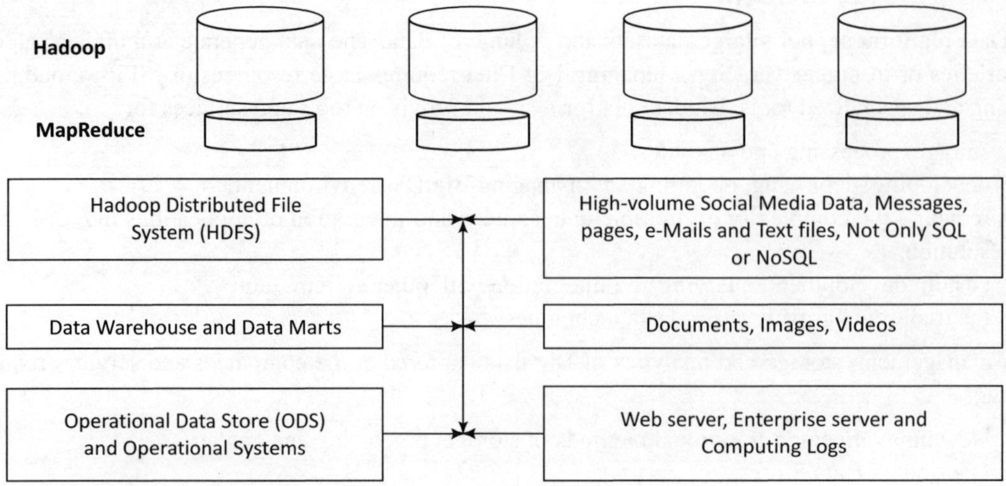

Figure 1.8 Hadoop based Big Data environment

1.6.3.3 Big Data Stack

A stack consists of a set of software components and data store units. Applications, machine-learning algorithms, analytics and visualization tools use Big Data Stack (BDS) at a cloud service, such as Amazon EC2, Azure or private cloud. The stack uses cluster of high performance machines.

Table 1.5 gives Big Data management, storage and processing tools.

Table 1.5 Tools for Big Data environment

Types	Examples
MapReduce	Hadoop, Apache Hive, Apache Pig, Cascading, Cascalog, mrjob (Python MapReduce library), Apache S4, MapR, Apple Acunu, Apache Flume, Apache Kafka
NoSQL Databases	MongoDB, Apache CouchDB, Apache Cassandra, Aerospike, Apache HBase, Hypertable
Processing	Spark, IBM BigSheets, PySpark, R, Yahoo! Pipes, Amazon Mechanical Turk, Datameer, Apache Solr/Lucene, ElasticSearch
Servers	Amazon EC2, S3, GoogleQuery, Google App Engine, AWS Elastic Beanstalk, Salesforce Heroku
Storage	Hadoop Distributed File System, Amazon S3, Mesos

1.6.4 Big Data Analytics

DBMS or RDBMS manages the traditional databases. Data analysis need pre-processing of raw data and gives information useful for decision making. Analysis brings order, structure and meaning to the collection of data. Data is collected and analyzed to answer questions, test the hypotheses or disprove theories.

1.6.4.1 Data Analytics Definition

Data Analytics can be formally defined as the statistical and mathematical data analysis that clusters, segments, ranks and predicts future possibilities. An important feature of data analytics is its predictive, forecasting and prescriptive capability. Analytics uses historical data and forecasts new values or results. Analytics suggests techniques which will provide the most efficient and beneficial results for an enterprise. Data analysis helps in finding business intelligence and helps in decision making.

Data analysis can be defined as,

> "Analysis of data is a process of inspecting, cleaning, transforming and modeling data with the goal of discovering useful information, suggesting conclusions and supporting decision making." (*Wikipedia*)

1.6.4.2 *Phases in Analytics*

Analytics has the following phases before deriving the new facts, providing business intelligence and generating new knowledge.

1. *Descriptive analytics* enables deriving the additional value from visualizations and reports
2. *Predictive analytics* is advanced analytics which enables extraction of new facts and knowledge, and then predicts/forecasts
3. *Prescriptive analytics* enable derivation of the additional value and undertake better decisions for new option(s) to maximize the profits
4. *Cognitive analytics* enables derivation of the additional value and undertake better decisions.

Analytics integrates with the enterprise server or data warehouse.

Figure 1.9 shows an overview of a reference model for analytics architecture. The figure also shows on the right-hand side the Big Data file systems, machine learning algorithms and query languages and usage of the Hadoop ecosystem.

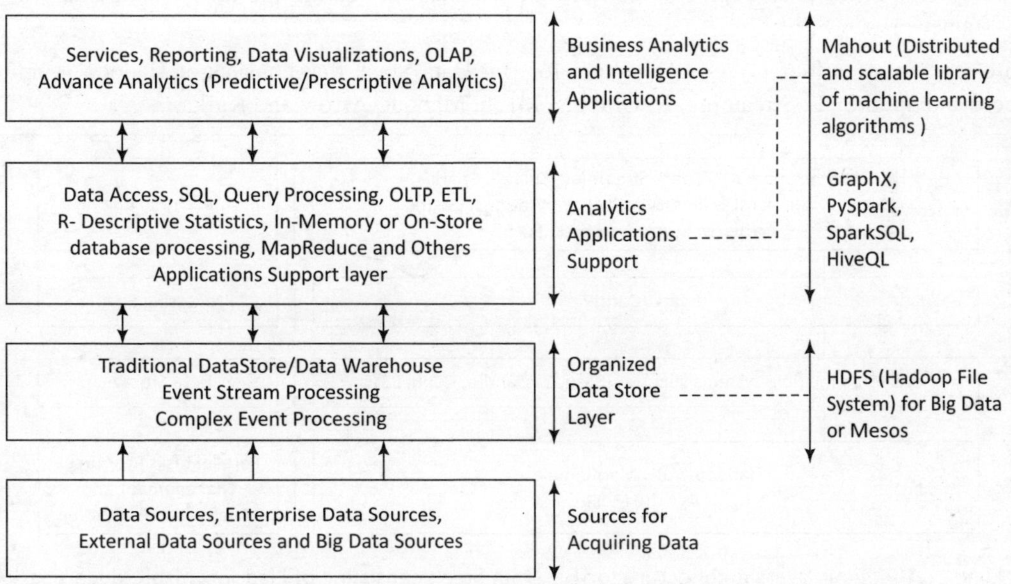

Figure 1.9 Traditional and Big Data analytics architecture reference model

The captured or stored data require a well-proven strategy to calculate, plan or analyze. When Big Data combine with high-powered data analysis, enterprise achieve valued business-related tasks. Examples are:

- Determine root causes of defects, faults and failures in minimum time.
- Deliver advertisements on mobiles or web, based on customer's location and buying habits.
- Detect offender before that affects the organization or society.

1.6.4.3 Berkeley Data Analytics Stack (BDAS)

BDAS consisting of the data processing, data management and resource management layers

The importance of Big Data lies in the fact that what one does with it rather than how big or large it is. Identify whether the gathered data is able to help in obtaining the following findings: 1) cost reduction, 2) time reduction, 3) new product planning and development, 4) smart decision making using predictive analytics and 5) knowledge discovery.

Big Data analytics need innovative as well as cost effective techniques. BDAS is an open-source data analytics stack for complex computations on Big Data.[11] It supports efficient, large-scale in-memory data processing, and thus enables user applications achieving three fundamental processing requirements; accuracy, time and cost.

Berkeley Data Analytics Stack (BDAS) consists of data processing, data management and resource management layers. Following list these:

1. Applications, AMP-Genomics and Carat run at the BDAS. Data processing software component provides in-memory processing which processes the data efficiently across the frameworks. AMP stands for Berkeley's Algorithms, Machines and Peoples Laboratory.
2. Data processing combines *batch*, *streaming* and *interactive* computations.
3. Resource management software component provides for sharing the infrastructure across various frameworks.

Figure 1.10 shows a four layers architecture for Big Data Stack that consists of Hadoop, MapReduce, Spark core and SparkSQL, Streaming, R, GraphX, MLib, Mahout, Arrow and Kafka.

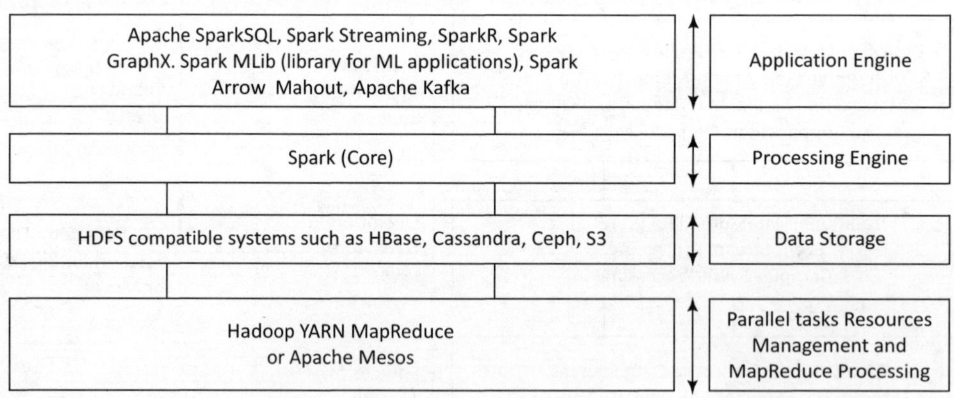

Figure 1.10 Four layers architecture for Big Data Stack consisting of Hadoop, MapReduce, Spark core and SparkSQL, Streaming, R, GraphX, MLib, Mahout, Arrow and Kafka

[11] https://amplab.cs.berkeley.edu/software/

Self-Assessment Exercise linked to LO 1.5

1. What are the traditional systems for data storage? How does in-memory columnar format help in OLAP? Give an example. ○●●
2. What are hierarchical and object oriented records? ○○●
3. What is enterprise server? How does enterprise server data store differ from a web server? ○●●
4. What are the functions of data integration software? How does application integration along with data integration help in business processes, intelligence and analytics? ○●●
5. What are the functions in SQL? List the differences between SQL data store and NoSQL data store. ●●●
6. How does a Big Data stack help in analytics tasks? ○●●
7. How does a Berkeley Data analytics stack help in analytics tasks? ○○●

1.7 BIG DATA ANALYTICS APPLICATIONS AND CASE STUDIES

LO 1.6

Big Data use cases, applications and case studies in various fields, such as marketing, sales and healthcare

Many applications such as social network and social media, cloud applications, public and commercial web sites, scientific experiments, simulators and e-government services generate Big Data. Big Data analytics find applications in many areas. Some of the popular ones are marketing, sales, health care, medicines, advertising etc. Following subsections describe these use cases, applications and case studies.

1.7.1 Big Data in Marketing and Sales

Data are important for most aspect of marketing, sales and advertising. Customer Value (CV) depends on three factors – quality, service and price. Big data analytics deploy large volume of data to identify and derive intelligence using predictive models about the individuals. The facts enable marketing companies to decide what products to sell.

A definition of marketing is the creation, communication and delivery of *value* to customers. Customer (desired) value means what a customer desires from a product. Customer (perceived) value means what the customer believes to have received from a product after purchase of the product. Customer value analytics (CVA) means analyzing what a customer really needs. CVA makes it possible for leading marketers, such as Amazon to deliver the consistent customer experiences. Following are the five application areas in order of the popularity of Big Data use cases:

1. CVA using the inputs of evaluated purchase patterns, preferences, quality, price and post sales servicing requirements
2. Operational analytics for optimizing company operations
3. Detection of frauds and compliances
4. New products and innovations in service
5. Enterprise data warehouse optimization.

An example of fraud is borrowing money on already mortgage assets. Example of timely compliances means returning the loan and interest installments by the borrowers.

A few examples in service-innovation are as follows: A company develops software and then offers services like Uber. Another example is of a company which develops software for hiring services, and then offers costly construction machinery and equipment. That service company might be rendering the services by hiring themselves from the multiple sources and locations of big construction companies.

Big data is providing marketing insights into (i) most effective content at each stage of a sales cycle, (ii) investment in improving the customer relationship management (CRM), (iii) addition to strategies for increasing customer lifetime value (CLTV), (iv) lowering of customer acquisition cost (CAC). Cloud services use Big Data analytics for CAC, CLTV and other metrics, the essentials in any cloud-based business

Big Data revolutionizes a number of areas of marketing and sales. Louis Columbus[12] recently listed the ways of usages. (Refer online content for solution of Practice Exercise 1.14.)

Contextual marketing means using an online marketing model in which a marketer sends to potential customers the targeted advertisements, which are based on the search terms during latest browsing patterns usage by customers.

For example, if a customer is searching an airline for flights on a specific date from Delhi to Bangalore, then a smart travel agency targeting that customer through advertisements will show him/her, at specific intervals, better options for another airline or different but cheap dates for travel or options in which price reduction occurs gradually.

The following example explains the use of search engine optimization.

EXAMPLE 1.14

Why does the search engine at a company product website of a travel agency need optimization?

SOLUTION

Consider a travel agency website offers search results for flights between two destinations *A* and *C*, which do not connect directly. The search shows the results in order of increasing travel cost through stopover at an intermediate airport *B*. Assume that search results show up just mechanically, without embedding intelligence and optimization. The customers find uncomfortable solutions with such searches. The searches show the cheaper options but sometimes show results such as the customer would reach C through stopover at B after 8 hours or even sometimes on the next day.

The searches at that travel agency do not consider stopover options at different Bs, options available in different airlines to cut short travel time from B to C at cheaper costs, or newly introduced flights. The searches therefore need optimization for parameters of travel cost, multiple intermediate stopovers and airlines that will provide maximum customer convenience as well as cost.

Big data algorithms and advanced analytics techniques enable price optimization for a given product or service, and pricing decisions, especially in the commodity driven industries where products are inelastic. Inelastic product means a situation in which the service, required quantity or supply of a product remains unaffected by the price changes.

1.7.1.1 Big Data Analytics in Detection of Marketing Frauds

Big data deployment in fraud detection related to marketing

Fraud detection is vital to prevent financial loses to users. Fraud means someone deceiving deliberately. For example, mortgaging the same assets to multiple financial institutions, compromising customer data and transferring customer

[12] https://www.forbes.com/sites/louiscolumbus/2016/05/09/ten-ways-big-data-is-revolutionizing-marketing-and-sales/#5e90bc21cff3

information to third party, falsifying company information to financial institutions, marketing product with compromising quality, marketing product with service level different from the promised, stealing intellectual property, and much more.

Big Data analytics enable fraud detection. Big Data usages has the following features–for enabling detection and prevention of frauds:

1. Fusing of existing data at an enterprise data warehouse with data from sources such as social media, websites, blogs, e-mails, and thus enriching existing data
2. Using multiple sources of data and connecting with many applications
3. Providing greater insights using querying of the multiple source data
4. Analyzing data which enable structured reports and visualization
5. Providing high volume data mining, new innovative applications and thus leading to new business intelligence and knowledge discovery
6. Making it less difficult and faster detection of threats, and predict likely frauds by using various data and information publicly available.

1.7.1.2 Big Data Risks

Large volume and velocity of Big Data provide greater insights but also associate risks with the data used. Data included may be erroneous, less accurate or far from reality. Analytics introduces new errors due to such data.

> Big Data large volume, velocity and veracity data provide greater insights for data security, privacy, increasing costs, and bad analytics and bad data risks associates

Big Data can cause potential harm to individuals. For example, when someone puts false or distorted data about an individual in a blog, Facebook post, WhatsApp groups or tweets, the individual may suffer loss of educational opportunity, job or credit for his/her urgent needs. A company may suffer financial losses.

Five data risks, described by Bernard Marr are data security, data privacy breach, costs affecting profits, bad analytics and bad data.[13] (Solutions in online content accompanying the book for Practice Exercise 1.15)

Companies need to take risks of using Big Data and design appropriate risk management procedures. They have to implement robust risk management processes and ensure reliable predictions. Corporate, society and individuals must act with responsibility.

1.7.1.3 Big Data Credit Risk Management

Financial institutions, such as banks, extend loans to industrial and household sectors. These institutions in many countries face credit risks, mainly risks of (i) loan defaults, (ii) timely return of interests and principal amount. Financing institutions are keen to get insights into the following:

1. Identifying high credit rating business groups and individuals,
2. Identifying risk involved before lending money
3. Identifying industrial sectors with greater risks
4. Identifying types of employees (such as daily wage earners in construction sites) and businesses (such as oil exploration) with greater risks
5. Anticipating liquidity issues (availability of money for further issue of credit and rescheduling credit installments) over the years.

[13] https://www.linkedin.com/pulse/5-biggest-risks-big-data-bernard-marr

The insight using Big Data decreases the default rates in returning of loan, greater accuracy in issuing credit and faster identification of the non-payment or fraud issues of the loan receiving entities. (Example of fraud is using the same assets for drawing credit from two or more institutions or hiding earlier outstanding loans and loan defaults.)

One innovative way to manage credit risks and liquidity risks is use of available data and Big Data. High volume of data analysis gives greater insight into the default patterns, emerging patterns and thus credit risks.

Big Data analytics monitors social media, interactions data, contact addresses, mobile numbers, website, financial status, activities or job changes to find the emerging credit risk that may affect a customer loan returning capacity. Digital footprints across social media provide a valuable alternative data source for credit risk analysis. The data companies assist in rating the customer in application processing and also during the period of repayment of a loan. Friends on Facebook and their credit rating, comments and assets posted also help in determining the risks.

The data insights from the analytics lead to credit and liquidity risk management and faster reactions. Three benefits are (i) minimize the non-payments and frauds, (ii) identifying new credit opportunities, new customers and revenue streams, thereby broadening the company high credit rating customers base and (iii) marketing to low risk businesses and households.

1.7.1.4 Big Data And Algorithmic Trading

Wikipedia gives a definition of algorithm trading as follows: "Algorithmic trading is a process for executing orders utilizing automated and pre-programmed trading instructions to account for variables such as price, timing and volume. It makes use of complex formulas, combined with mathematical models and human oversight, to make decisions to buy or sell financial securities on an exchange." (*Investopedia.com*) Complex mathematics computations enable algorithmic trading and business investment decisions to buy and sell. The input data are insights gathered from the risk analysis of market data. Big data bigger volume, velocity and variety in the trading provide an edge over other trading entities

1.7.2 Big Data and Healthcare

Big Data analytics in health care use the following data sources: (i) clinical records, (ii) pharmacy records, (3) electronic medical records (4) diagnosis logs and notes and (v) additional data, such as deviations from person usual activities, medical leaves from job, social interactions. Healthcare analytics using Big Data can facilitate the following:

> Big Data large volume, velocity and veracity data provide greater insights in health care systems and medicine

1. Provisioning of value-based and customer-centric healthcare,
2. Utilizing the 'Internet of Things' for health care
3. Preventing fraud, waste, abuse in the healthcare industry and reduce healthcare costs (Examples of frauds are excessive or duplicate claims for clinical and hospital treatments. Example of waste is unnecessary tests. Abuse means unnecessary use of medicines, such as tonics and testing facilities.)
4. Improving outcomes
5. Monitoring patients in real time.

Value-based and customer-centric healthcare means cost effective patient care by improving healthcare quality using latest knowledge, usages of electronic health and medical records and improving coordination among the healthcare providing agencies, which reduce avoidable overuse and healthcare costs.

Healthcare Internet of Things create unstructured data. The data enables the monitoring of the devices data for patient parameters, such as glucose, BP, ECGs and necessities of visiting physicians.

Prevention of fraud, waste, and abuse uses Big Data predictive analytics and help resolve excessive or duplicate claims in a systematic manner. The analytics of patient records and billing help in detecting, anomalies such as overutilization of services in short intervals, different hospitals in different locations simultaneously, or identical prescriptions for the same patient filed from multiple locations.

Improving outcomes is possible by accurately diagnosing patient conditions, early diagnosis, predicting problems such as congestive heart failure, anticipating and avoiding complications, matching treatments with outcomes and predicting patients at risk for disease or readmission.

Patient real-time monitoring uses machine learning algorithms which process real-time events. They provide physicians the insights to help them make life-saving decisions and allow for effective interventions. The process automation sends the alerts to care providers and informs them instantly about changes in the condition of a patient.

1.7.3 Big Data in Medicine

Big Data analytics deploys large volume of data to identify and derive intelligence using predictive models about individuals. Big Data driven approaches help in research in medicine which can help tpatients. Big Data offers potential to transform medicine and the healthcare system—Dr. Eric Schadt and Sastry Chilukuri.[14]

Following are some findings: building the health profiles of individual patients and predicting models for diagnosing better and offer better treatment,

1. Aggregating large volume and variety of information around from multiple sources the DNAs, proteins, and metabolites to cells, tissues, organs, organisms, and ecosystems, that can enhance the understanding of biology of diseases. Big data creates patterns and models by data mining and help in better understanding and research,
2. Deploying wearable devices data, the devices data records during active as well as inactive periods, provide better understanding of patient health, and better risk profiling the user for certain diseases,

1.7.4 Big Data in Advertising

The impact of Big Data is tremendous on the digital advertising industry. The digital advertising industry sends advertisements using SMS, e-mails, WhatsApp, LinkedIn, Facebook, Twitter and other mediums.

> Big data real time analytics for faster insights, emerging trends and patterns, and gain actionable insights for facing competitions from similar products in digital advertising and building relationships

Big Data technology and analytics provide insights, patterns and models, which relate the media exposure of all consumers to the purchase activity of all consumers using multiple digital channels. Big Data help in identity management and can provide an advertising mix for building better branding exercises.

Big Data captures data of multiple sources in large volume, velocity and variety of data unstructured and enriches the structured data at the enterprise data warehouse. Big data real time analytics provide emerging trends and patterns, and gain actionable insights for facing competitions from similar products. The data helps digital advertisers to discover new relationships, lesser competitive regions and areas.

Success from advertisements depend on collection, analyzing and mining. The new insights enable the personalization and targeting the online, social media and mobile for advertisements called hyper-localized advertising.

---

[14] https://www.mckinsey.com/industries/pharmaceuticals-and-medical-products/our-insights/the-role-of-big-data-in-medicine

Nielson Inc. CEO, Mitch Barns described Big Data's big impact on the future of advertising. Advertising nowadays limits no longer to TV, radio and print. Advertisers use along with these multiple devices and mediums. For example, advertisement of the introduction of new courses by an institution or introduction of new flights by an Airline needs media other than TV and requires targeted and cost effective solutions.

Advertising on digital medium needs optimization. Too much usage can also effect negatively. Phone calls, SMSs, e-mail-based advertisements can be nuisance if sent without appropriate researching on the potential targets. The analytics help in this direction. The usage of Big Data after appropriate filtering and elimination is crucial enabler of BigData Analytics with appropriate data, data forms and data handling in the right manner.

Self-Assessment Exercise linked to LO 1.6

1. How do data inputs help in Big Data based Customer value analytics? ○○●
2. How does Big Data help in credit risk management in financial institutions? ○○●
3. How does Big Data Analytics enable prevention of fraud, waste and abuse of healthcare system? ○●●
4. Why does Big Data offer the potential to transform the medicine and healthcare system? ○●●
5. Why are the Cloud services used for Big Data Analytics for customer acquisition, customer lifetime value analytics and other metrics? ●●●

KEY CONCEPTS

3Vs
4Vs
application integration
Big Data analytics
Big Data characteristics
Big Data types
Business intelligence
Business process
cloud
cost of acquisition
credit risk
CSV data format
customer value
data
data analytics
data architecture
database
data cleaning
data consumption
data cube
data ingestion
data integration
data management
data mining
data patterns
data pre-processing
data source
data store
data warehouse
descriptive analytics
distributed database
ELT
Enterprise server
ETL
event analytics
Hadoop
Hash-key value pair
in-memory column format
in-memory row format
JSON data format
key-value pair
knowledge discovery
logic machine
machine learning
Management Information Services
Massively Parallel Processing
multi-dimensional data cube
multi structured data
Noise
NoSQL
OLAP
OLTP
online analytic processing
Outlier
predictive analytics
prescriptive analytics
RDBMS
real-time analytics
semi-structured data
SQL
stream analytics
structured data
web data

Learning Outcomes

LO 1.1

- Data is raw information, usually in the form of facts or statistics that one can analyze or that one can use for further calculations and computations.
- Data are structured, semi-structured, multi-structured and unstructured.
- Four types of Big Data: Social networks and web data, transactions and business processes data, machine generated data and human generated data.
- Analytics helps in gathering, organizing, analyzing and reporting meaningful patterns in data. Analytics leads to communicate to user the meaningful patterns in data, helps data visualization, predictions and knowledge discovery. .
- Big Data is a collection of datasets very large and /or complex that traditional data processing applications are inadequate and has 3Vs or 4Vs as characteristics—volume, velocity, variety and veracity.

LO 1.2

- Scalability is the capability of a system to handle increasing workloads. Analytics scalability for Big Data uses distributed computing model. Scalability means multiple independent computational tasks submitted to multiple computing nodes which function coherently.
- Analytic scalability for Big Data deploys parallel computing, massive parallel processing, cloud computing, cluster or grid computing.

LO 1.3

- Big Data architecture provides the logical and/or physical layout/structure of how big data will be stored, accessed and managed.
- Data architecture design consists of five logical layers: data sources identification, ingestion and acquisition, data storage, data processing and consumption, such as applications, analysis, visualizations, business processes, business intelligence, knowledge discovery.
- Management functions enable controlling, protecting, delivering and enhancing the value of data and information assets.

LO 1.4

- Data sources are data-repositories, such as RDBMS and spreadsheets from which the application seeks the data. Data sources are machines which drive data from data creating programs or form data store.
- High quality data means data with five R's: Relevancy, recency, range, robustness and reliability.
- Data-Store exports after pre-processing the data from data sources, servers, computers and service to the cloud. Cloud services and platforms can be sourced from IBM, Microsoft, Oracle, Google, Amazon, Rackspace, TCS and Tata Communications.
- Big Data applications use cloud services: Hadoop Cloud Service (IBM BigInsight, Microsoft Azure HD Insights, Oracle Big Data Cloud Services and SQL on Hadoop. SQL used are Apache SparkSQL, GoogleSQL, IBM BigSQL, HPE Vertica, Microsoft Polybase, Oracle Big Data SQL or Google BigQuery).

LO 1.5

- Traditional systems use structured or semi-structured data, tables, RDBMS such as DB2, MySQL, JSON and XML represent semi-structured data and are best suited for representing object oriented records or hierarchical data records.
- Big Data systems use new innovative non-traditional methods of storage, processing and analytics. They use distributed Data Stores. Big Data tools use scalable as well as elastic virtualized platform (cloud computing), huge volume of Data Stores, massive parallelism, high-speed networks and graph databases. Analytics deploy social network messages and pages for Big Data analytics.
- Big Data storage can deploy Hadoop distributed file system, MongoDB, NoSql data stores. For example, HBase, Cassandra. HDFS are open source storage systems.

LO 1.6

- Data are important for most aspects of marketing and sales, credit risks management, fraud detection, healthcare, medicine and advertising.
- Big data analytics deploy a large volume of data to identify and derive intelligence using predictive models about individuals.
- Big Data analytics enables fraud detection and helps manage credit risks and liquidity risks.
- Big Data analytics also uses social media, interactions data, contact addresses, mobile numbers, website, financial status, activities or job changes for credit risk analysis.

Objective Type Questions

Select one correct-answer option for each questions below:

1.1 Data are usually required for: ○○●
(a) Calculation
(b) Planning
(c) Input to a software tool
(d) Calculate, plan, analyze and visualize something, obtaining intelligence or discover new knowledge

1.2 *Web data* is (i) data present at web servers, (ii) data accessible using the Internet, (iii) data which can be used in mobile and web applications, (iv) information in the form of documents and other web resources, (v) data at documents and resources which are accessible from the Internet such that each resource identifies by an URL of the data server store, and (vi) data in the documents interlink by hypertext links, and accessed using the Internet. ○●●
(a) all are true (b) all except ii
(c) all except iii and iv (d) ii to vi

1.3 Big Data analytics (i) deal with a large amount of data, (ii) manage, organize, process, analyze, share using traditional software tools running on require hundreds of computing nodes and large volume of storage devices, (iii) deal with fast generation of needed data, (iv) results in quick processing, analysis and usages, and has increased complexity due to multi-structured, (v) need processing of complex applications with large datasets, and (vi) deal with variety of data, various forms and formats, such as sensors, machine generated data, social media data ○○●
(a) iii to vii (b) all except ii
(c) all except vi (d) all

1.4 Big Data has (i) structured, semi-structured, and unstructured data formats, (ii) unstructured data format, (iii) stores as column-oriented, record-based, graph-based, hashed or key/value pairs, (iv) stores as column-oriented, row-oriented, and graph-based, (v) batch or real time processing needs, and (vi) real time processing needs. ○●●

(a) i, iii and v (b) ii to v
(c) ii, iv and vi (d) all except ii

1.5 Data architecture design considers: ○○●

(a) Four design layers with the lowest being identification of internal and external data sources
(b) Four design layers with the lowest being ingestion strategy and acquisition, and next identification of internal and external data sources.
(c) Five layers with data consumption for analytics, business processes, business intelligence, data mining, pattern recognition and knowledge discovery
(d) Five layers with data storage, processing and analytics being the highest layer

1.6 Data sources: ○●●

(i) In the Microsoft Applications are of two types: machine data sources and file data sources.
(ii) In the Oracle applications are of three types: file data sources, database data sources and logic-machine data sources which use the network functions or a server.
(iii) In the IBM applications are of three types: machine data sources, database instances data sources and file data sources.
(iv) Can be sensors, sensor networks, devices, controllers, intelligent edge nodes in industrial M2M and signals from the machines.
(v) Data is of high quality if they enable all the required operations, analysis, decisions, planning, and knowledge discovery.
(vi) A definition for high quality data can be five R's: Relevancy, recency, range, robustness and reliability.
(vii) Data noise, outliers, missing-values and duplicate-values affect the data quality. Applications such as analytics, data visualization and data mining need data cleaning, integrity, enrichment, editing, reduction and/or wrangling.

(a) all (b) all except ii, v and vi
(c) all except vi (d) all except ii and iii

1.7 NoSQL features are: ○●●

(i) The systems do not use the concept of joins (in distributed data storage systems)
(ii) Data written at one node and replicates to multiple nodes, therefore identical and fault-tolerant, and can be partitioned
(iii) Can offer relaxation in one or more of the ACID properties
(iv) Out of three properties (consistency, availability and partitions), two are at least present for the application/service/process.

(a) i, ii and iii (b) i to iv
(c) all except iii (d) all except ii

1.8 Big Data platform should enable the following: ○○●

(i) Storage, processing and analytics
(ii) Developing, deploying, operating and managing a Big Data environment in an enterprise
(iii) Reducing the complexity of multiple data sources and integrate the applications into one cohesive solution
(iv) Custom development, querying and integration with other systems involve the complexity
(v) Needs traditional as well as new and innovative techniques.

(a) i to iii (b) all except v
(c) all except iv (d) all are true

1.9 *Vertical scalability* means scaling up by: ○○●
(a) Using the giving system resources and increasing the systems analytics, reporting and visualization capabilities requiring additional ways to solve problems of greater complexities
(b) Adding computers in parallel
(c) Adding computers serially
(d) Adding computers in serially as well as parallel

1.10 *Grid Computing* refers to (i) distributed computing, in which a group of computers from several locations are connected with each other to achieve a common task, (ii) remotely connected computers using Internet, (iii) computer resources heterogeneously and geographically disperse, (iv) a group of computers that might spread over remotely forming a grid, (v) computing using cloud, and (vi) computations and no under-performance even on failure of any of the participating nodes. ○●●
(a) all (b) all except ii, v and vi
(c) all except vi (d) all except ii and iii

1.11 Cloud computing environment (i) performs parallel and distributed computing for processing and analyzing large datasets on computing nodes, (ii) is on-demand service (iii) enables software, infrastructure and platform resource pooling, (iv) has scalability, (v) has no accountability, and (vi) has restricted network access. ○●●
(a) all are true (b) all except v
(c) i to iv (d) all except vi

1.12 Predictive analytics (i) predicts the trends, (ii) enable undertaking of the preventive maintenance in future from the earlier analyzes of equipment and device failure rates, (iii) enable managing the future campaigns and adopting integrated marketing strategy using previous studies of effect of campaigns at different media types, regions, targeted age groups, (iv) predicts by identifying patterns, clusters with similar behaviour, and (v) predicts based on earlier anomalous features detection, anomaly detection and filtering. ○○●
(a) i to iii (b) all except iv
(c) all except v (d) all are true

1.13 Automatic Chocolate Vending Machines company can use for selling (i) event analytics followed next by predictive analytics, (ii) manage each flavour supply-chain maintenance with optimization, (iii) manage the regular preventive maintenance of the machines, (iv) predict about changes in user preferences for chocolates in general and for specific flavours and (v) predict future festive season sales, (vi) visualize with finer and coarse granulates and multi-dimensional data cubes, (vii) predicts declining or rising sales, and (viii) plan strategies for boosting sales. ●●●
(a) iv, v and vii (b) all except iii and viii
(c) all (d) all except vi

1.14 Use Cases for Marketing and Sales Application areas are: (i) customer value analytics using the inputs of evaluated purchase patterns preferences, quality, price and post sales servicing requirements, (ii) operational analytics for company operations optimization, (iii) detection of frauds and compliances, (iv) new products and services innovation, and (v) enterprise Data Warehouse Optimization. ○●●
(a) ii to v
(b) all except ii
(c) all five and have popularity in order from (i) to (v)
(d) all except iii

1.15 Big Data usage risks are: (i) data security risk, (ii) data privacy risk, (iii) cost affecting the profits, (iv) bad analytics results, (v) bad data, and (vi) data filtering. ○○●

(a) i and ii (b) all except iii
(c) all except v (d) all are true except vi

1.16 Automotive Maintenance Service Center Application in a company can (i) use analytics followed by predictive analytics, (ii) predict failure of components from periodic analysis of data, (iii) provide emergency services, (iv) improve the quality of components in future cars, (v) record driver rash driving habits and issue warnings, (vi) understand customer preferences, (vii) manage regular preventive maintenance of the automobile, (viii) visualization with finer and coarse granulates and multi-dimensional data cubes for maintenance needs, (viii) predict declining or rising sales, and (ix) plan strategies for boosting sales. ●●●
(a) i to vii (b) all except iv and vii
(c) all except vi, viii and ix (d) all except vii and viii

Review Questions

1.1 Describe the data, web data and Big Data. **(LO 1.1)** ○○●

1.2 Draw a diagram showing evolution of Big Data and their characteristics over the time as size, complexity increased and as unstructured data increased. **(LO 1.1)** ●●●

1.3 What do you mean by 3Vs characteristics of Big Data? What are the challenges faced from large growth in volume of data? **(LO 1.1)** ○●●

1.4 What do you mean by analytical scalability? What are vertical scalability and horizontal scalability? **(LO 1.2)** ○○●

1.5 Explain uses of massive parallel processing and cluster computing in Big Data scenario. **(LO 1.2)** ○●●

1.6 Describe grid computing features. Compare these with cluster computing. **(LO 1.2)** ○○●

1.7 Define Big Data architecture. Draw five layers in architecture design and explain functions in each layer. **(LO 1.3)** ○○●

1.8 What do you mean by data management? List the data management functions. **(LO 1.3)** ○●●

1.6 What are the data sources considered in Microsoft Storage applications, IBM databases and Oracle Data Stores? **(LO 1.4)** ●●●

1.9 What do you mean by the data noise, outliers, duplicate data and data anomaly? Why does the filtering require during pre-processing? Explain the following data processing steps: inspecting, cleaning, transforming, modeling and visualizing data. **(LO 1.4)** ○●●

1.10 Show using a figure how data store export using machine data sources and file data sources, computers, web servers, web services, Amazon, Rackspace and Hadoop cloud services. **(LO 1.4)** ●●●

1.11 How do the table rows in MySQL database export to Amazon AWS and Rackspace? **(LO 1.4)** ●●●

1.12 Define distributed databases. How do they differ from distributed Data Stores? Describe features of distributed database databases. **(LO 1.6)** ○●●

1.13 How does the data analytics enable predictive, forecasting and prescriptive capabilities? How does the data analytics enable use of historical data to forecast potential values or results? Describe methods of analytics results reporting and visualization. **(LO 1.6)** ●●●

1.14 What are the requirements for data management, storage and analytics of captured Big data at the Companies and services? **(LO 1.6)** ○●●

1.15 Explain traditional and Big Data analytics architecture reference models. **(LO 1.6)** ●●●

1.16 Describe ways of usages of Big Data analytics in marketing, sales and advertising. **(LO 1.6)** ○○●

1.17 What are the risks in Big Data usages? How does Big Data used in credit risk management? **(LO 1.6)** ○●●

1.18 Describe ways of usages of Big Data analytics in healthcare systems and medicine. **(LO 1.6)** ○●●

Practice Exercises

1.1 Diagrammatically show sources of structured, semi-structured, multi-structured and unstructured data. **(LO 1.1)** ○○●

1.2 Give examples of data resources at the enterprise server of an education institution. **(LO 1.1)** ○○●

1.3 List the unstructured data forms used in 'Automotive Components and Predictive Automotive Maintenance Services'. **(LO 1.1)** ○●●

1.4 List usages of Big Data analytics in a company for car manufacturing, marketing, sales and maintenance of car service centres. **(LO 1.1)** ●●●

1.5 Estimate how many massively parallel processing nodes will be required to process data at 4 Tera instructions per second when a single processor processes 1 Gega instructions per second. Assume 10% time is taken up in inter-process communications. **(LO 1.2)** ○○●

1.6 Show architectural design layers in 'Automotive Components and Predictive Automotive Maintenance Services'. **(LO 1.3)** ○●●

1.7 Take examples given in Examples 1.9. Consider example of a table in a student examination grade sheet for a semester. Fill the fields with presume values for two students in the same semester in the same course. Create CSV and JSON files. What are the benefits you can foresee in using JSON file in this case? **(LO 1.4)** ●●●

1.8 Take a student grade sheet in a semester examination in a course. Fill the presumed values for a student. Now create the hash and key-value pairs associated with a hash in traditional data. **(LO 1.5)** ●●●

1.9 Give details of the features of IBM IIS and Oracle Data Integrator. **(LO 1.5)** ○○●

1.10 Give details of features of integration and application integration solutions: Microsoft SQL-Server Integration-Services (SSIS), Informatica and Pentaho data-integration, SAS data-management advanced and SAP® BusinessObjects™ Integration. **(LO 1.5)** ○●●

1.11 What are the analytics phases? Take example of automotive maintenance and services. How will the results of analytics be used? **(LO 1.5)** ○●●

1.12 How will RDBMS make tables for the sales data of ACVMs? **[Refer Example 1.6(i)] (LO 1.5)** ○○●

1.13 Write five applications for NoSQL Databases? **(LO 1.5)** ○●●

1.14 Give details of Louis Columbus ten ways using which Big Data analytics is revolutionizing marketing and sales. **[Section 1.7.1] (LO 1.6)** ○○●

1.15 Describe five data risks, described by Bernard Marr. **[Section 1.7.1.2] (LO 1.6)** ○○●

Chapter 2

Introduction to Hadoop

LEARNING OBJECTIVES

After studying this chapter, you will be able to:

- **LO 2.1** Get conceptual understanding of Hadoop core, components of Hadoop ecosystem, and streaming and pipe interfaces for inputs to MapReduce
- **LO 2.2** Get understanding of Hadoop Distributed File System (HDFS), and physical-organiza¬tion of nodes for computing at clusters of large-scale files
- **LO 2.3** Get knowledge of MapReduce Daemon framework, and MapReduce programming model
- **LO 2.4** Get knowledge of functions of Hadoop YARN, management and scheduling of resources, and parallel processing of the application-tasks
- **LO 2.5** Get introduced to functions of Hadoop ecosystem-tools

RECALL FROM CHAPTER 1

Requirements for Big Data processing and analytics are:

1. Huge volume of data stores
2. Flexible, scalable and distributed storage and computations
3. Distributed data blocks and tasks, and processing at the clusters
4. Mapping of the data at the physical nodes
5. Reducing the complexity of multiple data sources, and sending the computational results to the applications
6. Developing, deploying, operating and managing in Big Data environment of an enterprise

7. Integration of solutions into a cohesive solution
8. Uses of large resources of MPPs, cloud, specialized tools and parallel processing and use of high speed networks [Section 1.5.3].

Big Data store should also manage the variety of data formats. Hadoop is scalable and parallel computing platform to handle Big Data (Section 1.6.3.1, Figure 1.8). Hadoop distributed file system design is for storing and analytics of Big Data. HDFS packages Big Data in a distributed data store along with processing using a programming model.

This chapter focuses on Hadoop, its ecosystem, HDFS based programming model, MapReduce, Yarn, and introduces to ecosystem components, such as AVRO, Zookeeper, Ambari, HBase, Hive, Pig and Mahout.

2.1 INTRODUCTION

A programming model is *centralized* computing of data in which the data is transferred from multiple distributed data sources to a central server. Analyzing, reporting, visualizing, business-intelligence tasks compute centrally. Data are inputs to the central server.

> Programming models of centralized computing of data, and the distributed computing of data sets at the multiple computing and data nodes

An enterprise collects and analyzes data at the enterprise level. The computations are at an enterprise server or data warehouse integrated with the applications (Figure 1.6). An example is computations using Oracle application integration architecture (Section 1.6.1.7). The computing nodes need to connect to a central system through high-speed networks.

Assume that a centralized server does the function of collection, storing and analyzing. For example, at an ACVM Company enterprise server. The data at the server gets collected from a large number of ACVMs which the company locates in multiple cities, areas and locations. The server also receives data from social media (Example 1.6 (i)). Applications running at the server does the following analysis:

1. Suggests a strategy for filling the machines at minimum cost of logistics
2. Finds locations of high sales such as gardens, playgrounds etc.
3. Finds days or periods of high sales such as Xmas etc.
4. Finds children's preferences for specific chocolate flavors
5. Finds the potential region of future growth
6. Identifies unprofitable machines
7. Identifies need of replicating the number of machines at specific locations.

Another programming model is distributed computing that uses the databases at multiple computing nodes with data sharing between the nodes during computation. Distributed computing in this model requires the cooperation (sharing) between the DBs in a transparent manner. Transparent means that each user within the system may access all the data within all databases as if they were a single database. A second requirement is location independence. Analysis results should be independent of geographical locations. The access of one computing node to other nodes may fail due to a single link failure.

The following example shows why the simply scaling out and division of the computations on a large number of processors may not work well due to data sharing between distributed computing nodes.

EXAMPLE 2.1

Consider a jigsaw Puzzle Ravensburger Beneath the Sea (5000 pieces). Children above 14 years of age will assemble the pieces in order to solve the puzzle. What will be the effect on time intervals for solution in three situations, when 4, 100 and 200 children simultaneously attempt the solution.

SOLUTION

Let the time taken by a single child to solve the puzzle be T. Assume 4 children sit together and solve the puzzle by dividing the tasks. Each child assembles one-fourth part of the picture for which they pick the pieces from a common basket (Distributed computing and centralized data model).

Alternatively, each child assembles one-fourth part of the picture for which the pieces are distributed in four baskets. The child in case does not find a piece in his/her basket, then searches for it in another basket (Distributed databases and distributed computing tasks with data sharing model).

Partitioning of assembling jobs into four has an issue. A child may complete his/her part much later than the remaining children. Beneath-the-sea portion is too complex, while upper-depth-sea portion is just plain. The children combine all four parts and finally complete the puzzle. Each one has to look into the other three parts to find a match and complete the task. Time taken to solve the puzzle is [$T/4 + T_I$ (4) + T_C (4)], where T_I (4) is the time taken in seeking from others the pieces not available to a child during intermediate phases, and T_C (4) in combining the results of the four children. Scaling factor is slightly less than 4. The proposed distributed model works well.

Assume a second situation in which 100 children assemble their parts of 50 pieces each, and finally combine all 100 parts and complete the puzzle. Each child must seek a piece, not available with her/him during the intermediate phase. Combining also becomes difficult and a time-consuming exercise compared to the four children case because each child now matches the results with the remaining 99 counterparts to arrive at the final solution. The time taken to solve the puzzle is [$T/100 + T_I$ (100) + T_C (100)], where T_I (100) and T_C (100) are the time taken in seeking pieces not available with the child and combining results of 100 children, respectively. Scaling is by factor less than 100. The distributed model has issues like sharing pieces, seeking pieces not available and combining issues. Issues are at the intermediate as well as at the end stages.

If 200 children attempt to solve the puzzle simultaneously at the same time then finally combining all 200 portions of the Beneath the Sea, the integration of 200 portions will be tedious and will be a far more time-consuming exercise than with 4 or 100. The time taken to solve the puzzle is [$T/200 + T_I$ (200) + T_C (200)], where T_I (200) and T_C (200) is the time taken in seeking the pieces not available and combining, respectively. Scaling up is by factor much less than 200 and may even be less than even 100. The distributed model with pieces sharing between the children is unsatisfactory because T_I (200) + T_C (200) < T/200.

Problem of inter-children interactions exponentially grows with the number of children in the proposed distributed model with seeking pieces in intermediate phases. Time TI becomes significantly high.

Alternatively, the picture parts and corresponding pieces of each part distribute to each participating child distinctly (Distributed computing model with no data sharing). Time TI taken in seeking a piece not available with him/her is zero. The time taken in joining the assembled picture portions is only at the end. Problem of inter-children interactions during solving the puzzle does not exist.

Traditionally, a program when executes calls the data inputs. Centralized computing model requires few communication overheads. Distributed computing model requires communication overheads for seeking data from a remote source when not available locally, and arrive at the final result. The completion of computations will take more and more time when the number of distributed computing nodes increase.

Distributed pieces of codes as well as the data at the computing nodes Transparency between data nodes at computing nodes do not fulfil for Big Data when distributed computing takes place using data sharing between local and remote. Following are the reasons for this:

- Distributed data storage systems do not use the concept of joins.
- Data need to be fault-tolerant and data stores should take into account the possibilities of network failure. When data need to be partitioned into data blocks and written at one set of nodes, then those blocks need replication at multiple nodes. This takes care of possibilities of network faults. When a network fault occurs, then replicated node makes the data available.
- Big Data follows a theorem known as the CAP theorem. The CAP states that out of three properties (consistency, availability and partitions), two must at least be present for applications, services and processes.

Recall Table 1.2. Consider distributed computing model which requires no sharing between data nodes. The model is equivalent to distribution of the picture's parts and corresponding pieces of each part to each participating child distinctly. Multiple tasks of an application also distribute, run using machines associated with multiple data nodes and execute at the same time in parallel.

The application tasks and datasets needed for computations distribute at a number of geographic locations and remote servers. The enterprise uses MPPs or computing clusters when datasets are too large. Application is divided in number of tasks and sub-tasks. The sub-tasks get inputs from data nodes at the same cluster. The results of sub-tasks aggregate and communicate to the application. The aggregate results from each cluster collect using APIs at the application.

(i) Big Data Store Model

A model for Big Data store is as follows:

Data store in file system consisting of data blocks (physical division of data). The data blocks are distributed across multiple nodes. Data nodes are at the racks of a cluster. Racks are scalable. A Rack has multiple data nodes (data servers), and each cluster is arranged in a number of racks.

Data Store model of files in data nodes in racks in the clusters Hadoop system uses the data store model in which storage is at clusters, racks, data nodes and data blocks. Data blocks replicate at the DataNodes such that a failure of link leads to access of the data block from the other nodes replicated at the same or other racks.

(ii) Big Data Programming Model

Big Data programming model is that application in which application jobs and tasks (or sub-tasks) is scheduled on the same servers which store the data for processing.

> Big Data programming model: application jobs run on the same servers which store the data for processing, and parallel running of the jobs

Job means running an assignment of a set of instructions for processing. For example, processing the queries in an application and sending the result back to the application *is a job*. Other example is instructions for sorting the examination performance data is a job.

Job scheduling means assigning a job for processing following a schedule. For example, scheduling after a processing unit finishes the previously assigned job, scheduling as per specific sequence or after a specific period.

Hadoop system uses the programming model, where jobs or tasks are assigned and scheduled on the same servers which hold the data. Hadoop is one of the widely used technologies. Google and Yahoo use Hadoop. Hadoop creators created a cost-effective method to build search indexes. Facebook, Twitter and LinkedIn use Hadoop. IBM implemented BigInsights and uses licensed Apache Hadoop. Oracle implements Hadoop system with Big Data Appliance, IBM with Infosphere and Microsoft with Big Data solutions.

Following are important key terms and their meaning.

Cluster Computing refers to computing, storing and analyzing huge amounts of unstructured or structured data in a distributed computing environment. Each cluster forms by a set of loosely or tightly connected computing nodes that work together and many of the operations can be timed (scheduled) and can be realized as if from a single computing system. Clusters improve the performance, provide cost-effective and improved node accessibility compared to a single computing node. Each node of the computational cluster is set to perform the same task and sub-tasks, such as MapReduce, which software control and schedule.

Data Flow (DF) refers to flow of data from one node to another. For example, transfer of output data after processing to input of application.

Data Consistency means all copies of data blocks have the same values.

Data Availability means at least one copy is available in case a partition becomes inactive or fails. For example, in web applications, a copy in the other partition is available. Partition means parts, which are active but may not cooperate as in distributed databases (DBs).

Resources means computing system resources, i.e., the physical or virtual components or devices, made available for specified or scheduled periods within the system. Resources refer to sources such as files, network connections and memory blocks.

Resource management refers to managing resources such as their creation, deletion and controlled usages. The manager functions also includes managing the (i) availability for specified or scheduled periods, (ii) prevention of resource unavailability after a task finishes and (iii) resources allocation when multiple tasks attempt to use the same set of resources.

Horizontal scalability means increasing the number of systems working in coherence. For example, using MPPs or number of servers as per the size of the dataset. Processing different datasets of a large data store *running similar application* deploys the horizontal scalability.

Vertical scalability means scaling up using the giving system resources and increasing the number of tasks in the system. For example, extending analytics processing by including the reporting, business processing (BP), business intelligence (BI), data visualization, knowledge discovery and machine learning (ML) capabilities which require additional ways to solve problems of greater complexities and greater processing, storage and inter-process communication among the resources. Processing different datasets of a large data store *running multiple application* tasks deploys vertical scalability.

Ecosystem refers to a system made up of multiple computing components, which work together. That is similar to a biological ecosystem, a complex system of living organisms, their physical environment and all their inter-relationships in a particular unit of space.

Distributed File System means a system of storing files. Files can be for the set of data records, key-value pairs, hash key-value pairs, relational database or NoSQL database at the distributed computing nodes, accessible after referring to their resource-pointer using a master directory service, look-up tables or name-node server.

Hadoop Distributed File System means a system of storing files (set of data records, key-value pairs, hash key-value pairs or applications data) at distributed computing nodes according to Hadoop architecture and accessibility of data blocks after finding reference to their racks and cluster. NameNode servers enable referencing to data blocks.

Scalability of storage and processing means the execution using varying number of servers according to the requirements, i.e., bigger data store on greater number of servers when required and on smaller data when smaller data used on limited number of servers. Big Data Analytics require deploying the *clusters using the servers or cloud* for computing as per the requirements.

Utility Cloud-based Services mean infrastructure, software and computing platform services similar to utility services, such as electricity, gas, water etc. Infrastructure refers to units for data-store, processing and network. The IaaS, SaaS and PaaS are the services at the cloud (Section 1.3.3).

This chapter describes on Hadoop's core components, such as MapReduce, HDFS and YARN, and Hadoop ecosystem components, such as HBase, Hive, Pig, and Mahout. Section 2.2 describes Hadoop, its ecosystem components, streaming and pipe functions. Section 2.3 describes Hadoop physical architecture, Hadoop distributed file system (HDFS) basics. The section describes how to organize the nodes for computations using large-scale file system. Section 2.4 gives a conceptual understanding of MapReduce Daemon and functioning of Hadoop MapReduce framework.

Section 2.5 describes Hadoop YARN for managing of resources along with application tasks. Section 2.6 describes the Hadoop ecosystem interactions, analytics application support with AVRO, Zookeeper, Ambari, HBase, Hive, Pig and Mahout.

2.2 HADOOP AND ITS ECOSYSTEM

LO 2.1

Hadoop core, components of Hadoop ecosystem, streaming and pipe interfaces for inputs to MapReduce

Apache initiated the project for developing storage and processing framework for Big Data storage and processing. Doug Cutting and Machael J. Cafarelle the creators named that framework as Hadoop. Cutting's son was fascinated by a stuffed toy elephant, named Hadoop, and this is how the name Hadoop was derived.

The project consisted of two components, one of them is for data store in blocks in the clusters and the other is computations at each individual cluster in parallel with another.

Hadoop components are written in Java with part of native code in C. The command line utilities are written in shell scripts.

Hadoop is a computing environment in which input data stores, processes and stores the results. The environment consists of clusters which distribute at the cloud or set of servers. Each cluster consists of a string of data files constituting data blocks. The toy named Hadoop consisted of a stuffed elephant. The Hadoop system cluster stuffs files in data blocks. The complete system consists of a scalable distributed set of clusters.

Infrastructure consists of cloud for clusters. A cluster consists of sets of computers or PCs. The Hadoop platform provides a low cost Big Data platform, which is open source and uses cloud services. Tera Bytes of data processing takes just few minutes. Hadoop enables distributed processing of large datasets (above 10 million bytes) across clusters of computers using a programming model called MapReduce. The system characteristics are scalable, self-manageable, self-healing and distributed file system.

Scalable means can be scaled up (enhanced) by adding storage and processing units as per the requirements. Self-manageable means creation of storage and processing resources which are used, scheduled and reduced or increased with the help of the system itself. Self-healing means that in case of faults, they are taken care of by the system itself. Self-healing enables functioning and resources availability. Software detect and handle failures at the task level. Software enable the service or task execution even in case of communication or node failure.

The hardware scales up from a single server to thousands of machines that store the clusters. Each cluster stores a large number of data blocks in racks. Default data block size is 64 MB. IBM BigInsights, built on Hadoop deploys default 128 MB block size. Hadoop framework provides the computing features of a system of distributed, flexible, scalable, fault tolerant computing with high computing power. Hadoop system is an efficient platform for the distributed storage and processing of a large amount of data.

Hadoop enables Big Data storage and cluster computing. The Hadoop system manages both, large-sized structured and unstructured data in different formats, such as XML, JSON and text with efficiency and effectiveness. The Hadoop system performs better with clusters of many servers when the focus is on horizontal scalability. The system provides faster results from Big Data and from unstructured data as well.

Yahoo has more than 100000 CPUs in over 40000 servers running Hadoop, with its biggest Hadoop cluster running 4500 nodes as of March 2017, according to the Apache Hadoop website. Facebook has 2 major clusters: a cluster has 1100-machines with 8800 cores and about 12 PB raw storage. A 300-machine cluster with 2400 cores and about 3 PB (1 PB = 10^{15} B, nearly 2^{50} B) raw-storage. Each (commodity) node has 8 cores and 12 TB (1 TB = 10^{12}, nearly 2^{40} B = 1024 GB) of storage.

2.2.1 Hadoop Core Components

Figure 2.1 shows the core components of the Apache Software Foundation's Hadoop framework.

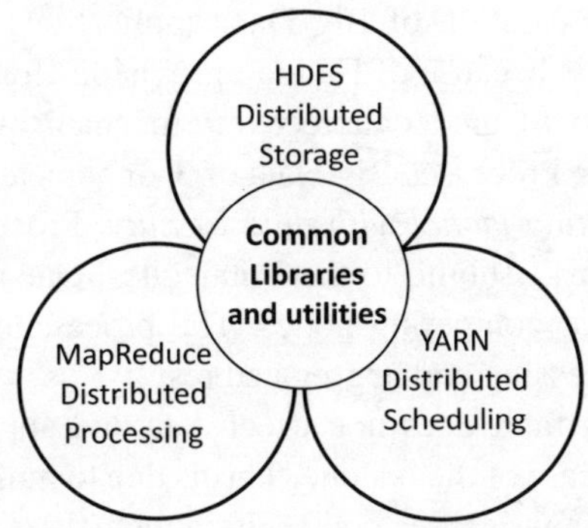

Figure 2.1 Core components of Hadoop

The Hadoop core components of the framework are:

1. Hadoop Common – The common module contains the libraries and utilities that are required by the other modules of Hadoop. For example, Hadoop common provides various components and interfaces for distributed file system and general input/output. This includes serialization, Java RPC (Remote Procedure Call) and file-based data structures.
2. Hadoop Distributed File System (HDFS) – A Java-based distributed file system which can store all kinds of data on the disks at the clusters.
3. MapReduce v1 – Software programming model in Hadoop 1 using Mapper and Reducer. The v1 processes large sets of data in parallel and in batches.
4. YARN – Software for managing resources for computing. The user application tasks or sub-tasks run in parallel at the Hadoop, uses scheduling and handles the requests for the resources in distributed running of the tasks.

5. MapReduce v2 – Hadoop 2 YARN-based system for parallel processing of large datasets and distributed processing of the application tasks.

2.2.1.1 Spark

Spark is an open-source cluster-computing framework of Apache Software Foundation. Hadoop deploys data at the disks. Spark provisions for in-memory analytics. Therefore, it also enables OLAP and real-time processing. Spark does faster processing of Big Data.

Spark has been adopted by large organizations, such as Amazon, eBay and Yahoo. Several organizations run Spark on clusters with thousands of nodes.

Spark is now increasingly becoming popular. Chapters 5 to 9 will describe Spark and its components in detail.

2.2.2 Features of Hadoop

Hadoop features are as follows:

1. *Fault-efficient scalable, flexible and modular design* which uses simple and modular programming model. The system provides servers at high scalability. The system is scalable by adding new nodes to handle larger data. Hadoop proves very helpful in storing, managing, processing and analyzing Big Data. Modular functions make the system flexible. One can add or replace components at ease. Modularity allows replacing its components for a different software tool.
2. *Robust design of HDFS*: Execution of Big Data applications continue even when an individual server or cluster fails. This is because of Hadoop provisions for backup (due to replications at least three times for each data block) and a data recovery mechanism. HDFS thus has high reliability.
3. *Store and process Big Data*: Processes Big Data of 3V characteristics.
4. *Distributed clusters computing model with data locality*: Processes Big Data at high speed as the application tasks and sub-tasks submit to the DataNodes. One can achieve more computing power by increasing the number of computing nodes. The processing splits across multiple DataNodes (servers), and thus fast processing and aggregated results.
5. *Hardware fault-tolerant*: A fault does not affect data and application processing. If a node goes down, the other nodes take care of the residue. This is due to multiple copies of all data blocks which replicate automatically. Default is three copies of data blocks.
6. *Open-source framework*: Open source access and cloud services enable large data store. Hadoop uses a cluster of multiple inexpensive servers or the cloud.
7. *Java and Linux based*: Hadoop uses Java interfaces. Hadoop base is Linux but has its own set of shell commands support.

Hadoop provides various components and interfaces for distributed file system and general input/output. This includes serialization, Java RPC (Remote Procedure Call) and file-based data structures in Java.

HDFS is basically designed more for batch processing. Streaming uses standard input and output to communicate with the Mapper and Reduce codes. Stream analytics and real-time processing poses difficulties when streams have high throughput of data. The data access is required faster than the latency at DataNode at HDFS.

YARN provides a platform for many different modes of data processing, from traditional batch processing to processing of the applications such as interactive queries, text analytics and streaming analysis.

These different types of data can be moved in HDFS for analysis using interactive query processing tools of Hadoop ecosystem components, such as Hive or can be provided to online business processes with the help of Apache HBase.

2.2.3 Hadoop Ecosystem Components

Hadoop ecosystem refers to a combination of technologies. Hadoop ecosystem consists of own family of applications which tie up together with the Hadoop. The system components support the storage, processing, access, analysis, governance, security and operations for Big Data.

> Hadoop ecosystem: AVRO, ZooKeeper, Pig, Hive, Sqoop, Ambari, Mahout, Spark, Flink and Flume

The system enables the applications which run Big Data and deploy HDFS. The data store system consists of clusters, racks, DataNodes and blocks. Hadoop deploys application programming model, such as MapReduce and HBase. YARN manages resources and schedules sub-tasks of the application.

HBase uses columnar databases and does OLAP. Figure 2.2 shows Hadoop core components HDFS, MapReduce and YARN along with the ecosystem. Figure 2.2 also shows Hadoop ecosystem. The system includes the application support layer and application layer components– AVRO, ZooKeeper, Pig, Hive, Sqoop, Ambari, Chukwa, Mahout, Spark, Flink and Flume. The figure also shows the components and their usages.

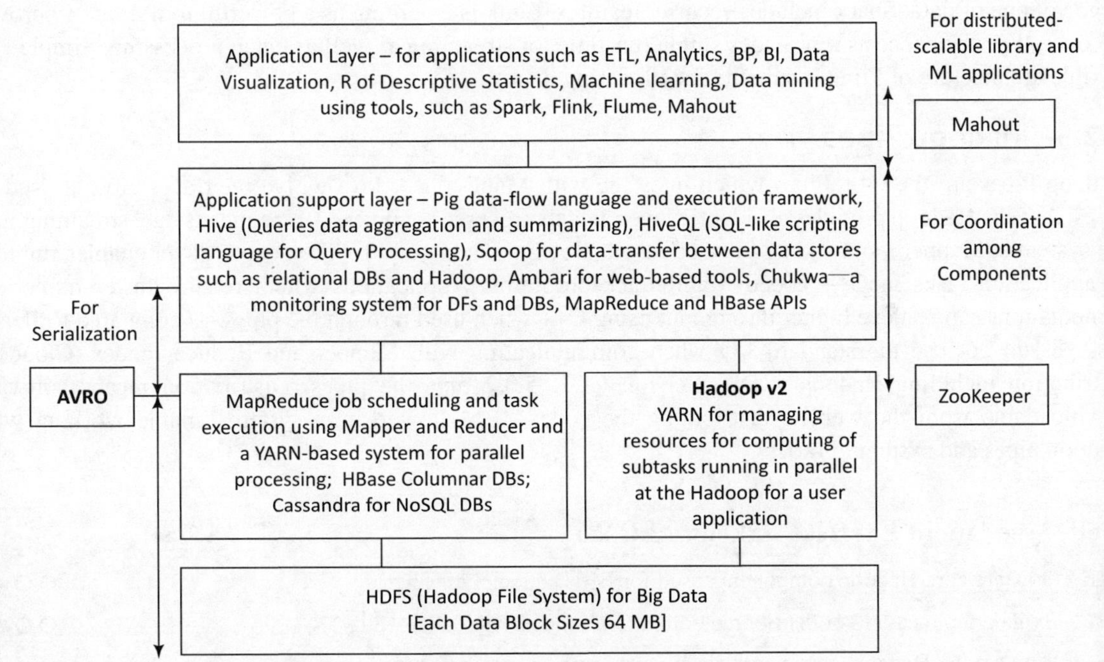

Figure 2.2 Hadoop main components and ecosystem components

The four layers in Figure 2.2 are as follows:

(i) Distributed storage layer
(ii) Resource-manager layer for job or application sub-tasks scheduling and execution
(iii) Processing-framework layer, consisting of Mapper and Reducer for the MapReduce process-flow

(iv) APIs at application support layer (applications such as Hive and Pig). The codes communicate and run using MapReduce or YARN at processing framework layer. Reducer output communicate to APIs (Figure 2.2).

AVRO enables data serialization between the layers. *Zookeeper* enables coordination among layer components.

The holistic view of Hadoop architecture provides an idea of implementation of Hadoop components of the ecosystem. Client hosts run applications using Hadoop ecosystem projects, such as Pig, Hive and Mahout.

Most commonly, Hadoop uses Java programming. Such Hadoop programs run on any platform with the Java virtual-machine deployment model. HDFS is a Java-based distributed file system that can store various kinds of data on the computers.

2.2.4 Hadoop Streaming

HDFS with MapReduce and YARN-based system enables parallel processing of large datasets. Spark provides in-memory processing of data, thus improving the processing speed. Spark and Flink technologies enable in-stream processing. The two lead stream processing systems and are more useful for processing a large volume of data. Spark includes security features. Flink is emerging as a powerful tool. Flink improves the overall performance as it provides single run-time for streaming as well as batch processing. Simple and flexible architecture of Flink is suitable for streaming data.

2.2.5 Hadoop Pipes

Hadoop Pipes are the C++ Pipes which interface with MapReduce. Java native interfaces are not used in pipes. Apache Hadoop provides an adapter layer, which processes in pipes. A pipe means data streaming into the system at Mapper input and aggregated results flowing out at outputs. The adapter layer enables running of application tasks in C++ coded MapReduce programs. Applications which require faster numerical computations can achieve higher throughput using C++ when used through the pipes, as compared to Java.

Pipes do not use the standard I/O when communicating with Mapper and Reducer codes. Cloudera distribution including Hadoop (CDH) version CDH 5.0.2 runs the pipes. Distribution means software downloadable from the website distributing the codes. IBM PowerLinux systems enable working with Hadoop pipes and system libraries.

Self-Assessment Exercise linked to LO 2.1

1. How are core Hadoop components used for Big Data analytics? ○○●
2. Explain the meaning of distributed computing model with data locality? ○○●
3. Why are the Hadoop system and ecosystem components shown in the four layers? Explain by an example. ●●●
4. Differentiate between MapReduce v1 and MapReduce v2. ○●●

Note: ○○● Level 1 & Level 2 category
○●● Level 3 & Level 4 category
●●● Level 5 & Level 6 category

2.3 HADOOP DISTRIBUTED FILE SYSTEM

LO 2.2

Hadoop Distributed File System (HDFS), and physical-organization of nodes for computing at clusters of large-scale files

Big Data analytics applications are software applications that leverage large-scale data. The applications analyze Big Data using massive parallel processing frameworks. HDFS is a core component of Hadoop. HDFS is designed to run on a cluster of computers and servers at cloud-based utility services. HDFS stores Big Data which may range from GBs (1 GB = 2^{30} B) to PBs (1 PB = 10^{15} B, nearly the 2^{50} B). HDFS stores the data in a distributed manner in order to compute fast. The distributed data store in HDFS stores data in any format regardless of schema. HDFS provides high throughput access to data-centric applications that require large-scale data processing workloads.

2.3.1 HDFS Data Storage

Hadoop data store concept implies storing the data at a number of *clusters*. Each cluster has a number of data stores, called *racks*. Each rack stores a number of DataNodes. Each DataNode has a large number of *data blocks.* The racks distribute across a cluster. The nodes have processing and storage capabilities. The nodes have the data in data blocks to run the application tasks. The data blocks *replicate by default at least on three DataNodes* in same or remote nodes. Data at the stores enable running the distributed applications including analytics, data mining, OLAP using the clusters. *A file, containing the data divides into data blocks. A data block default size is 64 MBs* (HDFS division of files concept is similar to Linux or virtual memory page in Intel x86 and Pentium processors where the block size is fixed and is of 4 KB).

Hadoop HDFS features are as follows:

(i) *Create*, *append*, *delete*, *rename* and *attribute* modification functions
(ii) Content of individual file cannot be modified or replaced but appended with new data at the end of the file
(iii) Write once but read many times during usages and processing
(iv) Average file size can be more than 500 MB.

The following is an example how the files store at a Hadoop cluster.

EXAMPLE 2.2

Consider a data storage for University students. Each student data, *stuData* which is in a file of size less than 64 MB (1 MB = 2^{20}B). A data block stores the full file data for a student of stuData_idN, where N = 1 to 500.

(i) How the files of each student will be distributed at a Hadoop cluster? How many student data can be stored at one cluster? Assume that each rack has two DataNodes for processing each of 64 GB (1 GB = 2^{30}B) memory. Assume that cluster consists of 120 racks, and thus 240 DataNodes.
(ii) What is the total memory capacity of the cluster in TB ((1 TB = 2^{40}B) and DataNodes in each rack?
(iii) Show the distributed blocks for students with ID= 96 and 1025. Assume default replication in the DataNodes = 3.
(iv) What shall be the changes when a stuData file size ≤ 128 MB?

SOLUTION

(i) Data block default size is 64 MB. Each students file size is less than 64MB. Therefore, for each student file one data block suffices. A data block is in a DataNode. Assume, for simplicity, each rack has two nodes each of memory capacity = 64 GB. Each node can thus store 64 GB/64MB = 1024 data blocks = 1024 student files. Each rack can thus store 2 × 64 GB/64MB = 2048 data blocks = 2048 student files. Each data block default replicates three times in the DataNodes. Therefore, the number of students whose data can be stored in the cluster = number of racks multiplied by number of files divided by 3 = 120 × 2048/3 = 81920. Therefore, the maximum number of 81920 stuData_IDN files can be distributed per cluster, with N = 1 to 81920.

(ii) Total memory capacity of the cluster = 120 × 128 MB = 15360 GB = 15 TB. Total memory capacity of each DataNode in each rack = 1024 × 64 MB = 64 GB.

(iii) Figure 2.3 shows a Hadoop cluster example, and the replication of data blocks in racks for two students of IDs 96 and 1025. Each stuData file stores at two data blocks, of capacity 64 MB each.

(iv) Changes will be that each node will have half the number of data blocks.

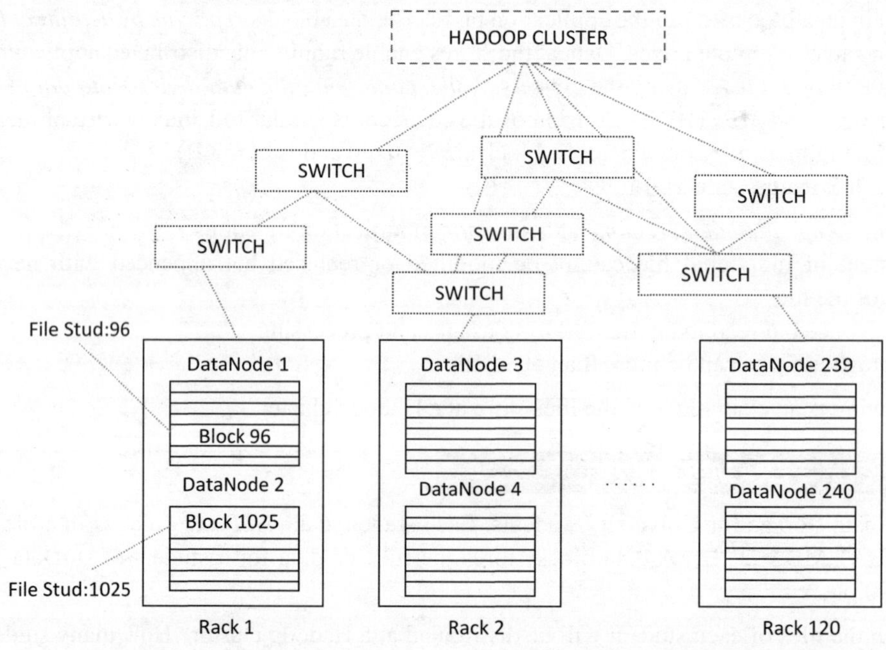

Figure 2.3 A Hadoop cluster example, and the replication of data blocks in racks for two students of IDs 96 and 1025

2.3.1.1 *Hadoop Physical Organization*

> Identification of data-blocks, DataNodes and Racks using MasterNodes and NameNodes for processing the data at slave nodes

The conventional file system uses directories. A directory consists of folders. A folder consists of files. When data processes, the data sources identify by pointers for the resources. A data-dictionary stores the resource pointers. Master tables at the dictionary store at a central location. (Section 1.5.1 for the details). The centrally stored tables enable administration easier when the data sources change during processing.

Similarly, the files, DataNodes and blocks need the identification during processing at HDFS. HDFS use the NameNodes and DataNodes. A NameNode stores the file's meta data. Meta data gives information about the file of user application, but does not participate in the computations. The DataNode stores the actual data files in the data blocks.

Few nodes in a Hadoop cluster act as NameNodes. These nodes are termed as MasterNodes or simply masters. The masters have a different configuration supporting high DRAM and processing power. The masters have much less local storage. Majority of the nodes in Hadoop cluster act as DataNodes and TaskTrackers. These nodes are referred to as slave nodes or slaves. The slaves have lots of disk storage and moderate amounts of processing capabilities and DRAM. Slaves are responsible to store the data and process the computation tasks submitted by the clients.

Figure 2.4 shows the client, master NameNode, primary and secondary MasterNodes and slave nodes in the Hadoop physical architecture.

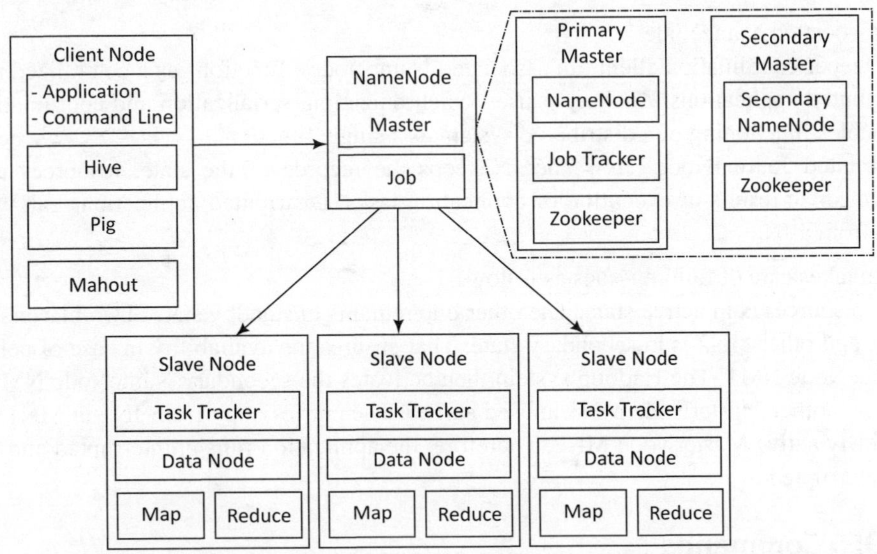

Figure 2.4 The client, master NameNode, MasterNodes and slave nodes

Clients as the users run the application with the help of Hadoop ecosystem projects. For example, Hive, Mahout and Pig are the ecosystem's projects. They are not required to be present at the Hadoop cluster. A single MasterNode provides HDFS, MapReduce and Hbase using threads in small to medium sized clusters. When the cluster size is large, multiple servers are used, such as to balance the load. The secondary NameNode provides NameNode management services and Zookeeper is used by HBase for metadata storage.

The MasterNode fundamentally plays the role of a coordinator. The MasterNode receives client connections, maintains the description of the global file system namespace, and the allocation of file blocks. It also monitors the state of the system in order to detect any failure. The Masters consists of three components NameNode, Secondary NameNode and JobTracker. The NameNode stores all the file system related information such as:

- The file section is stored in which part of the cluster
- Last access time for the files
- User permissions like which user has access to the file.

Secondary NameNode is an alternate for NameNode. Secondary node keeps a copy of NameNode meta data. Thus, stored meta data can be rebuilt easily, in case of NameNode failure. The JobTracker coordinates the parallel processing of data.

Masters and slaves, and Hadoop client (node) load the data into cluster, submit the processing job and then retrieve the data to see the response after the job completion.

2.3.1.2 *Hadoop 2*

Single NameNode failure in Hadoop 1 is an operational limitation. Scaling up was also restricted to scale beyond a few thousands of DataNodes and few number of clusters. Hadoop 2 provides the multiple NameNodes. This enables higher resource availability. Each MN has the following components:

- An associated NameNode
- Zookeeper coordination client (an associated NameNode), functions as a centralized repository for distributed applications. Zookeeper uses synchronization, serialization and coordination activities. It enables functioning of a distributed system as a single function.
- Associated JournalNode (JN). The JN keeps the records of the state, resources assigned, and intermediate results or execution of application tasks. Distributed applications can write and read data from a JN.

The system takes care of failure issues as follows:

One set of resources is in active state. The other one remains in standby state. Two masters, one MN1 is in active state and other MN2 is in secondary state. That ensures the availability in case of network fault of an active NameNode NM1. The Hadoop system then activates the secondary NameNode NM2 and creates a secondary in another MasterNode MN3 unused earlier. The entries copy from JN1 in MN1 into the JN2, which is at newly active MasterNode MN2. Therefore, the application runs uninterrupted and resources are available uninterrupted.

2.3.2 HDFS Commands

Figure 2.1 showed Hadoop common module, which contains the libraries and utilities. They are common to other modules of Hadoop. The HDFS shell is not compliant with the POSIX. Thus, the shell cannot interact similar to Unix or Linux. Commands for interacting with the files in HDFS require /bin/hdfs dfs <args>, where args stands for the command arguments. Full set of the Hadoop shell commands can be found at Apache Software Foundation website. `-copyToLocal` is the command for copying a file at HDFS to the local. `-cat` is command for copying to standard output (stdout). All Hadoop commands are invoked by the bin/Hadoop script. `% Hadoop fsck / -files -blocks` Table 2.1 gives the examples of command usages.

Table 2.1 Examples of usages of commands

HDFS shell command	Example of usage
-mkdir	Assume stu_filesdir is a directory of student files in Example 2.2. Then command for creating the directory is `$Hadoop hdfs-mkdir/user/stu_filesdir` creates the directory named stu_files_dir
-put	Assume file stuData_id96 to be copied at stu_filesdir directory in Example 2.2. Then `$Hadoop hdfs-put stuData_id96 /user/ stu_filesdir` copies file for student of id96 into stu_filesdir directory
-ls	Assume all files to be listed. Then `$hdfs hdfs dfs-ls` command does provide the listing.
-cp	Assume stuData_id96 to be copied from stu_filesdir to new students' directory newstu_filesDir. Then `$Hadoop hdfs-cp stuData_id96 /user/stu_filesdir newstu_filesDir` copies file for student of ID 96 into stu_filesdir directory

Self-Assessment Exercise linked to LO 2.2

1. (i) What does the create, append, delete, rename and attribute modification methods mean in the HDFS? (ii) Why is the content of an individual file not modified or replaced but appended at the end of the file? (iii) Why is the *write once but read many times* concept used in HDFS? ○○●
2. What are the functions of NameNode, DataNode, slave node and MasterNode? ○○●
3. What are the benefits of multiple MasterNodes? ○●●
4. What are the usages of meta data? ○●●
5. Make a data-store model using HDFS for SGPs, SGPAs and CGPAs of each student. Assume 50 UG and 10 PG courses offered at the university. Total intake capacity is 5000 each year. Each student information can extend up to 64 MB. How will the files of 5000 students be stored using HDFS? What shall be the minimum memory requirements in 20 years? (SGP means subject grade point awarded to a student, SGPA semester grade point average, and CGPA cumulative grade-point average.) ●●●

2.4 MapReduce FRAMEWORK AND PROGRAMMING MODEL

LO 2.3

MapReduce Daemon Framework and MapReduce Programming model for parallel processing very large data

Figure 2.4 showed MapReduce functions as integral part of the Hadoop physical organization. MapReduce is a programming model for distributed computing.

Mapper means software for doing the assigned task after organizing the data blocks imported using the keys. A key specifies in a command line of Mapper. The command maps the key to the data, which an application uses.

Reducer means software for reducing the mapped data by using the aggregation, query or user-specified function. The reducer provides a concise cohesive response for the application.

Aggregation function means the function that groups the values of multiple rows together to result a single value of more significant meaning or measurement. For example, function such as count, sum, maximum, minimum, deviation and standard deviation.

Querying function means a function that finds the desired values. For example, function for finding a best student of a class who has shown the best performance in examination.

MapReduce allows writing applications to process reliably the huge amounts of data, in parallel, on large clusters of servers. The cluster size does not limit as such to process in parallel. The parallel programs of MapReduce are useful for performing large scale data analysis using multiple machines in the cluster.

Features of MapReduce framework are as follows:

1. Provides automatic parallelization and distribution of computation based on several processors
2. Processes data stored on distributed clusters of DataNodes and racks
3. Allows processing large amount of data in parallel
4. Provides scalability for usages of large number of servers
5. Provides MapReduce batch-oriented programming model in Hadoop version 1
6. Provides additional processing modes in Hadoop 2 YARN-based system and enables required parallel processing. For example, for queries, graph databases, streaming data, messages, real-time OLAP and ad hoc analytics with Big Data 3V characteristics.

The following subsection describes Hadoop execution model using MapReduce Framework.

2.4.1 Hadoop MapReduce Framework

MapReduce provides two important functions. The distribution of job based on client application task or users query to various nodes within a cluster is one function. The second function is organizing and reducing the results from each node into a cohesive response to the application or answer to the query.

The processing tasks are submitted to the Hadoop. The Hadoop framework in turns manages the task of issuing jobs, job completion, and copying data around the cluster between the DataNodes with the help of JobTracker (Figure 2.4).

Daemon refers to a highly dedicated program that runs in the background in a system. The user does not control or interact with that. An example is MapReduce in Hadoop system [Collins English language dictionary gives one of Daemon meaning as 'a person who concentrates very hard or is very skilled at an activity and puts in lot of energy into it'].

MapReduce runs as per assigned Job by JobTracker, which keeps track of the job submitted for execution and runs TaskTracker for tracking the tasks. MapReduce programming enables job scheduling and task execution as follows:

A client node submits a request of an application to the JobTracker. A JobTracker is a Hadoop daemon (background program). The following are the steps on the request to MapReduce: (i) estimate the need of resources for processing that request, (ii) analyze the states of the slave nodes, (iii) place the mapping tasks in queue, (iv) monitor the progress of task, and on the failure, restart the task on slots of time available. The job execution is controlled by two types of processes in MapReduce:

1. The Mapper deploys map tasks on the slots. Map tasks assign to those nodes where the data for the application is stored. The Reducer output transfers to the client node after the data serialization using AVRO.
2. The Hadoop system sends the Map and Reduce jobs to the appropriate servers in the cluster. The Hadoop framework in turns manages the task of issuing jobs, job completion and copying data around the cluster between the slave nodes. Finally, the cluster collects and reduces the data to obtain the result and sends it back to the Hadoop server after completion of the given tasks.

The job execution is controlled by two types of processes in MapReduce. A single master process called JobTracker is one. This process coordinates all jobs running on the cluster and assigns map and reduce tasks to run on the TaskTrackers. The second is a number of subordinate processes called TaskTrackers. These processes run assigned tasks and periodically report the progress to the JobTracker.

Figure 2.4 showed the job execution model of MapReduce. Here the JobTracker schedules jobs submitted by clients, keeps track of TaskTrackers and maintains the available Map and Reduce slots. The JobTracker also monitors the execution of jobs and tasks on the cluster. The TaskTracker executes the Map and Reduce tasks, and reports to the JobTracker.

2.4.2 MapReduce Programming Model

MapReduce program can be written in any language including JAVA, C++ PIPEs or Python. Map function of MapReduce program do mapping to compute the data and convert the data into other data sets (distributed in HDFS). After the Mapper computations finish, the Reducer function collects the result of map and generates the final output result. MapReduce program can be applied to any type of data, i.e., structured or unstructured stored in HDFS.

The input data is in the form of file or directory and is stored in the HDFS. The MapReduce program performs two jobs on this input data, the Map job and the Reduce job. They are also termed as two phases—Map phase and Reduce phase. The map job takes a set of data and converts it into another set of data. The individual elements are broken down into tuples (key/value pairs) in the resultant set of data. The reduce job takes the output from a map as input and combines the data tuples into a smaller set of tuples. Map and reduce jobs run in isolation from one another. As the sequence of the name MapReduce implies, the reduce job is always performed after the map job.

> MapReduce and YARN based resource scheduling splits the jobs into subtasks which run across number of servers in parallel.

The MapReduce v2 uses YARN based resource scheduling which simplifies the software development. Here, the jobs can be split across almost any number of servers. For example, the ACVM Company can find the number of chocolates KitKat, Milk, Fruit and Nuts, Nougat and Oreo sold every hour at the number of ACVMs installed all over in the multiple cities on separate servers [Refer Example 1.6(i)]. A server maps the keys for KitKat and another for Oreo. It requires time to scan the hourly sales log sequentially. By contrast, MapReduce programmer can split the application task among multiple sub-tasks, say one hundred sub-tasks, where each sub-task processes the data of the selected set of ACVMs. The results of all the sub-tasks then aggregate to get the final result, hourly sales figures of each chocolate flavor from all ACVMs of the company. Finally, the aggregated hourly results appear from the hourly log of transactions filed at Hadoop DataNodes. The company enterprise server runs analytics and applications consider the results as if from a single server application. The following example shows the usage of HDFS and the map and reduce functions.

EXAMPLE 2.3

Consider Example 1.6(i) of ACVMs selling KitKat, Milk, Fruit and Nuts, Nougat and Oreo chocolates. Assume 24 files are created every hour for each day. The files are at file_1, file_2, …., file_24. Each file stores as key-value pairs as hourly sales log at the large number of machines.

(i) How will the large number of machines, say 5000 ACVMs hourly data for each flavor sales log store using HDFS? What will be the strategy to restrict the data size in HDFS?

(ii) How will the sample of data collected in a file for 0-1,1-2, … 12-13,13-14, 15-16, up to 23-24 specific hour-sales log for sales at a large number of machines, say 5000?

(iii) What will be the output streams of map tasks for feeding the input streams to the Reducer?

(iv) What will be the Reducer outputs?

SOLUTION

5000 machines send sales data every hour for KitKat, Milk, Fruit and Nuts, Nougat and Oreo chocolates, i.e., a total of 5 flavors. Assume each sales data size = 64 B, then data bytes 64 × 5 × 5000 B = 1600000 B will accumulate (append) each hour in a file.

Sales data are date-time stamped key-value pairs. Each of 24 hour hourly log files will use initially 24 data blocks at a DataNode and replicated at three DataNodes. A data file in one year will accumulate 1600000 × 24 × 365 B = 14016000000 B = nearly 16 GB. Each data block can store 64 MB. Therefore, 16 GB/64 MB = 250 data blocks in each file each year.

However, hourly and daily sales analytics is required only for managing supply chain for chocolate fill service and finding insight into sales during holidays and festival days compared to other days. Therefore, a strategy can be designed to replace the hourly sales data each month and create new files for monthly sales data.

A file sample-data of key-value pairs for hour-sales log in file_16 for sales during 15:00-16:00 will be as follows:

```
ACVM_id10KitKat, 23
ACVM_id2206Milk, 31
ACVM_id2Oreo, 36
ACVM_id10FruitNuts, 18
ACVM_id16Nougat, 8
.
.
.
ACVM_id1224KitKat, 48
ACVM_id4837Nougat, 28
.
```

Map tasks will map the input streams of key values at files, file_1, file_2, ... file_23, file_24 every hour. The resulting 5000 key value pairs maps each hour with keys for ACVM_idNKitKats (N = 1 to 5000). The output stream from Mapper will be as follows:

```
(ACVM_id10KitKat, 0), (ACVM_id1224KitKat, 3),..., ..,  ...,... ,.., ..,
..., ....,....,... ,..., .., ...
```

Hourly 5 output streams of mapped tasks for all chocolates of all 5000 machines will be input to the reduce task.

The Reducer processes each hour using 5 input streams, sums all machines sales and generates one output (ACVMs_KitKat, 109624), (ACVMs_Milk, 128324), (ACVMs_FruitNuts, 9835), (ACVMs_Nougat, 2074903), and (ACVMs_Oreo, 305163). The reduced output serializes and is input to the analytics applications each hour.

Chapter 4 describes MapReduce programming in detail.

Self-Assessment Exercise linked to LO 2.3

1. Why is mapping required when processing the stored data at HDFS? ○○●
2. How do Jobracker and TaskTracker function? ○○●

3. How does MapReducer along with the YARN resources manager enable faster processing of an application?
4. Consider HDFS DataNodes in a cluster. Draw a diagram depicting 10 data nodes storing the data of 4 groups of students. Using the diagram, show the execution of MapReduce sub-tasks for each group in parallel on the DataNodes in a cluster.

2.5 HADOOP YARN

LO 2.4

Hadoop YARN for management and scheduling of resources for parallel running of application tasks

YARN is a resource management platform. It manages computer resources. The platform is responsible for providing the computational resources, such as CPUs, memory, network I/O which are needed when an application executes. An application task has a number of sub-tasks. YARN manages the schedules for running of the sub-tasks. Each sub-task uses the resources in allotted time intervals.

YARN separates the resource management and processing components. YARN stands for Yet Another Resource Negotiator. An application consists of a number of tasks. Each task can consist of a number of sub-tasks (threads), which run in parallel at the nodes in the cluster. YARN enables running of multi-threaded applications. YARN manages and allocates the resources for the application *sub-tasks* and submits the resources for them at the Hadoop system.

2.5.1 Hadoop 2 Execution Model

Figure 2.5 shows the YARN-based execution model. The figure shows the YARN components—Client, Resource Manager (RM), Node Manager (NM), Application Master (AM) and Containers.

Figure 2.5 also illustrates YARN components namely, Client, Resource Manager (RM), Node Manager (RM), Application Master (AM) and Containers.

List of actions of YARN resource allocation and scheduling functions is as follows:

- A MasterNode has two components: (i) Job History Server and (ii) Resource Manager(RM).
- A Client Node submits the request of an application to the RM. The RM is the master. One RM exists per cluster. The RM keeps information of all the slave NMs. Information is about the location (Rack Awareness) and the number of resources (data blocks and servers) they have. The RM also renders the Resource Scheduler service that decides how to assign the resources. It, therefore, performs resource management as well as scheduling.
- Multiple NMs are at a cluster. An NM creates an AM instance (AMI) and starts up. The AMI initializes itself and registers with the RM. Multiple AMIs can be created in an AM.
- The AMI performs role of an Application Manager (ApplM),. that estimates the resources requirement for running an application program or sub-task. The ApplMs send their requests for the necessary resources to the RM. Each NM includes several containers for uses by the subtasks of the application.
- NM is a slave of the infrastructure. It signals whenever it initializes. All active NMs send the controlling signal periodically to the RM signaling their presence.

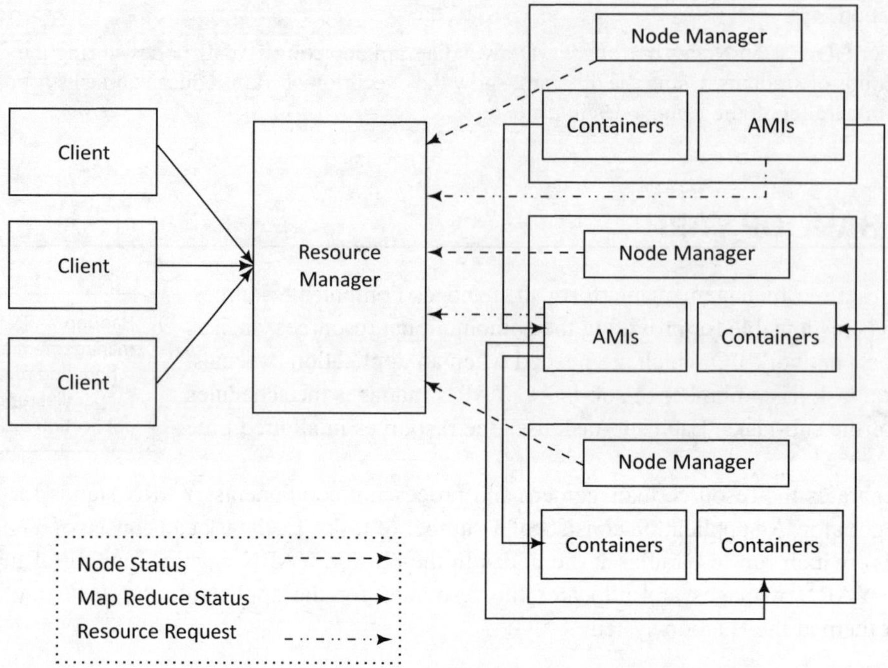

Figure 2.5 YARN-based execution model

- Each NM assigns a container(s) for each AMI. The container(s) assigned at an instance may be at same NM or another NM. ApplM uses just a fraction of the resources available. The ApplM at an instance uses the assigned container(s) for running the application sub-task.
- RM allots the resources to AM, and thus to ApplMs for using assigned containers on the same or other NM for running the application subtasks in parallel.

Self-Assessment Exercise linked to LO 2.4

1. What are the resources required for running an application? How they are allocated? ○○●
2. List the functions of YARN. ○○●
3. Explain using Example 2.3, how the Application Master coordinates the execution of all tasks submitted for an application and requests for appropriate resource containers to execute the task. ●●●
4. List the functions of Client, Resource Manager, Node Manager, Application Master and Containers ○●●

2.6 HADOOP ECOSYSTEM TOOLS

LO 2.5

Functions of Hadoop ecosystem – System tools at application support layer: AVRO, Zookeeper, Ambari, HBase, Hive, Pig and Mahout

A simple framework of Hadoop enabled development of a number of open-source projects has quickly emerged (Figure 2.2). They solve very specific problems related to distributed storage and processing model. Table 2.2 gives the functionalities of the ecosystem tools and components.

Table 2.2 Functionalities of the ecosystem tools and components

Ecosystem Tool	Functionalities
ZooKeeper – Coordination service	Provisions high-performance coordination service for distributed running of applications and tasks (Sections 2.3.1.2 and 2.6.1.1)
Avro— Data serialization and transfer utility	Provisions data serialization during data transfer between application and processing layers (Figure 2.2 and Section 2.4.1)
Oozie	Provides a way to package and bundles multiple coordinator and workflow jobs and manage the lifecycle of those jobs (Section 2.6.1.2)
Sqoop (SQL-to-Hadoop) – A data-transfer software	Provisions for data-transfer between data stores such as relational DBs and Hadoop (Section 2.6.1.3)
Flume – Large data transfer utility	Provisions for reliable data transfer and provides for recovery in case of failure. Transfers large amount of data in applications, such as related to social-media messages (Section 2.6.1.4)
Ambari – A web-based tool	Provisions, monitors, manages, and viewing of functioning of the cluster, MapReduce, Hive and Pig APIs (Section 2.6.2)
Chukwa – A data collection system	Provisions and manages data collection system for large and distributed systems
HBase – A structured data store using database	Provisions a scalable and structured database for large tables (Section 2.6.3)
Cassandra – A database	Provisions scalable and fault-tolerant database for multiple masters (Section 3.7)
Hive – A data warehouse system	Provisions data aggregation, data-summarization, data warehouse infrastructure, ad hoc (unstructured) querying and SQL-like scripting language for query processing using HiveQL (Sections 2.6.4, 4.4 and 4.5)
Pig – A high-level dataflow language	Provisions dataflow (DF) functionality and the execution framework for parallel computations (Sections 2.6.5 and 4.6)
Mahout –A machine learning software	Provisions scalable machine learning and library functions for data mining and analytics (Sections 2.6.6 and 6.9)

The following subsections describe the Hadoop Ecosystem tools.

2.6.1 Hadoop Ecosystem

Consider ZooKeeper, Oozie, Sqoop and Flume.

2.6.1.1 Zookeeper

Designing of a distributed system requires designing and developing the coordination services. Apache Zookeeper is a coordination service that enables synchronization across a cluster in distributed applications (Figure 2.2). The coordination service manages the jobs in the cluster. Since multiple machines are involved, the race condition and deadlock are common problems when running a distributed application.

Zookeeper in Hadoop behaves as a centralized repository where distributed applications can write data at a node called JournalNode and read the data out of it. Zookeeper uses synchronization, serialization and coordination activities. It enables functioning of a distributed system as a single function.

ZooKeeper's main coordination services are:

1 Name service – A name service maps a name to the information associated with that name. For example, DNS service is a name service that maps a domain name to an IP address. Similarly, name keeps a track of servers or services those are up and running, and looks up their status by name in name service.
2 Concurrency control – Concurrent access to a shared resource may cause inconsistency of the resource. A concurrency control algorithm accesses shared resource in the distributed system and controls concurrency.
3 Configuration management – A requirement of a distributed system is a central configuration manager. A new joining node can pick up the up-to-date centralized configuration from the ZooKeeper coordination service as soon as the node joins the system.
4 Failure – Distributed systems are susceptible to the problem of node failures. This requires implementing an automatic recovering strategy by selecting some alternate node for processing (Using two MasterNodes with a NameNode each).

2.6.1.2 Oozie

Apache Oozie is an open-source project of Apache that schedules Hadoop jobs. An efficient process for job handling is required. Analysis of Big Data requires creation of multiple jobs and sub-tasks in a process. Oozie design provisions the scalable processing of multiple jobs. Thus, Oozie provides a way to package and bundle multiple coordinator and workflow jobs, and manage the lifecycle of those jobs.

The two basic Oozie functions are:

- Oozie workflow jobs are represented as Directed Acrylic Graphs (DAGs), specifying a sequence of actions to execute.
- Oozie coordinator jobs are recurrent Oozie workflow jobs that are triggered by time and data availability.

Oozie provisions for the following:

1. Integrates multiple jobs in a sequential manner
2. Stores and supports Hadoop jobs for MapReduce, Hive, Pig, and Sqoop
3. Runs workflow jobs based on time and data triggers
4. Manages batch coordinator for the applications
5. Manages the timely execution of tens of elementary jobs lying in thousands of workflows in a Hadoop cluster.

2.6.1.3 Sqoop

The loading of data into Hadoop clusters becomes an important task during data analytics. Apache Sqoop is a tool that is built for loading efficiently the voluminous amount of data between Hadoop and external data repositories that resides on enterprise application servers or relational databases. Sqoop works with relational databases such as Oracle, MySQL, PostgreSQL and DB2.

Sqoop provides the mechanism to import data from external Data Stores into HDFS. Sqoop relates to Hadoop eco-system components, such as Hive and HBase. Sqoop can extract data from Hadoop or other ecosystem components.

Sqoop provides command line interface to its users. Sqoop can also be accessed using Java APIs. The tool allows defining the schema of the data for import. Sqoop exploits MapReduce framework to import and export the data, and transfers for parallel processing of sub-tasks. Sqoop provisions for fault tolerance. Parallel transfer of data results in parallel results and fast data transfer.

Sqoop initially parses the arguments passed in the command line and prepares the map task. The map task initializes multiple Mappers depending on the number supplied by the user in the command line. Each map task will be assigned with part of data to be imported based on key defined in the command line. Sqoop distributes the input data equally among the Mappers. Then each Mapper creates a connection with the database using JDBC and fetches the part of data assigned by Sqoop and writes it into HDFS/Hive/HBase as per the choice provided in the command line.

2.6.1.4 Flume

Apache Flume provides a distributed, reliable and available service. Flume efficiently collects, aggregates and transfers a large amount of streaming data into HDFS. Flume enables upload of large files into Hadoop clusters.

The features of flume include robustness and fault tolerance. Flume provides data transfer which is reliable and provides for recovery in case of failure. Flume is useful for transferring a large amount of data in applications related to logs of network traffic, sensor data, geo-location data, e-mails and social-media messages.

Apache Flume has the following four important components:

1. **Sources** which accept data from a server or an application.
2. **Sinks** which receive data and store it in HDFS repository or transmit the data to another source. Data units that are transferred over a **channel** from source to sink are called events.
3. **Channels** connect between sources and sink by queuing event data for transactions. The size of events data is usually 4 KB. The data source is considered to be a source of various set of events. Sources listen for events and write events to a channel. Sinks basically write event data to a target and remove the event from the queue.
4. **Agents** run the sinks and sources in Flume. The interceptors drop the data or transfer data as it flows into the system.

2.6.2 Ambari

Apache Ambari is a management platform for Hadoop. It is open source. Ambari enables an enterprise to plan, securely install, manage and maintain the clusters in the Hadoop. Ambari provisions for advanced cluster security capabilities, such as Kerberos Ambari.

2.6.2.1 Features

Features of Ambari and associated components are as follows:

1. Simplification of installation, configuration and management
2. Enables easy, efficient, repeatable and automated creation of clusters

3. Manages and monitors scalable clustering
4. Provides an intuitive Web User Interface and REST API. The provision enables automation of cluster operations.
5. Visualizes the health of clusters and critical metrics for their operations
6. Enables detection of faulty node links
7. Provides extensibility and customizability.

2.6.2.2 Hadoop Administration

Hadoop large clusters pose a number of configuration and administration challenges. Administrator procedures enable managing and administering Hadoop clusters, resources and associated Hadoop ecosystem components (Figure 2.2). Administration includes installing and monitoring clusters.

Ambari also provides a centralized setup for security. This simplifies the administering complexities and configures security of clusters across the entire platform. Ambari helps automation of the setup and configuration of Hadoop using Web User Interface and REST APIs.

IBM BigInsights provides an administration console. The console is similar to web UI at Ambari. The console enables visualization of the cluster health, HDFS directory structure, status of MapReduce tasks, review of log records and access application status. Single harmonized view on console makes administering the task easier. Visualization can be up to individual components level on drilling down. Nodes addition and deletion are easy using the console.

The console enables built-in tools for administering. Web console provides a link to server tools and open-source components associated with those.

2.6.3 HBase

Similar to database, HBase is an Hadoop system database. HBase was created for large tables. HBase is an open-source, distributed, versioned and non-relational (NoSQL) database. Features of HBase features are:

1. Uses a partial columnar data schema on top of Hadoop and HDFS.
2. Supports a large table of billions of rows and millions of columns.
3. Provides small amounts of information, called sparse data taken from large data sets which are storing empty or presently not-required data. For example, yearly sales data of KitKats from the data of hourly, daily and monthly sales (Example 2.3).
4. Supports data compression algorithms.
5. Provisions in-memory column-based data transactions.
6. Accesses rows serially and does not provision for random accesses and write into the rows.
7. Provides random, real-time read/write access to Big Data.
8. Fault tolerant storage due to automatic failure support between DataNodes servers.
9. Similarity with Google BigTable.

HBase is written in Java. It stores data in a large structured table. HBase provides scalable distributed Big Data Store. HBase data store as key-value pairs.

HBase system consists of a set of tables. Each table contains rows and columns, similar to a traditional database. HBase provides a primary key as in the database table. Data accesses are performed using that key.

HBASE applies a partial columnar scheme on top of the Hadoop and HDFS. An HBase column represents an attribute of an object, such as hourly sales of KitKat, Milk, Fruit and Nuts, Nougat and Oreo sold every hour at an ACVM (Example 2.3).

The following example shows a structured table considering Examples 1.6 and 2.3.

EXAMPLE 2.4

Recapitulate Examples 1.6 and 2.3. Consider ACVMs selling KitKat, Milk, Fruit and Nuts, Nougat and Oreo chocolates. Following is the table for hourly sales of chocolates at multiple ACVMs.

ACVM_ID	Date (DT) mmddyy	Hour (hr)	KitKat Hourly Sale (KKHS)	Milk Hourly Sale(MHS)	Fruit and Nuts Hourly Sale (FNHS)	Nougat Hourly Sale (NHS)	Oreo Hourly Sale (OHS)
2206	121217	16	28	23	38	8	50
10	121217	16	29	14	44	15	38
1224	121217	16	40	41	23	37	8
16	121217	46	13	25	7	8	74
28	121217	16	52	22	16	28	7
-	-	-	-	-	-	-	-
-	-	-	-	-	-	-	-

(i) How does the HBase store the table?
(ii) How will the records created using shell command 'put'?

SOLUTION

Format of the HBase that stores rows line by line is:

```
Row-Key Column-Family: {Column-Qualifier: Version: Value}
```

HBase data model specifies the *column qualifiers*. For example, column qualifiers are DT, HR, KKHS, MHS, FNHS, NHS and OHS. Version corresponds to a number reflecting the time stamp which identifies the data of columns uniquely. Version is a number reflecting server time-stamp by default. Value is the *value* in the column field for the qualifier. The first row stores in the HBase as follows:

```
ACVM_id: '2206' {'DT':1600080000024: '121217', 'HR': 1600008007319:
'16', 'KKHS': 1600081010821: '28', 'MHS': 1600082010582: '23', 'FNHS':
1600082018001: '38', 'NHS': 1600080158868: '8', 'OHS': 1600038028229: '50'}
```

Write similarly for other rows of hourly sales table.

The records are put in rows and columns as follows:

```
hbase (main) 001:0> put 'ACVM_id', '2206', 'DT', '121217', 'HR', '16',
'HourlySales: KKHS','28' 0 row(s) in 021120 seconds
hbase (main) 002:0> put 'ACVM_id', '2206', 'HourlySales: MHS', '23' 0
row(s) in 001120 seconds
hbase (main) 003:0> put 'ACVM_id', '2206', 'HourlySales: FNHS','38' 0
row(s) in 021120 seconds
hbase (main) 004:0> put 'ACVM_id', '2206', 'HourlySales: NHS', '8' 0
row(s) in 001120 seconds
hbase (main) 005:0> put 'ACVM_id', '2206', 'HourlySales: OHS', '50' 0
row(s) in 001120 seconds
```

2.6.4 Hive

Apache Hive is an open-source data warehouse software. Hive facilitates reading, writing and managing large datasets which are at distributed Hadoop files. Hive uses SQL. Hive puts a partial SQL interface in front of Hadoop.

Hive design provisions for batch processing of large sets of data. An application of Hive is for managing weblogs. Hive does not process real-time queries and does not update row-based data tables.

Hive also enables data serialization/deserialization and increases flexibility in schema design by including a system catalog called Hive Metastore. HQL also supports custom MapReduce scripts to be plugged into queries.

Hive supports different storage types, such as text files, sequence files (consisting of binary key/value pairs) and RCFiles (Record Columnar Files), ORC (optimized row columnar) and HBase.

Three major functions of Hive are data summarization, query and analysis. Hive basically interacts with structured data stored in HDFS with a query language known as HQL (Hive Query Language) which is similar to SQL. HQL translates SQL-like queries into MapReduce jobs executed on Hadoop automatically.

Sections 4.4 and 4.5 will describe the Hive and HiveQL in detail.

2.6.5 Pig

Apache Pig is an open source, high-level language platform. Pig was developed for analyzing large-data sets. Pig executes queries on large datasets that are stored in HDFS using Apache Hadoop. The language used in Pig is known as Pig Latin.

Pig Latin language is similar to SQL query language but applies on larger datasets. Additional features of Pig are as follows:

(i) Loads the data after applying the required filters and dumps the data in the desired format.
(ii) Requires Java runtime environment for executing Pig Latin programs.
(iii) Converts all the operations into map and reduce tasks. The tasks run on Hadoop.
(iv) Allows concentrating upon the complete operation, irrespective of the individual Mapper and Reducer functions to produce the output results.

Section 4.6 will describe the usages of Pig in detail.

2.6.6 Mahout

Mahout is a project of Apache with library of scalable machine learning algorithms. Apache implemented Mahout on top of Hadoop. Apache used the MapReduce paradigm. Machine learning is mostly required to enhance the future performance of a system based on the previous outcomes. Mahout provides the learning tools to automate the finding of meaningful patterns in the Big Data sets stored in the HDFS.

Mahout supports four main areas:

- Collaborative data-filtering that mines user behavior and makes product recommendations.
- Clustering that takes data items in a particular class, and organizes them into naturally occurring groups, such that items belonging to the same group are similar to each other.
- Classification that means learning from existing categorizations and then assigning the future items to the best category.
- Frequent item-set mining that analyzes items in a group and then identifies which items usually occur together.

Section 6.9 will describe Mahout architecture and usages.

Self-Assessment Exercise linked to LO 2.5

1. Why is ZooKeeper required to behave as a centralized repository where the distributed applications can write the data? ○○●
2. What are the functions which Ambari perform? How does Ambari enable administering of clusters and Hadoop components? ○●●
3. Make a table of ecosystem tools and their functions which are required for analyzing performances from SGPs, SGPAs and CGPAs of each student. Assume that programmes are Master of Science in Computer Science, Master of Computer Appliations and Master of Technology in Computer Science. ●●●
4. What are the activities which Mahout supports in the Hadoop system? ○○●

KEY CONCEPTS

active node
administering cluster
Ambari
application master
AVRO
Chukawa
cluster
columnar data
container
data Block
data node
data replication
Flink
Flume
Hadoop
Hadoop Common
Hadoop pipes
Hadoop streaming
HBase
HDFS
Hive
Mahout
managing cluster
Mapper
MapReduce
node manager
Oozie
parallel tasks
Pig
primary master
Rack
Reducer
resource
resource manager
resource scheduling
row-based data
secondary master
serialization
shell command
slave node
Spark
standby node
synchronization
YARN
ZooKeeper

Learning Outcomes

LO 2.1

- Hadoop is an open-source framework that uses cloud-based utility computing services. Tera Bytes of data processing takes just a few minutes.

- Hadoop system has features of fault tolerant, scalable, flexible, modular design and distributed clusters computing model with data locality.
- Hadoop core components are Hadoop Common, that uses the libraries and utilities, HDFS, MapReduce and YARN.
- Hadoop ecosystem includes the application support layer and application layer components – AVRO, ZooKeeper, Sqoop, Ambari, Chukwa, Flink and Flume, Pig, Hive, Spark and Mahout.
- HDFS with MapReduce YARN-based system enables parallel processing of large data sets.

LO 2.2

- HDFS is a Java-based distributed file system that can store various types of data.
- Hadoop stores the data in a number of *clusters*. Each cluster has a number of Data Store called *Racks*. Each Rack stores a number of DataNodes. Each DataNode has a large number of *Data Blocks.* The data blocks *replicate by default at least on three DataNodes* in the same or remote nodes.
- Files, data blocks and DataNodes need identification during processing at Hadoop DataNodes. The concept of the NameNode and DataNode associate the HDFS. A NameNode stores meta data for the files.
- Meta data gives information about the file of user application, but does not participate in the computations. DataNode stores the actual data files in the data blocks.
- Provision for multiple NameNodes enables higher resources availability.

LO 2.3

- MapReduce functions are an integral part of Hadoop physical organization.
- MapReduce is a programming model for distributed computing. MapReduce allows writing applications to process huge amounts of data, in parallel, on large clusters of servers reliably.
- The parallel programs of MapReduce are useful for performing large-scale data analysis using multiple CPUs at nodes in a cluster.

LO 2.4

- YARN separates the resource management and processing components. An application consists of a number of tasks and each task can consist of a number of sub-tasks (threads), which run in parallel. YARN enables running of multi-threaded applications. YARN manages and allocates the resources for the application *sub-tasks* and submits the resources for them at the Hadoop.
- YARN schedules and handles the resource requests of large scale, distributed applications.

LO 2.5

- Avro is a data transfer utility which provisions a system which enables data serialization for transfer between the application and processing layers.
- ZooKeeper is a coordination service for the distributed running of applications and tasks.
- Sqoop is a data-transfer software for data-transfer between data stores and relational DBs.
- Ambari is a web-based tool which provisions, monitors, manages, viewing of functioning of clusters, MapReduce, Hive and Pig APIs.
- Cassandra is a database which provisions a scalable and fault-tolerant database for multiple masters.
- Chukwa is a data collection system for large and distributed systems.

- HBase is a structured data store using database that provisions for a scalable and structured database for large tables.
- Hive is a data warehouse system which provisions for queries, data aggregation, summarizing, infrastructure-like enterprise data warehouse, data summarization, ad hoc (unstructured) querying and HiveQL which is SQL-like scripting language.
- Pig is a high-level dataflow language which provisions for dataflow functionality and the execution framework for parallel computations.
- Mahout is a software library for the machine learning algorithms.

Objective Type Questions

Select one correct-answer option for each questions below:

2.1 Programming model for Big Data is (i) centralized computing of input results of the applications from multiple computing nodes, (ii) the distributed computing of an application at the same time. Data sets and the application run at the MPPs at a number of geographic locations and remote servers. (iii) Distributed computing of the data sets using application tasks at the multiple computing nodes. (iv) Computing of the application codes transferred to the multiple nodes which store data sets and compute at cluster. ○●●

(a) i (b) ii to iv
(c) iii and iv (d) iv

2.2 Core components of Hadoop are (i) Hadoop Common which contains the libraries and utilities required by other modules of Hadoop, (ii) a Java-based distributed file system, (iii) MapReduce, (iv) YARN, (v) AVRO and ZooKeeper, (vi) Pig, Hive, Sqoop and (v) Ambari. ○○●

(a) all are true (b) (i) to (iv)
(c) all except vi (d) ii to vi

2.3 (i) HDFS design is for batch processing and cannot be used for stream analytics. (ii) Spark can be used for Hadoop stream analytics. (iii) YARN has made it possible to process applications, such as interactive queries, text analytics and streaming analysis. (iv) Flume can be used stream analytics. (v) Spark and Flink technologies are the most suitable for in-stream processing. ○○●

(a) all except iv (b) all except ii
(c) all except i (d) all

2.4 Hadoop distributed file system: (i) identifies the file by directories and folders which associate with file system, (ii) identifies the data sources for processing and uses the resource pointers which store in the data dictionary, (iii) identifies the data block using data dictionary master tables stored at a central location, (iv) identifies using centralized tables, and (v) identifies from file meta data at the application. ○●●

(a) none (b) ii to v
(c) ii, iv and v (d) all except ii

2.5 (i) HDFS uses the client, master NameNode, primary and secondary MasterNodes and slave nodes. (ii) YARN components use Client, Resource Manager (RM), Node Manager (RM), Application Master (AM) and Containers. (iii) YARN uses the client, master NameNode, primary and secondary MasterNode and slave nodes. (iv) MapReduce v2 when Hadoop uses YARN-based system, which enables parallel processing of large data sets. (v) Slaves are responsible to store the data and process the computation tasks submitted by the clients. ●●●

(a) Only i (b) all except ii ad iv.
(c) all except iii (d) all

2.6 (1) Hadoop shell commands are (i) – copyToLocal for copying a file at HDFS to the local and (ii) – cat for copying to standard output (stdout). (2) When file stuData_id96 to be copied at stu_filesdir directory, then command is (iii) $Hadoop hdfs-put stuData_id96 /user/ stu_filesdir, and (iv) $Hadoop hdfs-cp stuData_id96 /user/ stu_filesdir. ●●●

(a) ii to iv (b) i to iii
(c) all (d) only i and iii

2.7 (i) NM is a slave of the infrastructure. (ii) AM signals whenever it initializes. (iii) All active AMs send the controlling signal periodically to the RM when signaling their presence. (iv) NM accepts the request and queues up the resources for application program or sub-tasks. When the requested resources become available on slave nodes, (v) the RM grants the Application Master usage permission for the specific intervals for the containers on specific slave NMs. The systems do not use the concept of joins (in distributed data storage systems), and (vi) A Client Node submits request of an application to the RM. The RM is the master. ○●●

(a) all except ii to iv (b) all
(c) only iii and iv (d) ii to iv

2.8 HBASE (i) applies a partial columnar scheme on top of the MapReduce. It is (ii) an open-source, distributed, versioned, non-relational (NoSQL) database, (iii) written in Java, (iv) stores large unstructured table and (v) provisions for the scalable distributed Big Data Store. Data stores as key-value pairs and (vi) consists of a set of tables. Each table contains rows and columns. Therefore, it is similar to a traditional database and (vii) provisions a primary key as in the database table. ○○●

(a) i to iii (b) all except v
(c) all except i and iv (d) all

2.9 (i) Ambari is a structured data store using database that provisions for a scalable and structured database for large tables. (ii) Zookeeper in Hadoop behaves as a centralized repository where distributed applications can put data at a node. (iv) Cassandra is a data collection system for large and distributed systems. (v) Zookeeper is a coordination service that enables synchronization across a cluster in distributed applications. ●●●

(a) all (b) only ii and iii
(c) all except ii and iii (d) none

2.10 (i) Ambari is a web-based tool which provisions, monitors, manages, viewing of cluster functioning. (ii) Ambari and BigInsights have provisions for viewing. Their uses are for administering the Hadoop. (iii) Avro is a data transfer utility between application and application support layer. (iii) Cassandra is a database which provisions a scalable and fault-tolerant database for multiple masters. (iv) Chukwa is a data collection system for large and distributed systems. (v) HBase is a structured data store using database that provisions for a scalable and structured database for large tables. ○○●

(a) all correct except iii (b) all except iii and v
(c) all except iv (d) all except ii and iii

2.11 (i) Hadoop 1 and 2 provisions for multiple NameNodes. (ii) Each MasterNode (MN) has NameNode, Avro coordination client, and JournalNode (JN). (iii) A JN keeps the records of the state, resources required, intermediate results or cluster tasks execution. (iv) Application tasks and subtasks at the cluster can write data and read data from a JN. ○●●

(a) all correct except iii (b) all except iii and iv
(c) all except ii (d) only iv

2.12 (i) Oozie provides a way to package and bundle multiple coordinator and workflow jobs and manage the lifecycle of those jobs. (ii) Flink provisions for reliable data transfer and provides for recovery in case of failure. Transfers large amount of data in applications. (iii) Chukwa provisions data serialization during data transfer between application and processing layers. (iv) Sqoop provisions for data transfer between data stores such as relational DBs and Hadoop. (v) Chukwa provisions and manages data collection system for large and distributed systems. ●●●

(a) all correct except iii (b) all except iii and v

(c) all except iv (d) all except ii and iii

Review Questions

2.1 Why is the application program layer different from support layer in Big Data platform? Explain the Hadoop features. **(LO 2.1)** ○○●

2.2 List Hadoop two core components. Describe their usages. **(LO 2.1)** ○○●

2.3 Explain using a diagram the distributed storage, resource manager layer, processing framework and application APIs layers in Hadoop. **(LO 2.1)** ○○●

2.4 Give the meanings of Hadoop distributed file system, clusters, Racks, DataNodes, Data Blocks, MasterNode, NameNode and metadata of files. Explain these. **(LO 2.2)** ○●●

2.5 How do multiple NameNodes ensure high availability of Data in HDFS? **(LO 2.2)** ○○●

2.6 How does MapReduce function as a programming model for distributed computing? **(LO 2.3)** ○●●

2.7 How does MapReduce enables process huge amounts of data, in parallel, on large clusters of servers reliably. **(LO 2.3)** ○●●

2.8 List the resources required to run an application. How does the separation of resource management and processing components help the number of tasks and sub-tasks (threads) when running in parallel? **(LO 2.4)** ●●●

2.9 How does YARN resource manager do the following: (i) keep track of the active node managers and available resources and (ii) allocate the containers to the appropriate sub-tasks and monitors the Application Master? **(LO 2.4)** ●●●

2.10 Why are AVRO and Zookeeper essential in Hadoop programming for Big Data applications? **(LO 2.5)** ○●●

Practice Exercises

2.1 Recapatulate Example 2.3. Assume a company collects data from a large number of automatic chocolate vending machines (ACVMs) distributed over a large number of geographic locations in the cities and areas in each city. Each ACVM sells five different flavors of chocolates: KitKat, Milk, Fruit and Nuts, Nougat and Oreo. When will the centralized processing and analytics model and when will Hadoop programming be used? Each machine communicates data for the analytics every hour to the company's central data warehouse. **(LO 2.1)** ○○●

2.2 Make a data store model using HDFS for SGPs, SGPAs and CGPAs of each student in 50 UG and 10 PG offerred at the university with 5000 students intake capacity each year. Each student information can extend up to 64 MB. **(LO 2.2)** ○●●

2.3 Recapatilate Example 1.6 of a Automotive Components and Predictive Automotive Maintenance Services (ACPAMS) company which renders customer services for maintenance and servicing of (Internet) connected cars and its components. Assume that number of centres are 8192 ($=2^{13}$), number of car serviced by each centre per day equals 32 ($==2^5$). Each car has 256 ($=2^8$) components, which requires maintenance or servicing in the company's car. The service centre also collects feedback after every service and send responses to customer requests. The feedback and responses text takes on average 128 B($=2^7$ B) and each service or responses records in a report of average 512 B ($= 2^9$) text. The company stores the centres data for maximum 10 years and follows last-in first-out data replacement policy. How will the files of ACPAMS be stored using HDFS? What shall be the minimum memory requirement during 10 years? **(LO 2.2)** ●●●

2.4 Consider a car company selling five models of car: *Jagaur Land Rover*, *Hexa*, *Zest*, *Nexon* and *Safari Storme*. Assume each day the model sells at 600 show rooms with average 400 car sales average per week in a year. The files for each model are at file_1, file_2, …., file_5. Each file stores as the key-value pairs the daily sales log at the company large number of showrooms. ●●●

(i) Calculate how and how much will the showrooms weekly each model sales-log store using HDFS?

(ii) Write the sample of data collected in a file for day 1, 2, …., 365 starting January 1 from the showrooms.

(iii) What will be the output streams of map tasks for feeding the input streams to the Reducer?

(iv) What will be the Reducer outputs? **(LO 2.3)**

2.5 Recapitulate a list of actions of YARN resource allocation and scheduling functions in Section 2.5.1 Figure 2.5. Show the directions of sequences and step number over each arrow, to show the sequence of action to allocation of a container. **(LO 2.4)** ○○●

2.6 Recapitulate Practice Exercise 2.4, Consider a car company selling Jaguar Land Rover, Hexa, Zest, Nexon and Safari Storme models of car. Following is the table for the weekly sales log at the multiple car company showrooms. ○●●

CCSR_id	Date (DT) mmddyy	*Jagaur Land Rover* Weekly Sales (JLRWS)	*Hexa* Weekly Sales (HWS)	*Zest* Weekly Sales (ZWS)	*Nexon* Weekly Sales (NWS)	*Safari Storme* Weekly Sales (SSWS)
220	121217	28	23	138	148	50
10	121217	49	34	164	115	38
122	121217	40	141	123	37	88
16	121217	13	25	127	158	174
28	121217	12	122	116	128	57
-	-	-	-	-	-	-
-	-	-	-	-	-	-

(i) How the HBase stores the table in five weeks.

(ii) How will the records created using shell command 'put' for 35 entries given above? **(LO 2.5)**

Chapter 3

NoSQL Big Data Management, MongoDB and Cassandra

LEARNING OBJECTIVES

After studying this chapter, you will be able to:

- **LO 3.1** Get conceptual understanding of NoSQL data stores, Big Data solutions, schema-less models, and increased flexibility for data manipulation
- **LO 3.2** Get knowledge of NoSQL data architecture patterns namely, key-value pairs, tabular, column family, BigTable, Record Columnar (RC), Optimized Row Columnar (ORC) and Parquet, document, object and graph data stores, and the variations in architectural patterns
- **LO 3.3** Get conceptual understanding of NoSQL data store management, applications and handling problems in Big Data
- **LO 3.4** Solve Big Data analytics using shared-nothing architecture, choosing a distribution model among master-slave and peer-to-peer models, and get the knowledge of four ways by which the NoSQL handles the Big Data problems
- **LO 3.5** Apply the MongoDB databases and query commands
- **LO 3.6** Use the Cassandra databases, data model, clients, and integrate them with Hadoop

RECALL FROM PREVIOUS CHAPTERS

Big Data use new tools for processing and analysis of large volume of data. Big Data sources are Hadoop or Spark compatible file system, structured, unstructured or NoSQL data Store (Table 1.1). Big Data distributed computing uses shared-nothing paradigm, *no in-between data sharing and inter-processor communication*. (Table 1.2)

Chapter 1 introduced NoSQL. NoSQL data stores can store semi-structured or unstructured data. NoSQL stands for No-SQL or Not Only SQL. NoSQL databases can coexists with SQL databases. NoSQL data applications do not integrate with SQL databases applications. NoSQL databases store Big Data. Examples of NoSQL data stores are key-value pairs, hash key, JSON files, BigTable, HBase, MongoDB, Cassandra, and CouchDB (Section 1.6.2.1).

This chapter focuses on providing detailed concepts of NoSQL data architectural patterns, management of Big Data, data distribution models, handling of Big Data problems using NoSQL, MongoDB for document and Cassandra for columnar stores.

3.1 INTRODUCTION

Big Data uses distributed systems. A distributed system consists of multiple data nodes at clusters of machines and distributed software components. The tasks execute in parallel with data at nodes in clusters. The computing nodes communicate with the applications through a network.

Following are the features of distributed-computing architecture (Chapter 2):

1. *Increased reliability and fault tolerance*: The important advantage of distributed computing system is reliability. If a segment of machines in a cluster fails then the rest of the machines continue work. When the datasets replicate at number of data nodes, the fault tolerance increases further. The dataset in remaining segments continue the same computations as being done at failed segment machines.
2. *Flexibility* makes it very easy to install, implement and debug new services in a distributed environment.
3. *Sharding* is storing the different parts of data onto different sets of data nodes, clusters or servers. For example, university students huge database, on sharding divides in databases, called shards. Each shard may correspond to a database for an individual course and year. Each shard stores at different nodes or servers.
4. *Speed*: Computing power increases in a distributed computing system as shards run parallelly on individual data nodes in clusters independently (no data sharing between shards).
5. *Scalability*: Consider sharding of a large database into a number of shards, distributed for computing in different systems. When the database expands further, then adding more machines and increasing the number of shards provides horizontal scalability. Increased computing power and running number of algorithms on the same machines provides vertical scalability (Section 1.3.1).
6. *Resources sharing*: Shared resources of memory, machines and network architecture reduce the cost.
7. *Open system* makes the service accessible to all nodes.
8. *Performance*: The collection of processors in the system provides higher performance than a centralized computer, due to lesser cost of communication among machines (Cost means time taken up in communication).

The demerits of distributed computing are: (i) issues in troubleshooting in a larger networking infrastructure, (ii) additional software requirements and (iii) security risks for data and resources.

Big Data solutions require a scalable distributed computing model with shared-nothing architecture. A solution is Big Data store in HDFS files. NoSQL data also store Big Data, and facilitate random read/write accesses. The accesses are sequential in HDFS data.

HBase is a NoSQL solution (Section 2.6.3). Examples of other solutions are MongoDB and Cassandra. MongoDB and Cassandra DBMSs create HDFS compatible distributed data stores and include their specific query processing languages.

Following are selected key terms used in database systems.

Class refers to a template of program codes that is extendable. Class creates instances, called objects. A class consists of initial values for member fields, called *state* (of variables), and implementations of member functions and methods called behavior. An implementation means program codes along with values of arguments in the functions and methods (Java Class uses methods, C++ functions.) An abstract class consists of at least one abstract member or method.

Object is an instance of a class in Java, C++, and other object-oriented languages. Object can be an instance of another object (for example, in JavaScript).

Tupple is an ordered set of data which constitutes a record. For example, one row record in a table. A row in a relational database has column fields or attributes. Example of a tupple is (JLRWSale, Week 1, 138, Week 2, 232, …, week 52, 186) in an RDBMS table. Here, JLRWSale means Jaguar Land Rover Weekly Sale. (JLRWSale, Week 1, 138) is also a tupple, and gives JLR week 1 sales = 138. (Week 2, 232, …, week 52, 186) means week 2 sales = 232 abd 52 sales = 186 JLRs.

Transaction means execution of instructions in two interrelated entities, such as a query and the database.

Database transactional model refers to a model for transactions, such as the one following the ACID (Section 3.2) or BASE properties (Section 3.2.3).

MySQL refers to a widely used open-source database, which excels as a content management server.

Oracle refers to a widely used object-relational DBMS, written in the C++ language that provides applications integration with service-oriented architectures and has high reliability. Oracle has also released the NoSQL database system.

DB2 refers to a family of database server products from IBM with built-in support to handle advanced Big Data analytics.

Sybase refers to database server based on relational model for businesses, primarily on UNIX. Sybase was the first enterprise-level DBMS in Linux.

MS SQL server refers to a Microsoft-developed RDBMS for enterprise-level databases that supports both SQL and NoSQL architectures.

PostgreSQL refers to an enterprise-level, object-relational DBMS. PostgreSQL uses procedural languages like Perl and Python, in addition to SQL.

This chapter describes NoSQL data architecture patterns, NoSQL for increasing the flexibility in data store architecture, NoSQL usages in Big Data management, and the solutions, such as MongoDB and Cassandra. Section 3.2 describes NoSQL data stores for Big Data usages, schema-less models, and increasing the flexibility for data manipulation. Section 3.3 describes NoSQL data-architecture patterns: Key-value stores, graph stores, column family stores, tabular stores, document stores, object data stores, and variations of NoSQL architectural patterns. Section 3.4 describes NoSQL for managing Big Data, solutions for Big Data, and types of Big Data problems. Section 3.5 describes use of shared-nothing architecture, choosing a distribution model, master-slave versus peer-to-peer, and four ways by which NoSQL handles Big Data problems. Sections 3.6 describes MongoDB and query commands used in the applications. Section 3.7 describes Cassandra databases, data-model, clients and integration with Hadoop and applications.

3.2 NOSQL DATA STORE

LO 3.1

NoSQL data store, Big Data solutions, schema-less models, and increasing flexibility for data manipulation

SQL is a programming language based on relational algebra. It is a declarative language and it defines the data schema . SQL creates databases and RDBMSs. RDBMS uses tabular data store with relational algebra, precisely defined operators with relations as the operands. Relations are a set of tuples. Tuples are named attributes. A tuple identifies uniquely by keys called candidate keys.

Transactions on SQL databases exhibit ACID properties. ACID stands for atomicity, consistency, isolation and durability.

ACID Properties in SQL Transactions

Following are the meanings of these characteristics during the transactions.

Atomicity of transaction means all operations in the transaction must complete, and if interrupted, then must be undone (rolled back). For example, if a customer withdraws an amount then the bank in first operation enters the withdrawn amount in the table and in the next operation modifies the balance with new amount available. Atomicity means both should be completed, else undone if interrupted in between.

Consistency in transactions means that a transaction must maintain the integrity constraint, and follow the consistency principle. For example, the difference of sum of deposited amounts and withdrawn amounts in a bank account must equal the last balance. All three data need to be consistent.

Isolation of transactions means two transactions of the database must be isolated from each other and done separately.

Durability means a transaction must persist once completed.

Triggers, Views and Schedules in SQL Databases

Trigger is a special stored procedure. Trigger executes when a specific action(s) occurs within a database, such as change in table data or actions such as UPDATE, INSERT and DELETE. For example, a Trigger store procedure inserts new columns in the columnar family data store.

View refers to a logical construct, used in query statements. A View saves a division of complex query instructions and that reduces the query complexity. Viewing of a division is similar to a view of a table. View does not save like data at the table. Query statement when uses references to a view, the statement executes the View. Query (processing) planner combines the information in View definition with the remaining actions on the query. A query planner plans how to break a query into sub-queries for obtaining the required answer. View, hides the query complexity by dividing the query into smaller, more manageable pieces.

Schedule refers to a chronological sequence of instructions which execute concurrently. When a transaction is in the schedule then all instructions of the transaction are included in the schedule. Scheduled order of instructions is maintained during the transaction. Scheduling enables execution of multiple transactions in allotted time intervals.

Join in SQL Databases

SQL databases facilitate combining rows from two or more tables, based on the related columns in them. *Combining* action uses *Join* function during a database transaction. *Join* refers to a clause which combines. Combining the products (AND operations) follows next the selection process. A Join operation does pairing of two tuples obtained from different relational expressions. Joins, if and only if a given Join condition satisfies. Number of Join operations specify using relational algebraic expressions. SQL provides JOIN clause, which retrieves and joins the related data stored across multiple tables with a single command, Join. For example, consider an SQL statement:

```
Select KitKatSales From TransactionsTbl INNER JOIN ACVMSalesTbl ON
TransactionsTbl.KitKatSales = TransactionsTbl.KitKatSales;
```

The statement selects those records in a column named `KitKatSales` which match the values in two tables: one `TransactionsTbl` and other `ACVMSalesTbl`.

Relational databases and RDBMS developed using SQL have issues of scalability and distributed design. This is because all tuples need to be on the same data node. The database has an issue of indexing over distributed nodes. They do not model the hierarchical, object-oriented, semi-structured or graph databases.

Database Tables have relationships between them which are represented by related fields. RDBMS allows the Join operations on the related columns. The traditional RDBMS has a problem when storing the records beyond a certain physical storage limit. This is because RDBMS does not support horizontal scalability (Section 1.3.1).

For example, consider sharding a big table in a DBMS into two. Assume writing first 0.1 million records (1 to 100000) in one table and from 100001 in another table. Sharding a database means breaking up into many, much smaller databases that share nothing, and can distribute across multiple servers. Handling of the Joins and managing data in the other related tables are cumbersome processes, when using the sharding.

The problem continues when data has no defined number of fields and formats. For example, the data associated with the choice of chocolate flavours of the users of ACVM in Example 1.6(i). Some users provide a single choice, while some users provide two choices, and a few others want to fill three best flavours of their choice.

User Id	Choice
1	Dairy Milk
2	Dairy Milk, KitKat
3	KitKat, Snicker, Munch

Defining a field becomes tough when a field in the database offers choice between two or many. This makes RDBMS unsuitable for data management in Big Data environments as well as data in their real forms.

SQL compliant format means that database tables constructed using SQL and they enable processing of the queries written using SQL. 'NoSQL' term conveys two different meanings: (i) does not follow SQL compliant formats, (ii)"Not only SQL" use SQL compliant formats with variety of other querying and access methods.

3.2.1 NoSQL

A new category of data stores is NoSQL (means Not Only SQL) data stores. NoSQL is an altogether new approach of thinking about databases, such as schema flexibility, simple relationships, dynamic schemas, auto sharding, replication, integrated caching, horizontal scalability of shards, distributable tuples, semi-structures data and flexibility in approach.

Issues with NoSQL data stores are lack of standardization in approaches, processing difficulties for complex queries, dependence on eventually consistent results in place of consistency in all states.

3.2.1.1 Big Data NoSQL or Not-Only SQL

NoSQL DB does not require specialized RDBMS like storage and hardware for processing. Storage can be on a cloud. Section 1.6.2.1 introduced NoSQL data storage system. NoSQL records are in non-relational data store systems. They use flexible data models. The records use multiple schemas.

> NoSQL or Not Only SQL is a Class of non-relational data storage systems, flexible data models and multiple schema.

NoSQL data stores are considered as semi-structured data. Big Data Store uses NoSQL. Figure 1.7 showed co-existence of data store at server or cloud with SQL, RDBMS with NoSQL and Big Data at Hadoop, Spark, Mesos, S3 or compatible Clusters. However, no integration takes place with applications that are based on SQL. NoSQL data store characteristics are as follows:

1. NoSQL is a class of non-relational data storage system with flexible data model. Examples of NoSQL data-architecture patterns of datasets are key-value pairs, name/value pairs, Column family Big-data store, Tabular data store, Cassandra (used in Facebook/Apache), HBase, hash table [Dynamo (Amazon S3)], unordered keys using JSON (CouchDB), JSON (PNUTS), JSON (MongoDB), Graph Store, Object Store, ordered keys and semi-structured data storage systems.
2. NoSQL not necessarily has a fixed schema, such as table; do not use the concept of Joins (in distributed data storage systems); Data written at one node can be replicated to multiple nodes. Data store is thus fault-tolerant. The store can be partitioned into unshared shards.

Features in NoSQL Transactions NoSQL transactions have following features:

(i) Relax one or more of the ACID properties.
(ii) Characterize by two out of three properties (consistency, availability and partitions) of CAP theorem, two are at least present for the application/service/process.
(iii) Can be characterized by BASE properties (Section 3.2.3).

Big Data NoSQL solutions use standalone-server, master-slave and peer-to-peer distribution models.

Big Data NoSQL Solutions NoSQL DBs are needed for Big Data solutions. They play an important role in handling Big Data challenges. Table 3.1 gives the examples of widely used NoSQL data stores.

Table 3.1 NoSQL data stores and their characteristic features

NoSQL Data store	Description
Apache's HBase	HDFS compatible, open-source and non-relational data store written in Java; A column-family based NoSQL data store, data store providing BigTable-like capabilities (Sections 2.6 and 3.3.3.2); scalability, strong consistency, versioning, configuring and maintaining data store characteristics
Apache's MongoDB	HDFS compatible; master-slave distribution model (Section 3.5.1.3); document-oriented data store with JSON-like documents and dynamic schemas; open-source, NoSQL, scalable and non-relational database; used by Websites Craigslist, eBay, Foursquare at the backend
Apache's Cassandra	HDFS compatible DBs; decentralized distribution peer-to-peer model (Section 3.5.1.4); open source; NoSQL; scalable, non-relational, column-family based, fault-tolerant and tuneable consistency (Section 3.7) used by Facebook and Instagram

(Contd.)

NoSQL Data store	Description
Apache's CouchDB	A project of Apache which is also widely used database for the web. CouchDB consists of Document Store. It uses the JSON data exchange format to store its documents, JavaScript for indexing, combining and transforming documents, and HTTP APIs
Oracle NoSQL	Step towards NoSQL data store; distributed key-value data store; provides transactional semantics for data manipulation, horizontal scalability, simple administration and monitoring
Riak	An open-source key-value store; high availability (using replication concept), fault tolerance, operational simplicity, scalability and written in Erlang

CAP Theorem Among C, A and P, two are at least present for the application/service/process. *Consistency* means all copies have the same value like in traditional DBs. *Availability* means at least one copy is available in case a partition becomes inactive or fails. For example, in web applications, the other copy in the other partition is available. ***Partition*** means parts which are active but may not cooperate (share) as in distributed DBs.

1. *Consistency in distributed databases* means that all nodes observe the same data at the same time. Therefore, the operations in one partition of the database should reflect in other related partitions in case of distributed database. Operations, which change the sales data from a specific showroom in a table should also reflect in changes in related tables which are using that sales data.
2. *Availability* means that during the transactions, the field values must be available in other partitions of the database so that each request receives a response on success as well as failure. (Failure causes the response to request from the replicate of data). Distributed databases require transparency between one another. Network failure may lead to data unavailability in a certain partition in case of no replication. Replication ensures availability.
3. *Partition* means division of a large database into different databases without affecting the operations on them by adopting specified procedures.

Partition tolerance: Refers to continuation of operations as a whole even in case of message loss, node failure or node not reachable.

Brewer's CAP (Consistency, Availability and Partition Tolerance) theorem demonstrates that any distributed system cannot guarantee C, A and P together.

1. Consistency– All nodes observe the same data at the same time.
2. Availability– Each request receives a response on success/failure.
3. Partition Tolerance–The system continues to operate as a whole even in case of message loss, node failure or node not reachable.

Partition tolerance cannot be overlooked for achieving reliability in a distributed database system. Thus, in case of any network failure, a choice can be:

- Database must answer, and that answer would be old or wrong data (AP).
- Database should not answer, unless it receives the latest copy of the data (CP).

The CAP theorem implies that for a network partition system, the choice of consistency and availability are mutually exclusive. CA means consistency and availability, AP means availability and partition tolerance and CP means consistency and partition tolerance. Figure 3.1 shows the CAP theorem usage in Big Data Solutions.

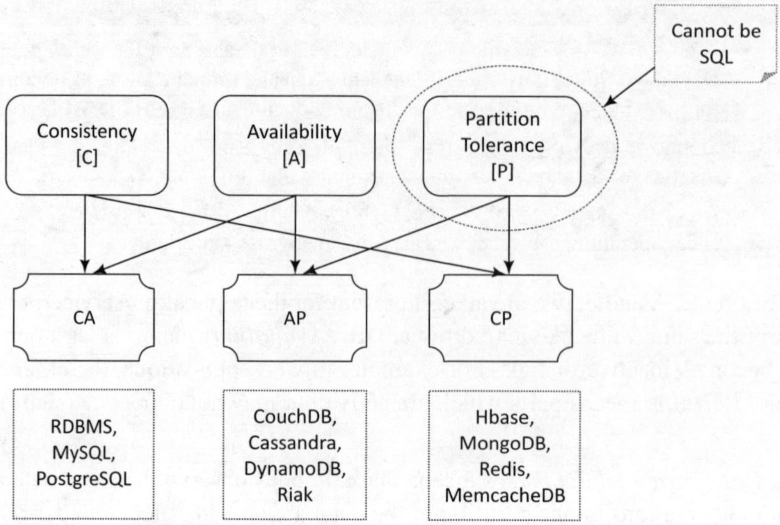

Figure 3.1 CAP theorem in Big Data solutions

3.2.2 Schema-less Models

Schema of a database system refers to designing of a structure for datasets and data structures for storing into the database. NoSQL data not necessarily have a fixed table schema. The systems do not use the concept of Join (between distributed datasets). A cluster-based highly distributed node manages a single large data store with a NoSQL DB.

Data written at one node replicates to multiple nodes. Therefore, these are identical, fault-tolerant and partitioned into shards. Distributed databases can store and process a set of information on more than one computing nodes.

NoSQL data model offers relaxation in one or more of the ACID properties (Atomicity, consistence, isolation and durability) of the database. Distribution follows CAP theorem. CAP theorem states that out of the three properties, two must at least be present for the application/service/process. (Section 3.2.1).

Figure 3.2 shows characteristics of Schema-less model for data stores. ER stands for entity-relation modelling.

Relations in a database build the connections between various tables of data. For example, a table of subjects offered in an academic programme can be connected to a table of programmes offered in the academic institution. NoSQL data stores use non-mathematical relations but store this information as an aggregate called metadata.

Metadata refers to data describing and specifying an object or objects. Metadata is a record with all the information about a particular dataset and the inter-linkages. Metadata helps in selecting an object, specifications of the data and, usages that design where and when. Metadata specifies access permissions, attributes of the objects and enables additions of an attribute layer to the objects. Files, tables, documents and images are also the objects.

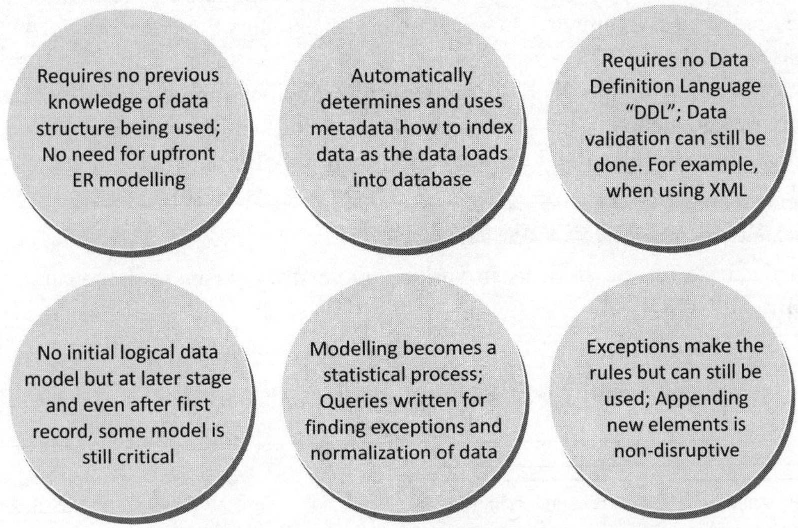

Figure 3.2 Characteristics of Schema-less model

3.2.3 Increasing Flexibility for Data Manipulation

Consider database 'Contacts'. They follow a fixed schema. Now consider students' admission database. That also follow a fixed schema. Later, additional data is added as the course progresses. NoSQL data store characteristics are schema-less. The additional data may not be structured and follow fixed schema. The data store consists of additional data, such as documents, blogs, Facebook pages and tweets.

NoSQL data store possess characteristic of increasing flexibility for data manipulation. The new attributes to database can be increasingly added. Late binding of them is also permitted.

BASE is a flexible model for NoSQL data stores. Provisions of BASE increase flexibility.

BASE Properties BA stands for basic availability, S stands for soft state and E stands for eventual consistency.

1. *Basic availability* ensures by distribution of shards (many partitions of huge data store) across many data nodes with a high degree of replication. Then, a segment failure does not necessarily mean a complete data store unavailability.
2. *Soft state* ensures processing even in the presence of inconsistencies but achieving consistency eventually. A program suitably takes into account the inconsistency found during processing. NoSQL database design does not consider the need of consistency all along the processing time.
3. *Eventual consistency* means consistency requirement in NoSQL databases meeting at some point of time in future. Data converges eventually to a consistent state with no time-frame specification for achieving that. ACID rules require consistency all along the processing on completion of each transaction. BASE does not have that requirement and has the flexibility.

BASE model is not necessarily appropriate in all cases but it is flexible and is an alternative to SQL-like adherence to ACID properties. Example 3.11 (Section 3.3.5) explains the concept of BASE in transactions using graph databases.

Schema is not a necessity in NoSQL DB, implying information storage flexibility. Data can store and retrieve without having knowledge of how a database stores and functions internally.

Following is an example to understand the increasing flexibility for data manipulation.

EXAMPLE 3.1

Use examples of database for the students in various university courses to demonstrate the concept of increasing flexibility in NoSQL DBs.

SOLUTION

Figure 3.3 shows increasing flexibility concept using additional data models.

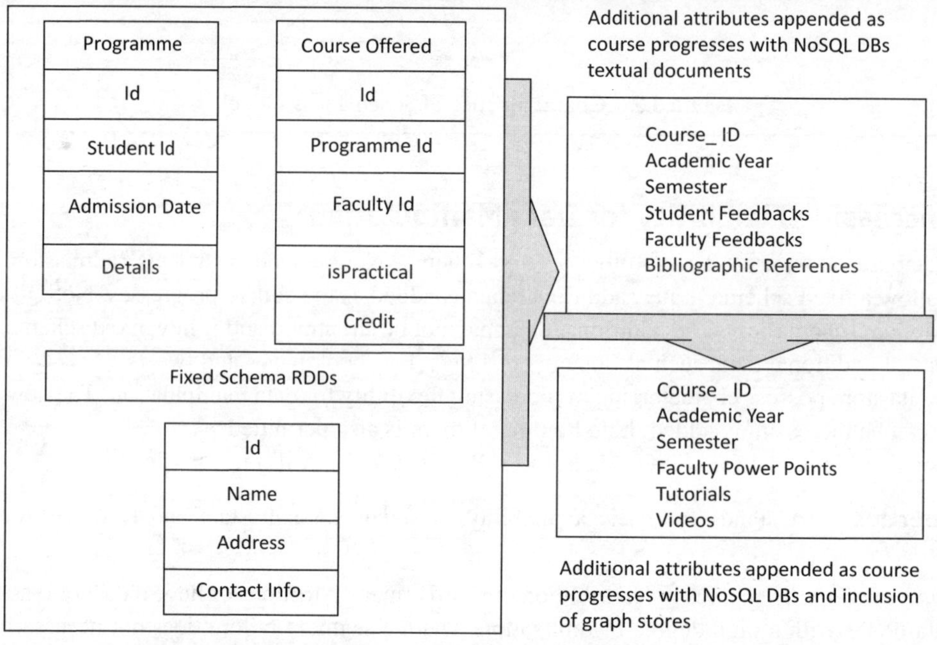

Figure 3.3 Increasing flexibility in NoSQL DB of students

Self-Assessment Exercise linked to LO 3.1

1. Explain when will you use the following: MongoDB, Cassandra, CouchDB, Oracle NoSQL and Riak. ●●●
2. How does CAP theorem hold in NoSQL databases? ○○●

3. How do ACID and BASE properties differ? ○●●
4. Why is the consistency not enforcable in NoSQL distributed databases during a transaction processing? ○●●
5. List characteristics of NoSQL data store. ○○●
6. Why is metadata a must when using NoSQL data store? ○○●

3.3 NOSQL DATA ARCHITECTURE PATTERNS

LO 3.2

NoSQL data-architecture patterns, namely key-value pairs, column family, BigTable, RC, ORC, Parquet, and tabular data stores, document stores, object data stores, graph databases, and data stores with variations in architectural patterns

NoSQL data stores broadly categorize into architectural patterns described in the following subsections:

3.3.1 Key-Value Store

The simplest way to implement a schema-less data store is to use key-value pairs. The data store characteristics are high performance, scalability and flexibility. Data retrieval is fast in key-value pairs data store. A simple string called, key maps to a large data string or BLOB (Basic Large Object). Key-value store accesses use a primary key for accessing the values. Therefore, the store can be easily scaled up for very large data. The concept is similar to a hash table where a unique key points to a particular item(s) of data. Figure 3.4 shows key-value pairs architectural pattern and example of students' database as key-value pairs.

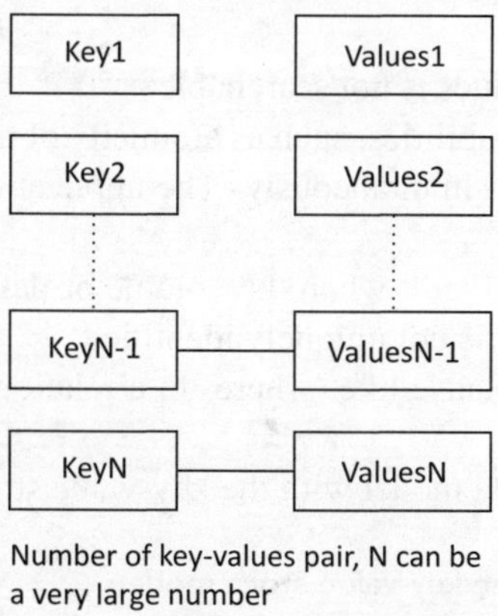

Key	Value
"Ashish"	"Category: Student; Class: B.Tech.; Semester: VII; Branch: Engineering; Mobile:9999912345"
"Mayuri"	"Category: student; class: M.Tech.; Mobile:8888823456"

Figure 3.4 Example of key-value pairs in data architectural pattern

Note: ○○● Level 1 & Level 2 category
○●● Level 3 & Level 4 category
●●● Level 5 & Level 6 category

Advantages of a key-value store are as follows:

1. Data Store can store any data type in a value field. The key-value system stores the information as a BLOB of data (such as text, hypertext, images, video and audio) and return the same BLOB when the data is retrieved. Storage is like an English dictionary. Query for a word retrieves the meanings, usages, different forms as a single item in the dictionary. Similarly, querying for key retrieves the values.
2. A query just requests the values and returns the values as a single item. Values can be of any data type.
3. Key-value store is eventually consistent.
4. Key-value data store may be hierarchical or may be ordered key-value store.
5. Returned values on queries can be used to convert into lists, table-columns, data-frame fields and columns.
6. Have (i) scalability, (ii) reliability, (iii) portability and (iv) low operational cost.
7. The key can be synthetic or auto-generated. The key is flexible and can be represented in many formats: (i) Artificially generated strings created from a hash of a value, (ii) Logical path names to images or files, (iii) REST web-service calls (request response cycles), and (iv) SQL queries.

The key-value store provides client to read and write values using a key as follows:

(i) `Get(key)`, returns the value associated with the key.
(ii) `Put (key, value)`, associates the value with the key and updates a value if this key is already present.
(iii) `Multi-get (key1, key2, .., keyN)`, returns the list of values associated with the list of keys.
(iv) `Delete(key)`, removes a key and its value from the data store.

Limitations of key-value store architectural pattern are:

(i) No indexes are maintained on values, thus a subset of values is not searchable.
(ii) Key-value store does not provide traditional database capabilities, such as atomicity of transactions, or consistency when multiple transactions are executed simultaneously. The application needs to implement such capabilities.
(iii) Maintaining unique values as keys may become more difficult when the volume of data increases. One cannot retrieve a single result when a key-value pair is not uniquely identified.
(iv) Queries cannot be performed on individual values. No clause like 'where' in a relational database usable that filters a result set.

Table 3.2 gives a comparison between traditional relational data model with the key-value store model.

Table 3.2 Traditional relational data model vs. the key-value store model

Traditional relational model	Key-value store model
Result set based on row values	Queries return a single item
Values of rows for large datasets are indexed	No indexes on values
Same data type values in columns	Any data type values

Typical uses of key-value store are: (i) Image store, (ii) Document or file store, (iii) Lookup table, and (iv) Query-cache.

Riak is open-source Erlang language data store. It is a key-value data store system. Data auto-distributes and replicates in Riak. It is thus, fault tolerant and reliable. Some other widely used key-value pairs in NoSQL DBs are Amazon's DynamoDB, Redis (often referred as Data Structure server), Memcached and its flavours, Berkeley DB, upscaledb (used for embedded databases), project Voldemort and Couchbase.

Concept of Hash Key The following example explains the hash and key-value pairs associated with a hash in traditional data.

EXAMPLE 3.2

Consider an example. Assume that student name is key, $\underline{k}$. Each student grade sheet entry has a number of values or set of (secondary) key-value pairs. For example, semester grade point average (SGPAs) values and cumulative grade point average (CGPA) value. How will the hash function be used?

SOLUTION

A hash function generates an index, I_k for k. I_k should ideally be unique and should uniquely map to k. I_k is a number with few digits only, compared to a number of characters (0-255 bytes) in the main key k used as input for the hash function. Assume that total 20 numbers of entries are present between slots indices between 00 to 99. Student name may consist of several characters, but index will be just two digits.

Hash table refers to using associated key-value pairs. A set of pairs retrieve by using a hash key. The hash key is a computed index using hash function for a column. The analytics may use the hash table. The table contains hash keys in the table-columns. The entries (values) across an array of slots (also called buckets). The buckets correspond to the key for the pairs at column. The values are in the associated rows of that column.

3.3.2 Document Store

Characteristics of Document Data Store are high performance and flexibility. Scalability varies, depends on stored contents. Complexity is low compared to tabular, object and graph data stores.

Following are the features in Document Store:

1. Document stores unstructured data.
2. Storage has similarity with object store.
3. Data stores in nested hierarchies. For example, in JSON formats data model [Example 3.3(ii)], XML document object model (DOM), or machine-readable data as one BLOB. Hierarchical information stores in a single unit called *document tree*. Logical data stores together in a unit.
4. Querying is easy. For example, using section number, sub-section number and figure caption and table headings to retrieve document partitions.
5. No object relational mapping enables easy search by following paths from the root of document tree.
6. Transactions on the document store exhibit ACID properties.

Typical uses of a document store are: (i) office documents, (ii) inventory store, (iii) forms data, (iv) document exchange and (v) document search.

The demerits in Document Store are incompatibility with SQL and complexity for implementation. Examples of Document Data Stores are CouchDB and MongoDB.

Real-life Datasets Section 10.3 will describe a very large real-life dataset for Big Data analytics as an examples. An application later analyses the structures in csv, json or other, and creates data stores in new forms (Sections 10.3.2 to 10.3.4). Runs in next step ETL, analytics or other functions. (Sections 10.4 to 10.6). This feature is called late binding (schema-on-read, or schema-on-need).

CSV and JSON File Formats CSV data store is a format for records [Example 1.9 and Example 3.3(i)]. CSV does not represent object-oriented databases or hierarchical data records. JSON and XML represent semistructured data, object-oriented records and hierarchical data records. *JSON* (Java Script Object Notation) refers to a language format for semistructured data. JSON represents object-oriented and hierarchical data records, object, and resource arrays in JavaScript.

The following example explains the CSV and JSON object concept and aspects of CSV and JSON file formats.

EXAMPLE 3.3

Assume Preeti gave examination in Semester 1 in 1995 in four subjects. She gave examination in five subjects in Semester 2 and so on in each subsequent semester. Another student, Kirti gave examination in Semester 1 in 2016 in three subjects, out of which one was theory and two were practical subjects. Presume the subject names and grades awarded to them.

(i) Write two CSV files for cumulative grade-sheets for both the students. Point the difficulty during processing of data in these two files.

(ii) Write a file in JSON format with each student grade-sheet as an object instance. How does the object-oriented and hierarchical data record in JSON make processing easier?

SOLUTION

(i) Two CSV file for cumulative grade-sheets are as follows:

CSV file for Preeti consists of the following nine lines each with four columns:

Semester, Subject Code, Subject Name, Grade

1, CS101, ""Theory of Computations"", 7.8.
1, CS102,1, ""Computer Architecture"", 7.8.
....
2, CS204, ""Object Oriented Programming"", 7.2.
2, CS205, ""Data Analytics"", 8.1.

The CSV file for Kirti consist of following five lines each with five columns: Semester, Subject Type, Subject Code, Subject Name, Grade

1, Theory, EL101, ""Analog Electronics"", 7.6.
1, Theory, EL102,1, ""Principles of Analog Communication"", 7.5.
1, Theory, EL103, ""Digital Electronics"", 7.8.
1, Practical, CS104, ""Analog ICs"", 7.2
1, Practical, CS105, ""Digital ICs"", 8.4

A column head is a key. Number of key-value pairs are (4 × 9) = 36 for preetiGradeSheet.csv and (5 × 5) = 25 for kirtiGradeSheet.csv. Therefore, when processing student records, merger of both files into a single file will need a program to extract the key-value pairs separately, and then prepare a single file.

(ii) JSON gives an advantage of creating a single file with multiple instances and inheritances of an object. Consider a single JSON file, *studentGradeSheets.json* for cumulative grade-sheets of many students. *Student_Grades* object is top in the hierarchy. Each *student_name* object is next in the hierarchy with object consisting of student name, each with number of instances of subject codes, subject types, subject titles and grades awarded. Each student name object-instance extends in student grades object-instances.

Part of the file construct can be as follows:

```
     0: {
              _id: 0,
  masterfile: "Students_Grades",
  instancetype: "single",
  mandatory: true,
  "description": "Uniquely identifies student grade master file Object
  Students_Grades "
   "resourcedefs": {
     "1": {
       _id:1,
        name: "studentName",
        instancetype: "multiple",
      "description": "Identifies a semester of the studentName and"
            resourcedefs: {
            "200" {
            _id:200
              studentName: "Kirti"
                instancetype: "single"
                resourcedefs: {
                   "201" {
        _id:201
         semester: "1",
         subjectType: "Theory",
          subjectCode: "EL101",
           subjectName: "Analog Electronics"
           Grade: 7.6
            type: "string",
            "description": "instance Grade for a subject Analog Electronics"
              }
      "202": {
    _ id:202,
              "203" {_id:203
     semester: "1",
     subjectType: "Theory"
    subjectCode: "EL102"
     subjectName: "Principles of Analog Communication"
    Grade: 7.5, type = "string"
```

```
                    }
        { .........
                         }
            {... .
                              }
     }
```

XML (eXtensible Markup Language) is an extensible, simple and scalable language. Its self-describing format describes structure and contents in an easy to understand format. XML is widely used. The document model consists of root element and their sub-elements. XML document model has a hierarchical structure. XML document model has features of object-oriented records. XML format finds wide uses in data store and data exchanges over the network. An XML document is semi-structured.

Document store appears quite similar to a key-value store and an object store. They are complex in implementation and are SQL incompatible. They have no object-relational layer for mapping and thus enable agile development of text analytics. No sharding of data takes place into the tables. Although the values stored as documents, follows structure and encoding of the managed data

The database stores and retrieves documents, such as XML, JSON, BSON (Binary-encoded Script Object Notation (for objects)). The documents are self-describing, hierarchical tree-structured consisting of maps, collections and scalar values. The documents stored are similar to each other but do not have to be the same. Some of the popular document data stores are CouchDB, MongoDB, Terrastore, OrientDB and RavenDB.

Certain NoSQL DBs enable ACID rule-based transactions also. Examples of document data stores are MongoDB, Apache Couchbase and MarkLogic.

CouchDB uses the JSON store data, HTTP APIs for connectivity, JavaScript for the query language and MapReduce for processing.

Document JSON Format CouchDB Database Apache CouchDB is an open-source database. Its features are:

1. CouchDB provides mapping functions during querying, combining and filtering of information.
2. CouchDB deploys JSON Data Store model for documents. Each document maintains separate data and metadata (schema).
3. CouchDB is a multi-master application. Write does not require field locking when controlling the concurrency during multi-master application.
4. CouchDB querying language is JavaScript. Java script is a language which documents use to transform.
5. CouchDB queries the indices using a web browser. CouchDB accesses the documents using HTTP API. HTTP methods are Get, Put and Delete (Section 3.3.1).
6. CouchDB data replication is the distribution model that results in fault tolerance and reliability.

Document JSON Format—MongoDB Database MongoDB Document database provides a rich query language and constructs, such as database indexes allowing easier handling of Big Data.

Example of Document in Document Store:

```
{
    "id": "1001"
```

```
    "Student Name":
  {
  "First": "Ashish",
  "Middle": "Kumar",
  "Last": "Rai"
     }
  "Category": "Student",
  "Class": "B.Tech.",
  "Semester": "VII",
  "Branch": "Computer Engineering",
  "Mobile": "12345"
  }
```

The document store allows querying the data based on the contents as well. For example, it is possible to search the document where student's first name is "Ashish". Document store can also provide the search value's exact location. The search is by using the document path. A type of key accesses the leaf values in the tree structure. Since the document stores are schema-less, adding fields to documents (XML or JSON) becomes a simple task.

Document Architecture Pattern and Discovering Hierarchical Structure Following is example of an XML document in which a hierarchical structure discovers later. Figure 3.5 shows an XML document architecture pattern in a document fragment and document tree structure.

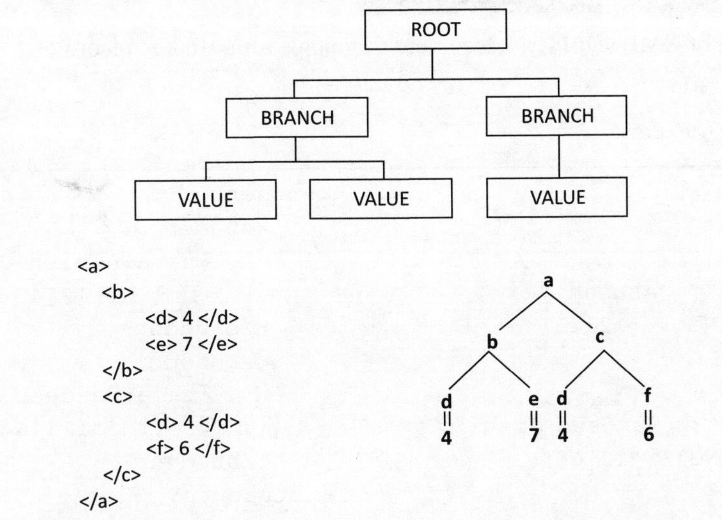

(a) XML document fragment (b) Tree representation of fragment

Figure 3.5 XML document architecture pattern

The document store follows a tree-like structure (similar to directory structure in file system). Beneath the root element there are multiple branches. Each branch has a related path expression that provides a way to navigate from the root to any given branch, sub-branch or value.

XQuery and XPath are query languages for finding and extracting elements and attributes from XML documents. The query commands use sub-trees and attributes of documents. The querying is similar as in SQL for databases. XPath treats XML document as a tree of nodes. XPath queries are expressed in the form of XPath expressions. Following is an example of XPath expressions:

EXAMPLE 3.4

Give examples of XPath expressions. Let outermost element of the XML document is *a*.

SOLUTION

An XPath expression */a/b/c* selects *c* elements that are children of *b* elements that are children of element *a* that forms the outermost element of the XML document.

An XPath expression */a/b[c=5]* selects elements *b* and *c* that are children of *a* and value of *c* element is *5*.

An XPath expression /a[b/c]/d selects elements c and d where c is child of *b* and *b* and *d* are children of *a*.

XML and JSON both are designed to form a simple and standard way of describing different kinds of hierarchical data structures. They are popularly used for storing and exchanging data. The following example explains the concept of Document Store in JSON and XML for hierarchical records.

EXAMPLE 3.5

Give the structures of XML and JSON document fragments for a student record.

SOLUTION

Following are the structures:

```
{
    "students": [
    {
      "name": "Ashish Jain",
      "rollNo": "12345"
    },
    {
      "name": "Sandeep Joshi",
      "rollNo": "12346"
    }
    ]
}
```

(a) JSON

```
<students>
    <student>
        <name>Ashish Jain</name>
        <rollNo>12345</rollNo>
    </student>
    <student>
        <name>Sandeep Joshi</name>
        <rollNo>12346</rollNo>
    </student>
</students>
```

(b) XML equivalent

When compared with XML, JSON has the following advantages:

- XML is easier to understand but XML is more verbose than JSON.
- XML is used to describe structured data and does not include arrays, whereas JSON includes arrays.
- JSON has basically key-value pairs and is easier to parse from JavaScript.
- The concise syntax of JSON for defining lists of elements makes it preferable for serialization of text format objects.

Document Collection A collection can be used in many ways for managing a large document store. Three uses of a document collection are:

1. Group the documents together, similar to a directory structure in a file-system. (A directory consists of grouping of file folders.)
2. Enables navigating through document hierarchies, logically grouping similar documents and storing business rules such as permissions, indexes and triggers (special procedure on some actions in a database).
3. A collection can contain other collections as well.

3.3.3 Tabular Data

Tabular data stores use rows and columns. Row-head field may be used as a key which access and retrieves multiple values from the successive columns in that row. The OLTP is fast on in-memory row-format data.

Oracle DBs provide both options: columnar and row format storages. Generally, relational DB store is *in-memory row-based data*, in which a key in the first column of the row is at a memory address, and values in successive columns at successive memory addresses. That makes OLTP easier. All fields of a row are accessed at a time together during OLTP. Different rows are stored in different addresses in the memory or disk. In-memory row-based DB stores a row as a consecutive memory or disk entry. This strategy makes data searching and accessing faster during *transactions* processing.

In-memory column-based data has the keys (row-head keys) in the first column of each row at successive memory addresses. The next column of each row after the key has the values at successive memory addresses. The values in the third column of each row are at the next memory addresses in succession, and so on up to N columns. The N can be a very large number. The column-based data makes the OLAP easier. All fields of a column access together. All fields of a set of columns may also be accessed together during OLAP. Different rows are stored in different addresses in the memory or disk, but each row values are now not at successive addresses. In-memory column-based DB store a column as a consecutive memory or disk entry. This strategy makes the analytics processing fast.

Following subsections describe NoSQL format data stores based on tabular formats.

3.3.3.1 Column Family Store

Columnar Data Store A way to implement a schema is the divisions into columns. Storage of each column, successive values is at the successive memory addresses. Analytics processing (AP) In-memory uses columnar storage in memory. A pair of row-head and column-head is a key-pair. The pair accesses a field in the table.

All values in successive fields in a column consisting of multiple rows save at consecutive memory addresses. This enables fast accesses during in-memory analytics, which includes CPU accesses and analyses using memory addresses in which values are cached from the disk before processing. The OLAP (on-line AP) is also fast on in-memory column-format data. An application uses a combination of row head and a column head as a key for access to the value saved at the field.

Column-Family Data Store Column-family data-store has a group of columns as a column family. A combination of row-head, column-family head and table-column head can also be a key to access a field in a column of the table during querying. Combination of row head, column families head, column-family head and column head for values in column fields can also be a key to access fields of a column. A column-family head is also called a super-column head.

Examples of columnar family data stores are HBase, BigTable, HyperTable and Cassandra. The following example explains a column-family data store and why OLAP is fast in-memory column data store in memory:

EXAMPLE 3.6

Consider Example 1.6(i). Assume in-memory columnar storage. Data for a large number of ACVMs with an ACVM_ID each, store in column 1. Data for each day sales at each ACVM for KitKat, Milk, Fruit and Nuts, Nougat and Oreo store in Columns 2 to 6. Each row has six cells (ID +five sales data).

(i) How do the column key values store in memory?
(ii) How do the values store in the memory in columnar storage format?
(iii) How does analytics of each day's sales help?
(iv) Why do in-memory columnar storage result in fast computations during analytics?
(v) How are a column family and column-family head (key) specified?
(vi) How do a column-families group specify?
(vii) How do row groups form? What is the advantage of division into sub-groups?

SOLUTION

Assume the following columnar storage at memory:

(i) Column and row keys
Addresses 1000, 2000, 3000, …., 6000 save the column keys. Address 1000 stores string 'ACVM_ID'. Then the adresses 1001, 1002, …., 1999 store the row keys, means ACVM_IDs.
Chocolate name of five flavours store at addresses 2000, 3000, 4000, 5000, and 6000.

(ii) Column field values
Column 1 ACVM_IDs store at address 1001 to 1999 for 999 ACVMs. Sales in a day for KitKat, Milk, Fruit and Nuts, Nougat and Oreo store at addresses 2001 to 2999, 3001 to 3999, 4001 to 4999, 5001 to 5999, and 6001 to 6999.
Table 3.3 gives sample values in the columns for a day's sales data. The table also gives the keys for row groups, rows (ACVM_IDs), a column family group, two column families and five column heads for 5 flavours of chocolates. The table gives a row group of just 100 rows, just for the sale of assumption.
Figure 3.6 shows fields in columnar storage and addresses in memory. The figure shows ACVM_IDs as well as each day's sales of each flavour of chocolate at 999 ACVMs. Following are the addresses assigned to the values in fields of Table 3.3:

Table 3.3 Each day's sales of chocolates on 999 ACVMs

		Nestle Chocolate Flavours Group				
		Popular Flavours Family		Costly Flavours Family		
	ACVM_ID	KitKat	Milk	Fruit and Nuts	Nougat	Oreo
Row-group_1 for IDs 1 to 100	1	360	150	500	101	222
	2	289	175	457	145	317
	....	....	....		....	....
Row-group_m for IDs 901 to 999	....	....	....		....	....
	998	123	201	385	199	310
	999	75	215	560	108	250

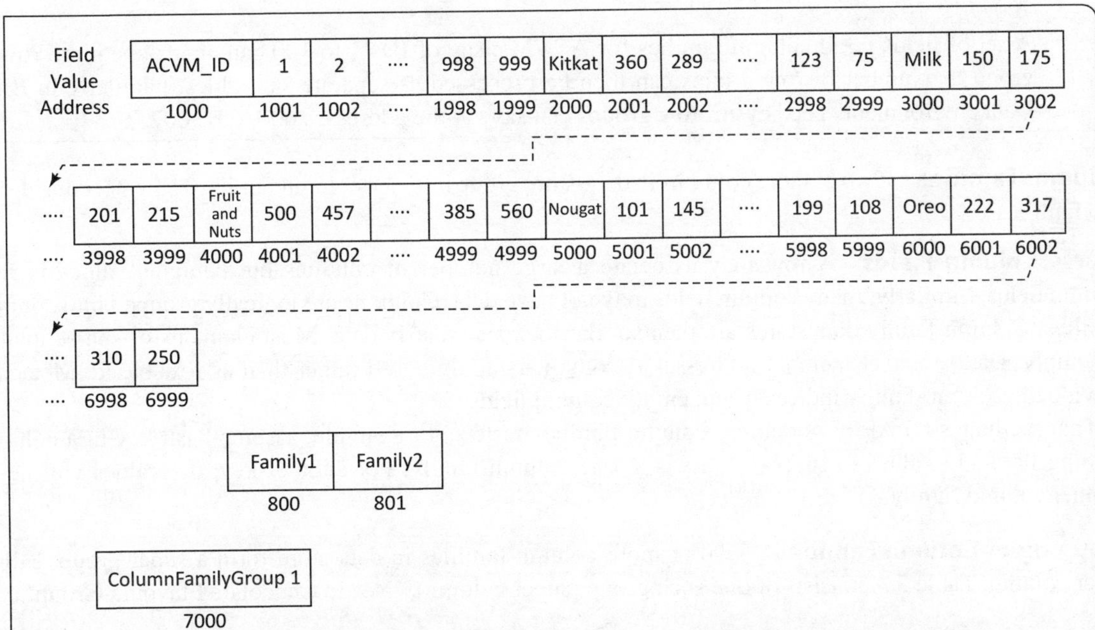

Figure 3.6 Fields in columnar storage and addresses in memory.

(iii) An analytics application computes the results, such as (a) total sales of each flavour, KitKat, Milk, Fruit and Nuts, Nougat and Oreo, each day, (b) Each ACVM requirement for refilling at each ACVM each day, (c) ID of maximum sales of chocolates each day, (d) cluster of ACVMs showing highest sales, classification of ACVMs as low, moderate and high sales.

(iv) Consider first address of sales data for KitKat, $address_{0,\ kk}$ = 1001 of machine ID, ACVMId at $address_0$ =1000. Total sales at all 999 ACVMs in a day requires the sum of values between address 1001 to 1999. Increment to the next address is fast when compared to the case when during the

execution the value addresses compute from a table of pointers for them. When values are in the row storage format, the chocolate KitKat sales data at the machines will be at addresses 1001, 1007, 1013, ... The table of pointers or computations of address$_{0, kk}$ + n × N + 1, where N is number of columns for each row, is required, and n = 0, 1, 2, ..., 998, 999. The processing takes longer compared to instruction for increment of pointed address to next memory address.
Therefore, analytics of (a), (b), (c) and (d) is quicker fast in case of In-memory columnar storage compared to row format storage in memory.

(v) Columns in Table 3.3 for KitKat and Milk form a group as one family. Columns for Fruit and Nuts, Nougat, and Oreo form a group as second family. The key for one family is 'Popular Flavours Family' and second family is 'Costly Flavours Family'. The keys of column families can save at the addresses 800, 801, ...

(vi) Two column-families in Table 3.3, Popular Flavours Family and Costly Flavours Family form a super group, 'Nestle Chocolate Flavours'. The key for super group of column-families group is 'Nestle Chocolate Flavours'. The keys of column-family super groups can save at the addresses 700, 701, 702, ...

(vii) A set of fields in all column families for ACVMs, say of IDs 1 to 100 can be grouped into row-group_1. Number of row-groups can then be processed as separate sub-tables, parallelly in Big Data environment. The keys of row groups can save at the addresses 600, 601, 602, ...

Columns Families Two of more columns in data-store group into one column family. Table 3.3 considered two families.

Sparse Column Fields A row may associate a large number of columns but contains values in few column fields. Similarly, many column fields may not have data. Columns are logically grouped into column families. Column-family data stores are then similar to sparse matrix data. Most elements of sparse matrix are empty. Data stores at memory addresses is columnar-family based rather than as row based. Metadata provide the column-family indices of not empty column fields.

That facilitates OLAP of not empty column families faster. For example, assume hash key in a column heading field and values in successive rows at one column family. For another key, the values will be in another column family.

Grouping of Column Families Two or more column-families in data store form a super group, called super column. Table 3.3 consists of one such group (super column), 'Nestle Chocolate Flavours Group'.

Grouping into Rows When number of rows are very large then horizontal partitioning of the table is a necessity. Each partition forms one row-group. For example, a group of 1 million rows per partition. A row group thus has all column data store in the memory for in-memory analytics. Practically, row groups are chosen such that memory required for the group is above, say 10 MB and below the maximum size which can cached and buffered in memory, say 1 GB for in-memory analytics.

Data caching, buffering in memory and storing back at disk takes time. So frequent disk accesses remain controlled. Therefore, minimum row-group size of 10 MB is practical (Table 3.3 considered a row group of just 100 rows for the purpose of explaining the addressing and use of keys in a columnar-family data store).

Characteristics of Columnar Family Data Store Columnar family data store imbibes characteristics of very high performance and scalability, moderate level of flexibility and lower complexity when compared to the object and graph databases. Advantages of column stores are:

1. *Scalability*: The database uses row IDs and column names to locate a column and values at the column fields. The interface for the fields is simple. The back-end system can distribute queries over a large number of processing nodes without performing any Join operations. The retrieval of data from the distributed node can be least complicated by an intelligent plan of row IDs and columns, thereby increasing performance. Scalability means addition of number of rows as the number of ACVMs increase in Example 1.6(i). Number of processing instructions is proportional to the number of ACVMs due to scalable operations.
2. *Partitionability*: For example, large data of ACVMs can be partitioned into datasets of size, say 1 MB in the number of row-groups. Values in columns of each row-group, process in-memory at a partition. Values in columns of each row-group independently parallelly process in-memory at the partitioned nodes.
3. *Availability*: The cost of replication is lower since the system scales on distributed nodes efficiently. The lack of Join operations enables storing a part of a column- family matrix on remote computers. Thus, the data is always available in case of failure of any node.
4. *Tree-like columnar structure* consisting of column-family groups, column families and columns. The columns group into families. The column families group into column groups (super columns). A key for the column fields consists of three secondary keys: column-families group ID, column-family ID and column-head name.
5. *Adding new data at ease*: Permits new column *Insert* operations. Trigger operation creates new columns on an Insert. The column-field values can add after the last address in memory if the column structure is known in advance. New row-head field, row-group ID field, column-family group, column family and column names can be created at any time to add new data.
6. *Querying all the field values* in a column in a family, all columns in the family or a group of column-families, is fast in in-memory column-family data store.
7. *Replication of columns*: HDFS-compatible column-family data stores replicate each data store with default replication factor = 3.
8. *No optimization for Join*: Column-family data stores are similar to sparse matrix data. The data do not optimize for Join operations.

Column-family data store in a format in which store set of column family field-values which are not empty (null or zero). Metadata of the matrix consists of hash keys that reference each set distinctly.

Typical uses of column store are: (i) web crawling, (ii) large sparsely populated tables and (iii) system that has high variance.

HDFS is highly reliable for very long running queries. However, IO operations are slow. Columnar storage is a solution for faster IOs. Columnar storage in memory stores the data actually required for the IOs. Only columns needing the access load during execution. Also, a columnar-object data store can be compressed or encoded. The encoding is according to the data type. Also, the executions of different columns or column partitions can be in parallel at the cluster data-nodes.

3.3.3.2 BigTable Data Store

Examples of widely used column-family data store are Google's BigTable, HBase and Cassandra. Keys for *row key*, *column key*, *timestamp* and *attribute* uniquely identify the values in the fields (Refer Example 2.4)

Following are features of a BigTable:

1. Massively scalable NoSQL. BigTable scales up to 100s of petabytes.
2. Integrates easily with Hadoop and Hadoop compatible systems.

3. Compatibility with MapReduce, HBase APIs which are open-source Big Data platforms.
4. Key for a field uses not only row_ID and Column_ID (for example, ACVM_ID and KitKat in Example 3.6) but also timestamp and attributes. Values are ordered bytes. Therefore, multiple versions of values may be present in the BigTable.
5. Handles million of operations per second.
6. Handle large workloads with low latency and high throughput
7. Consistent low latency and high throughput
8. APIs include security and permissions
9. BigTable, being Google's cloud service, has global availability and its service is seamless.

The following example explains the use of rowID, ColumID and Column attributes in BigTable formats.

EXAMPLE 3.7

Consider Example 3.6. Consider column fields which have keys to access a field not only by row ID and Column ID but also include the timestamp and attributes in a row. Show the column-keys for accessing column fields of a column.

SOLUTION

Table 3.4 gives keys for each day's sales of KitKat chocolates at ACVMs. First row-headings are the column-keys.

Table 3.4 Each day's sales of KitKat chocolates at ACVMs

Column-keys →

ACVM_ID	KitKatSalesDate	Timestamp	KitKatSalesNumber

3.3.3.3 RC File Format

Hive uses Record Columnar (RC) file-format records for querying. RC is the best choice for intermediate tables for fast column-family store in HDFS with Hive. Serializability of RC table column data is the advantage. RC file is DeSerializable into column data. A table such as that shown in Example 3.6 can be partitioned into row groups. Values at each column of a row group store as the RC record. The RC file records store data of a column in the row group (*Serializability* means query or transaction executable by series of instructions such that execution ensures correct results).

The following example explains the use of row groups in the RC file format for column of a row group:

EXAMPLE 3.8

Consider Example 3.6. Practically, row groups have millions of rows and in-memory between 10 MB and 1 GB. Assume two row groups of just two rows each. Consider the following values given in Table 3.3.

Row-group_1 for IDs 1 to 2					
1	360	150	500	101	222
2	289	175	457	145	317

Row-group_m for IDs 998 to 999					
998	123	201	385	199	310
999	75	215	560	108	250

Make a file in RC format.

SOLUTION

The values in each column are the records in file for each row group. Each row-group data is like a column of records which stores in the RC file.

Row group_1		Row group_m	
1, 2;		998, 999;	← ACVM_ID
360, 289;		123, 75;	← KitKat
….		…	← Milk
….		…	← Fruit and Nuts
		…	← Nougat
222, 317;		310, 250;	← Oreo

RC file for row group_1 will consists of records 1, 2; 360, 289; …, 222, 317; on serialization of column records. RC file for row group_m will consists of 998, 999; 123, 75; …, 310, 250;

3.3.3.4 *ORC File Format*

An ORC (Optimized Row Columnar) file consists of row-group data called stripes. ORC enables concurrent reads of the same file using separate RecordReaders. Metadata store uses Protocol Buffers for addition and removal of fields.[1]

ORC is an intelligent Big Data file format for HDFS and Hive.[2] An ORC file stores a collections of rows as a row-group. Each row-group data store in columnar format. This enables parallel processing of multiple row-groups in an HDFS cluster.

An ORC file consists of a stripe the size of the file is by default 256 MB. Stripe consists of indexing (mapping) data in 8 columns, row-group columns data (contents) and stripe footer (metadata). An ORC has two sets of columns data instead of one column data in RC. One column is for each map or list size and other values which enable a query to decide skipping or reading of the mapped columns. A mapped column has contents required by the query. The columnar layout in each ORC file thus, optimizes for compression and enables skipping of data in columns. This reduces read and decompression load.

Lightweight indexing is an ORC feature. Those blocks of rows which do not match a query skip as they do not map on using indices data at metadata. Each index includes the aggregated values of minimum, maximum, sum and count using aggregation functions on the content columns. Therefore, contents-column key for accessing the contents from a column consists of combination of row-group key, column mapping key, min, max, count (number) of column fields of the contents column. Table 3.5 gives the keys used to

[1] https://cwiki.apache.org/confluence/display/Hive/LanguageManual +ORC#LanguageManualORC-ORCFileFormat

[2] http://www.semantikoz.com/blog/orc-intelligent-big-data-file-format-hadoop-hive/

access or skip a contents column during querying. The keys are Stripe_ID, Index-column key, and contents-column name, min, max and count.

Table 3.5 Keys to access or skip a content column in ORC file format

	Index Column 1				Index Column 2
	Index column 1 key 1				Index column 2 key 1
	Contents-Column name	Contents Minimum value	Contents Maximum value	Count (number) of content-column fields	
	...	...	...	...	
Stripe_ID	...	...	...	...	
	Index column 1 key 2				Index column 2 key 2
	Column-name	Minimum value	Maximum value	Count of number of column fields	
	...	...	...	...	
	...	...	...	...	

Consider Example 3.6. ORC key to access during a query consist of not only column head 'KitKat' (Table 3.3) but also column minimum and maximum sales on an ACVM, count of number of fields in values 'KitKat'. Analytics operations frequently need these values. Ready availability of these values from the index data itself improves the throughput in Big Data HDFS environment. These values do not need to compute again and again using aggregation functions, such as min, max and count.

An ORC thus, optimizes for reading serially the column fields in HDFS environment. The throughput increases due to skipping and reading of the required fields at contents-column key. Reading less number of ORC file content-columns reduces the workload on the NameNode.

3.3.3.5 Parquet File Formats

Parquet is nested hierarchical columnar-storage concept. Nesting sequence is the table, row group, column chunk and chunk page. Apache Parquet file is columnar-family store file. Apache Spark SQL executes user defined functions (UDFs) which query the Parquet file columns (Section 5.2.1.3). A programmer writes the codes for an UDF and creates the processing function for big long queries.

A Parquet file uses an HDFS block. The block stores the file for processing queries on Big Data. The file compulsorily consists of metadata, though the file need not consist of data.

The Parquet file consists of row groups. A row-group columns data process in-memory after data cache and buffer at the memory from the disk. Each row group has a number of columns. A row group has N_{col} columns, and row group consists of N_{col} column chunks. This means each column chunk consists of values saved in each column of each row group.

A column chunk can be divided into pages and thus, consists of one or more pages. The column chunk consists of a number of interleaved pages, N_{pg}. A page is a conceptualized unit which can be compressed or encoded together at an instance. The unit is minimum portion of a chunk which is read at an instance for in-memory analytics.

An ORC array <int> has two columns, one for array size and the other for contents. Parquet format file does not consist of extra column per nesting level. Similarly, ORC has two columns, one is for each Map,

List size, min, max and the second is for the contents. Parquet format file does not consist of extra column per nesting level, just one column per leaf in the schema.

[Parquet in English means 'a floor covering made of small rectangular wooden blocks (tiles) fitted together in a pattern. Similarly, Parquet objects have pages as the tiles. Pages build a column chunk. Column chunks build a row group. Row groups build the table. A page is like a tile consisting of column fields. The values read or write at an instance or used for encoding or compression. The values are not read separately from a page.]

Table 3.6 gives the keys used to access or skip the contents page. Three keys are: (i) row-group_ID, (ii) column-chunk key and (iii) page key.

Table 3.6 Combination of keys for content page in the Parquet file format

<table>
<tr><td rowspan="8">Row-group_ID</td><td colspan="4">Column Chunk 1 key</td></tr>
<tr><td>Page 1 key</td><td>Page 2 key</td><td>"""</td><td>Page m key</td></tr>
<tr><td>..</td><td>...</td><td>...</td><td>...</td></tr>
<tr><td>..</td><td>...</td><td>...</td><td>...</td></tr>
<tr><td colspan="4">Column Chunk 2 key</td></tr>
<tr><td>Page 1key</td><td>Page 2 key</td><td>"""</td><td>Page key m'</td></tr>
<tr><td>..</td><td>...</td><td>...</td><td>...</td></tr>
<tr><td>..</td><td>...</td><td>...</td><td>...</td></tr>
</table>

3.3.4 Object Data Store

An object store refers to a repository which stores the:

1. Objects (such as files, images, documents, folders, and business reports)
2. System metadata which provides information such as filename, creation_date, last_modified, language_used (such as Java, C, C#, C++, Smalltalk, Python), access_permissions, supported query languages)
3. Custom metadata which provides information, such as subject, category, sharing permissions.

Metadata enables the gathering of metrics of objects, searches, finds the contents and specifies the objects in an object data-store tree. Metadata finds the relationships among the objects, maps the object relations and trends. Object Store metadata interfaces with the Big Data. API first mines the metadata to enable mining of the trends and analytics. The metadata defines classes and properties of the objects. Each Object Store may consist of a database. Document content can be stored in either the object store database storage area or in a file storage area. A single file domain may contain multiple Object Stores.

Data definition and manipulation, DB schema design, database browsing, DB administration, application compilation and debugging use a programming language.

Eleven Functions Supporting APIs An Object data store consists of functions supporting APIs for: (i) scalability, (ii) indexing, (iii) large collections, (iv) querying language, processing and optimization (s), (v) Transactions, (vi) data replication for high availability, data distribution model, data integration (such as with relational database, XML, custom code), (vii) schema evolution, (viii) persistency, (ix) persistent object life cycle, (x) adding modules and (xi) locking and caching strategy.

Object Store may support versioning for collaboration. Object Store can be created using IBM 'Content Platform Engine'. Creation needs installing and configuring the engine (Engine is software which drives forward.). Console of the engine makes creation of process easy. Amazon S3 and Microsoft Azure BLOB support the Object Store.

Amazon S3 (Simple Storage Service) S3 refers to Amazon web service on the cloud named S3. The S3 provides the Object Store. The Object Store differs from the block and file-based cloud storage. Objects along with their metadata store for each object store as the files. S3 assigns an ID number for each stored object. The service has two storage classes: Standard and infrequent access. Interfaces for S3 service are REST, SOAP and Bit Torrent. S3 uses include web hosting, image hosting and storage for backup systems. S3 is scalable storage infrastructure, same as used in Amazon e-commerce service. S3 may store trillions of objects.

The following example lists Object Store development platforms:

EXAMPLE 3.9

List the functions of Minio, Riak, VERSANT Object Database (VOD), GEMSTONE, Amazon S3 and Microsoft Azure BLOB that support using Object Store APIs.

SOLUTION

1. An open-source multi-clouds object storage server is Minio, which is API compatible with Amazon S3 API and number of widely used public and private clouds. Compatibility enables data export to S3 and usages of APIs.
2. Riak CS (Cloud Storage) is object storage management software on top of Riak. It models on open-source distributed-database which is Amazon-compliant. This means database exports to S3 and use S3 APIs.
3. VOD consists of 11 functions supporting APIs listed above. VOD enables use by multiple concurrent users. VOD supports cross-platform operating systems (OSs), such as Linux, Windows NT, AIX, HP-UX and Solaris (both 32 and 64 bits for all platforms).
4. GEMSTONE Object DB APIs development language is SmallTalk. The platform supports in-memory DBs, object-oriented processing and distributed caches. GEMSTONE provides cross platform support, OSs AIX, Linux, MacOS and Solaris.

3.3.4.1 Object Relational Mapping

The following example explains object relational mapping.

EXAMPLE 3.10

How does an HTML object and XML based web service relate with tabular data stores?

SOLUTION

Figure 3.7 shows the object relational mapping of HTML document and XML web services store with a tabular data store.

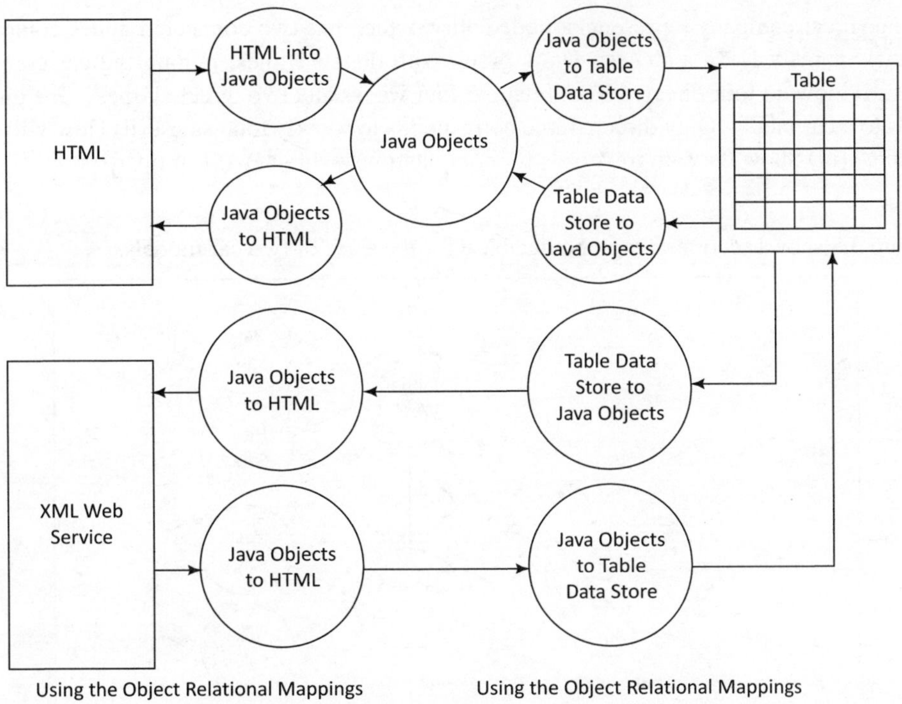

Figure 3.7 HTML document and XML web services

3.3.5 Graph Database

One way to implement a data store is to use graph database. A characteristic of graph is high flexibility. Any number of nodes and any number of edges can be added to expand a graph. The complexity is high and the performance is variable with scalability. Data store as series of interconnected nodes. Graph with data nodes interconnected provides one of the best database system when relationships and relationship types have critical values.

Data Store focuses on modeling *interconnected* structure of data. Data stores based on graph theory relation $\mathcal{G} = (\mathcal{E}, \mathcal{V})$, where $\mathcal{E}$ is set of edges $e_1, e_2, \ldots$ and $\mathcal{V}$ is set of vertices, $v_1, v_2, \ldots, v_n$.

Nodes represent entities or objects. Edges encode relationships between nodes. Some operations become simpler to perform using graph models. Examples of graph model usages are social networks of connected people. The connections to related persons become easier to model when using the graph model.

The following example explains the graph database application in describing entities relationships and relationship types.

EXAMPLE 3.11

Let us assume a car company represents a node entity, which has two connected nodes comprising two model entities, namely Hexa and Zest. Draw graph with directed lines, joining the car company with two entities. (i) How do four directed lines relate to four weeks and two directed lines? One directed line corresponds to a car model. Only directed line corresponds to weekly total sales. (ii) How will the yearly sales compute? (iii) Show the path traversals for computations exhibit BASE properties.

SOLUTION

(i) Figure 3.8 shows section of a graph database for the sales of two car models.

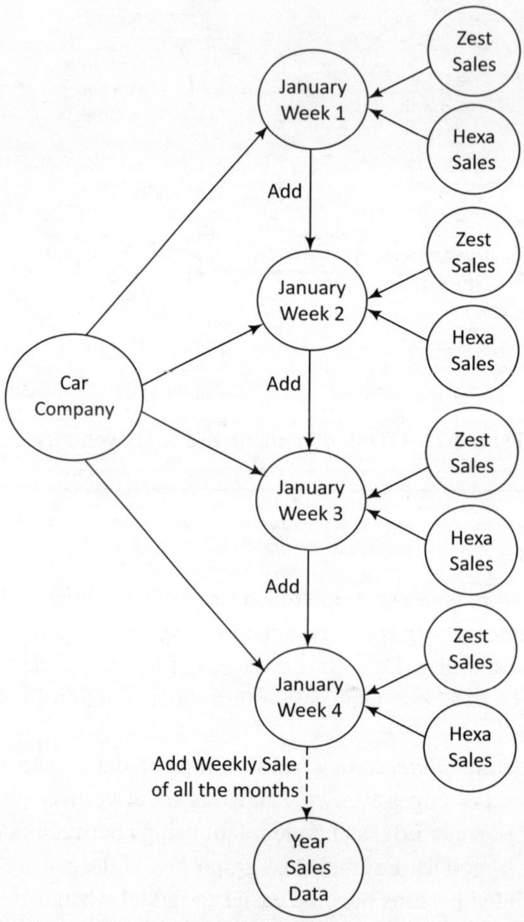

Figure 3.8 Section of the graph database for car-model sales

(ii) The yearly sales compute by path traversals from nodes for weekly sales to yearly sales data.

(iv) The path traversals exhibit BASE properties because during the intermediate paths, consistency is not maintained. Eventually when all the path traversals complete, the data becomes consistent.

Graph databases enable fast network searches. Graph uses linked datasets, such as social media data. Data store uses graphs with nodes and edges connecting each other through relations, associations and properties.

Querying for data uses graph traversal along the paths. Traversal may use single-step, path expressions or full recursion. A relationship represents key. A node possesses property including ID. An edge may have a label which may specify a role.

Characteristics of graph databases are:

1. Use specialized query languages, such as RDF uses SPARQL
2. Create a database system which models the data in a completely different way than the key-values, document, columnar and object data store models.
3. Can have hyper-edges. A hyper-edge is a set of vertices of a hypergraph. A hypergraph is a generalization of a graph in which an edge can join any number of vertices (not only the neighbouring vertices).
4. Consists of a collection of small data size records, which have complex interactions between graph-nodes and hypergraph nodes. Nodes represent the entities or objects. Nodes use Joins. Node identification can use URI or other tree-based structure. The edge encodes a relationship between the nodes.

When a new relationship adds in RDBMS, then the schema changes. The data need transfer from one field to another. The task of adding relations in graph database is simpler. The nodes assign internal identifiers to the nodes and use these identifiers to join the network. Traversing the joins or relationships is fast in graph databases. It is due to the simpler form of graph nodes. The graph data may be kept in RAM only. The relationship between nodes is consistent in a graph store.

Graph databases have poor scalability. They are difficult to scale out on multiple servers. This is due to the close connectivity feature of each node in the graph. Data can be replicated on multiple servers to enhance read and the query processing performance. Write operations to multiple servers and graph queries that span multiple nodes, can be complex to implement.

Typical uses of graph databases are: (i) link analysis, (ii) friend of friend queries, (iii) Rules and inference, (iv) rule induction and (v) Pattern matching. Link analysis is needed to perform searches and look for patterns and relationships in situations, such as social networking, telephone, or email records (Sections 9.4 and 9.5). Rules and inference are used to run queries on complex structures such as class libraries, taxonomies and rule-based systems.

Examples of graph DBs are Neo4J, AllegroGraph, HyperGraph, Infinite Graph, Titan and FlockDB. Neo4J graph database enable easy usages by Java developers. Neo4J can be designed fully ACID rules compliant. Design consists of adding additional path traversal in between the transactions such that data consistency is maintained and the transactions exhibit ACID properties.

Spark provides a simple and expressive programming model that includes supports to a wide range of applications, including graph computation. Chapter 8 describes Graph Databases.

3.3.6 Variations of NoSQL Architectural Patterns

Six data architectures are SQL-table, key-value pairs, in-memory column-family, document, graph and object. Selected architecture may need variations due to business requirements. Business requirements are ease of using an architecture and long-term competitive advantage. The following example explains the requirements for the database of students of a University that offers multiple courses in their various academic programmes for several years:

EXAMPLE 3.12

List the selection requirements for the database of University students in successive years. The University runs various Under Graduate and Post Graduate programmes. Students are registered to Multiple courses in a programme.

SOLUTION

Following are the selection requirements:

1. Scalability: Since the University archives the data for several years, data store should be scalable.
2. Search ability: Search of required information needs to be fast.
3. Quarrying ability: All applications need to query the data. Query retrieves the required data among the Big Data of several years.
4. Security: Database needs security and fault tolerance.
5. Affordability: Open source is a requirement.
6. Interoperability: Needs ease in search from different platforms. Search from any computer operating system, such as Windows, Mac, Linux, Android and iOS should be feasible.
7. Importability: Database needs to import data from other platforms, such as import of slides, video lectures, tutorials, e-books, webinars should be facilitated in store.
8. Transformability: Queries may be written in one language and may require transformation to another language, such as HTML.

Analysis of the above requirements suggests the document architecture pattern will be more suitable.

Kelly-McCreary, co-founder of 'NoSQL Now' suggested that when selecting a NoSQL-pattern, the pattern may need change and require variation to another pattern(s). Some reasons for this are:

1. Focus changing from performance to scalability
2. Changing from modifiability to agility
3. Greater emphasis on Big Data, affording capacity, availability of support, ability for searching and monitoring the actions

Steps for selecting a NoSQL data architectural pattern can be as follows:

1. Select an architecture
2. Perform a use-case driven difficulty analysis for each of the six architectural patterns. Difficulties may be low, medium or high in the following processes: (i) ingestion, (ii) validation of structure and its fields, (iii) updating process using batch or record by record approach, (iv) searching process using full text or by changing the sorting order, and (v) export the reports or application results in HTML, XML or JSON.
3. Estimate the total efforts for each architecture for all business requirements.

Process the choice of architecture using trade-off. For example, between the MongoDB document data store and Cassandra column-family data store.

Self-Assessment Exercise linked to LO 3.2

1. Compare traditional relational model and key-value pairs model. ○○●

2. When will you use the document data store? ○○●
3. Why is metadata must in a NoSQL Data Store? ○●●
4. How do interactions among graph nodes and hypergraph nodes differentiate? ○●●
5. List and compare the features of BigTable, RC, ORC and Parquet data stores. ●●●
6. What are the characteristics of the object data store model? ○○●
7. Data architecture pattern can be selected from among the six architectures, namely relational SQL table, OLAP-suitable in-memory column, key-value pairs, column-family, document and graph DBs. Explain with an example, how and when each of these is used. ○●●

3.4 NoSQL TO MANAGE BIG DATA

LO 3.3

NoSQL data store management, applications and handling problems in Big Data

The following subsections describe how to use a NoSQL data store to manage Big Data.

3.4.1 Using NoSQL to Manage Big Data

NoSQL (i) limits the support for Join queries, supports sparse matrix like columnar-family, (ii) characteristics of easy creation and high processing speed, scalability and storability of much higher magnitude of data (terabytes and petabytes).

NoSQL sacrifices the support of ACID properties, and instead supports CAP and BASE properties (Sections 3.2.1.1 and 3.2.3). NoSQL data processing scales horizontally as well vertically.

3.4.1.1 NoSQL Solutions for Big Data

Big Data solution needs scalable storage of terabytes and petabytes, dropping of support for database Joins, and storing data differently on several distributed servers (data nodes) together as a cluster. A solution, such as CouchDB, DynamoDB, MongoDB or Cassandra follow CAP theorem (with compromising the consistency factor) to make transactions faster and easier to scale. A solution must also be partitioning tolerant.

Characteristics of Big Data NoSQL solution are:

1. *High and easy scalability*: NoSQL data stores are designed to expand horizontally. Horizontal scaling means that scaling out by adding more machines as data nodes (servers) into the pool of resources (processing, memory, network connections). The design scales out using multi-utility cloud services.
2. *Support to replication*: Multiple copies of data store across multiple nodes of a cluster. This ensures high availability, partition, reliability and fault tolerance.
3. *Distributable*: Big Data solutions permit sharding and distributing of shards on multiple clusters which enhances performance and throughput.
4. *Usages of NoSQL servers* which are less expensive. NoSQL data stores require less management efforts. It supports many features like automatic repair, easier data distribution and simpler data models that makes database administrator (DBA) and tuning requirements less stringent.
5. *Usages of open-source tools*: NoSQL data stores are cheap and open source. Database implementation is easy and typically uses cheap servers to manage the exploding data and transaction while RDBMS

databases are expensive and use big servers and storage systems. So, cost per gigabyte data store and processing of that data can be many times less than the cost of RDBMS.

6. *Support to schema-less data model*: NoSQL data store is schema less, so data can be inserted in a NoSQL data store without any predefined schema. So, the format or data model can be changed any time, without disruption of application. Managing the changes is a difficult problem in SQL.
7. *Support to integrated caching*: NoSQL data store support the caching in system memory. That increases output performance. SQL database needs a separate infrastructure for that.
8. *No inflexibility* unlike the SQL/RDBMS, NoSQL DBs are flexible (not rigid) and have no structured way of storing and manipulating data. SQL stores in the form of tables consisting of rows and columns. NoSQL data stores have flexibility in following ACID rules.

3.4.1.2 Types of Big Data Problems

Big Data problems arise due to limitations of NoSQL and other DBs. The following types of problems are faced using Big Data solutions.

1. Big Data need the scalable storage and use of distributed servers together as a cluster. Therefore, the solutions must drop support for the database Joins
2. NoSQL database is open source and that is its greatest strength but at the same time its greatest weakness also because there are not many defined standards for NoSQL data stores. Hence, no two NoSQL data stores are equal. For example:
   (i) No stored procedures in MongoDB (NoSQL data store)
   (ii) GUI mode tools to access the data store are not available in the market
   (iii) Lack of standardization
   (iv) NoSQL data stores sacrifice ACID compliancy for flexibility and processing speed.

A comparison of NoSQL with SQL/RDBMS shows that NoSQL data model are schema-less, no pre-defined schema, multiple data architecture patterns, complex to implement vertical scalability, variable consistency and very week adherence to ACID rules. Table 3.7 gives a comparison.

Table 3.7 Comparison of NoSQL with SQL/RDBMS

Features	NoSQL Data store	SQL/RDBMS
Model	Schema-less model	Relational
Schema	Dynamic schema	Predefined
Types of data architecture patterns	Key/value based, column-family based, document based, graph based, object based	Table based
Scalable	Horizontally scalable	Vertically scalable
Use of SQL	No	Yes
Dataset size preference	Prefers large datasets	Large dataset not preferred
Consistency	Variable	Strong
Vendor support	Open source	Strong
ACID properties	May not support, instead follows Brewer's CAP theorem or BASE properties	Strictly follows

Self-Assessment Exercise linked to LO 3.3

1. Why does Big Data need scalable storage and uses distributed servers together as a cluster? ○●●
2. Why does Big Data solution possess CAP or BASE and may drop support for ACID properties? ○●●
3. Why does a Big Data solution drop support for the database Joins? ○○●
4. Compare NoSQL data stores with SQL databases. ○○●

3.5 SHARED-NOTHING ARCHITECTURE FOR BIG DATA TASKS

LO 3.4

Shared-nothing architecture, choosing a distribution model, master-slave versus peer-to-peer, and knowledge of four ways by which NoSQL handles the Big Data problems

The columns of two tables relate by a relationship. A relational algebraic equation specifies the relation. Keys share between two or more SQL tables in RDBMS. Shared nothing (SN) is a cluster architecture. A node does not share data with any other node.

Big Data store consists of SN architecture. Big Data store, therefore, easily partitions into shards. A partition processes the different queries on data of the different users at each node independently. Thus, data processes run in parallel at the nodes. A node maintains a copy of running-process data. A coordination protocol controls the processing at all SN nodes. An SN architecture optimizes massive parallel data processing.

Data of different data stores partition among the number of nodes (assigning different computers to deal with different users or queries). Processing may require every node to maintain its own copy of the application's data, using a coordination protocol. Examples are using the partitioning and processing are Hadoop, Flink and Spark.

The features of SN architecture are as follows:

1. *Independence*: Each node with no memory sharing; thus possesses computational self-sufficiency
2. *Self-Healing*: A link failure causes creation of another link
3. *Each node functioning as a shard*: Each node stores a shard (a partition of large DBs)
4. No network contention.

3.5.1 Choosing the Distribution Models

Big Data requires distribution on multiple data nodes at clusters. Distributed software components give advantage of parallel processing; thus providing horizontal scalability. Distribution gives (i) ability to handle large-sized data, and (ii) processing of many read and write operations simultaneously in an application. A resource manager manages, allocates, and schedules the resources of each processor, memory and network connection. Distribution increases the availability when a network slows or link fails. Four models for distribution of the data store are given below:

3.5.1.1 Single Server Model

Simplest distribution option for NoSQL data store and access is Single Server Distribution (SSD) of an application. A graph database processes the relationships between nodes at a server. The SSD model suits well for graph DBs. Aggregates of datasets may be key-value, column-family or BigTable data stores which require sequential processing. These data stores also use the SSD model. An application executes the data sequentially on a single server. Figure 3.9(a) shows the SSD model. Process and datasets distribute to a single server which runs the application.

3.5.1.2 Sharding Very Large Databases

Figure 3.9(b) shows sharding of very large datasets into four divisions, each running the application on four *i*, *j*, *k* and *l* different servers at the cluster. DB_i, DB_j, DB_k and DB_l are four shards.

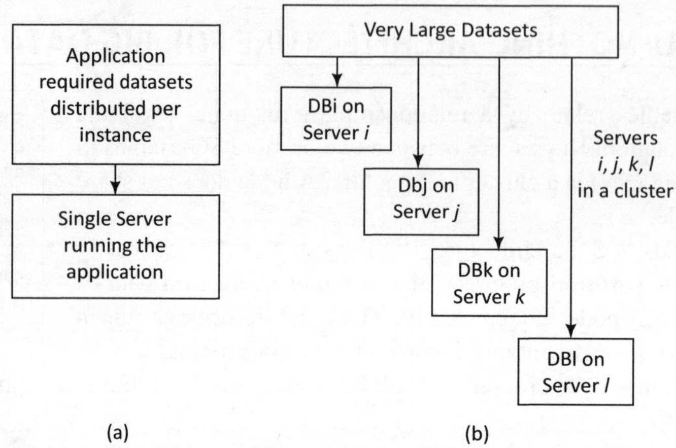

Figure 3.9 (a) Single server model (b) Shards distributed on four servers in a cluster.

The application programming model in SN architecture is such that an application process runs on multiple shards in parallel. Sharding provides horizontal scalability. A data store may add an auto-sharding feature. The performance improves in the SN. However, in case of a link failure with the application, the application can migrate the shard DB to another node.

3.5.1.3 Master-Slave Distribution Model

A node serves as a master or primary node and the other nodes are slave nodes. Master directs the slaves. Slave nodes data replicate on multiple slave servers in Master Slave Distribution (MSD) model. When a process updates the master, it updates the slaves also. A process uses the slaves for read operations. Processing performance improves when process runs large datasets distributed onto the slave nodes. Figure 3.10 shows an example of MongoDB. MongoDB database server is *mongod* and the client is *mongo*.

Master-Slave Replication Processing performance decreases due to replication in MSD distribution model. Resilience for read operations is high, which means if in case data is not available from a slave node, then it becomes available from the replicated nodes. Master uses the distinct write and read paths.

Complexity Cluster-based processing has greater complexity than the other architectures. Consistency can also be affected in case of problem of significant time taken for updating.

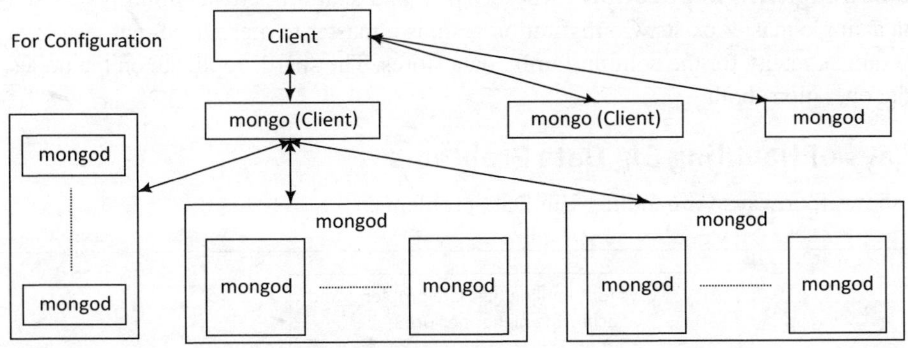

Figure 3.10 Master-slave distribution model. Mongo is a client and mongod is the server

3.5.1.4 *Peer-to-Peer Distribution Model*

Peer-to-Peer distribution (PPD) model and replication show the following characteristics: (1) All replication nodes accept read request and send the responses. (2) All replicas function equally. (3) Node failures do not cause loss of write capability, as other replicated node responds.

Cassandra adopts the PPD model. The data distributes among all the nodes in a cluster.

Performance can further be enhanced by adding the nodes. Since nodes read and write both, a replicated node also has updated data. Therefore, the biggest advantage in the model is consistency. When a write is on different nodes, then write inconsistency occurs.

Figure 3.11 shows the PPD model.

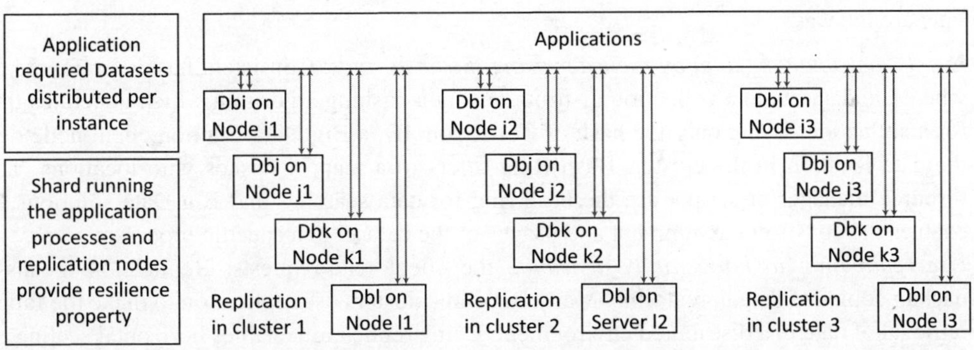

Figure 3.11 Shards replicating on the nodes, which does read and write operations both

3.5.1.5 *Choosing Master-Slave versus Peer-to-Peer*

Master-slave replication provides greater scalability for read operations. Replication provides resilience during the read. Master does not provide resilience for writes. Peer-to-peer replication provides resilience for read and writes both.

Sharing Combining with Replication Master-slave and sharding creates multiple masters. However, for each data a single master exists. Configuration assigns a master to a group of datasets. Peer-to-peer and sharding use same strategy for the column-family data stores. The shards replicate on the nodes, which does read and write operations both.

3.5.2 Ways of Handling Big Data Problems

Figure 3.12 shows four ways for handling Big Data problems.

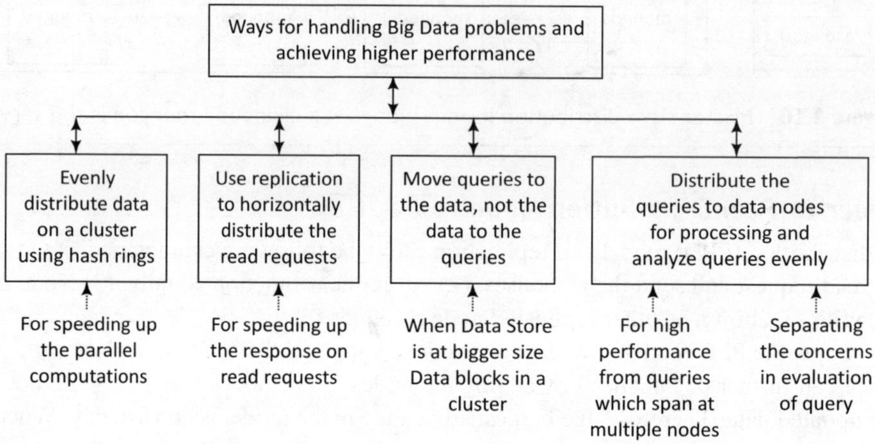

Figure 3.12 Four ways for handling big data problems

Following are the ways:

1. *Evenly distribute the data on a cluster using the hash rings*: Consistent hashing refers to a process where the datasets in a collection distribute using a hashing algorithm which generates the pointer for a collection. Using only the hash of Collection_ID, a Big Data solution client node determines the data location in the cluster. Hash Ring refers to a map of hashes with locations. The client, resource manager or scripts use the hash ring for data searches and Big Data solutions. The ring enables the consistent assignment and usages of the dataset to a specific processor.
2. *Use replication to horizontally distribute* the client read-requests: Replication means creating backup copies of data in real time. Many Big Data clusters use replication to make the failure-proof retrieval of data in a distributed environment. Using replication enables horizontal scaling out of the client requests.
3. *Moving queries to the data, not the data to the queries:* Most NoSQL data stores use cloud utility services (Large graph databases may use enterprise servers). Moving client node queries to the data is efficient as well as a requirement in Big Data solutions.
4. *Queries distribution to multiple nodes*: Client queries for the DBs analyze at the analyzers, which evenly distribute the queries to data nodes/ replica nodes. High performance query processing requires usages of multiple nodes. The query execution takes place separately from the query evaluation (The evaluation means interpreting the query and generating a plan for its execution sequence).

Self-Assessment Exercise linked to LO 3.4

1. List pros and cons of distribution using sharding. ●●●
2. List characteristics of master-slave distribution model. ○○●
3. List the benefits of peer-to-peer nodes data distribution model. ○●●
4. How is a hash ring used in the distribution of Big Data? ●●●

3.6 MongoDB DATABASE

LO 3.5

MongoDB databases and query commands

MongoDB is an open source DBMS. MongoDB programs *create* and *manage* databases. MongoDB manages the collection and document data store. MongoDB functions do querying and accessing the required information. The functions include viewing, querying, changing, visualizing and running the transactions. Changing includes updating, inserting, appending or deleting.

MongoDB is (i) non-relational, (ii) NoSQL, (iii) distributed, (iv) open source, (v) document based, (vi) cross-platform, (vii) Scalable, (viii) flexible data model, (ix) Indexed, (x) multi-master (Section 3.5.1.3), and (xi) fault tolerant. Document data store in JSON-like documents. The data store uses the dynamic schemas.

The typical MongoDB applications are content management and delivery systems, mobile applications, user data management, gaming, e-commerce, analytics, archiving and logging.

Features Following are features of MongoDB:

1. *MongoDB data store* is a physical container for collections. Each DB gets its own set of files on the file system. A number of DBs can run on a single MongoDB server. DB is default DB in MongoDB that stores within a data folder. The database server of MongoDB is *mongod* and the client is *mongo*.
2. *Collection* stores a number of MongoDB documents. It is analogous to a table of RDBMS. A collection exists within a single DB to achieve a single purpose. Collections may store documents that do not have the same fields. Thus, documents of the collection are schema-less. Thus, it is possible to store documents of varying structures in a collection. Practically, in an RDBMS, it is required to define a column and its data type, but does not need them while working with the MongoDB.
3. *Document model* is well defined. Structure of document is clear, Document is the unit of storing data in a MongoDB database. Documents are analogous to the records of RDBMS table. Insert, update and delete operations can be performed on a collection. Document use JSON (JavaScript Object Notation) approach for storing data. JSON is a lightweight, self-describing format used to interchange data between various applications. JSON data basically has key-value pairs. Documents have dynamic schema.
4. MongoDB is a document data store in which one collection holds different documents. Data store in the form of JSON-style documents. Number of fields, content and size of the document can differ from one document to another.
5. *Storing of data* is flexible, and data store consists of JSON-like documents. This implies that the fields can vary from document to document and data structure can be changed over time; JSON has a standard structure, and scalable way of describing hierarchical data (Example 3.3(ii)).

6. *Storing of documents* on disk is in BSON serialization format. BSON is a binary representation of JSON documents. The mongo JavaScript shell and MongoDB language drivers perform translation between BSON and language-specific document representation.
7. *Querying, indexing, and real time aggregation* allows accessing and analyzing the data efficiently.
8. *Deep query-ability*—Supports dynamic queries on documents using a document-based query language that's nearly as powerful as SQL.
9. No complex Joins.
10. *Distributed DB* makes availability high, and provides horizontal scalability.
11. *Indexes on any field* in a collection of documents: Users can create indexes on any field in a document. Indices support queries and operations. By default, MongoDB creates an index on the _id field of every collection.
12. *Atomic operations on a single document* can be performed even though support of multi-document transactions is not present. The operations are alternate to ACID transaction requirement of a relational DB.
13. *Fast-in-place updates*: The DB does not have to allocate new memory location and write a full new copy of the object in case of data updates. This results into high performance for frequent update use cases. For example, incrementing a counter operation does not fetch the document from the server. Here, the increment operation can simply be set.
14. *No configurable cache*: MongoDB uses all free memory on the system automatically by way of memory-mapped files (The operating systems use the similar approach with their file system caches). The most recently used data is kept in RAM. If indexes are created for queries and the working dataset fits in RAM, MongoDB serves all queries from memory.
15. *Conversion/mapping* of application objects to data store objects not needed

Dynamic Schema Dynamic schema implies that documents in the same collection do not need to have the same set of fields or structure. Also, the similar fields in a document may contain different types of data. Table 3.8 gives the comparison with RDBMS.

Table 3.8 Comparison of RDBMS and MongoDB databases

RDBMS	MongoDB
Database	Data store
Table	Collection
Column	Key
Value	Value
Records / Rows / Tuple	Document / Object
Joins	Embedded Documents
Index	Index
Primary key	Primary key (_id) is default key provided by MongoDB itself

Any relational DB has a typical schema design that shows the number of tables and the relationship between these tables. While in MongoDB, there is no concept of relationship.

Replication Replication ensures high availability in Big Data. Presence of multiple copies increases on different database servers. This makes DBs fault-tolerant against any database server failure. Multiple copies of data certainly help in localizing the data and ensure availability of data in a distributed system environment.

MongoDB replicates with the help of a replica set. A replica set in MongoDB is a group of mongod (MongoDb server) processes that store the same dataset. Replica sets provide redundancy but high availability. A replica set usually has minimum three nodes. Any one out of them is called primary. The primary node receives all the write operations. All the other nodes are termed as secondary. The data replicates from primary to secondary nodes. A new primary node can be chosen among the secondary nodes at the time of automatic failover or maintenance. The failed node when recovered can join the replica set as secondary node again. Replica set starts a mongod instance by specifying – replSet option before running these commands from mongo (MongoDb Client). Table 3.9 gives the commands used for replication (*Recoverability* means even on occurrences of failures; the transactions ensure consistency).

Table 3.9 MongoDB Client commands related to replica set

Commands	Description
rs.initiate ()	To initiate a new replica set
rs.conf ()	To check the replica set configuration
rs.status ()	To check the status of a replica set
rs.add ()	To add members to a replica set

Figure 3.13 shows a replicated dataset after creating three secondary members from a primary member.

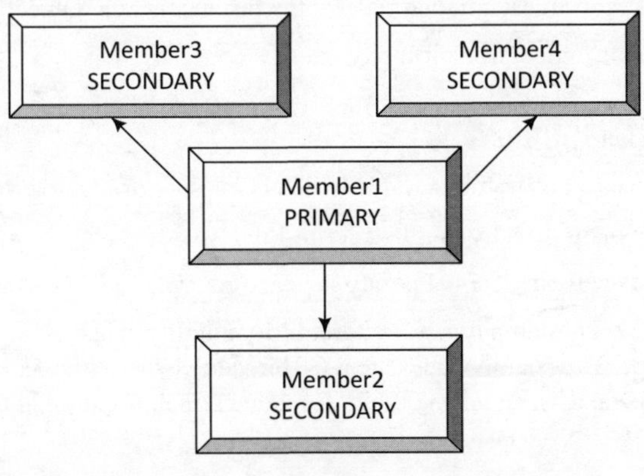

Figure 3.13 Replicated set on creating secondary members

Auto-sharding Sharding is a method for distributing data across multiple machines in a distributed application environment. MongoDB uses sharding to provide services to Big Data applications.

A single machine may not be adequate to store the data. When the data size increases, do not provide data retrieval operation. Vertical scaling by increasing the resources of a single machine is quite expensive. Thus, horizontal scaling of the data can be achieved using sharding mechanism where more database servers can be added to support data growth and the demands of more read and write operations.

Sharding automatically balances the data and load across various servers. Sharding provides additional write capability by distributing the write load over a number of mongod (MongoDB Server) instances. (Figure 3.10) Basically, it splits the dataset and distributes them across multiple DBs, called shards on the different servers. Each shard is an independent DB. The whole collection of shards forms a single logical DB. If a DB has a 1 terabyte dataset distributed amongst 20 shards, then each shard contains only 50 Giga Byte of data.

A shard stores lesser data than the actual data and handles lesser number of operations in a single instance. For example, to insert data into a collection, the application needs to access only the shard that contains the specified collection. A cluster can thus easily increase its capacity horizontally.

Data Types Table 3.10 gives data types which MongoDB documents support.

Table 3.10 Data types which MongoDB documents support

Type	Description
Double	Represents a float value.
String	UTF-8 format string.
Object	Represents an embedded document.
Array	Sets or lists of values.
Binary data	String of arbitrary bytes to store images, binaries.
Object id	ObjectIds (MongoDB document identifier, equivalent to a primary key) are: small, likely unique, fast to generate, and ordered. The value consists of 12-bytes, where the first four bytes are for timestamp that reflects the instance when ObjectId creates.
Boolean	Represents logical true or false value.
Date	BSON Date is a 64-bit integer that represents the number of milliseconds since the Unix epoch (Jan 1, 1970).
Null	Represents a null value. A value which is missing or unknown is Null.
Regular Expression	RegExp maps directly to a JavaScript RegExp
32-bit integer	Numbers without decimal points save and return as 32-bit integers.
Timestamp	A special timestamp type for internal MongoDB use and is not associated with the regular date type. Timestamp values are a 64-bit value, where first 32 bits are time, t (seconds since the Unix epoch), and next 32 bits are an incrementing ordinal for operations within a given second.
64-bit integer	Number without a decimal point save and return as 64-bit integer.
Min key	MinKey compare less than all other possible BSON element values, respectively, and exist primarily for internal use.
Max key	MaxKey compares greater than all other possible BSON element values, respectively, and exist primarily for internal use.

Rich Queries and Other DB Functionalities MongoDB offers a rich set of features and functionality compared to those offered in simple key-value stores. They can be comparable to those offered by any RDBMS. MongoDB has a complete query language, highly-functional secondary indexes (including text search and geospatial), and a powerful aggregation framework for data analysis. MongoDB provides functionalities and features for more diverse data types than a relational DB, and at scale. Table 3.11 gives a comparison of features.

Table 3.11 Comparison of features MongoDB with respect to RDBMS

Features	RDBMS	MongoDB
Rich Data Model	No	Yes
Dynamic Schema	No	Yes
Typed Data	Yes	Yes
Data Locality	No	Yes
Field Updates	Yes	Yes
Complex Transactions	Yes	No
Auditing	Yes	Yes
Horizontal Scaling	No	Yes

The ability to derive a document-based data model is also a distinct advantage of MongoDB. The method of storing data in the form of BSON (Binary JSON) helps to store the data in a very rich way while can hold arrays and other documents.

MongDB Query Language and Database Commands Table 3.12 gives MongoDB commands for querying the DBs.

Table 3.12 MongoDB querying commands

Command	Functionality
Mongo	Starts MongoDB; (*mongo is MongoDB client). The default database in MongoDB is test.
db.help ()	Runs help. This displays the list of all the commands.
db.stats ()	Gets statistics about MongoDB server.
Use <database name)	Creates database
Db	Outputs the names of existing database, if created earlier
Dbs	Gets list of all the databases
db.dropDatabase ()	Drops a database
db.database name.insert ()	Creates a collection using insert ()
db.<database name>. find ()	Views all documents in a collection
db.<database name>.update ()	Updates a document
db.<database name>.remove ()	Deletes a document

Following explains the sample usages of the commands:

To Create database Command `use` – use command creates a database; For example, Command `use lego` creates a database named *lego*. (A sample database is created to demonstrate subsequent queries. The Lego is an international toy brand). Default database in MongoDB is *test*.

To see the existence of database Command `db` – `db` command shows that *lego* database is created.

To get list of all the databases Command `show dbs` – This command `shows` the names of all the databases.

To drop database Command `db.dropDatabase()` – This command drops a database. Run `use lego` command before the `db.dropDatabase()` command to drop *lego* Database. If no database is selected, the default database *test* will be dropped.

To create a collection Command `insert()` – To create a collection, the easiest way is to insert a record (a document consisting of keys (Field names) and Values) into a collection. A new collection will be created, if the collection does not exist. The following statements demonstrate the creation of a collection with three fields (ProductCategory, ProductId and ProductName) in the *lego*:

```
db.lego.insert
(
        {
                "ProductCategory": "Airplane",
                "ProductId": 10725,
                "ProductName": "Lost Temple"
        }
)
```

To add array in a collection Command `insert()` - Insert command can also be used to insert multiple documents into a collection at one time.

```
db.lego.insert
(
        [
                {
                        "ProductCategory": "Airplane",
                        "ProductId": 10725,
                        "ProductName": "Lost Temple"
                },
                {
                        "ProductCategory": "Airplane",
                        "ProductId": 31047,
                        "ProductName": "Propeller Plane"
                },
                {
                        "ProductCategory": "Airplane",
                        "ProductId": 31049,
                        "ProductName": "Twin Spin Helicopter"
                }
        ]
)
```

To view all documents in a collection Command `db.<database name>.find()` - Find command is equivalent to select query of RDBMS. Thus, "`Select * from lego`" can be written as `db.lego.find()` in MongoDB. MongoDB created unique objecteId ("_id") on its own. This is the primary key of the collection. Command `db.<database name>.find().pretty()` gives a prettier look.

To update a document Command `db.<database name>.update()`- Update command is used to change the field value. By default, multi attribute is false. If {multi: true} is not written then it will update only the first document.

To delete a document Command `db.<database name>.remove()`- Remove command is used to delete the document. The query `db.<database name>.remove(("ProdctID":10725))` removes the document whose productId is 10725.

Self-Assessment Exercise linked to LO 3.5

1. Compare MongoDB and RDBMS? ○○●
2. Give example that demonstrates the uses of various data types of MongoDB. ○●●
3. List the functions of MongoDB query language and database commands. ○●●
4. How will you consider MongoDB as complete query language, which imbibes highly-functional secondary indices (including text search and geospatial), and provides a powerful aggregation framework for data analysis? ●●●

3.7 CASSANDRA DATABASES

LO 3.6

Cassandra databases, data-model and clients, and integration with the Hadoop

Cassandra was developed by Facebook and released by Apache. Cassandra was named after Trojan mythological prophet Cassandra, who had classical allusions to a curse on oracle. Later on, IBM also released the enhancement of Cassandra, as open source version. The open source version includes an IBM Data Engine which processes No SQL data store. The engine has improved throughput when workload of read-operations is intensive.

Cassandra is basically a column family database that stores and handles massive data of any format including structured, semi-structured and unstructured data.

Apache Cassandra DBMS contains a set of programs. They *create* and *manage* databases. Cassandra provides functions (commands) for querying the data and accessing the required information. Functions do the viewing, querying and changing (update, insert or append or delete), visualizing and perform transactions on the DB.

Apache Cassandra has the distributed design of Dynamo. Cassandra is written in Java. Big organizations, such as Facebook, IBM, Twitter, Cisco, Rackspace, eBay, Twitter and Netflix have adopted Cassandra.

Characteristics of Cassandra are (i) open source, (ii) scalable (iii) non-relational (v) NoSQL (iv) Distributed (vi) column based, (vii) decentralized, (viii) fault tolerant and (ix) tuneable consistency.

Features of Cassandra are as follows:

1. Maximizes the number of writes – writes are not very costly (time consuming)
2. Maximizes data duplication
3. Does not support Joins, group by, OR clause and aggregations
4. Uses Classes consisting of ordered keys and semi-structured data storage systems
5. Is fast and easily scalable with write operations spread across the cluster. The cluster does not have a master-node, so any read and write can be handled by any node in the cluster.
6. Is a distributed DBMS designed for handling a high volume of structured data across multiple cloud servers

7. Has peer-to-peer distribution in the system across its nodes, and the data is distributed among all the nodes in a cluster (Section 3.5.1.4).

Data Replication Cassandra stores data on multiple nodes (data replication) and thus has no single point of failure, and ensures availability, a requirement in CAP theorem. Data replication uses a replication strategy. Replication factor determines the total number of replicas placed on different nodes. Cassandra returns the most recent value of the data to the client. If it has detected that some of the nodes responded with a stale value, Cassandra performs a read repair in the background to update the stale values.

Components at Cassandra Table 3.13 gives the components at Cassandra and their description.

Table 3.13 Components of cassandra

Component	Description
Node	Place where data stores for processing
Data Center	Collection of many related nodes
Cluster	Collection of many data centers
Commit log	Used for crash recovery; each write operation written to commit log
Mem-table	Memory resident data structure, after data written in commit log, data write in mem-table temporarily
SSTable	When mem-table reaches a certain threshold, data flush into an SSTable disk file
Bloom filter	Fast and memory-efficient, probabilistic-data structure to find whether an element is present in a set, Bloom filters are accessed after every query.

Scalability Cassandra provides linear scalability which increases the throughput and decreases the response time on increase in the number of nodes at cluster.

Transaction Support Supports ACID properties (Atomicity, Consistency, Isolation, and Durability).

Replication Option Specifies any of the two replica placement strategy names. The strategy names are Simple Strategy or Network Topology Strategy. The replica placement strategies are:

1. Simple Strategy: Specifies simply a replication factor for the cluster.
2. Network Topology Strategy: Allows setting the replication factor for each data center independently.

Data Types Table 3.14 gives the data types built into Cassandra, their usage and descriptions

Table 3.14 Data types built into Cassandra, their usage and description

CQL Type	Description
ascii	US-ASCII character string
bigint	64-bit signed long integer
blob	Arbitrary bytes (no validation), BLOB expressed in hexadecimal
boolean	True or false
counter	Distributed counter value (64-bit long)
decimal	Variable-precision decimal integer, float

(Contd.)

CQL Type	Description
double	64-bit IEEE-754 *double precession* floating point integer, float
float	32-bit IEEE-754 *single precession* floating point integer, float
inet	IP address string in IPv4 or IPv6 format, used by the python-cql driver and CQL native protocols
int	32-bit signed integer
list	A collection of one or more ordered elements
map	A JSON-style array of literals: {literal: literal, literal: literal ...}
set	A collection of one or more elements
text	UTF-8 encoded string
timestamp	Date plus time, encoded as 8 bytes since epoch integers, strings
varchar	UTF-8 encoded string
varint	Arbitrary-precision integer

Cassadra Data Model Cassandra Data model is based on Google's BigTable (Section 3.3.3.2). Each value maps with two strings (row key, column key) and timestamp, similar to HBase (Example 2.4). The database can be considered as a sparse distributed multi-dimensional sorted map. Google file system splits the table into multiple tablets (segments of the table) along a row. Each tablet, called META1 tablet, maximum size is 200 MB, above which a compression algorithm used. META0 is the master-server. Querying by META0 server retrieves a META1 tablet. During execution of the application, caching of locations of tablets reduces the number of queries.

Cassandra Data Model consists of four main components: (i) Cluster: Made up of multiple nodes and keyspaces, (ii) Keyspace: a namespace to group multiple column families, especially one per partition, (iii) Column: consists of a column name, value and timestamp and (iv) Column-family: multiple columns with row key reference. Cassandra does keyspace management using partitioning of keys into ranges and assigning different key-ranges to specific nodes.

Following Commands prints a description (typically a series of DDL statements) of a schema element or the cluster:

DESCRIBE CLUSTER
DESCRIBE SCHEMA
DESCRIBE KEYSPACES
DESCRIBE KEYSPACE <keyspace name>
DESCRIBE TABLES
DESCRIBE TABLE <table name>
DESCRIBE INDEX <index name>
DESCRIBE MATERIALIZED VIEW <view name>
DESCRIBE TYPES
DESCRIBE TYPE <type name>
DESCRIBE FUNCTIONS

DESCRIBE FUNCTION <function name>
DESCRIBE AGGREGATES
DESCRIBE AGGREGATE <aggregate function name>

Consistency Command CONSISTENCY shows the current consistency level. CONSISTENCY <LEVEL> sets a new consistency level. Valid consistency levels are ANY, ONE, TWO, THREE,QUORUM, LOCAL_ONE, LOCAL_QUORUM, EACH_QUORUM, SERIAL AND LOCAL_SERIAL. Following are their meanings:

1. ALL: Highly consistent. A write must be written to commitlog and memtable on all replica nodes in the cluster.
2. EACH_QUORUM: A write must be written to commitlog and memtable on quorum of replica nodes in all data centers.
3. LOCAL_QUORUM: A write must be written to commitlog and memtable on quorum of replica nodes in the same center.
4. ONE: A write must be written to commitlog and memtable of at least one replica node.
5. TWO, THREE: Same as One but at least two and three replica nodes, respectively.
6. LOCAL_ONE: A write must be written for at least one replica node in the local data center.
7. ANY: A write must be written to at least one node.
8. SERIAL: Linearizable consistency to prevent unconditional update.
9. LOCAL_SERIAL: Same as Serial but restricted to the local data center.

Keyspaces A keyspacc (or kcy spacc) in a NoSQL data store is an object that contains all column families of a design as a bundle. Keyspace is the outermost grouping of the data in the data store. It is similar to relational database. Generally, there is one keyspace per application. Keyspace in Cassandra is a namespace that defines data replication on nodes. A cluster contains one keyspace per node.

Create Keyspace Command `CREATE KEYSPACE` <Keyspace Name> `WITH replication = {'class':` '<Strategy name>', 'replication_factor': '<No. of replicas>'`}AND durable_writes =` '<TRUE/FALSE>';

`CREATE KEYSPACE` statement has attributes replication with option class and replication factor, and durable_write.

Default value of *durable_writes* properties of a table is set to true. That commands the Cassandra to use Commit Log for updates on the current Keyspace true or false. The option is not compulsory.

1. ALTER KEYSPACE command changes (alter) properties, such as the number of replicas and the durable_writes of a keyspace: ALTER KEYSPACE <Keyspace Name> WITH replication = {'class': '<Strategy name>', 'replication_factor': '<No. of replicas>'};
2. DESCRIBE KEYSPACE command displays the existing keyspaces.
3. DROP KEYSPACE command drops a keyspace:
4. Re-executing the drop command to drop the same keyspace will result in configuration exception.
5. Use KEYSPACE command connects the client session with a keyspace.

Cassandra Query Language (CQL) Table 3.15 gives the CQL commands and their functionalities.

Table 3.15 CQL commands and their functionalities

Command	Functionality
CQLSH	A command line shell for interacting with Cassandra through CQL
HELP	Runs help. This displays the list of all the commands
CONSISTENCY	Shows the current consistency level
EXIT	Terminate the CQL shell
SHOW HOST	Displays the host
SHOW VERSION	Displays the details of current cqlsh session such as host, Cassandra version, or data type assumptions
CREATE KEYSPACE <Keyspace Name>	Creates keyspace with a name
DESCRIBE KEYSPACE <Keyspace Name>	Displays the keyspace with a name
ALTER KEYSPACE <Keyspace Name>	Modifies keyspace with a name
DROP KEYSPACE <Keyspace Name>	Deletes keyspace with a name
CREATE (TABLE | COLUMNFAMILY)	Creates a table or column family
COLLECTIONS	Lists the Collections

The following example provides the sample usages of the commands.

EXAMPLE 3.13

Give the examples of usages of various CQL commands.

SOLUTION

(1) Create Table Command: CREATE TABLE command creates a table in the current keyspace:

```
CREATE (TABLE | COLUMNFAMILY) <tablename> ('<column-definition>',
'<column-definition>') (WITH <option> AND <option>);
```

Primary key is a column used to uniquely identify a row. Therefore, defining a primary key is compulsory while creating a table. A primary key is made of one or more columns of a table. *Example*: Create a table *ProductInfo* in the keyspace *lego*, with primary key field *ProductId*.

```
Use lego;
Create table ProductInfo(ProductId int primary key, ProductType
text);
```

(2) Describe Tables Command: DESCRIBE TABLE Command displays all the tables in the current keyspace:

```
DESCRIBE TABLE <TABLE NAME>;
```

Example: Display the details of a table *ProductInfo*:

```
DESCRIBE TABLE ProductInfo;
```

(3) Alter Tables Command:

```
ALTER TABLE Command ALTER (TABLE | COLUMNFAMILY) <tablename> (ADD |
DROP) <column name>
```

The above command adds a column in the table or to delete a column of the table:
Example: Add a column dateOfManufacturing in the table *ProductInfo*:

```
ALTER TABLE ProductInfo add dateOfManufacturing timestamp;
```

* timestamp is a datatype used for date fields.

(4) Cassandra CURD Operations: (CURD—Create, Update, Read and Delete data into tables) :

(a) Insert Command:
INSERT command creates data in a table:

```
INSERT INTO <tablename> (<column1 name>, <column2 name>....)
VALUES (<value1>, <value2>....) USING <option>
```

(b) Update Command:
UPDATE command updates data in a table. The following keywords are used while updating data in a table:
Where – This clause is used to select the row to be updated.
Set – Set the value using this keyword.
Must – Includes all the columns composing the primary key.
If a given row is unavailable, then UPDATE creates a new row.

```
UPDATE <tablename>  SET <column name> = <new value> <column name>
= <value>.... WHERE <condition>
```

[A WHERE clause can be used only on the columns that are a part of primary key or have a secondary index on them.]

(c) Select Command
SELECT command reads the data from a table. The command can read a whole table, a single column, or a particular cell:

```
SELECT <column name(s)> FROM <Table Name>
```

To select all records:

```
SELECT * FROM <Table Name>
```

To select records that fulfils required condition:

```
SELECT <column1, column2,..> FROM <Table Name> where <Condition>
```

Example: Select Product Type, Product Id, Product Name, and Product Cost of Product whose ProductId is 31047:

```
SELECT Product Type, Product Id, Product Name, and Product Cost
from ProductInfo where ProductId = 31047;
```

(d) Delete Command
DELETE command deletes data from a table:

```
DELETE FROM <identifier> WHERE <condition>;
```

Example: Delete row from a table where Product id is 31047:

```
DELETE FROM ProductInfo WHERE ProductId = 31047;
```

(5) Creating a Table with List
CREATE Table command is used for creating a table with a list.
The following query creates a table with two columns, one is the primary key and the other has multiple items (List):

```
CREATE TABLE data (<column name>, <data type> PRIMARY KEY, <column
name list<data type>);
```

Example : Create a sample table *ContactInfo* with three columns: *Sno*, *name* and *EmailId*. To store multiple Email Ids, use a list:

```
create table ContactInfo (Sno int Primary key, Name text, emailId
list <text>);
```

(6) Insert Command for inserting data into a list
INSERT Command also inserts data into a list. To insert data into the elements in a list, enter all the values separated by a comma within square braces []:

```
INSERT INTO <table name> (column1, column2,) VALUES (value1, value2,
[list value1, list value2,…])
```

Example: Insert data of three persons into the *ContactInfo* Table:

```
Insert into ContactInfo (Sno, Name, EmailId) values
(1, 'Rahul',['rahul@gmail.com', 'rahul@yahoo.com']);

Insert into ContactInfo (Sno, Name, EmailId) values (1,
'Geetika',['geetika@gmail.com', 'geetika@yahoo.com']);

Insert into ContactInfo (Sno, Name, EmailId) values (1,
'Deepika',['deepika@gmail.com', 'deepika@yahoo.com']);
```

(7) Update Command for updating Data into a List
UPDATE command also updates data into a list:

```
UPDATE <table Name> SET <New data> where <condition>.
```

Example : Add one more email Id to the *emailId* list in *ContactInfo* table :

```
UPDATE ContactInfo SET emailId = emailId +['preeti@ymail.com'] where
SNo=1.
```

Cassandra Client A relational database client connects to DB server using drivers. Java JDBC driver API enables storing and retrieving data. Cassandra has peer-to-peer distribution architecture. Several instances require the clients. The driver enables the use of different languages for connecting to DBs. Cassandra does not include the drivers.

A client-generation layer enables the database interactions. AVRO project provides the client generation layer. Third party sources provide Cassandra clients in Java, Ruby, C#, Python, Perl, PHP, C++, Scala and other languages. The Cassandra client can be included in the applications.

Cassandra Hadoop Support Cassandra 2.1 has Hadoop 2 support. The setup and configuration overlays a Hadoop cluster on the Cassandra nodes. A server is configured for the NameNode and JobTracker. Each Cassandra node then installs the TaskTracker and Data Node.

The nodes in the Cassandra cluster can read data from the data in the Data Node in HDFS as well as from Cassandra. A client application sends the MapReduce input to Job Tracker/Resource Manager. RM/JobTracker sends a MapReduce request of job to the Task Trackers/Node Managers and clients such as MapReduce and Pig. The Reducer output writes to Cassandra. The client gets the results from Cassandra.

Self-Assessment Exercise linked to LO 3.6

1. List the differences between Cassandra, Google BigTable and HBase data models. ○○●
2. Compare Cassandra and RDBMS. ○○●
3. List the data types used in Cassandra. ○●●
4. How are the Cassandra query language and database commands used? ○●●
5. List the components in Casandra and their uses. ○○●
6. Write the syntax to create keyspace in Cassandra. State when the ALTER keyspace is used. ●●●
7. How are the Cassandra CQL collections used? ●●●

KEY CONCEPTS

ACID properties
aggregation
application
availability
BASE
BigTable
BLOB
BSON
CAP theorem
Cassandra
client
cluster
column family
consistency
data architecture pattern
database
data model
data node
data tree
data type
deserialization
distributed database
distribution model
document data store
DynamoDB
fixed table schema
hash ring
hierarchal record
indexing
Java object
Join
JSON
key-value pair
keyspace
Master-slave
MongoDB
Multi-master DB
NoSQL
object data store
OLAP
pattern
peer-to-peer
Persistency
Querying
RDBMS
relationship map
replication
Scalability
schema-less
serialization
server
sharding
shared nothing
sorted keys
SQL
transaction
XML
XPath

Learning Outcomes

LO 3.1

- A new category of data stores is NoSQL (Not Only SQL) databases. NoSQL is an altogether new approach of thinking about data stores.
- NoSQL data model offers relaxation in one or more of the ACID properties, instead follows CAP theorem and BASE.
- NoSQL DBs possess greater flexibility for data manipulation (compared to SQL).
- NoSQL data does not need fixed schema. The data model may drop support to Joins in Big Data environment.

LO 3.2

- Key-value pairs data store can be used as Big Data NoSQL database.
- Key-value pair is a simplest way to implement a schema-less data store. The pairs can store any data type in the value field. The store uses a primary-key access; therefore, the store can be easily scaled up to large data, and data retrieves fast using keys as the indices.
- NoSQL DB also stores the hierarchical information in a single unit, called *document* store. 'Document' stores unstructured data. Data stores in nested hierarchies. Data have no object-relational layer for the mapping. Document data store can be at multiple NameNodes and thus enables higher resources availability.
- Column-family data stores are similar to sparse matrix data. Columns are logically grouped into column families. Column families can logically group as super column. Data stores in memory are column-based than row-based. This facilitates faster OLAP processing. The table can be partitioned into row groups (or stripes). Data stores can be in columnar data RC, ORC and Parquet formats.
- An object data store consists of functions for supporting using APIs.
- Graph database with interconnected data nodes provides one of the best database systems. They enable fast network searches.
- A selected architecture needs variations due to business requirements. Business requirements are easy to use and have long-term competitive advantage.

LO 3.3

- Big Data solution emphasizes on scalable storage of a much higher magnitude of data (of terabytes and petabytes) by dropping support for database Joins, storing data differently and using several distributed servers (data nodes) together as a cluster.
- Big Data NoSQL solution provides high scalability, supports replication, no schema or no fixed data model, support integrated caching: not inflexible like SQL/RDBMS DBs and have flexibility in following ACID rules.

LO 3.4

- SN architecture features are independence, self-healing and no network contention. Each node data functions as a shard of the DB.

- Distribution models are (i) single server, (ii) sharding, (iii) master-slave, (iv) multi-master (v) peer-to-peer, and (vi) hash ring based.

LO 3.5

- MongoDB is (i) non-relational, (ii) distributed, (iii) open source, (iv) NoSQL, (v) document-based, (vi) Cross-platform, (vii) scalable, (viii) flexible, (ix) indexed, (x) deep querying ability, (xi) scalable multi-master data store with no single points of failure and (xii) provisions the data modeling flexibility.
- Querying, indexing and real-time aggregation functions access and analyze the data efficiently, and conversion/mapping of application objects to database objects is not needed.

LO 3.6

- Cassandra is (i) open source, (ii) scalable (iii) non-relational (iv) peer-to-peer distributed system (v) NoSQL (vi) column-based, (vii) decentralized, (viii) fault tolerant and (ix) tunable consistency.
- Cassandra Data model is based on Google's BigTable. Each value maps with two strings (row key, column key) and timestamp, similar to HBase.
- Cassandra data model consists of four main components: (i) Cluster: made up of multiple nodes and keyspaces, (ii) Keyspace: a namespace to group multiple column families, especially one per partition, (iii) Column: consists of a column name, value and timestamp and (iv) Column-family: multiple columns with row key reference.

Objective Type Questions

Select one correct-answer option for each questions below:

3.1 Big Data NoSQL data store (i) transactions show ACID properties, (ii) used in distributed environment, (iii) NoSQL DBs possess increasing flexibility for data manipulation, (iv) follows a fixed data storage schema (v) use the concept of Joins, and (vi) must follow CAP theorem. ○○●

(a) ii and iii (b) all
(c) ii, iii and vi (d) iii and iv

3.2 High scalability, flexibility and performance and low complexity are the characteristics of (i) key-value pair, (ii) document (iii) column-family, and (iv) graph databases. ○○●

(a) only i and ii (b) only i
(c) only ii (d) iii and iv

3.3 The advantages of a key-value store are: (i) can store any data type in the value field, (ii) stores the information as a BLOB of data (such as, text, hypertext, images, video and audio), but does not return the same BLOB when data is retrieved, (iii) scalability, (iv) reliability, (v) portability, and (vi) low operational cost. ○●●

(a) all except i (b) all
(c) all except ii (d) ii to vi

3.4 An object data store consists of functions for supporting (i) scalability, (ii) indexing, (iii) large collections, (iv) querying language, processing and optimization (s), (v) transactions, (vi) data replication for high availability, data distribution model, data integration (such as with relational database, XML, custom code), (vii) schema evolution, (viii) persistency, (ix) persistent object life cycle, (x) adding modules, (xi) locking and caching strategy, and (xii) object store may support versioning for collaboration. ●●●

(a) i to v, ix to xiii (b) all
(c) all except viii, ix ad xii (d) all except iii, vi and viii

3.5 Graph database with interconnected data nodes (i) provides one of the best data store system, (ii) provides one of the highly complex data store system, (iii) enables fast network searches, (iv) uses linked datasets, (v) used in social media data, (vi) consists of small data size records with complex interactions between graph nodes but not between the hypergraph nodes (vii) uses graph with nodes and edges connecting each other through the relations, associations and properties, and (viii) BASE properties. ○●●
(a) i, iii, iv and viii (b) ii to v
(c) ii to vi (d) all except vi

3.6 Selecting a NoSQL data architectural pattern can be as follows: (i) performing a use-case driven difficulty analysis for all architectural patterns. Assign the difficulties level, such as low, medium or high in the following processes (iii) ingestion, (iv) validation of structure and its fields, (v) updating process using near real-time approach, (vi) searching process using partial text or by changing the sorting order, (vii) exporting the reports or application results in HTML, XML or JSON, and estimating total efforts for each architecture for all the business requirements. ●●●
(a) all (b) all except v and vi
(c) i to v (d) all except ii

3.7 Big Data solution emphasizes on scalable storage of a much higher magnitude of data (of terabytes and petabytes) by (i) supporting database Joins, (ii) storing data differently and using several distributed servers (Data Nodes) together as a cluster, (iii) must perform transactions using ACID properties, (iv) implementing CAP theorem without compromising the consistency factor) to make transactions faster and easier to scale, and (v) must be partitioning tolerant. ○○●
(a) ii and v (b) all except i, iii
(c) all except iii and iv (d) all

3.8 Big Data NoSQL solution: (i) have high and easily scalability, (ii) supports replication, (iii) use multiple copies of data store across multiple nodes of the cluster, (iii) maintains NoSQL Servers, (iv) NoSQL data store implementation is easy and typically uses cheap servers to manage the exploding data and transaction while RDBMS databases are expensive and it uses big servers and storage systems, and (v) storing and processing data cost per gigabyte in the case of NoSQL can be many times more than the cost of RDBMS. ○○●
(a) i, ii and v (b) all except i, iii
(c) all except iii and iv (d) i to iv

3.9 Big Data NoSQL-solution should be (i) schema-less or not fixed data model, (ii) without any predefined schema, (iii) the format or data model can be changed any time, (iv) without application disruption and (v) with change in management, (v) support integrated caching, and (vi) not inflexible like SQL/RDBMS DBs. ○○●
(a) i to v (b) all
(c) all except iii (d) i to iv

3.10 A Big Data solution does the following: (i) unevenly distributes data on a cluster, (ii) distributes using token rings, (iii) uses replication and vertical distribution of the client read requests, (iv) creates backup copies of data in batches, (v) moves queries to the data, and data to queries, (vi) distributes queries to multiple nodes, and (vii) query execution takes place separately from query evaluation. ○●●
(a) ii to iv (b) vi and vii
(c) none (d) iv to vii

3.11 MongoDB is (i) non-relational, (ii) distributed, (iii) open source, (iv) NoSQL, (v) document-based, (vi) cross-platform, (vii) scalable, (viii) data modeling inflexibility, (ix) indexed, and (x) scalable multi-master data store with no single point of failure. ○○●

(a) all except viii (b) all except v and vi
(c) i to vi (d) i to vii

3.12 MongoDB features are: (i) document model is well defined, (ii) structure of document is clear, stores documents on disk in the (iii) BSON serialization format, (iv) JSON format, and (v) querying, indexing, real-time aggregation and allows accessing and analyzing the data efficiently. ○○●

(a) all (b) i, iii and iv
(c) all except iv (d) iii, iv and v

3.13 Cassandra data model is based on (i) Google's BigTable. Each value maps with two strings (row key, column key) and timestamp, similar to HBase, (ii) graph database (iii) distributed (iv) NoSQL (v) column-based, (vi) centralized, (vii) fault tolerant and (vii) tuneable consistency. ●●●

(a) all (b) i, iii and iv
(c) all except i (d) all except ii and vi

3.14 Cassandra data model consists of four main components: (i) Cluster: made up of multiple nodes and keyspaces, (ii) Keyspace: a namespace to group multiple column families, especially one per partition, (iii) Column: consists of a column name, value and timestamp, (iv) Column-family: multiple columns with row key reference, (v) provides a prompt in Cassandra query language shell (CQLSh) that allows keying and execution of commands in Cassandra Query Language (CQL). ○●●

(a) i to iii (b) ii and iii
(c) all (d) i, ii and iv

3.15 Cassandra features are as follows: (i) maximizes the number of writes – writes are not very costly (time consuming), (ii) maximizes data duplication, (iii) does not support Joins, group by, OR clause and aggregations, (iv) uses Classes consisting of ordered keys and semi-structured data storage systems, (v) is fast and easily scalable with write operations spread across the cluster, and (vi) the cluster does not have a master node, so any read and write can be handled by any node in the cluster. ○○●

(a) all except i and iii (b) all
(c) all except iv (d) all except iii and vi

Review Questions

3.1 When should data store be NoSQL instead of relational database? Why do Big Data analytics use NoSQL data stores? **(LO 3.1)** ○○●

3.2 How does NoSQL data store possess increasing flexibility in adding data? **(LO 3.1)** ○○●

3.3 How does CAP theorem apply in distributed data models? How is it applicable to NoSQL systems? What is eventual consistency in NoSQL stores? **(LO 3.1)** ○○●

3.4 Compare NoSQL databases with SQL databases in terms of the data model, schema, type of data architecture patterns, scalability, use of SQL Joins, data size preferences, consistency, ACID properties and top IT companies support. **(LO 3.1)** ●●●

3.5 Describe the pros and cons of (i) key-value data store, (ii) document data store, (iii) object data store, and (iii) graph database. **(LO 3.2)** ○●●

3.6 Why should the column-family data store be used for the student grade-sheets of a semester examinations showing semester subject grade-points (SGPs) (between 1 and 10) and semester grade point averages (SGPAs)? What does sparse data mean in student grade-sheets columnar data. **(LO 3.2)** ○●●

3.7 Describe the characteristics of column-family data stores. How do they suit the OLAP operations? How does BigTable store the data? **(LO 3.2)** ○●●

3.8 Describe the pros and cons of (i) RC, (ii) ORC and (iii) Parquet file format data stores. ○○●

3.9 Describe graph database characteristics. How are BASE properties exhibited in graph DBs? **(LO 3.2)** ●●●

3.10 How are replication and sharding used? Explain how does sharding help in minimizing the downtime? **(LO 3.3)** ○●●

3.11 What are the features of shared-nothing (SN) architecture? How does Big Data Store SN system partition? How does a partition process the different queries? **(LO 3.4)** ●●●

3.12 Describe four ways for handling Big Data problems. **(LO 3.4)** ○○●

3.13 Explain MongoDB commands for querying the DBs? How can one achieve transaction and locking in MongoDB? How will MongoDB command be used to insert a document in a database called 'Toys' and collection called 'Train'? **(LO 3.5)** ○●●

3.14 Discuss the cluster and failover model in Cassandra. Compare the peer-to-peer model that Cassandra supports with the master-slave model that other data stores, such as MongoDB support. What are the pros and cons of each model? **(LO 3.5)** ●●●

3.15 What are the important design considerations when using a column-family data store like Cassandra? List and explain usages of data types built into Cassandra. **(LO 3.6)** ○●●

3.16 List and explain usages of Cassandra Query Language (CQL) commands and their functionalities. How does the table data store create using CQL? **(LO 3.6)** ●●●

Practice Exercises

3.1 List ten examples where NoSQL data stores are required. **(LO 3.1)** ○○●

3.2 Show the increasing flexibility in NoSQL DB of car company by appending customer post-sales feedbacks, maintenance and service centre feedbacks about the models, and the customer region-wise preference analysis reports. **(LO 3.1)** ○○●

3.3 A company manufactures and sells car through large number of showrooms. Each car showroom records in main table and transaction tables. ○●●

Assume that each week company records the car sells. The table data are as follows:

Show-room ID (SR_ID)	Week Num-ber (counting 1.1.2018) (wkNum)	*Jagaur Land Rover Sales Number (JLRSNum)*	*Hexa Sales Number (HSNum)*	*Zest Sales Number (ZSNum)*	*Nexon Sales Number (NSNum)*	*Safari Storme Sales Number (SSSNum)*
124	1	2	8	4	7	10
125	1	1	7	9	6	9
126	1	1	9	4	8	3

Jagaur Land Rover Cost Rs. (JLRC)	*Hexa Cost* Rs. (HC)	*Zest Cost* Rs. *(ZC)*	*Nexon Cost* Rs. (NC)	*Safari Storme Cost* Rs. *(SSC)*
20 M	0.8 M	0.75 M	0.7 M	1 M

Write the (key/values) pairs in a week that estimate the total sales per week per showroom. **(LO 3.2)**

3.4 Recall Practice Exercise 2.6 and Exercise 3.3. Consider a car company selling Jagaur Land Rover, Hexa, Zest, Nexon and Safari Storme models of Car. Assign IDs as keys in rows 1 to 999999 and cloumn 1, row 0 column head is 'show room ID' ●●●

Assume key (at column-head) row 0 corresponds to Jagaur Land Rover Weekly Sales (JLRWS) in cloumn 2. JLRWS values for different showrooms are in successive rows from row 1 to 999999. The values save in same column at successive memory addresses starting from address 1000000. How the total showrooms sales calculation of JLRWS will be faster than row format? How will the addresses be assigned? **(LO 3.2)**

3.5 Geographic Information Systems (GIS), like Google Maps stores geographic information in BigTable. How will the values be retrieved during the following: (a) Identification of a location using its longitude and latitude coordinates, (b) Storage of items once, and then provides multiple access paths (queries) to let one view the data. **(LO 3.2)** ●●●

3.6 Using graph database model, how will the followings store: student id, contact info, admission info, and five courses each in four semesters and SGPs, SGPAs and CGPAs at the end of each semester and division awarded? **(LO 3.2)** ●●●

3.7 Recall Example 3.12 which listed selection requirements for the data architecture pattern the database of University students. Write logical reasons for each. **(LO 3.2)** ○○●

3.8 Listed selection requirements for the data architecture pattern for the ACVMs Chocolate sales data [Table 3.3]. **(LO 3.3)** ○●●

3.9 Give two examples each of usages of single server, sharding, master-slave and peer-to- peer distribution models. **(LO 3.4)** ○○●

3.10 Make a table in which left column gives the outputs using MongoDB querying commands. Fill the right column of the table giving action on the command. **(LO 3.5)** ○●●

3.11 Complete the following table fields for actions directed by Cassandra these command. ●●●

Actions directed by the command	Code
Create a Table with Set: **Table name**: ContactInfo **Fields**: Sno (primary key), Name, set of Contact numbers)	
Inserting 3 Datasets in table ContactInfo, and read them	
Updating a set, adding one more contact number to person with Sno = 1, and reading all the data.	

Collections: Map Collection

Actions directed by the command	Code
Create a Table with Map **Table name**: ContactInfo **Fields**: Sno (primary key), Name, Map of address)	
Inserting 3 Datasets in table ContactInfo, and read them	
Updating a Map, adding one more address to person with Sno = 1, and reading all the data.	

(LO 3.6)

3.12 Recapitulate Practice Exercise 3.3. Consider car company selling *Jagaur Land Rover*, *Hexa*, *Zest*, *Nexon* and *Safari Storme* models of cars. How will the CQL commands be used to create the table for weekly sales log at multiple car company showrooms? ●●●

CCSR_ id	Date (DT) mmddyy	*Jagaur Land Rover* Weekly Sales (JLRWS)	*Hexa* Weekly Sales (HWS)	*Zest* Weekly Sales (ZWS)	*Nexon* Weekly Sales (NWS)	*Safari Storme* Weekly Sales (SSWS)
220	121217	28	23	138	148	50
10	121217	49	34	164	115	38
122	121217	40	141	123	37	88
16	121217	13	25	127	158	174
28	121217	12	122	116	128	57
-	-	-	-	-	-	-
-	-	-	-	-	-	-

(LO 3.6)

Chapter 4

MapReduce, Hive and Pig

LEARNING OBJECTIVES

After studying this chapter, you will be able to:

- **LO 4.1** Get understanding of MapReduce, map tasks using the key-value store, grouping by keys, reduce tasks using combiners, and coping with node failures
- **LO 4.2** Get knowledge of composing MapReduce programs for calculations, such as counting, summing, and algorithms for relational algebraic operations, projections, unions, intersections, natural joins, grouping, aggregation operations and the matrix multiplication
- **LO 4.3** Get understanding of Hive, architecture, installation, comparison of Hive data store with traditional databases
- **LO 4.4** Apply HiveQL for querying, sorting, aggregating, querying scripts, MapReduce Joins and sub-queries
- **LO 4.5** Get knowledge of Pig architecture, Grunt shell commands, data model, Pig Latin, developing scripts and extensibility using UDFs.

RECALL FROM EARLIER CHAPTERS

Hadoop stores and processes data on large clusters (thousands of nodes) of commodity hardware. Hadoop is a software framework for writing distributed applications. Hadoop processes Big Data (multi-terabyte datasets) in parallel and in a reliable and fault-tolerant way. The Hadoop distribution model is a method in which both computations and the data distribute and handle large-sized data. (Section 2.3)

MapReduce functions are an integral part of the Hadoop physical organization. MapReduce is a programming model for the distributed computing environment. Applications using MapReduce v2, process huge amounts of data, in parallel, on a large number of data nodes reliably (Sections 2.4 and 2.5).

Figure 2.2 showed the main components and the ecosystem components of Handoop, such as AVRO, Zookeeper, Ambari, HBase, Hive, Pig and Mahout (Section 2.6).

This chapter focuses on details of MapReduce, Hive and Pig programming and their use in Big Data applications.

4.1 INTRODUCTION

The data processing layer is the application support layer, while the application layer is the data consumption layer in Big-Data architecture design (Figure 1.2). When using HDFS, the Big Data processing layer includes the APIs of Programs such as **MapReduce** and **Spark**.

The application support layer includes HBase which creates column-family data store using other formats such as key-value pairs or JSON file (Section 3.3.3). HBase stores and processes the columnar data after translating into MapReduce tasks to run in HDFS.

The support layer also includes Hive which creates SQL-like tables. Hive stores and processes table data after translating it into MapReduce tasks to run in HDFS. Hive creates SQL-like tables in Hive shell. Hive uses HiveQL processes queries, ad hoc (unstructured) queries, aggregation functions and summarizing functions, such as functions to compute maximum, minimum, average of selected or grouped datasets. HiveQL is a restricted form of SQL.

The support layer also includes Pig. Pig is a data-flow language and an execution framework (Section 2.6.4). Pig enables the usage of relational algebra in HDFS. MapReduce is the processing framework and YARN is the resource managing framework (Section 2.6.5).

Figure 4.1 shows Big Data architecture design layers: (i) data storage, (ii) data processing and data consumption, (iii) support layer APIs for MapReduce, Hive and Pig running on top of the HDFS Data Store, and (v) application tasks. Pig is a dataflow language, which means that it defines a data stream and a series of transformations.

Hive and Pig are also part of the ecosystem (Figure 4.1). Big Data storage and application-support APIs can use Hive and Pig for processing data at HDFS. Processing needs mapping and finding the source file for data. File is in the distributed data store. Requirement is to identify the needed data-block in the cluster. Applications and APIs run at the data nodes stored at the blocks.

The smallest unit of data that can be stored or retrieved from the disk is a block. HDFS deals with the data stored in blocks. The Hadoop application is responsible for distributing the data blocks across multiple nodes. The tasks, therefore, first convert into map and reduce tasks. This requirement arises because the mapping of stored values is very important. The number of map tasks in an application is handled by the number of blocks of input files.

Suppose stored files have key-value pairs. Mapping tells us whether the key is in file or in the value store, in a particular cluster and rack. Reduce task uses those values for further processing such as counting, sorting or aggregating.

Application sub-task assigned for processing needs only the outputs of reduce tasks. For example, a query needs the required response for a data store. In Example 2.3, a sub-task may just need total daily sales of specific chocolate flavours to compute the analytics and data visualization.

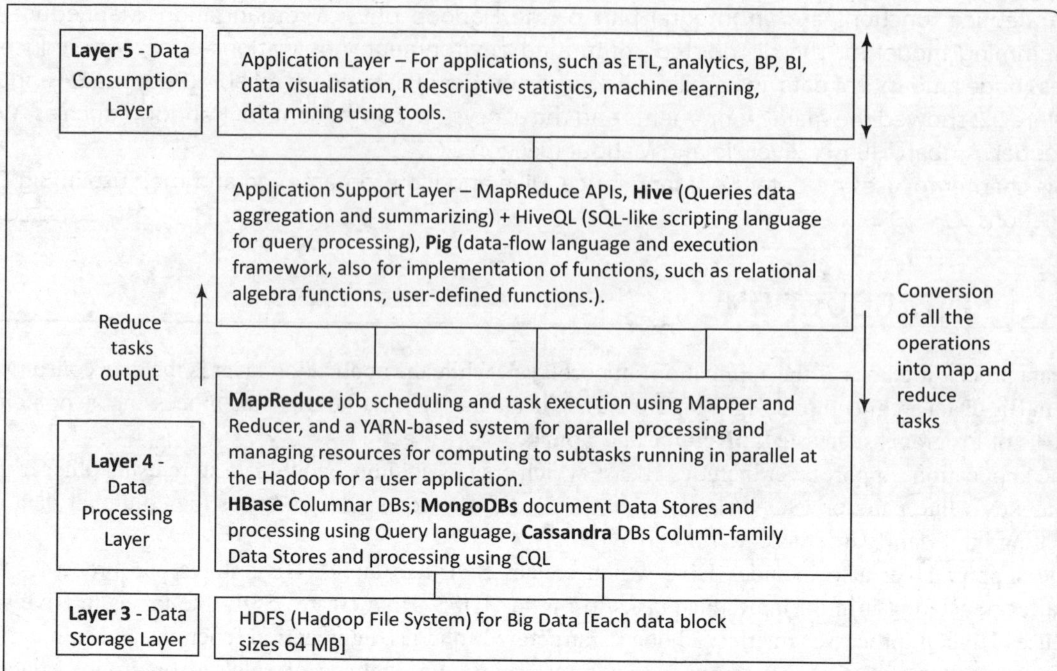

Figure 4.1 Big Data architecture design layers

A reader must learn the following new selected key terms and their meanings besides the key terms given in the previous three chapters.

MapReduce programming model refers to a programming paradigm for processing Big Data sets with a parallel and distributed environment using map and reduce tasks.

YARN refers to provisioning of running and scheduling parallel programs for map and reduce tasks and allocating parallel processing resources for computing sub-tasks running in parallel at the Hadoop for a user application. The YARN resources management enables large-scale data analytics using multiple machines (data nodes) in the HDFS cluster.

Script refers to a small program (codes up to few thousand lines of code) in a language used for purposes such as query processing, text processing, or refers to a small code written in a dynamic high-level general-purpose language, such as Python or PERL.

SQL-like scripting language means a language for writing script that processes queries similar to SQL. SQL lets us: (i) write structured queries for processing in DBMS, (ii) create and modify schema, and control the data access, (iii) create client for sending query scripts, and create and manage server databases, and (iv) view, query and change (update, insert or append or delete) databases.

NoSQL DBs refers to DBs with no prior fixed schema, schema-less models, and databases which possess increasing flexibility for data manipulation.

NoSQL data model refers to ones offering relaxation in one or more of the ACID properties (Atomicity, Consistence, Isolation and Durability) of the database. A theorem known as CAP (Consistency, Availability and Partitions) states that out of three properties, at least two must be present for the application/service/process. NoSQL relies upon another model known as the BASE model. This model has three principles: Basic availability (the availability of data even in the presence of multiple failures), Soft state (data consistency is the developer's problem and should not be handled by the database), Eventual consistency (when no new changes occur on existing data, eventually all accesses to that data will return the last updated value).

Data-architecture patterns refer to formats used in NoSQL DBs. The examples are Key-Value Data Stores, Object Data Stores, Column family Big Data Stores, Tabular Data Stores and Document Stores.

Key-Value Data Store refers to a simplest way to implement a schema-less database. A string called key maps to values in a large data string or BLOB (basic large object). Key-value stores use primary key access. Therefore, the storage easily scales up and data retrievals are fast.

Object Data Store refers to a repository which stores the (i) objects (such as files, images, documents, folders and business reports), (ii) system metadata which provides information such as filename, creation_date, last_modified, language_used (such as Java, C, C#, C++, Smalltalk, Python), access_permissions, supported Query languages, and (iii) Custom metadata which provides information such as subject, category and sharing permission.

Tabular Data Store refers to table, column-family or BigTable like Data Store.

Column family Big Data store refers to a storage in logical groups of column families. The storage may be similar to columns of sparse matrix. They use a pair of row and column keys to access the column fields.

BigTable Data Store is a popular column-family based Data Store. Row key, column key and timestamp uniquely identify a value. Google BigTable, HBase and Cassandra DBs use the BigTable Data Store model.

Document Store means a NoSQL DB which stores hierarchical information in a single unit called document. Document stores data in nested hierarchies; for example in XML document object model, JSON formats data model or machine-readable data as one BLOB.

Tuple means an ordered list of elements. An n-tuple relates to set theory, a collection (sequence) of "n" elements. Tuples implement the records.

Collection means a well-defined collection of distinct objects in a set, the objects of a set are the elements. That also means a store within a single DB to achieve a single purpose. A collection may be analogous to a table of RDBMS. A collection in a database also refers to storage of a number of documents. A collection may store documents which do not have the same fields. Thus, documents in the collection are schema-less. Thus, it is possible to store documents of varying structures in a collection.

Aggregate refers to collection of data sets in the key value, column family or BigTable data stores which usually require sequential processing.

Aggregation function refers to a function to find counts, sum, maximum, minimum, other statistical or mathematical function using a collection of datasets, such as column or column-family.

Sequence refers to an enumerated collection of objects, (the repetitions can be there) which contain members similar to a set. Sequence length equals the number of elements (can also be infinite). Sequence should reflect an order which matters, unlike a set.

Document refers to a container for the number of collections. The container can be a unit of storing data in a database, such as MongoDB.

Projection refers to a unary operation (single input or operand) written as $\Pi_{attr1,\ attr2,\ ...,\ attrn}$ where *(attr1, attr2, ..., attrn)* is a set of n attribute names. Projection returns a set obtained by selecting only the n attributes. A generalized projection includes a method using attribute values. $\Pi_{student\_Id,\ sum\ (GPA),\ sum\ (SGPA)}$.

Natural join is where two tables join based on all common columns. Both the tables must have the same column name and the data type.

Inner join is the default natural join. It refers to two tables that join based on common columns mentioned using the ON clause. Inner Join returns all rows from both tables if the columns match.

Node refers to a place for storing data, data block or read or write computations.

Data center in a DB refers to a collection of related nodes. Many nodes form a data center or rack.

Cluster refers to a collection of many nodes.

Keyspace means a namespace to group multiple column families, especially one per partition.

Indexing to a field means providing reference to a field in a document of collections that support the queries and operations using that index. A DB creates an index on the _id field of every collection.

This chapter describes MapReduce programming, Hive and Pig APIs in the MapReduce programming model and the HDFS data storage environment. Section 4.2 describes the MapReduce paradigm, map tasks using key-value pairs, grouping by keys and reduce tasks using partitioning and combiners in the application execution framework. Section 4.3 describes algorithms for using MapReduce. Section 4.4 describes Hive, architecture, installation and comparison with traditional databases. Section 4.5 describes HiveQL, querying the data, sorting and aggregating, scripts, joins and sub-queries. Section 4.6 introduces Pig architecture, grunt shell commands, data model, Pig Latin, developing scripts and extensibility using UDFs.

4.2 MapReduce MAP TASKS, REDUCE TASKS AND MapReduce EXECUTION

LO 4.1

MapReduce, map tasks using the key-value store, grouping by keys, reduce tasks using combiners, and coping with node failures

Big data processing employs the MapReduce programming model. A Job means a MapReduce program. Each job consists of several smaller units, called MapReduce tasks. A software execution framework in MapReduce programming defines the parallel tasks. The tasks give the required result. The Hadoop MapReduce implementation uses Java framework.

Figure 4.2 shows MapReduce programming model.

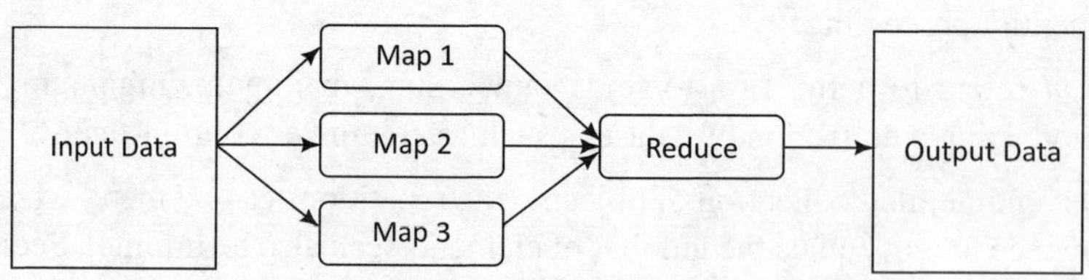

Figure 4.2 MapReduce Programming Model

The model defines two important tasks, namely Map and Reduce. Map takes input data set as pieces of data and maps them on various nodes for parallel processing. The reduce task, which takes the output from the maps as an input and combines those data pieces into a smaller set of data. A reduce task always run after the map task (s).

Many real-world situations are expressible using this model. Such Model describes the essence of MapReduce programming where the programs written are automatically parallelize and execute on a large cluster.

EXAMPLE 4.1

How can a car company quickly compute an aggregation function using the number of cars of a specific car-model sold at the company showrooms as input? Use the concept of division of an application task into a number of sub-tasks (running in parallel).

SOLUTION

The company's showrooms sell a specific model. Assume the analysis requires us to find the aggregate number N. The N computes by counting the number of cars of that model which have been sold over a specific period (Practice Exercise 3.3). N is a very large number. The application process will require a long time to count this sequentially from the sales figures.

The programming-model splits the application task into number of n sub-tasks, running in parallel. Each sub-task thus takes up and counts N/n sales entries for the car-model. Each sub-task fetches the items containing information of car sales separately. The results of all the application sub-tasks later combine at the end to send the result to the application. High volumes of data (Big Data) need the splitting and parallel processing of the tasks.

MapReduce simplifies software development practice. It eliminates the need to write and manage parallel codes. The YARN resource managing framework takes care of scheduling the tasks, monitoring them and re-executing the failed tasks. Following explains the concept:

EXAMPLE 4.2

How does MapReduce enable query processing quickly in Big Data problems?

SOLUTION

MapReduce provides two important functions for query processing. The distribution of task based on user's query to various nodes within the cluster is the first function. The other function is organizing and reducing the results from each node into a cohesive answer to a query.

The input data is in the form of an HDFS file. The output of the task also gets stored in the HDFS. The compute nodes and the storage nodes are the same at a cluster, that is, the MapReduce program and the HDFS are running on the same set of nodes. This configuration results in effectively scheduling of the sub-tasks on the nodes where the data is already present. This results in high efficiency due to reduction in network traffic across the cluster.

A user application specifies locations of the input/output data and translates into map and reduces functions. A job does implementations of appropriate interfaces and/or abstract-classes. These, and other job parameters, together comprise the job configuration. The Hadoop job client then submits the job (jar/executable etc.)

and configuration to the JobTracker, which then assumes the responsibility of distributing the software/configuration to the slaves by scheduling tasks, monitoring them, and provides status and diagnostic information to the job-client. Figure 4.3 shows MapReduce process when a client submits a job, and the succeeding actions by the JobTracker and TaskTracker.

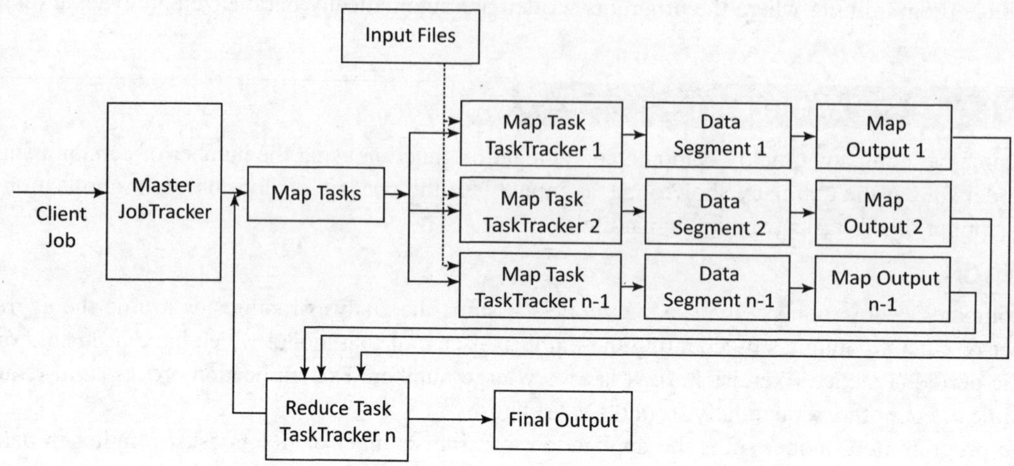

Figure 4.3 MapReduce process on client submitting a job

JobTracker and Task Tracker MapReduce consists of a single master JobTracker and one slave TaskTracker per cluster node. The master is responsible for scheduling the component tasks in a job onto the slaves, monitoring them and re-executing the failed tasks. The slaves execute the tasks as directed by the master.

The data for a MapReduce task is initially at input files. The input files typically reside in the HDFS. The files may be line-based log files, binary format file, multi-line input records, or something else entirely different. These input files are practically very large, hundreds of terabytes or even more than it.

Most importantly, the MapReduce framework operates entirely on key, value-pairs. The framework views the input to the task as a set of (key, value) pairs and produces a set of (key, value) pairs as the output of the task, possibly of different types (Section 2.4.2). Example 2.3 explained the process of converting input files into key-values.

4.2.1 Map-Tasks

Map task means a task that implements a map(), which runs user application codes for each key-value pair (**k1**, **v1**). Key **k1** is a set of keys. Key **k1** maps to a group of data values (Section 3.3.1). Values **v1** are a large string which is read from the input file(s).

The output of map() would be zero (when no values are found) or intermediate key-value pairs (**k2**, **v2**). The value **v2** is the information for the transformation operation at the reduce task using aggregation or other reducing functions.

Reduce task refers to a task which takes the output **v2** from the map as an input and combines those data pieces into a smaller set of data using a *combiner*. The reduce task is always performed after the map task.

The *Mapper* performs a function on individual values in a dataset irrespective of the data size of the input. That means that the Mapper works on a single data set. Figure 4.4 shows logical view of functioning of map().

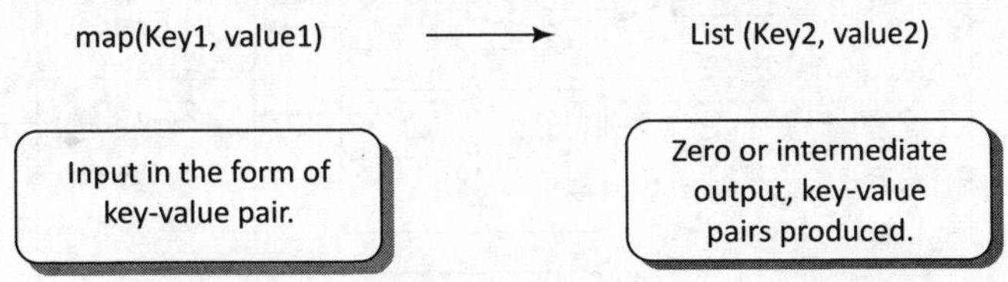

Figure 4.4 Logical view of functioning of map()

Hadoop Java API includes Mapper class. An abstract function map() is present in the Mapper class. Any specific Mapper implementation should be a subclass of this class and overrides the abstract function, map().

The Sample Code for Mapper Class

```
public class SampleMapper extends Mapper<k1, V1, k2, v2>
{
    void map (k1 key, V1 value, Context context) throws IOException,
    InterruptedException
   {..}
}
```

Individual Mappers do not communicate with each other.

Number of Maps The number of maps depends on the size of the input files, i.e., the total number of blocks of the input files. Thus, if the input files are of 1TB in size and the block size is 128 MB, there will be 8192 maps. The number of map task N_{map} can be explicitly set by using *setNumMapTasks(int)*. Suggested number is nearly 10-100 maps per node. N_{map} can be set even higher.

4.2.2 Key-Value Pair

Each phase (Map phase and Reduce phase) of MapReduce has key-value pairs as input and output. Data should be first converted into key-value pairs before it is passed to the Mapper, as the Mapper only understands key-value pairs of data (Section 3.3.1).

Key-value pairs in Hadoop MapReduce are generated as follows:

InputSplit – Defines a logical representation of data and presents a Split data for processing at individual map().

RecordReader – Communicates with the InputSplit and converts the Split into records which are in the form of key-value pairs in a format suitable for reading by the Mapper. RecordReader uses TextInputFormat by default for converting data into key-value pairs. RecordReader communicates with the InputSplit until the file is read.

Figure 4.5 shows the steps in MapReduce key-value pairing.

Generation of a key-value pair in MapReduce depends on the dataset and the required output. Also, the functions use the key-value pairs at four places: map() input, map() output, reduce() input and reduce() output.

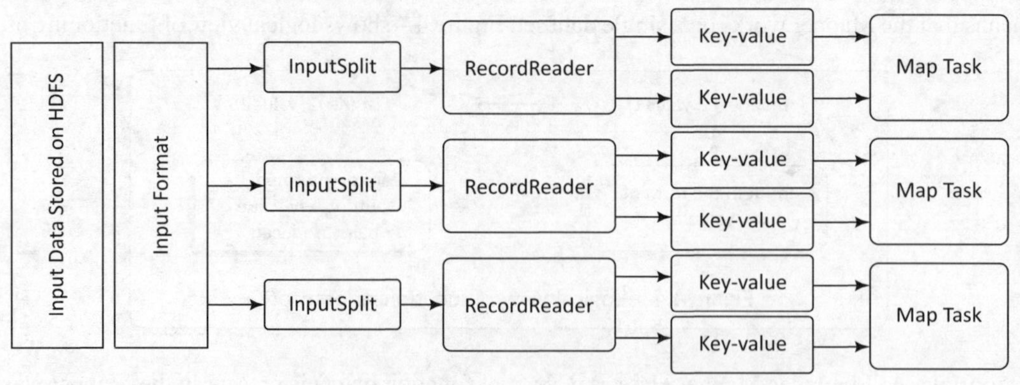

Figure 4.5 Key-value pairing in MapReduce

4.2.3 Grouping by Key

When a map task completes, Shuffle process aggregates (combines) all the Mapper outputs by grouping the key-values of the Mapper output, and the value **v2** append in a list of values. A "Group By" operation on intermediate keys creates **v2**.

Shuffle and Sorting Phase

Here, all pairs with the same group key (**k2**) collect and group together, creating one group for each key. So, the Shuffle output format will be a List of <**k2**, List (**v2**)>. Thus, a different subset of the intermediate key space assigns to each reduce node. These subsets of the intermediate keys (known as "partitions") are inputs to the reduce tasks.

Each reduce task is responsible for reducing the values associated with partitions. HDFS sorts the partitions on a single node automatically before they input to the Reducer.

4.2.4 Partitioning

The Partitioner does the partitioning. The partitions are the semi-mappers in MapReduce. Partitioner is an optional class. MapReduce driver class can specify the Partitioner. A partition processes the output of map tasks before submitting it to Reducer tasks. Partitioner function executes on each machine that performs a map task. Partitioner is an optimization in MapReduce that allows **local partitioning** before reduce-task phase. Typically, the same codes implement the Partitioner, Combiner as well as reduce() functions. Functions for Partitioner and sorting functions are at the mapping node. The main function of a Partitioner is to split the map output records with the same key.

4.2.5 Combiners

Combiners are semi-reducers in MapReduce. Combiner is an optional class. MapReduce driver class can specify the combiner. The combiner() executes on each machine that performs a map task. Combiners optimize MapReduce task that locally aggregates before the shuffle and sort phase. Typically, the same codes implement both the combiner and the reduce functions, combiner() on map node and reducer() on reducer node.

The main function of a Combiner is to consolidate the map output records with the same key. The output (key-value collection) of the combiner transfers over the network to the Reducer task as input.

This limits the volume of data transfer between map and reduce tasks, and thus reduces the cost of data transfer across the network. Combiners use grouping by key for carrying out this function. The combiner works as follows:

(i) It does not have its own interface and it must implement the interface at reduce().

(ii) It operates on each map output key. It must have the same input and output key-value types as the Reducer class.

(iii) It can produce summary information from a large dataset because it replaces the original Map output with fewer records or smaller records.

4.2.6 Reduce Tasks

Java API at Hadoop includes Reducer class. An abstract function, reduce() is in the Reducer. Any specific Reducer implementation should be subclass of this class and override the abstract reduce().

Reduce task implements reduce() that takes the Mapper output (which shuffles and sorts), which is grouped by key-values (k2, v2) and applies it in parallel to each group. Intermediate pairs are at input of each Reducer in order after sorting using the key. Reduce function iterates over the list of values associated with a key and produces outputs such as aggregations and statistics. The reduce function sends output zero or another set of key-value pairs (k3, v3) to the final the output file. Reduce: {(k2, list (v2) -> list (k3, v3)}

Sample Code for Reducer Class

```
public class ExampleReducer extends Reducer<k2, v2, k3, v3>
{
    void reduce (k2 key, Iterable<v2> values, Context context) throws
    IOException, InterruptedException
    {...}
}
```

4.2.7 Details of MapReduce Processing Steps

Execution of MapReduce job does not consider how the distributed processing implements. Rather, the execution involves the formatting (transforming) of data at each step.

Figure 4.6 shows the execution steps, data flow, splitting, partitioning and sorting on a map node and reducer on reducer node.

Example 2.3 described sales data of the five types of chocolates in a large number of ACVMs (Automatic Chocolate Vending Machines). The example gave answers to the following: (i) how hourly data log for each flavor sales on large number of ACVMs save using HDFS, (ii) how the sample of data-collect in a file each for 0-1,1-2, … 12-13,13-14, 15-16, ... for up to 23-24 specific hour sales, (iii) what will be output streams of map tasks which are the input streams to the reduce() tasks, and (iv) what will be the Reducer outputs.

Let us explore another example, Automotive Components and Predictive Automotive Maintenance Services (ACPAMS). ACPAMS is an application of (Internet) connected cars which renders services to customers for maintenance and servicing of (Internet) connected cars [Chapter 1 Example 1.6(ii)].

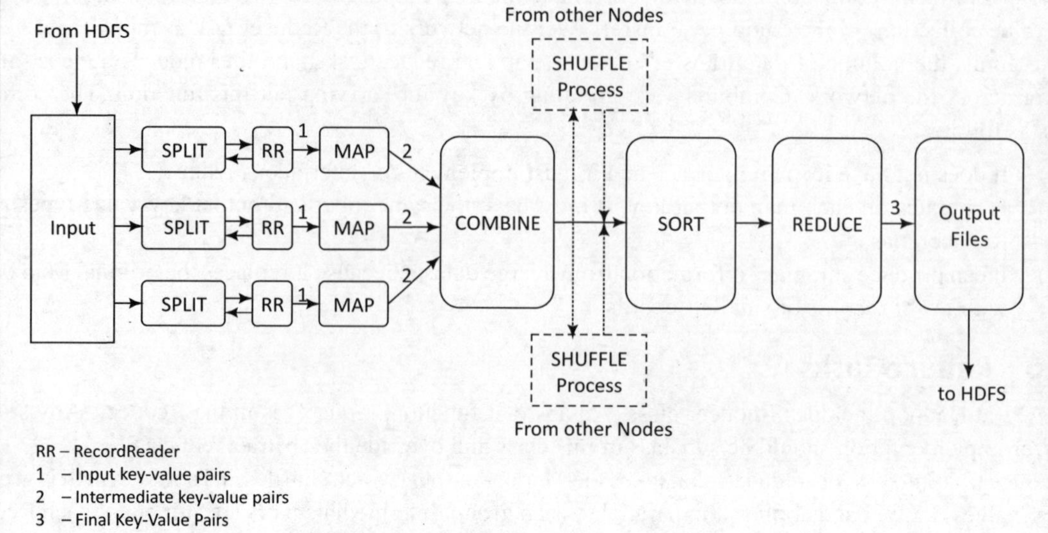

Figure 4.6 MapReduce execution steps

EXAMPLE 4.3

Describe the MapReduce processing steps of a task of ACPAMS.

SOLUTION

Figure 4.7 shows processing steps of an ACPAMS task in MapReduce. Steps are inputs, mapping, combining, shuffling and reducing for the output to application task.

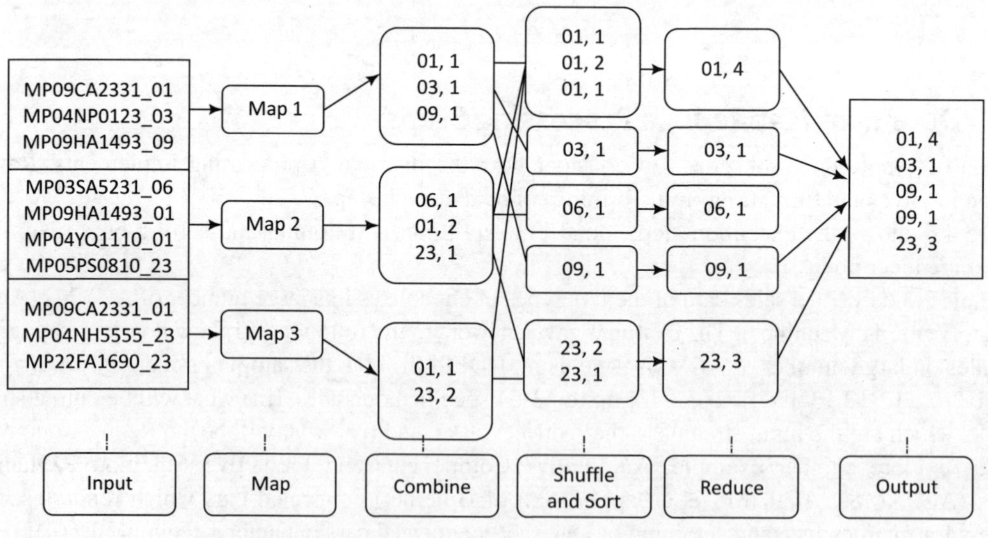

Figure 4.7 MapReduce processing steps in ACPAMS application

The *application* submits the inputs. The execution framework handles all other aspects of distributed processing transparently, on clusters ranging from a single node to a few thousand nodes. The aspects include scheduling, code distribution, synchronization, and error and fault handling.

The following example explains how the ACPAMS company receives alerts/messages.

EXAMPLE 4.4

Describe the MapReduce processing steps to illustrate how the ACPAMS receives alerts/messages.

SOLUTION

The ACPAMS Company can receive the alerts/messages every hour from several sensors of the automotive components installed in the number of cars. A server maps the keys for filling fuel, changing of the coolant, etc. It requires a lot of time to scan the hourly maintenance log sequentially because there are a million cars registered for the ACPAMS service. Each car is equipped with nearly 50 sensor-based components sending alerts/message every minute. By contrast, the MapReduce programmer can split the application task among multiple subtasks, say one hundred sub-tasks, and each sub-task processes the data of a selected set of a Service users.

The results of all the sub-tasks aggregate and produce the final result for hourly maintenance requirement of each component of the cars registered at ACPAMS Company. Finally, the aggregated hourly results appear from the hourly log of transactions files at Hadoop data nodes. The whole system maintains transparency, without knowing the presence of a distributed parallel system processing data of a hundred million records. Table 4.1 gives examples of assigning Ids to alerts/messages.

Table 4.1 Examples of Alert/MessageId (say, total 50 Ids, i.e., one for each sensor component)

Alert/ MessageId	Details
01	Fuel fill-in request
02	Filter requirement
03	Alignment and balancing requirement
04	Engine oil less
05	Coolant Change request

Assumption: Let 60 files for each hour create every day. The files are file_1, file_2, ..., file_60. Each file saves as a key-value pair at the large number of the company's machines. The log contains information in the following format:

```
maintenance service Id:(<CarRegistrationNumber>_<alert/messsageId>)
```

Thus, every line entry becomes the key, and the value will be the instance number.

Sample data of one of such file out of 60 files (file_10) saved as hour-maintenance-service log for the maintenance service during 15:00-16:00 will be as follows:

MP09CA2331_01
MP04NP0123_03

MP09HA1493_01
MP03SA5231_06
.
.
MP09CA2331_04
MP09CC4614_01
.

(i) The input files are using *NLineInputFormat* input format.
(ii) Map tasks will map the input streams of key values at files, file_1, file_2, ... file_59, file_60 every hour.
(iii) The map function *extracts* the alert/message Id from each line of the input files. They are the values after underscore in each line.
(iv) The resulting 1 million × 50 key-value pairs (since there are 50 sensors assumed per car) map each hour with keys for RegistrationNumber_N (N = 1 to 50). The output stream from Mapper will be as follows:
(01, 1), (03, 1), (01, 1), .., .., ...,

The (key, value) contains (alert/message Id, the instance number)

Mapper in ACPAMS

Input	Set of data	MP09CA2331_**01** MP04NP0123_**03** MP09HA1493_**09** MP03SA5231_**06** MP09HA1493_**01** MP04YQ1110_**01** MP05PS0810_**23** MP09CA2331_**01** MP04NH5555_**23** MP22FA1690_**23**
Output	Convert into another set of data (Key, Value) **Key** – Alert/Message Id **Value** – Number of instance	(01,1), (03,1), (09,1), (06,1), (01,1), (01,1), (23,1), (01,1), (23,1), (23,1)

Combiner in ACPAMS

Input	Key-Value Pairs (output of Mapper)	(01,1), (03,1), (09,1), (06,1), (01,1), (01,1), (23,1), (01,1), (23,1), (23,1)
Output	Key-Value Pairs (Group-By-key at node itself)	(01,1), (03,1), (09,1), (06,1), **(01,2)**, (23,1), (01,1), **(23,2)**

Shuffle in ACPAMS

Input	Key-Value Pairs (output of Combiner)	(01,1), (03,1), (09,1), (06,1), (01,2), (23,1), (01,1), (23,2)
Output	Key-Value Pairs (moved to other nodes based on key value)	(01,1), (01,2), (01,1) (03,1) (09,1) (06,1) (23,1), (23,2)

Sort in ACPAMS

Input	Key-Value Pairs (output of Shuffler)	(01,1), (01,2), (01,1) (03,1) (09,1) (06,1) (23,1), (23,2)
Output	Key-Value Pairs (Sort as per key)	(01,1), (01,2), (01,1) (03,1) (06,1) (09,1) (23,1), (23,2)

Reducer – Takes the output from Map (after the sort phase) as an input and combines the data tuples into a smaller set of tuples. Following are some examples of Reduce function in Alert/Message Count.

Input (output of map())	Set of Tuples	(01,1), (01,2), (01,1) (03,1) (06,1) (09,1) (23,1), (23,2)
Output	Converts into a smaller set of tuples (By using the aggregate function)	(01,4) (03,1) (06,1) (09,1) (23,3)

The output of the reduce(), which is the final result of MapReduce Job provides a number of alert or messages at an hourly basis for the complaint raised by each component of the cars registered at the ACPAMS Company. Then the analyst decides which components need maintenance on high to low priority. The report of ACAMPS helps the company in improving the manufacturing of its car components.

The following example gives pseudocodes for an algorithm:

EXAMPLE 4.5

Write pseudocodes for MapReduce algorithm for the ACPAMS.

SOLUTION

Figure 4.8 gives pseudocodes for the ACPAMS algorithm in MapReduce.

```
class Mapper {
    method Map (file id a; file f) {
        for all term i ∈ file f do {
            t = Substring (i, 2, After_)
            Emit (term t, count 1)}}}

class Reducer {
    method Reduce (term t, counts [c1, c2,…..]) {
        sum ← 0
        for all count c ∈ counts [c1, c2, ……] do {
        sum ← sum + c}
        Emit (term t, count sum)}}
```

Figure 4.8 Pseudocodes for the ACPAMS algorithm in MapReduce

Emit( ) function is for output in MapReduce. The Mapper emits an intermediate key-value pair for each alert/message in a document. The Reducer sums up all counts for each alert/message.

4.2.8 Coping with Node Failures

The primary way using which Hadoop achieves fault tolerance is through restarting the tasks. Each task nodes (TaskTracker) regularly communicates with the master node, JobTracker. If a TaskTracker fails to communicate with the JobTracker for a pre-defined period (by default, it is set to 10 minutes), a task node failure by the JobTracker is assumed. The JobTracker knows which map and reduce tasks were assigned to each TaskTracker.

> Node failure occurs when the TaskTracker fails to communicate with the JobTracker for a pre-defined period. The JobTracker restarts the TaskTracker for coping with the node failure.

If the job is currently in the mapping phase, then another TaskTracker will be assigned to re-execute all map tasks previously run by the failed TaskTracker. All completed map tasks also need to be assigned for re-execution if they belong to incomplete jobs. This is because the intermediate results residing in the failed TaskTracker file system may not be accessible to the reduce task.

If the job is in the reducing phase, then another TaskTracker will re-execute all reduce tasks that were in progress on the failed TaskTracker.

Once reduce tasks are completed, the output writes back to the HDFS. Thus, if a TaskTracker has already completed nine out of ten reduce tasks assigned to it, only the tenth task must execute at a different node.

Map tasks are slightly more complicated. A node may have completed ten map tasks but the Reducers may not have copied all their inputs from the output of those map tasks. Now if a node fails, then its Mapper outputs are inaccessible. Thus, any complete map tasks must also be re-executed to make their results available to the remaining reducing nodes. Hadoop handles all of this automatically. MapReduce does not use any task identities to communicate between nodes or which reestablishes the communication with other task node. Each task focuses on only its own direct inputs and knows only its own outputs. The failure and restart processes are clean and reliable.

The failure of JobTracker (if only one master node) can bring the entire process down; Master handles other failures, and the MapReduce job eventually completes. When the Master compute-node at which the JobTracker is executing fails, then the entire MapReduce job must restart. Following points summarize the coping mechanism with distinct Node Failures:

(i) Map TaskTracker failure:
- Map tasks completed or in-progress at TaskTracker, are reset to idle on failure
- Reduce TaskTracker gets a notice when a task is rescheduled on another TaskTracker

(ii) Reduce TaskTracker failure:
- Only in-progress tasks are reset to idle

(iii) Master JobTracker failure:
- Map-Reduce task aborts and notifies the client (in case of one master node).

Self-Assessment Exercise linked to LO 4.1

1. Show MapReduce process diagrammatically to depict a client submitting a job, the workflow of JobTracker and TaskTracker, and TaskTrackers creating the outputs. ○○●
2. Assume an input file size of 10 TB and a data block size of 128 MB. How many map tasks are required? Assume that each node does 100 maps. How many nodes are involved in processing? How will you change the number of map tasks per node to 120 using a Java statement? ○●●
3. Explain function of Group By, partitioning and combining using one example for each. ●●●
4. How does the data convert to (key, value) pairs before passing to the Mapper? How do the InputSplit and RecodReader function? ○●●
5. How are the failures of Map TaskTracker, Reduce TaskTracker and Master JobTracker handled in MapReduce? ○○●
6. How does the execution framework handle all aspects of distributed processing after a client node submits the job to the designated node of a cluster (the JobTracker)? Explain the concept using a diagram. ●●●

Note: ○○● Level 1 & Level 2 category
○●● Level 3 & Level 4 category
●●● Level 5 & Level 6 category

4.3 COMPOSING MapReduce FOR CALCULATIONS AND ALGORITHMS

LO 4.2

Composing MapReduce programs for calculations, such as counting and summing; and algorithms for relational algebraic operations, such as projections, unions, intersections, natural joins, grouping, aggregation operations and matrix multiplication

The following subsections describe the use of MapReduce program composition in counting and summing, algorithms for relational algebraic operations, projections, unions, intersections, natural joins, grouping and aggregation, matrix multiplication and other computations.

4.3.1 Composing Map-Reduce for Calculations

The calculations for various operations compose are:

Counting and Summing Assume that the number of alerts or messages generated during a specific maintenance activity of vehicles need counting for a month. Figure 4.8 showed the pseudocode using emit() in the map() of *Mapper* class. *Mapper* emits 1 for each message generated. The reducer goes through the list of 1s and sums them. Counting is used in the data querying application. For example, count of messages generated, word count in a file, number of cars sold, and analysis of the logs, such as number of tweets per month. Application is also in business analytics field.

Sorting Figure 4.6 illustrated MapReduce execution steps, i.e., dataflow, splitting, partitioning and sorting on a map node and reduce on a reducer node. Example 4.3 illustrated the sorting method. Many applications need sorted values in a certain order by some rule or process. *Mappers* just emit all items as values associated with the sorting keys which assemble as a function of items. *Reducers* combine all emitted parts into a final list.

Finding Distinct Values (Counting unique values) Applications such as web log analysis need counting of unique users. Evaluation is performed for the total number of unique values in each field for each set of records that belongs to the same group. Two solutions are possible:

(i) The *Mapper* emits the dummy counters for each pair of field and groupId, and the *Reducer* calculates the total number of occurrences for each such pair.

(ii) The *Mapper* emits the values and groupId, and the *Reducer* excludes the duplicates from the list of groups for each value and increments the counter for each group. The final step is to sum all the counters emitted at the *Reducer*. This requires only one MapReduce job but the process is not scalable, and hence has limited applicability in large data sets.

Collating Collating is a way to collect all items which have the same value of function in one document or file, or a way to process items with the same value of the function together. Examples of applications are producing inverted indexes and extract, transform and load operations.

Mapper computes a given function for each item, produces value of the function as a key, and the item itself as a value. *Reducer* then obtains all item values using group-by function, processes or saves them into a list and outputs to the application task or saves them.

Filtering or Parsing Filtering or parsing collects only those items which satisfy some condition or transform each item into some other representation. Filtering/parsing include tasks such as text parsing, value extraction and conversion from one format to another. Examples of applications of filtering are found in data validation, log analysis and querying of datasets.

Mapper takes items one by one and accepts only those items which satisfy the conditions and emit the accepted items or their transformed versions. *Reducer* obtains all the emitted items, saves them into a list and outputs to the application.

Distributed Tasks Execution Large computations divide into multiple partitions and combine the results from all partitions for the final result. Examples of distributed running of tasks are physical and engineering simulations, numerical analysis and performance testing.

Mapper takes a specification as input data, performs corresponding computations and emits results. *Reducer* combines all emitted parts into the final result.

Graph Processing using Iterative Message Passing Graph is a network of entities and relationships between them. A node corresponds to an entity. An edge joining two nodes corresponds to a relationship. Path traversal method processes a graph. Traversal from one node to the next generates a result which passes as a message to the next traversal between the two nodes. Cyclic path traversal uses iterative message passing.

Web indexing also uses iterative message passing. Graph processing or web indexing requires calculation of the state of each entity. Calculated state is based on characteristics of the other entities in its neighborhood in a given network. (State means present value. For example, assume an entity is a course of study. The course may be Java or Python. Java is a state of the entity and Python is another state.)

A set of nodes stores the data and codes at a network. Each node contains a list of neighbouring node IDs. MapReduce jobs execute iteratively. Each node in an iteration sends messages to its neighbors. Each neighbor updates its state based on the received messages. Iterations terminate on some conditions, such as completion of fixed maximal number of iterations or specified time to live or negligible changes in states between two consecutive iterations.

Mapper emits the messages for each node using the ID of the adjacent node as a key. All messages thus group by the incoming node. *Reducer* computes the state again and rewrites a node new state.

Cross Correlation Cross-correlation involves calculation using number of tuples where the items co-occur in a set of tuples of items. If the total number of items is N, then the total number of values = N × N. Cross correlation is used in text analytics. (Assume that items are words and tuples are sentences). Another application is in market-analysis (for example, to enumerate, the customers who buy item x tend to also buy y). If N × N is a small number, such that the matrix can fit in the memory of a single machine, then implementation is straightforward.

Two solutions for finding cross correlations are:

(i) The *Mapper* emits all pairs and dummy counters, and the *Reducer* sums these counters. The benefit from using combiners is little, as it is likely that all pairs are distinct. The accumulation does not use in-memory computations as N is very large.

(ii) The *Mapper* groups the data by the first item in each pair and maintains an associative array ("stripe") where counters for all adjacent items accumulate. The *Reducer* receives all stripes for the leading item, merges them and emits the same result as in the pairs approach.

[Stripe means a set of arrays associated with a dataset or a set of rows that belong to a common key with each row having a number of columns.]

The grouping:

- Generates fewer intermediate keys. Hence, the framework has less sorting to do.
- Greatly benefits from the use of combiners.
- In-memory accumulation possible.

- Enables complex implementations.
- Results in general, faster computations using stripes than "pairs".

4.3.2 Matrix–Vector Multiplication by MapReduce

Numbers of applications need multiplication of n × n matrix **A** with vector **B** of dimension **n**. Each element of the product is the element of vector **C** of dimension **n**. The elements of **C** calculate by relation, $c_i = \sum_{j=1}^{n} a_{ij} b_j$. An example of calculations is given below.

$$\text{Assume } \mathbf{A} = \begin{vmatrix} 1 & 5 & 4 \\ 2 & 1 & 3 \\ 4 & 2 & 1 \end{vmatrix} \text{ and } \mathbf{B} = \begin{vmatrix} 4 \\ 1 \\ 3 \end{vmatrix}. \quad \ldots (4.1)$$

$$\text{Multiplication } \mathbf{C} = \mathbf{A} \times \mathbf{B} = \begin{bmatrix} 1 \times 4 + 5 \times 1 + 4 \times 3 \\ 2 \times 4 + 1 \times 1 + 3 \times 3 \\ 4 \times 4 + 2 \times 1 + 1 \times 3 \end{bmatrix}$$

$$\text{Hence, } \quad \mathbf{C} = \begin{bmatrix} 21 \\ 18 \\ 21 \end{bmatrix} \quad \ldots (4.2)$$

Algorithm for using MapReduce: The Mapper operates on **A** and emits row-wise multiplication of each matrix element and vector element ($a_{ij} \times b_j \; \forall$ i). The Reducer executes sum() for summing all values associated with each i and emits the element c_i. Application of the algorithm is found in linear transformation.

4.3.3 Relational–Algebra Operations

Explained ahead are the some approaches of algorithms for using MapReduce for relational algebraic operations on large datasets.

4.3.3.1 *Selection*

Example of Selection in relational algebra is as follows: Consider the attribute names (ACVM_ID, Date, chocolate_flavour, daily_sales). Consider relation

R = {(524, 12122017, KitKat, 82), (524, 12122017, Oreo, 72), (525, 12122017, KitKat, 82), (525, 12122017, Oreo, 72), (526, 12122017, KitKat, 82), (526, 12122017, Oreo, 72)}.

Selection $\sigma_{ACVM\_ID <= 525}$ (*R*) selects the subset *R*= {(524, 12122017, KitKat, 82), (524, 12122017, Oreo, 72), (525, 12122017, KitKat, 82), (525, 12122017, Oreo, 72)}.

Selection $\sigma_{chocolate\_flavour = Oreo}$ selects the subset {(524, 12122017, Oreo, 72), (525, 12122017, Oreo, 72), (526, 12122017, Oreo, 72)}.

The test() tests the attribute values used for a selection after the binary operation of an attribute with the value(s) or value in an attribute name with value in another attribute name and the binary operation by which each tuple selects. Selection may also return *false* or *unknown*. The test condition then does not select any.

The *Mapper* calls test() for each tuple in a row. When test satisfies the selection criterion then emits the tuple. The *Reducer* transfers the received input tuple as the output.

4.3.3.2 *Projection*

Example of *Projection* in relational algebra is as follows:

Consider attribute names (ACVM_ID, Date, chocolate_flavour, daily_sales).

Consider relation R = {(524, 12122017, KitKat, 82), (524, 12122017, Oreo, 72)}.

Projection $\Pi_{ACVM\_ID}(R)$ selects the subset {(524)}.

Projection, $\Pi_{chocolate\_flavour,\ 0.5*\ daily\_sales}$ selects the subset {(KitKat, 0.5 × 82), (Oreo, 0.5 × 72)}.

The test() tests the presence of attribute (s) used for projection and the factor by an attribute needs projection.

The *Mapper* calls test() for each tuple in a row. When the test satisfies, the predicate then emits the tuple (same as in selection). The *Reducer* transfers the received input tuples after eliminating the possible duplicates. Such operations are used in analytics.

4.3.3.3 *Union*

Example of Union in relations is as follows: Consider,

R1 = {(524, 12122017, KitKat, 82), (524, 12122017, Oreo, 72)}

R2 = {(525, 12122017, KitKat, 82), (525, 12122017, Oreo, 72)}

and R3 = {(526, 12122017, KitKat, 82), (526, 12122017, Oreo, 72)}

Result of Union operation between R1 and R3 is:

R1 **U** R3 = {(524, 12122017, KitKat, 82), (524, 12122017, Oreo, 72), (526, 12122017, KitKat, 82), (526, 12122017, Oreo, 72)}

The *Mapper* executes all tuples of two sets for union and emits all the resultant tuples. The *Reducer* class object transfers the received input tuples after eliminating the possible duplicates.

4.3.3.4 *Intersection and Difference*

Intersection Example of Interaction in relations is as follows: Consider,

R1 = {(524, 12122017, Oreo, 72)}

R2 = {(525, 12122017, KitKat, 82)}

and R3 = {(526, 12122017, KitKat, 82), (526, 12122017, Oreo, 72)}

Result of Intersection operation between R1 and R3 are

R1 $\cap$ R3 = {(12122017, Oreo)}

The *Mapper* executes all tuples of two sets for intersection and emits all the resultant tuples. The *Reducer* transfers only tuples that occurred twice. This is possible only when tuple includes primary key and can occur once in a set. Thus, both the sets contain this tuple.

Difference Consider:

R1 = {(12122017, KitKat, 82), (12122017, Oreo, 72)}

and R3 = {(12122017, KitKat, 82), (12122017, Oreo, 25)}

Difference means the tuple elements are not present in the second relation. Therefore, difference set_1 is R1 – R3 = (12122017, Oreo, 72) and set_2 is R3 – R1 = (12122017, Oreo, 25).

The *Mapper* emits all the tuples and tag. A tag is the name of the set (say, set_1 or set_2 to which a tuple belongs to). The *Reducer* transfers only tuples that belong to set_1.

Symmetric Difference Symmetric difference (notation is $A \Delta B$ (or $A \ominus B$)] is another relational entity. It means the set of elements in exactly one of the two relations A or B. R3 ⊖ R1 = (12122017, Oreo, 25).

The *Mapper* emits all the tuples and tag. A tag is the name of the set (say, set_1 or set_2 this tuple belongs to). The *Reducer* transfers only tuples that belong to neither set_1 or set_2.

4.3.3.5 Natural Join

Consider two relations R1 and R2 for tuples a, b and c. Natural Join computes for R1 (a, b) with R2 (b, c). Natural Join is R (a, b, c). Tuples b joins as one in a Natural Join. The *Mapper* emits the key-value pair (b, (R1, a)) for each tuple (a, b) of R1, similarly emits (b, (R2, c)) for each tuple (b, c) of R2.

The *Mapper* is mapping both with Key for b. The *Reducer* transfers all pairs consisting of one with first component R1 and the other with first component R2, say (R1, a) and (R2, c). The output from the key and value list is a sequence of key-value pairs. The key is of no use and is irrelevant. Each value is one of the triples (a, b, c) such that (R1, a) and (R2, c) are present in the input list of values.

The following example explains the concept of join, how the data stores use the INNER Join and NATURAL Join of two tables, and how the Join compute quickly.

EXAMPLE 4.6

An SQL statement "`Transactions INNER JOIN KitKatStock ON Transactions.ACVM_ID = KitKatStock.ACVM_ID`"; selects the records that have matching values in two tables for transactions of KitKat sales at a particular ACVM. One table is KitKatStock with columns (KitKat_Quantity, ACVM_ID) and second table is Transactions with columns (ACVM_ID, Sales_Date and KitKat_SalesData).

1. What will be INNER Join of two tables KitKatStock and Transactions?
2. What will be the NATURAL Join?

SOLUTION

1. The INNER JOIN gives all the columns from the two tables (thus the common columns appear twice). The INNER JOIN of two tables will return a table with five column: (i) KitKatStock. Quantity, (ii) KitKatStock. KitKat_ACVM_ID, (iii) Transactions.ACVM_ID, (iv)Transactions. KitKat_SalesDate, and (v) Transactions.KitKat_SalesData.
2. The NATURAL JOIN gives all the unique columns from the two tables. The NATURAL JOIN of two tables will return a table with four columns: (i) KitKatStock.Quantity, (ii) KitKatStock. ACVM_ID, (iii) Transactions.KitKat_SalesDate, and (iv) Transactions.KitKat_SalesData.

Values accessible by key in the first table KitKatStock merges with Transactions table accessible by the common key ACVM_ID.

NATURAL JOIN gives the common column once in the output of a query, while INNER JOIN gives common columns of both tables.

Join enables fast computations of the aggregate of the number of chocolates of specific flavour sold.

4.3.3.6 Grouping and Aggregation by MapReduce

Grouping means operation on the tuples by the value of some of their attributes after applying the aggregate function independently to each attribute. A Grouping operation denotes by <grouping attributes> $\Im$ <function-list> (R). Aggregate functions are count(), sum(), avg(), min() and max().

Assume *R*= {(524, 12122017, KitKat, 82), (524, 12122017, Oreo, 72), (525, 12122017, KitKat, 82), (525, 12122017, Oreo, 72), (526, 12122017, KitKat, 82), (526, 12122017, Oreo, 72)}. Chocolate_flavour $\mathfrak{I}$ count ACVM_ID, sum (daily_sales (chocolate_flavour)) will give the output (524, KitKat, sale_month), (525, KitKat, sale_month), ... and (524, Oreo, sale_month), (525, Oreo, sale_month), ... for all ACVM_IDs.

The *Mapper* finds the values from each tuple for grouping and aggregates them. The *Reducer* receives the already grouped values in input for aggregation.

4.3.4 Matrix Multiplication

Consider matrices named A (i rows and j columns) and B (j rows and k columns) to produce the matrix C; (i rows and k columns). Consider the elements of matrices $\mathcal{A}$, $\mathcal{B}$ and $\mathcal{C}$ as follows:

$$\mathcal{A} = \begin{matrix} a_{11}\ a_{12} \ldots a_{1j} \\ a_{21}\ a_{22} \ldots a_{2j} \\ \ldots\ldots \\ \ldots\ldots \\ a_{i1}\ a_{i2} \ldots a_{ij} \end{matrix} \qquad \mathcal{B} = \begin{matrix} b_{11}\ b_{12} . b_{1k} \\ b_{21}\ b_{22} . b_{2k} \\ \ldots\ldots \\ \ldots\ldots \\ b_{j1}\ b_{i2} . b_{jk} \end{matrix} \qquad \mathcal{C} = \begin{matrix} c_{11}\ c_{12} . c_{1k} \\ c_{21}\ c_{22} . c_{2k} \\ \ldots\ldots \\ \ldots\ldots \\ c_{i1}\ c_{i2} . c_{ik} \end{matrix} \quad \ldots (4.3)$$

$\mathcal{A}.\mathcal{B} = \mathcal{C}$; Each element evaluates as follow:

$$C_{ik} = \text{Sum } (a_{ij} \times b_{jk})_{j=1 \text{ to } j}.\ v_a = a_{ij} \text{ and } v_b = b_{jk} \quad \ldots (4.4)$$

First row of $\mathcal{C}$

$\mathcal{C}$ first column element = ($a_{11}b_{11}$+ $a_{12}b_{21}$ +.... + $a_{1j}.b_{j1}$). Second column element = ($a_{11}b_{12}$+ $a_{12}b_{22}$+.... + $a_{1j}.b_{j2}$). The kth column element = ($a_{11}b_{1k}$+ $a_{12}b_{2k}$+.... + a_{1j} b_{jk}).

Second row of $\mathcal{C}$

$\mathcal{C}$ first column element = ($a_{21}b_{11}$+ $a_{22}b_{21}$ +.... + $a_{2j}.b_{j1}$). Second column element = ($a_{21}b_{12}$+ $a_{22}b_{22}$+.... + $a_{2j}.b_{j2}$). The kth column element = ($a_{21}b_{1k}$+ $a_{22}b_{2k}$+.... + a_{2j}. b_{jk}).

The ith row of $\mathcal{C}$

$\mathcal{C}$ first column element = ($a_{i1}b_{11}$+ $a_{i2}b_{21}$ +.... + $a_{ij}.b_{j1}$). Second column element = ($a_{i1}b_{12}$+ ai_2b_{22}+.... + $a_{ij}.b_{j2}$). The kth column element = ($a_{i1}b_{1k}$+ $a_{i2}b_{2k}$+.... + $a_{ij}.b_{jk}$).

Consider two solutions of matrix multiplication.

Matrix Multiplication with Cascading of Two MapReduce Steps

Table 4.2 gives the names, attributes, relations R_A, R_B and R_C, tuples in $\mathcal{A}$, $\mathcal{B}$, $\mathcal{C}$, natural Join of R_A and R_B, keys and values, and seven steps for multiplication of $\mathcal{A}$ and $\mathcal{B}$.

Table 4.2 Seven steps for multiplication of $\mathcal{A}$ and $\mathcal{B}$ for cascading of two MapReduce Steps

Step	Step description	Matrix $\mathcal{A}$	Matrix $\mathcal{B}$	Matrix $\mathcal{C} = \mathcal{A}.\mathcal{B}$
1	Name	A	B	C
2	Specify attributes of (Key, Value pairs of each element [row number, column number, value]	(I, J, v_a)	(J, K, v_b)	(I, K, v_c)
3	Specify relations	**R_A** = A (I, J, v_a)	**R_B** = A (J, K, v_b)	**R_C** = A (I, K, v_c)

(*Contd.*)

Step	Step description	Matrix $\mathcal{A}$	Matrix $\mathfrak{B}$	Matrix $\mathfrak{C} = \mathcal{A} . \mathfrak{B}$
4	Consider tuples of $\mathcal{A}$, $\mathfrak{B}$ and $\mathfrak{C}$	(i, j, a_{ij})	(j, k, b_{jk}).	(i, k, c_{ik})
5	Find natural Join of R_A and R_B = Matrix elements (a_{ij}, b_{jk}) [j is common in both]	-	-	tuples (i, j, k, v_a, v_b)
6	Get tuples for finding Product $\mathfrak{C}$			Four-component tuple (i, j, k, $v_a \times v_b$)
7	Grouping and aggregation of tuples with attributes I and K			<I, K> $\Im$ SUM ($v_a \times v_b$).

The product $\mathcal{A}\mathfrak{B}$ = Natural join of tuples in the relations R_A and R_B followed by grouping and aggregation. Natural Join of A (I, J, v_a) and B (J, K, v_b), having only attribute J in common = Tuples (i, j, k, v_a, v_b) from each tuple (i, j, v_a) in $\mathcal{A}$ and tuples (j, k, v_b) in $\mathfrak{B}$.

1. *MapReduce tasks for Steps 5 and 6*: Five-component tuple represents the pair of matrix elements (a_{ij}, b_{jk}). Requirement is product of these elements. That means four-component tuple (i, j, k, $v_a \times v_b$), from equation (4.4) for elements C_{ik} = Sum $(a_{ij}.b_{jk})_{j=1 \text{ to } j}$.
   (a) Mapper Function: (i) *Mapper* emits the key-value pairs (j, (A, i, a_{ij})) for each matrix element a_{ij}, and (ii) *Mapper* emits the key-value pair (j, (B, k, b_{jk})) for each matrix element a_{ij}.
   (b) Reduce Function: Consider the tuples of $\mathcal{A}$ = (A, i, a_{ij}) for each key j, consider tuples of $\mathfrak{B}$ = (B, k, b_{jk}) for each key j. Produce a key-value pair with key equal to (i, k) and value = $a_{ij} \times b_{jk}$. A and B are just the names, may be represented by 0101 and 1010.

2. *Next MapReduce Steps 7*: Perform <I, K> $\Im$ SUM ($v_a \times v_b$). That means do grouping and aggregation, with I and K as the grouping attributes and the sum of $v_a \times v_b$ as the aggregation.
   (c) The *Mapper* emits the key-value pairs (i, k, v_c) for each matrix element of C inputs with key i and k, and v_c from earlier task of the reducer $v_a \times v_b$.
   (d) *Reducer* groups (i, k, v_c) in C using [C, i, k, sum (v_c)] from aggregated values of v_c from sum (v_c). Aggregation uses the same memory locations as used by elements v_c. C is just the name, may be represented by 1111.

Matrix Multiplication with One MapReduce Step MapReduce tasks for Steps 5 to 7 in a single step.

(e) Map Function: For each element a_{ij} of $\mathcal{A}$, the *Mapper* emits all the key-value pairs [(i, k), (A, j, a_{ij})] for k = 1, 2, . . ., up to the number of columns of $\mathfrak{B}$. Similarly, emits all the key-value pairs [(i, k), (B, j, b_{jk})] for i = 1, 2, . . ., up to the number of rows of $\mathcal{A}$. for each element b_{jk} of $\mathfrak{B}$.

(f) Reduce Function: Consider the tuples of $\mathcal{A}$ = (A, i, a_{ij}) for each key j. Consider tuples of $\mathfrak{B}$ = (B, k, b_{jk}) for each key j. Emits the key-value pairs with key equal to (i, k) and value = sum of ($a_{ij} \times b_{jk}$) for all values j.

Memory required in one step MapReduce is large as compared to two steps in cascade. This is due to the need to store intermediate values of v_c and then sum them in the same *Reducer* step.

Self-Assessment Exercise linked to LO 4.2

1. How does MapReduce program implement counting, filtering and parsing? ○○●
2. How does MapReduce collate all items which have the same value? ○○●
3. How does MapReduce perform graph analysis in a network of computing nodes to build a spanning tree information at a particular node? ○●●
4. How does MapReduce program collate and process items with the same value of the function together in an ETL operation? ●●●
5. How does MapReduce program implement <grouping attributes> ℑ <function-list> (R)? ○●●

4.4 HIVE

LO 4.3

Hive, architecture, installation, comparison of Hive data store with traditional databases

Hive was created by Facebook. Hive is a data warehousing tool and is also a data store on the top of Hadoop. An enterprise uses a data warehouse as large data repositories that are designed to enable the tracking, managing, and analyzing the data. (Section 1.6.1.7) Hive processes structured data and integrates data from multiple heterogeneous sources. Additionally, also manages the constantly growing volumes of data.

Figure 4.9 shows the main features of Hive.

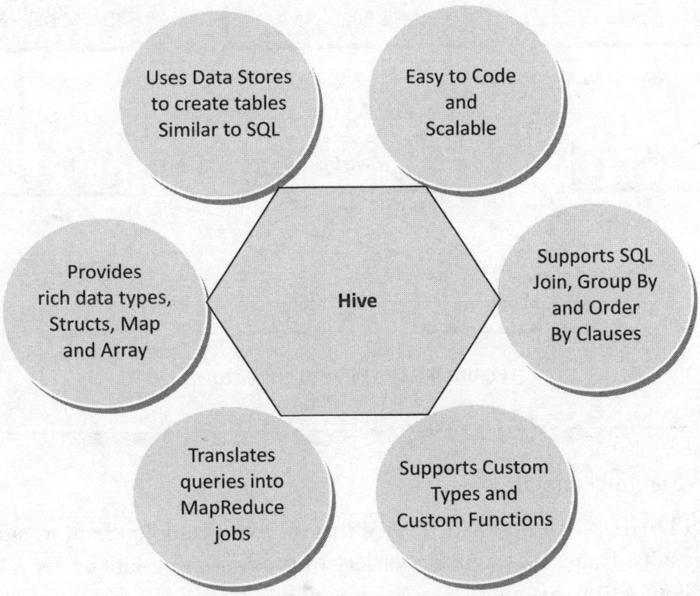

Figure 4.9 Main features of Hive

Hive Characteristics

1. Has the capability to translate queries into MapReduce jobs. This makes Hive scalable, able to handle data warehouse applications, and therefore, suitable for the analysis of static data of an extremely large size, where the fast response-time is not a criterion.
2. Supports web interfaces as well. Application APIs as well as web-browser clients, can access the Hive DB server.
3. Provides an SQL dialect (Hive Query Language, abbreviated HiveQL or HQL).

Results of HiveQL Query and the data load in the tables which store at the Hadoop cluster at HDFS.

Limitations

Hive is:

1. Not a full database. Main disadvantage is that Hive does not provide update, alter and deletion of records in the database.
2. Not developed for unstructured data.
3. Not designed for real-time queries.
4. Performs the partition always from the last column.

4.4.1 Hive Architecture

Figure 4.10 shows the Hive architecture.

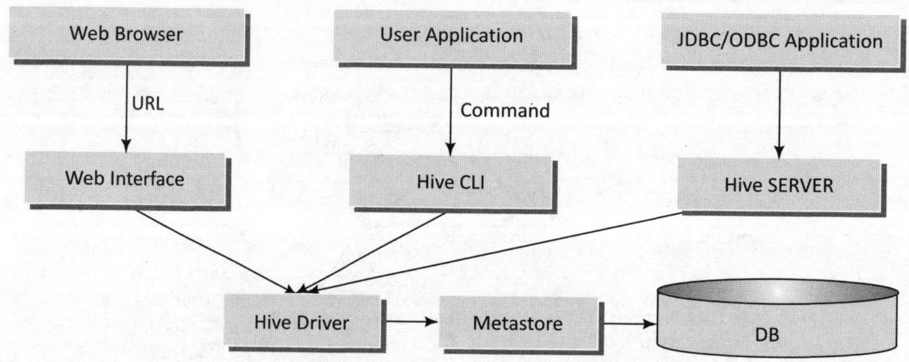

Figure 4.10 Hive architecture

Components of Hive architecture are:

- **Hive Server (Thrift)** – An optional service that allows a remote client to submit requests to Hive and retrieve results. Requests can use a variety of programming languages. Thrift Server exposes a very simple client API to execute HiveQL statements.
- **Hive CLI (Command Line Interface)** – Popular interface to interact with Hive. Hive runs in local mode that uses local storage when running the CLI on a Hadoop cluster instead of HDFS.

- **Web Interface** – Hive can be accessed using a web browser as well. This requires a HWI Server running on some designated code. The URL *http:// hadoop:<port no.> / hwi* command can be used to access Hive through the web.
- **Metastore** – It is the system catalog. All other components of Hive interact with the Metastore. It stores the schema or metadata of tables, databases, columns in a table, their data types and HDFS mapping.
- **Hive Driver** – It manages the life cycle of a HiveQL statement during compilation, optimization and execution.

4.4.2 Hive Installation

Hive can be installed on Windows 10, Ubuntu 16.04 and MySQL. It requires three software packages:

- Java Development kit for Java compiler (Javac) and interpreter
- Hadoop
- Compatible version of Hive with Java– Hive 1.2 onward supports Java 1.7 or newer.

Steps for installation of Hive in a Linux based OS are as follows:

1. Install Javac and Java from Oracle Java download site. Download jdk 7 or a later version from http://www.oracle.com/technetwork/java/javase/downloads/jdk7-downloads-1880260.html, and extract the compressed file.
   All users can access Java by Make java available to all users. The user has to move it to the location "/usr/local/" using the required commands
2. Set the path by the commands for jdk1.7.0_71, export JAVA_HOME=/usr/local/jdk1.7.0_71, export PATH=$PATH: $JAVA_HOME/bin
   (Can use alternative install /usr/bin/java usr/local/java/bin/java 2)
3. Install Hadoop http://apache.claz.org/hadoop/common/hadoop-2.4.1/
4. Make shared HADOOP, MAPRED, COMMON, HDFS and all related files, configure HADOOP and set property such as replication parameter.
5. Name the yarn.nodemanager.aux-services. Assign value to mapreduce_shuffle. Set namenode and datanode paths.
6. Download http://apache.petsads.us/hive/hive-0.14.0/. Use ls command to verify the files $ tar zxvf apache-hive-0.14.0-bin.tar.gz, $ ls
   OR
   Hive archive also extracts by the command apache-hive-0.14.0-bin apache-hive-0.14.0-bin.tar.gz. , $ cd $HIVE_HOME/conf, $ cp hive-env.sh.template hive-env.sh, export HADOOP_HOME=/usr/local/hadoop
7. Use an external database server. Configure metastore for the server.

4.4.3 Comparison with RDBMS (Traditional Database)

Hive is a DB system which defines databases and tables. Hive analyzes structured data in DB. Hive has certain differences with RDBMS. Table 4.3 gives a comparison of Hive database characteristics with RDBMS.

Table 4.3 Comparison of Hive database characteristics with RDBMS

Characteristics	Hive	RDBMS
Record level queries	No Update and Delete	Insert, Update and Delete
Transaction support	No	Yes
Latency	Minutes or more	In fractions of a second
Data size	Petabytes	Terabytes
Data per query	Petabytes	Gigabytes
Query language	HiveQL	SQL
Support JDBC/ODBC	Limited	Full

4.4.4 Hive Data Types and File Formats

Hive defines various primitive, complex, string, date/time, collection data types and file formats for handling and storing different data formats. Table 4.4 gives primitive, string, date/time and complex Hive data types and their descriptions.

Table 4.4 Hive data types and their descriptions

Data Type Name	Description
TINYINT	1 byte signed integer. Postfix letter is Y.
SMALLINT	2 byte signed integer. Postfix letter is S.
INT	4 byte signed integer
BIGINT	8 byte signed integer. Postfix letter is L.
FLOAT	4 byte single-precision floating-point number
DOUBLE	8 byte double-precision floating-point number
BOOLEAN	True or False
TIMESTAMP	UNIX timestamp with optional nanosecond precision. It supports java.sql.Timestamp format "YYYY-MM-DD HH:MM:SS.fffffffff"
DATE	YYYY-MM-DD format
VARCHAR	1 to 65355 bytes. Use single quotes (' ') or double quotes (" ")
CHAR	255 bytes
DECIMAL	Used for representing immutable arbitrary precision. DECIMAL (precision, scale) format
UNION	Collection of heterogeneous data types. `Create union`
NULL	Missing values representation

Table 4.5 gives Hive three Collection data types and their descriptions.

Table 4.5 Collection data-types and their descriptions

Name	Description
STRUCT	Similar to 'C' struc, a collection of fields of different data types. An access to field uses dot notation. For example, struct ('a', 'b')
MAP	A collection of key-value pairs. Fields access using [] notation. For example, map ('key1', 'a', 'key2', 'b')
ARRAY	Ordered sequence of same types. Accesses to fields using array index. For example, array ('a', 'b')

Table 4.6 gives the file formats and their descriptions.

Table 4.6 File formats and their descriptions

File Format	Description
Text file	The default file format, and a line represents a record. The delimiting characters separate the lines. Text file examples are CSV, TSV, JSON and XML (Section 3.3.2).
Sequential file	Flat file which stores binary key-value pairs, and supports compression.
RCFile	Record Columnar file (Section 3.3.3.3).
ORCFILE	ORC stands for Optimized Row Columnar which means it can store data in an optimized way than in the other file formats (Section 3.3.3.4).

Record columnar file means one that can be partitioned in rows and then partitioned with columns. Partitioning in this way enables serialization.

4.4.5 Hive Data Model

Table 4.7 below gives three components of Hive data model and their descriptions.

Table 4.7 Components (also called data units) of Hive Data Model

Name	Description
Database	Namespace for tables
Tables	Similar to tables in RDBMS Support filter, projection, join and union operations The table data stores in a directory in HDFS
Partitions	Table can have one or more partition keys that tell how the data stores
Buckets	Data in each partition further divides into buckets based on hash of a column in the table. Stored as a file in the partition directory.

4.4.6 Hive Integration and Workflow Steps

Hive integrates with the MapReduce and HDFS. Figure 4.11 shows the dataflow sequences and workflow steps between Hive and Hadoop.

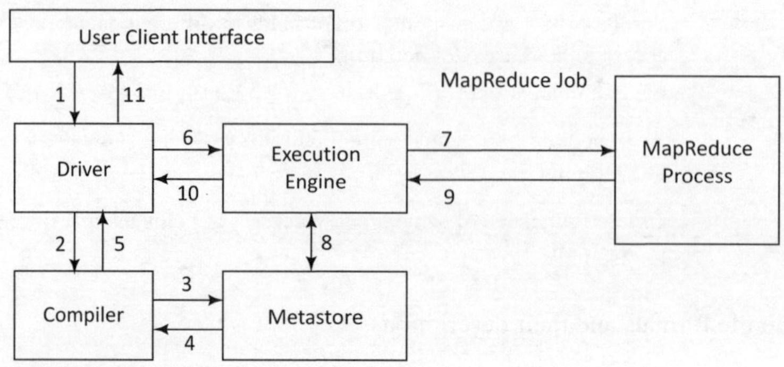

Figure 4.11 Dataflow sequences and workflow steps

Steps 1 to 11 are as follows:

STEP No.	OPERATION
1	**Execute Query**: Hive interface (CLI or Web Interface) sends a query to Database Driver to execute the query.
2	**Get Plan**: Driver sends the query to query compiler that parses the query to check the syntax and query plan or the requirement of the query.
3	**Get Metadata**: Compiler sends metadata request to Metastore (of any database, such as MySQL).
4	**Send Metadata**: Metastore sends metadata as a response to compiler.
5	**Send Plan:** Compiler checks the requirement and resends the plan to driver. The parsing and compiling of the query is complete at this place.
6	**Execute Plan:** Driver sends the execute plan to execution engine.
7	**Execute Job:** Internally, the process of execution job is a MapReduce job. The execution engine sends the job to JobTracker, which is in Name node and it assigns this job to TaskTracker, which is in Data node. Then, the query executes the job.
8	**Metadata Operations:** Meanwhile the execution engine can execute the metadata operations with Metastore.
9	**Fetch Result:** Execution engine receives the results from Data nodes.
10	**Send Results:** Execution engine sends the result to Driver.
11	**Send Results:** Driver sends the results to Hive Interfaces.

4.4.7 Hive Built-in Functions

Hive supports a number of built-in functions. Table 4.8 gives the return types, syntax and descriptions of the examples of these functions.

Table 4.8 Return types, syntax, and descriptions of the functions

Return Type	Syntax	Description
BIGINT	round(double a)	Returns the rounded BIGINT (8 Byte integer) value of the 8 Byte double-precision floating point number a
BIGINT	floor(double a)	Returns the maximum BIGINT value that is equal to or less than the double.
BIGINT	ceil(double a)	Returns the minimum BIGINT value that is equal to or greater than the double.
double	rand(), rand(int seed)	Returns a random number (double) that distributes uniformly from 0 to 1 and that changes in each row. Integer seed ensured that random number sequence is deterministic.
string	concate(string str1, string str2, ...)	Returns the string resulting from concatenating str1 with str2, ...
string	substr(string str, int start)	Returns the substring of str starting from a start position till the end of string str.
string	substr(string str, int start, int length)	Returns the substring of str starting from the start position with the given length.
string	upper(string str), ucase (string str)	Returns the string resulting from converting all characters of str to upper case.
string	lower(string str), lcase(string str)	Returns the string resulting from converting all characters of str to lower case.
string	trim(string str)	Returns the string resulting from trimming spaces from both ends. trim ('12A34 56') returns '12A3456'
string	ltrim(string str); rtrim(string str)	Returns the string resulting from trimming spaces (only one end, left or right hand side or right-handside spaces trimmed). ltrim('12A34 56') returns '12A3456' and rtrim(' 12A34 56 ') returns '12A3456'.
string	rtrim(string str)	Returns the string resulting from trimming spaces from the end (right hand side) of str.
int	year(string date)	Returns the year part of a date or a timestamp string.
int	month(string date)	Returns the month part of a date or a timestamp string.
int	day(string date)	Returns the day part of a date or a timestamp string.

Following are the examples of the returned output:

SELECT floor(10.5) from marks; Output = 10.0

SELECT ceil(10.5) from marks; Output = 11.0

Self-Assessment Exercise linked to LO 4.3

1. How does Hive install? What are the features of Hive? What are the components of the Hive architecture? ○○●
2. Give reasons for Hive provided with distinct integer types: TINYINT, SMALLINT, INT and BIGINT. ○●●
3. How does Hive use text, sequential, RC and ORC files? ○●●
4. How does the Hive use Collection data types: STRUCT, MAP and ARRAY? ●●●
5. How does Hive integrate with MapReduce and HDFS? ○○●
6. Give one example each of usages of round(), floor(), ceil(), rand() and upper() built-in functions in Hive. ○○●

4.5 HiveQL

LO 4.4

HiveQL for querying, sorting, aggregating, querying scripts, and MapReduce scripts for Joins and sub-queries

Hive Query Language (abbreviated HiveQL) is for querying the large datasets which reside in the HDFS environment. HiveQL script commands enable data definition, data manipulation and query processing. HiveQL supports a large base of SQL users who are acquainted with SQL to extract information from data warehouses.

HiveQL Process Engine	HiveQL is similar to SQL for querying on schema information at the Metastore. It is one of the replacements of traditional approach for MapReduce program. Instead of writing MapReduce program in Java, we can write a query for MapReduce job and process it.
Execution Engine	The bridge between HiveQL process Engine and MapReduce is Hive Execution Engine. Execution engine processes the query and generates results same as MapReduce results. It uses the flavor of MapReduce.

The subsections ahead give the details of data definition, data manipulation and querying data examples.

4.5.1 HiveQL Data Definition Language (DDL)

HiveQL database commands for data definition for DBs and Tables are CREATE DATABASE, SHOW DATABASE (list of all DBs), CREATE SCHEMA, CREATE TABLE. Following are HiveQL commands which create a table:

CREATE [TEMPORARY] [EXTERNAL] TABLE [IF NOT EXISTS] [<database name>.] <table name>
[(<column name> <data type> [COMMENT <column comment>], ...)]
[COMMENT <table comment>]
[ROW FORMAT <row format>]
[STORED AS <file format>]

Table 4.9 gives the row formats in a Hive table.

Table 4.9 Hive Table Row Formats

DELIMITED	Specifies a delimiter at the table level for structured fields. This is default. Syntax: FIELDS TERMINATED BY, LINES TERMINATED BY
SERDE	Stands for Serializer/Deserializer. SYNTAX: SERDE 'serde.class.name'

HiveQL database commands for data definition for the DBs and Tables are CREATE DATABASE, SHOW DATABASE (list of all DBs), CREATE SCHEMA, CREATE TABLE.

The following example uses HiveQL commands to create a database `toys_companyDB`.

EXAMPLE 4.7

How do you create a database named toys_companyDB and table named toys_tbl?

SOLUTION

```
$HIVE_HOME/binhive – service cli
hive>set hive.cli.print.current.db=true;
hive> CREATE DATABASE toys_companyDB
hive>USE toys_companyDB
hive (toys_companyDB)> CREATE TABLE toys_tbl (
>puzzle_code STRING,
>pieces SMALLINT
>cost FLOAT);
hive (toys_company)> quit;
&ls/home/binadmin/Hive/warehouse/toys_companyDB.db
```

The following example uses the command CREATE TABLE to create a table toy_products.

EXAMPLE 4.8

How do you create a table toy_products with the following fields?

Field	Data type
ProductCategory	string
ProductId	int
ProductName	string
ProductPrice	float

SOLUTION

```
CREATE TABLE IF NOT EXISTS toy_products (ProductCategory String, ProductId int, ProductName String, ProductPrice float)
  COMMENT 'Toy details'
  ROW FORMAT DELIMITED
  FIELDS TERMINATED BY '\t'
  LINES TERMINATED BY '\n'
  STORED AS TEXTFILE;
```

The option IF NOT EXISTS, Hive ignores the statement in case the table already exists.

Consider the following command:

A command is

```
CREATE DATABASE|SCHEMA [IF NOT EXISTS] <database name>;
```

IF NOT EXISTS is an optional clause. The clause notifies the user that a database with the same name already exists. SCHEMA can be also created in place of DATABASE using this command

A command is written to get the list of all existing databases.

```
SHOW DATABASES;
```

A command is written to delete an existing database.

```
DROP (DATABASE|SCHEMA) [IF EXISTS] <database name> [RESTRICT|CASCADE];
```

The following example gives the sample usages of the commands.

EXAMPLE 4.9

Give examples of usages of database commands for CREATE, SHOW and DROP.

SOLUTION

```
CREATE DATABASE IF NOT EXISTS toys_companyDB;
SHOW DATABASES;
default toys_companyDB
```

*Default database is test.

```
Delete dtabase using the command:
Drop Database toys_companyDB.
```

4.5.2 HiveQL Data Manipulation Language (DML)

HiveQL commands for data manipulation are USE <database name>, DROP DATABASE, DROP SCHEMA, ALTER TABLE, DROP TABLE, and LOAD DATA.

The following is a command for inserting (loading) data into the Hive DBs.

```
LOAD DATA [LOCAL] INPATH '<file path>' [OVERWRITE] INTO TABLE <table
name> [PARTITION (partcol1=val1, partcol2=val2 ...)]
```

LOCAL is an identifier to specify the local path. It is optional. OVERWRITE is optional to overwrite the data in the table. PARTITION is optional. val1 is value assigned to partition column 1 (partcol1) and val2 is value assigned to partition column 2 (partcol2).

Command	Functionality	Script Example
LOAD DATA	Insert data in a table	LOAD DATA LOCAL INPATH '/home/user/ jigsaw_puzzle_info.txt' OVERWRITE INTO TABLE toy_tbl;

The following is an example for usages of data manipulation commands, INSERT, ALTER, and DROP.

EXAMPLE 4.10

Consider an example of a toy company selling Jigsaws. Consider a text file named jigsaw_puzzle_info.txt in */home/user* directory. The file is text file with four fields: Toy-category, toy-id, toy-name, and Price in US$ as follows:

```
puzzle_Garden 10725 Fantasy 1.35
puzzle_Jungle 31047 Animals 2.85
puzzle_School 81049 Nursery 4.45
```

How will you use (i) LOAD (insert), (ii) ALTER and (iii) DROP commands?

SOLUTION

(i) Insert the data of this file into a table using the following commands:
LOAD DATA LOCAL INPATH '/home/user/ jigsaw_puzzle_info.txt'
OVERWRITE INTO TABLE jigsaw_puzzle;

(ii) Alter the table using the following commands:
ALTER TABLE <name> RENAME TO <new name>
ALTER TABLE <name> ADD COLUMNS (<col spec> [, <col spec> ...])
ALTER TABLE <name> DROP [COLUMN] <column name>
ALTER TABLE <name> CHANGE <column name> <new name> <new type>
ALTER TABLE <name> REPLACE COLUMNS (<col spec> [, <col spec> ...])
The following query renames the table from jigsaw_puzzle to toy_tbl:
ALTER TABLE jigsaw_puzzle RENAME TO toy_tbl;
The following query renames the column name ProductCategory to ProductCat:
ALTER TABLE toy_tbl CHANGE ProductCategory ProductCat String;
The following query renames data type of ProductPrice from float to double:
ALTER TABLE toy_tbl CHANGE ProductPrice ProductPrice Double;
The following query adds a column named ProductDesc to the toy_tbl table:
ALTER TABLE toy_tbl ADD COLUMNS (ProductDesc String COMMENT 'Product Description');
The following query deletes all the columns from the toy_tbl table and replaces it with ProdCat and ProdName columns:
ALTER TABLE toy_tbl REPLACE COLUMNS (ProductCategory INT ProdCat Int, ProductName STRING ProdName String);

(iii) The following query deletes a column named ProductDesc from the toy_tbl table:
ALTER TABLE toy_tbl DROP COLUMN ProductDesc;
A table DROP using the following command: DROP TABLE [IF EXISTS] table_name;
The following query drops a table named jigsaw_puzzle:
DROP TABLE IF EXISTS jigsaw_puzzle;

4.5.3 HiveQL For Querying the Data

Partitioning and storing are the requirements. A data warehouse should have a large number of partitions where the tables, files and databases store. Querying then requires sorting, aggregating and joining functions.

Querying the data is to SELECT a specific entity *satisfying* a condition, *having* presence of an entity or selecting specific entity using GroupBy .

```
SELECT [ALL | DISTINCT] <select expression>, <select expression>, ...
FROM <table name>
[WHERE <where condition>]
[GROUP BY <column List>]
[HAVING <having condition>]
[CLUSTER BY <column List>| [DISTRIBUTE BY <column List>] [SORT BY <column
List>]]
[LIMIT number];
```

4.5.3.1 Partitioning

Hive organizes tables into partitions. Table partitioning refers to dividing the table data into some parts based on the values of particular set of columns. Partition makes querying easy and fast. This is because `SELECT` is then from the smaller number of column fields. Section 3.3.3.3 described RC columnar format and serialized records. The following example explains the concept of partitioning, columnar and file records formats.

EXAMPLE 4.11

Consider a table **T** with eight-column and four-row table. Partition the table, convert in RC columnar format and serialize.

SOLUTION

Firstly, divide the table in four parts, t_{r1}, t_{r2}, t_{r3} and t_{r4} horizontally row-wise. Each sub-table has one row and eight columns. Now, convert each sub-table t_{r1}, t_{r2}, t_{r3} and t_{r4} into columnar format, or RC File records [Recall Example 3.7 on how RC file saves each row-group data in a format using SERDE (serializer/des-serializer)].

Each sub-table has eight rows and one column. Each column can serially send data one value at an instance. A column has eight key-value pairs with the same key for all the eight.

Table Partitioning

Create a table with Partition using command:

```
CREATE [EXTERNAL] TABLE <table name> (<column name 1> <data type 1>,
…....)
PARTITIONED BY (<column name n> <data type n> [COMMENT <column comment>],
...);
```

Rename a Partition in the existing Table using the following command:

```
ALTER TABLE <table name> PARTITION partition_spec RENAME TO PARTITION
partition_spec;
```

Add a Partition in the existing Table using the following command:

```
ALTER TABLE <table name> ADD [IF NOT EXISTS] PARTITION partition_spec
[LOCATION 'location1'] partition_spec [LOCATION 'location2'] ...;
```

```
partition_spec:(p_column = p_col_value, p_column = p_col_value, ...)
```

Drop a Partition in the existing Table using the following command:

```
ALTER TABLE <table name> DROP [IF EXISTS] PARTITION partition_spec, PARTITION
partition_spec;
```

The following example explains concept of add, rename and drop a partition.

EXAMPLE 4.12

How will you add, rename and drop a partition to a table, toys_tbl?

SOLUTION

(i) Add a partition to the existing toy table using the command:

```
ALTER TABLE toy_tbl ADD PARTITION (category='Toy_Airplane') location
'/Toy_Airplane/partAirplane';
```

(ii) The following query renames a partition:

```
ALTER TABLE toy_tbl PARTITION (category='Toy_Airplane') RENAME TO
PARTITION (name='Fighter');
```

(iii) Drop a Partition in the existing Table using the command:

```
ALTER TABLE toy_tbl DROP [IF EXISTS] PARTITION (category='Toy_
Airplane');
```

The following example explains how querying is facilitated by using partitioning of a table. A query processes faster when using partition. Selection of a product of a specific category from a table during query processing takes lesser time when the table has a partition based on a category.

EXAMPLE 4.13

Assume that following file contains toys_tbl.

```
/table/toy_tbl/file1
Category, id, name, price
Toy_Airplane, 10725, Lost Temple, 1.25
Toy_Airplane, 31047, Propeller Plane, 2.10
Toy_Airplane, 31049, Twin Spin Helicopter, 3.45
Toy_Train, 31054, Blue Express, 4.25
Toy_Train, 10254, Winter Holiday Toy_Train, 2.75
```

A table *toy_tbl* contains many values for categories of toys. Query is required to identify all toy_airplane fields. Give reasons why partitioning reduces query processing time.

SOLUTION

Here, a table named toy_tbl contains several toy details (category, id, name and price). Suppose it is required to identify all the airplanes. A query searches the whole table for the required information. However, if a partition is created on the toy_tbl, based on category and stores it in a separate file, then it will reduce the query processing time.

Let the data partitions into two files, file 2 and file 3, using category.

```
/table/toys/toy_airplane/file2
toy_airplane, 10725, Lost Temple, TP, 1.25
toy_airplane, 31047, Propeller Plane, 2.10
toy_airplane, 31049, Lost Temple, 3.45
/table/toys/toy_train/file3
Toy_Train, 31054, Blue Express, 4.25
Toy_Train, 10254, Winter Holiday Toy_Train, 2.75
```

Advantages of Partition

1. Distributes execution load horizontally.
2. Query response time becomes faster when processing a small part of the data instead of searching the entire dataset.

Limitations of Partition

1. Creating a large number of partitions in a table leads to a large number of files and directories in HDFS, which is an overhead to NameNode, since it must keep all metadata for the file system in memory only.
2. Partitions may optimize some queries based on Where clauses, but they may be less responsive for other important queries on grouping clauses.
3. A large number of partitions will lead to a large number of tasks (which will run in separate JVM) in each MapReduce job, thus creating a lot of overhead in maintaining JVM start up and tear down (A separate task will be used for each file). The overhead of JVM start up and tear down can exceed the actual processing time in the worst case.

4.5.3.2 Bucketing

A partition itself may have a large number of columns when tables are very large. Tables or partitions can be sub-divided into buckets. Division is based on the hash of a column in the table.

Consider bucketed column C_{bucket_i}. First, define a hash_function **H**() according to type of the bucketed column. Let the total number of buckets = $N_{buckets}$. Let C_{bucket_i} denote i^{th} bucketed column. The hash value h_i = hashing function $\mathbf{H}(C_{bucket\_i})$ *mod* ($N_{buckets}$).

Buckets provide an extra structure to the data that can lead to more efficient query processing when compared to undivided tables or partition. Buckets store as a file in the partition directory. Records with the same bucketed column will always be stored in the same bucket. Records kept in each bucket provide sorting ease and enable Map task Joins. A Bucket can also be used as a sample dataset.

CLUSTERED BY clause divides a table into buckets. A coding example on Buckets is given below:

EXAMPLE 4.14

A table *toy_tbl* contains many values for categories of toys. Assume the number of buckets to be created = 5. Assume a table for `Toy_Airplane` of product code 10725.

1. How will the bucketing enforce?
2. How will the bucketed table partition `toy_airplane_10725` create five buckets?
3. How will the bucket column load into `toy_tbl`?
4. How will the bucket data display?

SOLUTION

#Enforce bucketing

```
set hive.enforce.bucketing=true;
```

#Create bucketed Table for toy_airplane of product code 10725 and create cluster of 5 buckets

```
CREATE TABLE IF NOT EXISTS toy_airplane_10725(ProductCategory
STRING, ProductId INT, ProductName STRING, PrdocutMfgDate YYYY-MM-
DD, ProductPrice_US$ FLOAT) CLUSTERED BY (Price) into 5 buckets;
```

Load data to bucketed table.

```
FROM toy_airplane_10725 INSERT OVERWRITE TABLE toy_tbl SELECT
ProductCategory, ProductId, ProductName, PrdocutMfgDate,
ProductPrice;
```

- To display the contents for Price_US$ selected for the ProductId from the second bucket.

```
SELECT DISTINCT ProductId FROM toy_tbl_buckets TABLE FOR
10725(BUCKET 2 OUT OF 5 ON Price_US$);
```

4.5.3.3 *Views*

A program uses functions or objects. Constructing an object instance enables layered design and encapsulating the complexity due to methods and fields. Similarly, Views provide ease of programming. Complex queries simplify using reusable Views. A HiveQL View is a logical construct.

A View provisions the following:

- Saves the query and reduces the query complexity
- Use a View like a table but a View does not store data like a table
- Hive query statement when uses references to a view, the Hive executes the View and then the planner combines the information in View definition with the remaining actions on the query (Hive has a query planner, which plans how a query breaks into sub-queries for obtaining the right answer.)
- Hides the complexity by dividing the query into smaller, more manageable pieces.

4.5.3.4 *Sub-Queries (Using Views)*

Consider the following query with a nested sub-query.

EXAMPLE 4.15

A table *toy_tbl* contains many values for categories of toys. Assume a table for Toy_Airplane of product code 10725. Consider a nested query:

```
FROM (
SELECT * toy_tbl_Join people JOIN Toy_Airplane
    ON (Toy_Airplane.ProductId= productId.id) WHERE productId=10725
    ) toys_ catalog SELECT prdocutMfgDate WHERE prdocutMfgDate = '2017-10-23';
```

Create a View for using that in a nested query.

SOLUTION

```
# create a view named toy_tbl_MiniJoin
CREATE VIEW toy_tbl_MiniJoin AS
    SELECT * toy_tbl_Join people JOIN Toy_Airplane
    ON (Toy_Airplane.ProductId= productId.id) WHERE productId=10725
    ) toys_ catalog SELECT prdocutMfgDate WHERE prdocutMfgDate = '2017-10-23';
```

4.5.4 Aggregation

Hive supports the following built-in aggregation functions. The usage of these functions is same as the SQL aggregate functions. Table 4.10 lists the functions, their syntax and descriptions.

Table 4.10 Aggregate functions, their return type, syntax and descriptions

Return Type	Syntax	Description
BIGINT	count(*), count(expr)	Returns the total number of retrieved rows.
DOUBLE	sum(col), sum(DISTINCT col)	Returns the sum of the elements in the group or the sum of the distinct values of the column in the group.
DOUBLE	avg (col), avg (DISTINCT col)	Returns the average of the elements in the group or the average of the distinct values of the column in the group.
DOUBLE	min (col)	Returns the minimum value of the column in the group.
DOUBLE	max(col)	Returns the maximum value of the column in the group.

Usage examples are:

Example: SELECT ProductCategory, count (*) FROM toy_tbl GROUP BY ProductCategory;
Example: SELECT ProductCategory, sum(ProductPrice) FROM toy_tbl GROUP BY ProductCategory;

4.5.5 Join

A JOIN clause combines columns of two or more tables, based on a relation between them. HiveQL Join is more or less similar to SQL JOINS. Following uses of two tables show the Join operations.

Table 4.11 gives an example of a table named *toy_tbl* of Product categories, ProductId and Product name.

Table 4.11 Table of Product categories, Product Id and Product name

ProductCategory	ProductId	ProductName
Toy_Airplane	10725	Lost temple
Toy_Airplane	31047	Propeller plane
Toy_Airplane	31049	Twin spin helicopter
Toy_Train	31054	Blue express
Toy_Train	10254	Winter holiday Toy_Train

Table 4.12 gives an example of a table named *price* of ID or Product ID and ProductCost.

Table 4.12 Table of ID and Product Cost

Id	ProductPrice
10725	100.0
31047	200.0
31049	300.0
31054	450.0
10254	200.0

Different types of joins are follows:

JOIN
LEFT OUTER JOIN
RIGHT OUTER JOIN
FULL OUTER JOIN

JOIN Join clause combines and retrieves the records from multiple tables. Join is the same as OUTER JOIN in SQL. A JOIN condition uses primary keys and foreign keys of the tables.

```
SELECT t.ProductId, t.ProductName, p.ProductPrice
FROM toy_tbl t JOIN price p
ON (t.ProductId = p.Id);
```

LEFT OUTER JOIN A LEFT JOIN returns all the values from the left table, plus the matched values from the right table, or NULL in case of no matching JOIN predicate.

```
SELECT t.ProductId, t.ProductName, p.ProductPrice
FROM toy_tbl t LEFT OUTER JOIN price p
ON (t.ProductId = p.Id);
```

RIGHT OUTER JOIN A RIGHT JOIN returns all the values from the right table, plus the matched values from the left table, or NULL in case of no matching join predicate.

```
SELECT t.ProductId, t.ProductName, p.ProductPrice
FROM toy_tbl t RIGHT OUTER JOIN price p
ON (t.ProductId = p.Id);
```

FULL OUTER JOIN HiveQL FULL OUTER JOIN combines the records of both the left and the right outer tables that fulfill the JOIN condition. The joined table contains either all the records from both the tables, or fills in NULL values for missing matches on either side.

```
SELECT t.ProductId, t.ProductName, p.ProductPrice
FROM toy_tbl t FULL OUTER JOIN price p
ON (t.ProductId = p.Id);
```

4.5.6 Group by Clause

GROUP BY, HAVING, ORDER BY DISTRIBUTE BY, CLUSTER BY are HiveQL clauses. An example of using the clauses is given below:

EXAMPLE 4.16

How do SELECT statement uses GROUP BY, HAVING, DISTRIBUTE BY, CLUSTER BY? How does clause GROUP BY used in queries on toy_tbl?

SOLUTION

(i) Use of SELECT statement with WHERE clause is as follows:

```
SELECT [ALL | DISTINCT] <select expression>, <select expression>, ...
FROM <table name>
[WHERE <where condition>]
[GROUP BY <column List>]
[HAVING <having condition>]
[CLUSTER BY <column List>| [DISTRIBUTE BY <column List>] [SORT BY
<column List>]]
[LIMIT number];
```

(ii) Use of the clauses in queries to toy_tbl is as follows:

```
SELECT * FROM toy WHERE ProductPrice > 1.5;
SELECT ProductCategory, count (*) FROM toy_tbl GROUP BY
ProductCategory;
SELECT ProductCategory, sum(ProductPrice) FROM toy_tbl GROUP BY
ProductCategory;
```

Self-Assessment Exercise linked to LO 4.4

1. What are the results after execution of the following command? ○○●

```
CREATE TABLE IF NOT EXISTS toy_products (ProductCategory
String, ProductId int, ProductName String, ProductPrice
float)
COMMENT 'Toy details'
ROW FORMAT DELIMITED
FIELDS TERMINATED BY '\t'
LINES TERMINATED BY '\n'
STORED AS TEXTFILE;
```

2. What do the following statements mean? ○●●

```
ALTER TABLE <puzzle_info> RENAME TO <jigsaw_puzzle_info>
ALTER TABLE <jigsaw_puzzle_info> ADD COLUMNS (<puzzle_code_
name>[,<pieces> [,<puzzle_cost> [, ...])
ALTER TABLE <jigsaw_puzzle_info> DROP [COLUMN] <puzzle_cost_
US$>
```

3. How do you create partitions and buckets in a Hive database? ○○●
4. Consider sales table for all five car models at a large number of showrooms. How are the sales figures of a specific model queried? ○●●

5. Explain the meaning of the following statements:

```
SELECT [ALL | DISTINCT] <select expression>, <select
expression>, ...
FROM <table name>
[WHERE <where condition>]
[GROUP BY <column List>]
[HAVING <having condition>]
[CLUSTER BY <column List>| [DISTRIBUTE BY <column List>]
[SORT BY <column List>]]
[LIMIT number];
```

4.6 PIG

LO 4.5

Pig, architecture, Grunt shell commands, data model, Pig Latin, developing scripts, and extensibility using UDFs

Apache developed Pig, which:

- Is an abstraction over MapReduce
- Is an execution framework for parallel processing
- Reduces the complexities of writing a MapReduce program
- Is a high-level dataflow language. Dataflow language means that a Pig operation node takes the inputs and generates the output for the next node
- Is mostly used in HDFS environment
- Performs data manipulation operations at files at data nodes in Hadoop.

1. Applications of Apache Pig

Applications of Pig are:

- Analyzing large datasets
- Executing tasks involving adhoc processing
- Processing large data sources such as web logs and streaming online data
- Data processing for search platforms. Pig processes different types of data
- Processing time sensitive data loads; data extracts and analyzes quickly. For example, analysis of data from twitter to find patterns for user behavior and recommendations.

2. Features

(i) Apache PIG helps programmers write complex data transformations using scripts (without using Java). Pig Latin language is very similar to SQL and possess a rich set of built-in operators, such as group, join, filter, limit, order by, parallel, sort and split. It provides an interactive shell known as Grunt to write Pig Latin scripts. Programmers write scripts using Pig Latin to analyze data. The scripts are internally converted to Map and Reduce tasks with the help of the component known as Execution Engine, that accepts the Pig Latin scripts as input and converts these scripts into MapReduce jobs. Writing MapReduce tasks was the only way to process the data stored in HDFS before the Pig.

(ii) Creates user defined functions (UDFs) to write custom functions which are not available in Pig. A UDF can be in other programming languages, such as Java, Python, Ruby, Jython, JRuby. They easily embed into Pig scripts written in Pig Latin. UDFs provide extensibility to the Pig.
(iii) Process any kind of data, structured, semi-structured or unstructured data, coming from various sources.
(iv) Reduces the length of codes using multi-query approach. Pig code of 10 lines is equal to MapReduce code of 200 lines. Thus, the processing is very fast.
(v) Handles inconsistent schema in case of unstructured data as well.
(vi) Extracts the data, performs operations on that data and dumps the data in the required format in HDFS. The operation is called ETL (Extract Transform Load).
(vii) Performs automatic optimization of tasks before execution.
(viii) Programmers and developers can concentrate on the whole operation without a need to create mapper and reducer tasks separately.
(ix) Reads the input data files from HDFS or the data files from other sources such as local file system, stores the intermediate data and writes back the output in HDFS.
(x) Pig characteristics are data reading, processing, programming the UDFs in multiple languages and programming multiple queries by fewer codes. This causes fast processing.
(xi) Pig derives guidance from four philosophies, live anywhere, take anything, domestic and run as if flying. This justifies the name Pig, as the animal pig also has these characteristics. Table 4.13 gives differences between Pig and MapReduce.

Table 4.13 Differences between Pig and MapReduce

Pig	MapReduce
A dataflow language	A data processing paradigm
High level language and flexible	Low level language and rigid
Performing Join, filter, sorting or ordering operations are quite simple	Relatively difficult to perform Join, filter, sorting or ordering operations between datasets
Programmer with a basic knowledge of SQL can work conveniently	Complex Java implementations require exposure to Java language
Uses multi-query approach, thereby reducing the length of the codes significantly	Require almost 20 times more the number of lines to perform the same task
No need for compilation for execution; operators convert internally into MapReduce jobs	Long compilation process for Jobs
Provides nested data types like tuples, bags and maps	No such data types

Table 4.14 gives differences between Pig and SQL.

Table 4.14 Differences between Pig and SQL

Pig	SQL
Pig Latin is a procedural language	A declarative language
Schema is optional, stores data without assigning a schema	Schema is mandatory
Nested relational data model	Flat relational data model
Provides limited opportunity for Query optimization	More opportunity for query optimization

Pig and Hive codes, both create MapReduce jobs when execute. Hive in some cases, operates on HDFS in a similar way Apache Pig does. Table 4.15 gives a few significant points that set Pig apart from Hive.

Table 4.15 Differences between Pig and Hive

Pig	Hive
Originally created at Yahoo	Originally created at Facebook
Exploits Pig Latin language	Exploits HiveQL
Pig Latin is a dataflow language	HiveQL is a query processing language
Pig Latin is a procedural language and it fits in pipeline paradigm	HiveQL is a declarative language
Handles structured, unstructured and semi-structured data	Mostly used for structured data

3. Pig Architecture

Firstly, Pig Latin scripts submit to the Apache Pig Execution Engine. Figure 4.12 shows Pig architecture for scripts dataflow and processing in the HDFS environment.

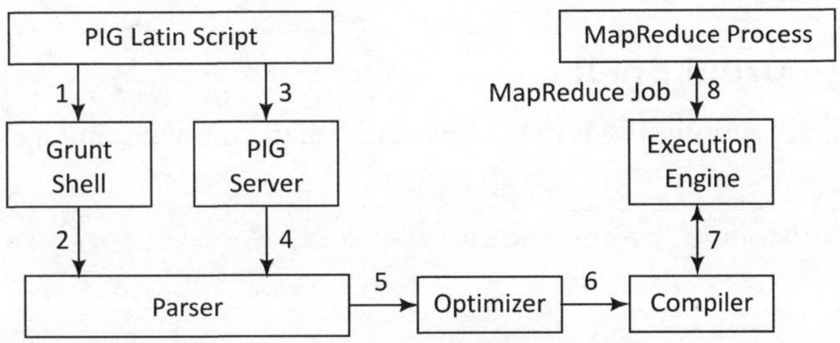

Figure 4.12 Pig architecture for scripts dataflow and processing

The three ways to execute scripts are:

1. **Grunt Shell:** An interactive shell of Pig that executes the scripts.
2. **Script File:** Pig commands written in a script file that execute at Pig Server.
3. **Embedded Script**: Create UDFs for the functions unavailable in Pig built-in operators. UDF can be in other programming languages. The UDFs can embed in Pig Latin Script file.

Parser A parser handles Pig scripts after passing through Grunt or Pig Server. The Parser performs type checking and checks the script syntax. The output is a Directed Acyclic Graph (DAG). Acylic means only one set of inputs are simultaneously at a node, and only one set of output generates after node operations. DAG represents the Pig Latin statements and logical operators. Nodes represent the logical operators. Edges between sequentially traversed nodes represent the dataflows.

Optimizer The DAG is submitted to the logical optimizer. The optimization activities, such as split, merge, transform and reorder operators execute in this phase. The optimization is an automatic feature. The optimizer reduces the amount of data in the pipeline at any instant of time, while processing the extracted data. It executes certain functions for carrying out this task, as explained as follows:

PushUpFilter: If there are multiple conditions in the filter and the filter can be split, Pig splits the conditions and pushes up each condition separately. Selecting these conditions at an early stage helps in reducing the number of records remaining in the pipeline.

PushDownForEachFlatten: Applying flatten, which produces a cross product between a complex type such as a tuple, bag or other fields in the record, as late as possible in the plan. This keeps the number of records low in the pipeline.

ColumnPruner: Omitts never used columns or the ones no longer needed, reducing the size of the record. This can be applied after each operator, so that the fields can be pruned as aggressively as possible.

MapKeyPruner: Omitts never used map keys, reducing the size of the record.

LimitOptimizer: If the limit operator is immediately applied after *load* or *sort* operator, Pig converts the load or sort into a limit-sensitive implementation, which does not require processing the whole dataset. Applying the limit earlier reduces the number of records.

Compiler The compiler compiles after the optimization process. The optimized codes are a series of MapReduce jobs.

Execution Engine Finally, the MapReduce jobs submit for execution to the engine. The MapReduce jobs execute and it outputs the final result.

4.6.1 Apache Pig – Grunt Shell

Main use of Grunt shell is for writing Pig Latin scripts. Any shell command invokes using sh and ls. Syntax of **sh** command is:

```
grunt> sh shell command parameters
```

Syntax of **ls** command:

```
grunt> sh ls
```

Grunt shell includes a set of utility commands. Included utility commands are `clear`, `help`, `history`, `quit` and `set`. The shell includes commands such as `exec`, `kill` and `run` to control the Pig from the Grunt shell.

4.6.2 Installing Pig

Following are the steps for installing Pig:

1. Download the latest version from – https://pig.apache.org/
2. Download the tar files and create a Pig directory

```
$ cd Downloads/
$ tar zxvf pig-0.15.0-src.tar.gz
$ tar zxvf pig-0.15.0.tar.gz
$ mv pig-0.15.0-src.tar.gz/* /home/Hadoop/Pig/
```

3. Configure the Pig

```
export PIG_HOME = /home/Hadoop/Pig
export PATH = $PATH:/home/Hadoop/pig/bin
export PIG_CLASSPATH = $HADOOP_HOME/conf
```

4.6.3 Pig Latin Data Model

Pig Latin supports primitive data types which are atomic or scalar data types. Atomic data types are int, float, long, double, char [], byte []. The language also defines complex data types. Complex data types are tuple, bag and map. Table 4.16 gives data types and examples.

Table 4.16 Data types and examples

Data type	Description	Example
bag	Collection of tuples	{(1,1), (2,4)}
tuple	Ordered set of fields	(1,1)
map (data map)	Set of key-value pairs	[Number#1]
int	Signed 32-bit integer	10
long	Signed 64-bit integer	10L or 10l
float	32-bit floating point	22.7F or 22.7f
double	64-bit floating point	3.4 or 3.4e2 or 3.4E2
chararray	Char [], Character array	data analytics
bytearray	BLOB (Byte array)	ff00

A simple atomic value is known as a field. For example, 'Oreo' or '10' are fields. Atomic means non-divisible. NULL denotes an unknown or non-existent value in Pig Latin.

Tuple Tuple is a record of an ordered set of fields. A tuple is similar to a row in a table of RDBMS. The elements inside a tuple do not necessarily need to have a schema associated to it. A tuple represents by '()' symbol. For example, (1, Oreo, 10, Cadbury)

Indices of the fields access the fields in each tuple. Tuples are ordered, like $1 from above tuple will return a value 'Oreo'.

Figure 4.13 shows Pig data model with fields, Tuple and Bag.

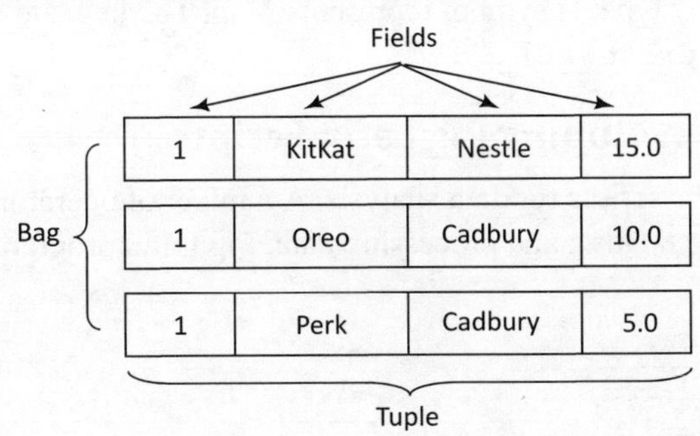

Figure 4.13 Pig Data Model with fields, Tuple and Bag

Bag A bag is an unordered set of tuples. A bag can contain duplicate tuples as it is not mandatory that they need to be unique. Each tuple can have any number of fields (flexible schema). A bag can also have tuples with different data types.

{} symbol represents a bag. It is similar to a table in RDBMS, but unlike a table in RDBMS, it is not necessary that every tuple contains the same number of fields or that the fields in the same position (column) have the same type. For example, {(Oreo, 10), (KitKat, 15, Cadbury)}

There are two types of bag: outer bag or relations and inner bag. Outer bag or relation is a bag of tuples. Here relations are similar as relations in relational databases. To understand it better let us take an example: {(Oreo, Cadbury), (KitKat, Nestle), (Perk, Cadbury)}. This bag explains the relation between the Chocolate brand and their brand company.

A bag can be a field in a relation; in that context, it is known as an inner bag. Thus, an inner bag contains a bag inside a tuple. Figure 4.14 shows a relation and keys and their values: (Cadbury, {(Oreo, 10), (Perk,5)}) (Nestle {(Kitkat,15)})

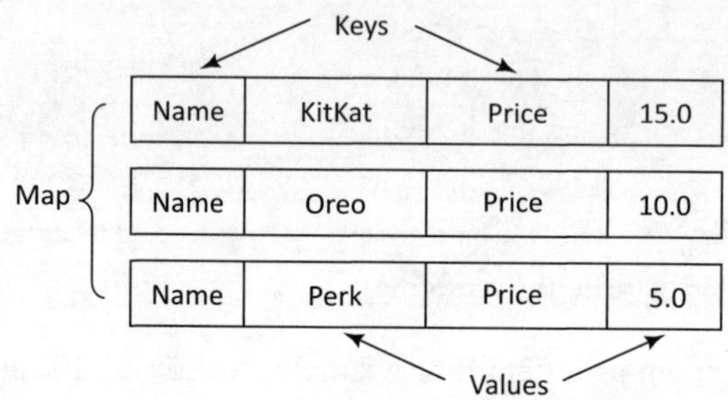

Figure 4.14 Relation and corresponding keys and their values (key-value pairs)

Relation A relation is a bag of tuples. The relations in Pig Latin are unordered (there is no guarantee that tuples are processed in any particular order).

Map A map (or data map) is a set of key-value pairs. The key needs to be of type chararray and should be unique (similar to a column name). Map can be indexed and value associated with it can be accessed from the keys. The value might be of any type. [] symbol represents Map. The key and value separate by '#' symbol. For example, `[type#Oreo, price#10]`

4.6.4 Pig Latin and Developing Pig Latin Scripts

Pig Latin enables developing the scripts for data analysis. A number of operators in Pig Latin help to develop their own functions for reading, writing and processing data. Pig Latin programs execute in the Pig run-time environment.

Pig Latin

Statements in Pig Latin:

1. Basic constructs to process the data.
2. Include schemas and expressions.
3. End with a semicolon.
4. LOAD statement reads the data from file system, DUMP displays the result and STORE stores the result.

5. Single line comments begin with - - and multiline begin with /* and end with */
6. Keywords (for example, LOAD, STORE, DUMP) are not case-sensitive.
7. Function names, relations and paths are case-sensitive.

Figure 4.15 shows the order of processing Pig statements—Load, dump and store.

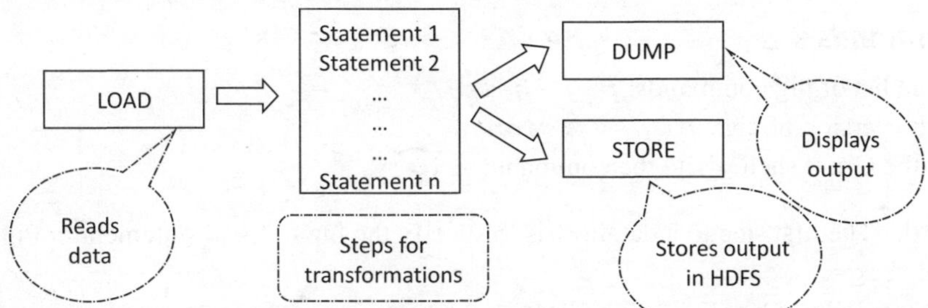

Figure 4.15 Order of processing Pig statements—Load, dump, and store

Operators in Pig Latin

Arithmetic Operators	+	-	*	/	%
Used for	Addition	Subtraction	Multiplication	Division	Remainder

Comparison Operators	==	!=	<	>	≤	≥
Used for	Equality	Not equal	Less than	Greater than	Less than and equal to	Greater than and equal to

Boolean Operators	AND	OR	NOT
Used for	Logical AND	Logical OR	Logical NOT

4.6.4.1 *Apache Pig Execution*

Pig Execution Modes Local Mode: All the data files install and run from a local host using the local file system. Local mode is mostly used for testing purpose.

COMMAND: `pig -x local`

MapReduce Mode: All the data files load or process that exists in the HDFS. A MapReduce job invokes in the back-end to perform a particular operation on the data that exists in the HDFS when a Pig Latin statement executes to process the data.

COMMAND: `pig -x mapreduce or pig`

Pig Latin Script Execution Modes

- Interactive Mode – Using the Grunt shell.
- Batch Mode – Writing the Pig Latin script in a single file with .pig extension.
- Embedded Mode – Defining UDFs in programming languages such as Java, and using them in the script.

4.6.4.2 Commands

- To get the list of pig commands: `pig -help;`
- To get the version of pig: `pig -version.`
- To start the Grunt shell, write the command: `pig`

LOAD Command The first step to a dataflow is to specify the input. Load statement in Pig Latin loads the data from `PigStorage`.

To load data from HBase: `book = load 'MyBook' using HBaseStorage();`

For reading CSV file, `PigStorage` takes an argument which indicates which character to use as a separator. For example, `book = LOAD 'PigDemo/Data/Input/myBook.csv' USING PigStorage (,);`

For reading text data line by line: `book = LOAD 'PigDemo/Data/Input/myBook.txt' USING PigStorage() AS (lines: chararray);`

To specify the data-schema for loading: `book = LOAD 'MyBook' AS (name, author, edition, publisher);`

Store Command Pig provides the store statement for writing the processed data after the processing is complete. It is the mirror image of the load statement in certain ways.

By default, Pig stores data on HDFS in a tab-delimited file using PigStorage:

```
STORE processed into '/PigDemo/Data/Output/Processed';
```

To store in HBaseStorage with a *using* clause: `STORE processed into 'processed' using HBaseStorage();`

To store data as comma-separated text data, PigStorage takes an argument to indicate which character to use as a separator: `STORE processed into 'processed' using PigStorage(',');`

Dump Command Pig provides dump command to see the processed data on the screen. This is particularly useful during debugging and prototyping sessions. It can also be useful for quick adhoc jobs.

The following command directs the output of the Pig script on the display screen:

```
DUMP processed;
```

Relational Operations

The relational operations provided at Pig Latin operate on data. They transform data using sorting, grouping, joining, projecting and filtering. Followings are the basic relational operators:

Foreach FOREACH gives a simple way to apply transformations based on columns. It is Pig's projection operator. Table 4.17 gives examples using FOREACH.

Table 4.17 Applying transformations on columns using FOREACH operator

Load an entire record, but then remove all but the name and phone fields from each record	`A = load 'input' as (name: chararray, rollno: long, address: chararray, phone: chararray, preferences: map []);` `B = foreach A generate name, phone;`
Tuple projection using dot operator	`A = load 'input' as (t:tuple (x:int, y:int));` `B = foreach A generate t.x, t.$1;`
Bag projection	`A = load 'input' as (b:bag{t:(x:int, y:int)});` `B = foreach A generate b.x;`
Bag projection	`A = load 'input' as (b:bag{t:(x:int, y:int)});` `B = foreach A generate b.(x, y);`

Add all integer values	`A = load 'input' as (x:chararray, y:int, z:int);`
	`A1 = foreach A generate x, y + z as yz;`
	`B = group A1 by x;`
	`C = foreach B generate SUM(A1.yz);`

Filter FILTER gives a simple way to select tuples from a relation based on some specified conditions (predicate). It is Pig's *select* command.

Loads an entire record, then selects the tuples with marks more than 75 from each record	`A = load 'input' as (name:chararray, rollno:long, marks:float);` `B = filter A by marks > 75.0;`
Find name (chararray) that do not match a regular expression by preceding the text without a given character string. Output is all names that do not start with P.	`A = load 'input' as (name:chararray, rollno:long, marks:float);` `B = filter A by not name matches 'P.*';`

Group GROUP statement collects records with the same key. There is no direct connection between group and aggregate functions in Pig Latin unlike SQL.

Collects all records with the same value for the provided key into a bag. Then it can pass to aggregate function, if required or do other things with that.	`A = load 'input' as (name: chararray, rollno:long, marks: float);`
	`grpd = group A by marks;`
	`B = foreach grpd generate name, COUNT(A);`

Order by ORDER statement sorts the data based on a specific field value, producing a total order of output data.

The syntax of order is similar to group. Key indicates by which the data sort.	`A = load 'input' as (name: chararray, rollno: long, marks: float);` `B = order A by name;`
To sort based on two or more keys (For example, first sort by, then sort by), indicate a set of keys by which the data sort. No parentheses around the keys when multiple keys indicate in order	`A = load 'input' as (name:chararray, rollno:long, marks:float);` `B = order A by name, marks;`

Distinct DISTINCT removes duplicate tuples. It works only on entire tuples, not on individual fields:

Removes the tuples having the same name and city.	`A = load 'input' as (name: chararray, city: chararray);` `B = distinct A;`

Join JOIN statement joins two or more relations based on values in the common field. Keys indicate the inputs. When those keys are equal, two tuples are joined. Tuples for which no match is found are dropped.

Join selects tuples from one input to put together with tuples from another input.	`A = load 'input1' as (name:chararray, rollno:long);`
	`B = load 'input2' as (rollno:long, marks:float);`
	`C = join A by rollno, B by rollno`

Also based on multiple keys join. All cases must have the same number of keys, and they must be of the same or compatible types.	`A = load 'input1' as (name: chararray, fathername: chararray, rollno: long);`
	`B = load 'input2' as (name: chararray, rollno: long, marks: float);`
	`C = join A by (name, rollno), B by (name, rollno)`

Pig also supports *outer joins*. Tuples which do not have a match on the other side are included, with null values being filled for the missing fields in outer joins. Outer joins can be *left, right or full*. A left outer join means tuples from the left side will be included even when they do not have a match on the right side. Similarly, a *right* outer join means tuples from the right side will be included even when they do not have a match on the left side. A full outer join implies tuples from both sides are taken even when they do not have matches.

Limit LIMIT gets the limited number of results.

Outputs only first five tuples from the relation.	`A = load 'input' as (name: chararray, city: chararray);` `B = Limit A 5;`

Sample SAMPLE offers to get a sample of the entire data. It reads through all of the data but returns only a percentage of rows on random basis. Thus, results of a script with sample will vary with every execution. The percentage it will return is expressed as a double value, between 0 and 1. For example, 0.2 indicates 20%.

Outputs only 10% tuples from the relation	`A = load 'input' as (name:chararray, city: chararray);` `B = sample A 0.1;`

Split SPLIT partitions a relation into two or more relations

Outputs A relation A splits into two relations P and Q	`A = load 'input' as (name:chararray, rollno:long, marks:float);` `Split A into P if marks >50.0, Q if marks ≤ 50.0;`

Parallel PARALLEL statement is for parallel data processing.

Any relational operator in Pig Latin can attach PARALLEL. However, it controls only reduce-side parallelism, so it makes sense only for operators that force a reduce phase, such as group, order, distinct, join or limit.

Generating MapReduce job with 10 reducers	`A = load 'input' as (name: chararray, marks: float);` `B = group A by marks parallel 10;`

EVAL Functions Following are the evaluation functions:

Function Name	Description
AVG	Compute the average of the numeric values in a in a single-column bag
SUM	Compute the sum of the numeric values in a single-column bag
MAX	Get the maximum of numeric values or chararrays in a single-column bag
MIN	Get the minimum of numeric values or chararrays in a single-column bag
COUNT and COUNT_STAR	Count the number of tuples in a bag
CONCAT	Concatenate two fields. The data type of the two fields must be the same, either chararray or bytearray.
DIFF	Compare two fields in a tuple
IsEmpty	Check if a bag or map is empty (has no data)
SIZE	Compute the number of elements based on the data type
TOKENIZE	Split a string and output a bag of words

Piggy Bank *Pig users* share their functions from Piggy Bank. *Register* is keyword for using Piggy bank functions.

User-Defined Functions (UDFs) A programmer defines UDFs which perform functionalities not present as built-in Pig function. A programmer can use UDFs for filtering data or performing further analysis. A programmer can write UDF using a programming language, such as Java, Python, Ruby, Jython or JRuby.

A UDF should extend a Filter function or Eval function and must contain a core method called *exec*, which contains a Tuple.

The UDF class extends the *EvalFunc* class which is the base for all Eval functions. All evaluation functions extend the Java class '*org.apache.pig.EvalFunc*'. It is parameterized with the return type of the UDF which is a Java String in this case.

Filter functions are Eval functions that return a Boolean value. The UDF class when extends the *FilterFunc* class can be used anywhere a Boolean expression is appropriate, including the FILTER operator or Bincond expression.

The following example gives the codes for developing a user-defined function (UDF) returning Boolean after checking the age.

EXAMPLE 4.17

Write a UDF 'IsCorrectAge' which checks if the age given is correct or not. UDF should return a Boolean value: True or False. If the Tuple is null or zero then also it should return False. Use Java. Create a JAR file and then export. Later register the JAR file. The JAR files are in the library files of Apache Pig at the time of loading.

SOLUTION

Followings are the codes for the user-defined function `IsCorrectAge`.

```
public class IsCorrectAge extends FilterFunc {
@Override
    Public Boolean exec (Tuple tuple) throws IOException {
    if (tuple == null || tuple.size() == 0) {
            return false;
    }
    try {
            Object object= tuple.get(0);
            if (object == null) {
                    return false;
            }
            Int i = (Integer) object;
            if (i == 18 || i == 20 || i == 21 || i == 25) {
                    return true;
            }
            else {
                    return false;
            }
    } catch (ExecException e) {
            throw new IOException(e);
    }
    }
}
```

Once `IsCorrectAge` create, the following command registers a JAR file into the library of JAR files:

```
register myudf.jar;
```

A = load 'input' as (name chararray, age int);

```
X = filter A by IsCorrectAge(age);
```

Self-Assessment Exercise linked to LO 4.5

1. How does Apache Pig execution engine function for faster data processing? ○○●
2. List the Grunt shell commands and the use of each command. ○●●
3. When is Hive and when is Pig used? ○○●
4. How are tuple and map used? ○●●
5. How are projections used? ○●●

6. Write the functions of GROUP, JOIN, FILTER, LIMIT, ORDER BY, PARALLEL, SORT and SPLIT. ●●●
7. How will a UDF return the difference of maximum and minimum sales from sales data values in Pig Latin? ●●●

KEY CONCEPTS

aggregation	having()	partitioning
bag	Hive	Pig
BLOB	Hive data units	Piggy Bank
bucketing	Hive File Format	Pig Latin
collating	HiveQL	projection
collection data type	inner Join	querying table
combining	InnerSplit	RCFile
command line interface	intersection	RecordReader
composing	iterative message passing	relation
cross correlation	JobTracker	relational operator
data definition	key-value pair	right join
data manipulation language	left Join	sequential file
deserializer	managed table	serializer
diagnostic operator	map (a Pig data type)	shuffle and store
difference	MapReduce metadata	sorting
dynamic partition	Metastore	SQL-like script
EVAL	natural Join	static partition
filtering	ORC	tuple
graph processing	outer Join	user-defined function
Group By	parallel tasks	views
grouping by keys	parsing	

Learning Outcomes

LO 4.1

1. An *application* consists of a number of tasks. A MapReduce program for an application task is termed as a job. Each job consists of several smaller units, called MapReduce tasks. They run in parallel for the application task. MapReduce programming is a software execution framework that defines the parallel tasks, the results combine and application obtains the consolidated result.
2. MapReduce implements a data model, which represents data as key-value pairs.

3. Reduce task implements using Reducer function that takes Mapper output (which is shuffled and sorted), that is grouped key-value data (k2, v2) and applies it in parallel to each group. Another set of key-value pairs (k3, v3) are the final output file.
4. Coping with node failures is done by the TaskTracker, which when fails to communicate with the JobTracker for a pre-defined period, the JobTracker restarts.

LO 4.2

1. MapReduce functions have a number of applications:
   (a) Counting, summing, run algorithms for the relational algebra operations, projections, union, intersection, natural Join, grouping and aggregation.
   (b) Collating, filtering and parsing. Collating is a method to collect all the items which have same value of function.
   (c) Graph processing using iterative message passing.
   (d) Web Indexing also uses the method of iterative message-passing. A state of each entity calculates based on characteristics of the other entities in its neighborhood in a given network of entities and relationships between them.
   (e) Multiplication of matrix with a vector and of matrix with a matrix.
2. When multiplying two matrices, two cascaded MapReduce operations require much less memory than a single step MapReduce.

LO 4.3

1. Apache Hive is an open-source data-warehouse software. Data summarization, analysis and querying are major functions of Hive. Hive facilitates reading, writing and managing large datasets residing in distributed Hadoop files using SQL-like scripts. Hive supports serialization, deserialization and user-defined functions.
2. Hive includes a system catalog, called Hive Metastore. Hive provides increased flexibility in schema design.
3. Hive supports primitive and collection data types. Hive supports text files, sequence Files (consisting of binary key/value pairs), RCFiles (Record Columnar Files), ORC (optimized row columnar) and HBase file format types. Hive considers database, tables, partitions, bucketed tables and buckets as data units.

LO 4.4

1. HiveQL has SQL-like script statements for (i) data definition, (ii) data manipulation, (iii) creating, dropping, and using the databases and tables, (iv) selection by where, GroupBy and Having clauses.
2. The partitions are must in large dataset tables in the databases of a data warehouse. Hive command creates partitions. HiveQL commands create buckets, views and sub-queries.
3. HiveQL has the command provision for join, sorting and aggregation.
4. HiveQL plug-ins the custom MapReduce scripts into queries.

LO 4.5

1. Pig is an open-source high-level language platform. Pig applications are mainly for analyzing large datasets. Pig executes queries in the HDFS environment. Processes any kind of data: structured, semi-structured or unstructured data from various sources.

2. Pig language used is known as Pig Latin. Pig Latin programming is in Java. Pig is SQL-like query language applied on a larger dataset, and provides additional features. Pig Grunt shell enables development. Pig Grunt shell enable development of Pig Latin scripts.
3. Pig converts all the operations into Map and Reduce tasks that process on Hadoop efficiently. Programmers write scripts using Pig Latin to analyze data. The scripts internally convert into Map and Reduce tasks.
4. Pig application is ETL operations (Extract, Transform and Load). The language allows a detailed step-by-step procedure by which the data must be transformed. Pig is designed to handle any kind of data. Pig programming language can handle inconsistent schema data as well.
5. Helps programmers write complex data transformations without knowing Java. Possess a rich set of built-in data types, such as Bag (collection of tuples) and Map (set of key-value pairs). Possess a rich set of built-in operators, such as group, join, filter, limit, order by, parallel, sort and split.
6. Allows programmers to write User-Defined Functions (UDF) to write custom functions in other programming languages, such as Java, Python, Ruby, Jython or JRuby. UDF easily embeds in Pig scripts and provides extensibility to Pig.

Objective Type Questions

Select one correct-answer option for each of the following questions:

4.1 (i) A user application specifies the input/output data locations, (ii) The application supplies map and reduce functions by the implementation of appropriate interfaces and/or abstract classes, (iii) Application task configures the job and specifies other job parameters, (iv) Map takes output dataset as pieces of data from the Reducer and maps them on various nodes for parallel processing, and (v)The reduce task, which takes the input at Mapper combines those data pieces into a smaller set of data. ○○●

(a) ii and iii (b) all
(c) i, ii and iii (d) i, iv and v

4.2 (i) MapReduce implies, the reduce task is mostly performed after the map task, (ii) Map takes input dataset as pieces of data and maps them on various nodes for sequential processing, (iii) MapReduce framework may not operate entirely on (key-value) pairs, and (iv) The framework views the output to the task as a set of (key, value) pairs and produces a set of (key, value) pairs as the input of the task, possibly of different types. ●●●

(a) none (b) only iv
(c) only ii (d) all

4.3 (i) Partitioner does the partitioning, (ii) The partitions are the semi-mappers in MapReduce, (iii) Combiners are semi-reducers in MapReduce, (iv) Combiners process the input of map tasks before submitting it to Reducer tasks, (v) Reduce task implements using Reduce function (or Reducer) that takes Mapper output (which is shuffled and sorted), that is (grouped key-value data) (k2, v2) and applies it in parallel to each group, and (vi) Reduce function iterates over the list of values associated with a key and produces outputs, such as aggregations and statistics. ○●●

(a) all except ii and iii (b) all
(c) i to v (d) all except iv

4.4 MapReduce program composes the (i) Count, (ii) find distinct values, (iii) search unique value, (iv) group using attributes, and does aggregating, (v) summing, (vi) relational-algebra operations, (vii) projections, (viii) union, (ix) intersection, (x) difference, (xi) natural Join, (xii) multiplication of two matrices, and (xiii) multiplication of matrix and vector. ○○●

(a) all except ii, iii, iv, xii and xiii (b) all
(c) all except ii to vi (d) all except xii and xiii

4.5 (i) Graph processing needs iterative message passing, (ii) Graph processing uses are in web indexing, (iii) A state of each entity calculates based on characteristics of the other entities in its neighborhood in a given network of entities and relationships between them, (iv) Mapper class emit() emits the messages for each node using ID of the non-adjacent node as a key, (v) All messages groups by the incoming node, and (vi) Reducer class method computes the state again and rewrites a node with the new state. ●●●
(a) i, iii, iv and vi (b) i to v
(c) ii to vi (d) All except iv

4.6 Hive (i) does not have commands to update or delete using the record level queries, (ii) does not support transactions on the DB, (iii) supports to create, drop and use functions, (iv) latency for query operations is much less than a second for Big Data of petabytes, and (v) provides limited JDBC/ODBC connectivity functions. ○●●
(a) i, iii, iv and vi (b) iii to v
(c) ii to vi (d) All except iv

4.7 Hive architecture consists of (i) Hive Server, (ii) CLI, (iii) web interface, (iv) metastore, and (v) Hive driver. (vi) Usages of Hive metastore are to provide names of tables, databases, columns in a table. ○○●
(a) ii to v (b) all
(c) ii to iv (d) i, ii, iv, v

4.8 HiveQL data manipulation commands are (i) USE, (ii) DROP DATABASE, (iii) DROP SCHEMA, (iv) ALTER TABLE, (v) DROP TABLE, (vi) DELETE TABLE, (vii) DELETE DATABASE, (viii) INSERT TABLE, (ix) INSERT DATABASE, and (x) LOAD DATA. ○●●
(a) all except ii, iii and v (b) all except i, iii
(c) all except vi to ix (d) i to iv

4.9 HiveQL (i) Join clause combines and retrieves the records from multiple tables, (ii) Join is same as OUTER JOIN in SQL, (iii) JOIN condition uses primary keys and foreign keys of the tables, (iv) JOIN clause combines the columns of two or more tables, based on a related column between them, (v) JOIN is same as SQL JOIN, (vi) A LEFT JOIN returns all the values from the left table, plus the matched values from the right table, or NULL in case of no matching JOIN predicate, (vii) A RIGHT JOIN returns all the values from the right table, plus not matched values from the left table, or NULL in case of no matching join predicate, (viii) FULL OUTER JOIN combines the records of both the left and the right outer tables those fulfill the JOIN condition, and (ix) the joined table contains either all the records from both the tables, or fills in NULL values for missing matches on either side. ○○●
(a) all except v and vii (b) all
(c) all except iii and x (d) i to vii

4.10 Pig (i) reads the input data files from HDFS or the data files from other sources such as the local file system, (ii) stores the intermediate data and writes back the output in HDFS, (iii) processes any kind of data: structured, semi-structured or unstructured data coming from various sources, (iv) allows programmers to write User-Defined Functions (UDFs) to write custom functions, (v) UDFs written in several other programming languages, (vi) UDF easily embed in Pig scripts written in Linux, (vii) exploits multi-query approach, thereby reducing the length of codes; ten lines is equal to MapReduce code of two hundred lines, which enables spreads processing, and (viii) Pig read data, processing, programming the UDFs in multiple languages and programming multiple queries by fewer code enabling fast processing are guided by four philosophies: live anywhere, take anything, domestic and run like flying. ●●●
(a) i to vi (b) all except vi
(c) all except iii to v (d) all

4.11 Pig (i) helps programmers write complex data transformations using scripts (without using Java) that possess a rich set of built-in operators such as (ii) Bag, (iii) BLOB, (iv) Map, (v) Group, (vi) Join, (vii) Filter, (viii) Limit, (ix) Order by, (x) parallel, (xi) sort and (xii) split. ○○●
(a) all except i
(b) all except i, x and xii
(c) all except ii, iii and iv
(d) ii to ix and xi

4.12 *Pig* (i) is a dataflow language, (ii) low level language, (iii) performs Join, filter, sorting or ordering operations, (iv) uses multi-query approach, thereby increasing the length of the codes, (v) no need for compilation, (vi) on execution, operators convert internally into a MapReduce job, (vii) provides nested data types like tuples, bags, and maps. *MapReduce* on the other hand, (viii) is a data processing paradigm, (ix) relatively difficult to perform Join, filter, sorting or ordering operations between datasets, (x) Complex Java implementations require exposure to Java language, (xi) Jobs have a long compilation process, and (xii) nested data types, such as tuples, buckets and views. ●●●
(a) all except ii, iv and xii
(b) all except v, x, xi and xii
(c) i to x
(d) all except vi and xi

Review Questions

4.1 List and explain the features of the MapReduce programming model? How does MapReduce program enable parallel processing? **(LO 4.1)** ○○●

4.2 How does a Map task implement using key-value pairs in an input file? What are the uses of Shuffle in processing the aggregates for all the Mapper output by grouping key values of the Mapper output and the value which gets appended in a list of values? **(LO 4.1)** ●●●

4.3 How does 'Group By' operate for creating Mapper output? What are the roles of partitioning and combining? **(LO 4.1)** ○●●

4.4 How does MapReduce program find the distinct values and count the unique values? **(LO 4.2)** ○○●

4.5 How does the MapReduce implement the relational algebraic functions, union, projection, difference, intersection, natural join, grouping and aggregation? Explain each with an example. **(LO 4.2)** ●●●

4.6 How do MapReduce tasks implement a matrix multiplication by a vector? **(LO 4.2)** ○●●

4.7 Describe the Hive architecture components. Why are HiveQL, SQL-like scripts used in place of RDBMS, such as MySQL for Big Data? **(LO 4.3)** ○●●

4.8 What are the types of built-in functions available in Hive? What are the uses of each of these? **(LO 4.3)** ○○●

4.9 Why should partitions be created in databases and tables in Hive data warehouse for very large datasets? **(LO 4.4)** ○●●

4.10 What are aggregation commands provisioned in HiveQL? What are the partitioning commands? **(LO 4.4)** ○●●

4.11 An enterprise needs to create and use a Hive data warehouse with very large databases and tables. Why are the usages of RCFile and ORCFile formats, creation of large number of partitions, buckets and views required in the databases and tables? **(LO 4.4)** ●●●

4.12 What are the differences between Pig programming model with MapReduce, relational database and Hive programming models? **(LO 4.5)** ○○●

4.13 Describe Pig data types and operators: Group, Join, Filter, Limit, Order by, parallel, sort and split. **(LO 4.5)** ○○●

4.14 Describe usages of Pig operations: parallel, split and defining a UDF. Give one example of each. **(LO 4.5)** ○●●

Practice Exercises

4.1 MapReduce program imports the following at the beginning: ○○●

```
import org.apache.hadoop.fs.Path
import org.apache.hadoop.mapreduce.Mapper
import org.apache.hadoop.mapreduce.Job
import org.apache.hadoop.mapreduce.Reducer
import org.apache.hadoop.io.Text
import org.apache.hadoop.mapreduce.lib.input.FileInputFormat
import org.apache.hadoop.mapreduce.lib.output.FileOutputFormat
import org.apache.hadoop.fs.Path
```

What are the functions that each Class provides in the program? **(LO 4.1)**

4.2 A company manufactures and sells cars through a large number of showrooms. Each car showroom records in main table and transaction tables. Recapitulate Practice Exercise 3.3 Table data. Describe the steps for composing MapReduce program parallel tasks for calculating aggregated annual sales of each model for all showrooms. **(LO 4.2)** ●●●

4.3 Recapitulate Section 4.3.4. Consider that two MapReduce cascaded programs multiply 3 × 4 matrix A with another matrix 4 × 6 matrix B. Calculate the number of tuples in each matrix, tuples after natural join. List each step for using these tuples, grouping and aggregation of tuples with attributes. Now calculate these numbers again for 8192 × 4096 matrix multiplication by 4096 × 32768 matrix. **(LO 4.2)** ○●●

4.4 Install Hive and demonstrate usages of each data type and collection types listed in Tables 4.6 and 4.7. **(LO 4.3)** ○●●

4.5 Create a HiveQL table for grade-sheet of your five-course semester examination with SGPA (Semester Grade Point average) in a semester. Now, write commands to create partitions in the table in RCFile formats. How will the table serialize? **(LO 4.4)** ○●●

4.6 Insert the Hive-table above in all University students' data warehouse. Write commands for joining four tables for four-semester examinations. How will that be used for calculating CGPA (Cumulative Grade Point average)? **(LO 4.4)** ●●●

4.7 Recapitulate Examples 4.10 to 4.13. Create a HiveQL data warehouse for toys_company manufacturing 1600 different toys and 2000 puzzle product categories, up to 20 product types for each, and each puzzle product of product types 100, 200, 400, 800, 1600, 2400 and 500 pieces. **(LO 4.4)** ●●●

4.8 Recapitulate Example 1.6. Create Pig user-defined functions (UDFs) for selecting the sales of each flavour of chocolate from the multiple ACVMs. **(LO 4.5)** ○○●

4.9 Select and list the Pig data types, operations and their usages during processing the data tables created in Practice Exercise 4.7. **(LO 4.5)** ○○●

Chapter 5

Spark and Big Data Analytics

LEARNING OBJECTIVES

After studying this chapter, you will be able to:

- **LO 5.1** Get understanding of the Spark architectural features, software stack components and their functions
- **LO 5.2** Get knowledge of analysis steps using Spark, Spark along with Python, advanced features, UDFs, vectorized UDFs, grouped vectorized UDFs and Python analytics libraries
- **LO 5.3** Get understanding of the methods of downloading Spark, getting started in programming with Spark, Spark shell, Spark context, developing and testing codes, programming with RDDs and the applications of MLib
- **LO 5.4** Get understanding of the ETL processes using built-in functions, operators and ETL pipelines
- **LO 5.5** Get Introduced to analytics, data/information reporting and visualizing methods

RECALL FROM EARLIER CHAPTERS

CHAPTER 1

Spark, Spark SQL and Apache Drill are advanced processing methods for Big Data. They also enable real-time processing. Berkeley Data Analytics Stack (BDAS) is an open-source data analytics stack. The stack consists of number of software components and frameworks for complex computations using Big Data.

CHAPTER 2

The four layers of the Hadoop ecosystem are:

1. Data store layer: Stores Big Data HDFS.
2. Data processing layer: Processes the stored data using programs, such as MapReduce, YARN, HBase and Cassandra.
3. Applications support layer: APIs supporting the processing of applications at the data processing layer, such as Pig, Hive, HiveQL, Sqoop, Ambari, Chukwa.
4. Applications layer: Tools such as Spark, Flink, Flume, Mahout, and Processes ETL, Analytics, BP, BI, Data Visualization, R-Descriptive Statistics, Machine learning, Data mining (Section 2.2.3 and Figure 2.3).

CHAPTER 3

When the Big Data Store is at clusters HDFS, the applications access the data sequentially. When it is using NoSQL databases, the data read/write access by applications is random-access. The access to a resource is as per the specified resource pointer (address) for the access.

CHAPTER 4

MapReduce tasks processes in parallel and in a distributed environment. A program composes the MapReduce tasks for the calculations and uses the relational-algebraic operations, 'grouping by' and aggregation functions (Section 4.3).

Hive creates databases which load into the enterprise data warehouse. Hive composes the queries and does data aggregation and summarization (Section 4.4). HiveQL functions query the DBs, tables, partitions and buckets, and executes the SQL like operations and UDFs (Section 4.5).

Pig functions executes query on large datasets which are stored in HDFS. Pig programming model enables writing complex data transformations without knowing Java [due to a rich set of built-in functions and operators such as group, join, filter, limit, order by, parallel, sort and split, and possessing of a rich set of built-in data types such as Bag (collection of tuples) and Map (set of key-value pairs)] (Section 4.6).

This chapter focuses on Apache Spark using the data sources at HDFS, any Hadoop compatible data source, such as HBase, Cassandra and Ceph, or Object Store S3. Spark provides in-memory, distributed and faster cluster-computing, and consists of APIs in Java, Scala, Python and R.

5.1 INTRODUCTION

Pig or Hive are high-level scripting languages that are used with the Apache Hadoop. They have SQL like commands for queries. The commands before executing, translate to Map and Reduce parallel-tasks. They process the queries, built-in functions, aggregation operations and User Defined Functions (UDFs). They enable ease in programming for these functions. They run ETL processes using Big Data Store.

Pig and Hive programs use complex data types and operations. The scripts and programs use the datasets distributed in the HDFS Data Store.

Applications such as data analytics, stream analytics and graph analytics, and machine learning require the following:

In-memory processing: In-memory processing is fast when compared to processing data most of the times, from the disk or remotely distributed nodes. This is because the processor takes much less time in accessing the memory compared to the disk or remote data node. In-memory processing also facilitates real-time processing and streaming data analysis. DAG-based acyclic data flow further boosts the *processing speed.*

Application tasks processing Framework: Application tasks require processing in a framework which uses HDFS as well Hadoop compatible data sources, such as HBase, Cassandra, Ceph, cloud-based Objects Store Service or Amazon S3. The tasks require support which facilitates running the Hive, Pig, and other Hadoop ecosystem tools in Java, Python, R and Scala. APIs using Python shell and Scala shell facilitate the interactive running of the applications. Many applications such as statistical, mathematical and graph analytics, and machine learning algorithms require APIs designed in these languages.

These features ease the programming for complex analytics, machine learning and other solutions.

Advent of Apache® Spark™

Berkeley's Algorithms, Machines and Peoples Laboratory (AMP) developed Berkeley Data Analytics Stack (BDAS) which support efficient, large-scale in-memory data processing, and includes applications fulfilling three fundamental processing requirements: accuracy, time and cost. AMP first developed Spark in 2009 and later passed on the project to Apache. A new version is Spark 2.3.1.

Apache® Spark™ uses in-memory data processing. Thus, processing is fast since there is no delay. The reason is that processor in-memory read and write operations are fast compared to read from disk and write to disk. Apache® Spark™ uses the DAGs and acyclic data-flows, and data from HDFS compatible data sources and cloud-based Data Stores. It provides APIs for programming in R, Python, Java and Scala.

Open Source Analytics Tools

Following are the tools:

1. R and its library provide various statistical analysis functions. R now analyses large data sets also since R integrates with Big Data platforms, such as Spark.
2. Python is a widely used language due to its analysis and statistics libraries, such as numpy, scipy, scikit-learn, pandas, StatsModel.
3. Storm is for real-time continuous data streams.
4. Pig is a data flow language with SQL like operations and uses UDFs. Pig enables easy coding compared to MapReduce for the complex tasks.
5. Hive is for creation of data warehouse, integration of databases and applications, and uses SQL like scripts and UDFs. Coding is easy compared to MapReduce.

Pandas is an open source Python package, and consists of BSD-licensed library functions using the Panda (Panel Data). (5.3.2.1) The Pandas give high performance, easy-to-use data structures and data analysis tools. Pandas enrich the Python programming language.

The most popular open source analytics tools are Apache Spark, Python, R, Apache Pig and Hive, according to a study.

Spark is for high volume unstructured data. Spark seamlessly integrates with Spark SQL which uses the structured data, Spark Streaming is for streaming data, Spark GraphX for graph databases, Spark MLib for machine-learning library, and Spark Arrow for columnar in-memory analytics. Spark provides easy programmability with inclusion of APIs for programmers to develop applications in Python, R, Java or Scala.

Reader needs to learn the following new select key term, and their meanings besides the ones given in the previous chapters:

User Defined Functions (UDFs) refer to custom functions which are not built-in a programming language but user adds them and they can be written in a language, such as Java, Python, Ruby, Jython, JRuby or Scala. They easily embed into scripts written in that programming language. Examples of languages with provisions of UDFs are Hive, Pig and Spark. The UDFs provide extensibility to the programming language.

Vectorized UDFs (VUDFs) refer to custom functions using series data-structure (meaning one dimensional array or tuples).

Grouped Vectorized UDFs (GVUDFs) refer to custom functions written using DataFrame as inputs.

DataFrame in Spark refers to a distributed collection of data that organizes into the named columns. The concept of the DataFrame in Spark is similar to database table in a relational database. The data frame concept in R is the basis of the data frame concept in Spark. Scala and Java APIs for DataFrames are just dataset of rows.

SchemaRDD is the name of Spark DataFrame in the earlier versions of Spark.

SerDe refers to Serializer/Deserializer functions (methods). Java syntax is SERDE, 'serde.class.name'. SerDe use in codes for obtaining records from unstructured data. The serializer function saves the records and the deserializer function loads (extracts) the records.

Data pipeline means data collected from various data sources passes through in-between phases (stages) of processing. The output of each stage is the input to the next in the pipeline. Processing in-between uses a chain of function calls in an application or process, such as ETL.

Graph refers to a non-linear data structure with properties attached to each vertex and edge. Computations perform at each node in a graph structure using path traversals between the vertices (Section 8.2).

Directed Acyclic Graph (DAG) refers to a directed graph with no cyclic traversal. Here, one set of inputs simultaneously applies at a DAG node input, and after the operations (computations) at the node, only one set of outputs is generated. The node represents the statements and operators, which execute at the node in the graph.

Nested tables in databases refer to one column tables. Oracle RDBMS uses PL/SQL. A database stores the rows of a nested table in no particular order. While the SQL assigns the rows in consecutive subscripts starting at 1 so that each row accesses like an array element, PL/SQL accesses a nested table in no order.

Parquet refers to nested hierarchical columnar storage in group of rows, wherein each row has a number of columns, each column has one chunk, and each chunk has a number of pages.

In-memory refers to data read from the memory during computations and data written to the memory at same data node, thus ensuring fasten memory accesses. Disk accesses and remote node accesses make computations slow.

Columnar in-memory analytics refers to usages of optimized layout columnar tables (nested tables, Hive ORC tables). That provides the easier data locality using successive memory addresses. The CPUs and GPUs provide higher performance for native vectorized optimization during analytics and OLAP. Apache Arrow™ enables usages of in-memory columnar analysis and grouped vectorized UDFs.

ETL (Extract, Transform and Load) refers to operations on a database or Data Store using a tool or program (maximum) to code up to few thousand lines of code. ETL tools pull the data from various data sources and store (load) it in the appropriate Data Store after applying the required transformation operation.

Shell means an environment to write and run programming scripts; for example the scripts for query processing similar to SQL.

Schema refers to a blueprint for organization or structuring of a database or table or dataset. The blueprint tells how the database constructs. A construction may use division of the data into rows. Relational-database construction may use the division into database tables. Schema for a database is defined as set of formulae, called integrity constraints, imposed. (Formulae may be just sentences.)

SQL refers to a language for (i) writing structured queries for processing using a relational database; (ii) schema creation, schema modifications and data access control; (iii) creating client for sending query scripts, creating server databases and managing the databases; and (iv) viewing, querying and changing (update, insert or append or delete) the databases.

Metastore refers to the system objects, files, catalog, schema or tables, databases, columns in a table, their data types, and mapping with HDFS or any other storage formats. Metastore provides access to them during computation.

Cassandra refers to a distributed DBMS designed for handling a high volume of structured data across multiple servers. Cassandra is HDFS compatible. Cassandra DBs distribution model is peer-to-peer distribution in a system across its nodes. Data distributes among all the nodes in a cluster.

Software stack refers to a group of programs. Stack programs work in tandem (together or in conjunction) and produce a result. Software stack also refers to any set of applications that works in a specific and defined order. For example, LAMP is a software stack that consists of a group of open source components, namely Linux, Apache, MySQL, Perl, PHP or Python.

Ad hoc query refers to a "for this purpose" query, "on the fly" query or a "just so" query. It's the kind of SQL query that is loosely used when required. For example, `var newSqlQuery = "SELECT * FROM table WHERE id = " + toy_puzzleId`. It will be different each time this code executes, depending on the value of toy_puzzleId (Example 4.7).

This chapter focusses on Spark and data analysis with Spark. Section 5.2 introduces Spark architecture features, software stack components and their functions. Section 5.3 describes steps in data analysis with Spark and using Spark with advanced Python features. Section 5.4 describes methods of downloading Spark, programming with RDDs, Spark shell and developing and testing Spark codes, and applications of MLib. Section 5.5 describes ETL processes using the built-in functions and operators, and ETL pipelines. Section 5.6 describes data analytics, data reporting and data visualization.

5.2 SPARK

LO 5.1

Spark architectural features, software stack components, and their functions

Apache® Spark™ is a *fast and general compute engine*. Apache® Spark™ powers the analytics applications up to 100 times faster. It supports *HDFS compatible data*. Spark has a simple and *expressive programming model*.

Expressive program model implements a *number* of mathematical and logic operations with smaller and easier written codes which a compiler as well as programmer can understand easily. The model, therefore, gives programming ease for a wide range of applications. Applications of expressive codes are in analytics, Extract Transform Load (ETL), Machine Learning (ML), stream processing and graph computations.

Spark runs on both Windows and UNIX-like systems, such as Linux and Mac OS. Java is essential for running Spark applications. Executing a spark application on a computer system therefore requires setting a JDK path using JAVA_HOME environment variable or system variable, PATH. Spark 2.3.1 runs on Java 8+, Python 2.7+/3.4+ and R 3.1+, and Scala 2.11.x. The multiple languages, Python and Scala shells provide *great ease in programming for complex analytics, machine learning* and other solutions.

Following subsections describe Spark and introduce data analysis using Spark.

5.2.1 Introduction to Big Data Tool—Spark

Figure 5.1 shows the main components in the Apache Software Foundation's Spark framework, which includes data storage, APIs and resources management bonded with functions in Spark core.

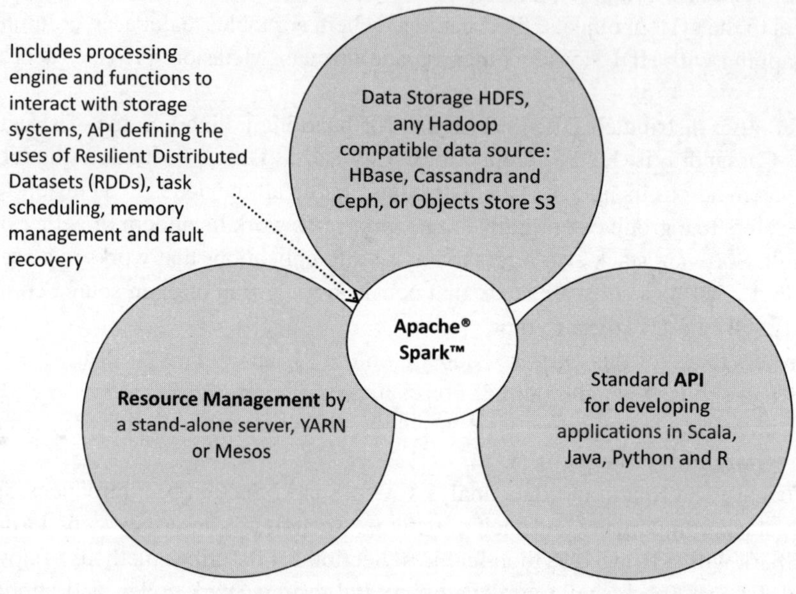

Figure 5.1 Main components of the Spark architecture

Main components of the Spark architecture are:

1. Spark HDFS file system for data storage: Storage is at an HDFS or Hadoop compatible data source (such as HDFS, HBase, Cassandra, Ceph), or at the Objects Store S3
2. Spark standard API enables the creation of applications using Scala, Java, Python and R
3. Spark resource management can be at a stand-alone server or it can be on a distributed computing framework, such as YARN or Mesos.

Ceph refers to an open source, scalable object, block, file storing unified system. Ceph provides for dynamic replication and redistribution. Ceph provides HDFS compatible mechanisms for Big data in petabytes or exabytes. An application uniquely accesses the object, block and file stores in a system using Ceph. Ceph is highly reliable.

Apache Mesos is an open source project developed at University of Berkeley, and now passed to Apache. It manages computing clusters. Its implementation is in C++. Apache released a stable version 1.3.0 of Mesos in June 2017. Apache Mesos enables fine-grained sharing of CPU, RAM, IOs and other across frameworks. Mesos offers them **resource**. Each resource contains a list of agents. Each agent has the Hadoop and MapReduce executers.

S3 (Simple Storage Service) refers to an Amazon web service on the cloud named S3 which provides Object Stores for data (Section 3.3.4).

5.2.1.1 Features of Spark

Figure 5.2 shows the main features of Spark.

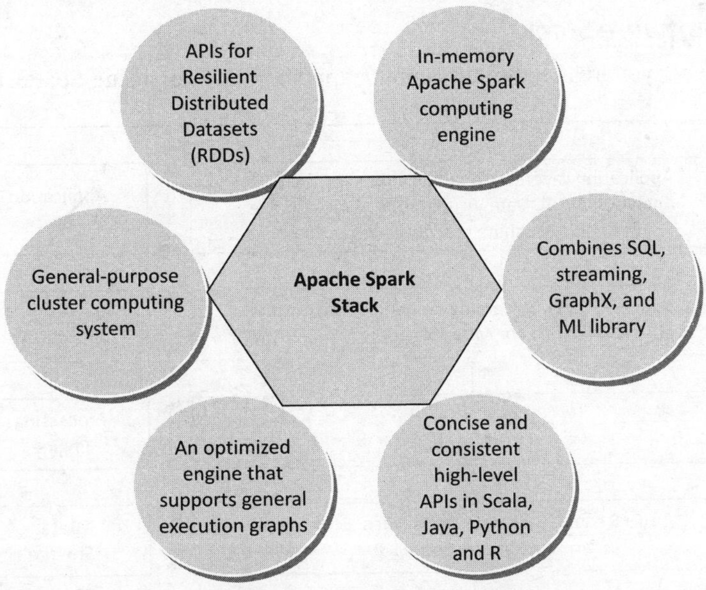

Figure 5.2 Main features of Spark

The features of Spark:

1. Spark provisions for creating applications that use the complex data. In-memory Apache Spark computing engine enables up to 100 times performance with respect to Hadoop.
2. Execution engine uses both in-memory and on-disk computing. Intermediate results save in-memory and spill over to disk.
3. Data uploading from an Object Store for immediate use as a Spark object instance. Spark service interface sets up the Object Store.
4. Provides high performance when an application accesses memory cache from the disk.
5. Contains API to define Resilient Distributed Datasets (RDDs). RDD is a programming abstraction. RDD is the core concept in Spark framework. RDD represents a collection of Object Stores distributed across many compute nodes for parallel processing. Spark stores data in RDD on different partitions. A table has partitions into columns or rows. Similarly, an RDD can also be considered as a table in a database that can hold any type of data. RDDs are also fault tolerant.
6. Processes any kind of data, namely structured, semi-structured or unstructured data arriving from various sources.

7. Supports many new functions in addition to Map and Reduce functions.
8. Optimizes data processing performance by slowing the evaluation of Big Data queries.
9. Provides concise and consistent APIs in Scala, Java and Python. Spark codes are in Scala and run on JVM environment.
10. Supports Scala, Java, Python, Clojure and R languages.
11. Provides powerful tool to analyze data interactively using shell which is available in either Scala (which runs on the Java VM and is thus a good way to use existing Java libraries) or Python. The tool also provides for learning the usages of API.

5.2.1.2 Spark Software Stack

Figure 5.3 shows a five-layer architecture for running applications when using Spark stack.

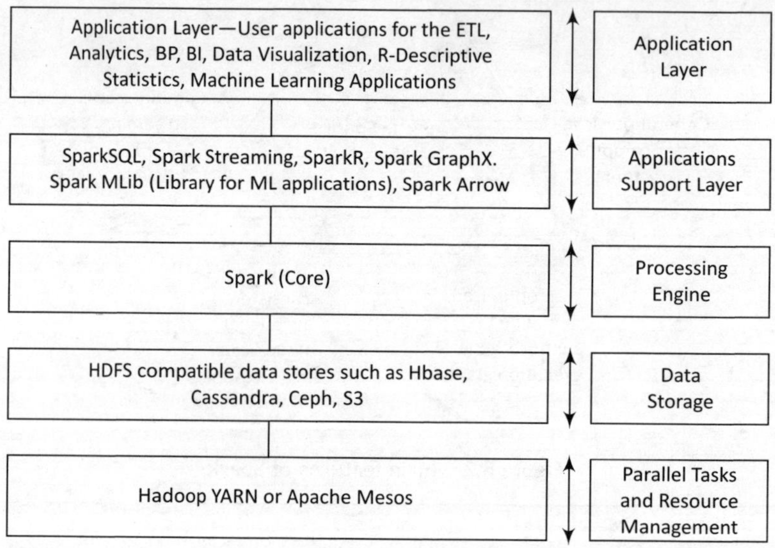

Figure 5.3 Five-layer architecture for running applications using Spark stack

The main components of Spark stack are SQL, Streaming, R, GraphX, MLib and Arrow at the applications support layer. Spark core is the processing engine. Data Store provides the data to the processing engine. Hadoop, YARN or Mesos facilitates the parallel running of the tasks and the management and scheduling of the resources.

Spark Stack

Spark stack imbibes generality to Spark. Grouping of the following forms Spark stack:

Spark SQL for the structured data. The SQL runs the queries on Spark data in the traditional business analytics and visualization applications. Spark SQL enables Spark datasets to use JDBC or ODBC API. HQL queries also run in Spark SQL. Runs UDFs for inline SQL, distributed DataFrames, Parquet, Hive and Cassandra Data Stores.

Spark Streaming is for processing real-time streaming data. Processing is based on micro-batches style of computing and processing. Streaming uses the DStream which is basically a series of RDDs, to process the real-time data.

SparkR is an R package used as light-weight front end for Apache Spark from R. Spark API uses SparkR through the RDD class. A user can interactively run the jobs from the R shell on a cluster. An RDD API is in the distributed lists in R.

Spark MLib is Spark's scalable machine learning library. It consists of common learning algorithms and utilities. MLib includes classification, regression, clustering, collaborative filtering, dimensionality reduction and optimization primitives. MLib applies in recommendation systems, clustering and classification using Spark.

Spark GraphX is an API for graphs. GraphX extends the Spark RDD by introducing the Resilient Distributed Property. GraphX computations use fundamental operators (e.g., subgraph, joinVertices and aggregateMessages). GraphX uses a collection of graph algorithms for programming. Graph analytics tasks are created with ease using GraphX.

Spark Arrow for columnar in-memory analytics and enabling usages of vectorised UDFs (VUDFs). The Arrow enables high performance Python UDFs for SerDe and data pipelines.

Self-Assessment Exercise linked to LO 5.1

1. How does Spark process as a fast and general compute engine? What does expressive programming model mean? ●●●
2. List the main components of Spark stack and the functions of each. ○●●
3. List the advanced provisions in Spark SQL compared to HiveQL. ○●●
4. List the main features of Spark? ○○●

5.3 INTRODUCTION TO DATA ANALYSIS WITH SPARK

LO 5.2

Steps in data analysis with Spark, using Spark with Python advanced features, UDFs, vectorized UDFs, group vectorized UDFs and Python libraries for the analysis

"The process of methodically applying statistical and/or logical techniques to describe and demonstrate, summarize and recap, and assess data is called Data Analysis."

For examples, consider a car company. Assume that company sells five models of cars. Each model is available in 16 different colours and shades. Sales are processed through a large number of showrooms, all over the country. An analyses of annual sales and annual profits model-wise, colour-wise, region-wise and showroom-wise help the company in discovering useful information and making suggestive conclusions. The company does predictive analytics from the results of the analyses and decides the future strategies for manufacturing, sales and out-reaches to customers on the basis of the results of the analytics.

Note: ○○● Level 1 & Level 2 category
○●● Level 3 & Level 4 category
●●● Level 5 & Level 6 category

Figure 5.4 shows the steps between acquisition of data from different sources, applications of the analyzed data, and application support by Spark for the analyses.

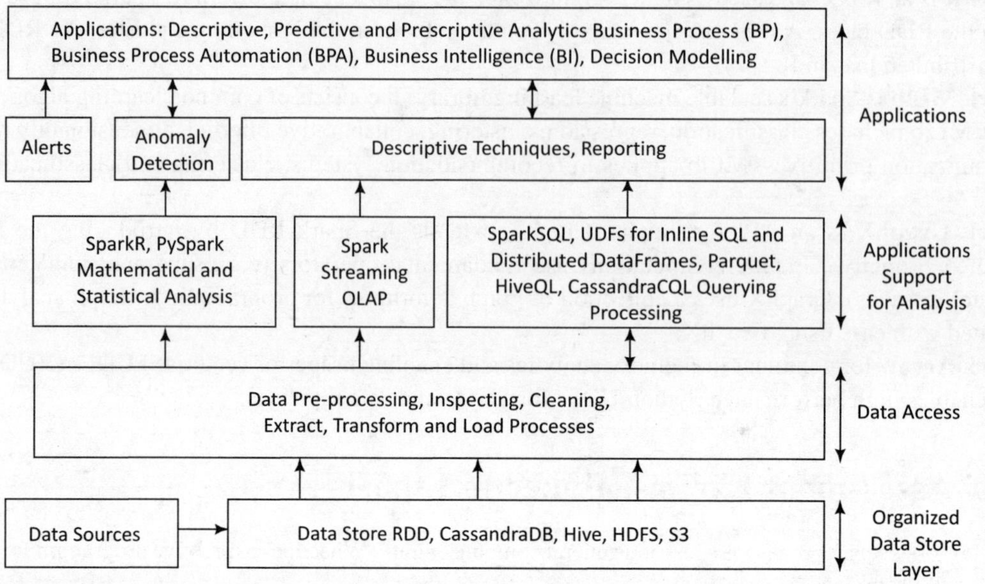

Figure 5.4 Steps between acquisition of data from different sources and its applications

Following are the steps for analyzing the data:

1. Data Storage: Store of data from the multiple sources after acquisition. The Big Data storage may be in HDFS compatible files, Cassandra, Hive, HDFS or S3.
2. Data pre-processing: This step requires:
   (a) dropping out of range, inconsistent and outlier values,
   (b) filtering unreliable, irrelevant and redundant information,
   (c) data cleaning, editing, reduction and/or wrangling,
   (d) data-validation, transformation or transcoding.
3. Extract, transform and Load (ETL)) for the analysis
4. Mathematical and statistical analysis of the data obtained after querying relevant data needing the analysis, or OLAP,
5. Applications of analyzed data, for example, descriptive, predictive and prescriptive analytics, business processes (BPs), business process automation (BPA), business intelligence (BI), decision modelling and knowledge discovery.

5.3.1 Spark SQL

Spark SQL is a component of Spark Big Data Stack. Spark SQL components are DataFrames (SchemaRDDs), SQLContext and JDBC server. Spark SQL at Spark does the following:

1. Runs SQL like scripts for query processing, using *catalyst optimizer* and *tungsten execution engine*

2. Processes structured data
3. Provides flexible APIs for support for many types of data sources
4. ETL operations by creating ETL pipeline on the data from different file-formats, such as JSON, Parquet, Hive, Cassandra and then run ad-hoc querying.

Spark SQL has the following features for analysis:

1. SparkR, PySpark, Python, Java and other language support for coding for data analysis.
2. Provisioning of JDBC and ODBC APIs: Applications in Java and Microsoft programs (such as Excel) need to connect to databases using JDBC (Object Database Connectivity) and ODBC (Object Database Connectivity). Spark APIs enable that connectivity,
3. Spark SQL enables users to extract their data from different formats, such as Hive, JSON and Parquet, and then transform that into required formats for ad hoc querying. [Ad hoc query is a query 'just for this purpose' or query 'on the fly.' For example, var newToyQuery = "SELECT * FROM table WHERE id = " + toy_puzzleId. The result will be different each time this code executes, depending on the value of toy_puzzleId.
4. Spark SQL processing support inclusion of Hive. Hive support enables the use of Hive tables, database and data warehouse, UDFs and SerDe (serialization and deserialization).
5. Spark SQL supports HiveQL and Cassandra CQL for query processing.
6. Spark Streaming for support to OLTP and structured streaming.

Figure 5.5 shows the connectivity of applications with Spark SQL which connects to Object Stores in different formats.

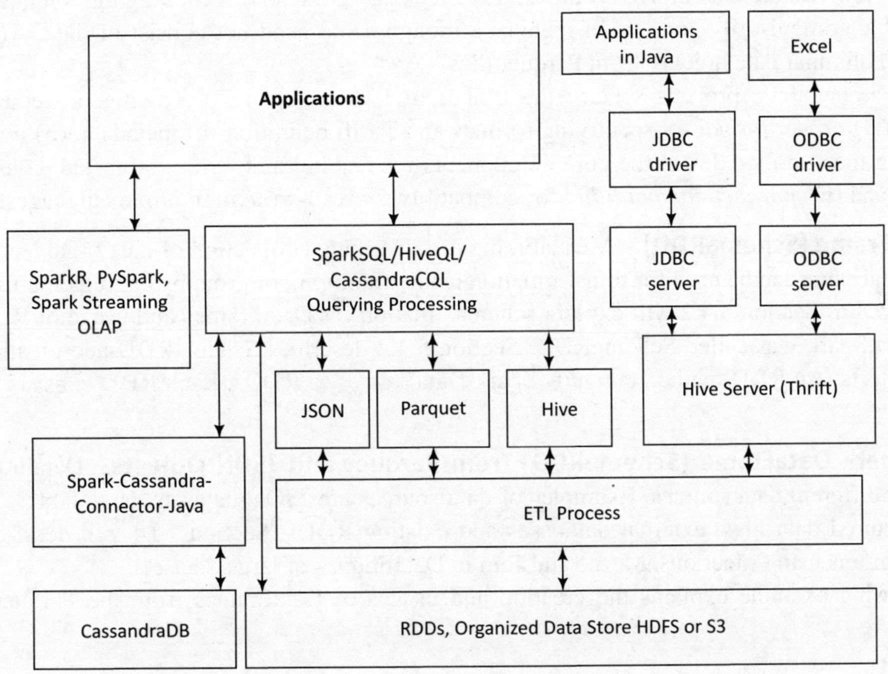

Figure 5.5 Connectivity between the applications and Spark SQL

JDBC Server An application reads the data tables in RDBMS using a JDBC client (JDBC API at the application). Many applications in Java connect to databases using JDBC driver and server. Spark SQL API provides JDBC connectivity. Command for using JDBC server is as follows:

```
./sbin/start-thriftserver.sh -- master sparkMaster
```

Hive Server (Thrift) enables a remote Hive client or JDBC driver to send a request to Hive and the server sends response to that (Section 4.4.1). The requests can be in Scala, Java, Python or R.

JSON, Hive, Parquet Objects Section 3.3.2 explained JSON object data formats and files. Section 4.4 explained Hive, HiveQL database and QL commands for data definition of databases, tables, columns, partitions and views, and their querying.

HDFS is highly reliable for very long running queries. However, IO operations are slow. Columnar storage is a solution for faster IOs. Columnar storage stores the data portion, presently required for the IOs. Load-only columns access during processing. Also, a columnar object Data Store can be compressed or encoded according to the data type. Also, executions of different columns or column partitions can be in parallel at the data nodes.

Section 3.3.3.3 and Section 3.3.3.4 described record columnar (RC) file, and optimized row columnar (ORC) file formats respectively. Hive RC file records store in columns and can be partitioned into row groups. An ORC file consists of row-groups row data called stripes. ORC enables concurrent reads of the same file using separate RecordReaders.[1] Metadata stored using protocol buffers for addition and removal of fields.

Parquet is a nested hierarchical columnar storage concept. Apache Parquet file is a columnar storage file (Section 3.3.3.5). The file uses an HDFS block. The block saves the file for running big long queries on Big Data. Each file compulsorily consists of metadata, though a file need not consist of data. An application retrieves the columnar data quickly from Parquet files.

Apache Parquet three projects specify the usages of files for query processing or applications. The projects are (i) *parquet-format* for specifying formats and Thrift definitions of metadata, (ii) *parquet-mr* for implementing the sub-modules in the core components for reading and writing a nested, column-oriented data stream, and (iii) *parquet-compatibility* for compatibly for read-write in multiple languages.

Spark DataFrame (SchemaRDD) A DataFrame is a distributed collection of data organized into named columns. DataFrame can be used for transformation using filter, join, or groupby aggregation functions.

Example 5.8 in Section 5.4.2 will explain schema creation for DataFrames and usage of RDDs. Earlier, DataFrame in Spark was called SchemaRDD. Section 5.4.2 describes SchemaRDD and creation of RDDs from row objects. An RDD method converts Spark DataFrames to RDDs. Each RDD consists of a number of row objects.

Creating Spark DataFrame (SchemaRDD) from Parquet and JSON Objects DataFrames can be created from different data sources. Examples of data sources are JSON datasets, Hive tables, Parquet row groups, structured data files, external databases and existing RDDs. Section 10.4 will describe Hive and PySpark programs using functions, Merge and Join in DataFrames of large datasets.

The following example explains the creation and usages of DataFrames from the Parquet and JSON objects:

[1] https://cwiki.apache.org/confluence/display/Hive/LanguageManual+ORC#LanguageManualORC-ORCFileFormat

EXAMPLE 5.1

Assume a table toyPuzzleTypeCostTbl with four columns. Figure 5.6 shows the sample table toyPuzzleTypeCostTbl. The columns are puzzle type, puzzle code, number of puzzle pieces and puzzle cost. DataFrame1 named toyPuzzleTypeCodes consists of columns 1 and 2. DataFrame2 named toyPuzzleCodesCost consists of Columns 2 and 4. The table consists of multiple rows in each row group. The dashed lines point to the columns in the two data frames.

toyPuzzleTypeCostTbl

	puzzleType	puzzleCode	puzzlePieces	puzzleCost
Row Group1	puzzle_ Garden	10725	100	1.35
	puzzle_ Garden	10825	200	1.35
	puzzle_ Garden	10975	400	1.35
	...	...	...	...
Row Group2	puzzle_Jungle	31047	300	2.85
	puzzle_Jungle	31047	300	2.85
	...	...	...	...
Row Group3	puzzle_ School	81409	800	0.90
	...	...	...	....
	puzzle_Forest	...	...	...

DataFrame toyPuzzleTypeCodes Columns 1 and 2

DataFrame toyPuzzleCodesCost Columns 2 and 4

Figure 5.6 Sample table toyPuzzleTypeCostTbl rows, row groups and DataFrames

(i) Create a sqlContext from a given SparkContext 'sc'.

(ii) Create a four columns DataFrame using the Parquet file named "toyPuzzleTypeCostTbl".

(iii) How will a DataFrame create using a JSON file format file "toyPuzzleTypeCostTbl"? Create two DataFrames using Java and SqlContext, one with columns for puzzle type and puzzle code, and the other for puzzle code and cost.

(iv) How will two DataFrames join using puzzle code as a join key to create a DataFrame of three columns, 1, 2 and 4?

SOLUTION

(i) The following statement creates sqlContext from Spark Context *sc*:

```
SqlContext sqlContext = new org.apache.spark.sql.SQLContext(sc)
```

(ii) The following statement creates a DataFrame named toyTypeCost:

```
DataFrame toyTypeCost = sqlContext.
parquetFile("toyPuzzleTypeCostTbl")
```

[DataFrame created will have four columns.]

(iii) DataFrame creates using Load() method at the sqlContext.

```
# To display the contents of Table: "toyPuzzleTypeCostTbl"
  spark.sql ("SELECT * FROM toyPuzzleTypeCostTbl ")
# To create DataFrame toyPuzzleTypeCostTbl
  DataFrame toyPuzzleTypeCostTbl = sqlContext.Load
("toyPuzzleTypeCostTbl", "json")
```

The following statements create two DataFrames using DataFrame toyPuzzleTypeCostTbl. One frame of two columns, 1 and 2, puzzle type and puzzle code:

```
DataFrame toyTypeCodes = toyPuzzleTypeCostTbl.
select(toyPuzzleTypeCostTbl ['puzzleType'], toyPuzzleTypeCostTbl
['puzzleCode'])
```

Second frame of two columns, 2 and 4, puzzle code and puzzle cost

```
DataFrame toyCodesCost = toyPuzzleTypeCostTbl.
select(toyPuzzleTypeCostTbl ['puzzleCode'], toyPuzzleTypeCostTbl
['puzzleCost'])
```

(iv) DataFrame1 (toyTypeCodes) has two columns, 1 and 2, as *puzzleType* and *puzzleCode*, respectively. The frame joins dataFrame2 (toyCodesCost) column 4 as *puzzleCost* and resultant is a joined new-dataFrame ***toyTypeCodesCost*** consisting of columns 1, 2 and 4. Join key is *puzzleCode*. Following statements use join() method and joining key.
Format of the statement is

```
dataFrame. join (dataframe1, dataframe2.col ("JoinKey") =
dataframeNew ("JoinKey")
```

and the statement is

```
dataFrame.join(toyTypeCodes, toyCodesCost.col("puzzleCode"). equalTo
(toyTypeCodesCost ("puzzleCode")))
```

Using HiveQL for Spark SQL Spark SQL programming provides two contexts, SQLContext and HiveContext. While using HiveContext, then, commands access the Hive Server only and use HiveQL commands. SQLContext is a subset of Spark SQL. SQLContext does not need the HiveServer (Thrift). Therefore, when needing access to the HiveServer, specify the HiveContext. HiveQL is recommended for Spark SQL. Many resources are available in Hive readily and can directly be used.

Use of Aggregation and Statistical Functions Aggregation functions can be used for analysis. Hive consists of count (*), count (expr); sum (col), sum (DISTINCT col), avg (col), avg (DISTINCT col), min (col) and DOUBLE max(col) (Table 4.10). The statistical functions stdev(), sampleStdev(), variance, sampleVariance() can be used for analysis with DataFrames in input.

Consider the example below to find sum of the sales of the Jaguar Land Rover model and trace the showroom that recorded the best sales.

EXAMPLE 5.2

Recall Practice Exercise 3.11. Consider the annual car sales data in the following format:

CarShowroomsCumulativeYearlySales

Car ShowroomID (csID)	Date (DT) mmddyy	*Jagaur Land Rover* Sale (JLRDS)	*Hexa* Sale (HDS)	*Zest* Sales (ZDS)	*Nexon* Sale (NDS)	*Safari Storme* Sale (SSDS)
220	....	..	...	....	...	...
10	121217	49	34	164	115	38
122	121217	40	141	123	37	88
-	-	-	-	-	-	-
-	-	-	-	-	-	-

(i) Find the **Jagaur Land Rover** annual sale figure over all showrooms.

(ii) Find the showroom ID and Land Rover sales figure for the showroom giving *maximum Jaguar Land Rover sales*.

SOLUTION

(i) The following query returns the sum of the **Jagaur Land Rover** annual sale in column 3 of the table:

```
SELECT sum (JLRDS)FROM CarShowroomsCumulativeYearlySales
```

(ii) The following nested query statement returns the csID and maximum annual sale value for Land Rover:

```
SELECT csID, saleJL (max (map (csID, ID, JLRDS, saleJL))) FROM
CarShowroomsCumulativeYearlySales
```

5.3.2 Using Python Advanced Features with Spark SQL

Python is a general purpose, interpreted, interactive, object oriented and high level programming language. Python defines the basic data types, containers, lists, dictionaries, sets, tuples, functions and classes. Python Standard Library is very extensive. The libraries for regular expressions, documentation generation, unit testing, web browsers, threading, databases, CGI, email, image manipulation and a lot of other functionalities are available in Python.

Python programming is a strong combination of performance and features in the same bundle of codes. Spark SQL binds with Python easily. Python has the expressive program statements. Spark SQL features together with Python help a programmer to build challenging applications for Big Data. The following example explains the use of PySpark, Python along with the Spark SQL:

EXAMPLE 5.3

(i) How is HiveContext and Spark SQL used?

(ii) How does PySpark use a row object?

(iii) Assume a JSON file, *toyTypeProductTbl* of row objects. Assume the use of a row object *toyPuzzleProduct* for query (Table 4.13). How do a file load and query sent to the file?

	ProductCategory	ProductId	ProductName
Row Object1	Toy_Airplane	10725	Lost Temple
Row Object2	Toy_Airplane	....	....
Row Object3	.....	.....	......

SOLUTION

(i) Import Spark SQL using the following statement:

```
Import Spark SQL
```

(ii) Then use the following command for importing a row object, toyPuzzleTypeCost:

```
# Now use the variable named hiveCtx using Hive Context from
# sc statement using statement
hiveCtx = HiveContext (sc)
from pyspark.sql import HiveContext, toyPuzzleTypeCost
```

(iii) A file loads using hiveCtx and input loads at the file

```
input = hiveCtx.jsonFile(toyTypeProductTbl)
input.registerTempTable ("toyPuzzleProduct")
```

The queries raised for finding Product_ID_Name using SELECT command.

```
Product_ID_Name = hiveCtx.sql  ("SELECT ID, name FROM toyPuzzleProduct
ORDER BY ProductCategory")
```

5.3.2.1 *Python Libraries for Analysis*

NumPy and SciPy are open source downloadable libraries for numerical (Num) analysis and scientific (Sci) computations in Python (Py). Python has open source library packages, NumPy, SciPy, Scikit-learn, Pandas and StatsModel, which are widely used for data analysis. Python library, matplotlib functions plot the mathematical functions.

Spark added a Python API support for UDFs. The functions take one row at a time. That requires overhead (additional codes) for SerDe. Earlier data pipelines first defined the UDFs in Java or Scala, and then invoked them from Python. Spark 2.3 provisions for vectorized UDFs (VUDFs) and Apache Arrow facilitates VUDFs, which enables high performance Python UDFs for SerDe and data pipelines.

NumPy NumPy includes (i) N-dimensional array object, array and vector mathematics; (ii) linear algebraic functions, Fourier transform and random number functions; (iii) sophisticated (broadcasting) functions; and (iv) tools for integrating with C/C++ and Fortran codes.

NumPy provides multi-dimensional efficient containers of generic data and definitions of arbitrary data types. NumPy integrates easily with a wide variety of databases. NumPy provides import, export (load/save) files, creation of arrays, inspection of properties, copying, sorting and reshaping, addition and removal of elements in the arrays, indexing, sub-setting and slicing of the arrays, scalar and vector mathematics (such as +, –, ×, ÷, power, sqr, sin, log, ceil – round up to nearest int, floor – round down up to the nearest int, round – round to nearest integer). NumPy also provides statistical functions.

Table 5.1 gives the examples of NumPy functions for data analysis problems.

Table 5.1 Examples of NumPy functions for data analysis problems

Function	Description	Function	Description
np.loadtxt('file.txt')	Loads a text file	np.mean(arr, axis = 0)	Returns mean along a specific axis
np.genfromtxt('file.csv', delimiter= ',')	Loads a csv file with comma as the delimiter between records	np.sum(); np.min(),	Returns the sum and minimum of the array
np.savetxt('file.txt,' arr, delimiter= ' ')	Saves a text file which is an array of strings separated by a space each.	np.max(arr, axis = 0)	Returns the maximum along a specific axis
np.genfromtxt('file.csv', arr, delimiter= ',')	Saves a CSV file which is an array of strings separated by a comma each.	np.var(arr)	Returns the variance of array
arr.sort()	Sorts an array	np.std(arr, axis = 0)	Returns the standard deviation of a specific axis
np.add (arr1, arr2)	Performs a vector addition of array 1 and array 2	np.corr()	Returns the correlation coefficient

SciPy SciPy adds on top of NumPy. It includes MATLAB files and special functions, such as routines for numerical integration and optimization. SciPy defines some useful functions for computing distances between a set of points.

SciPy includes (i) interactions with NumPy, (ii) creation of dense and open mesh grids, (iii) shape manipulation functions, (iv) polynomial and vectoring functions, (v) real and imaginary functions, and casting an object to a data type, and (vi) matrix creation and matrices routines and usages of spark matrices.

Table 5.2 gives few examples of SciPy functions for scientific computational problems.

Table 5.2 Examples of SciPy functions for data analysis problems

Function	Description	Function	Description
np.c_[b, c]	Create Stacked column-wise array	np.cast ['f'] (np.pi)	Casts an object into a data type
b.flatten()	Flattens the array	from numpy import polyID p = polyID ([2, 3, 4])	Creates a polynomial object p
np.vsplit (c, 2) and np.hsplit (d, 2)	Functions for vertically splitting and horizontally splitting the array at the end of the second index	A.I, A.T, A.H	Inverses, transposes, and conjugate transposes the matrix, A

(Contd.)

Function	Description	Function	Description
linalg.det(A)	Returns the determinate of A	np.select ([c<4], [c*2])	Returns values from a list of arrays depending on the conditions
np.img(c)	Returns the imaginary part of the array elements	A = np.matrix ([3, 4], [5, 6])	Creates a matrix

Panda Panda derives its name from usages of a data structure called Panel. The first three characters *Pan* in Panda stand for the term 'panel'. The next two characters *da* in Panda stand for data. The Panda package considers three data structures: Series, DataFrame and Panel.

DataFrame is a container for Series. Panel is a container for DataFrame objects. The Panel objects can be inserted or removed similar to as in a dictionary. DataFrame may be a DataFrame of statistical or observed datasets. The data need not be labeled. This means datasets, objects and DataFrames can be placed into a Panda data structure without labels.

Panel is a container for three-dimensional data. Panel is a widely used term in econometrics. Three axes describe operations involving panel data. For example, panel data in econometric analysis. Items can be considered as along axis 0 of an inside DataFrame (set of columns). Index (rows) of each of the DataFrames correspond to axis 1 (major axis). Columns of each of the DataFrames correspond to axis 2 (minor axis). Panel 4D consists of labels as 0 - axis, items - axis 1, major axis - axis 2 and minor axis - axis 3.

Figure 5.7 shows the main features of Pandas package.

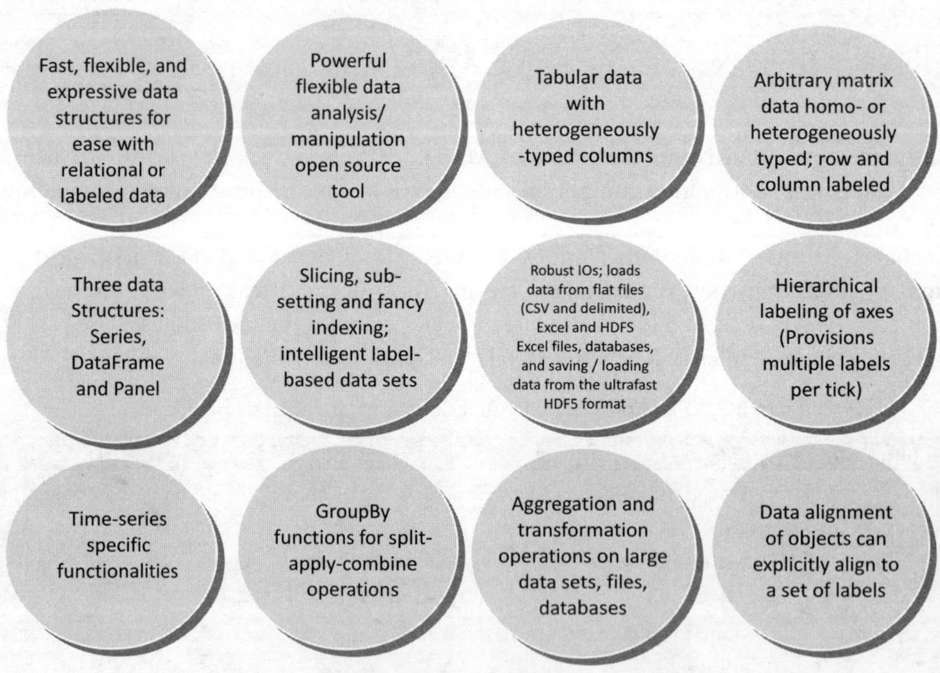

Figure 5.7 Main features of Panda for data analysis

Pandas package includes the following provisions:

1. Database style DataFrames merge, join, and concatenation of objects
2. RPy interface for R functions plus additional functions
3. Panda ecosystem has statistics, machine learning, integrated development environment (IDE), API and several out of core features
4. SQL like features: SELECT, WHERE, GROUPBY, JOIN, UNION, UPDATE and DELETE
5. GroupBy feature of split-apply-combine with the steps as: (i) an object such as table, file or document splits into groups, (ii) iterate through the groups and select a group for aggregation, transformation and/or filtration. The instance method can be dispatched and applied in a manner similar to the aggregation/transformation function
6. Size mutability, which means that columns can be inserted and deleted from DataFrame and higher dimensional objects
7. Slicing and dicing a collection of DataFrame objects. The names of axes can be somewhat arbitrary in a Panel. (Arbitrary means the axes need not be named a1, a2, …, an, and can be year, car model, sales, …). If slicing function slices the first dimension, the lower dimension objects are obtained.

5.3.2.2 User-Defined Functions (UDFs)

The functions take one row at a time. This requires overhead for SerDe. Data exchanges take place between Python and JVM. Earlier the data pipeline (between data and application) defined the UDFs in Java or Scala, and then invoked them from Python while using Python libraries for analysis or other application. SparkSQL UDFs enable registering of themselves in Python, Java and Scala.

The SQL calls the UDFs. This is a very popular way to expose advanced functionality to SQL users. User codes call the registered UDFs into the SQL statements without writing the detailed codes. The following example demonstrates how a UDF is created in PySpark.

EXAMPLE 5.4

Recapitulate Example 5.1 table, `toyPuzzleTypeCostTbl`. Create a UDF, `udfCostPlus()` in pandas. The table column `puzzleCost` creates using jigsaw_puzzle_info.txt from an RDD. Write a UDF which increases the costs in the column, `puzzle_cost_USD` by 10%. (The UDF takes one row at a time as input.)

SOLUTION

Following are the Python statements

```
from pyspark.sql.functions import udf
```

[Use udf to define a row at a time udf.]

```
@udfCostPlus('float')
```

[Input and output costs are two values both for a single float variable, v.]

```
def plusTenPercent(v):
return v + 0.1 × v;
df.withColumn('v4', puzzle_cost_USD (df.v))
```

[Data Frame `df` has v4 as `puzzleCost` in the fourth column.]

Dataset at Example 5.2 consists of car sales data. Column 1 represents car showroom ID. The ID key is present in all date fields on which the sales were recorded during the year. Corresponding to an ID, column 3 has the Jaguar Land Rover sales figures in more than 300 rows for more than 300 dates. Sales figures of four other models are in columns 4, 5, 6 and 7.

The product sales analysis is widely performed in many businesses. Writing a UDF for analysis of sales once and using it for different products whenever and wherever desired reduces coding efforts. This also integrates new functions (UDFs) in higher level language with their lower level language implementations. Also, writing UDFs are helpful when built-in functionalities in a currently used tool needs additional functionalities.

A UDF using aggregation function max() calculates the Land Rover sales and traces the showroom giving *maximum Jaguar Land Rover sales*. The UDF is of great help to perform similar analyses on different models of the car.

Java class can be created user defined method (UDF) `productSalesAnalysis()`. Python scripts can also create the UDF to find that sales point ID and total yearly sale for that sales point from which the total is highest for a product. The UDF will be reusable not only for car sales analysis but also for analysis of sales of many companies, such as ACVM or Toy Company.

Python provides a register function: `hiveContext (sc).registerFunction()`. The command can be `hiveContext (sc). registerFunction ("csIDn1", int: bestYearlySalesModel1, LongType (), ("csIDn2", int: bestYearlySalesModel2, LongType (), ...)`. csIDn1 is car-showroom ID1, bestYearlySalesModel1 is best yearly sale of model 1.

5.3.2.3 *Vectorized User Defined Functions (VUDFs)*

Python UDFs express data in detail. Therefore, Python UDFs, block-level UDFs with block-level arguments and return types, conversions or transformations are widely used in ETL or ML applications. Spark Arrow facilates columnar in-memory analytics, which results in high performance of Python UDFs, SerDe and data pipelines.

VUDFs use series data structure (meaning one-dimensional array or tuples). Spark 2.3 (2018) provisions for using vectorized UDFs (VUDFs). Apache Arrow 0.8.0 (release date December 18, 2017) facilitates usages of VUDFs. Pandas UDF, *pandas_UDF* uses the function to create a VUDF with (i) pandas.Series as input to the UDF, (ii) pandas.Series as output from the UDF, (iii) no grouping using GroupBy, (iv) output size same as input, and (v) returns the same data types as specified type in return pandas.Series.

The following example explains the use of VUDF.

EXAMPLE 5.5

Recapitulate Example 5.1 `toyPuzzleTypeCostTbl`. Create a vectorized UDF (VUDF). First define a pandas_UDFCostPlus for increasing cost puzzle_cost_USD of toys in puzzle_Costs RDD created from jigsaw_puzzle_info.txt,.

SOLUTION

Following are the Python statements from pyspark.sql.functions import pandas_udf:

```
from pyspark.sql.functions import pandas_udf
```

[Use pandas_udf to define a vectorized udf.]

```
@pandas_udfCostPlus ('float')
```

[Input/output are both a pandas.Series of elements with data type *float*.]

```
def vectorized_plusTenPercent (v):
 return v4 + 0.1
df.withColumn('v4', vectorized_ plusTenPercent (df.v))
```

[Use udf to define a DataFrame vudf.]

5.3.2.4 *Grouped Vectorized UDFs (GVUDFs)*

Grouped Vectorized UDFs (GVUDFs) use Panda library *split-apply-combine pattern* in data analysis. The GVUDF group function operates on all the data for a group, such as operate on all the data, "for each car showroom, compute yearly sales".

GVUDF steps are:

1. Splits a Spark DataFrame into groups based on the conditions specified in the groupby operator
2. Applies a vectorized user-defined function (pandas.DataFrame -> pandas.DataFrame) to each group
3. Combines into new group
4. Returns the results as a new Spark DataFrame

Pandas GVUDF, *pandas_GVUDF*, (i) uses the function similar to pandas_VUDF, (ii) pandas.DataFrame as input to the GVUDF, (ii) pandas.DataFrame as output from the GVUDF, (iii) grouping semantics defined using clause GroupBy, (iv) output size can be any and can be grouped and can be distinct from input, and (v) returns data type is a StructType. The type defines a column name and the type of the returned pandas. DataFrame.

The following example explains GVUDF for adding 10% in a cost of group of rows for toy products.

EXAMPLE 5.6

Add 10% cost in each value of item cost in a group of rows. Use GVUDF to define a `DataFrame` `costTenPercetPlus` GVUDF.

SOLUTION

Following are the Python statements from pyspark.sql.functions import pandas_udf:

```
from pyspark.sql.functions import pandas_udf
```

[Use pandas_udf to define a grouped vectorized udf.]

```
@pandas_udf(df.schema)
# Input/output are both a pandas.DataFrame
def costTenPercetPlus (pdf):
 return pdf.assign(v=add(pdf.v + 0.1×pdf.v))
df.groupby('id').apply(costTenPercetPlus)
```

5.3.3 Data Analysis Operations

Examples of operations required in the above analysis are given below:

1. Filtering single and multiple columns
2. Creating a top-ten list with values or percentages
3. Setting up sub-totals
4. Creating multiple-field criteria filters
5. Creating unique lists from repeating field data
6. Finding duplicate data with specialized arrays, and using the remove duplicates command and removing outliers
7. Multiple key sorting
8. Counting the number of unique items in a list
9. Using SUMIF and COUNTIF functions
10. Working with database functions, such as DSUM and DMAX
11. Converting lists to tables.

5.3.3.1 Removing Outliers for Data Quality Improvement for Analysis

Outliers are data which appear as they do not belong to the data set. The Outliers are generally results of human data-entry errors, programming bugs, some transition effect or phase lag in stabilizing the data value to the true value.

The actual outliers need to be removed from the data set. For example, missing decimal in the cost of a toy US$ 1.85 will make the cost 100 times more for a single toy. The result will thus be affected by a small or large amount. When valid data is identified as an outlier, then also the results are affected.

The statistical mean is computed from the product of each observed value *v* of *Values* with probability (or weight) P and then taking the average. The variance equals the difference of a value with respect to the mean, then square that, and then average the results. Standard deviation is just the square root of the variance.

The following example explains the Python codes for removing outliers.

EXAMPLE 5.7

How will you remove outliers in values in a column?

SOLUTION

Transform RDD string or other to numeric data so that statistical methods compute and remove those who have larger distanceNumerics.

```
distanceNumerics = distances.map (PySpark string: float (string))
stats = distanceNumerics.stats()
```

[stats() means a statistical function, such as mean(), stdev()]'

```
statdev = std.stdev()
mean = stats.mean()
reasonableDistances = distanceNumerics.filter (PySpark values: maths.fabs
(values-mean) < 3 xstdev)
```

[Assume that distances that are reasonable are less than three times the standard deviation. Distance means difference with respect to mean or peak value.]

```
print reasonableDistances.collect()
```

[Print the values within reasonable distances.]

Self-Assessment Exercise linked to LO 5.2

1. What are the steps between acquisition of data from different sources, applications of analyzed data, and applications support by Spark for analyses? ○○●
2. What are the different sources from which the DataFrames are created for query processing? ○●●
3. What are grouped vectorized UDFs? How do they differ from UDFs? ●●●
4. List the actions of the count(*), count(expr); sum(col), sum(DISTINCT col), avg(col), avg(DISTINCT col), min(col) and DOUBLE max(col) aggregation functions. ○○●
5. How is a four-column DataFrame created using a parquetFile? ○●●
6. List the actions of each statement in codes given in Example 5.7. ●●●

5.4 DOWNLOADING SPARK, AND PROGRAMMING USING RDDs AND MLIB

LO 5.3

Downloading Spark, getting started in programming with Spark, Spark shell, Spark context, developing and testing the codes, Programming with the RDDs, and applications of MLib

The following subsections describe downloading of Spark, getting started in programming with RDDs and introduces Machine learning with the MLib:

5.4.1 Downloading, Installing Spark and Getting Started

Spark 2.3.1 uses Scala 2.11.x API when using compatible Scala version 2.11.x. Initially select the choices for the download: (i) *Choose a Spark Release*: 2.3.1 (June, 2018), (ii) *Choose a package type*: pre-built for Hadoop 2.7 or later, (iii) *Choose a download type*: Direct Download, and (iv) *Verify this release using the* 1.2.0 signatures and checksums.

Spark new versions run on Java 8+, Python 2.7+/3.4+ and R 3.1+. Programmers using Scala 2.11 download the Spark source package and build the Scala 2.11 support in that.

Downloading Steps for downloading are:

(i) Programmer gets Spark from the Apache Spark project website http://spark.apache.org/downloads.html.

Assume that Spark version is 2.3.1. Spark uses HDFS and YARN client libraries in Hadoop. Built-in libraries are available for Spark SQL, Spark Streaming, MLib and GraphX (graph). Spark 2.3.1 is pre-packaged with Hadoop 2.7. When a download is pre-packaged for no Hadoop version, then install Hadoop from the site http://apache.claz.org/hadoop/common/hadoop-2.7/. The make shared HADOOP, MAPRED, COMMON, HDFS and all related files, configure HADOOP and set property such as replication parameter. Name the yarn.nodemanager.aux-services. Assign value to mapreduce_shuffle. Set namenode and datanode paths.

```
export HADOOP_HOME=/usr/local/hadoop
```

Download that from http://spark.apache.org/downloads.html and unzip using the command:

```
$ tar -xvzf ~/spark-2.3.1-bin-hadoop2.7.tgz
$ ls
```

Set Path by the commands:

```
$ cd $SPARK_HOME/conf
$ cp spark-env.sh.template spark-env.sh
```

Spark artifacts host at Maven Central. Maven dependency adds using the following coordinates:

```
groupID: org.apache.spark
artifactID: spark-core_2.2

version 2.2.1
```

Scala and Java users can include Spark in their projects using its Maven coordinates and later pointing to a Java installation or with Java installed in the system PATH.

(ii) When using Python and running the Python shell, use command:

```
cd spark-2.3.1-bin-hadoop2.7
. /bin/pyspark
```

Python users can also install Spark from PyPI. Python has provision of compound data types. Python provides lists, known as arrays in other languages. Lists can be indexed, sliced and manipulated with built-in Python functions. Spark Python shell is bin/pyspark.

(iii) Programmers requiring Hive databases and HiveQL, do so by the command:

```
apache-hive-0.14.0-bin apache-hive-0.14.0-bin.tar.gz
```

and extracts the Hive archive.

(iv) Programmers can also use an external database server. This requires configuration of Metastore for that server.

(v) When using Scala interactive shell running on JVM, install Javac and Java from Oracle Java download site. Download Jdk 8 or a later version from http://www.oracle.com/technetwork/java/javase/downloads/jdk8-downloads-xxxxx.html and extract the compressed file.

```
update-alternatives --Install /usr/bin/java java usr/local/java/bin/java 8
```
[2,3]

(vi) Make Java available to all the users to access Java. Move download to the location "/usr/local/" using the required commands. Set the path by the commands:

```
export JAVA_HOME=/usr/local/jdk8u152
export PATH=$PATH: $JAVA_HOME/bin
```

(vii) When using Scala, run the shell by the command:

```
cd spark-2.2.1-bin-hadoop2.7
./bin/spark-shell
```

Spark Core Concept: Driver and Context A Spark application consists of a driver program that executes various operations in parallel on a cluster. The driver program contains the main function of an application and defines distributed databases on the cluster, and then applies operations to them.

---

[2] https://www.tecmint.com/install-java-jdk-jre-in-linux/

[3] https://www.vultr.com/docs/how-to-manually-install-java-8-on-ubuntu-16-04

A driver program can be the Spark shell itself. A driver program accesses Spark through an object, SparkContext which represents a connection to a computing cluster. The Spark shell automatically creates the SparkContext, referred by *sc*.

A driver program uses the *sc*. The driver program distributes to multiple worker nodes (machines) in a cluster. Each worker node has an executor (machine). The executor executes multiple tasks in parallel.

A driver program manages executors. For example, when method *count*() executes then different executors count the elements in different ranges of an RDD. For example, elements (columns) in RDD for a table in the rows 1 to 100 count on one executor, 101 to 200 on another, and so on. An executor may run four tasks, by dividing the range into four parts.

Testing the Installation Use "README.md". It is main documentation file. The total number of lines is 127 and the first line is '# Apache Spark'

```
>>> mainDocLines = sc.textFile(README.md) [RDD named mainDocLines creates.]
>>> mainDocLines.count()
127
```

If 127 is displayed, it means the installation of Apache Spark and Python is successful.

Alternatively, create a text file jigsaw_puzzle_info.txt in Example 4.10 given below.

Write a line counting program:

```
>>> toycostsDocLines = sc.textFile(jigsaw_puzzle_info.txt)
[RDD named toycostsDocLines creates.]
>>> toycostsDocLines.count()
```

Test shows successful installation, if the number of lines matches.

Spark Supported File Formats Table 5.3 describes the Spark supported file formats and their descriptions.

Table 5.3 File formats and their descriptions

File Format	Description
Text File	Saves unstructured data. Text file is the default file format. A line represents a record. The delimiting characters separate the lines. Text file examples are CSV, TSV, JSON and XML.
Sequence File	Saves structured data. Like a flat file which stores binary key-value pairs, supports compression. Example of application is HDFS file format used for key-value pairs.
Object File	Saves structured data in Object Store. An Object file transfers by serialization; for example, using Java Serialization. Applications save data from a Spark job which shared code consumes or saves data onto cloud object store service S3.
Protocol buffer	Saves structured data in protocol buffer. An application in a programming language requires efficient and fast protocol buffer.
JSON	Saves semi-structured data in text-based format. Programming language libraries mostly require one per line. [(Section 3.3.2 and Section 1.6.1 Example 1.12 (ii)]
CSV	Saves structured data in text-based format, such as spreadsheet

5.4.2 Programming with RDDs

Spark Resilient Distributed Dataset (RDD) is a collection of objects distributed on many computing nodes. Each RDD can split into multiple partitions, which may be computed in parallel on different nodes of a cluster.

Characteristics of RDDs

1. fault-tolerant abstraction which enables In-Memory cluster computations,
2. immutable (thus read-only) and partitioned distributed collection of objects,
3. have interface which enables transformations that apply the same to many data objects,
4. create only through the deterministic operations on either (i) data in stable Data store such as file or (ii) operations on other RDDs,
5. are parallel data structures,
6. enable efficient execution of iterative algorithms,
7. enable efficient execution of interactive data-mining,
8. the commands to them enable the intermediate-results explicitly persist in memory, and
9. the command to them controls the partitioning so that placement of data optimizes and partitions can be manipulated using operators.

Spark RDD is immutable (not capable of or not susceptible to change). A new RDD creates on *transform* and *action* commands. Commands create RDDs in two ways: (i) load an external dataset as a distributed collection of objects, or (ii) use a driver (program) for distributing a collection of objects.

Two operations, *transform* and *action* can be performed on an RDD. Each dataset represents an object. The transform-command invokes the methods using the objects to create new RDD(s). Action is an operation that (i) returns a value into a program or (ii) exports data to a Data Store. Transform and action are different because of the way in which Spark computes RDDs. Transform operations create RDDs from each other. The action command does the computation when a first-time action takes place on an RDD and returns a value or sends data to a Data Store.

The following example explains the command for creation of the RDD, and transform and action commands for operations on the RDD textFile.

EXAMPLE 5.8

Recapitulate Example 4.10 of a toy company selling Jigsaws. Consider a text file named jigsaw_puzzle_info.txt in */home/user* directory. The three lines in the text file are:

```
puzzle_code_Garden 10725 pieces 100 puzzle_cost_USD 1.35
puzzle_code_Jungle 31047 pieces 300 puzzle_cost_USD 2.85
puzzle_code_School 81049 pieces 800 puzzle_cost_Cents 90
```

(i) How will you create RDD puzzle_Costs from jigsaw_puzzle_info.txt? Use Spark Context (sc).

(ii) A new RDD must have the lines having the string "puzzle_cost_USD". How will you use transform command to get new RDD textFile, puzzle_cost_USD? How many lines will puzzle_cost_USD possess?

(iii) How will an action command display first line from the filtered text?

SOLUTION

(i) RDD creates from text file at Spark Core using the following command:[4],[5]

```
>>> puzzle_Costs = sc.textFile("jigsaw_puzzle_info.txt")
```

[sc stands for SparkContext.]
Alternatively, without using sc then create RDD using the following command:

```
puzzle_Costs = spark.read.textFile("jigsaw_puzzle_info.txt").rdd
```

(ii) A *transformation* command is filter(). The following statement does the transformation using filter():

```
>>>puzzle_cost_USD = puzzle_Costs.filter (pyspark line: "puzzle_cost_
USD" in line)
```

`puzzle_cost_USD` RDD will have first two lines only. (Third line has the cost in cents.)

(iii) An *action* command to get the first line is first(). The following statement does the *action* using first():

```
>>> puzzle_Costs_USD.first()
```

The result puzzle_cost_USD first line will display as follows:

```
## puzzle_code_Garden 10725 pieces 100 puzzle_cost_USD 1.35
```

Examples of Transform Commands Examples of the transform command are filter(), map(), mapValues(), flatMap(), sort(), pratitionBy(), groupByKey(), reduceByKey(), aggregateByKey(), pipe(), coalesce(), sample(), union(), join(), cogroup(), and crossProduct().

Examples of Action Commands Examples of the action command are: reduce(), collect() [Returns the elements themselves], count() [Returns the number of elements in the dataset], first(), take(), countByKey(), lookup() [used when RDDs hash/range partitioned], foreach() and save() [Returns the dataset to a Data store].

RDDs Persistence Command `persist` enables the RDDs to reuse intermediate results in later operations. The following example explains the command, `persist` for an RDD, and action command `count()`.

EXAMPLE 5.9

Recapitulate Example 5.8 (ii) of a toy company selling Jigsaws. The RDD has two lines after filter().

(i) How will the intermediate results be used?

(ii) What will be the output of action commands count() and first()?

SOLUTION

(i) RDD persist command saves intermediate results of actions using the following command:

```
>>> puzzle_Costs_USD.persist
```

[4] https://data-flair.training/blogs/create-rdds-in-apache-spark/

[5] http://data-flair.training/forums/topic/how-to-create-rdd

(ii) The *action* command count() will do the action as follows:

```
>>> puzzle_Costs_USD.count()
2
```

[The result will display 2 as two lines remained after filter() in Example 5.8(ii).]
Action for display first line will be use the command:

```
>>> puzzle_Costs_USD.first()
```

The result puzzle_cost_USD first line will display as follows:

```
## puzzle_code_Garden 10725 pieces 100 puzzle_cost_USD 1.35
```

Removing Data Spark auto-monitors the usages of caches. Spark removes the caches using 'least recently used partitions removed first' strategy. A programmer can use RDD.unpersist() to remove caches.

RDDs Partitioning and Parallelizing Spark RDD partitioning enables execution of each partition in parallel.

```
puzzle_cost_USD = sc.parallelize(["puzzle_cost_USD", ""puzzle_cost_USD"])
```

DataFrame (SchemaRDD) SchemaRDD is similar to a table in a traditional database. SchemaRDD in earlier Spark versions is now named as DataFrame. The schema is blueprint for the organization of data in an RDD (similar to traditional database schema). The blueprint tells how the RDD constructs. The SchemaRDD returns on the queries loading or execution. A SchemaRDD is composed of row objects. The SchemaRDD has additionally the 'Data Type' information for each column. A row object wraps the arrays of basic data types.

Table 5.4 provides Spark data types and their descriptions. These are similar to HiveQL.

Table 5.4 Spark data types and their descriptions

Data Type Name	Description
TINYINT	1 byte signed integer. Postfix letter is Y
SMALLINT	2 bytes signed integer. Postfix letter is S
INT	4 bytes signed integer
BIGINT	8 byte signed integer. Postfix letter is L
FLOAT	4 byte single-precision floating-point number
DOUBLE	8 byte double-precision floating-point number
BOOLEAN	True or False
TIMESTAMP	UNIX timestamp with optional nanosecond precision. It supports java.sql.Timestamp format "YYYY-MM-DD HH:MM:SS.ffffffff" Java has `java.SQL.TimeStamp` and Python has `datetime.Datetime`
DATE	YYYY-MM-DD format

(Contd.)

Data Type Name	Description
STRING	Use single quote (' ') or double quote (" "). Python, Java and Scala use string, String and String, respectively to define a string variable.
VARCHAR	1 to 65355 bytes use single quotes (' ') or double quotes (" ")
CHAR	255 bytes
DECIMAL	Used for representing immutable arbitrary precision. DECIMAL (precision, scale) format Java has `java.Math.BigDecimal` and Python `decimal.Decimal`.
UNION	Collection of heterogeneous data types.
NULL	Missing values representation

Table 5.5 provides three Collection data types available in Spark SQL and HiveQL and their descriptions.

Table 5.5 Three Collection data types: STRUCT, MAP and ARRAY and their descriptions (same as HiveQL)

Name	Description
STRUCT	Similar to 'C' struct. Fields are accessed using dot notation. For example, struct `('a', 'b')` An example is row object STRUCT<Col1:Col1_Type, ...>. Python, Java and Scala have structures named Row.
MAP <KEY_TYPE, VAL_TYPE>	A collection of key-value pairs. Fields are accessed using [] notation. For example, `map ('key1', 'a', 'key2', 'b')`. Scala and Java use Map and Python `dict`
ARRAY <DATA TYPE>	Ordered sequence of same types. Fields are accessed using array index. For example, `array ('a', 'b')`. Scala uses `Seq`, Java `List` and Python `list`, `tuple` or `array`.

Row objects represent records inside SchemaRDDs and are simply fixed-length arrays of fields. A SchemaRDD example is given below:

EXAMPLE 5.10

Recapitulate Example 4.10 of a toy company selling Jigsaws. Consider the following table object named toyPuzzleTypeCostTbl and row objects named toyPuzzleTypeCost.

toy_type	puzzle_code	pieces	puzzle_cost_USD
puzzle_ Garden	10725	100	1.35
puzzle_ Jungle	31407	300	2.85
puzzle_ School	81049	800	1.37

(i) What will be the SchemaRDD for the table as array of rows with four columns each?
(ii) Which command will be used to access a row for puzzle_School?
(iii) What is an alternative method to create Schema RDD for row objects toyPuzzleTypeCost from toyPuzzleTypeCostTbl?

SOLUTION

(i) SchemaRDD will be as follows:

```
|-- toyPuzzleTypeCostTbl: ARRAY (nullable = true)
```

[The table is an array of rows. An array may not have any element.]
|-- element: STRUCT toyPuzzleTypeCost (containsNull = false)
[The data type of element (row) of the array named toyPuzzleTypeCostTbl is a STRUCT named toyPuzzleTypeCost.]

```
|-- toyPuzzleTypeCost: STRUCT (toy_type: STRING, puzzle_code:
STRING, pieces: SMALLINT, puzzle_cost_USD: FLOAT)
```

[The array element is a data structure of four columns of data types STRING, STRING, SMALLINT and FLOAT, respectively.]

```
|- - toy_type: STRING (nullable = false)
|- - puzzle_code: STRING (nullable = false)
|- - pieces: SMALLINT (nullable = false)
|- - puzzle_cost_USD: FLOAT (nullable = false)
```

(ii Command to access the row having key puzzle_School in Python is:

```
toyPuzzleTypeCostTbl.map(toyPuzzleTypeCost: puzzle_School).
```

[The returned data type will be STRUCT.]

(iii) Python commands to create toyPuzzleTypeCostTbl RDD are:

```
toyPuzzleTypeCostRDD = sc.parallelize([Row (toy_type = "puzzle_
Garden", puzzle_code= "10725", pieces = 100, puzzle_cost_USD =
1.35)]
```

[Created row `toyPuzzleTypeCost` RDD with a tuple using parallelize method of Spark Context, *sc*]

```
toyPuzzleTypeCostSchemaRDD= HiveContext(sc).inferSchema
(toyPuzzleTypeCostRDD)
```

[Created row-schema, `toyPuzzleTypeCostSchemaRDD` using method, inferSchema of Hive Context inbuilt in Spark Context, *sc*]

```
toyPuzzleTypeCostSchemaRDD.registerTempTable ("toyPuzzleTypeCostTbl")
```

[Created RDD using registerTempTable method for the row object schema. Table toyPuzzleTypeCostTbl creates toyPuzzleTypeCostSchemaRDD.]

Numeric Operations on RDD Spark provides several descriptive statistics operations on RDDs containing numeric data. Table 5.6 provides description of numeric RDD operations available in Spark.

Table 5.6 Numeric RDD Operations

Method	Description
count()	Returns the number of elements in an RDD. Returns BIGINT of 8 bytes. For example, Command toyPuzzleTypeCostTbl.count() returns 12 in the table in Example 5.10.
sum()	Returns the sum of the elements
mean()	Returns the sum of the elements divided by the number of elements
min()	Returns the minimum value of the elements
max()	Returns the maximum value of the elements
stdev()	Returns the statistical parameter, standard deviation of the elements
sampleStdev()	Returns the statistical parameter, standard deviation of a sample of the elements
variance()	Returns the statistical parameter, variance of the elements
sampleVariance()	Returns the statistical parameter, variance of a sample of the elements

Shared Variables The variables in HDFS have multiple copies in the data nodes of a cluster. While mapping or reducing functions for execution on a cluster node, the operations take place on separate copies of all variables used in the function. These copies also updated, but the copies or changes do not pass on to the driver program. Usages of read and write instructions for the variables are inefficient.

Broadcast variables and accumulators enable the implementation of shared variables.

Broadcast Variables Spark also attempts to distribute broadcast variables using efficient broadcast algorithms to reduce communication cost. Broadcast variables are created from a value denoted by a variable *v* and running method `sc.broadcast` (*v*). The broadcast variable is a wrapper around *v*.

EXAMPLE 5.11

Recapitulate Example 5.8 (ii) of a toy company selling Jigsaws. The RDD has two lines after filter(). How will you use the intermediate results and execute action commands count() and first()?

SOLUTION

Recapitulate Example 5.10. Python code accesses the value of the broadcast variable as follows:

```
>>> broadcastVar = sc.broadcast([("puzzle_Garden", "10725", 100, 1.35)])
```

The result will be: <pyspark.broadcast.Broadcast object at 0x102789f10>. The value can be accessed by calling the value method as follows:

```
>>> broadcastVar.value
```

Result will be [("puzzle_Garden", "10725", 100, 1.35)]

Accumulators

Spark supports accumulators of numeric type. A programmer can provide additional support to other data types. Accumulators are special variables. They add the values using associative and commutative operations. They also support parallel run: for example, in `count()` or `sum()`.

An accumulator variable creates from an initial value *v*. Later the value accumulates into that using += operator. For example, in `count()` initial value is `0`. The command to create accumulating variable is `sc.accumulator(v)`.

EXAMPLE 5.12

Recapitulate Example 5.10. How does Python code access the value of the accumulator variable?

SOLUTION

Python code accumulates the value using variable *v* as follows:

```
>>> accumColumns = sc.broadcast(0)
>>> accumColumns
```

The result will be <Accumulator id = 0, value = 0>.
When following command executes:

```
>>> sc.parallelize([1.35,2.85,1.37]).foreach(x: accumColumns.add(x))
```

The result will be 5.57.

5.4.3 Machine Learning with MLib

Apache MLib is a component of Spark that is open source downloadable from Apache Spark website. Figure 5.8 shows the main usages of MLib (machine learning library).

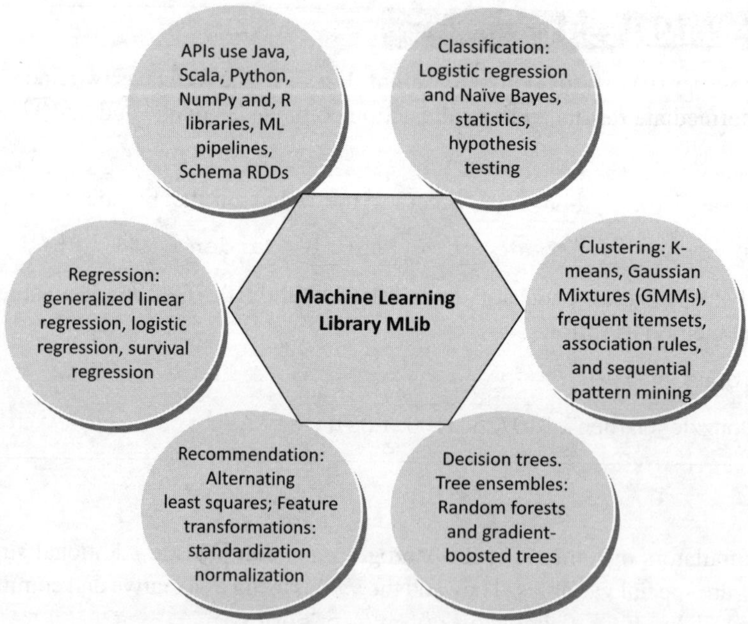

Figure 5.8 Main usages of MLib machine learning library

Spark Support ML pipelines. An ML pipeline means data taken from data sources, passes through the machine learning programs in between and the output becomes input to the application. Decision tree, knowledge discovery, clustering and mining are examples of ML pipeline application.

Spark 2.3 supports Python UDFs, VUDFs, block-level UDFs with block-level arguments and return types, complex object types (array map and structure), and conversions or transformations of object types. These features are widely used for the ML applications.

ML datasets are RDDs, thus use HDFS, HBase or local files. MLib APIs are interoperable with Spark SQL. MLib Python implementation adds Python APIs. MLib interoperates with NumPy in Python.

Chapter 6 will describe ML algorithms in detail.

Self-Assessment Exercise linked to LO 5.3

1. What are the steps for downloading a Spark version? ○○●
2. List the Spark supported file formats and their usages. ○●●
3. Write the use of transform commands in RDD programming, filter(), map(), mapValues(), flatMap(), sort(), pratitionBy(), groupByKey(), reduceByKey(), aggregateByKey(), pipe(), coalesce(), sample(), union(), join(), cogroup(), and crossProduct(). ●●●
4. How do broadcast variables and accumulators enable the implementation of shared variables? ○●●
5. Create, using inferSchema method of HiveContext inbuilt in Spark Context *sc*, row-schema `toyPuzzleTypeCostSchemaRDD`. ●●●
6. What does machine learning mean? What are the main usages of MLib? ○○●

5.5 DATA ETL (EXTRACT, TRANSFORM AND LOAD) PROCESS

LO 5.4

ETL processes using built-in functions and operators, and ETL pipelines

The ETL process combines the following three functions into one:

1. Extract which does the acquisition of data from Data Store querying or from another program,
2. Transform which does the change of data into a desired file, columnar, tabular or other. Transformation converts the previous form of the extracted data into a new form. Transformation occurs by using rules or lookup tables. Transformation uses the functions, namely join(), groupBy(), cogroup(), filter(), map(), mapValues(), flatMap(), sort(), pratitionBy(), groupByKey(), reduceByKey(), aggregateByKey(), pipe(), coalesce(), sample(), union(), crossProduct(). Spark 2.3 includes transformation functions on complex objects like arrays, maps and set of columns. Pandas provide powerful transformation UDFs, VUDFs and GVUDFs.
3. Load which does the process of placing transformed data into another Data Store or data warehouse for usage by an application or for analysis.

Python, Spark SQL and HiveQL support ETL programming and extracting by query-processing and text processing.

5.5.1 Composing Spark Program Steps for ETL

Spark 2.3 ETL Pipeline Apache Spark 2.3+ includes usage of UDFs, VUDFs and Data Source API v2. These facilitate the creation of ETL pipelines easily. Figure 5.9 shows an ETL pipeline using Spark SQL for ETL Process and Data Source API v2 in Spark 2.3.

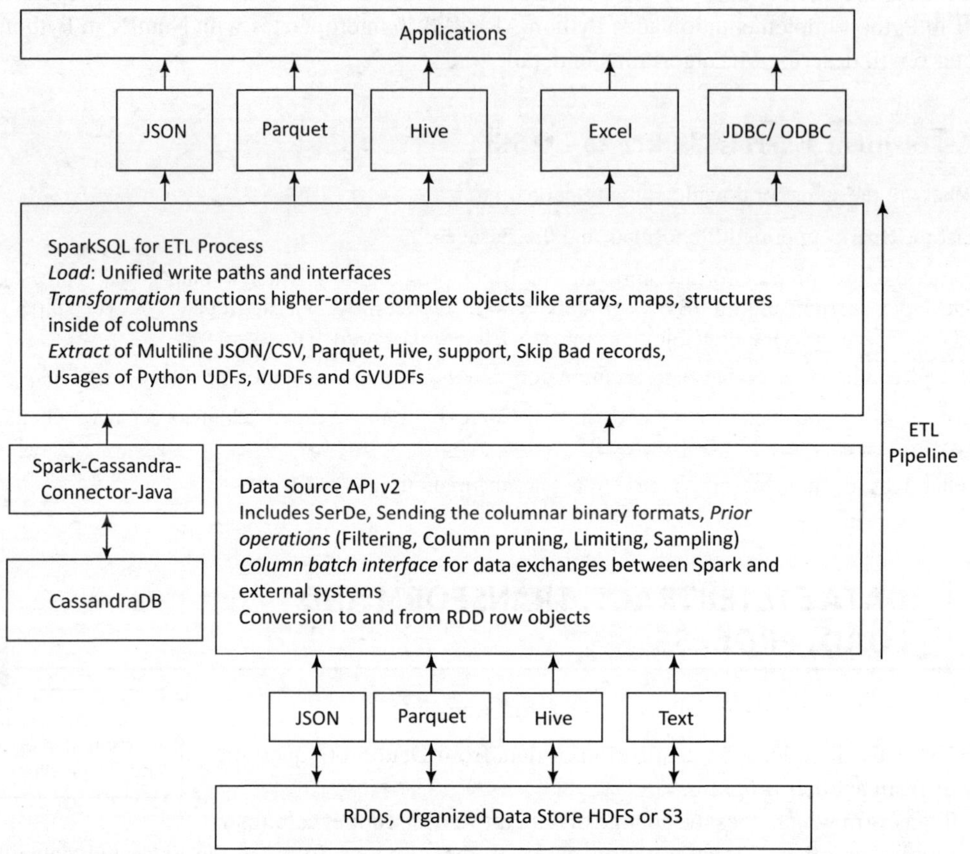

Figure 5.9 ETL pipeline using Spark SQL

Extract

Skipping Corrupt or Bad Records or Files A record can sometimes be bad. For example, "toyPuzzle_ Type", toyPuzzle_Airplane. Here the data type in schema is string, but quotes are missing in toyPuzzle_Airplane. Use the following command to ignore bad records or file: `spark.sql.files.ignoreCorruptFiles = true`.

Spark supports parser for text file formats in JSON and CSV with three modes: PERMISSIVE, DROPMALFORMED OR FAILFAST. Reading data requires a parser in a SELECT for querying or load for extraction process.

Extract and Load: Multi-line JSON/CSV Support *Load and Save files:* SerDe uses codes for obtaining records from unstructured data. Save process uses serializer codes and Loading (extracting) process uses deserializer.

The following example explains the codes for sequence File, JSON and CSV file load and save functions for obtaining records/rows/files.

EXAMPLE 5.13

Using Python,

(i) How does a sequence file load?
(ii) How does a text file 'jigsaw_puzzle_info.txt' load? (Example 4.10)
(iii) How does a file productCodesCosts save as a TextFile in Python?
(iv) How does a JSON studentSemGrades file load?
(v) Assume record field names are "StuName, "rollNum", "enrollNum", "SemID", "courseID", "subjectID", "subjectType", "SemSubjGrade" in a CSV file line. How does StuSemRecord(line) load from a JSON file 'studentSemGrades'?
(vi) How does StuSemRecord(line) save as CSV format file?

SOLUTION

(i) Load a sequence file using the following statement:

```
val data= sc.sequenceFile(inFile "org.apache.hadoop.io.Text", "org.
apache.hadoop.io.IntWritable")
```

(ii) Load a text file jigsaw_puzzle_info.txt using the following statement:

```
hiveCtx.textFile
(file:///home/PySpark/hive/'jigsaw_puzzle_info.txt')
```

(iii) Save the text file productCodesCosts using the following statement:

```
productCodesCosts.saveAsTextFile(outputFile)
```

(iv) Load an unstructured JSON file `studentSemGrades` using the following statement:

```
import json
studentGradesData = input.map (hiveCtx: json.loads(studentSemGrades))
```

(v) Load `StuSemRecord(line)` from a CSV file `'studentSemGrades'` using the following statement:

```
import stringIO
import csv
..
..
def StuSemRecord(line): """Parse a CSV line"""
reader = csv.DictReader (input, fieldNames = ["StuName, "rollNum",
"enrollNum", "SemID", "courseID", "subjectID", "subjectType",
"SemSubjGrade"])
return reader.next()
```

```
input = hiveCtx.textFile(inputFile).map(StuSemRecord)
```

(vi) Save `StuSemRecord(line)` from a CSV file `'studentSemGrades' using following statement:`

```
def writeStuSemRecords(records) """Write a CSV line"""
output =scv.DictWriter(output, fieldNames = ["StuName, "rollNum",
"enrollNum", "SemID", "courseID", "subjectID", "subjectType",
"SemSubjGrade"])
for record in records
writer.writerow(record)
return [output.getvalue()]
hiveCtx.mapPartitions(writeStuSemRecords).saveAsTextFile
(outputFile)
```

Transformation The following example explains Spark SQL transformations in Spark 2.3. The example shows complex objects, nested tables (one column rows) and array transformations and uses the DataframeWriter API.

EXAMPLE 5.14

Use Spark 2.13 SQL APIs and DataframeWriter API.

(i) How does a table-column schema create for a nested table (single Column table) tbl_puzzleCost? (Example 5.1) Text file is 'jigsaw_puzzle_info.txt'. (Example 4.10)

(ii) How does the value filter using a row from table 'tbl_puzzleCost' for a puzzle costing above USD 1.00? (Example 5.1)

(iii) How does yearlySales compute from table for Jaguar Land Rover Yearly sales, JLRDS (Example 5.2) from CarShowroomsCummulativeYearlySales table?

(iv) CREATE Hive-SerDe table. Create a table similar to one in Example 5.1. Use DataframeWriter API.

(iv) CREATE Hive-SerDe table. Create a table similar to one in Example 5.1. Use Hive.

SOLUTION

(i) Table schema for a nested table (single Column table) `tbl_puzzleCost` creates:

```
FROM tbl_puzzleCost;
tbl_nested
|-- key: string (nullable = false)
|-- values: array (nullable = false)
|-- element: float (containsNull = false)
```

(ii) The following Spark SQL statement filters an array or row or nested table, tbl_puzzleCost:

```
SELECT FILTER(values, v4 -> v4 > 1.00) AS v4
FROM tbl_puzzleCost;
```

(iii) The following Spark SQL aggregation function for the sum of an array or row or nested table elements, `JLRDS in CarShowroomsCummulativeYearlySales row tbl_JLDR`:

```
SELECT REDUCE (values, (value, JLRDS) -> value + JLRDS) AS
yearlyJLRSales FROM tbl_JLRDS;
```

(iv) The following statements create a Hive-SerDe table using the DataframeWriter:

```
CREATE Hive-serde tables
df.write.format("hive")
.option("fileFormat", "avro")
saveAsTable("tbl_puzzleTypeCodeCosts")
CREATE TABLE tbl_puzzleTypeCodeCosts (puzzleType STRING, puzzleCode
STRING, puzzlePieces SMALLINT, puzzleCost FLOAT)
STORED AS ORC
```

(v) The following statements create a table using Hive:

```
CREATE TABLE tbl_puzzleTypeCodeCosts (puzzleType STRING, puzzleCode
STRING, puzzlePieces SMALLINT, puzzleCost FLOAT)
USING hive
OPTIONS (fileFormat 'ORC')
```

Self-Assessment Exercise linked to LO 5.4

1. What are the three ETL functions in Data Store? ○○●
2. How do line records *extract* from a multiline JSON file? ○●●
3. How do values filter from a column 'puzzleCost' for puzzle costing below USD 1.00? ○●●
4. What are the program steps for creating a Hive-SerDe table using the DataframeWriter? ●●●

5.6 INTRODUCTION TO ANALYTICS, REPORTING AND VISUALIZING

LO 5.5

Analytics, data/information reporting and visualizing methods

"Analytics is the process of discovering, interpreting, and communicating significant patterns in data. Simply put, analytics helps us see insights and meaningful data that we might not otherwise detect."
(*Oracle.com*)

Analytics needs interpretation, reporting of meaningful patterns and gaining insight into new knowledge. Visualization is an effective method for examining the interpretations of reports. The subsections ahead introduce analytics, reporting and visualization methods.

5.6.1 Introduction to Analytics

Some examples of open source tools for analytics are Python, R, Apache Spark, Apache Storm, Pig and Hive. Examples of commercial tools are SAS, Tableau, Excel, QlikView and Splunk. Figure 5.10 shows a framework for applications and analytics using Spark.

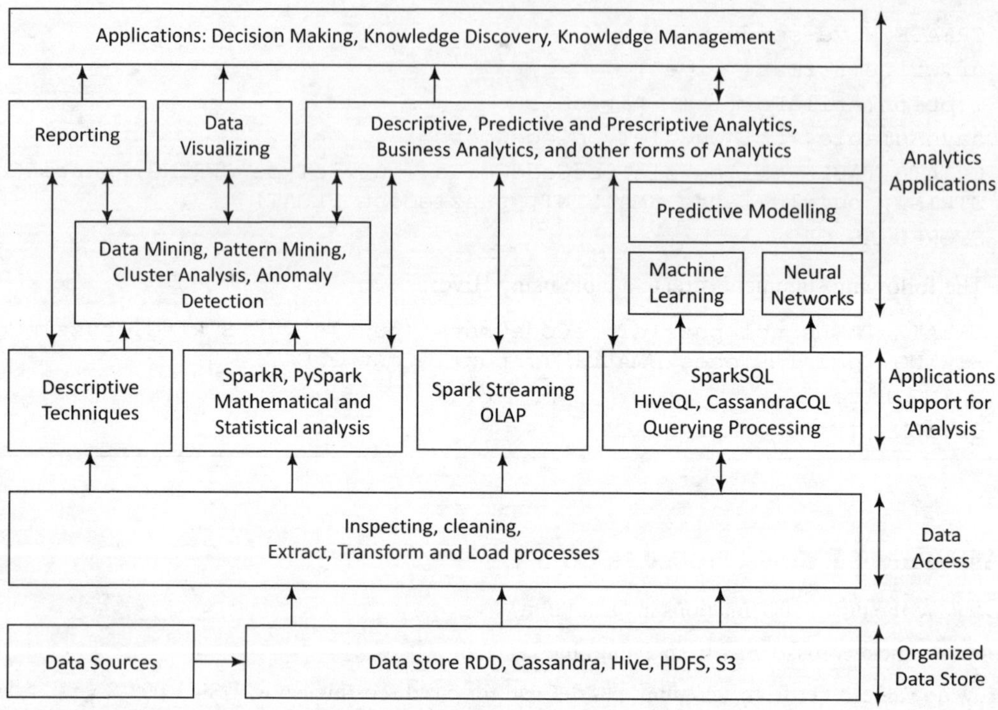

Figure 5.10 Processing framework for applications and Big Data analytics using Spark

Spark Stack provides support to applications for analysis of huge data from multiple sources and Data Stores. Analytics also use machine learning and neural networks, which enable predictive modeling and decisions. Analytics use data mining, pattern mining, cluster analysis and detect anomalies.

Applications use the results derived from the descriptive, predictive and prescriptive analytics, business analytics and other forms of analytics. The applications also use the results derived from reporting and visualizations. Common applications are decision making about further actions required, knowledge discovery and knowledge management.

The example below explains the usages of analytics in different domains.

EXAMPLE 5.15

(i) How does analytics help a manufacturing company for toys and puzzles?

(ii) How does analytics helps a company for chocolates, which sells its products through ACVMs?

(iii) How does analytics help a manufacturing, sales and service company for cars of different models?

SOLUTION

(i) An analysis of sales figures for toys and puzzles, lets the toy company understand the preferences of children in different age groups, regions and income groups. The knowledge of preferences enables appropriate manufacturing, supply, sales, quality enhancement and promotion activities. The predictive analytics enable the company to take steps from the forecast about future growth, estimate the direction for future innovations in children toys and puzzles, and plan for the desired products mix in future.

The company organizes quizzes in schools of science, mathematics, geography and other subjects and awards brilliant students, as a part of promotional activity. The company also analyses the impact on sales after this activity.

(ii) Analysis of sales figures and machine-users data by the company for chocolates being sold through ACVMs lets the company understand the following: (a) users and their needs, (b) chocolate preferences for specific flavours among children and youth in different regions in the country, different areas of cities, age groups, and sales in specific periods in a year. Detailed analysis enables the appropriate manufacturing, supply-chain, sales, innovations and promotional activities.

The predictive analytics enable the company to know the predictions about growth in profits, sales, identify future installation-areas for ACVMs, design relocation strategy and understand directions of future innovations and promotional strategy, needs, and desired product-mix of the company. The company also analyzes the impact of rewarding chocolate buyers on birthdays, marriage anniversaries and festival periods. Company plans incentives for frequent buyers. The company also organizes quizzes in schools and colleges. Company rewards brilliant school students as a part of promotional strategy.

(ii) Analysis of sale figures, customer, and service center feedbacks by the company for cars in different models, lets the company understand the followings: (a) users preferences for the different models and colour shades, (b) car model's sales in different regions in the country, age groups, and sales in specific periods in a year. Detailed analysis enables the appropriate product mix, manufacturing, supply-chain management, competition, advertisement strategy, innovations in design and shades, and facilitates promotional activities.

Predictive analytics enables company to know the predictions about growth in profits, sales and competition; identify car showrooms future expansion in different regions, and understand the direction for future innovations, such as use of IoT for studies on functioning of car components and IoT based maintenance services. The company can plan future expansion in plant machinery and ideal future product-mix strategy of the company. The company can also analyze the impact of incentives to showrooms for higher sales growth, festive-period incentives to buyers, and organizing the cultural events in order to design appropriate promotional activities.

5.6.2 Data/Information Reporting

Reports are essential after any analysis. Some important reasons for generating reports are:

1. Provide cross-databases and the data sheets [Cross-database created by application/system software so as to enable access to different database formats.]
2. Enable accesses to multi-business system data

3. Provide multi-data source correlations
4. Present related businesses data integrated in a Data Store
5. Enable more data applications for business control and operations analysis.

Data Organization Guidelines for Reports Some guidelines for organizing data in reports are:

1. Must have abstract, context introduction and conclusion sections
2. Divide the contents in sections or split it into multiple sheets with one context in one sheet
3. Place similar items under the same heading or in the same column in case of spreadsheets
4. Insert figures, charts or graphical plots to enhance the readability of the report
5. Position critical data appropriately
6. Avoid blank text areas or rows and columns in case of sheets.

Data Format Guidelines Some guidelines for formatting data in reports are:

1. Use section and subsection headings or column labels to identify contents
2. Use appropriate font, alignment, format, pattern, border or capitalization style
3. Use text borders or cell borders to distinguish data
4. Maintain same formats for paragraphs, section headings, subsection headings and captions of table and figures.

Report Designer A report designer has three components: (i) report, (ii) Data Tools Platform/Web Tools Platform (DTP/WTP), and (iii) chart designers. Users can add a custom designer at their end. The designer outputs to process at a design engine, which communicates the outputs in XML format to the Report Engine. Figure 5.11 shows the features of the components of a report designer.

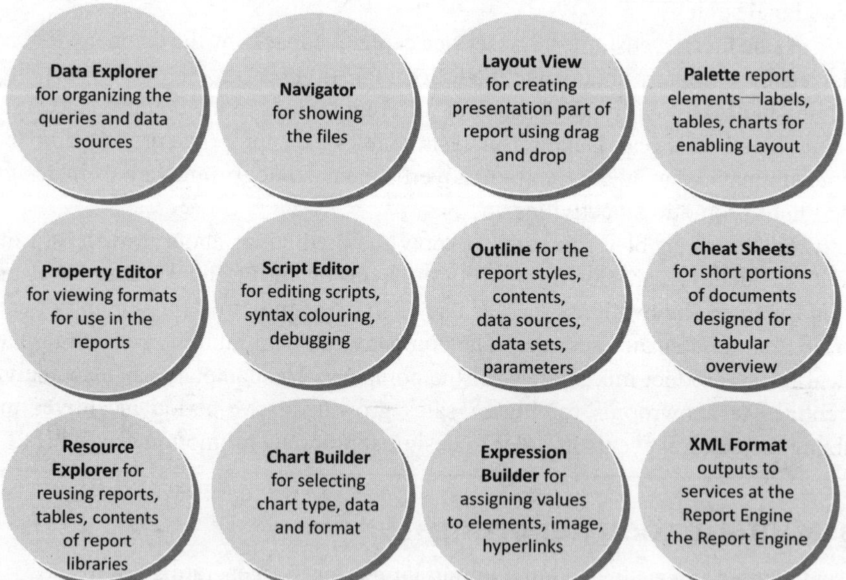

Figure 5.11 Features of the components of report designer

Open Source Eclipse Business Intelligence and Reporting Tool (BIRT)

BIRT is an open source software project created by the Eclipse Foundation. It's latest version is 4.8.0 was released in June 2018. BIRT includes Eclipse Report Designer (ERD), Eclipse Report Engine (ERE) and Eclipse Charting Engine (ECE). BIRT creates reports and enables data visualization of the reports. Reports can be embedded into rich Java, Java EE client and web applications.

Figure 5.12 shows the architecture of BIRT.

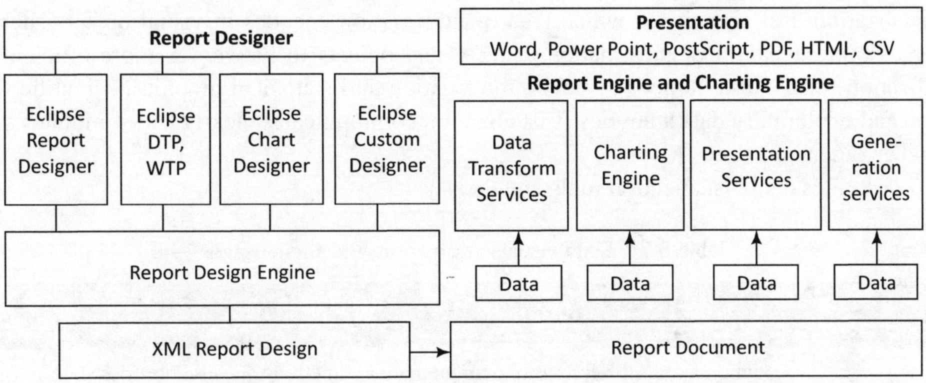

Figure 5.12 BIRT architecture design and report engine components

Data explorer creates views of multi-dimensional cubes from the datasets provided. Cubes enable building of dynamic cross-tables. A dimension in the view can be used to design report parameters.

Report Engine The figure shows that report document and data process occurs at four service plug-ins – data transformation, charting, presentation and generation services.

Transformation service plug-in presents the data after sorting, summarizing, filtering and grouping. The transformations are performed as per the needs of user. A program function performs the transformation in the ETL process, but BIRT does that for simple data sources, such as Java objects or flat files. BIRT does provision for complex operations, such as grouping on sums, percentages of overall totals.

Charting services at the engine generate the charts. The Charting Engine is used to design and generate the charts. A chart can be separate or embedded within the generated reports, such as BIRT reports. Charting engine API (CE API) in Java/Java EE adds charting capabilities to their applications. The design and report engines make use of CE API for generating the charts.

BIRT 'viewer' enables preview reports at an Apache Tomcat server included in the BIRT. The server fulfills the client request for preview. The outputs are web output as a single HTML document, paginated HTML, PDF, XLS, DOC, PPT, and Postscript. Additionally, the viewer has functionality for exporting the data to CSV, printing and Table of Contents.

5.6.3 Data Visualization

Data visualization is a technique that entails the creation and study of the visual representation of data, meaning "information that has been abstracted in some schematic form, including attributes or variables for the units of information". A primary goal of data visualization is to communicate information clearly and efficiently via statistical graphics, plots and information graphics. Data visualization tools have shifted the interpretation of data from dashboard displays to quick digestion of real-time analysis and custom analysis. (*Wikipedia*)

Data Display can be accessed via PC dashboards or mobile terminals and interpreted thereafter. Display improves the reading of reports. Reports include the functions for display of the analysis of a wide variety of charts, multi-dimensional analysis, real-time analytics, and slicing and dicing views of reports. Data visualization tools have completely changed the concept dashboard displays for interpretations.

Data visualization uses techniques which data or information encodes in visual objects such as points, lines or bars. Communication of information using visual objects to viewers is more efficient and clear. Data visualization relates to a number of fields: information and statistical graphics, scientific information visualization and exploratory data analytics. Visualization communicates clearly and stimulates the viewer's attention and engagement.

Table 5.7 describes data visualization tools and their usages.

Table 5.7 Data visualization tools and their usages

Data Visualization Tool	Description
matplotlib	Python matplotlib for plotting mathematical functions. Several libraries such as vispy, bokeh, seaborn, pygal, folium build up on matplotlib for data visualization.
Chart.js	A tiny widely used open source library that supports just six chart types: line, bar, radar, polar, pie and doughnut. Employs HTML5 canvas element for rendering charts. Not used when the application is big and complex.
Google Charts	Shows charts in HTML5/SVG and many charts including interactive charts and most commonly used chart types like bar, area, pie and gauges.
Tableau	Public version is open source. Tableau is an easy-to-learn popular data visualizing tool. Tableau communicates insights through data visualization. The charts easily embed in any web page. Supports a wide variety of charts, graphs, maps and other graphics. Tableau's visuals enable quick investigation of a hypothesis. Commercial version includes additional facilities for handling over a million rows.
D3.js	D3 (Data Driven Documents) is free and open source, deploys HTML, CSS and SVG, and shows the amazing charts and diagrams. It has rich features and is quite interactive.
FusionCharts	Includes over 90+ chart types, 965 maps, collection of business dashboards and live demos. The charts and maps are highly customizable and have attractive interactions. The tool supports to (i) JSON and XML data formats and (ii) export the charts in PNG, JPEG, SVG or PDF formats. FusionCharts is a commercial tool.
QlikView	Is a fast processing tool with usages for the intuitive GUIs, interactive plotting of data, slicing and dicing features in data visualizing, and creating highly useful visualizations and dashboards.
Splunk	Is a machine log analytic tool. It includes powerful visualization features and easy to use tool due to its web interface. Features are events list, table visualization, charts, gauges, maps, Trellis layout for visualizations, dashboard creation with XML and Drilldown and dashboard interactivity.

Self-Assessment Exercise linked to LO 5.5

1. What do the terms analytics and analysis mean? ○○●
2. List the functions of Report Designer. ○●●
3. List the services of the Report Engine. ○●●
4. Explain events list, table visualization, charts, gauges, maps, and Trellis layout for visualization. ●●●

KEY CONCEPTS

accumulator
ad hoc query
aggregation
analytics
BIRT
broadcast
Ceph
data visualization
DataFrame
data pipeline
data source
dicing
drill down analysis
ETL
ETL pipeline
GraphX
GroupBy
grouped VUDF
HDFS
HiveContext
Hive Server
immutability
JDBC
matplotlib
Mesos
metadata
metastore
MLib
ML pipeline
nested table
NumPy
ODBC
Outliers
Pandas
Parquet
PySpark
Python
query processing
RDD
RDD programming
Report Designer
Report Engine
S3
SchemaRDD
SciPy
SequenceFile
SerDe
slicing
Spark
SparkContext
Spark SQL
Spark Streaming
Tableau
transform
UDF
Vectorized UDF
Viewer

Learning Outcomes

LO 5.1

1. Apache® Spark™ is a *fast and general compute engine*. Apache® Spark™ powers analytics applications up to 100 times faster.
2. It supports HDFS compatible data. Spark has a simple and expressive programming model.

3. Spark standard API enables creation of the application APIs using Scala, Java, Python and R. Spark consists of software stack with Spark SQL, Spark Streaming, Spark Arrow, SparkR, MLib and GraphX components.

LO 5.2

1. Spark SQL is a Spark module for structured data; SQL runs the queries on Spark data in traditional business analytics and visualization applications. Spark SQL enables Spark datasets to use JDBC API or ODBC API.
2. DataFrames can be created from different data sources. Examples of data sources are JSON datasets, Hive tables, Parquet row groups, structured data files, external Data Stores and RDDs.
3. Spark and Python provide powerful Big Data analysis tools. Python provisions Python NumPy, SciPy, Pandas consists of advanced functions for analytics, and provides an Integrated Development Environment (IDE).
4. Python Pandas library functions provide database style DataFrames, Merge, join, and concatenation of objects, RPy interface for R functions plus additional functions, SQL like features: SELECT, WHERE, GROUPBY, JOIN, UNION, UPDATE and DELETE, size mutability which means columns can be inserted and deleted from DataFrame and higher dimensional objects. Pandas GroupBy feature of split-apply-combine enables group vectorized UDFs.

LO 5.3

1. Spark 2.3.1. Spark runs on Windows and UNIX-like systems, Linux, Mac OS. Spark runs on Java 8+, Python 2.7+/3.4+ and R 3.1+. Spark 2.3.1 uses Scala 2.11 API when using compatible Scala version 2.11.x.
2. Spark Resilient Distributed Dataset (RDD) is a collection of objects distributed on many computing nodes. Each RDD can split into multiple partitions, which may be computed in parallel on different nodes of the cluster.
3. Spark RDD is immutable (not capable of or not susceptible to change). A new RDD creates on *transform* and *action* commands.
4. Spark supports Python UDFs, VUDFs, block-level UDFs with block-level arguments and return types, complex object types, array map and structure conversions or transformations.
5. Spark MLib supports ML pipelines. MLib is widely used for the ML applications.

LO 5.4

1. Data ETL has three Data Store functions – Extract, Transform and Load. Applications using Spark 2.3 with Spark Arrow use the ETL data pipeline between data sources and applications.
2. *Extract* does the acquiring of data from a Data Store (by querying or another program). Transform does the change of data into a desired format. *Transform* uses join(), groupBy(), cogroup(), filter(), map(), mapValues(), flatMap(), sort(), pratitionBy(), groupByKey(), reduceByKey(), aggregateByKey(), pipe(), coalesce(), sample(), union(), crossProduct().
3. Load saves the transformed data into another Data Store for usage by an application or for analysis.

LO 5.5

1. Analytics is the discovery, interpretation and communication of meaningful patterns in data. Spark Stack provides support to applications for analysis of data from multiple sources and Data Stores. Analytics use

machine learning and neural networks, which enable predictive modeling and decisions based on the data. Analytics use data mining, pattern mining, clusters analysis and detect anomalies.

2. Reporting of results of analysis using appropriate tools is an essential step. Eclipse Foundation created BIRT. BIRT includes Eclipse Report Designer (ERD), Eclipse Report Engine (ERE) and Eclipse Charting Engine (ECE).
3. Data visualization is a technique that entails the creation and study of data using visual representations such as charts, plots and graphics. Examples of data visualization tools are matplotlib, Chart.js, Google charts, Tableau, D3.js, FusionCharts, QlikView and Splunk.

Objective Type Questions

Select one correct-answer option for each questions below:

5.1 Spark uses for data storage (i) HDFS file system, (ii) Hadoop compatible data source, such as HDFS, (iii) HBase, Cassandra and Ceph, and (iv) Amazon S3. Spark standard API enables creation of the application APIs in (v) Scala, (vi) Java, (vii) Python, (viii) Pandas. Spark resources management can be at (ix) stand-alone server, and (x) at a distributed computing framework, such as YARN and Mesos. ○●●

(a) all except iv, v and ix (b) all
(c) all except viii, ix and x (d) all except iii, viii and ix

5.2 Spark Stack includes (i) Spark SQL, (ii) Spark Streaming, (iii) Spark Arrow, (iv) SparkR, (v) MLib, (vi) GraphX, (vii) SparkContext, (viii) HiveContext and Pig, (ix) Cassandra, and (x) PySpark. ○○●

(a) all except viii and ix (b) all except iii and v
(c) all except viii and ix (d) ii, iii, vii, viii

5.3 Steps between acquisition of data from different sources, and applications of analyzed data, and applications support by Spark for the analyses are as follows: (i) Storage of data from the multiple sources after acquisition, (ii) Partitioning of tables, (iii) Data pre-processing, (iv) filtering unreliable, irrelevant and redundant information, (v) Extract, transform and load (ETL) for analysis using Python or Scala, (v) Mathematical and statistical analysis of the data obtained after querying relevant data needing in the analysis, and (vi) applications of analyzed data; for example, descriptive, predictive and prescriptive analytics. ○●●

(a) all except ii and iii (b) all except v and vi
(c) all except i and iv (d) all except ii

5.4 A Parquet file consists of (i) row groups and (ii) column groups. (iii) Each row can have number of columns, but each column has only one column chunk. (iv) A page is a conceptualized unit in a column chunk. (v) Only one page can store in a chunk. (vi) ORC array has two columns, one for array size and other for array dimensions. (vii) Parquet format file consists of an extra column per nesting level. ●●●

(a) all (b) i to v
(c) i, iii, iv (d) all except vi and vii

5.5 When using HiveQL and Spark SQL, the aggregation functions can be used for (i) analysis and (ii) filtering. Hive aggregation functions consist of (iii) count(*) and count(expr); (iv) sum(col), (v) sum (DISTINCT col), (vi) Avg (col), (vii) avg (DISTINCT col), (viii) GroupBy, with (vii) DataFrames as input. ○○●

(a) i, ii, iii, iv and vi (b) i to v
(c) all except ii and viii (d) all except v and vii

5.6 NumPy provides (i) one-dimensional efficient containers of generic data, (ii) definitions of non-arbitrary data-types, (iii) easy integration with a wide variety of Data Stores, (iv) import, export (load/save) files, (iv) creation of arrays, (v) inspection of properties, copying, sorting, and reshaping, (vi) addition and removal of elements in the arrays, indexing, sub-setting and slicing of the arrays, (vii) scalar and vector mathematics (such as +, −, ×, ÷, power, sqr, sin, log), (viii) recoil (round up to nearest int), and (ix) base (round down up to the nearest int), round (round to nearest integer). ○●●

(a) iii to vii (b) ii to v
(c) ii to viii (d) All except ix

5.7 Spark supports following file formats: (i) text files (ii) CSV, (iii) TSV, (iv) JSON, (v) doc file, (vi) XML, (vi) sequenceFiles (vii) ObjectFiles, and (viii) protocol buffers. ○○●

(a) all except v (b) all except iii and viii
(c) ii to iv and vi to vii (d) i, ii, iv, vi

5.8 An RDD (i) is a fault-tolerant abstraction, (ii) enables in-memory cluster computations, (iii) is mutable, (iv) partitioned distributed collection of objects, (v) enables efficient execution of non-interactive data mining, and (vi) RDDs create only through operations which are deterministic. ○●●

(a) all except ii to iv (b) all except i, iii
(c) all except vi (d) all except iii and v

5.9 Transform command examples are (i) filter(), (ii) reduce(), (iii) collect(), (iv) map(), (v) mapValues(), (vi) flatMap(), (vii) sort(), (viii) pratitionBy(), (ix) groupByKey(), (x) reduceByKey(), (xi) sample(), (xii) union(), (xiii) join(), (xiv) cogroup(), (xv) crossProduct(). Action command examples are (xvi) aggregateByKey(), (xvii) pipe(), (xviii) coalesce(), (xix) count(), and (xx) first(). ●●●

(a) all except ii, iii, xi, xvii i (b) all ii, iii, xvi, xvii and xviii
(c) all except iii and xiv (d) all xvi to xviii

5.10 DataFrames represent (i) ML datasets, thus uses HDFS, (ii) ML datasets, thus uses HBase or local files. (iii) MLib APIs are interoperable with Spark SQL. (iv) MLib Python implementation adds Python APIs. (v) MLib does not interoperate with NumPy in Python. ○○●

(a) i to iii (b) all except v
(c) all except ii (d) all

5.11 SerDe uses codes for obtaining the records from (i) structured data. (ii) A data saving process uses deserializer codes and (iii) Loading (extracting) process uses serializer. Apache Spark 2.3+ provisions for (iv) UDFs, (v) VUDFs and (vi) Data Source API v1. (vii) ETL pipeline refers to data collected from (viii) in-between processing using a chain of function calls. ○○●

(a) all except v and vi (b) all except i
(c) all except ii, iii and iv (d) iv, v, vii and viii

5.12 Spark Stack provides the (i) support to applications for the analysis of data, (ii) unstructured multiple sources, (iii) Data Stores. The (iv) analytics use machine learning algorithms, (v) neural networks, (vi) descriptive modeling, and (vii) enables decisions. Analytics use the algorithms for (viii) data mining, (ix) pattern mining (x) clustering, and (xi) anomaly detection. ●●●

(a) all except ii, v and vi (b) all except v and ix
(c) all except ii and vi (d) all except vi and xi

5.13 Process for preparing a report document and data consists of service plug-ins for (i) data transformation, (ii) charting, (iii) summarizing (iii) presentation, and (iv) generation services. Transform services plug-in presents the data after (v) sorting, (vi) filtering, and (vii) grouping. ○●●

(a) all except ii, v and vi (b) all except iii
(c) all except vii (d) all except vi and vii

5.14 Data visualizing tool Tableau is (i) open source completely, (ii) easy-to-learn data visualizing tool, (iii) communicates predictions through data visualization. (iv) The charts can be easily embed in any web page. (v) Supports a wide variety of charts and graphs, but not maps. (vi) Tableau's visuals enables quick investigation of a hypothesis. ○○●

(a) ii, iv and vi (b) all except iii
(c) all except i (d) all except iii and vi

Review Questions

5.1 What are the features present in the Spark architecture that enable fast computations and usages of expressive programming model? **(LO 5.1)** ●●●

5.2 Describe the functions of Spark SQL, Spark Streaming and GraphX? **(LO 5.1)** ○○●

5.3 How do Spark and Python provide a powerful Big Data analysis tool? **(LO 5.2)** ○●●

5.4 How does Parquet file usage differ from the usages of RCFile and ORCFile? **(LO 5.2)** ○●●

5.5 How does DataFrame create from JSON datasets and Hive tables? **(LO 5.2)** ●●●

5.6 What are the aggregation commands provisioned in Spark SQL? **(LO 5.2)** ○○●

5.7 How do NumPy, SciPy and Pandas Python libraries provision for advanced functions for analytics, and create an integrated development environment (IDE)? **(LO 5.2)** ○●●

5.8 How does the Spark version download, install, and start the use of SparkContext? **(LO 5.3)** ○○●

5.9 How does the Spark Resilient Distributed Dataset (RDD) programming collect the objects? **(LO 5.3)** ○○●

5.10 Explain method of creation of RDDs using the *transform* and *action* commands. **(LO 5.3)** ○○●

5.11 Describe the machine learning algorithms available in Spark MLib. **(LO 5.3)** ○○●

5.12 How does the Spark 2.3 with Spark Arrow enable the creation of the ETL data pipeline between data sources and applications? **(LO 5.4)** ○●●

5.13 How does a tool help in reporting of results of analysis? **(LO 5.5)** ○○●

5.14 What are the actions performed by the Eclipse Report Designer (ERD), Eclipse Report Engine (ERE) and Eclipse Charting Engine (ECE). **(LO 5.5)** ○●●

5.15 Define data visualization, statistical graphics, plots and information graphics. **(LO 5.5)** ○○●

5.16 How do the following visualization tools matplotlib, Chart.js, Google charts, Tableau, D3.js, FusionCharts, QlikView and Splunk differ? **(LO 5.5)** ●●●

Practice Exercises

5.1 List Spark stack components and give examples of their applications. **(LO 5.1)** ○○●

5.2 A company manufactures and sells cars through a large number of showrooms. Each car showroom keeps their records in a main table and transaction tables. Recapitulate table in Practice Exercise 3.3. Describe the steps for analyzing the sales from HDFS compatible files. **(LO 5.2)** ○●●

5.3 How does the Parquet file structure look like for a large number of student semester grade sheets? A semester grade sheet consists of University Name, Department Name, Student name, enrollment number, class, roll number, program of study, batch (for example 2017-2010), semester, subjects type (theory/practical/project/on-line), subject names, credit, credits awarded, semester grade point average (SGPA), cumulative grade point average (CGPA), and general performance analysis. **(LO 5.2)** ●●●

5.4 List the steps for downloading Spark and Python libraries for analytics and for creating Hive and PySpark contexts. **(LO 5.3)** ○○●

5.5 Compose the SchemaRDD for a table. The table, named toys_tbl is as follows: (Product categories, ProductId and Product name are three columns) **(LO 5.3)** ○●●

Table of Product Categories, ProductId and Product Name

ProductCategory	ProductId	ProductName
Toy_Airplane	10725	Lost Temple
Toy_Airplane	31047	Propeller Plane
Toy_Airplane	31049	Twin Spin Helicopter
Toy_Train	31054	Blue Express
Toy_Train	10254	Winter Holiday Toy_Train

5.6 Compose the SchemaRDD for grade sheets specified in Practice Exercise 5.3. **(LO 5.3)** ○●●

5.7 Write the RDD program steps for calculating SGPA and CGPA of a student program of study from file created in Practice Exercise 5.3. **(LO 5.3)** ○●●

5.8 Write the program steps for creating an ETL pipeline for monthly and yearly sales analysis from a table. The table consists of data of toys_company manufacturing 1600 different toys and 2000 puzzle product categories, up to 20 product types for each puzzle product of product types 100, 200, 400, 800, 1600, 2400 and 500 pieces. **(LO 5.4)** ●●●

5.9 List the steps for reporting using the BIRT tool on analysis of sales of the toy company in above Practice Exercise 5.7. **(LO 5.5)** ○○●

5.10 List the steps for viewing charts for analysis of sales of the toy company in above Practice Exercise 5.7. **(LO 5.5)** ○●●

Chapter 6

Machine Learning Algorithms for Big Data Analytics

LEARNING OBJECTIVES

After studying this chapter, you will be able to:

LO 6.1 Understand metric, feature and category variables, evaluate and estimate the relationships, outliers, variances, probability distribution, and the correlations between the variables in variables, items or entities

LO 6.2 Apply regression analysis using linear, non-linear and multiple regression models, K-Nearest Neighbours (KNN) distance measures, and predict the expected results

LO 6.3 Discover similar items and the similarities using distance measures

LO 6.4 Apply methods for Frequent-Itemsets Mining (FIM), market-basket model, association-rules mining, Apriori algorithm, and method of evaluation of Candidate Rules. Get knowledge of FIM and association rule applications and find the associations and similarities

LO 6.5 Apply methods of unsupervised machine-learning for clustering a collection, K-means, determine the number of clusters, and perform cluster diagnostics

LO 6.6 Apply methods of supervised machine-learning for classification; K-Nearest Neighbour (KNN) classifier, decision trees and Random-Forest, AdaBoost and other ensemble, Naïve Bayes classifiers, Artificial Neural Networks and SVM-based classifiers

LO 6.7 Design a recommender system using approaches of Collaborative Filtering (CF), Contents-based Filtering (CBF), Knowledge-based Filtering (KBF) and hybrid approaches for making recommendations

LO 6.8 Get knowledge of Apache Mahout Architecture, the ML algorithms for clustering, classification, collaborative filtering, and design recommender in Big Data environment

RECALL FROM EARLIER CHAPTERS

The most popular open-source analytics-tools are Apache Spark, Python, R, Apache Pig, and Hive, according to a study (Section 5.1). Spark with multiple languages, Python and Scala shells provide *great ease in programming for complex analytics, machine learning* and other solutions (Section 5.2).

Big Data analysis requires scalable distributed computations. Spark scalable MLib (machine-learning library) consists of the widely used ML algorithms and utility functions for large datasets. MLib includes the algorithms for optimization-primitives, regression, collaborative filtering, dimensionality reduction, cluster analysis, classification and recommender.

Uses of Machine Learning (ML) and Artificial Neural Networks (ANN) are in analytics, predictive modeling and decisions. The analytics methods include data mining, pattern mining, clusters analysis and detection of anomalies.

Apache Mahout consists of ML algorithms for Big Data analysis (Section 2.2.3 Figure 2.2).

This Chapter focusses on the ML methods of regression analysis based predictions, finding similarities, FIM, clustering, classifiers, recommenders, and introduces Mahout Architecture and features for the ML applications in Big Data analytics.

6.1 INTRODUCTION

Analytics uses the mathematical equations, formulae and models. Analytics also uses the statistics, AI, ML and DL, and predict the behaviour of entities, objects and events. Statistics refers to studying organization, analysis of a collection of data, making interpretations and presentation of analyzed results.

Artificial Intelligence (AI) refers to the science and engineering of making computers perform tasks, which normally require human intelligence. For example, tasks such as predicting future results, visual perception, speech recognition, decision making and natural language processing.

Two concepts in AI, '*machine learning*' and 'deep learning' provide powerful tools for advanced analytics and predictions.

Google-owned company *Deep Mind* developed an Artificial Intelligence (AI) program called AlphaZero, which played 100 chess games in 24 hours, and defeated Stockfish, the highest-rated chess program by 28 games to 0 with 72 games drawn. This was a historical moment. It became a milestone in the history of AI, ML and DL.

The former world champion, Garry Kasparov, noted that achievement of AlphaZero has history-shaping potential. "The ability of a machine to replicate and surpass centuries of human knowledge, is a world-changing tool". (Garry Kasparov, "*Deep Thinking — Where Artificial Intelligence Ends and Human Creativity Begins*", published by the author himself, 2017)

Machine Learning – Definition and Usage Examples

Machine Learning (ML) is a field of computer science based on AI which deals with learning from data in three phases, i.e. *collect*, *analyze* and *predict*. It does not rely on explicitly programmed instructions.

An ML program learns the behavior of a process. The program uses data generated from various sources for training. Learning from the outcomes from common inputs improves future performance from previous outcomes. Learning applies in many fields of research and industry. Learning from study of data enables efficient and logical decisions for future actions.

Advanced ML techniques use unsupervised, semi-supervised or supervised learning. Supervised learning uses a known dataset (called *training dataset*). Learning enables creation of a *model program* for evaluating outcomes. The program makes future predictions and leads to knowledge discovery. Supervised learning uses output datasets, which are used to train a machine (program) such that the program leads to the desired outputs. Unsupervised learning does not use output datasets to train a machine.

Deep Learning (DL) refers to structured learning (DSL) or hierarchical learning. DL methods are advanced methods, such as artificial neural networks (ANN) such as artificial neural networks (ANN) or neural nets, deep neural networks, deep belief networks and recurrent neural networks. Learning can be unsupervised, semi-supervised or supervised. Applications of DL and ANN include computer vision, speech recognition, Natural Language Processing (NLP), audio recognition, social network filtering, machine translation, bioinformatics and drug design. DL methods give results comparable to and in some cases superior to human experts.

The present chapter describes the ML methods and introduces Mahout Architecture, features and its ML applications. Section 6.2 describes methods of estimating relationships, outliers, variances, probability distribution, errors and correlations in variables, items and entities. Section 6.3 describes regression analysis using linear, non-linear and multiple-regressor models and KNN distance measures for making predictions. [Regressor means an independent (explanatory) variable in regression equation.]

Section 6.4 describes methods of finding similar items, similarities and filtering of similar items. Section 6.5 describes frequent-itemset mining by collaborative filtering of similar itemsets. Section 6.5 also describes associations and association rules mining. Section 6.6 describes methods of finding the clusters. Section 6.7 describes the classifiers for classifying data in datasets. Section 6.8 introduces recommendation system and collaborative, content, knowledge and hybrid recommendation approaches. Section 6.9 describes Apache Mahout and ML algorithms for Big Datasets.

The following sections use a convention for fonts when denoting an absolute value, mean value, function value, vector element, set member, entity or variable using a character or set of characters, entities or elements.

1. |u| represents absolute value of u, means value without sign. For example, consider |– 3| and |+ 3|, the value of both is 3.
2. $\bar{x}$ represents mean, average or expected value of x.
3. F (y, x) represents a function with an expression, which finds value of F from the given values of y and x. F (y, x) values depend on one or more dependent variables as a function of one or more independent variables. For example, F depends y as well as x is F (y, x) = 1/sqrt $\{(y + x)^2 + k^2\}$. The F also depends on constant k. Another example is y = F (x), for example, y = cos (x). F (x) represents a function F, which gives value of y, is a dependent variable. The x is an independent variable.
4. **V** denotes a vector **V** (V1, V2 …). V is in bold font. V1 and V2 are in text font and are elements 1 and 2 of **V**. The V consists of number of elements V1, V2 …
5. ||**U**|| represents length of vector **U**.
6. $\mathbb{S}$ denotes a set $\mathbb{S}$ (A, B, C …). Font $\mathbb{S}$ is in French script MT or distinct font for English S. The A, B and C are in text font (no bold), and are the members of $\mathbb{S}$. The members can be vectors or subsets. They, when denoted in bold, represent vector elements.

6.2 ESTIMATING THE RELATIONSHIPS, OUTLIERS, VARIANCES, PROBABILITY DISTRIBUTIONS AND CORRELATIONS

LO 6.1

Metric, feature and category variables, Relationships, outliers, variances, probability distribution, and the correlations between the variables, items, or entities

Methods of studying relationships use variables. Types of variables used are as follows:

Independent variables represent directly measurable characteristics. For example, year of sales figure or semester of study. Dependent variables represent the characteristics. For example, profit during successive years or grades awarded in successive semesters. Values of a dependent variable depend on the value of the independent variable.

Predictor variable is an independent variable, which computes a dependent variable using some equation, function or graph, and does a prediction. For example, predicts sales growth of a car model after five years from given input datasets for the sales, or predicts sentiments about higher sales of particular category of toys next year.

Outcome variable represents the effect of manipulation(s) using a function, equation or experiment. For example, CGPA (Cumulative Grade Points Average) of the student or share of profit to each shareholder in a year using profit as the dependent variable. CGPA of a student computes from the grades awarded in the semesters for which student completes his/her studies. A company declares the share of profit to each shareholder in a year after subtracting requirements of money for future growth from the profit.

Explanatory variable is an independent variable, which explains the behavior of the dependent variable, such as linearity coefficient, non-linear parameters or probabilistic distribution of profit-growth as a function of additional investment in successive years.

Response variable is a dependent variable on which a study, experiment or computation focuses. For example, improvement in profits over the years from the investments made in successive years or improvement in class performance is measured from the extra teaching efforts on individual students of a class.

Feature variable is a variable representing a characteristic. For example, apple feature red, pink, maroon, yellowish, yellowish green and green. Feature variables are generally represented by text characters. Numbers can also represent features. For example, red with 1, orange with 2, yellow with 3, yellowish green 4 and green 5.

Categorical variable is a variable representing a category. For example, car, tractor and truck belong to the same category, i.e., a four-wheeler automobile. Categorical variables are generally represented by text characters.

Independent and dependent variables may exhibit a relation or correlation. The relationships may be linear, nonlinear, positive, negative, direct, inverse, scattered or spread. A data point for dependent variable can be an outlier with no relationship.

Data analysis requires studying relationships graphically, mathematically and statistically, studying the outliers, anomalies, variances, correlations, features, categories and probability distributions using a set of variables, and other characteristics. The relationship involves some quantifiable independent variables and the resulting dependent variable or entity. The following subsections explain methods of estimating the relationships, outliers, variances, correlations and probability distributions between a set of variables.

6.2.1 Relationships—Using Graphs, Scatter Plots and Charts

A relationship between two or more quantitative dependent variables with respect to an independent variable can be well-depicted using graph, scatter plot or chart with data points, shown in distinct shapes. Conventionally, independent variables are on the x-axis, whereas the dependent variables on the y-axis in a graph. A line graph uses a line on an x-y axis to plot a continuous function.

A scatter plot is a plot in which dots or distinct shapes represent values of the dependent variable at the multiple values of the independent variable [Section 10.5]. Whether two variables are related to each other or not, can be derived from statistical analysis using scatter plots.

A data point is (x_i, y_i) when dependent variable value = y_i at the independent variable value = x_i. The i = 1, 2... n for number of data points = n. The i varies with the position of projection of the point on X-axis. Scatter plot represents data points by dots. The dot can also be a bubble, triangle, circle, cross or vertical bar. Size or colour of dot distinguishes the dependent variables on the same plot.

Another method is quantifying two or more dependent variables by columns of different widths with filled colours, shades or patterns. The width quantifies the dependent variable. The column-position quantifies the independent variable.

Examples of dependent variables are sales of five car models in a year, grades in five courses taken in a semester.

6.2.1.1 Linear and Non-linear Relationships

A linear relationship exists between two variables, say x and y, when a straight line ($y = a_0 + a_1.x$) can fit on a graph, with at least some reasonable degree of accuracy. The a_1 is the linearity coefficient. For example, a scatter chart can suggest a linear relationship, which means a straight line. Figure 6.1 shows a scatter plot, which fits a linear relationship between the number of students opting for computer courses in years between 2000 and 2017.

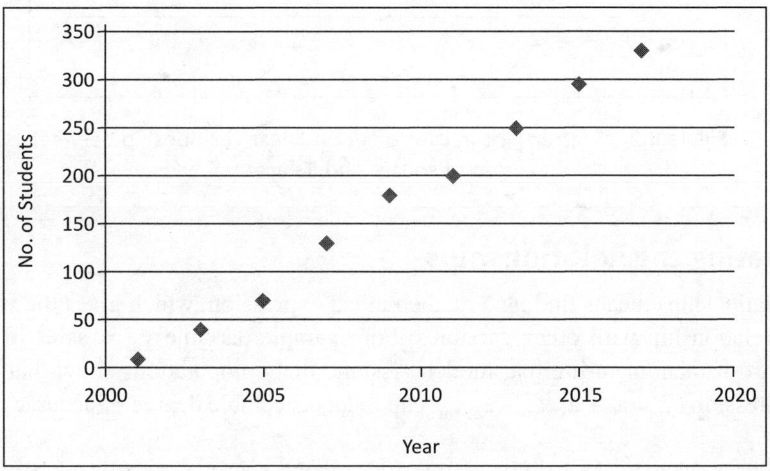

Figure 6.1 Scatter plot for linear relationship between students opting for computer courses in years between 2000 and 2017

A linear relationship can be positive or negative. A positive relationship implies if one variable increases in value, the other also increases in value. A negative relationship, on the other hand, implies when one increases in value, the other decreases in value. Perfect, strong or weak linearship categories depend upon the bonding between the two variables.

A non-linear relationship is said to exist between two quantitative variables when a curve ($y = a_0 + a_1.x + a_2.x^2 + \ldots$) can be used to fit the data points. The fit should be with at least some reasonable degree of accuracy for the fitted parameters, a_0, a_1, a_2 ... Expression for y then generally predicts the values of one quantitative variable from the values of the other quantitative variable with considerably more accuracy than a straight line.

Consider an example of non-linear relationship: The side of a square and its area are not linear. In fact, they have quadratic relationship. If the side of a square doubles, then its area increases four times. The relationship predicts the area from the side.

Figure 6.2 shows a scatter plot in case of a non-linear relationship between side of square and its area.

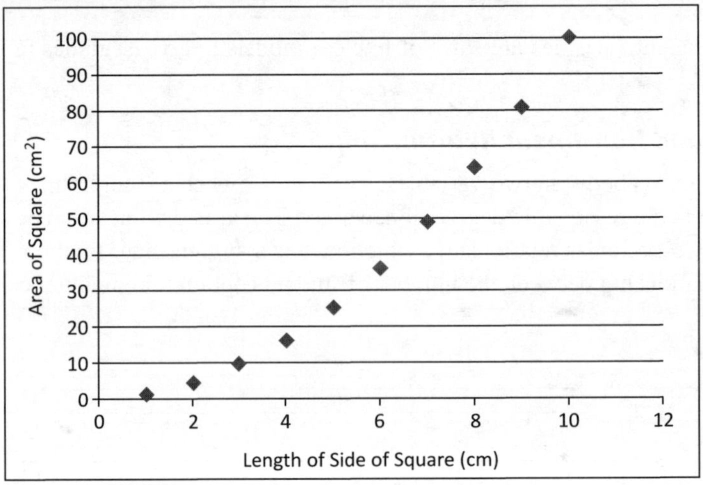

Figure 6.2 Scatter plot in case of a non-linear relationship between side of square and its area

6.2.2 Estimating the Relationships

Estimating the relationships means finding a mathematical expression, which gives the value of the variable according to its relationship with other variables. For example, assume y_m = sales of a car model *m* in x^{th} year of the start of manufacturing that model. Assume that computations show that the y_m relates by a mathematical expression ($y_m = a_0 + a_1.x_m + a_2.x_m^2$) up to an acceptable degree of accuracy, when $a_0 = 490$, $a_1 = 10$ and $a_2 = 5$.

Estimated first year sales, $y_m(1) = (490 + 10) = 500$, second year $y_m(2) = (490 + 10 \times 2 + 5 \times 2^2) = 530$, third year $y_m(3) = (490 + 10 \times 3 + 5 \times 3^2) = 565$, if fit with the desired accuracy, then the results are showing that the expression of y_m estimates the relationship between model *m* sales in next and other years. The y_m can also predict the sales in 6th or later years. Predictions are up to a certain degree of certainty.

6.2.3 Outliers

Outliers are data, which appear as they do not belong to the dataset (Section 5.3.3.1). Outliers are data points that are numerically far distant from the rest of the points in a dataset, are termed as outliers. Outliers show significant variations from the rest of the points (Section 1.5.2.2). Identification of outliers is important to improve data quality or to detect an anomaly. The estimating parameters mathematically, statistically, describing an outcome, predicting a dependent variable value, or taking the decisions based on the datasets given for the analysis are sensitive to the outliers.

There are several reasons for the presence of outliers in relationships. Some of these are:

- Anomalous situation
- Presence of a previously unknown fact
- Human error (errors due to data entry or data collection)
- Participants intentionally reporting incorrect data (This is common in self-reported measures and measures that involve sensitive data which participant doesn't want to disclose)
- Sampling error (when an unfitted sample is collected from population).

Population means any group of data, which includes all the data of interest. For example, when analysing 1000 students who gave an examination in a computer course, then the population is 1000. 100 games of chess will represent the population in analysis of 100 games of chess of a grandmaster.

Sample means a subset of the population. Sample represents the population for uses, such as analysis and consists of randomly selected data.

6.2.4 Variance

A random variable is a variable whose possible values are outcomes of a random phenomenon. A random variable is a function that maps the outcomes of unpredictable processes to numerical quantities. A random variable is also called stochastic variable or random quantity. Randomness can be around some expected mean value or outcome, and with some normal deviation.

Variance measures by the sum of squares of the difference in values of a variable with respect to the expected value. Variance can alternatively be a sum of squares of the difference with respect to value at an origin. Variance indicates how widely data points in a dataset vary. If data points vary greatly from the mean value in a dataset, the variance is large; otherwise, the variance is less. The variance is also a measure of dispersion with respect to the expected value.

A high variance indicates that the data in the dataset is very much spread out over a large area (random dataset), whereas a low variance indicates that the data is very similar in nature.

No variance is sometimes hard to understand in real datasets. The following example illustrates no variance:

EXAMPLE 6.1

Consider an examination where everyone gets the same grades. What does it signify?

SOLUTION

Some measurement problem may have taken place in a situation where either the semester examination questions were so easy that everyone got full marks, or it was so hard that everyone got a zero. Now consider the two types of examinations. After each examination, everyone gets the same score on the test, i.e., everyone gets 'A' grade in one test and everyone gets 'B' in the second test. This is again not telling much about the study or intelligent quotient of the students. Now, these no variance results signify the extreme case and hard to understand or explain. But in general, differences in scores are always found.

6.2.4.1 *Standard Deviation and Standard Error Estimates*

The variance is not a standalone statistical parameter. Estimations of other statistical parameters, such as standard deviation and standard error are also used.

Standard Deviation With the help of variance, one can find out the standard deviation. Standard deviation, denoted by σ, is the square root of the variance. The σ says, "On an average how far do the data points fall from the mean or expected outcome?" Though the interpretation is the same as variance but σ is squared rooted, therefore, less susceptible to the presence of outliers. The formulae for the population and the sample standard deviations are as follows:

$$\text{The Population Standard Deviation: } \sigma = \sqrt{\frac{1}{N-1}\sum_{i=1}^{N}(x_i - \mu)^2} \tag{6.1a}$$

$$\text{The Sample Standard Deviation: } \sigma = \sqrt{\frac{1}{S-1}\sum_{i=1}^{S}(x_i - \overline{x})^2}\,, \tag{6.1b}$$

where N is number of data points in population, S is number in the sample, μ is expected in the population or average value of x, and $\overline{x}$ is expected x in the sample.

Standard Error The standard error estimate is a measure of the accuracy of predictions from a relationship. Assume the linear relationship in a scatter plot of y (Figure 6.1). The scatter plot line, which fits, is defined as the line that minimizes the sum of squared deviations of prediction (also called the **sum of squares error**). The **standard error of the estimate** is closely related to this quantity and is defined below:

$$\sigma_{est} = \sqrt{\frac{\sum (y-y')^2}{N}}, \quad \text{... (6.2)}$$

where σ_{est} is the standard error in the estimate, y is an observed value, y′ is a predicted value, and N is the number of values observed. The standard error estimate is a measure of the dispersion (or variability) in the predicted values from the expression for relationship. Following are three interpretations from the σ_{est}:

1. When σ_{est} is small, most of the observed values (y) dots are fairly close to the fitting line in the scatter plot, and better is the estimate based on the equation of the line.
2. When the σ_{est} is large, many of the observed values are far away from the line.
3. When the standard error is zero, then no variation exists corresponding to the computed line for predictions. The correlation between the observed and estimation is perfect.

6.2.5 Probabilistic Distribution of Variables, Items or Entities

Probability is the chance of observing a dependent variable value with respect to some independent variable. Suppose a Grandmaster in chess has won 22 out of 100 games, drawn 78 times, and lost none. Then, probability P of winning P_w is 0.22, P of drawn game P_D is 0.78 and P of losing, $P_L = 0$. The sum of the probabilities is normalized to 1, as only one of the three possibilities exist.

Probability distribution is the distribution of P values as a function of all possible independent values, variables, situations, distances or variables. For example, if P is given by a function P(*x*), then P varies as

x changes. Variations in P(x) with x can be discrete or continuous. The values of P are normalized such that sum of all P values is 1. Assuming distribution is around the expected value $\bar{x}$, the standard normal distribution formula is:

$$P(x) = \frac{1}{\sigma\sqrt{2\pi}} e^{\frac{-(x-\bar{x})^2}{2\sigma^2}} \tag{6.3}$$

Normal distribution relates to Gaussian function. Figure 6.3 shows a PDF with normal distribution around $x = \bar{x}$ standard deviation = σ and variance = σ^2.

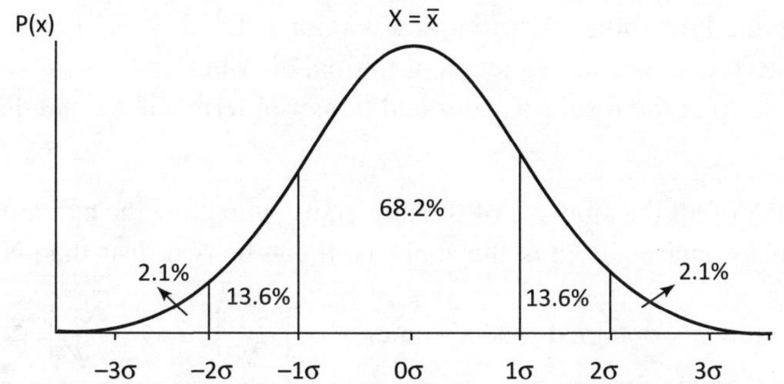

Figure 6.3 Probability distribution function as a function of x assuming normal distribution around $x = \bar{x}$ and standard deviation = σ

The figure also shows the percentages of areas in five regions with respect to the total area under the curve for P(x). The variance for probability distribution represents how individual data points relate to each other within a dataset. The variance is the average of the squared differences between each data value and the mean.

Moments (0, 1, 2 ...) refer to the expected values to the power of (0, 1, 2,) of random variable variance (Section 6.2.5.3). The variance is the second central moment of a distribution, which equals to the square of the standard deviation, and the covariance of the random variable with itself, and it is often represented by σ^2 or var (x). The variance is computed as follows:

$$\sigma^2 = \frac{\sum(x_i - \bar{x})^2}{N} \tag{6.4}$$

Assume that probability distribution (PDF) is normal, called Gaussian distribution, which is like a bell-shaped curve (Figure 6.3). The PDF of the normal distribution is such that 68% of area under the PDF is within ($\bar{x} + \sigma$) and ($\bar{x} - \sigma$), 95% of area under the PDF is within ($\bar{x} + 2\sigma$) and ($\bar{x} - 2\sigma$) and 99.7% is within ($\bar{x} + 3\sigma$) and ($\bar{x} - 3\sigma$).

Standard deviation and empirical rule help in computing the population distribution over 68%, 95% and 99.7% of data under normally distributed population. This further helps in forecasting. The following example explains the meaning of population, expected values, normalized probabilities, PDF and interpretation using mean value.

EXAMPLE 6.2

Assume that N students gave the examination. Let N_1 is number of students obtained grade pointer average = 1, N_2 got 2, …, N_{10} got 10. Highest-grade pointer is 10.0. Grade pointer obtained is not a random variable. Grade pointer variation is a random variable with an expected value and standard deviation.

Expected value among the distributed x_i values, where i varies discretely from 0.0 to 10.0 will depend on the expected performance of the student. If teaching in the class is very good and students prepare for the examination very well, then expected value of GPA is 8.0 for very good performing students and standard deviation found is 1.0.

(i) What do you mean by population? What do you mean by sample?
(ii) What will be the normalized probabilities?
(iii) How will you define Probability Distribution Function (PDF)?
(iv) How will you interpret the results in terms of normal distribution?
(v) When will you interpret the results as poor and poorer in terms of normal distribution?

SOLUTION

(i) Population is GPA of all the students of the university who gave the examination. Population size is N. Sample means datasets used in the analysis. It can be N or less than N students and GPA of each one.
(ii) Probability that students obtained grade pointer 1 is $\left(\frac{N_1}{N}\right)$, 2 is $\left(\frac{N_2}{N}\right)$, … on normalization of probability. ($N = N_1 + N_2 + \ldots.$)
(iii) PDF represents a curve for independent variable x between GPA = 0 and GPA = 10, such that the sum of all P values is 1, where P_i is the ratio of number of students getting GPA = i with respect to the total population N or the sample.

$$P(x) = \frac{1}{\sigma\sqrt{2\pi}} e^{\frac{-(x-\bar{x})^2}{2\sigma^2}} \tag{6.5}$$

between $x = 0$ and 10.0, where $\sigma = 1.0$ and $\bar{x} = 8.0$.
(iv) GPA value is 8.0 and standard deviation is 1.0, which means 68% of the students will get GPAs between 7.0 and 9.0, 95% between 6.0 and 10.0, and 99.7% between 5.0 and 10.0.
(v) The expected value of 3.0 (less than 3.0) and standard deviation of 1.0 means poor performance of students because 68% students get between 2.0 and 4.0. The expected value of 3.0– (less than 3.0, say 2.5) and standard deviation of 1.5 means poorer performance of students because 68% students get between 1.0 and 4.0.

6.2.5.1 *Kernel Functions*

A probability or weight can be represented by a kernel function[1] like a Gaussian or tri-cube function. (Kernel in English means some thing central and key (important) part. For example, the kernel inside a walnut's shell is important because it is the edible part. Kernel in an operating system is key or central component.)

Kernel function is a function which is a central or key part of another function. For example, Gaussian kernel function is the key part of the probability distribution function [Equation (6.5)]. Figure 6.3 shows the probability normal distribution, which is a Gaussian function based on the Gaussian kernel function.

A kernel function[1], K* defines as

$$K^*(u) = \lambda.K(\lambda.u), \tag{6.6a}$$

where $\lambda > 0$. Gaussian kernel function is

$$K^*(x) = \left[\frac{1}{(\sqrt{2\pi})}\right] e^{\left[-\frac{u^2}{2^2}\right]}, \tag{6.6b}$$

and when $u = \frac{\left\{\frac{x-\overline{x}}{2}\right\}}{\sigma}$, the distribution function is proportional to $P(x) = \frac{1}{\sigma\sqrt{2\pi}} e^{\frac{-(x-\overline{x})^2}{2\sigma^2}}$.

$\lambda = \left(\frac{1}{\sigma\sqrt{2}}\right)$ in Equation (6.3).

Tricube kernel function is:

$$K^*(u) = (70/81)\,(1 - |u|^3)^3 \lambda.K(\lambda.u), \tag{6.6c}$$

where $|u| \le 1$.

6.2.5.2 Moments

Moments (0, 1, 2, ...) refer to expected values to the powers of (0, 1, 2 ...) of random variable variance. 0th moment is 1, 1st moment = $E(x) = \overline{x}$ (expected value), 2nd moment is squared $V[(x_i - \overline{x})^2]$ = sum of product of $(x_i - \overline{x})^2$, and $P(x = x_i)$.

Here, P is the probability at $x = x_i$ when i is varying from 1 to n, for n values of random variable x. The rth moment is r^{th} power of variance $V[(x_i - \overline{x})^r]$. Moments are evaluated from the results obtained for the randomly distributed probabilistic values of the variable, such as sales. 1st moment assigns equal weight to variances of outliers and inliers, i.e., equal weight for variance of each. 2nd moment assigns higher weight to outliers compared to inliers. 3rd moment assigns greater weight to outliers compared to inliers. Moment can be defined with respected to the origin, and in that case, $\overline{x}$ is considered 0.

Let P is along y axis and variable x on x axis. Central moment means that moments compute taking $\overline{x}$ equals to variable x at x axis point where the probability curve partitions equally by a vertical axis, parallel to the y axis.

6.2.5.3 Unequal Variance Welch's t-test

A test in statistics is unequal-variance *t* test, also called Welch *t* test.

(i) The test assumes that two groups of data are sampled data which consist of Gaussian distributed populations (Equation (6.3)).

(ii) The test does not assume those two populations have the same standard deviation.

Unequal variances t-test is a two-sample location test. It tests the hypothesis that two populations have equal means. (*Hypothesis* means making assumption statements about certain characteristics of the population. For example, an assumption that most students of a specific professor will excel as a programmer. Hypothesis when tested for a decade may pass or fail depending up on whether the statistically significant results show that the students of that professor really excelled as programmers.)

[1] https://en.wikipedia.org/wiki/Kernel (statistics)

Welch's t-test is an adaptation of student's t-test in statistics. The t-test is more reliable when the two samples have unequal variances and unequal sample sizes.

6.2.5.4 Analysis of Variance (ANOVA)

An ANOVA test is a method which finds whether the fitted results are significant or not. This means that the test finds out (infer) whether to reject or accept the null hypothesis. Null hypothesis is a statistical test that means *the hypothesis that "no significant difference* exists between the specified populations". Any observed difference is just due to sampling or experimental error.

Consider two specified populations (datasets) consisting of yearly sales data of Tata Zest and Jaguar Land Rover models. The statistical test is for proving that yearly sales of both the models, means increments and decrements of sales are related or not. Null hypothesis starts with the assumption that no significant relation exists in the two sets of data (population).

The analysis (ANOVA) is for disproving or accepting the null hypothesis. The test also finds whether to accept another alternate hypothesis. The test finds that whether testing groups have any difference between them or not.

Analysis of variance (ANOVA) is a useful technique for comparing more than two populations, samples, observations or results of computations. It is used when multiple sample cases are involved. Variation between samples and also within sample items may exist. For example, compare the effect of three different types of teaching methodologies on students. This may be done by comparing the test scores of the three groups of 20 students each. This technique provides inferences about whether the samples have been drawn from populations having the same mean. It is done by examining the amount of variation within each of these samples, relative to the amount of variation between the samples.

F-test F-test requires two estimates of population variance— one based on variance between the samples and the other based on variance within the samples. These two estimates are then compared for F-test:

$$F = \frac{E1(V)}{E2(V)} \tag{6.7}$$

where $E1(V)$ is an estimate of population variance between the two samples and $E2(V)$ is an estimate of population variance within the two samples. Several different F-tables exist. Each one has a different level of significance. Thus, look up the numerator degrees of freedom and the denominator degrees of freedom to find the critical value.

The value of F calculated using the above-mentioned formula is to be compared to the critical value of F for the given degrees of freedom. If the F value calculated is equal or exceeds the critical value, then significant differences between the means of samples exist. This reveals that the samples are not drawn from the same population and thus null hypothesis is rejected.

6.2.5.5 No Relationship Case

Statistical relationship is a dependence or association between two random variables or bivariate data. Bivariate means 'two variables'. In other words, there are two types of data. Relationships between variables need to be studied and analyzed before drawing conclusions based on it. One cannot determine the right conclusion or association when no relationship between the variables exists.

6.2.6 Correlation

Correlation means analysis which lets us find the association or the absence of the relationship between two variables, *x* and *y*. Correlation gives the strength of the relationship between the model and the dependent variable on a convenient 0-100% scale.

R-Square *R* is a measure of correlation between the predicted values y and the observed values of *x*. *R-squared* (R^2) is a goodness-of-fit measure in linear-regression model. It is also known as the coefficient of determination. R^2 is the square of *R*, the coefficient of multiple correlations, and includes additional independent (explanatory) variables in regression equation.

Interpretation of *R*-squared The larger the R^2, the better the regression model fits the observations, i.e., the correlation is better. Theoretically, if a model shows 100% variance, then the fitted values are always equal to the observed values, and therefore, all the data points would fall on the fitted regression line.

Correlation differs from a regression analysis. Regression analysis predicts the value of the dependent predictor or response variable based on the known value of the independent variable, assuming a more or less mathematical relationship between two or more variables within the specified variances.

6.2.6.1 *Correlation Indicators of Linear Relationships*

Correlation is a statistical technique that measures and describes the 'strength' and 'direction' of the relationship between two variables. Let us explore the relations between only two variables. The significant questions are:

Does y increase or decrease with x? For example, expenditure increases with income or does the number of patients decrease with proper medication. (Direction)

(i) Suppose y does increase with x; then, how fast?
(ii) Is this relationship strong?
(iii) Can reliable predictions be made? That is, if one tells the income, can the expenditure be predicted?

Relationships and correlations enable training model on sample data using statistical or ML algorithms. Statistical correlation is measured by the coefficient of correlation. The most common correlation coefficient, called the *Pearson product-moment correlation coefficient*. It measures the strength of the linear association between variables. The correlation *r* between the two variables *x* and *y* is:

$$r = \left[\frac{1}{(n-1)}\right] \times \sum\left\{\left[\frac{(x_i - \overline{x})}{\sigma_x}\right] \times \left[\frac{(y_i - \overline{y})}{\sigma_y}\right]\right\}, \tag{6.8a}$$

where n is the number of observations in the sample, x_i is the *x* value for observation *i*, $\overline{x}$ is the sample mean of *x*, y_i is the *y* value for observation *i*, $\overline{y}$ is the sample mean of *y*, σ_x is the sample standard deviation of *x*, and σ_y is the sample standard deviation of *y*.

Summation is over all *n* values of *i*, $i = 1, 2, ..., n$.

[r^2 is square of sample correlation coefficient between the observed outcomes and the observed predictor values, and includes intercept on y-axis in case of linear regression.]

Use of Statistical Correlation Assume one sample dataset is $\{u_1, ..., u_n\}$ containing *n* values of a parameter *r*. The $r_{u,i}$ is *i*-th data point in dataset **u**. ($i = 1, 2, ..., n$). Another sample dataset is $\{v_1, ..., v_n\}$ containing *n* values of *r*. $r_{v,i}$ is *i*-th data point in dataset **v**. Let the correlation among two samples is being measured. Sample Pearson correlation metric c_r measures how well two sample datasets fit on a straight line.

$$c_r(u, v) = \frac{\sum_i (r_{u,i} - \bar{r}_u)(r_{v,i} - \bar{r}_v)}{\sqrt{\sum_i (r_{u,i} - \bar{r}_u)^2 \sum_i (r_{v,i} - \bar{r}_v)^2}} \quad \text{... (6.8b)}$$

where the summations are over the values of parameter in the datasets.

Three other similarities based on correlation are:

(i) Constrained Pearson correlation – It is a variation of Pearson correlation that uses midpoint instead of mean rate.

(ii) Spearman rank correlation – It is similar to Pearson correlation, except that the ratings are ranks.

(iii) Kendall's Γ correlation – It is similar to the Spearman rank correlation, but instead of using ranks themselves, only the relative ranks are used to calculate the correlation.

Numerical value of correlation coefficient ranges from +1.0 to −1.0. It gives an indication of both the strength and direction of the relationship between variables.

In general, a correlation coefficient $r > 0$ indicates a positive relationship; $r < 0$ indicates a negative relationship; $r = 0$ indicates no relationship (or that the variables are independent of each other and not related). Here $r = +1.0$ describes a perfect positive correlation and $r = -1.0$ describes a perfect negative correlation.

The closer the coefficients are to +1.0 and −1.0, the greater is the *strength* of the relationship between the variables.

Table 6.1 gives rough guidelines on the strength of the relationship (though many experts would somewhat disagree on the choice of boundaries).

Table 6.1 The strength of the relationship as a function of *r*

Value of r	Strength of relationship
−1.0 to −0.5 or 1.0 to 0.5	Strong
−0.5 to −0.3 or 0.3 to 0.5	Moderate
−0.3 to −0.1 or 0.1 to 0.3	Weak
−0.1 to 0.1	None or very weak

Correlation is only appropriate for examining the relationship between meaningful quantifiable data (such as, temperature, marks, score) rather than categorical data, such as gender, color etc. Figure 6.4 shows perfect and imperfect, linear positive and negative relationships, and the strength and direction of the relationship between variables

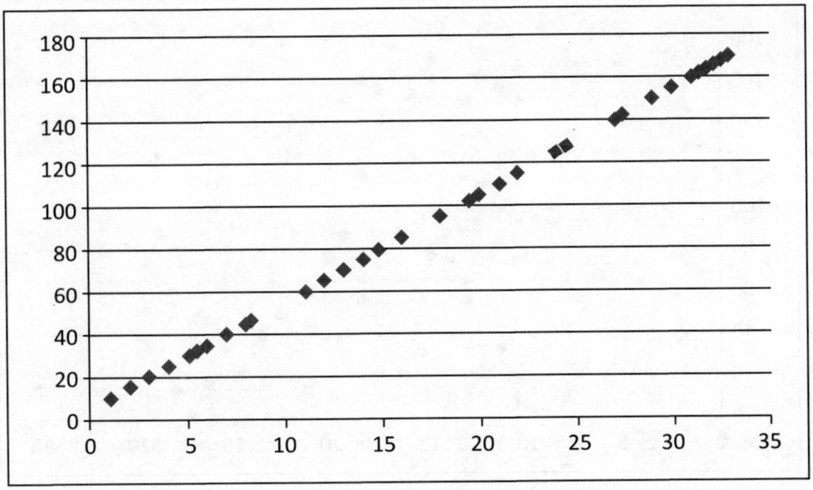

Perfect Positive Linear Relationship ($r = 1$)

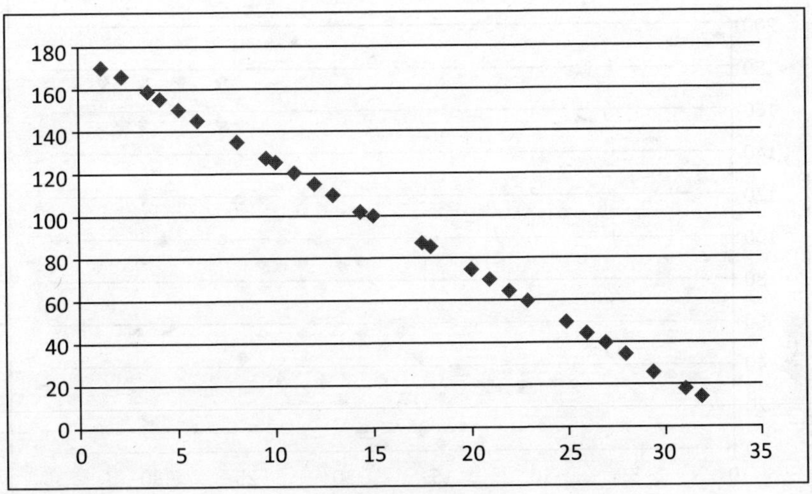

Perfect Negative Linear Relationship ($r = -1$)

Figure 6.4 *(Contd.)*

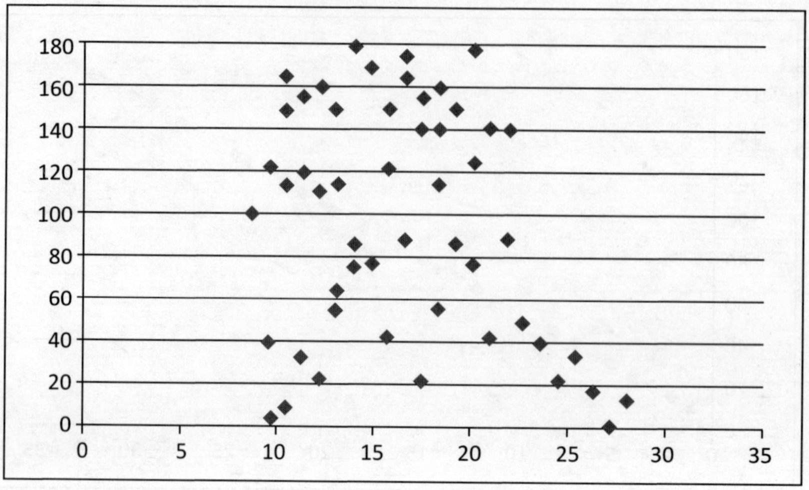

No Relationship ($r \sim 0$)

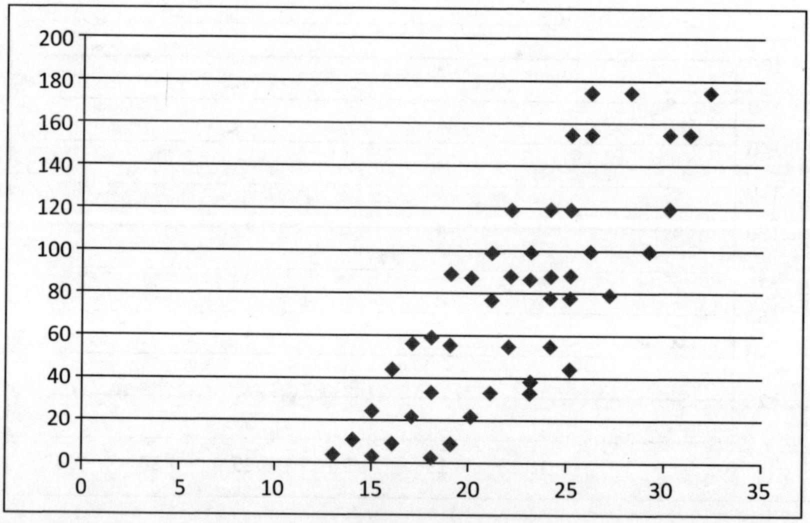

Positive Linear Relationship ($r = 0.9$)

Figure 6.4 Perfect and imperfect, linear positive and negative relationships, and the strength and direction of the relationship between variables

Self-Assessment Exercise linked to LO 6.1

1. Define non-linear relation. Plot on the same graph, a company car sales, y for its two models every year between 2012 to 2017, using the formula ($y_m = a_0 + a_1.x_m + a_2.x_m^2$). How will you predict the sales in 2010? Assume for first model $a_0 = 490$, $a_1 = 10$ and $a_2 = 5$. Assume for second model $a_0 = 4900$, $a_1 = 100$ and $a_2 = 50$. Assume, $x_m = 0$ for year 2011, $x_m = 1$ for 2012 and $x_m = 6$ for 2017. ●●●
2. How does the P(x) vary in normal distribution when expected mean is at $x = 6.0$ and standard deviation σ is 1.0? Show a plot of P(x) and x and points at deviations of 1.0, 2.0 and 3.0 (means at σ, 2σ and 3σ). ●●●
3. Define mean, variance and standard deviation. How do the 0th moment, 1st moment, 2nd moment and 3rd moment compute from the values and their probabilities? ○●●
4. When will you perform t-test and F-test? ○○●
5. What does variable R-squared mean? How is the correlation parameter between predicted valued and observed value evaluated? When do you use R, r, R^2 and when r^2? ○●●
6. Consider correlation r between two variables. How do you interpret $r > 0$, $r < 0$ and $r = 0$? ○○●
7. How is the inference made that two variables do not correlate? ○○●

6.3 REGRESSION ANALYSIS

LO 6.2

Regression analysis using linear and non-linear regression models, K-Nearest-Neighbours, and using distance measures for predictions

Correlation and regression are two analyses based on multivariate distribution. A multivariate distribution means a distribution in multiple variables.

Suppose a company wishes to plan the manufacturing of Jaguar cars for coming years. The company looks at sales data regressively, i.e., data of previous years' sales. Regressive analysis means estimating relationships between variables. Regression analysis is a set of statistical steps, which estimate the relationships among variables. Regression analysis may require many techniques for modeling and performing the analysis using multiple variables. The aim of the analysis is to find the relationships between a dependent variable and one or more independent, outcome, predictor or response variables. Regression analysis facilitates prediction of future values of dependent variables.

It helps to find how a dependent variable changes when variation is in an independent variable among a set of them, while the remaining independent variables in the set are kept fixed.

Non-linear regression equation is as follows:

$$y = a_0 + a_1.x + a_2.x^2 + a_3.x^3, \tag{6.9}$$

where number of terms on the right-hand side are 3 or 4. Linear regression means only the first two terms are considered. The following subsections describe regression analysis in detail.

6.3.1 Simple Linear Regression

Linear regression is a simple and widely used algorithm. It is a supervised ML algorithm for predictive analysis. It models a relationship between the independent predictor or explanatory, and the dependent

Note: ○○● Level 1 & Level 2 category
○●● Level 3 & Level 4 category
●●● Level 5 & Level 6 category

outcome or variable, y using a linearity equation.

$$y = f(a_0, a_1) = a_0 + a_1.x, \tag{6.10}$$

where a_0 is a constant and a_1 is the linearity coefficient.

Simple linear regression is performed when the requirement is prediction of values of one variable, with given values of another variable. The following example explains the meaning of linear regression.

EXAMPLE 6.3

How can a university student's GPA be predicted from his/her high school percentage (HSP) of marks?

SOLUTION

Consider a sample of ten students for whom their GPAs and high school scores, HSPs, are known. Assume linear regression. Then,

$$\text{GPA} = b_1.\text{ HSP} + A \quad \text{... (6.11)}$$

Figure 6.5 shows a simple linear regression plot for the relationship between the college GPA and the percentage of high school marks. Plot the values on a graph, with high school scores in percentage on the *x* axis and GPA on the y axis.

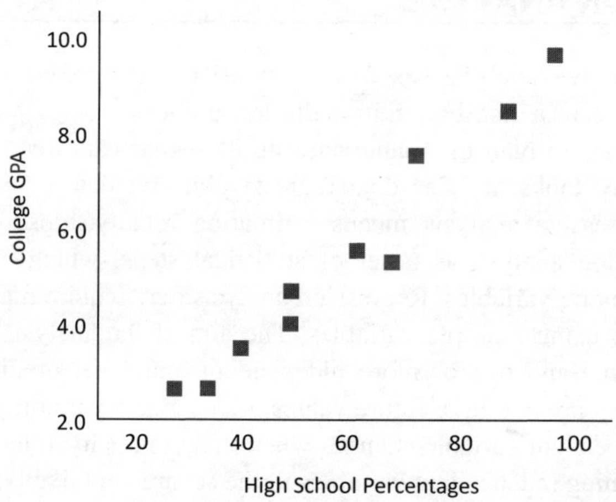

Figure 6.5 Linear regression relationship between college GPA and percentage of high school marks

Whenever a perfect linear relationship between GPA and high school score exists, all 10 points on the graph would fit on a straight line. However, this is never the case. Whenever an imperfect linear relationship exists between these two variables, a cluster of points on the graph, which slope upward, may be obtained. In other words, students who got more marks in high school should get more GPA in college as well.

One variable, denoted by x, is regarded as the predictor, explanatory or independent variable. The other variable, denoted by y, is regarded as the response, outcome or dependent variable.

The purpose of regression analysis is to come up with an equation of a line that fits through a cluster of points with minimal amount of deviation from the line. The best-fitting line is called the *regression line*. The deviation of the points from the line is called an 'error'. Once this regression equation is obtained, the GPA of a student in college examinations can be predicted provided his/her high school percentage is given. Simple linear regression is actually the same as a correlation between independent and dependent variables.

Figure 6.6 shows a simple linear regression with two regression lines with different regression equations. Looking at the scatter plot, two lines can fit best to summarize the relation between GPA and high school percentage.

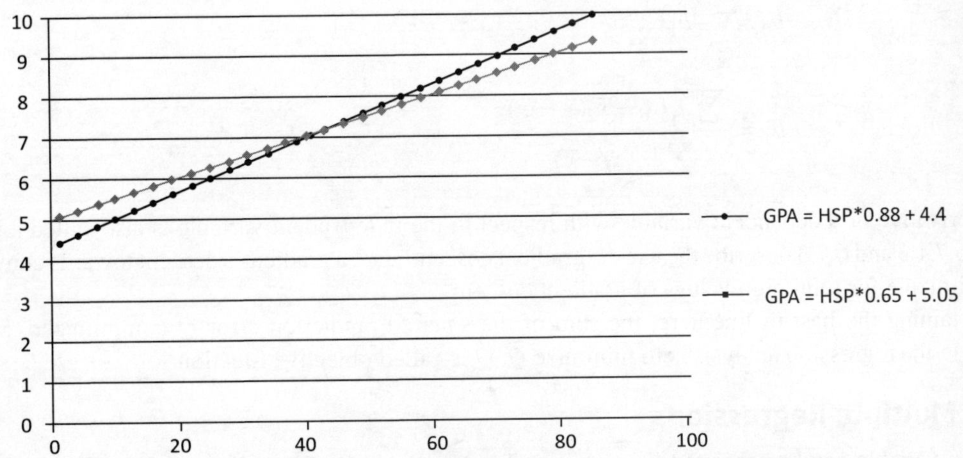

Figure 6.6 Linear regression relationship with two regression lines with different coefficient in regression equation

Following notations can be used for examining which of the two lines is a better fit:

1. y_i denotes the observed response for experimental unit i
2. x_i denotes the predictor value for experimental unit i
3. y_i' is the predicted response (or fitted value) for experimental unit i

Then, the equation for the best fitting line using a sum of the error estimating function is:

$$y_i' = a_0' + a_1'x_i, \tag{6.12}$$

where a_0' and a_1' are the coefficients in Equation (6.10). Use of the above equation to predict the actual response y_i, leads to a prediction error (or residual error) of size:

$$e_i = y_i - y_i' \tag{6.13}$$

6.3.2 Least Square Estimation

Assume n data-points, i = 1, 2, …, n. A line out of two lines (Figure 6.6) that fits the data *best* will be one for which the sum of the squares of the n prediction errors (one for each observed data point) is as small as possible. This is the 'least squares criterion', which says that the best fit is one, which 'minimizes the sum of the squared prediction errors'. This implies that when the equation of the best fitting line is:

$$y_i' = b_0 + b_1 x_i, \tag{6.14}$$

where b_0 and b_1 are the coefficients which minimize the errors. The coefficients values make the sum of the squared prediction errors as small as possible. Thus,

$$\text{Minimize } Q = \sum_{i=1}^{n} (y_i - y_i')^2 \tag{6.15}$$

Q is also called chi-square function. To minimize $Q = \sum_{i=1}^{n} (y_i - (b_0 + b_1 x_i))^2$, compute the derivative with respect to b_0 and b_1, set to 0, respectively, and get the 'least squares estimates' for b_0 and b_1 as follows:

$$b_0 = \bar{y} - b_1 \bar{x}, \tag{6.16}$$

and

$$b_1 = \frac{\sum_{i=1}^{n} (x_i - \bar{x})(y_i - \bar{y})}{\sum_{i=1}^{n} (x_i - \bar{x})^2} \quad \text{... (6.17)}$$

The derivative of a dependent variable with respect to the independent variable is also called a gradient. Sections 6.7.1.3 and 6.7.3 describe the use of 'gradient descent', i.e., a gradient's descent towards convergence when optimizing for minimum values of gradient descent.

For obtaining the best-fit line here, the sum of the squared prediction error Q is minimized. Since the objective in the regression analysis is to minimize Q, Q is called objective function.

6.3.3 Multiple Regressions

A criterion variable can be predicted from one predictor variable in simple linear regression. The criterion can be predicted by two or more variables in ***multiple regressions***. The following example explains the meaning of multiple regression and coefficients.

EXAMPLE 6.4

Recall Example 6.3 where an assumption that university examination GPA depends on past examination HSP was made. Now assume that GPA depends on HSP as well as internal assessment (IA) at the university.

(i) How will you predict a student GPA on the basis of the HSP and IA during university study?
(ii) What do the coefficients tell?

SOLUTION

(i) Regression analysis requirement is to find a linear combination of HSP and IA that best predicts overall GPA. Regression relation gives GPA:

$$\text{GPA} = b_1.\text{HSP} + b_2.\text{IA} + b_0, \tag{6.18}$$

where b_0, b_1 and b_2 are regression coefficients.

(ii) With multiple independent variables, the coefficients tell how much the dependent (response) variable is expected to increase when the independent (predictor) variable increases by unit value, holding all the other independent variables constant. Remember, the units by which the variables are measured differ for different models. For example, assume $y = 1 + 2x_1 + 3x_2$. When x_2 is constant, for each change of 1 unit in x_1, y changes 2 units.

Multiple regressions are used when two or more independent factors are involved. These regressions are also widely used to make short- to mid-term predictions to assess which factors to include and which to exclude. Multiple regressions can be used to develop alternate models with different factors.

More than one variable can be used as a predictor with multiple regressions. However, it is always suggested to use a few variables as predictors necessarily, to get a reasonably accurate forecast. The prediction takes the form:

$$y = a + c_1.x_1 + c_2.x_2 + \ldots + c_n.x_n, \tag{6.19}$$

where a is the intercept of line on the y axis (means value of y when all independent variable values = 0). The $c_1, c_2, \ldots,$ and c_n are coefficients, representing the contributions (weights) of the independent variables $x_1, x_2, \ldots, x_n$ in the calculation of y.

Multiple regression analysis, often referred to simply as regression analysis, examines the effects of multiple independent variables on the value of a dependent variable or outcome.

Statistical significance means that the observer can be confident that the findings are real, and not just a coincidence, for the given data. Regression calculates a coefficient for each independent variable and its statistical significance, to estimate the effect of each independent variable on the dependent variable. An example of a regression study is to examine the effect of education, experience, gender and social background on income.

6.3.4 Modelling Possibilities using Regression

Regressions range from simple models to highly complex equations. Two primary uses for regression are forecasting and optimization. Consider the following examples:

1. Using linear analysis on sales data with monthly sales, a company could forecast sales for future months.
2. For the funds that a company has invested in marketing a particular brand, an analysis of whether the investment has given substantial returns or not can be made.
3. Suppose two promotion campaigns are running on TV and Radio in parallel. A linear regression can confine the individual as well as the combined impact of running these advertisements together.
4. An insurance company exploits a linear regression model to obtain a tentative premium table using predicted claims to Insured Declared Value ratio.
5. A financial company may be interested in minimizing its risk portfolio and hence want to understand the top five factors or reasons for default by a customer.
6. To predict the characteristics of child based on the characteristics of their parents.
7. A company faces an employment discrimination matter in which a claim that women are being discriminated against in terms of salary is raised.
8. Predicting the prices of houses, considering the locality and builder characteristics in a locality of a particular city.
9. Finding relationships between the structure and the biological activity of compounds through their physical, chemical and physicochemical traits is most commonly performed with regression techniques.
10. To predict compounds with higher bioactivity within groups.

6.3.5 Predictions using Regression Analysis

Regression analysis is a powerful technique used for predicting the unknown value of a variable from the known value of another variable. Regression analysis is generally a statistical method to deal with the formulation of a mathematical model depicting the relationship amongst dependent and independent variables. The dependent variable is used for the purpose of prediction of the values. One or more variables whose values are hypothesized are called independent variables. The prediction for the dependent variable can be made by accurate selection of independent variables to estimate a dependent variable.

Two steps for predicting the dependent variable:

1. *Estimation step*: A function is hypothesized and the parameters of the function are estimated from the data collected on the dependent variable.
2. *Prediction step*: The independent variable values are then input to the parameterized function to generate predictions for the dependent variable.

Consider an example of data that contain two variables, viz., crop yield and rainfall. Assume that the yield depends on rainfall (in certain critical growth phases). Using past yield data as a function of rainfall, the crop yield can be predicted. The application of linear regression upon these two variables will generate a linear equation, $y = a + b.x$, where y and x variables denotes crop yield and rainfall, respectively. Constants, a and b are the model's parameters known as the intercept and slope of the equation.

6.3.6 K-Nearest-Neighbour Regression Analysis

Consider the saying, 'a person is known by the company he/she keeps.' Can a prediction be made using neighbouring data points? K-Nearest Neighbours (KNN) analysis is an ML based technique using the concept, which uses a subset of $K = 1, 2$ or 3 neighbours in place of a complete dataset. The subset is a training dataset.

Assume that population (all data points of interest) consist of k-data points. A data point independent variable is x_i, where $i = 1$ to k. K-Nearest Neighbours (KNN) is an algorithm, which is usually used for classifiers. However, it is useful for regression also. Predictions can use all k examples (global examples) or just K examples (K-neighbours with K = 1, 2 or 3). It predicts the unknown value y_p using predictor variable x_p using the available values at the neighbours. The training dataset consists of available values of y_{ni} at x_{ni} with $n_i = 1$ to K, where n_i is the K-the neighbour, means just the local examples.

A subset of training dataset restricts k to K-neighbours, where $K = 1, 2$ or 3. This means using local values near the predictor variable. $K = 1$ means the nearest neighbour data points. $K = 2$ means the next nearest neighbour data points (x_i, y_i). $K = 3$ means the next to next nearest neighbour data points (x_i, y_i).

First find all available neighbouring target (x_i, y_i) cases and then predict the numerical value to be predicted based on a similarity measure. Prediction methods are as follows:

(i) Simple interpolation, when predictor variable is outside the training subset
(ii) Extrapolation, when predictor variable is outside the training subset
(iii) Averaging, local linear regression or local-weighted regression.

KNN analysis assumes that weight is inversely proportional to the square of distance ($w \alpha D^{-2}$), inverse of the distance (αD^{-1}) or inverse of qth power of the distance (αD^{-q}) called Euclidean D_{Eu}, Manhattan D_{Ma} and Minkowski D_{Mi} distances, respectively. When predicting, a weight assignment may require computations using a kernel function[1] like a Gaussian or tri-cube function (Section 6.2.5.1) in cases where the dependent variable varies according to the kernel function.

Assume continuously varying values as a function of independent variables. Assume v denotes the number of variables, independent as well as dependent. The following equations give the KNN distances in *v-dimensional space* for the purpose of using weights.

Euclidean Distance The following equation computes the Euclidean distance D_{Eu}:

Sum of the squared Euclidean distance, $[D_{Eu}]^2 = \left[\sum_{i=1}^{v}(x_i - x_i')^2\right]$, and

$$\text{Euclidean distance } D_{Eu} = \left[\sum_{i=1}^{v}(x_i - x_i')^2\right]^{1/2} \tag{6.20a}$$

Sum is over v dimensions. If one independent and one dependent variable, then $v = 2$. For example, if $v = 2$ and two data points are (x_j, y_j) and (x_{j+1}, y_{j+1}), then Euclidean distance between the points is as follows:

$$\text{Euclidean distance } D_{Eu} = [(x_j - x_{j+1})^2 + (y_j - y_{j+1})^2]^{1/2} \tag{6.20b}$$

Euclidean distance for three variables $v = 3$ (two independent variables and one dependent variable case) consists of three terms on the right-hand side in Equation (6.20b).

Manhattan Distance The following equation computes the Manhattan distance D_{Ma}:

$$\text{Manhattan distance } D_{Ma} = \sum_{i=1}^{v}\left[|x_i - x_i'|\right] \tag{6.20c}$$

Manhattan distance for three variables $v = 3$ (two independent variables and one dependent variable case) consists of three terms on the right-hand side in Equation (6.20c).

Comparison between Euclidean and Manhattan Distances Basically, Euclidean distance is the direct path distance between two data points in v-dimensional metric spaces. Manhattan distance is the staircase path distance between them. Staircase distance means to move to the next point, first move along one metric dimension (say, x axis) from the first point, and then move to the next along another dimension (say, y axis).

When $v = 2$, Euclidean distance is the diagonal distance between the points on an x-y graph. Manhattan distances are faster to calculate as compared to Euclidean distances. Manhattan distances are proportional to Euclidean distances in case of linear regression.

Minkowski Distance The following equation computes the Minkowski distance D_{Mi}:

$$\text{Minkowski distance } D_{Mi} = \left\{\sum_{i=1}^{v}\left[(x_i - x_i')^q\right]\right\}^{1/q} \tag{6.20d}$$

Hamming Distance When predictions are on the basis of categorical variables, then use the Hamming distance. It is a measure of the number of instances in which corresponding values are found.

$$\text{Hamming Distance, } D_H = \sum_{i=1}^{v}|x_i - x_i'|, \tag{6.20e}$$

when $xi = x_i'$ then $D_H = 0$ and when x_i not equal to x_i' then $D_H = 1$. For example, Hamming distance $D_H = 1$ between 101001 11100 and 111001 11100 because just one substitution is needed, change second bit from 0 to 1 at 10th place from the right to left positioned bits. Hamming distance $D_H = 4$ between 111001 00000 and 011001 11100 because we need four substitutions, change 3rd, 4th, 5th and from 0 to 1 and 11th bit from 1 to 0

An application is in text analytics. Hamming distance $D_H = 3$ between 'Bank notes' and 'Java notes'. The distance = 3 because the required number of changes is 3 at B, n and k among two strings. Another application of Hamming distance is in counting the number of data points off from the regression curve (Refer Section 6.4.4.6). Another application is in counting the wrong or distinct characters when comparing two document sentences.

Normalization Concept Normalization factor in p-norm form in a v-dimensional space is

$$x_i = N^{-1} \cdot x_i \text{ where } N = \left(\sum_{i=1}^{v} |x_i|^p\right)^{1/p} \quad (6.21)$$

Here, x_i is i^{th} component of the vector **X**. The total number of components are v. Two-dimensional space $v = 2$, three-dimensional $v = 3$.

The following example explains the meaning of distances, use of Euclidean and Manhattan distances, use distances for predictions, and the KNN regression analysis.

EXAMPLE 6.5

Assume dataset $\mathbb{S}$ with two subsets of sets J_{spi} and Z_{spi} for sales and sales percent increase (SPI) for Jaguar Land Rover and Zest models of Tata Motors Company. Assume $\mathbb{S}$ is training dataset and consists of data points as per the following table.

Table 6.2 An example of two car models, Jaguar, and Zest (JLRS and ZS), sales and sales percent increase (SPI) in years between 2012 and 2018

Year Y	Number of years from the base year 2012 Y_b	Car model Jaguar sales, JLRS	Car model M, SPI over previous year (M, J_{spi})	Car model Zest sales, ZS	Car model SPI over previous year (M, Z_{spi})
2012	0	1000	(0, 5)	10000	(1, 3)
2013	1	1040	(0, 4)	10400	(1, 4)
2014	2	1123	(0, 8)	11232	(1, 8)
2015	3	1224	(0, 9)	12242	(1, 9)
2016	4	1298	(0, 6)	12977	(1, 6)
2017	5	1428	(0, 10)	13496	(1, 4)
2018	6	1541	(0, 8)	14576	(1, 8)

M = 0 means Jaguar Land Rover, and M = 1 means Zest.

(i) Draw two plots, one with scatter set of points with **Y** and **ZS**, which means columns 1 and 5 data, second plot between $\mathbf{Y_b}$ and $\mathbf{J_{spi}}$ with columns 2 and 4.

(ii) Find the Euclidean 2-NN distance between third and first row data points (2014, 11232) and (2012, 10000).

(iii) What is the Manhattan 2-NN distance between the third and first row data points (2014, 11232) and (2012, 10000)?

(iv) What are seven Hamming distance terms of Equation (6.20e) between fourth and six column vectors **Jspi** and **Zspi**? Interpret the summed D_{Ha}.

(v) Assume data point for JLRS as missing for 2015. How do you predict car sales in 2015 assuming missing row for 2015? Use Euclidean distances using 1-NN. How do the results differ when using 2-NN and 3-NN?

(vi) How do you predict car sales for 2011? Use Euclidean distances.

(vii) How will you use 1-NN, 2-NN and 3-NN for estimation regression coefficient?

(viii) How will you calculate Euclidean distances D_{Eu} between values $\mathbf{J_{spi}}$ in columns 4 for Yb = 3 and 5?

(ix) How will you calculate D_{Eu} between value for column 2 $Y_b = 0$ and column 2 Z_{spi} value in column 6 for $Y_b = 1$, 3 and 4?

SOLUTION

(i) Figure 6.7 shows scatter set of points one for **Y** and **ZS**, which means data points in columns 1 and 5, and second for $\mathbf{Y_b}$ and $\mathbf{J_{spi}}$, which means data points in columns 2 and 4.

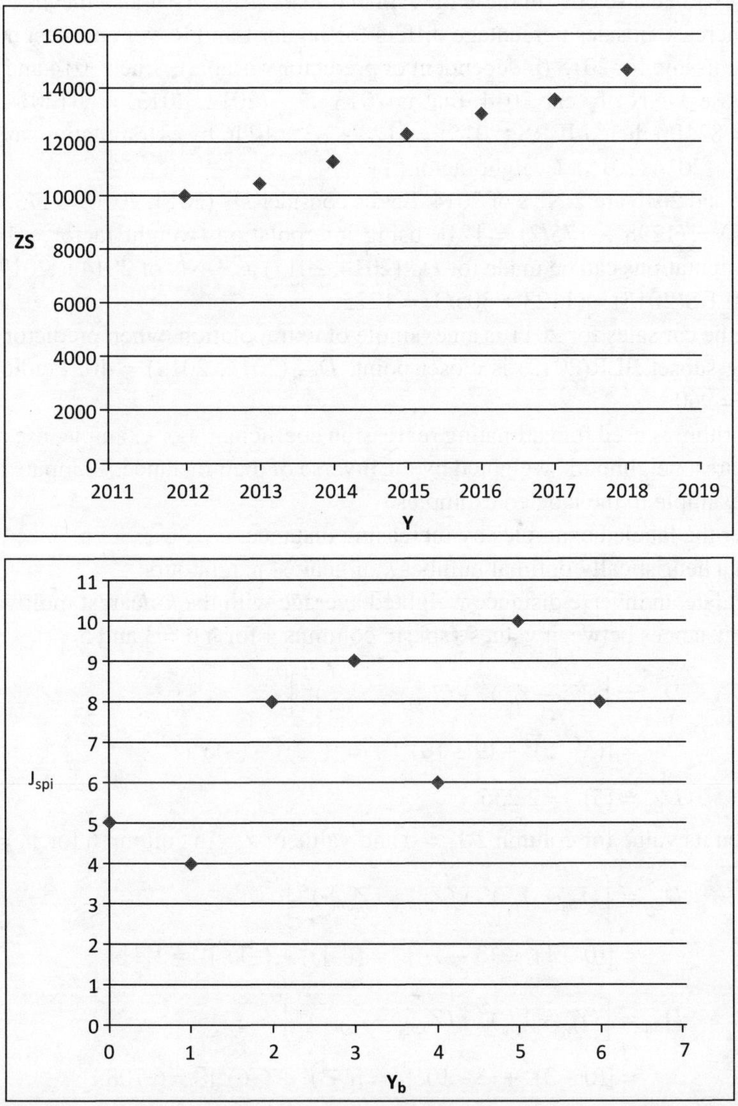

Figure 6.7 Scatter plots for two set of data points, one between **Y** and **ZS**, and second between $\mathbf{Y_b}$ and $\mathbf{J_{spi}}$

(ii) Using the equation, $D_{Eu} = [(x_j - x_{j+1})^2 + (y_j - y_{j+1})^2]^{½}$, find the Euclidean 2-NN distance between third and first row data points (2014, 11232) and (2012, 10000) $D_{Eu} = [(2014 - 2012)^2 + (11232 - 10000)^2]^{½} = [(2)^2 + (1232)^2]^{½} = 1232.001$.

(iii) Using the equation, $D_{Ma} = [(x_j - x_{j+1}) + (y_j - y_{j+1})]$. Manhattan 2-NN distance between third and first row data points (2014, 11232) and (2012, 10000) = [(2014 – 2012)+ (11232 – 10000)] = [2 + 1232] = 1234.

(iv) Hamming distances need to compute between fourth and six column vectors Jspi and Zspi are {1, 0, 0, 0, 0, 1, 0} because only in these the Jspi and Zspi differ. That also means that in two years out of seven, increase in sales percentage differs for Jaguar Land Rover and Zest models.

(v) Lets JLRS missing for 2015 (independent or predictor variable). Since 2014 and 2016 are its 1-NN. Let us choose 1-NN of year 2014, that is 2013. D_{Eu} (2014, 2013) = $\sqrt{\{(2014 - 2013)^2 + (1123 - 1040)^2\}}$ = 83. Predicted JLRS (2015) = 1123 + 83 = 1246 by extrapolation, assuming D_{Eu} (2014, 2013) = D_{Eu} (2014, 2015). (weight factors 1)
Years 2012 and 2016 are 2-NNs of 2014. Let us consider D_{Eu}(2014, 2016) = 175. Thus, the predicted JLRS(2015) = (1298 – 175/2) = 1210 using interpolation (weight factor = 1 per year change). Similar computations can be made for D_{Eu}(2014, 2017) as 3-NN of 2014 is 2017. D_{Eu} 3-NN = 305. Predicted JLRS(2015) = (1123 + 305/3) = 1225.

(vi) Predicting the car sales for 2011 is an example of extrapolation, when predictor variable is outside the training subset. JLR(2012) is closet point. D_{Eu} (2012, 2013) = 40. Predicted JLRS(2011) = 1000 – 40 = 960.

(vii) K-NN algorithm is used for estimating regression coefficient. For example, use a weighted average of the k-nearest neighbours, weighted by the inverse of their distance. Compute the Euclidean from the query example to the labeled examples.
   1. Order the labeled examples by increasing distance.
   2. Find a heuristically optimal number *k* of nearest neighbours.
   3. Calculate an inverse distance weighted average with the *k*-nearest multivariate neighbours.

(viii) Euclidean distances between values $\mathbf{Jspi_n}$ in columns 4 for Yb = 3 and 5

$$D_{Eu} = \left[(Y_{b_3} - Y_{b_5})^2 + (J_{spi_3} - J_{spi_5})^2\right]^{1/2}$$
$$= [(3-5)^2 + (9-10)^2]^{1/2} = [(-2)^2 + (-1)^2]^{1/2}$$
$$D_{Eu} = [5]^{½} = 2.236$$

(ix) D_{Eu} between its value for column 2 $Y_b = 0$ and value of Z_{spi} in column 6 for $Y_b = 1, 3$, and 4

$$D_{Eu} = \left[(Y_{b_0} - Y_{b_1})^2 + (Z_{spi_0} - Z_{spi_1})^2\right]^{1/2}$$
$$= [(0-1)^2 + (3-4)^2]^{½} = [(-1)^2 + (-1)^2]^{½} = 1.414$$
$$D_{Eu} = \left[(Y_{b_0} - Y_{b_3})^2 + (Z_{spi_0} - Z_{spi_3})^2\right]^{1/2}$$
$$= [(0-3)^2 + (3-9)^2]^{½} = [(-3)^2 + (-6)^2]^{½} = 6.708$$
$$D_{Eu} = \left[(Y_{b_0} - Y_{b_4})^2 + (Z_{spi_0} - Z_{spi_4})^2\right]^{1/2}$$
$$= [(0-4)^2 + (3-6)^2]^{½} = [(-4)^2 + (-3)^2]^{½} = 5.0$$

Self-Assessment Exercise linked to LO 6.2

1. How does regression analysis predict the value of the dependent variable in case of linear regression? ○○●
2. (i) Define objective function for least square fitting of coefficients in regression equation.
   (ii) How are the best-fitting regression coefficients evaluated? ○●●
3. When are multiple regressions used? How do multiple regressions predict intermediate term? How do multiple regressions assess which factors to include and which to exclude? How do multiple regressions help in developing alternate models with different factors? ●●●
4. How is KNN regression used for predicting, considering two variables and K = 3? Use training dataset given in Example 6.5. ○●●
5. How do KNN regression computations differ when using Euclidean and Manhattan distances? Consider two variables and K = 3. Use the training dataset given in Example 6.5. ○●●

6.4 FINDING SIMILAR ITEMS, SIMILARITY OF SETS AND COLLABORATIVE FILTERING

LO 6.3

Finding similar items, applications of Near-Neighbour search; Jaccard similarity of sets; similarity of documents; collaborative filtering as a similar-set problem; and Euclidean, Jaccard, Cosine, Edit and Hamming distances

Similar item search refers to a data mining method which helps in discovering items which have similarities in datasets. (*Data mining* means discovering previously unknown interesting patterns and knowledge from apparently unstructured data. The process of data mining uses the ML algorithms. Data mining enables analysis, categorization and summarization of data and relationships among data.)

The following subsections describe methods of finding similar items using similarities, application of near-neighbour search, Jaccard similarity of sets, similarity of documents, Collaborative Filtering (CF) as a similar-set problem, and the distance measures for finding similarities.

6.4.1 Finding Similar Items

An analysis requires many times to find similar items. For example, finding similar excellent performance of students in Python programming, similar showrooms of a specific car model which show high sales per month, recommending books on similar topic such as in Internet of Things by Raj Kamal from McGraw-Hill Higher Education, etc.

6.4.1.1 Application of Near Neighbour Search

Similar items can be found using Nearest Neighbour Search (NNS). The search finds that a point in a given set is most similar (closest) to a given point. A dissimilarity function having larger value means less similar. The dissimilarity function is used to find similar items.

NNS algorithm is as follows: Consider set $\mathbb{S}$ having points in a space **M**. Consider a queried point q $\in$**M**, which means q is member of M. k-NNS algorithm finds the k-closet (1-NN) points to q in $\mathbb{S}$.

Three problems with the Pearson similarities (6.2.6.1):

1. Do not consider the number of items in which two users' preferences overlap. (e.g., 2 overlap items ==> 1, more items may not be better.)

2. If two users overlap on only one item, no correlation can be computed.
3. The correlation is undefined if series of preference values are identical.

Greater distance means greater dissimilarity. Dissimilarity coefficient relates to a distance metric in metrics space in v-dimensional space. An algorithm computes Euclidean, Manhattan and Minkowski distances using Equations (6.20a) to (6.20d).

Distance metric is symmetric and follows triangular inequality. Meaning of triangular inequality can be understood by an example. Consider three vectors of lengths x, y, and z. Then, triangular inequality means $z < x + y$. It is similar to the theorem of inequality that the third side of a triangle is less than the sum of two other sides, and never equal. The theorem applies to v-dimensional space also. Dissimilarity can be asymmetric, i.e., triangular inequality is not true (Bergman divergence).

Consider a linear search (also referred as Naïve search) algorithm, Naïve, one of meaning is *simple* in English. Search requires computations of distances to every other point. The algorithm running time is large. The time function, O (v.c) which measures the efficiency of the search algorithm in terms of means v.c. The v is dimensionality of M and c is cardinality of S. Cardinality refers to the number of relationships. For example, one independent variable and two dependent variables in a relationship, then cardinality is 3. Cardinality in the context of databases means the uniqueness of values contained in a column fields.

Note: Space partitioning followed by the search algorithm is an efficient method using a k-d tree or R-tree data structure. Search is made after arranging the tree-like data structure. Space partitioning problems become complex in case of high dimensionality.

Naïve search algorithm outperforms space partitioning approaches when using high dimensional spaces **M** and high cardinality.[2]

The following example explains the NNS approach to find similar items.

EXAMPLE 6.6

Assume a set $\mathbb{S}$ consists of data of a large number of students. The dataset consists of grade points (GPs) in each of the five subjects of study in a semester. The total dataset is for six semesters. Each semester examination awards SGPAs (Semester Grade Point averages). CGPA_i (Cumulative GPA of ith semester) calculates after end of ith semester after adding the SGPAs of previous semesters. Assume that each student GP is on a 10-point scale. A student performance in a subject is high (H) if GP is 8.0 or close within ±1.0. A student performance in a subject is excellent (E) if GP is 9.0 or close by within ±1.0.

(i) How will you choose independent and dependent variables? What does metric space mean?
(ii) How will you define a metric space for finding similar performances in a specific subject? How will you define a metric space **M** for finding similar performance from SGPAs of the first semester? How will you define a metric space for finding similar performances from CGPAs of a semester?
(iii) What will you consider $\mathbb{S}$ for finding similarities by NNS?
(iv) What does nearest neighbour search mean when search is for students with similar excellent performance?
(v) How will you find students of similar excellent performance by the GPs of a subject, say Java Programming in the second semester?
(vi) How will you find similar excellent performances by the CGPA?

[2] Weber, Roger; Schek, Hans-J.; Blott, Stephen, 'A quantitative analysis and performance study for similarity search methods in high dimensional spaces'

(vii) How will you find similar high performances by the SGPA?

(viii) How will you compute Euclidian and Manhattan distances with respect to query point GP = 8.0 ±1.0? How will you compute dissimilarity?

(ix) What do you mean by dimensionality of **M**? What do you mean by cardinality of $\mathbb{S}$?

SOLUTION

(i) Independent variables are student ID, year of study, semester period, name and type (theory or practical) of five subjects. Dependent variables are GP, GPA, SGPA and CGPA. Metric space means a space in which variables are quantifiable. For example, GP, GPA, SGPA and CGPA.

(ii) Metric space for finding similar performances in a specific subject, Metric space M for finding similar performance in SGPA of first semester, Metric space for finding similar performances from CGPA of a semester:

(iii) Members of set $\mathbb{S}$ are input vectors, each having elements {studentID, CGPA [or SGPA, GPA, T_GPA (GPA of theory subject), P_GPA (GPA of practical subject)]} for each student for finding the similarities by NNS using three distances D1, D2, D3 of first, second and third nearest neighbours.

(iv) Nearest neighbour search for students with similar excellent performance means search of studentIDs awarded CGPA within the distance 1.0 from 9.0.

(v) Students of similar excellent performance by the GPs of a subject, say Java Programming, in the second semester means Student IDs with GPs in Java programming within the distance ±1.0 from 9.0.

(vi) Similar excellent performance by the CGPA means similar performance of students_IDs with CGPA within the distance ±1.0 from 9.0.

(vii) Similar high performance by the SGPA means similar performance of students_IDs with SGPA within the distance ±1.0 from 8.0.

(viii) Computation of Euclidian distances with respect query point GP = 8.0 ± 1.0
Computation of Manhattan distances with respect query point GP = 8.0 ± 1.0

(ix) Dimensionality of **M** equals the number of independent and dependent variables in metric space for which distances are quantifiable.
Cardinality of $\mathbb{S}$ means number of relationships, number of independent but unrelated and dependent unrelated variables. For example, subject_name and subject_type is related to each other. Therefore, subject_name and subject_type are counted as one variable when computing cardinality.

6.4.2 Jaccard Similarity of Sets

Let A and B be two sets. Jaccard similarity coefficient of two sets measures using notations in set theory as shown below:

$$J(A, B) = \frac{|A \cap B|}{|A \cup B|} \tag{6.22}$$

$A \cap B$ means the number of elements or items that are same in sets A and B. $A \cup B$ means the number of elements or items present in union of both the sets. Assume two set of students in two computer courses, Computer Applications CA, and Computer Science CS in a semester. Set CA 40 students opted for Java out of 60 students. Set CS 30 students opted for Java out of 50 students. Jaccard similarity coefficient

J_{java} (CA, CS) = 30/(60 + 50) × 100% = 27%. Two sets are sharing 27% of the members for Java course. (∩ is symbol for intersection in set theory. ∪ is symbol for union in set theory.)

6.4.2.1 *Similarity of Documents*

An application of Jaccard similarity coefficient is in Natural Language Processing (NLP) and text processing. It quantifies the similarity in documents. Computational steps are as follows:

1. Find Bag of Words (Section 9.2.1.4) and remove words such as is, are, does, at, in, ….
2. Assign weighting factor is the Term frequency and Inverse Document Frequency (TF-IDF). Consider the frequency of words in the document.
3. Find *k*-shingles. A shingle is a word of fixed length. The k-shingles are the number of times the similar shingles extracted from a document or text. Examples of a shingle are Java, GP, 8.0, Python, 80%, Programming.
4. Find *n*-grams. A gram is a contiguous sequence of fixed length item (word or set of characters, letters, words in pairs, triplets, quadruplets, ...) in a document or text. The n-grams are the number of times the similar items (1-grams, 2-grams, ..) extracted from a document or text. The 3-gram examples are Java GP 8.0, Python Programming 7.8, Big Data Analytics, 23A 240C 8LP, the numbers of which are extracted from the text.
5. Compute Jaccard similarity coefficient using Equation (6.22) between the documents.

A number of other methods exist for computing similarity of documents. One method is Latent Semantic Indexing method (LSI). The computational steps are as follows:

- Steps 1 and 2 are the same as above.
- Consider documents into word space. Reduce dimensionality of the projection space. An algebraic model is one that represents text documents as vectors or identifiers, such as how many times a word is present in a document, the index terms or deploy singular value decomposition method.
- Use Cosine Similarity measure between the documents.

Refer Section 9.2 for details on text analysis.

6.4.3 Collaborative Filtering as a Similar-Sets Finding Problem

An analysis requires finding similar sets using collaborative filtering. Collaborative filtering refers to a filtering algorithm, which filters the items sets that have similarities with different items in a dataset.

CF finds the sets with items having the same or close similarity coefficients. Following are some examples of applications of CF:

- Find those sets of students in computer application, and computer science who opt for the Java Programming subject in a semester.
- Find sets of students in Java Programming subjects to whom same teacher taught and they showed excellent performance.

An algorithm finds the similarities between the sets for the CF. Applications of CF are in many ML methods, such as association rule mining, classifiers, and recommenders.

6.4.4 Distance Measures for Finding Similar Items or Users

Distance measures compute the dissimilarities. Complement of dissimilarity gives similarity. The following subsections describe the distance measures.

6.4.4.1 *Definition of a Distance*

Distance can be defined in a number of ways. Distance is the measure of length of a line between two values in a two-dimensional map or graph. Set of Equations (6.20) measures distances.

For example, distance between (2014, 6%) and (2018, 8%) on a scatter plot when year is on the x axis and profit % on the y axis is Distance = $\sqrt{[(2014-2018)^2+(6-8)^2]} = \sqrt{(16+4)} = 4.47$, using Equation (6.20b). Distance can also be similarly defined in v-dimensional space using Equation (6.20a).

Distances between all members in a set of points can be computed in metrics space using a mathematical equation. Metrics space means measurable or quantifiable space. For example, profit and year on a scatter plot are in metric space of two dimensions. Probability distribution function values are in metric space.

Consider student-performance measures 'very good' and 'excellent'. These parameters are in non-metric space. How are they made measurable? They become measurable when very good is specified as grade point average 8.5 which implies that a score between 8.0 to 9.0 is very good, and define 9.5 which implies that a score between 9.0 to 10.0 is excellent on a 10-point scale.

Consider a chart between number of students passing in examination with best grades vs languages C++, Java, Node.js and Python. Languages are in non-metric space. They become measurable when numbers, say 0, 1, 2 and 3 are assigned for a language for the purpose of using distance measure for similarity analysis.

Distance can be defined as the reciprocal of weight in v-dimensional space. For example, a point at unit distance can be taken as weight w = 1, and a point at distance = 2, w = ½ and so on.

Distance can also be defined as dissimilarity coefficient in v-dimensional space. Greater distance means greater dissimilarity. Subtracting dissimilarity coefficient from 1 gives similarity coefficient. Many different algorithms exist to compute distance and thus similarity between entities, number of users or items. An algorithm computes the distances D_{Eu}, D_{Ma}, D_{Mi}, D_{Ha} [Equations (6.20a to e)] or any other distance metric, for example, Jaccard distance D_{Ja}, cosine distance D_{Cos}, edit distance D_{Ed}.

Jaccard similarity, Cosine similarity, edit distance or correlation methods are used to find out similarities between users.

6.4.4.2 *Euclidean Distance*

Euclidean distance $D_{Eu} = \left[\sum_{i=1}^{v}(x_i - x_i')^2\right]^{1/2}$, refer Equation (6.20a) in Section 6.3.6 for details.)

6.4.4.3 *Jaccard Distance*

Equation (6.22) gives J ($\mathcal{A}$, $\mathcal{B}$). Jaccard distance, D_{Ja} ($\mathcal{A}$, $\mathcal{B}$) measures the dissimilarity between two sets. It is equal to result of subtraction of Jaccard similarity coefficient J ($\mathcal{A}$, $\mathcal{B}$) from 1.

$$D_{Ja}(\mathcal{A}, \mathcal{B}) = 1 - J(\mathcal{A}, \mathcal{B}) \tag{6.23}$$

(Refer Section 6.4.2 for details.)

6.4.4.4 *Cosine Distance*

Cosine similarity is a measure of similarity in the inner-product space between two vectors of finite magnitudes. Cosine distance D_{Cos} is measure of dissimilarity between vectors. A measure of cosine distance is in terms of the angle between the vectors. Cosine similarity has low complexity. Cosine distance has applications in text mining, finding similarity of documents, and similarities in sparse vectors, column-vectors (fields) and matrices (Section 3.3.3.1).

Let **U** and **V** be two non-zero vectors, two documents in the vector space.

$$D_{\text{Cos}}(\mathbf{U}, \mathbf{V}) = \frac{\sum_i U_i V_i}{\sqrt{\sum_i U_i^2}\sqrt{\sum_i V_i^2}}, \tag{6.23a}$$

where U_i and V_i are components of **U** and **V**, respectively, and summation in numerator is over $i = 1$ to N, where N is the number of elements of the vectors.

No Triangular Inequality Property Cosine distances do not exhibit triangular inequality property, while the Euclidean distances exhibit triangular inequality (Section 6.4.1.1).

Vector Cosine-Based Similarity **Vector cosine similarity** in terms of angle ϕ between two vectors U and V is given by equation:

$$\phi_{\text{UV}} = \cos^{-1}(\mathbf{U}, \mathbf{V}) = \frac{\boldsymbol{U} \cdot \boldsymbol{V}}{[\|\boldsymbol{U}\| - \|\boldsymbol{V}\|]} \tag{6.23b}$$

Consider Example 6.5. Let each model have Sales Percentage Increase (SPI) values in successive years. The similarity between SPIs of two models, M_1 and M_2, is measured by treating each model as a vector of SPIs and computing the cosine of the angle formed by the SPI vectors.

Formally, if **P** is $m \times n$ SPI matrix for a model M, then the similarity between two models, M_i and Mj is defined as the cosine in the n-dimensional vectors space corresponding to the ith and j^{th} columns of **P**.

The following example illustrates computing of cosine and Euclidean similarities to find similar items.

EXAMPLE 6.7

Consider members of a dataset $\mathbb{S}$ in five-dimensional metric space. Assume $\mathbb{S}$ subsets are $\mathcal{JLR}$ and $\mathcal{Z}$. Data subset members consist of values in two column vectors $\mathbf{J_{spi}}$ and $\mathbf{Z_{spi}}$ of the elements SPIs. Data subset $\mathcal{JLR}$ consists of percentage increase in sales number in a year of Tata Jaguar Land Rovers cars, and $\mathcal{Z}$ consists of Zest cars SPIs. (Example 6.5) Assume dataset $\mathbb{S}$ consists of data points as per Table 6.2.

(i) Represent members of dataset $\mathbb{S}$ of table data points in five-dimensional metric space consisting of three independent variables Y, Y_b, M and two dependent variables J_{spi} and Z_{spi}.

(ii) Represent the members of six subsets for values in columns 1, 2, 3 and 5 as elements of vectors **Y**, $\mathbf{Y_b}$, and matrices (**M**, $\mathbf{J_{spi}}$) and (**M**, $\mathbf{Z_{spi}}$), respectively.

(iii) Represent the table data points in two-dimensional metric spaces (Y_b, Jspi) and (Y_b, Zspi).

(iv) Represent the table data points in three-dimensional metric space (Y_b, Jspi, Zspi).

(v) How will you calculate the cosine distance, cosine similarity and angle between the vectors $\mathbf{J_{spi}}$ and $\mathbf{Z_{spi}}$?

(vi) How will you calculate Euclidean similarity using six neighbour distances D_{Eu} starting from Z_{spi} for $Y_b = 0$ and Z_{spi} values in columns 6 for $Y_b = 1$ to 5?

SOLUTION

(i) $\mathbb{S}$\{2012, 0, (0,5), (1,3)\}, \{2013, 1, (0,4), (1,4)\}, \{2014, 2, (0,8), (1,8)\}, \{2015, 3, (0,9), (1,9)\}, \{2016, 4, (0,6), (1,6)\}, \{2017, 5, (0,10), (1,10)\}, \{2018, 6, (0,8), (1,8)\}

(ii) **Y** = \{2012, 2013, 2014, 2015, 2016, 2017, 2018\}, $\mathbf{Y_b}$ = \{0, 1, 2, 3, 4, 5, 6\}, (**M**, $\mathbf{J_{spi}}$ = \{(0,5), (0, 4), (0, 8), (0, 9), (0. 6), (0, 10), (0, 8)\}, and (**M**, $\mathbf{Z_{spi}}$) = \{(1, 3), (1, 4), (1, 8), (1, 9), (1, 6), (1, 4), (1, 7)\}

(iii) $(\mathbf{Y_b}, \mathbf{J_{spi}})$ = {(0,5), (0,4), (0,8), (0,9), (0,6), (0,10), (0,8)} and $(\mathbf{Y_b}, \mathbf{Z_{spi}})$ = {(0,3), (0,4), (0,8), (0,9), (0,6), (0,4), (0,8)}

(iv) $(\mathbf{Y_b}, \mathbf{J_{spi}}, \mathbf{Z_{spi}})$ = {{(0,5, 3), (1,4, 4), (2,8, 8), (3,9, 9), (4,6, 6), (5,10, 4), (6,8, 8)}.

(v) D_{cos} (**Jspi, Zspi**) = $\{(5 \times 3) + (4 \times 4) + (8 \times 8) + (9 \times 9) + (6 \times 6) + (10 \times 4) + (8 \times 8)\}/\sqrt{\{5^2 + 4^2 + 8^2 + 9^2 + 6^2 + 10^2 + 8^2\}} \times \sqrt{\{3^2 + 4^2 + 8^2 + 9^2 + 6^2 + 4^2 + 8^2\}} = 0.951$

Cosine similarity = 1 – D_{cos} (**Jspi, Zspi**) = 1– 0.951 = 0.049

Angle between **Jspi**, **Zspi** = $\cos^{-1}(D_{cos}) = 87.191$

(vi) Use Equation (6.20b) for the computations.

1. D_{Eu} $(Y_b = 0, Y_b = 1) = \sqrt{\{(0 - 1)^2 + (3 - 4)^2\}}$;
2. D_{Eu} $(Y_b = 1, Y_b = 2) = \sqrt{\{(1 - 2)^2 + (4 - 8)^2\}}$;
3. D_{Eu} $(Y_b = 2, Y_b = 3) = \sqrt{\{(2 - 3)^2 + (8 - 9)^2\}}$
4. D_{Eu} $(Y_b = 3, Y_b = 4) = \sqrt{\{(3 - 4)^2 + (9 - 6)^2\}}$
5. D_{Eu} $(Y_b = 4, Y_b = 5) = \sqrt{\{(4 - 5)^2 + (6 - 4)^2\}}$
6. D_{Eu} $(Y_b = 5, Y_b = 6) = \sqrt{\{(5 - 6)^2 + (4 - 8)^2\}}$

Euclidean similarity coefficient = 1 – √{Sum of all square of all six D_{Eu} values using 1-NN} divided by {√(6^2 + Sum of square of all six J_{spi} values)}

(vii) Euclidean similarity = $1 - \sqrt{\{2^2 + 17^2 + 2^2 + 10^2 + 5^2 + 17^2\}}/\{\sqrt{(6^2 + 386}\} = -0.305$

Differing Similarity Coefficients for SPIs Calculated from Cosine distances and Euclidean Distances The following section explains the use of cosine distance and the situations in which D_{Cos} does not find similarity correctly.

Consider a comparison between the cosine and Euclidean similarities when finding similar items. Several situations exist in which predictions from two computational approaches differ. The reason is that triangular inequality holds true for Euclidean distances, while does not hold true for cosine distances.

Certain dimensions have widely different values. For example, let us compare sales JLRS and ZS in column 3 and 5 of Table 6.2. ZS values are nearly ten times the value of JLRS values. A solution is normalizing the values in all dimensions by dividing with the mean values using Equation (6.21). However, that also may give differing and incorrect results using D_{Cos}.

Cosine singularity is found to exhibit correct results for similarities in text documents. Cosine similarity is very efficient to evaluate situations of sparse vectors and those where one needs to consider non-zero values in the dimensions.

Concept of Sparse and Dense Vectors Sparse vector uses a hash-map and consists of non-zero values. Hash-map is a collection, which stores data in (key-value) format (Section 3.3.1). Format is also called random access. Hashing means to convert a large value or string into shorter value or string so that indexing for searching is fast.

For example, assume a vector, which consists of array elements, (subject, number of students opting, average GPA).

1. Dense vectors have elements (Hive, 40, 8.0), (Java, 30, 8.5), (FORTRAN, 0, 0), (Pascal, 0, 0). Dense vector consists of all elements, whether the element value is 0 or not 0.
2. Sparse vectors will be two only with elements (4, 40, 8.0) and (3, 30, 8.5). Random access Sparse vector means access to elements (key, value pairs) using key. Sparse vector consists of elements for which key is such that value is not 0 (Section 3.3.1).

3. Sparse vector has an associated hash-map in form of a hash-table. First row— Pascal, 1, second row— FORTRAN, 2, third row— Java, 3 and fourth row— Hive.
4. Hashing is a process of assigning a small number or small-sized string indexing, searching and memory saving purposes. Hash process uses a hash function, which results into not-colliding values. In case of two colliding numbers, the process assigns a new number. Sequential access sparse vectors mean two parallel accessing vectors, i.e., one to access keys and the other for values.

6.4.4.5 Edit Distance

Edit distance D_{Ed} is a distance measure for dissimilarity between two set of strings or words. D_{Ed} equals the minimum number of inserts and deletes of characters needed to transform one set into another. Applications of edit distances are in text analytics and natural language processing, similarities in DNA sequences etc. DNA sequences are strings of characters.

Levenshtein suggested a method for finding edit distance, minimum number of operations of deletion, insertion or substitution of a character in a set of strings to transform one into another. The cost of substitution is taken as 2. Thus, edit distance from computation using that method is also called the Levenshtein method.[3]

6.4.4.6 Hamming Distance

If both **U** and **V** are vectors, Hamming distance D_{Ha} is equal to the number of different elements between these two vectors. Recall Example 6.5 (iv) for Hamming distance between **Jspi** and **Zspi**. Hamming similarity-coefficient between car models Jaguar Land Rover and Zest is (1– 2/7) = 0.7. [70%]

If **M** is a matrix, then D_{Ha} is equal to the number of different elements between the rows of **M** ignoring the columns.

D_{Ha} between two strings of equal length is the number of positions at which the corresponding characters differ. D_{Ha} is also equal to the minimum number of substitutions required to transform one string into the other. D_{Ha} is also equal to the minimum number of errors that need correction using transformation or substitution.

Hamming distance is therefore another distance measure for measuring the edit distance between two sets of strings, words or sequences.

Self-Assessment Exercise linked to LO 6.3

1. Why is triangular inequality in a distance measure important? ○○●
2. How will you compute Jaccard similarity coefficients between datasets for Jspi and Zspi . Use data Table 6.2 as the training dataset. ○○●
3. Why does similarity in documents computed? ○●●
4. Write applications of Euclidean, Jaccard, Cosine, Edit and Hamming distance measures. ○●●
5. Explain how Euclidean, Jaccard, Cosine and Hamming distance measures can be applied for analyzing the dataset given in Table 6.2? ●●●

[3] https://en.wikipedia.org/wiki/Levenshtein_distance

6.5 FREQUENT ITEMSETS AND ASSOCIATION RULE MINING

LO 6.4

Frequent Item-sets Mining (FIM), applications of FIM, market basket model, mining the association rules, use of Apriori algorithm, evaluation of candidate rules, applications of association rules, and finding the association and similarity

The following subsections describes frequent itemset mining, market basket model, association rules mining, and their applications.

6.5.1 Frequent Itemset Mining

Extracting knowledge from a dataset is the main goal of data analytics and data mining. Data mining mainly deals with the type of patterns that can be mined. A method of mining is Frequent Patterns (FPs) mining method. Frequent patterns occur frequently in transactional data.

Frequent itemset refers to a set of items that frequently appear together, for example, Python and Big Data Analytics. Students of computer science frequently choose these subjects for in-depth studies. *Frequent itemset* refers to a frequent itemset, which is a subset of items that appears frequently in a dataset.

Frequent Itemset Mining (FIM) refers to a data mining method which helps in discovering the itemsets that appear frequently in a dataset. For example, finding a set of students who frequently show poor performance in semester examinations. *Frequent subsequence* is a sequence of patterns that occurs frequently. For example, purchasing a football follows purchasing of sports kit. *Frequent substructure* refers to different structural forms, such as graphs, trees or lattices, which may be combined with itemsets or subsequences.

FIM is one of the popular techniques to extract knowledge from data. The technique has been an essential part of data analysis and data mining. The extraction is based on frequently occurring events. An algorithm specifies a given minimum frequency threshold for considering an itemset as frequent. The extraction generally depends on the specified threshold.

FIM finds the regularities in data. Frequent itemset mining is the preceding step to the association rule learning algorithm. Most often the algorithm is used for analyzing a business. For example, customers of supermarkets, mail order companies and online shops use FIM to find a set of products that are frequently bought together. This provides the knowledge of important pairs of items that occur much more frequently than the items bought independently. A sales person can learn the pattern of what should be bought together for sales.

The analysis results in:

- Improvement of arrangement of products in shelves and on catalog pages
- Marketing and sales promotion
- Planning of products that a store should stock up
- Support cross-selling (suggestion of other products) and product bundling.

6.5.2 Association Rule— Overview

An important method of data mining is association rule mining or association analysis. The method has been widely used in many application areas for discovering interesting relationships which are present in large datasets. The objective is to find uncovered relationships using some strong rules. The rules are termed as association rules for frequent itemsets. Mahout includes a 'parallel frequent pattern growth' algorithm. The method analyzes the items in a group and then identifies which items typically appear together (association) (Section 6.8). A formal statement of the association rule problem is:

Let $\mathfrak{I} = \{I_1, I_2, \ldots, I_d\}$ be a set of d distinct attributes, also called literals. Let $\mathfrak{T} = \{t_1, t_2, \ldots, t_n\}$ be set of n transactions and contain a set of items such that $\mathfrak{T} \subseteq \mathfrak{I}$. An association rule is an implication of the form, $X \rightarrow Y$, where X, Y belong to sets of items called itemsets ($X, Y \subset \mathfrak{I}$), and X and Y are disjoint itemsets ($X \cap Y = \emptyset$). Here, X is called antecedent, and Y consequent.

Explanation:

1. $\subseteq$ means 'subset of', $\subset$ means 'proper (strict) subset of', $\cap$ means intersection and $\emptyset$ means disjoint, no commonality in members.
2. Consider an If () then () form of a rule. The *If part* of the rule (*A*) is known as *antecedent* and the *THEN* part of the rule (B) is known as *consequent*. The condition is *antecedent*. Result is *consequent*.

6.5.3 Apriori Algorithm

Apriori algorithm is used for frequent itemset mining and association rule mining. Apriori algorithm is considered as one of the most well-known association rule algorithms. The algorithm simply follows a basis that any subset of a large itemset must be a large itemset. This basis can be formally given as the Apriori principle. The Apriori principle can reduce the number of itemsets needed to be examined. Apriori principle suggests if an itemset is frequent, then all of its subsets must also be frequent. For example, if itemset {A, B, C} is a frequent itemset, then all of its subsets {A}, {B}, {C}, {A, B}, {B, C} and {A, C} must be frequent. On the contrary, if an itemset is not frequent, then none of its supersets can be frequent. This results into a smaller list of potential frequent itemsets as the mining progresses.

Support is an indication of how popular an itemset is. That is the frequency of the itemset for appearing in a database.

Assume X and Y are two itemsets. Apriori principle holds due to the following property of support measure:

$$\forall X, Y: (X \subseteq Y) \rightarrow s(X) \geq s(Y) \tag{6.24}$$

Explanation: $\forall$ means for all, and $\subseteq$ means 'subset of' and can be 'equal to or included in'. Support of an itemset never exceeds the support of its subsets. This is known as the *anti-monotone property* of support.

The algorithm uses k-itemsets (An itemset which contains k items is known as a k-itemset) to explore (k+1)-itemsets in order to mine frequent itemsets from transactional database for the Boolean association rules (If Then rule is a Boolean association rule, as it checks if true or false).

The frequent itemset algorithm uses candidate generation process. The groups of candidates are then tested against the dataset. Apriori uses breadth-first search method and a hash tree structure to count candidate itemsets. Also, it is assumed that items within an itemset are kept in lexicographic order. The algorithm identifies the frequent individual items in the database and extends them to larger and larger itemsets as long as those itemsets are found in the database. The frequent itemsets provide the general trends in the database as well.

6.5.4 Evaluation of Candidate Rules

Apriori algorithm evaluates candidates for association as follows:

C_k: Set of candidate-itemsets of size k
F_l: Set of frequent itemsets of size k
F_1 = {large items}
for (k=1; F_k != 0; k++) *do* {
C_{k+1} = New candidates generated from F_k

for each transaction t in the database *do*
Increment the count of all candidates in C_{k+1} that are contained in t
F_{k+1} = Candidates in C_{k+1} with minimum support
}

Steps of the algorithm can be stated in the following manner:

1. Candidate itemsets are generated using only large itemsets of the previous iteration. The transactions in the database are not considered while generating candidate itemsets.
2. The large itemset of the previous iteration is joined with itself to generate all itemsets having size higher by 1.
3. Each generated itemset that does not have a large subset is discarded. The remaining itemsets are candidate itemsets.

Figure 6.8 shows Apriori algorithm process for adopting the subset of frequent itemsets as a frequent itemset.

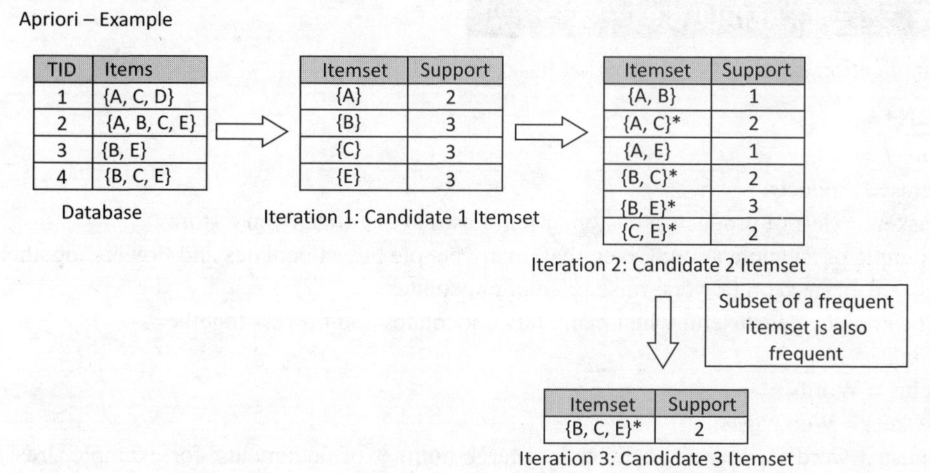

Figure 6.8 Apriori algorithm process for adopting the subset of frequent itemsets as a frequent itemset

It is observed in the Apriori example that every subset of a frequent itemset is also frequent. Thus, a candidate itemset in C_{k+1} can be pruned even if one of its subsets is not contained in F_k.

The Apriori algorithm adopts the fact that the subset of a frequent itemset is also a frequent itemset. The algorithm thus reduces the number of candidates being considered by only considering the itemsets whose support count is greater than the minimum support count. All infrequent itemsets are pruned if they have an infrequent subset.

Apriori algorithm also possesses certain disadvantages. The algorithm requires multiple scans of a database. The process for generation of a complex candidate exploits more time, space and memory. Therefore, Big Data analytics need alternatives to Apriori algorithm to cut down on the size of candidate pairs. Section 7.4 will describe Park, Chen and Yu (PCY), multistage and multihash algorithms.

6.5.5 Applications of Association Rules

FIM is a popular technique for market basket analysis.

6.5.5.1 *Market Basket Model*

Market basket analysis is a tool for knowledge discovery about co-occurrence of items. A co-occurrence means two or more things occur together. It can also be defined as a data mining technique to derive the strength of association between pairs of product items. If people tend to buy two products (say A and B) together, then the buyer of product A is a potential customer for an advertisement of product B.

The concept is similar to the real market basket where we select an item (product) and put it in a basket (itemset). The basket symbolizes the transactions. The number of baskets is very high as compared to the items in a basket. A set of items that is present in many baskets is termed as a frequent itemset. Frequency is the proportion of baskets that contain the items of interest.

Market basket analysis can be applied to many areas. The following example explains the market basket model using application examples.

EXAMPLE 6.8

Suggest application examples of the market basket model.

SOLUTION

Application 1:

1. Items = Products
   Baskets = Sets of products a customer purchases at one time from a store.
   Example of an application: Given that, many people buy chocolates and flowers together:
   - Run sales on flowers; raise price of chocolates.

   The knowledge is useful when many buy chocolates and flowers together.

Application 2:

2. Items = Words
   Baskets = Web pages
   Unusual words appearing together in a large number of documents, for example, ‘research’ and ‘plastic’ may provide interesting information.

Market basket analysis generates If-Then scenario rules. For example, if X occurs then Y is likely to occur too. If item A is purchased, then item B is likely to be purchased too. The rules are derived from the experience. This may be the result of frequencies of co-occurrence of items in past transactions.

The rules can be used in several analytical strategies. The rules can be written in format If {A} Then {B}. The *If* part of the rule (A) is known as *antecedent* and the *THEN* part of the rule (B) is known as *consequent*. The condition is *antecedent* and the result is *consequent*.

If-then rules about the contents of baskets: $\{p_1, p_2..., p_k\} \rightarrow$ q means, “If a basket contains all of $p_1, p_2...,$ p_k then it is *likely* to contain *q*.”

Scale of analysis:

- Amazon sells more than 12 million products and can store hundreds of millions of baskets.
- www has 1000 million words and several billion pages.

- 75 million credit card transactions in a month in India (RBI statistics of June, July 2016) at Point of Sales (POS) terminals.

Market basket analysis signifies shopping carts and supermarket shoppers at once. The analysis is the mining of transaction data to identify relations between different products. This is normally performed to identify products that a customer is likely to buy, given the products that they have already bought (or added to basket). The approach behind Amazon's users who bought a particular product also reviewed or bought other list of items is a well-known example of market basket analysis.

The applications of market basket analysis in various domains other than retail are:

> Applications of FIM in market analytics, medical analytics, web usage analytics, fraud detection, clickstream analytics

- Medical analytics: Market basket analysis can be used for conditions and symptom analysis. This helps in identifying a profile of illness in a better way. The analysis is also useful in genome analysis, molecular fragment mining, drug design and studying the role of biomarkers in medicine. The analysis can also help to reveal biologically relevant associations between different genes. Further, it can also help to find the effect of environment on gene expressions.
- Web usage analytics: FIM approaches can be used with viewing data on websites. The information contained in association rules can be exploited to learn about website browsing of visitor's behavior, developing website structure by making it more effective for visitors, or improving web marketing promotions. The results of this type of analysis can be used to inform website design (how items are grouped together) and to power recommendation engines (Section 6.8). Results are helpful in targeted marketing. For example, advertising content that people are probably interested in, based on past behavior of users.
- Fraud detection and technical dependence analysis: Extract knowledge so that normal behavior patterns may be obtained in illegal transactions from a credit card database in order to detect and prevent fraud. Another example can be to find frequently occurring relationships or FIM rules between the various parties involved in the handling of the financial claim. Some examples are:
    - Financial institutions to analyze credit card purchases of customers to build profiles for fraud detection purposes and cross-selling opportunities.
    - Insurance institution builds the profiles to detect insurance claim fraud. The profiles of claims help to determine if more than one claim belongs to a particular victim within a specified period of time.
- Click stream analysis or web link analysis: Click stream refers to a sequence of web pages viewed by a user. Analysis of clicks is the process of extracting knowledge from web logs. This helps to discover the unknown and potentially interesting patterns useful in the future. It facilitates an understanding of the behavior of website visitors. This knowledge can be used to enhance the way that web pages are interconnected or for increasing the sales of the commercial websites.
- Telecommunication services analysis: Market basket analysis can be used to determine the type of services being utilized and the packages customers are purchasing. This knowledge can be used to plan marketing strategies for customers who are interested in similar services. For example, telecommunication companies can offer TV Internet, and web-services by creating combined offers. The analysis might also be useful to determine capacity requirements.
- Plagiarism detection: It is the process of locating instances of similar content or idea within a work or a document. Plagiarism detection can find similarities among statements that may lead to similar

paragraphs if all statements are similar and that possibly lead to similar documents. Formation of relevant word and sentence sequences for detection of plagiarism using association rule mining technique is also very popular technique.

6.5.5.2 Finding Association

Association rules intend to tell how items of a dataset are associated with each other. The concept of association rules was introduced in 1993 for discovering relations between items in sales data of a large retailing company.

The following examples give rules between items found associated in the sales data of a retailer.

EXAMPLE 6.9

Suggest association rules between items found in the sales data of a retailer, and rules for course choice for a computer science student in college.

SOLUTION

1. {Bread} →{Butter}
   The rule suggests a relationship between the sales of bread and butter. A customer who buys bread also buys butter.
2. {Chocolates} → {a Gift Box}
   The rule suggests a that relationship between the sales of chocolates and empty gift boxes exists. A customer who buys chocolates also buys a gift box.
3. {Java programming} → {advanced web technology} and
   {Python programming} → {Big Data Analytics}
   The rules suggest relationships between Java and advanced web technology, and Python programming and data analytics. Students who opt for Java programming also want to learn advanced web technology, and those who opt for Python programming also opt for Big Data Analytics.
4. {Data Mining} → {Data Visualization}
   The rule may be that 90% of students who select data mining as a major subject will opt for the data visualization course as well.
5. {Computer Graphics, Modeling Techniques} → {Animation}
   The rule may be that students who study computer graphics and modeling techniques courses are likely to choose the course on animation in higher semesters.

Association analysis is applicable to several domains. Some of them are marketing, bioinformatics, web mining, scientific data analysis, and intrusion detection systems.

The applications might be to find: products that are often purchased together, types of DNA sensitive to a new drug, the possibility of classifying web documents automatically, geophysical trends or patterns in seismicity to predict earthquakes and automate the malicious detecting characteristics.

In medical diagnosis, for example, considering the co-morbid (co-occur) conditions can help in treating the patient in better way. This helps in improving patient care and medicine prescription.

6.5.5.3 *Finding Similarity*

Section 6.4 describes finding similarity of an item attribute, such as sales percentage increase using Euclidean or cosine similarity coefficients. Section 6.4.2 describes Jaccard similarity of sets. The similarity of sets applies to recommenders and collaborative filtering.

Let A and B be two itemsets. Jaccard similarity index of two itemsets is measured in terms of set theory using the following equation:

$$\text{Jaccard itemsets similarity index} = 1 - \frac{|A \cap B|}{|A \cup B|} \times 100\%. \qquad (6.25)$$

Explanation: $\cap$ means intersection, number of those elements or items which are the same in set $\mathcal{A}$ and $\mathcal{B}$. $\cup$ means union, number of elements or items present in union of A and B.

EXAMPLE 6.10

(i) How will you define similarity in purchase of a car model?

(ii) How will you specify frequent threshold for FIM? How will you use association rule to find and count the cities where more than threshold numbers buy a specific car model?

SOLUTION

(i) Assume two sets of car customers, youth $\mathcal{Y}$ and family $\mathcal{F}$. Assume in set $\mathcal{Y}$, 40 out of 100 youths and $\mathcal{F}$ 50 out of 200 families opted for the Tata Zest car model. Jaccard similarity index $J_{Zest}(\mathcal{Y}, \mathcal{F})$ = 40/ (100 + 200).100% = 13%. Two sets are sharing 13% of the members who purchased a Zest.

(ii) FIM involves finding similarity index in large number of sets after specifying the similarity index threshold which defines an itemset as frequent. Assume N sets of car customers, youth $\mathcal{Y}_1, \mathcal{Y}_2, \ldots, \mathcal{Y}_N$, and N′ sets of families $\mathcal{F}_1, \mathcal{F}_2, \ldots, \mathcal{F}_{N'}$ in N″ cities. Assume that meaning of frequent is that 10% or more of $\mathcal{Y}_i + \mathcal{F}_i$ buying Zest among the various car models. Assume all other models sell less than that in the cities. Here i = 1, 2, …, N″.

Let set $\mathcal{X}$ is a set, which has X_i as member if youth buy or if family buy the Zest car model frequently in the ith City. Initialize value, j = 0 for frequent item sets. Then association rule for the FIM in the present case is:

If (J_{Zest} ($\mathcal{Y}$, i, $\mathcal{F}$)>10%) Then (City X_i is a member of $\mathcal{X}$ and j = j + 1)} (6.26)

The rule is used for all cities for i = 1, 2, …, N′; Here j is the number of cities where frequent item set {Youth, Zest). FIM gives a set of j cities and youth, where youth buy Zest more than 10% of all car buyers.

Self-Assessment Exercise linked to LO 6.4

1. How does frequent itemset mining function mine the association rule? ○○●
2. Why does Apriori principle that 'if an itemset is frequent, then all of its subsets must also be frequent' hold true? ○●●
3. What are the features of Apriori principle that enable frequent itemsets mining? ●●●
4. How do you evaluate candidates for the associations? ○●●
5. How does concept of market basket model apply for frequent itemset mining? ○○●
6. List five examples where the assocation rule and count of frequent item sets apply. ○○●

6.6 CLUSTERING ANALYSIS

LO 6.5

Clustering a collection, cluster analysis, K-means and other methods, determining the number of clusters and cluster diagnostics

The following subsections describe clustering and cluster analysis methods.

6.6.1 Overview of Clustering

Clustering of *a collection* means 'a process (method) of grouping a collection of objects into subsets or clusters' according to their distinct characteristics in the group. Clustering forms one or more clusters, such that objects within one cluster are similar to each other while the objects belonging to different clusters are dissimilar. The process can assign restriction on further additions of similar objects or add further new dissimilarity conditions. This limits the number of objects in a cluster in a collection.

Clustering and cluster analysis need segmentation of a population into a number of subgroups using unsupervised techniques of data mining.

For example, consider a university course. Assume a cluster of students that has distinct characteristic, i.e., students mostly get high grade points (GPs) in semester examinations. Input datasets consist of university course students (GPs) in semester examinations. Clustering algorithm computes the cluster from the input datasets only. The following example gives the results of cluster analysis for students with high GPs in both theory and practical courses.

EXAMPLE 6.11

Consider a superset $\mathfrak{D}$ of all data of students enrolled $\mathfrak{S}$ in a university. $\mathfrak{D}$ consists of computer courses as members of set $\mathfrak{C}$. $\mathfrak{C}$ consists of GPs in a semester examination as members of subset $\mathfrak{S}$. $\mathfrak{S}$ consists of GPs as members of GPs in theory $\mathfrak{T}$ subjects as well as practical $\mathfrak{P}$ subjects.

Assume the following: Only one cluster with centroid exists at Theory GPA_T = 8.25 and Practical GPA_P = 8.25. The similarity criterion function is that GPAs in theory and practical both are high, i.e., (GPA_T, GPA_P) are within = (8.25 ± 1.75, 8.25± 1.75). The number criterion function is when 8% and above students in the set $\mathfrak{C}$, then a cluster of high GPA_T with high GPA_P exists. This means the circle that surrounds the points within the cluster has periphery diameter = 3.5, twice of 1.75.

How does a plot show a cluster of members in $\mathfrak{S}$ high GPAs in theory $\mathfrak{T}$ as well as practical $\mathfrak{P}$ subjects in number of university courses $\mathfrak{C}$?

SOLUTION

Consider plot of the P_GPAs and T_GPAs, GPAs in practical subjects as independent variable along the x axis and the GPAs in theory subjects as dependent variable along the y axis. Figure 6.9 shows cluster 1 and the results of cluster analysis of students with criterion 1. The cluster consists of students with high GPAs in theory $\mathfrak{T}$ as well as practical $\mathfrak{P}$ subjects in a number of university courses $\mathfrak{C}$ in a semester $\mathfrak{S}$.

Each dot in Figure 6.9 corresponds to a distinct enrolled student in university computer courses (set $\mathfrak{C}$) for semester examination (set $\mathfrak{S}$).

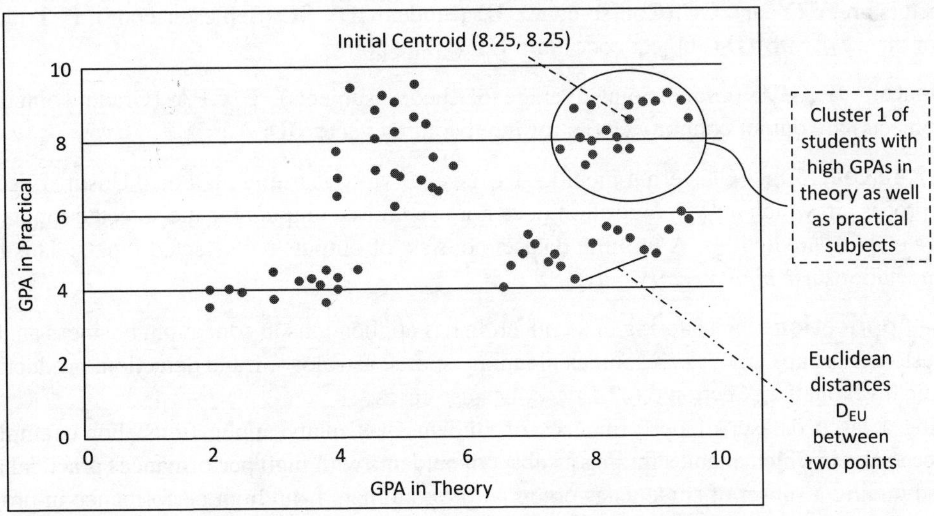

Figure 6.9 Result of cluster analysis of students' cluster I with high GPAs in theory subjects $\mathfrak{T}$ as well as practical subjects $\mathfrak{P}$ in a number of university courses $\mathfrak{C}$ and semesters

Partitions Example 6.11 considers one cluster. It considers one of the four possible partitions and assumes a starting centroid point= (8.25, 8.25). Opted criterion is considering distances up to 1.75 from a centroid for inclusion in the cluster of similar students. The figure also shows the centroid of the cluster at (8.25, 8.25) and a circle for criteria for the distances. Students in the cluster are those whose practical subject GPAs are between 6.5 and 10.0 and theory subject GPAs between 6.5 and 10.0.

Other three options can be as follows:

2— GPA in practical subjects between 4.5 and 6.0 and theory GPA between 6.5 and 10.0

3— GPA practical subjects between 6.5 and 10.0 and theory GPA between 4.5 and 6.0

4— GPA practical subjects below 4.5 and theory GPA below 4.5.

Centroid Figure 6.9 in Example 6.11 shows centroid (a central point of a cluster) GPAs of practical subjects (P_GPAs) and GPAs (T_GPAs) for data points of in subset $\mathfrak{S}$ of set of students $\mathfrak{C}$. Example 6.11 considers centroid as point for the student sub-groups where means of both the GPAs (P_GPAs) and GPAs (T_GPAs) are high (near 8.0).

Distance Metrics A distance metric is Euclidean distance, D_{Eu} (Equations 6.20a and b). A circle of radius corresponds to maximum D_{Eu} around the centroid when using the criterion of inclusion in the cluster (Figure 6.9). When D_{Eu} is used, then the boundary data points lie on the circle.

A distance metric is Manhattan distance, D_{Ma} (Equation 6.20c). When D_{MA} is used then the boundary points lie on a rectangle around the cluster.

Criterion Function Cluster 1 in the figure shows a circle, which specifies that all data points within the circle are at a distance 1.75 from the centroid 8.25. Criterion function for cluster 1 can also put addition criterion that more than 8% data points of all students in set $\mathfrak{C}$ fall inside the cluster and have practical $\mathfrak{P}$ and theory $\mathfrak{T}$ GPAs values (data points) (8.25± 1.75, 8.25± 1.75).

Input Vector Input column vectors of each data point in the figure have elements in the metric space. The column vectors are **Y** (Year), **CC** (Course-code), **ID** (Student-ID), **SC** (Semester-code), **P_T** (subject type (practical or theory)), **SubjID** (Subject code) **and GP** (grade point).

Output Vector **T_GPA** (Grade point average of theory subjects), **P_GPA** (Grade point average of practical subjects) are output column vectors for input column vector **ID.**

Unsupervised Learning Clustering methods use unsupervised learning methods. Unsupervised learning refers to a process in which an ML algorithm does not use known outputs for the selected inputs for taking decisions or making predictions. A training dataset consists of outputs for selected inputs. This means that cluster computations *use input vectors only.*

Clustering Applications Clustering of a collection has applications in education, business analysis, sales analysis, customer groups analysis, resources planning, sports, astrology, fraud detection, production control and scientific investigation. Section 6.6.2.1 describes use cases.

Clustering a large dataset of performances of students has many applications. For example, student performance analysis which enables finding a subset of students with high performances practical and theory subjects and finding a subset of students as potential programmers from high performance in programming subjects.

Clustering Algorithms Following are the categories of clustering algorithms:

1. Partitions/centroid based K-means (Section 6.6.1), K-medoids, Fuzzy k-means, Mean-shift clustering and other related methods
2. Connectivity and spectrum based hierarchical clustering (Section 6.6.2). When closeness relates to connectivity then spectral clustering
3. Probabilistic distribution based Latent-Dirichlet-Allocation (LDA) (Section 6.9), Gaussian Mixture Model (GMM), Expectation Maximization (EM) clustering and others, [Expectation Maximization (EM) algorithm uses a set of parameters that maximize the probability of the chosen PDF for data as a metric.]
4. Dimensionality reduction based Principal Component Analysis (PCA) (Section 6.9)
5. Density based Density-Based Spatial Clustering of Applications with Noise (DBSCAN)
6. Neural Networks/Deep Learning— Auto-encoders, self-organizing maps

The following Examples 6.12 and 6.13 explain the usages of clustering concept in two different cases.

EXAMPLE 6.12

How does clustering express the gene for a living cell that is undergoing a biological process?

SOLUTION

Genes are expressed differently whenever a living cell undergoes a biological process. Clustering of cells in the biological process enables the study of gene expression. This is required for understanding the underlying biological processes. This study is required to be carried out for different developmental phases, different body tissues, different clinical conditions and different organisms.

Recall Example 1.5. The following example explains how clustering analysis helps a ACVMs company.

EXAMPLE 6.13

(i) Recapitulate Example 1.6(i) of an ACVM Company. The company sells chocolates of say, five flavours. How does the clustering concept help the company to plan future strategies?

(ii) The ACVM company has to select new ACVMs in a city irrespective of whether these machines were installed or not previously. How does clustering guide the company?

SOLUTION

(i) The company wants to analyze sales performance of all flavours of chocolates in order to check which flavour sells widely or which ACVM needs filling frequently. The cluster analysis could further be extended for the sale of a particular flavour at many ACVMs in various cities. The clustering algorithm helps to find customer preferences in a specific set of regions.

The company needs to establish its sale points by putting its ACVMs in different regions. The location for installing ACVMs can be found using the clustering algorithm so that more of its customers receive a supply of their favourite flavours.

(ii) The demand for new sales point is to be analyzed. Firstly, regions of city where youth population is high, such as regions with hostels and the regions of minimum concentration of other vendors need to be identified. Clusters of sparse or subserviced areas and clusters of higher sales potential need to be first identified for installing new ACVMs. Finding these options of course may require mathematical or statistical analysis.

The above examples require a study of problems based on grouping objects of similar types or characteristics. This requires applying exploratory data mining techniques for statistical data analysis. These techniques are used in many fields, including ML, pattern recognition, image analysis, information retrieval and bioinformatics.

Difference With Respect to Classification Clustering finds only the similar objects. Classification differs from clustering in the sense that classification assigns a class to each distinct set of characteristics in the collection. For example, classification will assign four classes of students, as per four criterion functions. For example, a collection of students in Figure 6.9 can be classified into one of the four classes: (i) good overall performing students, (ii) poor performance in practical subjects, (iii) poor performance in theory, and (iv) poor performance in both type of subjects. Section 6.7 describes classification and classifying methods in detail.

Clustering on the other hand discovers a large number of close-by points which form a distinct set in a collection. How much large and how much close depends on the chosen criterion function.

The following subsections describe selected clustering algorithms.

6.6.2 K-Means

MacQueen (1967) developed K-means algorithm. This is one of the simplest unsupervised learning algorithms for clustering. The algorithm groups the objects based on the attributes (features) into k number of groups where k is a positive integer number.

The grouping of data results into k clusters ($\mathcal{C}_1$, $\mathcal{C}_2$, …, $\mathcal{C}_K$) represented by K centroids. A centroid is fundamentally a central representative of a cluster. The centroid of each cluster is the mean of all the instances belonging to that cluster. All objects of the cluster have similar characteristics, and fall within a criterion function specified for the cluster.

Criterion Function A criterion function assumes that at least p number of objects have similar characteristics, and are within the specified distances from a cluster centroid. A centroid may be assumed in the criterion, i.e., it is the one for which the sum of square of distances is least for all points of each cluster of a collection. The following example explains the use of K-means method.

EXAMPLE 6.14

How will you consider the criterion function in K-means method? Assume partitioning into k clusters. Assume the cluster problem similar to the one in Example 6.11.

SOLUTION

When partitioning N objects into k-clusters, the optimization of number of clusters and their centroid positions uses a criterion function. K-means method takes assumptions about similarity criterion. Assume that similarity is when T_GPAs are within 1.25 and P_GPAs also within 1.25. Assume that K-means method centroids, C1, C2, ..., Ck are ones for which the sum of square of distances is least for all points taken into the clusters, $\mathcal{C}_1$, $\mathcal{C}_2$ ..., $\mathcal{C}_k$, respectively. This means that the sum is 1.25 ×1.25 + 1.25 ×1.25 at the farthest point in an ith cluster.

Assume criterion that p = 0.08 × N, 8% of all students within a cluster.

K-means methods evaluates C1, C2, ... using the data points and criterion function assumptions. Considering Example 6.11, C_1 = (8.25, 8.25). Another cluster C_2 may evaluate to (8.25, 3.25). Number of objects in $\mathcal{C}_1$, $\mathcal{C}_2$ ... may evaluate and come out to be 18%, 10%, ... but at least 8%.

6.6.2.1 K-means Use Cases

Clustering can also provide a significant way to solve a number of real-life situations. The following are the use cases where K-means is fast and efficient:

- Identifying abnormal data items in a very large dataset. For example, identifying potentially fraudulent credit card transactions, risky loan applications and medical claim fraud detection.
- The feature similarities information helps the K-means algorithm to be used in an image retrieval system
- Applied to many use cases in healthcare and helps to better characterize sub-populations and diseases by medical conditions. Some examples include:
    - Finding diabetic/non-diabetic or hypertension/non-hypertension group structure from the input value.
    - Identifying similar patients based on their attributes to explore costs, treatments or results.
    - To forecast the possible type (cause) of future treatment or hospitalization of affected patients.
    - Help researchers discover new insights by segmenting patients and providing them with effective treatments.
- To find the segment of customers and customer category using the spending behavior characteristic.

6.6.2.2 Overview of the K-means Method

Computations are needed for finding the distances between the data and the corresponding cluster centroid. A distance is taken as Euclidean, squared Euclidean, Manhattan or Cosine distance (Equations (6.20a) to (6.20d) and Section 6.4.4).

Figure 6.10 shows the steps in K-means clustering.

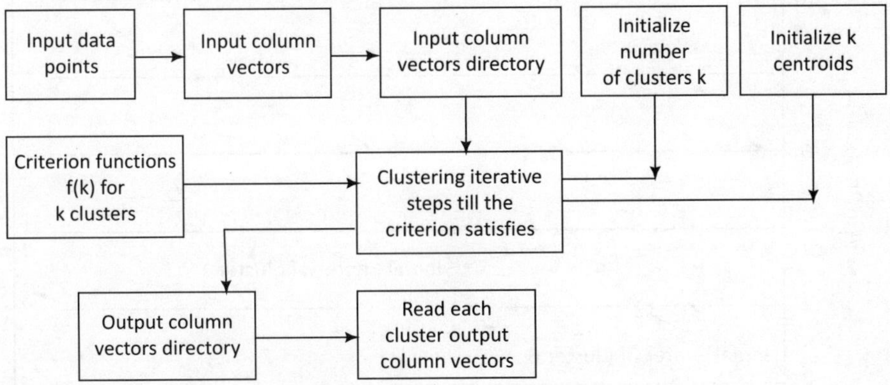

Figure 6.10 Steps in K-means clustering

K-means can be executed in the following steps:

1. Randomly initialize the k cluster centroid points (= C1, C2, ..., Ck) as partition centers which mean partitions with these cluster centroids.
2. Go through each of the data points and assign points to a cluster where the distance from a centroid is minimum.
3. Identify the centroid of the new cluster formed. It is the average of all the data points in a cluster. In other words, the algorithm calculates the average of all the points in a cluster, and moves the centroid to that average location.
4. The process is repeated until no change in the clusters takes place (or possibly until some other stopping condition is met).
5. Steps of iterative relocation algorithm:
   (1) Input: N (objects) and k (the number of clusters)
   (2) Output: A set of k clusters, which uses criterion-functions *f*(*k*) (For example, minimizing the sum of squared distances (Euclidean distances) for each cluster
   (3) Algorithm steps:
      (i) Initialize k centroids as the initial solution.
      (ii) (Re) compute memberships for the objects using the current cluster centroids
      (iii) Update centroid of the cluster according to new memberships of the objects.
      (iv) Repeat from Step (ii) until there is no object change the cluster centroid.

Iterative methods compute the centroid values for each cluster. Centroids are the concentration points for clusters. The mean or median are typical choices for a centroid metrics.

Figure 6.11 shows the iterative method actions in K-means clustering (Consider students GPA example similar to Example 6.11).

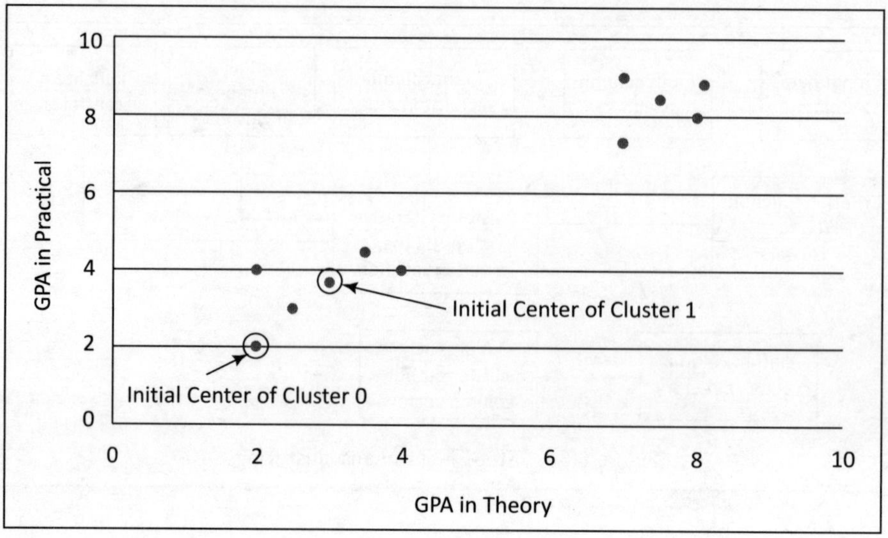

Figure 6.11 Iterative method actions in K-means clustering

Properties of K-means Clustering Algorithm The properties of K-means clustering algorithm are:

1. Number of clusters which form are always k clusters, where k is the number of partition centers.
2. Each cluster consists of at least one object in each cluster.
3. The clusters are flat (non-hierarchical) and they do not overlap.
4. Every member object of a cluster is closer to its cluster than any other cluster.

The algorithm has a number of variations, depending on the method for selecting the initial centroids, the choice for the measure of similarity, and the way that the centroid is computed. Most commonly, the Euclidean data exploits the mean as the centroid and selects the initial centroids randomly. The four other features of K-means clustering algorithm are as follows:

1. The K-means method is numerical, unsupervised, non-deterministic and iterative
2. The method is well suited if the clusters are globular
3. The centroid depends on the distance function that is measured by Euclidean distance (Sum of Squared distance (SSD)), cosine similarity or correlation
4. Centroid is the mean of the points in the cluster for SSD and cosine similarity; the median for Manhattan distance.

The K-means algorithm converges to a solution, which is typically a local minimum. The *space requirements* of the algorithm are O (n × d), where n is the number of points and d is the number of attributes. Here, only the data points are stored. The *time requirements* are O (n × k × I × d), where k is the number of clusters, and I is the number of iterations required for convergence. I is usually small as most of the convergence happens in the first few iterations.

Thus, the time required by K-means is efficient, as well as simple, as long as the number of clusters is significantly less than n.

O (f (n)) measures the efficiency of an algorithm in terms of function f (n). If f (n) = n^2, then the requirement of the algorithm is proportional to n^2. The requirement may be measured for memory or may be for run time. Space requirement O (n × d) means that memory taken by the algorithm is proportional to n × d. O is called as the big O notation.

Advantage of K-means is that computing the distances between points and group centres has linear complexity O (*n*). Disadvantages are (i) need to choose k, the number of groups/classes required to form the clusters, (ii) need to start and randomly choose the cluster centres, the results may be choice dependent. Thus, there is less consistency of the results compared to other methods.

6.6.2.3 K-medoids Algorithm

A medoid is similar to a mean or centroid, but restricts to members of the dataset. A dataset may have more than one medoid. The K-medoids algorithm initializes k data points as exemplars (centers), which shift iteratively for minimizing dissimilarities. The algorithm K-medoids does clustering using an algorithm, which has flavours of k-means algorithm and medoid-shift algorithm.

1. Step 1: Choose a set of medoids.
2. Step 2: Compute distances from each medoid to other points.
3. Step 3: Cluster the data points according to their similarities with the medoid.
4. Step 4: Optimize the set of medoids using iterative process.

The sum of pair of dissimilarities minimizes in K-medoids compared to minimizing the sum of squared Euclidean distances. The algorithm is based on partitioning technique of clustering, which clusters the data set of n objects into k clusters.

Use of medoid is in graphs and other non-metric spaces. Non-metric means non-quantifiable. Medoids mean the objects in a cluster or dataset such that average of dissimilarities minimizes taking all cluster members (objects). Recall that distance is a measure of dissimilarity. Computation of minimum dissimilarity considers minimum distances of all pairs of points within a cluster. Median is v-dimensional data point.

6.6.2.4 Determining the Number of Clusters

K-means algorithm finds k clusters in a given dataset. The K-means algorithm partitions the objects into k non-empty subsets. Thus, k signifies assumption about formation of a number of clusters. The data points represent the objects. Choice of k is either random or as per specific initial starting data points that the user specified.

A partition technique generates specific number of flat disjoint clusters (say, k clusters). Each object belongs to a specific cluster. Each object in a cluster is closer to the centroid than to the centroid of any other cluster. The centroid can be an arithmetic mean of the attribute values of all the objects in case of real-valued data. The centroid can be the rank value of the objects in case of categorical data. The iterative relocation algorithm is an excellent method for finding k partitions/clusters/centroids.

When partitioning n objects into k clusters, optimization uses a criterion function. For example, criterion that more than 10% of all students within (8.25± 1.25, 8.25± 1.25) GPAs in practical and theory belong to the same cluster (Example 6.11).

A useful tool for determining k is the silhouette value, s. A silhouette value computes from the similarity of an object with own cluster objects (means cohesion in the objects) instead of other clusters (means separation in the objects of all other clusters).

The s ranges from −1 to +1. Value −1 represents complete separation and +1 means complete cohesion. +1 means an object matches perfectly with an object in its own cluster and completely mismatches outside the cluster objects. When most objects of a cluster have high silhouette value, it means the cluster is well configured.

6.6.2.5 Diagnostics Method

Clustering validation tool does cross validation and validates initial centroid choices. A diagnostic tool uses the output of clustering for the decisions. For example, Microsoft Windows Server 2003 resource kit includes ClusDiag.exe, a tool for cluster diagnostics and verification tool for web files and events. It does basic verification and analyses configuration. It collects logs of files and events.

6.6.2.6 Reasons to Choose and Cautions

K-means algorithm finds k clusters in a given dataset, but one of the important questions is about the value of k to be selected. It is suggested to choose the value of k randomly or define it based on a domain requirement. However, if k + 1 clusters do not make significant change in the data points of clusters, from the case with k clusters do not increase one more cluster. Thus, select an optimal value of k such that introducing a new cluster may just be of little benefit.

Clustering explores similarities or cohesiveness in a significant number of objects or elements of the vectors. A point to remember is that improper criterion function can lead to erroneous results for clusters. One should be cautious while making predictions using current data points. For example, consider prediction from clustering analysis in Example 6.11. Clustering is not including teachers and resources availability for studying computer courses. Non-inclusion can lead to erroneous predictions.

6.6.3 Hierarchical Clustering

'Hierarchical clustering algorithms create a hierarchical decomposition of objects of a given data set using some criterion'. Figure 6.12 shows the original object points and one hierarchical cluster representation of those object points.

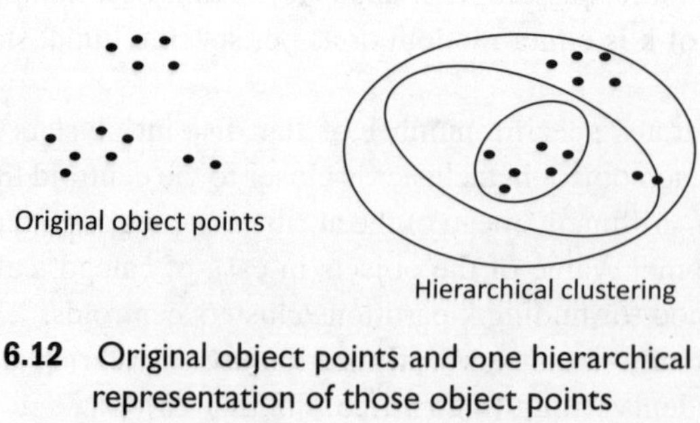

Figure 6.12 Original object points and one hierarchical cluster representation of those object points

EXAMPLE 6.15

How will you consider hierarchical clustering to solve the problem of ACVM owner for identifying distinct groups in their customer bases?

SOLUTION

Suppose the ACVM owner want to identify distinct groups in their customer bases, and then use this knowledge to develop targeted sales and marketing programs for a particular flavour of chocolate. They definitely require the formation of a hierarchy of nearest ACVMs targeting high sale campaigns for that flavour of chocolate. The hierarchical clustering may solve their problem efficiently. Recall Example 1.6. Figure 6.13 shows hierarchical clustering. The hierarchy is (i) clusters of $\mathcal{C}$ city-regions showing high sales per day and (ii) clusters of j set of regions $\mathcal{R}_1$ and $\mathcal{R}_2$ showing high total sales per day.

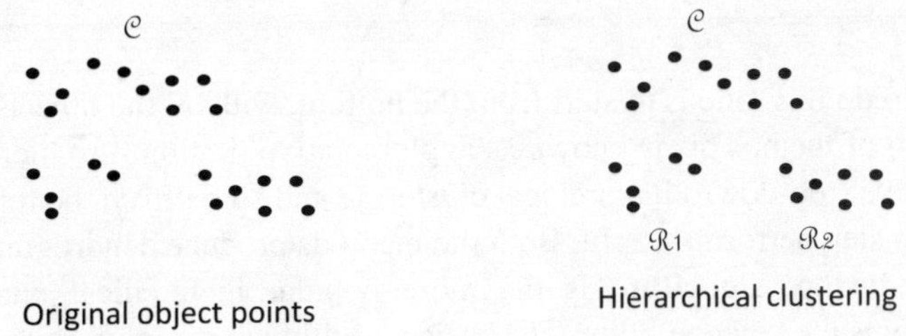

Figure 6.13 Hierarchical clustering of (i) original object points in city $\mathcal{C}$ showing high total sales per day, (ii) clusters of j set of regions $\mathcal{R}_1$ and $\mathcal{R}_2$ showing high total sales per day.

Hierarchical clusters may correspond to meaningful taxonomies as well. For example, evolutionary relationships among animals in biological sciences, and product catalogs in the web (online) world. It can also be used to represent file systems of any operating system.

Hierarchical clustering generally produces consistent results. The results of hierarchical algorithms are represented by a tree-structured graph known as a dendrogram. The dendrogram basically records the sequences of merges or splits.

The individual objects are arranged along the bottom of the dendrogram. They are referred to as leaf nodes. Object clusters are formed by joining individual objects or existing object clusters with the join point referred to as a node. Figure 6.14 shows dendrogram structure nodes. Each dendrogram node has a right and left sub-branch of clustered objects. The vertical axis is labeled as distance, and is used for distance measures between objects or object clusters. The height of the node represents the distance value between the right and left sub-branch clusters.

- Each node represents a group.
- Root node represents the group containing complete data set.
- Leaf node represents single object of the data set.
- Internal node has two children (sub-branches) representing the internal groups or leaf nodes (objects).

As the name implies, hierarchical clustering builds a hierarchy of clusters. Any number of clusters can be obtained by 'cutting' the dendrogram at the proper level.

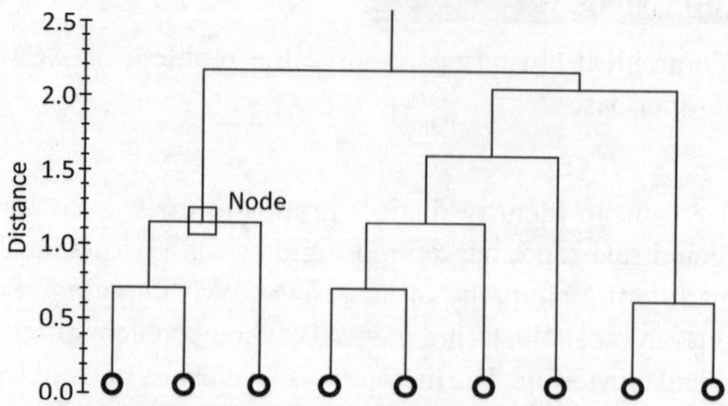

Figure 6.14 Dendrogram structure

There are two ways to do this: one is to start from the bottom, with all the objects as clusters and then, at each step, merge the two of them. This is known as agglomerative (bottom-up) hierarchical clustering. The other one is called divisive (top-down) hierarchical clustering and starts from the top, with all the objects in a big cluster, and at each step performs a split. Both the methods produce dendrograms.

Agglomerative Clustering Algorithm is the more popular hierarchical clustering technique. The computation of similarity is the key operation. The basic algorithm is straightforward.

1. Consider each data object as a cluster.
2. Compute the similarity between each pair of objects (cluster).
3. Repeat until only a single cluster remains:
   (i) Merge the two clusters having the smallest dissimilarity
   (ii) Update the similarities between a pair of clusters.

Online Contents (OLC) for BDACh06OLC6_1 for hierarchical clustering, which accompany this book describe in detail different approaches including agglomerative-divisive-distance measures for defining the distance between clusters in the different algorithms (Solution of Practice Exercise 6.12).

A dataset consisting of n object points the space and the time requirement for agglomerative hierarchical clustering is:

1. O (N^2) space to store the distance matrix, most of them are O (N^2) or more but one can stop at any arbitrary number of clusters.
2. O (n^3) time in most of the cases. There are n steps and at each step the size n^2 distance matrix must be updated and searched. The complexity can be reduced to O $(n^2 \log(n))$ time for some of the approaches by using appropriate data structures.

Advantage of hierarchical clustering is in finding the underlying finer structure. For example, resource planning for filling the ACVMs or for installing ACVMs in appropriate regions of the city (Figure 6.13).

Hierarchical clustering is not used in Big Data environment because of scalability and partition ability issues. Another disadvantage of hierarchical clustering in Big Data analytics is a large n and the time complexity of O (n^3) compared to O (n) linear complexity in K-means and GMM.

Self-Assessment Exercise linked to LO 6.5

1. Write meanings of partition, input vector, output vector, centroid and minimizing distance method. ○○●
2. Why is clustering an unsupervised machine learning method? ○○●
3. What does a machine learn during running of a clustering algorithm? ○○●
4. How do the cluster size and criterion function relate? ○●●
5. How is minimization performed using Euclidean squared distance for finding the cluster centroids? ○●●
6. Write effects of using in Euclidean squared, Euclidean distance and Manhattan distance used in K-means clustering on cluster size and centroid. How does it effect the cluster size? ●●●
7. Why does time complexity of K-means equal O (n)? ○●●
8. When is hierarchial clustering useful? ●●●

6.7 CLASSIFICATION

LO 6.6

K-nearest neighbour (KNN) classifier, decision trees, Random-Forest classifier, AdaBoost and other ensemble classifiers, Naïve Bayes classifier and SVM-based classifier

Classification refers to learning from existing categorizations and forming groups of objects showing similar characteristics. For example, categorize students good in theory and practical subjects both as 'very good'.

Classification is a supervised learning method. Classifier is an ML algorithm for classification, which decides usage of the experience, and emulates certain human decisions.

The classification techniques are used in many fields, including machine learning, pattern recognition, image analysis, information retrieval and bioinformatics. Classification is an exploratory data-mining method, which creates groups of objects of similar types or characteristics.

Consider an automatic chocolate vending machine (ACVM) for vending chocolates of say, five flavours. The chocolate company needs to establish its sale points by putting its ACVMs in a particular region. The location of putting these ACVMs can be found by a clustering algorithm so that all its ACVMs receive supply based on the analysis of customers favourite flavours.

The company surveys the sales performance of each flavour in order to check which flavour is giving wider sales, and needs enhanced supply frequency to ACVMs. The survey could be further extended for the sales promotion of a particular flavour in its various cities.

6.7.1 Concept of Classification

A classifier needs training, which means learning from existing categorizations and forming groups of objects showing similar characteristics. Training is a learning process which uses training dataset $\mathfrak{T}$ and generates a model program, M. *Training dataset* means a subset $\mathfrak{S}$ of an exemplary dataset which includes training variables. $\mathfrak{T}$ includes value of the target variables and predictors also. The training algorithm generates a 'Model', which is a program which gives the output vectors for taking the decision of the class to which the input vector belongs. (Remember, a set of data points can be represented by a vector in v-dimensional space.)

Figure 6.15 shows the steps during the learning phase of a classifier. The learning needs (i) training dataset $\mathfrak{T}$, which includes **P**, both as the inputs. The classifier consists of a training algorithm and creates a model program from inputs and outputs **ET** (estimated target variables). The algorithm creates a model program M for internal uses of a classifier and its copy M′. The M′ estimates target variable(s) are inputs to a decider **D** program to decide which data points to put in which class. It emulates certain human decisions for classification.

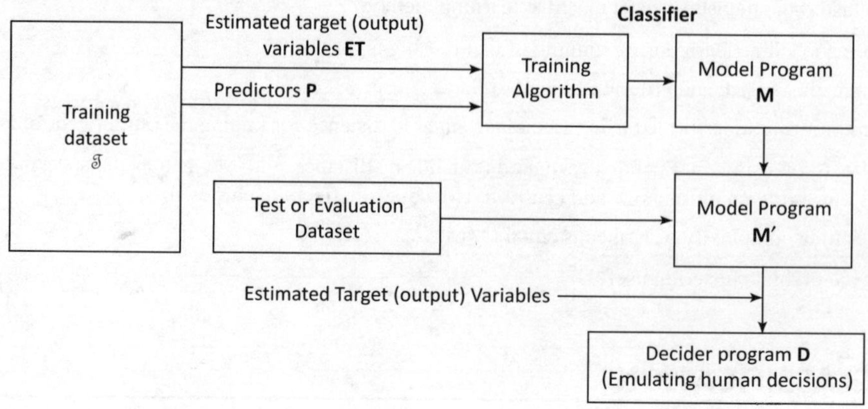

Figure 6.15 Steps during the learning phase of a classifier

A dataset for testing or evaluating tests the decisions of the Model and Decider. The test dataset is a subset, whose members are the input vectors, Predictors **P** and target output vectors (variables) **ET** for taking the decision for the class to which input vectors belong. If decision from model passes the test, then the model will predict correct decisions and the class from future inputs.

Predictor can be: (i) a continuous value, such as grade point; (ii) text, such as Java; (iii) string, such as 'GPA ≥ 8.0'; and (iv) a category, such as 'very good', 'potential researcher', 'high performance', 'Zest model', 'red apple'.

The following example gives the understanding of steps in classification of students with high GPs in both theory and practical courses. Consider a classifier for classifying 'very good performing students' and thus, who are potential innovators.

EXAMPLE 6.16

Recall Example 6.11. Consider the student ID, his/her T_GPAs in theory subjects and P_GPAs in practical subjects. GPAs means grade points average computed from grade points in the semester examination. Assume the data points similar to ones in Figure 6.9.

How will you specify: (i) training dataset, (ii) target variables, (iii) predictors (predictor variables), (iv) features, (v) training algorithm, (vi) model program, (vii) exemplary (Test) dataset, (viii) estimated target variables, and (ix) decider which categorizes and forms the classes (groups of objects) in a classifier? (x) What do you mean by field in a record of data points?

SOLUTION

(i) Training dataset: 75% of the student data consisting of student ID, his/her T_GPAs in theory subjects and P_GPAs in practical subjects.

(ii) Target means, a feature as a target variable which is found using learning examples. Target is to find whether a student group belongs to one with high GPA in theory and practical subjects, and both. Target variables are T_ GPAs and P_ GPAs.

(iii) Predictors (Predictor variables): Subject of study, subject-wise attendance in class, number of hours a student studies a subject etc.
(iv) Features: Gender, Age, Coaching (Yes/No), Residence (Rural/Urban), High T_ GPAs and P_ GPAs
(v) Training algorithm steps are as follows:
- Define a training set.
- Choose a learning algorithm. For example, Support Vector Machines, Naïve Bayes or Decision Trees.
- Complete the design. Run the algorithm.
- Evaluate the accuracy of the learned model from test dataset.

(vi) Model Program: Classification technique (or classifier) which systematically builds the classification model from an input dataset.
(vii) Test dataset: Remaining 25% of the student data consisting of student ID, his/her T_GPAs in theory subjects and P_GPAs in practical subjects.
(viii) Estimated target variables: GPA in semester examinations.
(ix) Record of data points: Record is a container for $\mathfrak{I}$ which consists of fields. For example, training grade sheets of the students is a record.
(x) Fields in the record: Fields are a part of a record. A field consists of a value, feature, characteristic, outcome or category. Example of input fields are T_GPA, P_GPA, Semester, High T_ GPAs and P_GPAs in input vectors at a student record. Example of feature variable fields are 'Excellent', 'Potential Programmer'.

6.7.1.1 Concept of Supervised Learning

Methods of ML are fundamentally driven by data. On the basis of data availability these methods are broadly classified into supervised learning and unsupervised learning. *Supervised learning r*efers to a case when an algorithm uses training data to take decisions or make predictions.

Supervised learning uses a known output dataset for the input dataset (called the training dataset). The Model (program) then learns to make predictions. The output datasets are used to train the machine and get the desired outputs. Test dataset tests the Model and Decider to verify themselves. The developed Model makes predictions for an unknown output for the further input datasets. However, in unsupervised learning, no output and input datasets are provided to train the machine.

Table 6.3 illustrates the difference between supervised and unsupervised learning.

Table 6.3 Supervised vs unsupervised learning

	Supervised Learning	Unsupervised Learning
Training set	Used	Not used
Input variables	Observations	Latent variables
Output variables	Observations	Observations
Labels	All data are labeled	All data are unlabeled
Goal	To approximate the mapping function exactly in a way that on new data input, it can predict the output variables for that data.	To model the underlying structure or distribution in the data in order to learn more about the data
Application examples	Classification and regression problems	Clustering and association problems

The following example shows how classification forms the groups of objects with similar characteristics from analysis of student performances in different courses.

EXAMPLE 6.17

Show the results of a classifier for classification of students showing potential as scientists and researchers, data architects and programmers after analysis of the GPAs in different courses, i.e., theory and practical.

SOLUTION

Figure 6.16 shows results of classification of student groups into courses as potential classification into classes (groups) of students in different courses as potential (1) scientists and researchers, (2) data architects and (3) programmers.

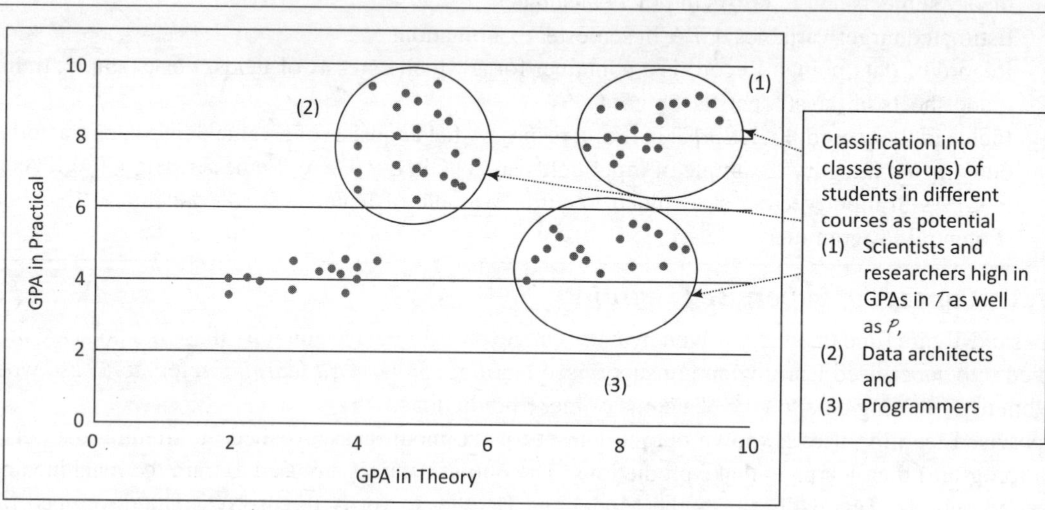

Figure 6.16 Classification on the basis of performances of the student groups

6.7.1.2 *Clustering and Classification Differences*

Clustering and **classification** differ as shown below, though both the methods characterize the objects into groups by one or more features. Classification is a supervised learning method, whereas clustering is an unsupervised learning method used to form groups of objects with similar characteristics.

Table 6.4 compares and highlights the characteristics of classification and clustering.

Table 6.4 Classification vs clustering

Property	Classification	Clustering
Supervision	Supervised learning	Unsupervised learning
Training set	Used	Not used

(Contd.)

Property	Classification	Clustering
Labels	All data are labeled	All data are unlabeled
Datasets	Consist of attributes and class labels	Consists of attributes
Process	Employs algorithms to categorize new data according to the observations of the training set	Statistical concepts are used. Datasets are split into sub-sets with similar features
Goal	To find which class a new object belongs to from a set of predefined classes	To group a set of objects in order to find the relationship between them

The category structure is known in classification task, whereas the clustering deals with object collections, whose class labels are unknown.

Examples of classification techniques include decision tree classifiers, rule-based classifiers, Support Vector Machines (SVM) and Naïve Bayes Classifier (Section 6.7.4). Each classifier employs a learning algorithm to build a model that best fits the relationship between the objects of a class.

6.7.1.3 *Classifiers*

Classifiers for Big Data analytics require parallel and scalable computations with shared-nothing architecture for efficiency. Parallel means computations of the same set of codes simultaneously on multiple data nodes (Section 1.2.1). Scalable means linear relation between data volume and the required total number of computation steps and thus, computational time. This means if 10 MB data require time = T for processing, then 100 MB will take 10T. Shared nothing means during computations, no inter-processor communications, thus processors spend no time on them (Example 2.1).

Naïve Bayes and complementary Naïve Bayes are efficient between medium to large datasets (>1 M up to 100 M), but mostly suitable for text data variables and medium to high overhead for training. **Random Forest** uses all four types of predictor variables: continuous, text, words or categorical. Random Forest is able to handle conditional and non-linear relationships and thus, the complex classification problems. It exhibits high performance computations *above 10 M dataset*.

Certain classifiers do sequential computations with shared architecture. For example, **Support Vector Machines** (SVMs). The SVM classifier is efficient for computational needs of small (0.1 M or less) to medium (< 1 M) datasets.

Stochastic Gradient Descent (SGD) algorithms, such as logistic regression are sequential, incremental efficient (fast) and used when computational needs are of small (< 0.1 M) to medium (< 10 M) dataset. Predictor variables can be of any of the four types. Section 6.7.3 describes SGD.

Hidden Markov and **multi-level perceptron** are also sequential algorithms. OLCs accompanying the book describe the *Hidden Markov* and *multi-level perceptron* (Solution of Practice Exercises 6.15 and 6.16).

6.7.2 K-Nearest Neighbour Classifier

Recall Sections 6.3.6 and 6.4.1.1 for applications of K-NN in regression and in similar items search (k is 1 for nearest neighbour, 2 for next to nearest and 3 for next to next nearest. Training dataset consists of k-closest examples in feature space. Feature space means, space with categorization variables (non-metric variable). For example, Grade A, B, C, D awarded in an examination are feature space variables. The k-NN learning is learning based on instances, and thus also works lazily because instance close to the input vector for test or prediction may take time to occur in the training dataset. An object classification criteria is majority vote. k-NN is also called the lazy algorithm. The following example explains this method.

EXAMPLE 6.18

Assume that when CGPA (cummulative grade point average) is 8.0 and above up to the maximum 10.0), a student performance is classified as A. When CGPA is 6.5 and above below 8.0, performance is B. When CGPA is 5.0 and above below 6.5, performance is C. When CGPA is 4.0 and above below 5.0, performance is D. When CGPA is less than 4.0, performance is F (poor).

A training dataset consists of data of 40 students. Training dataset consisting of vectors 1, 2, … to 40 are (StudentID1, 8.1, A), (StudentID2, 7.6, A), (StudentID3, 6.6, B), (StudentID3, 4.6, D), (StudentID4, 8.8, A), (StudentID2, 5.6, C), (StudentID5, 6.7, B), (StudentID6, 5.2, C), (StudentID7, 4.5, D), (StudentID8, 7.9, B), (StudentID9, 6.8, B), (StudentID10, 9.1, A), (StudentID11, 7.1, B), (StudentID12, 7.9, B), (StudentID13, 6.0, B), (StudentID14, 8.0, A), …

How will a 1-NN classifier classify a student of ID 250 with CGPA 7.2?

SOLUTION

The training algorithm will follow the following steps (Fig. 6.15):

(i) Find the distance for each value of CGPA, distances of CGPAs and the output variable class, A, B, C, D, or F from the training dataset of 40 students.
(ii) Assign frequencies for class = A, B, C, D, or F for each range of grade points.
(iii) Build and update the table with the additional datasets given of training, if required.

Table 6.5 gives guidelines of the table between the range of CGPA and frequency of output variables = A, B, C, D and F.

Table 6.5 Range of CGPAs and frequency of output variables = A, B, C, D and F.

CGPA Minimum	CGPA Maximum	Freq (A)	Freq (B)	Freq (C)	Freq (D)	Freq (F)
8.a	9.b or 10.0	> 0	0	0	0	0
6.c	7.d	0	> 0	0	0	0
5.e	6.f	0	0	> 0	0	0
4.g	4.h	0	0	0	> 0	0
0.i	3.j	0	0	0	0	> 0

The values of a, b, c, d, e, f, g, h, i and j build up gradually as the number of training input vectors and output vectors keep increasing, eventually 8.a reaching 8.0, 9.b reaching > 9.9 and so on. Time taken and the number of inputs and output vectors may be such that final output values may take a long time.

Model develops a program to read the table and compute output variable estimate for test dataset and unclassified input vector.

Decider Program: When input vector is for ID250, find the distance of 7.2 with the input vectors.ID1 distance is 0.9. Successive input vector distances from vector I1 to I40 are 0.9, 0.4, 0.6, 2.6,0.8, 1.6, 0.5, 2.0, 2.7, 0.5, 0.4, 1.9,0.1, …, Nearest neighbours have distances = 0.4 from studentID 250.Using CGPA range and student CGPA, the decider will output the predictor variable as B.

Classifier places that student in class B.

6.7.3 Stochastic Gradient Descent Method – Logistic Regression

Stochastic in English means a process or system connected with random probability, chance or randomness. *Gradient* equals to change in a function value with respect to a very small change in a parameter value. For example, in a function $y(x_1, x_2, ..., x_v)$ in v-dimensional space, gradient of y with respect to x_i equals differentiation of y with respect to $x_i = dy/dx_i$, where $i = 1, 2, ..., v$.

Gradient descent means decremental change in gradient. Gradient descent is used for reaching convergence for each value of x_i iteratively. It reaches a minimum value for each x during optimizing the set of parameters or values which are input to an objective or other function. The gradient descends iteratively to a minimum value. Incremental or decremental change means successive increment or decrement in x that leads to approach towards the optimum value of y.

Recall Section 6.3.3. It explained how the best fit could be reached by using the 'least squares criterion', which says that best fit is one, which 'minimizes the sum of the squared prediction errors.' Here, Object function $Q = \sum_{i=1}^{n}(y_i - y_i')^2$. Equation (6.15) is minimized to obtain coefficients of the regression equation (6.14), $y_i' = b_0 + b_1x_i$ which gives best fit, i.e., minimizes Q. To minimize $Q = \sum_{i=1}^{n}(y_i - (b_0 + b_1x_i))^2$, take the gradient (derivative) with respect to b_0 and b_1, set to 0, respectively, and get the 'least squares estimates' for b_0 and $b_1$from Equations (6.16) and (6.17).

The method is called logistic regression when we consider a generalized objective function as follows:

$$Q(y) = N^{-1}\left[\sum_{i=1}^{N} Q_i(y)\right], \tag{6.27}$$

where N is the number of data points summed using the input vector, Q_i is i-th observation of y for input variables y, being estimated such that the sum is minimized and parameters r coefficients are optimized.

Steps in an SGD algorithm are: (i) choose a starting input vector **Y** and a learning rate ε, i.e., the rate by which y decrements in next computations to get the minimum sum (Equation 6.27) and minimized regression coefficients for computing Y, and (ii) randomly change (scuffle) the exemplary input vectors and corresponding output vectors which are used as examples for learning. For i-th observation 1 to m, find

$$y = y - b_1.\nabla Q_i(y) \tag{6.28}$$

Here, ∇ is the mathematical symbol for gradient, which computes gradient of $Q_i(y)$. b_1 is the linear regression coefficient in Equation (6.28).

SGD classifier trains and learns the computation of objective function values and classifies based on predictor values for each class.

Logistic regression uses hash values for the features, which means training algorithm assigns each feature a hash value, which is used for indexing, search and predictor variable.

OLCs accompanying the book gives examples of the Stochastic gradient descent method for logistic regression and classification (Solution of Practice Exercise 6.13).

6.7.4 Decision Tree Algorithm

Tree-based learning algorithms are simpler and efficient supervised learning methods. They provide accurate, persistent and ease of analysis to predictive models. Tree-based algorithms are used for solving classification and regression problems. They are suitable for representing non-linear relationships as well. Some of examples of tree-based learning algorithms are decision trees, Random Forest and gradient boosting.

Following are the important terms related to Decision Trees:

1. *Root Node:* Represents the entire dataset.

2. *Splitting*: A process of dividing a node into two or more sub-nodes
3. *Decision Node:* When a sub-node splits into further sub-nodes
4. *Leaf/Terminal Node:* Nodes that do not split further
5. *Pruning:* Process of removing sub-nodes of a decision node (opposite of splitting)
6. *Branch/Sub-Tree:* A sub-section of the entire tree
7. *Parent Node:* A node divided into sub-nodes
8. *Child Node:* A node derived from a parent node.

Decision Tree is a supervised learning algorithm, having a desired response value that is mostly used in classification problems. Decision tree works for both categorical and continuous input and output variables.

The decision steps are as follows:

First, split the dataset when classifying a response variable. That is based on most significant splitter/differentiator in input variables into two or more subsets.

The decision trees segregate the datasets based on all values of three variables and identify the variable, which creates the best homogeneous sets of datasets (which are heterogeneous to each other). The following example explains how decision trees segregate student datasets based on all values of three variables.

EXAMPLE 6.19

Consider a dataset of 100 students with three variables Gender (Boy/Girl), Branch (CS/EC) and GPA score of previous year (8.0 to 10.0). 40 out of these 100 enrolled in coaching class for learning the programming. It is required to create a model to predict who will enroll in coaching class. (CS: Computer Science, EC means Electronics and Communication).

SOLUTION

First segregate the students who took admission in coaching classes based on each significant input variable and find which variable is most significant among the three (Gender, branch, GPA). Figure 6.17 suggests that variable GPA identifies the best homogeneous sets compared to the other two variables.

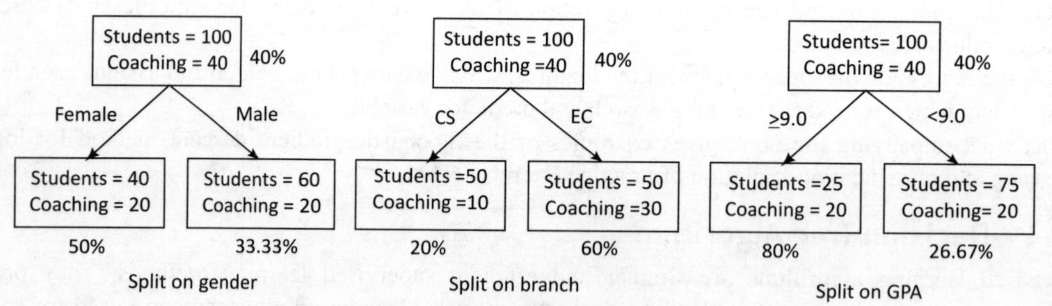

Figure 6.17 Example of decision trees for creating the best homogeneous sets of students

Types of decision tree are based on the type of response variables:

1. *Categorical-variable Decision Tree*: Decision tree, which has categorical response variable. For example, consider the above illustrated student problem, where the response variable is "Student will enroll in coaching class or not" and the answer is YES or NO.
2. *Continuous-variable Decision Tree:* Decision tree, which has continuous response variable.

Table 6.6 gives features of decision trees.

Table 6.6 Features of decision trees

Feature	Description
Application Examples	1. Identify the best combination of products and marketing strategies that target specific sets of consumers in a marketing area. 2. Customer behavior analysis, customer retention strategy planning 3. Fraud detection in industries 4. Diagnosis of diseases
Advantages	1. Decision tree output in the form of graphical representation is very easy to understand. 2. Useful in predicting significant response variable. 3. Not influenced by outliers and missing values to a fair degree as compared to other techniques of modeling. 4. Handles both numerical and categorical variables. 5. Decision tree is a non-parametric method. Thus, decision trees have no assumptions about space distribution and classifier structure.
Disadvantages	1. Over fitting is a problem associated with decision tree models. Setting constraints on model parameters and pruning solve this problem. 2. When the numerical variables are continuous, the decision tree loses information while categorizing the variables in different categories.

6.7.4.1 Evaluating a Decision Tree

Different decision-tree building algorithms are used. Each algorithm aims to search a variable, which gives the maximum information gain or divides the data in the most homogenous way.

For example, split on GPA in the above example suggests the student enrolls in coaching class more than the Gender of the student.

A decision tree exploits various metrics. For example, Gini index, chi-square and Entropy and Information Gain. Metrics find out the best split variables. A decision tree algorithm CART (Classification and Regression Tree) uses Gini index to split the node. The decision tree resulted by CART algorithm is a binary decision tree (each node will have only two child nodes).

The selection of two items from a population at random must be of the same class and the probability for this is 1 if the population is pure.

1. Gini index is used for categorical response variable "Success" (p) or "Failure" (q).
2. Generates binary splits only.

3. Higher the value of Gini, higher the homogeneity.

Steps to calculate Gini for a split.

1. Calculate Gini for sub-nodes, using formula sum of square of probability for success and failure $(p^2 + q^2)$.
2. Calculate Gini for split using weighted Gini score of each node of that split.

The following example explains the computation of Gini score and when the node split will take place on GPA.

EXAMPLE 6.20

(i) How will the split on Gender compute?
(ii) How will the split on GPA compute?

SOLUTION

(i) To find Split on Gender: Calculate,
Gini for sub-node Female = (0.5) × (0.5) + (0.5) × (0.5) =0.50
Gini for sub-node Male = (0.33) × (0.33) + (0.67) × (0.67) =0.5578
Weighted Gini for Split Gender = (40/100) × 0.50 + (60/100) × 0.5578 = 0.53468

(ii) Similarly, for Split on GPA: Calculate,
Gini for sub-node ≥9.0 = (0.80) × (0.80) + (0.20) × (0.20) = 0.68
Gini for sub-node <9.0 = (0.27) × (0.27) + (0.73) × (0.73) = 0.6058
Weighted Gini for Split Class = (25/100) × 0.68 + (75/100) × 0.6058 = 0.62435

Gini score for *Split on GPA* is higher than *Split on Gender*. Hence, the node split will take place on GPA.

The next category of algorithm is based on the chi-square. This finds the statistical significance between the differences between sub-nodes and parent node. The calculation is based on the sum of squares of standardized differences between observed and expected frequencies of the response variable.

The algorithm is used for categorical response variable "Success" or "Failure". The algorithm generates two or more splits.

The generated tree is known as CHAID (Chi-square Automatic Interaction Detector) which detects using the rule that "higher the value of chi-Square, higher is the statistical significance of differences between the sub-node and the Parent node". Calculation of chi-square of each node uses the term:

$$= \sqrt{\left(\frac{(\text{Observed} - \text{Expected})^2}{\text{Expected}}\right)} \qquad (6.29)$$

Steps to calculate chi-square for a split:

(i) Calculate the chi-square for an individual node.
(ii) Calculated the chi-square of Split using the sum of all chi-square of success and failure of each node of the split.

The following example explains chi-square calculation.

EXAMPLE 6.21

How will split compute for Gender and GPA using chi-square calculation?

SOLUTION

To find Split on Gender: Calculate,

Node	Enrolled in Coaching	Not Enrolled	Total	Expected to Enroll (40%)	Not Expected (60%)	Chi-square Enroll Coaching	Chi-square Not Enroll Coaching
Female	20	20	40	16	24	1.0	.82
Male	20	40	60	24	36	.82	.67
				Total Chi-square:		3.31	

To find Split on GPA: Calculate,

Node	Enrolled in Coaching	Not Enrolled	Total	Expected to Enroll (40%)	Not Expected (60%)	Chi-square Enroll Coaching	Chi-square Not Enroll Coaching
≥9.0	20	5	25	10	15	3.16	2.58
<9.0	20	55	75	30	45	1.83	1.49
				Total Chi-square:		9.06	

Chi-square also suggests the *GPA split* is more significant compare to *Gender* since Chi-square for GPA split is much higher than Chi-square for Gender split.

A category of algorithm is based on entropy computations and information gain. Entropy in thermodynamics is a measure of disorder or randomness of a system. Statistical studies suggest similar concept to characterize the (im) purity of an arbitrary dataset (randomness in dataset). A pure node requires less information to describe it, and an impure node requires more information. If the subset or the dataset is completely homogeneous, then the entropy is zero and if the sample is an equally divided (50% – 50%), it has entropy of one.

The formula for statistical entropy is:

$$H = \sum_{i=1}^{n} p_i \log_2 p_i \tag{6.30}$$

Here p is probability of success in that node. Entropy is used with categorical response variable. The split is decided when the entropy is lower than the parent node and other splits. The lesser the entropy value, the better split variable it is.

Steps to calculate entropy for a split:

1. Calculate entropy of parent node.
2. Calculate entropy of each individual node of split and calculate the weighted average of all sub-nodes available in split.

The following example explains the use of entropy computations for the dataset used to calculate Gini in Example 6.20.

EXAMPLE 6.22

How will you split and compute entropies for Gender and GPA using entropy calculation? How much is the information gain?

SOLUTION

1. Entropy for the parent node = – (40/100) $\log_2$ (40/100) – (60/100) $\log_2$ (60/100) = **0.971.** The node is impure.
2. Entropy for the female node = – (20/40) $\log_2$ (20/40) – (20/40) $\log_2$ (20/40) = 1 and for male node, – (20/60) $\log_2$ (20/60) – (40/60) $\log_2$ (40/60) = 0.92
3. Entropy for split Gender =Weighted entropy of sub-nodes = (40/100) × 1.0 + (60/100) × 0.92 = **0.95**
4. Entropy for GPA ≥ 9.0 node = – (20/25) $\log_2$ (20/25) – (5/25) $\log_2$ (5/25) = 0.72, and for GPA< 9.0, – (20/75) $\log_2$ (20/75) – (55/75) $\log_2$ (55/75) = 0.84.
5. Entropy for split GPA = (25/100) × 0.72 + (75/100) × 0.84 = **0.81**

Entropy for Split on GPA is the lower than entropy for Split on Gender, so the tree will split on GPA. Information gain from entropy as (1– Entropy).

The basics of decision trees and the decision-making process involved to select the best splits in modeling such tree structure is presented in this section. Decision tree can be applied on regression problems as well as classification problems.

6.7.4.2 Decision Trees in R

Multiple packages are available to implement decision tree in R programming, such as ctree and rpart. The rpart programs build classification or regression models using a two-phase procedure. The resultant models can be represented as binary trees.

First phase is the splitting process using a selected data variable. The process continues recursively either until the sub-groups reach a default minimum size or until no improvement can be made. The second phase consists of using cross-validation to trim back the full tree.

Regression analysis, time series analysis and Markov model use statistical techniques in ML algorithms for predictions. A regression algorithm is a supervised ML algorithm. This means that they predict the value for new data (output value) on learning from model dependencies and relationships between the target output and input features.

Six widely used ML Regression analysis algorithms are as follows:

1. Simple Linear Regression Model— Single input variable and multiple input linear regression
2. Multivariate Regression Algorithm
3. Multiple Regression Algorithm
4. Support Vector Machines Algorithm — Use epsilon-insensitivity (margin of tolerance) loss function to solve regression problems

5. Logistic Regression Classifier Algorithm — It uses SGD method (Table 6.8) and is used for classification (Section 6.7.3)
6. LASSO (Least Absolute Selection Shrinkage Operator) Algorithm

6.7.5 Naïve-Bayes Theorem – Naïve Bayes Classifier

Naïve Bayes is a simple classifier. It is the probabilistic and statistical classifier. It is based on Bayes theorem (from Bayesian statistics) with strong (Naïve) independence assumptions and maximum posteriori hypothesis. It is also a supervised learning technique, which uses non-parametric approach (Posteriori means at the back of something. For example, hypothesis). The classifier assumption is that features have strong independences.

The classifier exploits one of the most basic text classification techniques with a variety of applications in email spam detection, personal email sorting and document categorization.

The technique uses the probabilities of every feature belonging to each class to make a prediction. Makes simpler calculation of probabilities by assuming that the probability of a particular feature belonging to a given class value is independent of all other features. This type of assumption is termed as class conditional independence. The probabilities can be looked up in a single scan of the database and stored in a small table. This makes it a fast and space efficient method.

The use of this method is in decider program for the classifier. The training program trains on maximum likelihood which means maximum probability of occurrences.

Naïve Bayes is widely used for text classification. Vectorization of data points need one pass for vectorization and other for the algorithm. Since the method uses vector implicitly (for example, a bag of word as input), a single pass suffices (Pass means the number of times the input vectors are re-examined during training).

In addition, Naïve Bayes classifier requires a small amount of training data to estimate the parameters, viz., means and variances of the variables, which are necessary for classification. However, training needs high overheads and more time.

Section 9.2.1.3 will give details. A word contained (and its occurrences) represents text in a document. The bag-of-words model is commonly used methods of document classification where the (frequency of) occurrence of each word is used as a feature for training a classifier (Wikipedia). Section 9.2.2 will describe Naïve Bayes Analysis in detail.

Bayes theorem describes the conditional probability of an event. The theorem basis is that conditions that might be related to the event. The probability P (A|B) of Event A occurring and Event B has already occurred is given by the formula:

$$P(A|B) = P(A \text{ and } B)/P(B) = P(A \cap B)/P(B) \tag{6.31}$$

Probability of conditions A or B is equal to the probability of both A and B happening divided by Probability of B alone. ($\cap$ is symbol for intersection in set theory. $\cup$ is symbol for union in set theory).

Naïve Bayes classifiers are efficient in terms of CPU and memory consumption. The classifiers are not sensitive to irrelevant features. They have the ability to handle real and discrete data as well as streaming data well. The classifiers can also be trained very quickly. The only disadvantage is that they assume independence of features. Overall, Naïve Bayes outperforms by other classifiers most of the times and is used as a baseline in many researches.

6.7.6 Support Vector Machine Classifier

Support Vector Machine (SVM) is a method in a set of related *supervised learning method* that uses a vector, which has in general, *v* elements in v-dimensional space. The vector classifies the data points. Following is a brief introduction.

A data point in the space is represented by a vector. A data point represents by (x1, x2, ..., xn) in n-dimensional space. Consider two-dimensional space, with data points (x1, x2) and axes X1 and X2. Each data-point if considered as a vector element has two components, x1, and x2. (Two sets of words in text analysis). A *hyperplane* is a subspace of one dimension less than its ambient space in geometry. If a space is 3-dimensional, then its hyperplanes are the 2-dimensional planes. However, if the space is 2-dimensional, its hyperplanes are 1-dimensional which means lines.

The algorithm finds Support Vector (SV) to maximize boundary distances. Figure 6.18 shows car sales in different showrooms. A star corresponds to Jaguar sales in a year at different showrooms and dot corresponds to Zest sales of Tata Zest model. X1 axes in feature space and X2 is in metric spaces (sales number).

Figure 6.18 shows the separating hyperplanes using three hyperplanes A, B, and C for classification of data points. A hyperplane is equivalent to a line in case of 2-dimensional space.

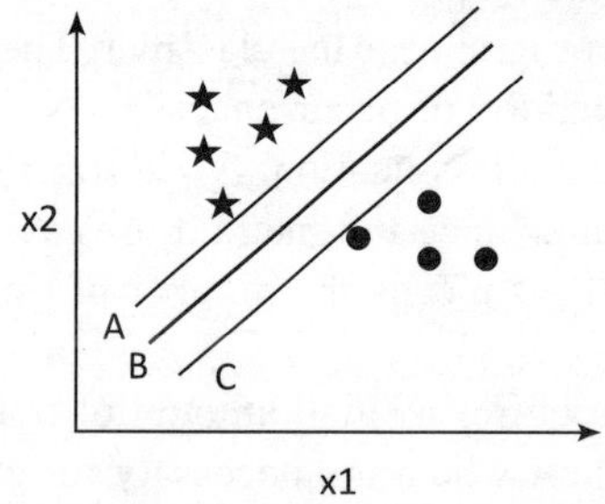

Figure 6.18 Three hyperplanes A, B, and C for classification of data points

The planes are iteratively chosen to maximize distances. SV curve can be specified by not only a plane, but also by a kernel function (such as Gaussian or tri-cube).

Both positive and negative support vectors can be used in features space. Negative SV means the features, which exclude in classification, are used by the classifier.

6.7.7 Random Forest Classifier

Random Forest (RF) uses all four categories of predictor variables. It is an ensemble learning method. Its applications are in classification as well as regression. RF has high overheads. Its architecture is based on a decision tree. The training program trains a regression tree or decision tree (Section 6.7 Figure 6.15).

RF uses a tree learning algorithm modified that selects, such that each candidate splits in the learning process and uses a random subset of features for learning (to take decisions).

For example, Let **I** (T) = Training input features or values and **O** [I (T)] = Output exemplary features or values of **I**. RF selects a bootstrap sample, randomly from input and output examples (T). Decision or regression tree **D** trains on the sample s = 1 to S of d_s (I_s, O_s).

Training algorithm uses bootstrap aggregating method. It puts tree learners in bags (containers). Training dataset input vectors and corresponding output variables bootstrap the sample repeatedly, and fits with the decision tree. The prediction variable can either be estimated by vote (frequency of correct decisions or regression) or by using the averaging formula, in Equation (6.27).

D(S) = Maximum vote frequency (s)/Total sample features or

$$D(S) = S^{-1}\left[\sum_{s=1}^{S} d_s(y)\right] \tag{6.32}$$

The advantage of RF is that it effectively programs the conditional relationships and non-linear functions, kernel or other complex functions. Its applications are when the data points are less than 10 M. It has parallel execution with shared nothing architecture.

6.7.8 AdaBoost and Other Ensemble Classifiers

AdaBoost means adaptive boosting. It builds a strong learner from a linear combination of weak learners.

It initially assumes uniform weight of training examples. Weight means importance of an example with respect to other examples. Assume a trainer algorithm using a sample (example) s in trained vector **T**. The T_s: $\varepsilon \rightarrow \{-1, 1\}$. It means training example T_s weight is – 1 or + 1 to start with. T_s is a week classifier, as it cannot generate a predictor variable and classify. Each classifier is considered sequentially. When its algorithm increases its weight, then other weights correspondingly reduce.

Now increase the weights of variables those T_e, which are misclassified and need greater importance. Assume weight of T_s is ε(s). Finally, the classifier adapts and forms linear combinations of those T_e whose weights were increased. The equation for Decider D(S) using the linear combination of features is given by:

$$D(S) = K\left[\sum_{s=1}^{S}\{\varepsilon(s)\times d_s(y)\}\right], \tag{6.33}$$

where $K = \sum_{s=1}^{S}\varepsilon(s)$ is the sum of the weights of each sample, and $d_s(y)$ is the feature of sample *s*.

OLCs accompanying the book will describe an example of application of AdaBoost.

Self-Assessment Exercise linked to LO 6.6

1. List the meaning of the terms, training example, input vector, predictor variable, continuous variable, categorical variable and feature hashing. ●●●
2. What is vectorization? How does a vector differ from a bag of words? ○●●
3. How does decision tree algorithm CART (Classification and Regression Tree) use the Gini index to split a node. How is the entropy calculated? ●●●
4. When will you use Naïve Bayes, Random Forest and Support vector Classifiers? ○●●
5. List features of the Naïve Bayes classifier. ○○●
6. How do parallel computations with shared nothing architectures help in efficient Big Data analysis? Which are the classifiers supporting these features? ○●●
7. How does AdaBoost generate a strong classifier? ○○●
8. What are the limitations of AdaBoost and Random Forest classifiers? ○○●

6.8 RECOMMENDATION SYSTEM

LO 6.7

Recommender system using collaborative filtering approach, and collaboration-based, contents based, knowledge based and hybrid approaches for recommendations

Recommender refers to a machine learning (ML) tool that enables recommendations after extractions of features in the itemsets from multiple datasets. Example is a product recommender, such as book recommender. Recommendation of a recommender enables the selection of the right product among the high recommendation products. A recommender's need arises because a customer finds it difficult to search the right product due to information overload. Figure 6.19 shows the steps in user-based collaborative filtering (CF) and content-based filtering (CBF) recommenders.

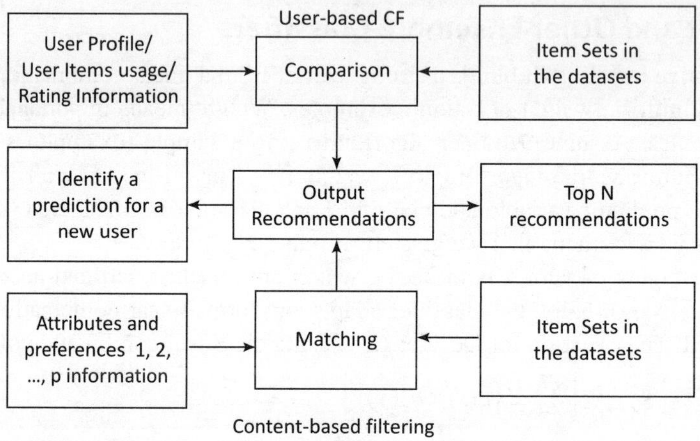

Figure 6.19 Steps in user-based CF and CBF recommenders

6.8.1 Collaborative Recommendation

A recommender generates by collaborative filtering (CF) and gives either prediction or recommendation (Figure 6.19). Prediction is a numerical value (Rij), suggesting the predicted score of item j for the user i. Recommendation can be a list of top-N items that the user will like the most.

Group forms for similar users which means in neighbourhoods. Similar means not distant. The recommender is an application of near-neighbour search method. The already rated items are significant in searching for a neighbour. Once a neighbour of a user is found, different algorithms can be used to combine the preference of neighbours to generate recommendations.

6.8.1.1 Collaborative Filtering

CF algorithm makes recommendations by calculating the similarities in itemsets in-between different items in the datasets. The algorithm predicts the likeliness of an item that it has not rated based on a set of historical preference judgments from a community of users.

CF is different from content-based filtering (CBF) which is built around the attributes of a given item (Figure 6.19). Item features do not capture everything. User's interests may change. CF on the other hand relies on the behavior of the users.

Top-N Recommendations A step in a CF system is to find Top-N Recommendations (Figure 6.19). Top-N recommendation is used to recommend a set of N top-ranked items that will be of interest to a certain user. For example, a user of a website recommends a list of books (or other products) that may be of his/her interest before leaving the website. Top-N recommendation techniques analyze the user-item matrix to discover relations between different users or items.

The two approaches to collaborative filtering are:

- Model-based collaborative filtering – Based on ML techniques (Section 6.8.2)
- Memory-based collaborative filtering – Based on similarity between users and items

Memory-based Collaborative Filtering Memory-based techniques are best suited to real-life applications due to their effectiveness. Memory-based collaborative filtering can be achieved through two approaches, i.e., one based on items, and the other on users, and termed as user-based and item-based approaches.

6.8.1.2 *User-Based Top-N Recommendation Algorithm*

An algorithm does the following:

Identify the k most similar users (nearest neighbours) to the active user using the *Pearson correlation* or vector space model. Every user is treated as a vector in the v-dimensional item space. The similarities between the active user and other users are computed between the vectors (Sections 6.3.6 and 6.4.4).

- The corresponding rows are aggregated in the user-item matrix, **R** to identify a set of items, $\mathcal{C}$, purchased by the group together with their frequencies.
- Recommend the top-N most frequent items in set $\mathcal{C}$ that the active user has not purchased.

Pearson correlation model: (i) Does not consider overlapping preferences of two users, (ii) Computation of only one item in case of two user overlapping preferences, (iii) Correlation does not give added weights when a series of preference values are equal. Pearson correlation using weights is an option to consider these issues.

User-based CF recommends items by finding similar users.

- Users who were interested in the past, are likely to agree again.
- Exploit the opinion of similar users to predict a user's opinion for an item
- Similarity between users is calculated by looking at their overlap in opinions for other items.

User-based nearest-neighbour CF Algorithm, performs the following steps:

- Calculate the similarity or weight, $w_{i,j}$, which reflects distance, correlation or weight, between two users or two items, i and j
- Identify a prediction for the new user by taking the weighted average of all the ratings of the user, item on a certain item or user, or using a simple weighted average
- Suggestions for Top-N recommendation
- The task to generate a top-N recommendation requires finding k most similar users or items (nearest neighbours) after computing the similarities
- Aggregate the neighbours to get the top-N most frequent items as the recommendation.

6.8.1.3 *Item-based Collaborative Filtering*

An item-based CF recommends items by finding similar items. Amazon initially developed the item-based method. The method calculates similarity between items and makes recommendations. Different items that are purchased together are involved to draw inferences about the relationship between items. The more often two items (say, chocolate, gift box and greeting card) appear in the same shopping cart or user history, they are considered as associated with one another. Association between two items specifies by the observations, such as when a customer adds a greeting card to the purchase cart, the algorithm will suggest things that are associated with items in the cart like chocolate and gift box, over things that are not associated, such as electronic items.

- Items that are purchased together in the past are likely to be selected again.
- Similarity between items is decided by looking at their overlap in the purchase pattern for items.

Exploit the full or a sample of the user-item database to generate a prediction. Users part of a group show similar interest. A prediction of preferences on new items for a new user (or active user) can be evaluated by identifying the neighbours.

Problems with User-based Collaborative Filtering Following are some problems associated with using user-based collaborative filtering:

- User Cold-Start Problem: The technique of filtering is based on user history, but what if the user history is not available? This is referred as the "cold start" problem, and it can apply both to new items and to new users. Not enough information exists about a new user to decide the similarity.
- Sparsity: Users have rated only a few items when recommending from a large dataset of itemsets. This makes it hard to find similar users.
- Scalability: For millions of ratings, computations become slow.

User-based vs Item-based Collaborative Filtering User-based similarity between users is dynamic. Pre-computing the user neighbourhood can lead to poor predictions. User similarities have a much vast domain. Item-based similarity between items is more static, and hence it enables pre-computation which improves online performance. An item-based similarity is more meaningful.

Let a user assign a rating to an item, such as a book on a topic. The similarity between two users of the items can be measured by treating each user as a vector of rating frequencies and computing the cosine of the angle formed by the frequency vectors. The basis of recommendation is similarity. (Vector cosine similarity between two sets of data points (vectors A and B) is given by Equation (6.23b)).

Formally, if **P** is an $m \times n$ user-item matrix, then the similarity between two items j and i is defined as the cosine of the angles between v-dimensional vectors corresponding to the i-th and j-th columns of matrix **P**.

Figure 6.20 shows prediction on an item and top 10 recommendation list for a user.

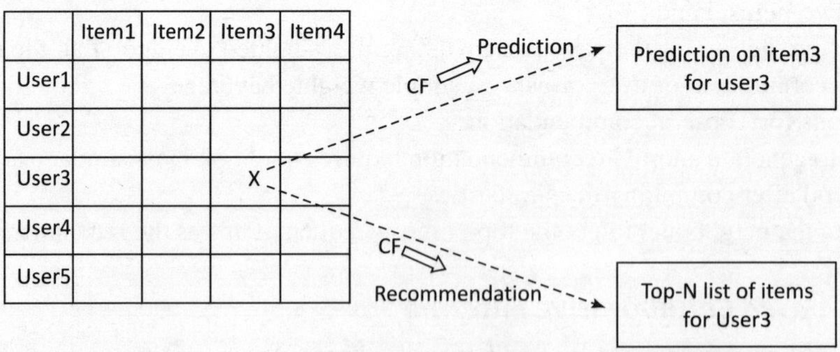

Figure 6.20 Prediction on an item and top 10 recommendation list for a user

6.8.1.4 *Computations of Prediction and Recommendation*

Next step in a collaborative filtering system is to obtain predictions or recommendations. A subset of nearest neighbours of the active user is chosen based on their similarities in the neighbourhood-based CF algorithm. A weighted aggregate of their ratings is used to generate predictions for the active user.

Weighted Sum of Others' Ratings Calculate a weighted average of all the ratings on a certain item i to make a prediction for the active user according to the following formula:

$$P_{a,i} = \bar{r}_a + \frac{\sum_{u \in U} (r_{u,j} - \bar{r}_u) \cdot w_{a,u}}{\sum_{u \in U} |w_{a,u}|}, \tag{6.34}$$

where $\bar{r}_a$ and $\bar{r}_u$ are the average ratings for the user a, and user u on all other rated items, and $w_{a,u}$ is the weight between the user a and user u. The summations are overall the users u ∈ U who have rated the item i.

Simple Weighted Average Use the simple weighted average to predict the rating $P_{u,i}$ for user u on item i in case of item-based prediction.

Item-based Top-N Recommendation Algorithms These algorithms consider the scalability problem of user-based top-N recommendation algorithms.

- Compute k most similar items for each item according to the similarities.
- Identify the set C as candidates of recommended items by taking the union of the k most similar items and removing each of the items in the set $\mathcal{U}$ that the user has already purchased.
- Calculate the similarities between each item of the set $\mathcal{C}$ and the set $\mathcal{U}$.
- The resulting set of the items in $\mathcal{C}$, sorted in decreasing order of the similarity, will be the recommended item-based Top-N list.

The combined distribution of a set of items may result into different from the distributions of the individual items in the set. The method can suggest sub-optimal recommendations in such cases. Higher-order item-based top-N recommendation algorithms can be used in such situations to consider all combinations of items.

6.8.2 Model for Recommendation Systems

Figure 6.15 showed model building approach for building classifier using machine learning. Similarly, a model building for recommender approach utilizes machine learning. They can quickly recommend a set of items since they use pre-computed models. They use the association rules, regression, clustering, neural network, Bayesian classifiers, decision trees and matrix completion techniques.

Matrix completion means filling the missing entries in sparse matrices. The recommender uses user-item matrices. The matrix completion algorithm uses an algorithm similar to principal component analysis (Section 6.9). A model-based technique analyzes the user-item matrix to identify relations between items. These relations are used to compare the list of top-N recommendations. Model-based techniques resolve the sparsity of data problems associated with recommendation systems.

A model-based recommender is an association-rule-based technique. The following example explains how the association rule (Section 6.5.2) applies in designing a recommender system for books.

EXAMPLE 6.23

How does association rule help in designing a recommender system for books?

SOLUTION

An online bookstore posts recommendations for buying books and suggests the offers after a buyer makes a purchase. For example, if a buyer selects the book 'Data Analytics', a list of related books, such as Data Mining, Statistical Concepts, Machine Learning, Big Data Analytics will be offered as recommendations for future purchase. The association rules suggests that when a book on data analytics is purchased, 25% of the times a book on Big Data analytics, 20% of the times a book on data mining, 20% of the times a book on statistical concepts, and 20% of the time a book on machine learning is bought along with it.

Association rules can also be used to plan market strategies for the store. For example, the book on Big Data analytics can be promoted for the sales of the other three books with or without a discount.

Websites and services such as Amazon, Facebook, YouTube and Google use association rules mining. The recommender looks at patterns of activities between different users and different products to produce the recommendations.

1. Online bookstore: 'Customer who bought this, also bought'.
2. Online shopping site: 'You may like this'.
3. Social web: Recommended applications, such as 'Jobs you may be interested' in....
4. Search engine: Similar advertising

6.8.3 Content Based Recommendation

Content-based filtering is built around the attributes and preferences of a given item. The recommender evaluates the contents or items on the preferences of others with a similar point of view. When anyone buys a product online, most websites automatically recommend other products that she/he may be interested to buy. Figure 6.19 illustrated these steps.

6.8.4 Knowledge-based Recommendation

A Knowledge-based Filtering (KBF) recommender builds on explicit knowledge about user preferences, the number of items of specific attributes and a criterion function for the recommendation means positive recommendation criterion for the given context.

Advantage of KBF recommender is that it applies in scenarios where CF and CBF have difficulties in uses. For example, cold start difficulty. Another advantage is applicability in complex domains, such as purchase of house, where ratings are mostly unavailable. Another advantage is applicability when using the conversations with experts.

A disadvantage is problem associated with acquiring difficulties for knowledge. A definitive recommendation in explicit form is difficult without full knowledge.

6.8.5 Hybrid Recommendation Approaches

Hybrid filtering is a combination of collaborative and content base filtering for recommendations. CF and CBF have following issues in making recommendations to new users.

CF Issues Three CF issues are (i) sparsity issue (Section 6.8.1.3), (ii) early rater issues, such as that several times a proper rating can be true if rendered after longer usages, and (iii) preference of a group of users does not account for low ratings by certain users.

CBF Issues Three CBF issues are (i) description of contents difficulties in format accessible to a new user, (ii) over-special need of new user, making recommendation outside the specialized information available, and (iii) difficulty in comparing subjective domains information.

Hybrid approach combines CF and CBF. The approach combines both types of information, applying both filters, CF and CBF.

Self-Assessment Exercise linked to LO 6.7

1. How does a recommender provide top 10 recommendations? ○○●
2. List the difference in approaches of recommender-based on user-based collaborative filtering (CF) and content-based filtering (CBF). ○●●
3. When is collaborative filtering used? ○●●
4. How does a model-based recommender use the association rule? ●●●
5. Compare knowledge-based filtering and content-based filtering. ○○●

6.9 APACHE MAHOUT MACHINE-LEARNING APPLICATIONS

LO 6.8

Apache Mahout architecture and components and their applications for clustering, classification, collaborative-filtering and recommender system

Big Data requires fast and efficient processing of very large datasets at the cluster of machines. Big Data analysis uses datasets with over 1 million data points. Mahout has high efficiency for above 10 M data points in shared-nothing environment. Mahout in sequential shared environment has higher time efficiency for less than 1 M data points.

Mahout computational tasks execute fast when using multiple machines as well as multi-core processing units, distributed over the cloud, tasks runs parallel, and run in shared nothing-computational environment.

Mahout requires installing JVM and integrated development environment (IDE). For example, Eclipse, installing Apache Maven and then the Mahout. (Maven in English means a person with good knowledge or understanding of a subject. Apache *Maven* is a build automation tool used primarily for Java projects).

Mahout is a scalable generalized tensor and linear algebra solving engine. Mahout vectors specify in three Java Classes: SequentialAccessSparseVector, RandomAccessSparseVector, and DenseVector (Section 6.4.4.4). Sequential access sparse means accessing two parallel vectors, one of keys and other of values. Random access means accessing vectors using key, index or hash followed by values, in any order.

Mahout is a tool from Apache Foundation that runs the ML algorithms on Big Data in a parallel computing environment. Mahout primarily focuses on clustering and classification, collaborative filtering and regression analysis. Mahout consists of tools to automate finding of meaningful patterns at big datasets stored in data store at HDFS.

Features of Mahout are as follows:

1. Mahout is designed on top of Apache Hadoop, using the supported algebraic platforms like fast computing Apache Spark paradigm and MapReduce (Spark is fast compared to MapReduce).
2. Offers effective and faster algorithms to analyze large datasets.
3. Contains several Spark and MapReduce enabled clustering implementations, such as k-means, fuzzy k-means, Canopy, Dirichlet and mean shift.
4. Supports distributed Naïve Bayes and complementary Naïve Bayes classification implementations,
5. Designed for a distributed computing environment, but includes contributions that run on a single node or on a non-Hadoop cluster also, such as 'Taste' collaborative-filtering recommender,
6. Mahout, besides collaborative filtering baser recommender, includes other recommenders also, say (i) SVD recommender (ii) KNN-item-based recommender (linear interpolation item based recommender), (iii) cluster-based recommender.
7. Exploits Apache Hadoop library to scale effectively in the cloud.
8. Includes APIs for distributed and in-core first and second moment routines, distributed row matrix (DRM), distributed and scalable libraries for matrix and vector, distributed and local principal component analysis (DSPCA and SPCA)and stochastic singular value decomposition (DSSVD and SSVD), singular value decomposition (SVD), Distributed Cholesky QR (thinQR), Distributed regularized Alternating Least Squares (DALS), Java libraries for common mathematics and statistical operations (focused on linear algebra) and primitive Java Collection Interfaces.
9. Provides an easy to use framework for processing large volume of data, hence is suitable in big data environment.

(*Principal Component Analysis* (PCA) means a linear transformation method for finding the directions of maximum variance in high-dimensional data and project those for transformation onto a smaller dimensional subspace while retaining most of the information. PCA identifies patterns in data sets and detect the correlation among the variables. When there is a strong correlation, then try for reducing the dimensionality. PCA applies in a number of use cases, such as stock market predictions, and the analysis of gene expression data.)

Mahout 0.13.0 released on 17 April 2017 enables easier implementations of most modern machine learning and deep learning algorithms. The versions include the open-source distributed scalable linear algebra library ViennaCL, the Java wrapper library interface JavaCPP and the graphics processor manufacturer, NVIDIA CUDA bindings directly into Mahout. The new version of Mahout makes it easier to run matrix mathematics on graphics cards (used in computers for fast graphic computations). Future versions of Mahout will include support for inclusion of native iterative solvers, according to Apache.

Mahout is used by big companies, such as Adobe, Facebook, LinkedIn, Foursquare, Twitter and Yahoo. The companies use Mahout for the following:

(i) Recommendation engine on Foursquare— Foursquare helps in finding out places, food, and entertainment available in a particular area
(ii) Pattern mining on Yahoo! as anti-spam
(iii) Research Gate, the professional network for scientists and researchers, uses Mahout's recommendation algorithms
(iv) Twitter uses Mahout's Latent-Dirichlet-Allocation (LDA) implementation for user interest modeling
(v) ADOBE AMP uses Mahout's clustering algorithms to increase video consumption by better user targeting.

Figure 6.21 shows Mahout architecture.

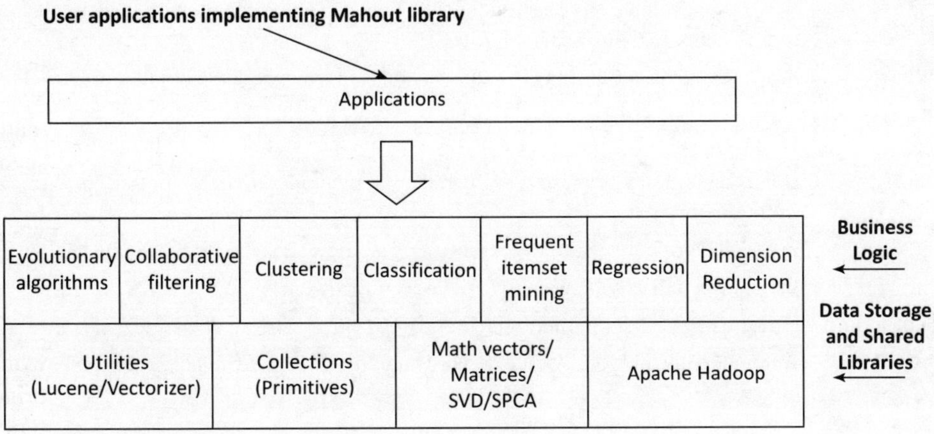

Figure 6.21 Mahout architecture

Mahout implements ML methods as:

1. **Collaborative Filtering** – Enables making automatic predictions about interests of a user. The methods consider the preferences from many users to make predictions (collaborating). Collaborative filtering methods are used by recommender systems and similar itemsets mining. For example, user-based, weighted matrix factorization SVD++, and parallel SGD (in sequentially in shared-data environment), item-based, matrix factorization with alternating least squares, matrix factorization with alternating least squares with implicit feedback, using parallel scalable shared nothing (MapReduce) as well as sequential algorithms. Some popular websites that make use of the collaborative filtering include Amazon, Netflix and iTunes.
2. **Clustering** – Take items in a particular class and organize them into groups, such that items belonging to the same group are similar to each other. Mahout includes the ML algorithms for k-means, fuzzy k-means, Canopy, Dirichlet, and mean-shift for the clusters analysis (Section 6.9).
3. **Classification** – Learns from existing categorizations and then assigns unclassified items to the best category. For example, Naïve Bayes and Random Forest using parallel scalable algorithm (parallel shared-nothing) and logistic regression, support vector, Hidden Markov model and multi-layer perceptron (sequentially shared data environment).
4. **Frequent Itemset Mining** – Analyses items in a group and identifies which items typically appear together.

Clustering algorithms are canopy, k-means, fuzzy k-means, streaming k-means and spectral clustering, using parallel scalable (MapReduce) as well as sequential algorithms. Table 6.7 gives brief descriptions of them.

Table 6.7 Clustering methods

Canopy clustering	Pre-processes the data before using a k-means or hierarchical clustering algorithm
K-means clustering	Deduces partition of *n* observations into *k* clusters in which each observation belongs to the cluster with the nearest mean
Mean shift clustering	Retrieves modes or clusters in 2-dimensional space, where the number of clusters is unknown
Fuzzy k-means	Discovers soft clusters where a particular point can fall into more than one cluster
Hierarchical clustering	Builds a hierarchy of clusters using either an *agglomerative* (bottom-up) or *divisive* (top-down) approach
Spectral clustering	Finds cluster points using Eigenvectors of matrices derived from the data
MinHash clustering	Estimates similarity between two datasets quickly
Dirichlet process clustering	Performs Bayesian mixture modeling
Latent Dirichlet Allocation	Automatically and jointly cluster words into *topics* and *documents* into mixtures of topics

Three other categories of Mahout algorithm belong to the collaborative filtering, classification or frequent itemset mining. Mahout provides two collaborative-filtering algorithms:

1. One is distributed item-based collaborative filtering. The method estimates a user's preference for an item based on the preferences for similar items and row matrices.
2. Other is collaborative filtering using a parallel matrix factorization. The method the items the user might prefer among a matrix of items which a user has not seen so far.

Table 6.8 Brief descriptions of collaboration filtering, Classification and frequent itemset Hadoop-compatible algorithms

Algorithm	Description
Collaborative Filtering	
Distributed item-based collaborative filtering	Estimates a user's preference for an item on the basis of the preferences for similar items and row matrices
Collaborative filtering using a parallel matrix factorization	Finding the items, the user might prefer among a matrix of items, which a user has not seen so far.
Classification	
Bayesian	Classifies objects into binary categories; Naïve Bayes classification.
Random Forests	Provides a collective learning method for classification (and regression) that operate by constructing a multitude of decision trees
Stochastic Gradient Descent (SGD)	Iterative learning algorithm in which each training example is used to pull the model slightly to give more closer to correct answer for that one example (Logistic regression algorithm uses the SGD)
Frequent Itemset Mining	
Parallel frequent pattern growth algorithm	Analyzes items in a group and then identifies which items typically appear together

Mahout Recommender Engine Mahout provides recommender engines of several types, such as (i) user-based recommenders, (ii) item-based recommenders, and (iii) several other algorithms. Mahout has a non-distributed, non-Hadoop-based recommender engine. A text document is the input and has user preferences for items. The output of this engine would be the estimated preferences of a particular user for other items. Five components in Mahout to build a recommender engine are as follows:

1. Data Model– The object of this class holds a file that contains the users, items and preferences details of a product.
2. User Similarity– A measure that returns a number representing how similar the given two users are.
3. Item Similarity– Defines a notion of similarity between two items.
4. User Neighbourhood– For finding the neighbourhood of a given user.
5. Recommender– Takes data model, neighbourhood and user similarity together to produce recommendations.

A data model is prepared from large datasets and is passed as an input to the recommender engine. The recommender engine generates the recommendations for a particular user.

Self-Assessment Exercise linked to LO 6.8

1. Why does Mahout compute faster in case of data points above 1M compared to sequential non-scalable programming? ○○●
2. List the features of Mahout 0.13 version and expected new version features. ○●●
3. List and differentiate between two Mahout collaborative-filtering algorithms, collaborative filtering using a parallel matrix factorization and and distributed item-based collaborative filtering. ○●●
4. Write meanings of distributed row matrix (DRM), distributed and scalable libraries for matrix and vector, distributed and local principal component analysis (DSPCA and SPCA) and stochastic singular value decomposition (DSSVD and SSVD), singular value decomposition (SVD). ○○●

KEY CONCEPTS

AdaBoost	confidence level	feature variable
ANOVA	correlation	frequent itemset
Apache Mahout	cosine similarity	Gini index
Apriori algorithm	data mining	hypothesis
Artificial intelligence	decision tree	interaction variable
association rules	dimension	Jaccard similarity
Bayesian classification	distance measure	K-mean
category variable	distribution function	K-NN
candidate rules	edit distance	kernel function
chi-square	entropy	Manhattan distance
classification	Euclidean distance	market basket model
clustering	explanatory variable	moment
collaborative filtering	F-test	multiple regression

multivariate regression
Naïve Bayes classifier
non-linear transformation
null hypothesis
objective function
outcome variable
outlier
Pearson correlation
population
predictor variable
probability distribution function
Random Forest
recommender
regression model
relationship
response variable
sample
scatter plot
similar itemsets
similarity
similarity coefficient
singular value decomposition
standard deviation
standard error of estimate
statistical inference
statistical significance
stochastic gradient descent
supervised learning
support vector
test dataset
training data
unequal variance
unsupervised learning
user neighbourhood
variable
variance
Welch's t-test

Learning Outcomes

LO 6.1

1. Mathematical and statistical methods estimate the relationships, outliers, variances, probability distribution and correlations in variables, items or entities. Scatter plot depicts the relationship between two variables, and suggests whether they have linear or non-linear relationship.
2. Variance means dispersion with respect to the expected. *Moments* (0, 1, 2, ...) refer to expected values to the powers of (0, 1, 2, …) of random-variable variance.
3. Correlation is a statistical technique that is used to measure and describe the strength and direction of the relationship between two variables.

LO 6.2

1. Linear and non-linear regression model-based analysis predicts the values of one variable, given the values of another variable. More than one variable can be used as predictor with multiple regressions.
3. Regression analysis is a powerful technique used for predicting the unknown value of a variable from the known value of another variable.
4. K-NN method uses Euclidean, Manhattan, Hamming and other distance measures for regression analysis. K-NN predicts using interpolation, extrapolation and averaging methods using weights.

LO 6.3

1. Methods of finding similar items and similarities are nearest neighbour search, Jaccard similarity and collaborative filtering.

2. The similar items and similarities use the distance measures. The distance measures are Euclidean, Jaccard, cosine, edit and Hamming distances.

LO 6.4

1. Frequent Itemset Mining (FIM) is one of the popular techniques to extract knowledge from the data. The technique has been an essential part of data analysis and mining. The extraction is based on frequently occurring events.
2. Market basket analysis is a tool of knowledge discovery about co-occurrence of items. A co-occurrence means two or more things happen together. It can also be defined as a data mining technique to derive strength of association between a pair of product items.
3. Objective of generation of association rules is to find uncovered relationships using some strong rules.
4. Apriori algorithm is used for frequent itemset mining and association rule mining. Apriori algorithm simply follows a basis that any subset of a large itemset must be a large itemset. This is called the Apriori principle, and can reduce the number of itemsets which an algorithm needs to examine. Apriori principle suggests, if an itemset is frequent, then all of its subsets must also be frequent.

LO 6.5

1. Cluster analysis means finding the grouping of the objects (datasets) of similar types or characteristics. ML algorithms methods are K-means, K-medoids, Fuzzy K-means, Canopy, and Dirichlet for clusters analysis.
2. A clustering algorithm finds k clusters in a given dataset using k centroids.

LO 6.6

1. Methods of machine learning are supervised and unsupervised learning. Clustering and classification differ. Clustering is identification of groups of similar objects. Classification means splitting the datasets into subsets with similar features using statistical concepts.
2. Classifiers use training datasets, input vectors, output vectors and predictor variables. Classifier algorithm components are training, model and decider programs.
3. Classfiers, for example Random Forest, use decision tree algorithms which evaluate decision tree.
4. Naïve Bayes is a simple, probabilistic and statistical classifier. Naïve Bayes classifier basis is Bayes' Theorem (from Bayesian statistics) with strong (Naïve) independence assumptions and maximum posteriori hypothesis. The classifier uses are in text and documents.
5. Classification methods are k-nearest neighbour, Stochastic Gradient Descent – Logistic Regression, Support Vector Machine, Random Forest and AdaBoost classifiers.

LO 6.7

1. Recommender system is a system that evaluates contents or items on the preferences of others with a similar point of view. The two approaches to collaborative filtering are (i) memory-based collaborative filtering – based on similarity between users and items, and (ii) model-based collaborative filtering – based on ML techniques.
2. Collaborative filtering predicts the likeliness of an item that she/he has not rated based on a set of historical preference judgments from a community of users.
3. Collaborative filtering builds around the attributes of a given item. Collaborative filtering relies on the behavior of the users.

LO 6.8

1 Apache Mahout is scalable generalized tensor and linear algebra solving engine, which runs the ML algorithms on Big Data in parallel computing environment. Mahout enables clustering, classification, collaborative filtering, regression and recommender. Mahout consists of tools to automate finding of meaningful patterns at big datasets stored in data store at HDFS.

2. Contains several Spark and MapReduce enabled clustering implementations, such as K-means, Fuzzy K-means, Canopy, Dirichlet, supports distributed Naïve Bayes and complementary Naïve Bayes classification implementations.

Objective Type Questions

Select one correct answer option for each of the following questions:

6.1 Mahout includes APIs for (i) distributed and in-core first and second moment routines, (ii) distributed row matrix (DRM), (iii) distributed and scalable libraries for tensor, matrix and vector, (iv) distributed and local principal component analysis and stochastic singular value decomposition, (v) distributed Cholesky QR (thinQR), (vi) distributed regularized alternating least squares, (vii) Java libraries for common mathematics and statistical operations, (viii) focuses on linear algebra for matrices and vectors, and (ix) primitive C++ and well as Java collections ○○●

(a) i to viii (b) all
(c) all except i and v (d) i to v, viii and ix

6.2 (i) Regression analysis is a technique used for predicting, (ii) predicts the unknown value of a variable from the known value of another variable. (iii) Regression analysis is a statistical method. (iv) Regression deals with the formulation of conceptual model depicting a relationship amongst dependent and independent variables. (v) The independent variable is used for the purpose of prediction of the values. (vi) More than one variable whose values are hypothesized are called independent variables. (vii) The prediction for the dependent variable can be made by accurate selection of the independent variables to estimate a dependent variable. ●●●

(a) none (b) all
(c) all except v and vi (d) iii to vii

6.3 (i) The standard error of the estimate is a measure of the dispersion (or variability) in the (ii) predicted values in a regression, (iii) probabilistic values in a regression. (iv) When the σ_{est} is small, most of the observed values (y) dots are close to the regression line in a scatter plot and better is the estimate based on the equation of the line. (v) When the σ_{est} is small, many of the observed values are far away from the regression line. (vi) When the standard error is zero, then no variation exists corresponding to the computed line. The correlation is perfect. ○○●

(a) iv (b) all
(c) all except ii to v (d) all except iii and v

6.4 (i) Coefficient values suggest which relationships in the model are statistically significant and (ii) the p-values in regression analysis suggest the nature of those relationships. (iii) The coefficients describe the mathematical relationship between each independent variable and the dependent variable. (iv) The p-values for the coefficients indicate whether these relationships are statistically significant. ○●●

(a) all except ii (b) iii and iv
(c) all (d) ii to iv

6.5 A hypothesis test requires (i) stating the hypotheses, (ii) null hypothesis, (iii) alternative hypothesis, (iv) F-test hypothesis, and (v) t-test hypothesis. Also required is (vi) preparing plan for the analysis. (vii) The analysis plan means how to use sample data to accept or reject the alternative hypothesis.

(a) i, iii, iv and vi
(b) i to v
(c) ii to vi
(d) i, ii, iii, vi

6.6 K-mean based algorithm (i) classifies or groups the objects based on the attributes (features) into k number of groups. k is a positive integer number. (ii) The grouping of data results into k clusters (C1, C2, . . ., CK), each has A centroid. (iii) Centroid is fundamentally a center representative of a cluster. (iv) The centroid of each cluster is calculated as the mean of all the instances belonging to that cluster. (v) The clusters are formed by maximizing the sum of squares of distances between the data and the corresponding cluster centroid.

(a) all except v
(b) i, ii, iii, v
(c) ii to v
(d) all except iii

6.7 (i) Clustering *finds* to which class a new object belongs to from the set of predefined classes. (ii) Classification *groups* a set of objects in order to find the relationship between them. Clustering and classification *differ* in terms of (iii) supervised and unsupervised learning, (iv) use of training datasets, no training datasets usage (v) labels (all the data labeled, unlabeled), (vi) datasets consisting of attributes and class labels, (vii) process algorithms (categorization of new data according to the observations of the training set, usages of statistical concepts and splitting of datasets sub-sets with similar features), respectively.

(a) all except i
(b) all except iii and iv
(c) all except i, iii
(d) all

6.8 Formal statement of the association rule problem is stated as: Let $I = \{I_1, I_2, ..., I_d\}$ be a set of d distinct attributes, also called literals. Let $T = \{t_1, t_2, ..., t_n\}$ be set of transactions and (i) contains a set of items such that $T \subseteq I$. (ii) An association rule is an implication of the form $X \rightarrow Y$, (iii) where X, Y belongs to sets of items called itemsets ($X, Y \subset I$), and (iv) X and Y are union of itemsets ($X \cup Y = \emptyset$). Here, (v) X is called consequent, and (vi) Y antecedent.

(a) i, ii and v
(b) all except i, v
(c) i to iii
(d) i to iv

6.9 Apriori algorithm is simple as (i) it follows a basis that any subset of a large itemset must be a large itemset, called Apriori principle. (ii) The Apriori principle can reduce the number of itemsets need to examine. (iii) Apriori principle suggests if itemset {A, B, C} is a frequent itemset, then all its subsets {A}, {B}, {C}, {A, B}, {B, C} and {A, C} need not be frequent. (iv) On contrary, if an itemset is not frequent, then none of its supersets can be frequent. (v) Apriori advantage is that the principle results in to a smaller list of potential frequent itemsets as mining progresses. (vi) The algorithm requires multiple scans of the database. (vii) The complex generation process for candidate exploits more time, space and memory.

(a) i to v
(b) all but vi and vii
(c) all except iii
(d) i to iv

6.10 (i) A recommender system is a system that evaluates contents or items on the preferences of others with a similar point of view. (ii) Collaborative filtering predicts the likeliness of an item that he/she has not rated based on a set of historical preference judgments from a community of users. (iii) Collaborative filtering is similar from content-based filtering, (iv) which is built around the attributes of a given item. (v) Item features capture everything. When user's interest changes then also the collaborative filtering does not on the other hand rely on the behavior of the users.

(a) i, ii, iv
(b) all except v
(c) all except iii
(d) all except i

6.11 Item-based collaborative filtering uses (i) full or (ii) a sample of the user-item database to (iii) generate a prediction. (iv) Users of a group shows dissimilar interest. (v) A prediction of preferences on new items for a new user (or active user) can be evaluated by identifying the neighbours. (vi) Jaccard Similarity, (vii) cosine similarity, (viii) edit-distance or (ix) correlation methods are used to find similarities between users. ○●●

(a) all except viii (b) all except iv
(c) i to vii (d) all except i

6.12 User-based nearest neighbour collaborative filtering algorithm, performs the following steps: (i) Calculate the similarity or weight $w_{i, j}$, which reflects distance, correlation or weight between two users or two items, i and j. (ii) Identify a prediction for the new user by taking the weighted average of all the ratings of the user or item on a certain item or user, or (iii) using variance. (iv) Suggest top-N recommendations. (v) The task to generate a top-N recommendation requires finding k most similar users or items (nearest neighbours) after computing the similarities, and (vi) aggregate the neighbours to get the top N most frequent items as the recommendation. ○○●

(a) all (b) i, iii and iv
(c) all except iv (d) all except iii

6.13 The decision trees (i) aggregate the datasets based on all values of three variables and identify the variable, which creates the (ii) best heterogeneous sets of datasets (which are (iii) homogeneous to each other). (iv) Decision tree output in the form of (v) graphical representation is very easy to understand. (vi) Useful in predicting significant response variable. (vii) Influenced by outliers and missing values to a fair degree as compared to other techniques of modeling. (viii) Handles both numerical and statistical variables. (ix) Decision tree is considered a non-parametric method. Thus, (x) decision trees have no assumptions about the space distribution and the classifier structure. ●●●

(a) all (b) iv, v, vi, viii, ix, and x
(c) all except i (d) all except i and x

6.14 Naïve Bayes is (i) simple, (ii) probabilistic and (iii) statistical classifier. (iv) The classifier base is Bayes theorem (from Bayesian statistics) with strong (Naïve) independence assumptions and maximum posteriori hypothesis. (v) It is an unsupervised learning technique, which uses non-parametric approach. (vi) The classifier exploits one of the most basic text classification techniques with a variety of applications in email spam detection, personal email sorting and document categorization. (vii) Classifier assumes class conditional dependence. ○●●

(a) all except vi and vii (b) all except ii
(c) All except v and vii (d) All except iii and vi

Review Questions

6.1 Describe the approaches used in linear, multivariate and multiple regression algorithms. **(LO 6.1)** ●●●

6.2 How are correlations indicators used for evaluating linear relationships? What do the strength and direction of the relationship describe? **(LO 6.1)** ○●●

6.3 How do Euclidean and Manhattan distances perform regression analysis and predictions? How do the weights apply? **(LO 6.2)** ●●●

6.4 How are Jaccard distance, cosine distance and edit distance used for finding similar items? **(LO 6.3)** ●●●

6.5 How does frequent pattern mining enable knowledge discovery from a large number of itemsets? **(LO 6.4)** ○○●

6.6 Describe the Apriori algorithm. **(LO 6.4)** ○○●

6.7 How are methods of collaborative filtering used? **(LO 6.4)** ○●●

6.8 How does clustering a large dataset help in knowledge discovery about the datasets? **(LO 6.5)** ○○●

6.9 Compare the characteristics features of K-means, K-medoids, Canopy and hierarchical clustering techniques. **(LO 6.5)** ●●●

6.10 What are the differences between clustering and classification algorithms, and between supervised and unsupervised learning? Explain functions of training, model and decider programs. **(LO 6.6)** ○●●

6.11 How is a decision tree used? **(LO 6.6)** ○●●

6.12 Compare the characteristic features of K-NN, SGD, Naïve Bayes, Random Forest, Support Vector and AdaBoost classifiers. **(LO 6.6)** ●●●

6.13 What are the steps in item-based collaborative filter when used for recommender? **(LO 6.7)** ○○●

6.14 List and explain the features of Mahout 0.13. List the machine learning algorithms, which Mahout implements. **(LO 6.8)** ○●●

6.15 How is principal component analysis used in machine learning algorithms? **(LO 6.8)** ○○●

6.16 How do algorithms provided in Mahout perform clustering and classification? **(LO 6.8)** ●●●

Practice Exercises

6.1 Consider student expected grades in an examination. Assume that grades have probabilistic distributions. Consider grade point as a variable. Assume that probability of student awarded grade point 1.0 is 1%, 2.0 is 4%, 3.0 is 8%, 4.0 is 16%, 5.0 is 24%, 6.0 is 26%, 7.0 is 11% and 8.0 is 10%. (i) What are the mean, variance and standard deviation? (ii) Compute the 0th moment, 1st moment, 2nd moment and 3rd moment. (iii) How do moment and variance relate? (iv) Interpret the parameters computed. **(LO 6.1)** ●●●

6.2 Recapitulate Practice Exercise 3.1. Consider a car company selling Jaguar Land Rover, Hexa, Zest, Nexon and Safari Storme models of cars. Table 6.9 gives a dataset for sales of these cars at 2000 showrooms for each date in 2017. Total 2000 × 365 rows per year. Total columns are 2000 × 365 × 7 per year. Variables for sales are denoted as x followed by day of the year (1 or 2, ..., 365) followed by the model_ID, (1, 2, 3, 4 or 5) in columns 3 to 7. Using interaction variables concept, list the steps to find whether any relationship between the monthly sales figures of car models exists or not. ○●●

Table 6.9 Sales data for cars of 5 models at 2000 showrooms for each date in 2017

CCSR_ id	Date (DT) mmddyy	Jaguar Land Rover-daily Sale (JLRDS)	Hexadaily Sales (HDS)	Zest-daily Sales (ZDS)	Nexon Weekly Sale (NWS)	Safari Storme Weekly Sale (SSWS)
0001	010117	x11	x12	x13	x14	x15
0001	010217	x21	x22	x23	x24	x25
0001	010317	x31	x32	x33	x34	x35

(Contd.)

CCSR_id	Date (DT) mmddyy	Jaguar Land Rover-daily Sale (JLRDS)	Hexadaily Sales (HDS)	Zest-daily Sales (ZDS)	Nexon Weekly Sale (NWS)	Safari Storme Weekly Sale (SSWS)
0001	010417	x41	x42	x43	x44	x45
.	.	.	.	.	.	-
.	.	.	.	.	.	-
.	.	.	.	.	.	.
2000	122717	x3631	x3632	x3633	x3634	x3635
2000	122817	x3631	x3632	x3633	x3634	x3635
2000	12 2917	x3631	x3632	x3633	x3634	x3635
2000	123017	x3641	x3642	x3643	x3644	x3645
2000	123117	x3651	x3652	x3653	x3654	x3655
.	.	.	.	.	.	-

(LO 6.1)

6.3 Show a simple linear regression chart for varying weekly sales of cars of a specific model, say Tata Zest all over the country. Plot the values on a graph, with week of the year on the x axis and weekly sales on the y axis. How are variance and moments 0, 1, 2 and 3 estimated? Assume the plot fits a line Sales at 52nd week = Sales at 1st week of the year + 0.001 × 52 × Sales at 1st week. How can the sales at 100th week be predicted from regression analysis? **(LO 6.2)** ○○●

6.4 List the steps to use the linear regression model to find the rate of monthly sales growth of each car model combined at all showrooms. **(LO 6.2)** ○○●

6.5 List the steps to prepare a new table. Table 6.10 gives yearly accumulated sales of each model from 2010 to 2017, i.e., total 8 rows for 8 years of accumulated yearly sales and total columns are 8 × 7 per year. Variables for sales are denoted as s followed by day of the year (1 or 2, ..., 8). Use values in each cell in terms of variable s. Table 6.9 format can be as shown below. ○●●

Table 6.10 Yearly sales data for cars of 5 models accumulated over all showrooms and all dates in a year during 2010 to 2017

S.No.	Year yyyy	Jaguar Land Rover daily Sale (JLRYS)	Hexa daily Sales (HYS)	Zest daily Sales (ZYS)	Nexon Weekly Sale (NYS)	Safari Storme Weekly Sale (SSYS)
1	2010	s11	s12	s13	s14	s15
2	2011	s21	s22	s23	s24	s25
3	2012	s31	s32	s33	s34	s35
4	2013	s41	s42	s43	s44	s45
5	2014	.	.	.	.	.
6	2015	.	.	.	.	.
7	2016	.	.	.	.	.
8	2017	s81	s82	s83	s84	s85

(LO 6.2)

6.6 List the steps to find regression coefficients in linear model and non-linear model, moments, variance and standard deviation of actual yearly sales vs estimates from the coefficient values for each car model. **(LO 6.2)** ●●●

6.7 List the steps to find regression coefficients using linear model and Euclidean distances. **(LO 6.2)** ●●●

6.8 List the steps in coding for determining the Jaccard, cosine and Euclidean similarity coefficients. **(LO 6.3)** ○●●

6.9 List the steps for finding the association, association rules, filtering the frequent itemsets for computer science books on two programming languages, Java and Python. **(LO 6.4)** ●●●

6.10 Assume a graph with price discount given between 0% to 40 % with respect to total sales realised to that customer. Show the dots for each customer. How will the company optimize the profit using that data and take pricing discount decisions using clustering algorithm. **(LO 6.5)** ○○●

6.11 Describe hierarchial approaches including agglomerative-divisive-distance measures to defining the distance between clusters in different algorithms. **(LO 6.5)** ○●●

6.12 List the steps in Schoastic Gradient Descent and logistic regression. Give an example of using SGD logistic regression. **(LO 6.6)** ○●●

6.13 List the steps in a AdaBoost classifier. Give an example of using SGD logistic AdaBoost. **(LO 6.6)** ○●●

6.14 List the steps for using the hidden Markov deep learning algorithm. Give an example of using the hidden Markov. **(LO 6.6)** ●●●

6.15 List the steps for using the multi-level perceptron deep learning algorithm. Give an example of using multi-level perceptron. **(LO 6.6)** ●●●

6.16 List the steps for cluster analysis and find whether clustering shows higher sales in certain group of showrooms in festive months, i.e., Octobers and Decembers in most of years compared to other months. **(LO 6.6)** ●●●

6.17 List the steps for the decision trees from the data in Table 6.9. **(LO 6.6)** ○○●

6.18 List the steps for collaborative recommendation, and mining the similar itemsets in the problem in Practice Exercise 6.6. **(LO 6.7)** ○●●

6.19 List the coding steps using Mahout 0.13 and Python libraries for the algorithms listed in Table 6.6. **(LO 6.8)** ●●●

Chapter 7

Data Stream Mining and Real-Time Analytics Platform—SparkStreaming

LEARNING OBJECTIVES

After studying this chapter, you will be able to:

LO 7.1 Get conceptual understanding of data stream, model, architecture, management, sources, querying and stream processing issues

LO 7.2 Get knowledge of methods of sampling, filtering and counting distinct elements in stream computing

LO 7.3 Get knowledge of methods of finding the frequent itemsets in a stream, handling the large datasets and mining the association-rules

LO 7.4 Get introduced to a real-time analytics platform—Apache SparkStreaming, and applications of real-time analytics to sentiments analysis, and the stock prices analysis

RECALL FROM EARLIER CHAPTERS

Apache® Spark™ is a fast and dynamic compute engine with in-memory processing. Processing requires *read* of instructions and data, and *write* of results. The in-memory data processing results in fast computations. In-memory *read* and *write* operations take place without any delay as compared to read from disk and write to disk operations. Fast computations also result due to the use of DAGs and acyclic dataflows. Spark processes the data stored at HDFS and compatible cloud stores, such as Ceph or S3. Spark has the APIs which facilitate programming in R, Python, Java and Scala (Section 5.1).

SparkStreaming is a software component in Spark stack. The software processes real-time streaming data using micro-batches. SparkStreaming processes DStream (or discretized stream) which consists of a series of RDDs as the real-time data.

This chapter focuses on streaming data concepts, stream analytics and real-time analytics.

7.1 INTRODUCTION

Data stream in general means continuously flowing data in sequences. A theoretical definition of stream is an unbounded sequence of data items and records, which may or may not be related, or correlated with each other. Examples of the stream are computer network traffic, data of stock quotations, online videos, telephone conversations, transactions in database and transmission of sensors data.

Streaming data originates from several sources. Examples include data and images from satellites, IoT devices, Internet websites and social media posts. Many applications require streaming data for various services. Processing of data stream helps extraction of knowledge-structures from the continuous, rapid flowing data stream.

Some important key terms and their meanings are given below:

Apache® Spark™ refers to a fast and general compute engine. Apache® Spark™ powers analytics applications up to 100 times faster. It supports HDFS compatible data. Spark has a simple and expressive programming model. The multiple languages, Python, and Scala shells provide *great ease in programming for complex analytics, machine learning,* and other solutions.

Spark software stack refers to SparkSQL, SparkStreaming, Spark Arrow, SparkR, MLib, and GraphX.

Scalability can refer to many different system parameters, such as how much added traffic can it handle, how easy is it to add more storage capacity, or even how many more transactions process.

This chapter describes methods of processing, analyzing, mining the streaming datasets and SparkStreaming—a real-time analytics platform for Big Data. Section 7.2 describes the concept, model, architecture, management of data stream and gives examples of sources. Section 7.3 describes stream computing aspects—sampling, filtering and counting distinct elements in a stream. Section 7.4 describes the methods of frequent itemset stream analytics, handling large datasets and association rule mining. Section 7.5 describes real-time analytics platform—Apache SparkStreaming, and case studies on real-time sentiment analytics and stock prices analytics.

7.2 DATA STREAM CONCEPTS AND DATA STREAM MANAGEMENT

LO 7.1

Data stream concept, modeling, architecture, management, sources, stream querying and issues

The following subsections describe the concept, model, architecture and management of data streams.

7.2.1 Data Stream Concepts

A stream is a sequence of data elements or symbols made available over time.

Data stream transmits from a source and receives at the processing end in a network.

An application processes a data stream differently. Processing is in micro-batches instead of processing batches. Processing of stream can be comprehended as filling milk in bottles on a conveyor belt and capping them, one at a time successfully rather than in a large batch at the same time.

Standard operations do not apply on stream as they may have unlimited or infinite data, and at an instance may not be available completely. Formally, streams are partial data (potentially unlimited), and not finite data. Programmers use the term "stream" in computer science in several ways. Some of these are:

(i) Stream is communication of bytes or characters over sockets in a computer network.

(ii) A program uses stream as an underlying data type in inter-process communication channels.

(iii) Stream Java class objects perform I/Os. Java encapsulates Stream Classes in java.io package. Java defines two types of streams: Byte Stream and Character Stream. Java has several IO classes for inputs and outputs, such as ObjectOutputStream, ObjectInputStream, and FilterOutputStream. A stream object is a logical interface to a file. That file can refer to a disk file, screen, keyboard, port, or a file on a secondary storage device.

(iv) A stream is a source or sink of data in UNIX. It usually comprises individual bytes or characters. Stream behaves as an abstraction when reading or writing files, or communicating over network sockets. UNIX recognizes three standard input and output streams called standard input (stdin), standard output (stdout) and standard error (stderr).

(v) A UNIX utility sed (stream editor) parses and transforms text using a simple compact programming language.

(vi) A Linux stream is a data transfer entity in a Linux shell that transfers data from one process to another through a pipe, or from one file to another as a redirect.

(vii) Perl and Python implement the stream as an iterator. An iterator is a useful abstraction of an input stream.

(viii) A stream is an abstraction of a construct that sends or receives an unknown number of bytes in some programming languages. C++ uses this abstraction to perform input and output. Here, a stream is an entity where a program can either insert or extract characters.

(ix) Oracle streams enable information sharing. A message is a unit of shared piece of information. Oracle streams can share the messages in the stream. The stream propagates information within a database or from one database to another.

(x) HTTP Live Streaming (also known as HLS) is an HTTP-based media streaming communication protocol implemented by Apple Inc. It is a part of Apple's QuickTime, Safari, OS X and iOS software.

Streaming is a term which is popular in the field of media as well. Here, streaming means listening to music or watching video in 'real time' instead of first downloading and then listening or viewing the content. The contents transmit in a compressed format over the Internet and the receiver plays the contents instantly. A continuous stream of data flows between the source and receiver ends, and is processed in real time.

7.2.2 Data Stream Model

Stream is data in motion. Three approaches for updating the end-points (sinks) are (i) non-overlapping, (ii) slow (batch processing) and (iii) fast (near real-time). Following are the different ways of modeling data stream, querying, processing and management.

(a) Graph model Stream can be modeled as a graph of nodes connected by the edges. The edges model the stream of data moving between the operators. The data processes at the node. Each node in the graph is an operator or adapter. The node can have inputs, zero inputs and outputs or zero outputs. One node output connects to the input of the next node. Figure 7.1 shows graph-based stream as data model for processing at an operator or adapter.

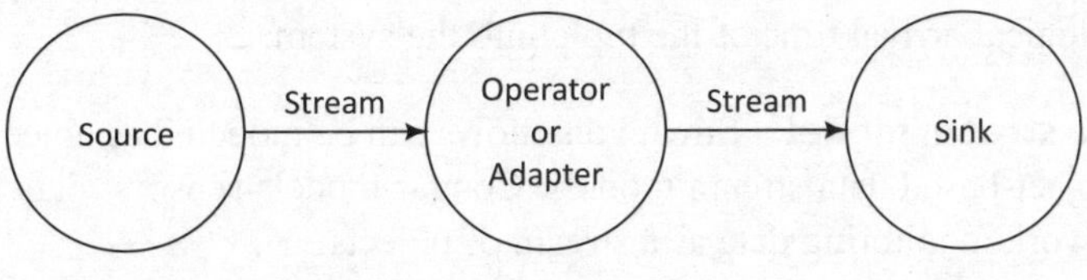

Figure 7.1 Graph-based stream data model for processing at an operator or adapter

(b) Relation-oriented stream-tuples model Stream dataflow can be modeled as tuples flow. Individual data items may be relational tuples in a data stream model.

Data sink may be Parquet nested column-oriented data stream or RDBMS row-oriented storage in tables. *Parquet* is nested hierarchical columnar-storage concept. Nesting sequence is table, row groups within a table, column chunk within the row groups, page chunks with the column chunk. Chunk pages are inside a column chunk, column chunks inside a row group and row groups inside a table (Section 3.3.3.5).

Examples of tuple model stream of data are Borealis, STREAM and TelegraphCQ. Figure 7.2 shows relational tuple-based data stream model. Arrow shows the stream *S* flowing from the source to sink. *S* consists of infinite (means unbounded) time-ordered multiple sets of tuples. Each tuple consists of (Timestamp τ, Key, Values). Sink is Parquet nested column-oriented or RDBMS tabular store.

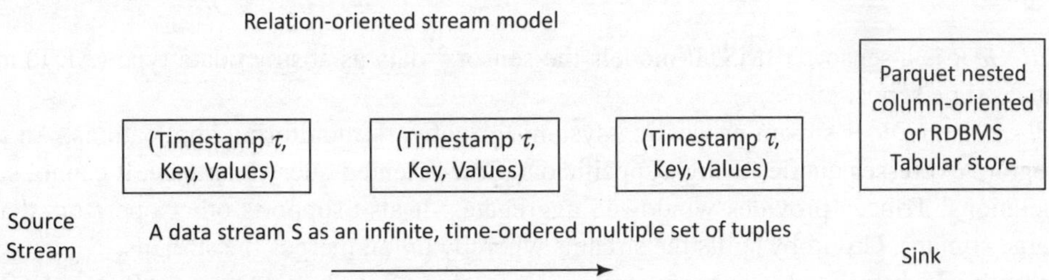

Figure 7.2 Relation-oriented stream-tuples model (Time stamp for real-time streaming data)

Stream dataflow can be modeled as Parquet nested sequences (Section 3.3.3.5). The sequences in data stream are page chunks nested in column chunks in each column. First the (i) page chunks, which nest in a column chunk, then (ii) page chunks of the next column chunk, then (iii) the remaining column chunks which nest at a row group in the table, then (iv) the next row group, and so on. Thus, all Parquet tabular data transfer as the stream in the column-oriented data stream.

Processing in data stream model can also include some data from conventional stored relations, if required. That means queries on data stream may perform join operations between data stream and stored relational data.

A data stream is a potentially unbounded and time-ordered sequence of data items (relational tuples) in the data stream model. The receiving software receives the sequences in order and sees the data items only once. Each tuple consists of a set of attributes, like a row in a database table. The tuples have a schema-like traditional database. One of the attributes in the tuple schema is a timestamp, usually represented by τ. The timestamp denotes the logical arrival time of the tuple into the system.

(c) Object-based data stream model Stream dataflows can be modeled as objects. Cougar and Tribeca are two examples of object-based data stream models. Cougar models sensors' data as a stream of objects. Tribeca models the network monitoring data as a stream of objects.

(d) XML-based data stream model NiagaraCQ is anXML-based data stream model. It provides scalable continuous query processing over XML documents. It performs operations over millions of simultaneous queries by dynamically grouping them according to their structural similarities.

(e) Window-based data stream model Stream data direction can be towards fixed window, sliding window or landmark window-sinks (end-points) [Window means a time window during which the data stream is looked at an instance. Suppose an application software queries streaming data at each successive 2^{20} time-units in time = T_{window}. Then, 2^{30} bits queried for 1 or 0 takes (2^{10} = 1024) × T_{window} time units (minimum). One time unit corresponds to a time interval in which a bit 1 or 0 can arrive in the stream. Application query caches the arriving bit in one time unit. Stream data unpredictably changes in both size and frequency, and thus it can happen in certain time units that no bits may be arriving. [2^{10} T_{window} time-units may receive less or much less than 2^{30} bits.]

Examples of stream processing modeling systems Examples of modeling systems for stream processing are:

1. *COUGAR* is a sensor DBMS. It models the sensors' data as abstract data type (ADT) and sensors data as time series.
2. *Tribeca* is an older stream processing system for network monitoring applications. An application program expresses queries using a specific dataflow-oriented query language. It cannot support join operations. Tribeca provides windowed aggregates. It also supports other operators that split and merge streams. Group-by splits the streams whereby union merges the streams.
3. *Borealis* is a distributed stream processing engine from Brandeis University, Brown University and MIT. Borealis builds on their previous engines, Aurora and Medusa for stream processing.

   Borealis, current version includes various modules, such as a stream processing engine. The version provides the core functionality of low latency in stream processing using a rich set of stream-oriented operators. Borealis includes coordinator, load manager, load shedder and fault tolerance modules. Also includes graphical query editor, system visualizer, and stream connection generator.
4. STREAM is a data stream management system developed at Stanford University. The project reinvestigated data management and query processing in the presence of multiple, continuous, rapid, time-varying data stream. The STREAM prototype supports continuous queries over stream as well as stored relations. To achieve this, STREAM supports three types of operators: stream-to-relation, relation-to-stream and relation-to-relation.
5. TelegraphCQ project developed at University of California, Berkeley, is a suite of technologies for continuously adaptive query processing. TelegraphCQ handles a large number of queries over high volume, highly variable data stream. It continuously processes the incoming data without any storage.

7.2.3 Architecture

Big Data stores at the:

(i) HDFS (Distributed at data nodes in clusters), or

(ii) DFS compatible data store, such as HBase, Cassandra, Ceph or S3 (Section 5.2).

Figure 7.3 shows a query processing architecture.

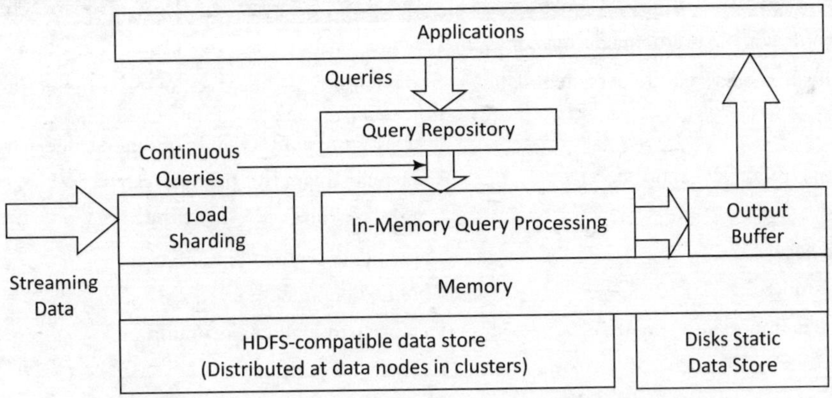

Figure 7.3 Data stream architecture for processing

Figure 7.3 shows that large data blocks in received stream store at HDFS compatible data store or static data at disk. Data shards load at memory from data store or disk for future uses (Section 3.2). The figure also shows that streaming data shards load at memory in real-time applications. A user application uses a query repository, which continuously sends queries for processing of the shards in-memory. The responses of queries save at an output buffer before they are finally retrieved by the application.

The processing model can also use hybrid architecture, referred as *lambda architecture* for processing streaming data and back-end jobs at the same time. The system manages stream flow over real-time data until data elements are pushed to a batch system. The data then become available to access and process as batch data from disk static data store or HDFS.

7.2.4 Data Stream Management System (DSMS)

Fundamentally basis of traditional data management systems are on the notion of determined and static data storage. The streaming data basis is altogether different. The data requires collection and parsing before using and deletion from the system.

Responses against the queries are precise in static DBMS. Streaming data can unpredictably change in both size and frequency, and thus results into approximate responses.

Management and processing of streaming data are different from traditional DBMSs. These systems build primarily on the concept of persistence and static data collections while the streaming data require parsing and processing at once when they arrive in the system.

Data Stream Management System (DSMS) is a data-intensive application in which the data models as a transient data stream. DSMS is an application program that manages streaming data. The usage of the program is different than using of persistent relations in DBMS.

Some popular applications of DSMS are network monitoring, telecommunications data management, web applications and sensor networks. Individual data items model as relational tuples in the data stream model. For example, data of network measurements, call records, web page visits, and sensor readings. Table 7.1 highlights the differences between DBMS and DSMS.

Table 7.1 Comparison between DBMS and DSMS

DBMS	DSMS
Stores sets of records with no pre-defined time concept	Provides on-line analysis of rapidly changing stream of data
Suitable for applications that require persistent data storage and complex querying	Suitable for real-time, continuous, ordered (arrival time or timestamp) sequence of data elements. Also, for data that is large to store entirely and continuous querying environment
Persistent relations (relatively static, stored)	Transient stream (on-line analysis)
One-time queries	Continuous queries
Requires random access	Implements sequential access
Unbounded disk storage	Bounded main memory
Only current state is important	Past or historical data is important
No real-time services requirements	Real-time requirements
Relatively low update rate	Very high arrival rate (usually in multi-GBs)
Assume precise data	Data get stale or imprecise later
Access plan determined by query processor, physical database design	Unpredictable data arrival and varying characteristics of the data

Traditional DBMSs do not directly support real-time continuous queries. The data is available on disk or memory for random access to them. Some or all input data that are to be operated on and arrive as one or more continuous data stream in the data stream model.

Data stream differs from the conventional stored relational model in the following ways:

- The data elements in the stream arrive in real time.
- Size of the data stream is unbounded.
- The data processes in the order in which the data elements arrive.
- The processed elements delete or archive.
- The buffer is relatively small than the size of the data stream and not accessible easily.

These are two types of data streams:

1. **Transactional data stream**: They carry data related to the interactions between different entities. For example:
   (i) ATM transactions – Withdrawals/deposits by users from bank accounts
   (ii) Telecommunication – Phone calls by callers to dialed numbers
   (iii) Web access by clients of resources at servers.
2. **Measurement data stream**: They carry data related to measured values or metric of entity states. For example:
   (i) Sensor networks – Traffic density values, presence, or absence of obstacles in the path
   (ii) IP network – IP packet in and out at router interfaces
   (iii) Climate data – Temperature and moisture records.

Many systems support handling of streams. Several major research projects relate to relation-oriented stream databases.

Following are examples of commercial databases for streams:

(i) **StreamBase** (commercial version of Aurora/Borealis)
(ii) **Truviso** (commercial version of TelegraphCQ); Cisco acquired it in May 2012 extending existing relational databases to build TelegraphCQ and Truviso syntaxes. They are extensions of PostgreSQL that incorporate data stream
(iii) **TIBCO** Business Events, Oracle Business Activity Monitoring

7.2.5 Example of Sources of Streams

The sources of streaming data range from simple computer programs to Internet of Things (IoT) applications. The sources of stream include sensory machines, satellites, instruments, IoT application areas, websites, published information from service providers and social media posts.

Some useful applications of data stream are:

1. Making data-driven marketing decisions in real time. It requires the use of data from trends analyses of real-time sales, and analysis of social media, and the sales distribution.
2. Monitoring and detection of potential failures of system using network management tool
3. Monitoring of industrial or manufacturing machinery in real time
4. A sensor network or IoT controlled by another entity, or a set of entities
5. Watching online video lectures, and rewinding or forwarding them
6. Subscribing to the daily news alerts, weather forecasting services or other similar subscription based services
7. Using location based services, such as finding nearest point-of-interest (POI)
8. Getting location-based advertisements or notifications
9. Watching on-demand movie, listening to online music, watching television
10. Navigation using GPS
11. Playing online games
12. Response stream from a web server
13. Using social networks, such as Facebook and Twitter
14. Traffic management, pollution control, flight traffic control, war field surveillance using sensor networks.

DSMS deals with streams and processes them differently from traditional data management systems. A traditional system builds primarily on the concept of persistence and static data collections. Streaming data requires traversing and processing at once before collection or deletion in the system.

7.2.6 Stream Queries

Data is static in a relational database. Thus, applications send queries to the database and obtain the results. They are one-time queries or transient queries. Data in stream changes frequently. The results of the queries against the stream also change. The queries are defined as continuous queries or persistent queries. They process continuously as data continue to arrive.

Their query processing results can be obtained in two forms. The results store and update when data arrives or they make data stream for the results themselves. For example, aggregation queries mostly use the first form, while join queries may use the stream form.

The queries may also be classified as predefined and ad hoc queries. Continuous queries are generally predefined and therefore register with the database server.

Ad hoc queries can be issued online along with the flowing data stream. They can be either one-time queries or continuous queries. Ad hoc queries make the design of a DSMS difficult. Firstly, they do not optimize since they're not known in advance. Secondly, they may require reference to an already streamed (or discarded) data for correct results.

Another issue related to queries in DBMS and DSMS is that the former mostly leads to exact query results while the later mostly approximate-query results.

Query Languages

1. **Relation-based** query language is based on SQL-like syntax. These languages provide better support for windows and ordering. Examples are Esper, CQL (STREAM), StreaQuel (TelegraphCQ), AQuery and GigaScope.
2. **Object-based** query languages are based on object-oriented stream modeling. These languages classify stream-elements according to type hierarchy. Examples are Tribeca and COUGAR.
3. **Procedure-based languages** are those where user functions (procedures) specify the dataflow. For example, Aurora provides graphical interface to users for constructing query plans.

Examples of query languages are given below:

STREAM Continuous Query Language (CQL) CQL developed at Stanford is an extension of SQL. The following example gives usages of CQL syntaxes.

EXAMPLE 7.1

Consider a network security monitoring system. (i) How does STREAM CQL create a stream? (ii) How does STREAM CQL remove a stream? (iii) How does STREAM CQL use time within the query?

SOLUTION

(i) Creating stream: CQL syntax is:

```
CREATE STREAM network_admin(
      communication_time TIMESTAMP,
      ticker_symbol VARCHAR (10),
      num_packets INTEGER,
      bytes_per_packet NUMERIC (9, 0)
);
```

(ii) Removing stream: CQL Syntax is:

```
DROP STREAM network_admin;
```

(iii) Actual data stream generally arrives over network and must be in a specific format for the database to use it.
STREAM CQL stream uses time within the query:

```
SELECT ticker_symbol,
SUM(num_packets * bytes_per_packet) / SUM(num_packets)
FROM network_admin [RANGE 5 MINUTES]
GROUPBY ticker_symbol;
```

The following example gives usages of Truviso syntaxes.

EXAMPLE 7.2

How does Truviso syntax create stream and use system-generated timestamps?

SOLUTION

(i) Create a stream with time stamp:

```
CREATE STREAM network_admin(
      communication_time TIMESTAMP CQTIME USER GENERATED,
      ticker_symbol VARCHAR (10),
      num_packets INTEGER,
      bytes_per_packet NUMERIC (7, 2)
);
```

(ii) Queries can be issued against both relations and stream. If a stream is involved, then it specifies the window as follows:

```
SELECT ticker_symbol,
SUM(num_packets * bytes_per_packet) / SUM(num_packets)
FROM network_admin< VISIBLE '5 MINUTES' >
GROUPBY ticker_symbol;
```

Example 7.3 explains usages of TelegraphCQ TIMESTAMP COLUMN modifier.

EXAMPLE 7.3

How is query in TelegraphCQ used by giving a separate window specification?

SOLUTION

TelegraphCQ has a separate window specification:

```
SELECT ticker_symbol,
SUM(num_packets * bytes_per_packet) / SUM(num_packets)
FROM network_admin
GROUPBY ticker_symbol WINDOW network_admin ['5 MINUTES'];
```

7.2.7 Stream Processing Issues

Stream processing refers to a method of continuous computation that takes place as data is flowing through the system. The processing can be helpful to gather statistics and/or monitor the streaming data. It can also, help in studying the source of streaming data and forecast the future behavior.

The unbounded size, frequency, velocity and variety of data in stream add challenges to the system. Following issues surface during stream processing:

Size of the streaming data not fixed Batch or static processing is a method of stored data processing. The calculations of execution time and usage of memory for algorithm are easy because processing of static data depends on the size. The size of streaming data size is variable and is rather unbounded. Therefore, algorithm works differently. Algorithms cannot iterate over the complete data. The processing can be possible on a piece of data comprising specific data elements or recent data elements.

Need of scalable processing Very high data volume requires scalable processing. As applications grow, their data processing needs also grow. Fulfilling demands of growing users can accelerate data processing requirements as the application demand grows.

Size is a vital aspect of scale that needs consideration in case of processing large datasets and distribution systems. System capacity need to increase for handling greater amounts of data, commonly referred as system scalability issue.

Variation in the frequency of data stream The frequency of data stream varies significantly over time. These variations are unpredictable or depend on social and public trends. For example, streaming data on social networks such as Facebook and Twitter can increase in volume during holidays or festivals. The variations can be periodic also, for example, in the evenings or weekends.

Need of near real-time processing The streaming data management systems require near real-time processing. Managing and processing data in motion is a typical capability of streaming data systems. The data requires processing when the data is in motion on place after the collection. The analogy can be found in sensor data processing. The computations need completion in real time. The processing needs to be fast for streaming sensor data.

Need of processing large data streams from different domains Data streams can vary with domain. The streams can source from several applications. Data arrives as large data streams from different domains. For example, satellite data, scientific instruments, sensors, social networks, stock data, process industries, traffic controls and network logs. Processing of variety (formats, types, compression) of data is another challenge.

Need of events-processing The processing may be required for different events representing measurements, such as position, particle mass, temperature, number of tweets per minute, stock update, number of items manufactured during last one hour, number of vehicles passed in an hour, number of login on Amazon on a festival day, etc.

Need of filtering to eliminate undesirable data elements Another important processing need is for searching the required data from a data stream and filtering the stream to eliminate undesirable data elements.

A restriction in data streaming systems is must. They should carry out relatively simple computations, say one record processing at an instance. The other requirements may be near real-time computations, at times in-memory and independent computations.

The processing function often provides the service to a system or a stream source. The function does not interact with system or source (one-way communication). They do not even provide any feedback of the system. Most stream-based systems are also subscriber-based systems.

7.2.8 Real-time Processing, Stream Processing and Batch Processing

A system is a real-time system if it provides the output guaranteed within hard "real-world" time deadlines. Software, which continuously processes a stream or stored stream, achieves nearly real-time performance. Time limitation is not a concern in stream processing. No fixed time deadline exists on the output of the system after receiving an input. These requirements for streaming data processing are reasonably different from batch processing. Data management and analysis are inclusive in batch processing.

7.2.9 Summarizing Streaming Processing Needs

Stream processing needs are:

(i) Computations are a function of a single data element or a smaller piece of recent data. They have no access to the complete data.
(ii) Processing algorithms must be relatively fast and simple
(iii) Need to complete each computation in near real-time while static processing has more latency
(iv) Computations are generally independent
(v) Asynchronous processing, i.e., the source of data does not interact with the stream processing system directly
(vi) Requirements of high-volume processing with low latency because no information exists about when the next data will arrives.

Self-Assessment Exercise linked to LO 7.1

1. List ten examples from two different domains for data streams. ○○●
2. How does a data-stream model as a relation-oriented stream tuples? What are the benefits of the relational tuples model? ●●●
3. Draw the data-stream processing architecture. ○○●
4. List the characteristics of Data Stream Management System (DSMS). ○●●
5. List the features of different types of data stream query languages. ○●●
6. What are the issues in data stream processing in case of data with high velocity and volume? ●●●

7.3 STREAM COMPUTING ASPECTS

LO 7.2

Stream computing aspects—sampling, filtering and counting distinct elements in a stream

Many applications require Big Data stream computing. Stream computing is a way to analyze and process Big Data in real time to gain current insights. Following subsections describe the methods of stream computing, sampling data in a stream, filtering of data in a stream and counting of distinct elements:

7.3.1 Stream Computing

Stream computing has many uses, such as financial sectors for business intelligence, risk management, marketing management, etc. Stream computing is also used in search engines and social network analysis.

Note: ○○● Level 1 & Level 2 category
○●● Level 3 & Level 4 category
●●● Level 5 & Level 6 category

The computing pulls the data from the stream, process the data, and streams it back out as a single flow. Such computing is required to process a huge amount of data at a high speed.

Usually, a Big Data stream computing implements in a distributed clustered environment, as the amount of data is enormous. Rate of receiving data in stream is high, and the results are required in real time to take appropriate decisions or to predict new trends in the immediate future.

Stream computing uses algorithms that analyze data in real time at high speed and with accuracy. Stream computing is one effective way to support Big Data by providing extremely low-latency velocities with massively parallel processing architectures.

Stream computing is becoming the fastest and most efficient way to obtain useful knowledge from Big Data. Organizations can react quickly when problems appear, or to predict new trends for the future.

The efficiency of data stream algorithms is measured using some fundamental characteristics:

1. Number of passes (scans) the algorithm must make over the stream
2. Available memory
3. Running time of the algorithm.

Data stream algorithms usually have limited memory availability. They may take certain action until the dataset arrives completely (for which the application is waiting). On the other hand, the usual online algorithms require action as soon as every piece of data arrives.

7.3.2 Sampling Data in a Stream

Sampling in data stream means the process of selecting a few data items from the incoming stream of data items for analysis. Methods of obtaining representative sample data items from a stream can be classified in two categories:

Obtaining a Representative Sample

Two categories of sampling methods are probabilistic and non-probabilistic. First category, probabilistic sampling is a statistical technique used for making a choice of data items for processing. The basis of the choice is the probability of sampling the data items. For example, if probability value chosen is 0.01, the method takes up 1 out of 100 data items for analysis.

Probabilistic sampling technique obtains the representative sample. The sample chosen is an actual representative of the population.

Five probabilistic sampling methods are simple random sampling, systematic sampling, cluster sampling, stratified sampling and multistage sampling.

Second category is non-probabilistic. Non-probability sampling uses arbitrary or purposive sample selection instead of sampling based on a randomized selection. This introduces bias and increases variance to the measurement data.

Reservoir sampling is a random sampling method. The method chooses a sample of limited data items from a list containing a very large number of items randomly. The list is larger than one that upholds in the main memory. An example of reservoir sampling method is given below:

EXAMPLE 7.4

Using the reservoir sampling method, illustrate the probability that the incoming item is stored in the main memory, while choosing a sample of limited data items from a very large number of items?

SOLUTION

Let k be the number of items selected from an infinite stream of data items. Suppose when processing a sequence of items, the program processes one at a time. Hence, for n items, the probability that a new item is in the main memory will be k/n. The algorithm works as:

```
Select the first k items in memory.
for (i > k) {
On the arrival of ith item, select a new item with probability (k/i)
Remove an old item at random, each with chance 1/k
with probability (1 - k/i), retain the old items instead of new item}
Thus,
Items ≤ k, the probability of item in memory is 1
Item = k+1 the probability will be k/ (k+1)
Item = k+2 the probability will be k/ (k+2)
```

Concise sampling and counting sampling are other uniform random sampling methods. Concise method is like the reservoir sampling method, with a difference that a value that appears once is stored as a singleton, whereas a value that appears more than once is stored as a (value, count) pair. This overcomes the restriction of sample size due to the size of the main memory. The method inserts a new data item in the sample with a probability of 1/n. If the new item is already present in sample, the count is incremented.

Counting sampling method is the refinement of concise sampling in terms of accuracy. The method maintains the sample in the case of deletion of data items as well. The method reverses the increment procedure by decrementing the count value upon deleting a value. The process may lead to converting back to singleton when a single value remains in the sample or even removing a singleton if that single value is removed.

General Sampling Problem

Some problems encountered while trying to find a sample of a data item from an infinite length data stream are:

(i) Unknown size of data set
(ii) Applications that need continuous analysis, such as surveillance analysis
(iii) Irregular data rates as in the case of data network analysis.

Varying the Sample Size

Sample size means the number of data items, with respect to the reference number of data items, chosen to make an inference or decision. A large sample size can generally give inference with greater accuracy. However, it may not be feasible to choose a large size.

Procedures for calculating sample sizes are (i) estimation, called confidence interval approach, and (ii) hypothesis testing. Statistics prescribes Chi-squared, T-test, Z-test, F-test, P value for testing the significance of a statistical inference.

The number of tables is available for sample size estimation for making inferences. Estimation is done for the minimum sample size required for accuracy in estimating the key proportions *P* of data items *D* for selection.

Some steps taken into consideration are: (i) a reasonable estimate of *P* to be measured in the study, (ii) the degree of accuracy *D* that is desired in the study, ~1% –5% or 0.01–0.05, and (iii) the confidence level *Z* needed from the inference, 95%.

7.3.3 Filtering of Stream

Filtering application identifies the sequence patterns in a stream. Stream filtering is the process of selection or matching instances of a desired pattern in a continuous stream of data.

For example, assume that a data stream consists of tuples. Following are the filtering steps: (i) Accept the tuples that meet a criterion in the stream, (ii) Pass the accepted tuples to another process as a stream and (iii) discard remaining tuples.

Several filtering techniques exist: Bloom Filter and its variants, Streaming Quotient Filter (SQF), Particle filter, Kalman filter, XML filters (such as XFilter, YFilter).

Conditional matching is simple to implement, even in case of streaming data when a tuple is matched with some desired value. For example, if the '*stock price* field value is greater than the maximum price in 52 weeks' in the stream of data, then that price filters out using a single 'if ' condition. The complexity of computation increases when one has to check duplication of records or match more than one tuple with a loose condition (can be or cannot be accepted). Then, the requirement is revisiting the record that becomes a memory-demanding computation.

The following subsections provide an overview of Bloom filter, one of the popular variants of Bloom filter (Counting Bloom Filter):

7.3.3.1 Filtering of Stream: The Bloom Filter Analysis

Bloom filter is a simple space-efficient data structure introduced by Burton Howard Bloom in 1970.[1] The filter matches the membership of an element in a dataset. The data structure is a probabilistic representation of a vector that supports membership queries. [Anand Rajaraman *et al.*[2]]

The filter, since then has been widely used in applications, such as database applications, intrusion detection systems, and query filtering and routing applications.

The filter is basically a bit vector of length *m* that represent a set $S = \{x_1, x_2, \ldots, x_n\}$ of *n* elements. Initially all bits are set to 0. Then, define *k* independent hash functions, $h_1, h_2, \ldots,$ and h_k. Each of which maps (hashes) some element *x* in set **S** to one of the *m* array positions with a uniform random distribution. Number *k* is constant, and much smaller than *m*. That is, for each element $x \in \mathbf{S}$, the bits $h_i(x)$ are set to 1 for $1 \le i \le k$. [∈ is symbol in set theory for 'contained in'.]

Figure 7.4 shows an example of a Bloom filter with k = 3. The filter is a bit vector of length 10. When a value x is inserted into the Bloom filter, the bits at position h1 (x), h2 (x) and h3 (x) are set to 1. To detect whether a value y is in the filter or not, the bits of position $h_1(y)$, $h_2(y)$ and $h_3(y)$ are thus checked.

---

[1] B. H. Bloom, Space/time trade-offs in hash coding with permissible errors. Communications of the ACM, 13(7):422–426, 1970.

[2] Anand Rajaraman and Jeffrey David Ullman in their book "Mining of Massive Datasets", Cambridge University Press, 2012.

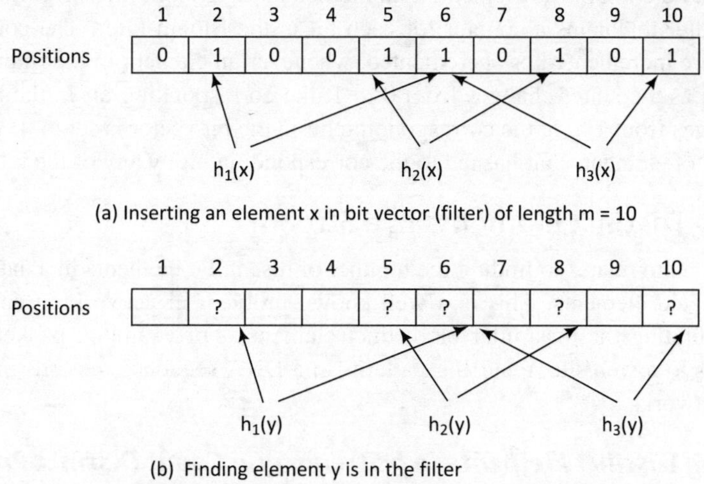

Figure 7.4 (a) Inserting an element x in bit vector (filter) of length m = 10, (b) finding an element y in an example of Bloom Filter

The operation results in setting a particular bit to 1 many of times, but only the first operation has an effect.

To check if an item y is in S, the bits at positions h_1 (y), h_2 (y), . . . , and h_k (y) are checked (Figure 7.4 (b)). If any of the bits is 0, undoubtedly y is not a member of S. If all h_i (y) are found to be 1, y may be in S. The bits may have by chance been set to 1 during the insertion of other elements. Thus, chance of incorrect assumption is present with some probability. This is a false positive, where the Bloom filter suggests that an element y is in S even though it is not.

It has been given in the literature that the probability of a false positive is equal to $(1 - e^{-kn/m})^k$.

7.3.3.2 Counting Bloom Filter: A Variant of Bloom Filter

Process of deleting a particular element in the Bloom filter requires that the corresponding positions computed by k hash functions in the bit vector, be set to zero. This may possibly concern other elements stored in the filter, which hash to any of these positions. For example, the bit position 6 is set to one by two hash functions h_1 (x) and h_3 (x) in Figure 7.4(a). Thus, it is not possible to delete an element stored in the filter.

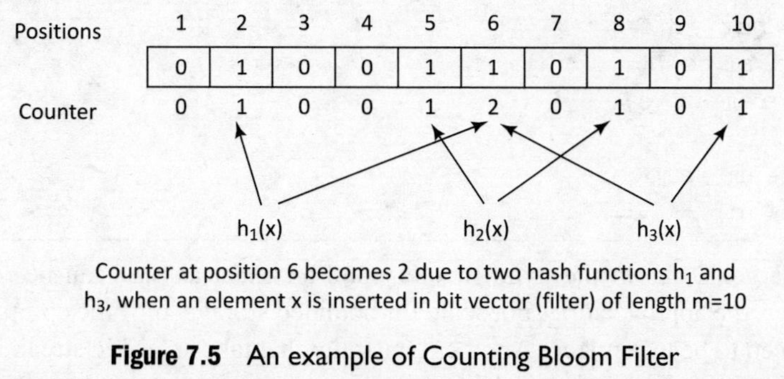

Figure 7.5 An example of Counting Bloom Filter

In order to perform deletion of the element, a method counting Bloom filter, a variant of Bloom filter be used. The counting filter maintains a counter for each bit in the Bloom filter. The counters corresponding to the k hash values are incremented or decremented, whenever an element in the filter is added or deleted, respectively. As soon as a counter changes from 0 to 1, the corresponding bit in the bit vector is set to 1. When a counter changes from 1 to 0, the corresponding bit in the bit vector is set to 0. The counter basically maintains the number of elements that hashed to the corresponding bit by any of the k hash functions.

7.3.4 Counting Distinct Elements in a Stream

The count-distinct problem relates to finding the number of dissimilar elements in a data stream. The stream of data contains repeated elements. This is a well-known problem in networking and databases. Several applications require finding the dissimilar or distinct elements. For example, packets passing through a router, unique visitors to a web site, recurring patterns in a DNA sequence, records in a large database, or elements of sensor networks.

7.3.4.1 *Counting Distinct Elements in a Stream and Count Distinct Problem*

If n possible elements a_1, a_2, …, and a_n are present then for an exact result n spaces are required. In the worst case, all n elements can be present. Let m be the number of distinct elements. The objective is to find an estimate of m using only s storage units, where $s \ll m$.

The example below gives an algorithm to compute distinct elements.

EXAMPLE 7.5

Assume data items set (A, B, B, C, C, D, B, A, A, D, C, B, C). Assume m is the number of distinct elements. (i) What are the distinct elements? (ii) Write an algorithm to compute m_t.

SOLUTION

(i) Number of distinct elements, m = |{A, B, C, D}| = 4

(ii) Assume D will contain the list of distinct elements, a_i where i = 0, 1, 2, …., m. Algorithm is as follows:

```
Initialize a Counter c = 0;

Initialize a data structure say, D in which insertion of an element
can be done easily (for example, hash table or search tree);

Repeat for each element ai of stream
{If ai is not in D
     add ai to D;
     increment c;
end if;}
until stream is over;
output m = c;
```

If m is not very large, D fits in the main memory and an exact answer can be retrieved as shown in Example 7.5. However, the approach does not scale for bounded storage, or if the computation performed for each element a_i is forced to be minimized. Another constraint that takes place in streaming data processing is that the algorithm only observes each input element once.

Several proposed streaming algorithms use a fixed number of storage units in such case; for example, bitmap algorithm. The algorithm uses a limited amount of memory for solving the counting distinct element problem.

The following example gives the bitmap algorithm to compute distinct elements.

EXAMPLE 7.6

(a) Write the bitmap algorithm for computing m, the number of distinct elements.
(b) Find m in the following data stream: A, B, B, D, A, A, E, B, H, B, A, F, D, E.

SOLUTION

(a) Assume a large binary array (bitmap) of size S with all members initializing to 0.
Choose a hash function h such that the value h(i) is uniformly distributed on [S]:
$\{1,..., n\} \rightarrow \{1,... ,S\}$.
Apply the hash function on every element (i) of data stream to compute h(i) and mark that position in the bitmap with a 1.
Count the number of positions in the bitmap with a 1 and call it p.

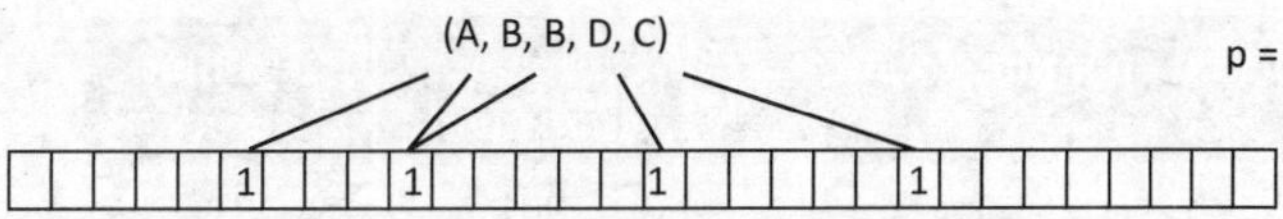

Thus, $m = S \cdot \ln\left(\frac{S}{S-p}\right)$, ... (7.1)

Let S = 4 and h(i) = i mod 4, such that:
h(A) = 1, h(B) = 2, h(C) = 3, h(D) = 0, h(E) = 1, and so on.
Thus the bitmap (drawn for h(i) = 1 in the following figure) will be:

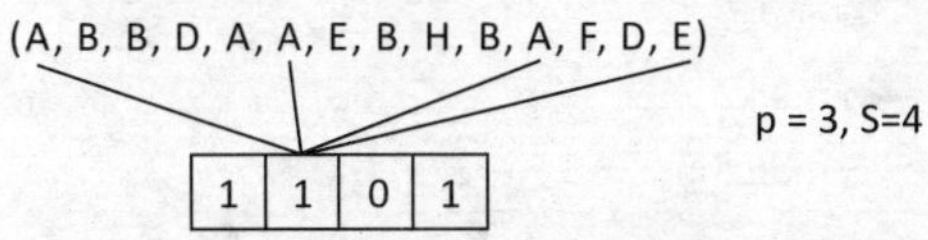

(b) Using equation (7.1), the estimated number of distinct elements = $4 \times \ln(4/(4-3)) = 5.55 \approx 6$

Streaming algorithms have several applications, such as monitoring packet flow in networks, counting the number of distinct elements in a stream, estimating the distribution of flow sizes and estimating the size of a join in databases.

7.3.4.2 The Flajolet–Martin Algorithm

Flajolet–Martin (FM) algorithm approximates the m, number of distinct (unique) elements, in a stream or a database in one pass. The stream consisting of n elements with m unique elements runs in O (n) time and needs O (log (m)) memory. Thus, the space consumption calculates with the maximum number of possible distinct elements in the stream, which makes it innovative.

Following are the features of the FM algorithm:[3,4]

(i) Hash-based algorithm.
(ii) Needs several repetitions to get a good estimate.
(iii) The more different elements in the data, the more different hash values are obtained
(iv) Different hash values suggest the chances of one of these values will be unusual [the unusual property can be that the value ends in many 0s (alternates also exist)].

The following example demonstrates an estimation of number of distinct elements in a stream using the FM algorithm:

EXAMPLE 7.7

Find an estimation of the number of distinct elements in the following stream:

s = 2, 3, 1, 2, 3, 4, 3, 1, 2, 3, 1, 4

SOLUTION

Consider a hash function, say f (a) = 7s + 2 mod 5

Now apply hash function on the input stream, perform the bit calculation and trailing zeroes, to get:

Apply hash function on input stream				Binary equivalent	Trailing zeroes
f(2)	7*2+ 2 mod 5	16 mod 5	1	001	0
f(3)	7*3+ 2 mod 5	23 mod 5	3	011	0
f(1)	7*1+ 2 mod 5	9 mod 5	4	100	2
f(2)	7*2+ 2 mod 5	16 mod 5	1	001	0
f(3)	7*3+ 2 mod 5	23 mod 5	3	011	0
f(4)	7*4+ 2 mod 5	30 mod 5	0	000	**0**
f(3)	7*3+ 2 mod 5	23 mod 5	3	011	0
f(1)	7*1+ 2 mod 5	9 mod 5	4	100	2
f(2)	7*2+ 2 mod 5	16 mod 5	1	001	0
f(3)	7*3+ 2 mod 5	23 mod 5	3	011	0
f(1)	7*1+ 2 mod 5	9 mod 5	4	100	2
f(4)	7*4+ 2 mod 5	30 mod 5	0	000	**0**

If output is zero, then trailing bits are also zero

(i) The maximum number of trailing zeros from the binary equivalent trailing zero values, r = 2.
(ii) The distinct value $R = 2^r = 2^2 = 4$
(iii) Therefore, R = 4 means there are four(4) distinct values as 2,3,1,4.

7.3.4.3 Combining Estimates— Space Requirements

Different hash functions result in different estimates of m (the number of distinct elements). Thus, one needs to combine all these estimates. Two ways for combining estimates are described below:

[3] Flajolet, P. and Martin, G. N, "Probabilistic counting algorithms for data base applications", Journal of Computer and System Sciences, 31(2), 182–209, 1985

[4] http://algo.inria.fr/flajolet/Publications/FlMa85.pdf

One way is to take the average of the values of R, computed from different hash functions. (Example 7.7) Taking the average can be over estimation, thus cannot be a good solution. Another way is to take the median of all the estimates (taking the median is almost correct, but is always a power of 2).

Therefore, combination of the two ways mentioned above can be a good way to combine the estimates. Thus, build the groups of hash function and take their average, then take the median of the averages.

Processing multiple data stream and combining limits using in-memory processing is feasible.

7.3.5 Estimating Moments

Recall Sections 6.2.4 and 6.2.5. Assume a random variable X where X refers to a variable, such as number of distinct elements x in data stream. Assume that variable x has probabilistic distribution in values around the mean value $\bar{x}$. Probabilistic distribution means probability of variable having value found = x varying with variable X. Expected value among the distributed X_i values where i varies from 0 to n will depend upon the expected distinct element count. Expected value will be m for expected number of distinct elements in the data stream, and much less than m for wide variance.

The variance is the square of the standard deviation in m from the expected value, the second central moment of a distribution, and the σ^2 or var (x) represents covariance of the random variable with itself. The method computes variance for formula:

$$\sigma^2 = \Sigma(x_i - \bar{x})^2/n \qquad \text{... (7.2)}$$

Moments (0, 1, 2 ...) refer to expected values to the powers of (0, 1, 2 ...) of random-variable variance (Section 6.2.5).

Let $P(x_i)$ is probability that $m = m_i$. Sum of probabilities P (m_i) over all possible n values of x is 1. 0th moment is always 1.

7.3.6 Counting of 1's in a Window

Streaming data are fundamentally continuously generated data. Continuous data stream may be infinite. A good example is network traffic analysis. Here, millions of packets arrive per second, and hundreds of concurrent queries are raised per second.

Infinite Stream Processing

Figure 7.3 showed data stream architecture for processing queries. Volume of data is too large that it cannot be stored. Hardly a chance exists to look at all of it. Stream processing is important for applications where new data arrives frequently. Important queries may be likely to ask about the most recent data or summaries of data.

Sliding Time Window Method for Data Stream Processing

The sliding window model for data stream algorithms is a popular model for infinite data stream processing. (Window refers to time interval during which stream raised and processed the queries). The receiving of data elements is taking place one by one. Statistical computations are over a sliding time-window of size N (not over the whole stream) in time-units. Window covers the most recent data items arrived. Assume that t is the time interval, which a query processing algorithm needs to cache a bit, 1 or 0. Then window time interval T_{window} for raising the queries and processing equals to $N \times t$.

Sliding window focuses on recent data and hence provides more significant and relevant data in real-world applications. The network traffic analysis, requires analysis based on the recent past. This is more informative and useful than analysis based on stale data.

A useful model of stream processing is the one in which queries are processed for a window of length N, where N corresponds to the most-recent elements received. Usually it is so that N is very large and cannot be stored on storage device, or there are so many streams that elements from windows for all cannot be stored.

Counting of 1's Problem

Recall Section 7.2.2 (e). Consider a counting problem. For a given stream of 0's and 1's, "How many 1s are present in the last k bits?" where $k \leq N$. The obvious solution is to store the most recent N bits. When new a bit comes in, discard the first bit. This will result into the exact answer. What happens if one cannot have enough memory to store N bits? For example, when the stream processor is processing, assume N is 1 Billion. Here, the solution can be an approximate answer. An algorithm called Datar-Gionis-Indyk-Motwani (DGIM) algorithm is a solution for such problem in counting.

7.3.6.1 DGIM algorithm

DGIM algorithm suggests that store just the O [$\log_2 (\log_2 N)$] bits per stream. The algorithm uses the concept of time buckets. A time window divides in a number of buckets. It is different from hash buckets.

Assume that N_b = time units of specific duration in which stream 1s and 0s arrive. When N time units elapse, the bucket ends. A bucket stores O (log2 N_b) bits, and the count of number of 1s between its beginning and end of the bucket (which is the size of the bucket) [O ($\log_2 (\log_2 N_b)$)]. A bucket in the DGIM algorithm is a record, which consists of (i) a timestamp placed at a position at which the rightmost bit (which is the most recent bit) arrives. Timestamp consists of O (log2 N_b) bits, [Suppose the number of bits 1s as well as 0s arrived in a given bucket time = $1024 \times 1024 \times 1024 = 2^{30}$, then the timestamp will be 11110 (= 30 decimal), and (ii) count cnt of 1s between beginning and rightmost bit, [Suppose cnt during that time = 2^{24}, then cnt = 11000 (= 24 decimal). Maximum value cnt = 29 when all bits arrived happens to be 1s and none 0s when the bucket time 2^{30} time units.] The algorithm prefixes cnt. The succeeding bucket of $2^{(2 \times cnt)}$ time units can be less than the earlier. Earlier arriving buckets are, therefore, not smaller than the later [Anand Rajaraman *et al.*[2]].

The size of the bucket restricts to the power of two. Buckets do not overlap in timestamps. Buckets are sorted by size (number of 1's). The algorithm uses either one or two buckets with the same power of 2 number of 1's. The error is just equal to the time taken in storing the bucket timestamps and cnt.

Suppose the last bucket has size $2^{(2 \times cnt)}$, then ($2^{cnt} - 1$) of its 1's are still within the window, an error of at most that much can be there. Minimum one bucket is of size not less than $2^{(2 \times cnt)}$. Thus, the error can be at most 50%.

Further extensions to the algorithm are also found in literature suggesting the use of the algorithm discussed in this section to handle aggregations more general than counting 1's in a binary stream. The next subsection discusses another important data stream algorithm using the sliding window model.

7.3.7 Decaying Windows

Anand Rajaraman *et al.*[2] describe the details of the decaying windows method. Decaying windows are useful in applications which need identification of most common elements. The use of the decaying window concept is when more weight assigns to recent elements.

The technique computes a smooth aggregation of all the 1's ever seen in the stream, with decaying weights. When it further appears in the stream, less weight is given.

The effect of exponentially decaying weights is to spread out the weights of the stream elements as far back in time as the stream flows.

Self-Assessment Exercise linked to LO 7.2

1. Why does processing of data stream require sampled datasets in place of all datasets? How is a representative sample taken from a stream?
2. What are the uses of mean, variance, moments, probability distribution and standard deviation in stream computing?
3. What is the information obtained after filtering of data stream?
4. How is the sliding window used for data stream processing?
5. Why is decaying window with decaying weights used for aggregation of all the 1's ever seen in a stream?

7.4 FREQUENT ITEMSETS

LO 7.3

Methods of frequent itemsets analytics and handling large datasets, association rule mining for finding and counting instances of presence of those itemsets

Frequent itemsets and frequent patterns have several uses. The following subsections describe the methods of finding frequent itemsets and handling of larger datasets in the main memory, and algorithms to count the instances of frequent itemsets in streams containing those sets:

7.4.1 Finding Frequent Itemsets

The computational model of finding frequent itemsets typically consists of mining the number of itemsets in a flat file system. Assume that a Department of Computer Science is offering five courses and students have different computer subjects. Figure 7.6 shows the organization of the courses.

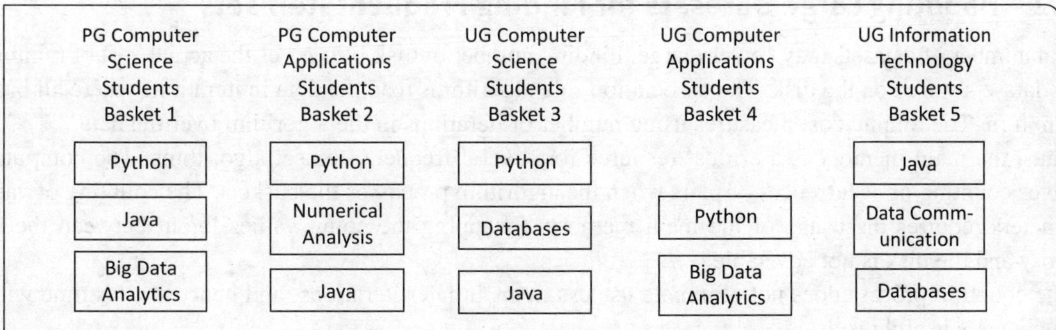

Figure 7.6 Courses organization

Let us define that if an itemset (subjects-set) is present in at least 3 out of 5 course baskets, then that subjects set is a frequent itemset [Use that criterion for finding whether Java and Python subjects set is the frequent itemset]. If the support threshold, S_{th} is raised to 0.8 (80%), then that subject set does not qualify as a frequent itemset. It is not necessary that an itemset is present in a basket once only, but its presence is counted as once only though the itemset may be present 2, 3 or more times.

Let us consider an association rule. Let us assume SS is a subject set. Let a subject is subj. Consider the association rule that SS $\rightarrow$ subj. It implies that if SS is present in a basket, then subj is likely to appear in that basket.

Frequent sets basket counting problem has many applications: If a sports shop is selling badminton racquets, then it is likely to sell shuttlecocks as well. A car company sells five models through thousands of car showrooms. It wants to analyze in what areas, the Jaguar as well as Zest cars are selling frequently, considering S_{th} = 80%.

Assume (Java, Python) is a subject set **SS**. The students in a computer course if taught Java subject for study, they may be taught Python as well. Association rules are (Java, Python) $\rightarrow$ Java and (Java, Python) $\rightarrow$ Python. Association rule mining means finding the course baskets in which both the association rules apply. Figure 7.6 shows 3 course baskets where both the pairs of rules apply. How does number 3 find? Assume m is number of course baskets and nB is number of baskets where that subject set taught. Following can be the association-rule mining method:

```
Initialize nB = 0;
For each i from 1 to m, [if (Java is a subject in a course-basket CB (i))
then if (Python is also a subject in CB (i)) then nB = nB + 1;]
if (nB>= Sth) then subject-set SS is frequent itemset.
```

The present example considers the number of associations, p just two. What about a frequent pattern in which p is ten or more. Remember that the number of items can be 12000K (Products at Amazon) or web pages at www with thousands of words on each page.

The ***goal of association rule mining*** is to discover items that are found together in sufficient number of baskets and to find dependencies among these items. This simply implies finding frequent itemsets.

7.4.2 Handling Large Datasets for Finding Frequent Itemsets

Actual number of datasets may be very large. Finding number of disk I/Os gives the actual cost of mining the large datasets stored on the disk. The association rule algorithms read the data in iterations where all baskets read in turn. The mining cost measures using number of iterations in the algorithm over the data.

Thus, the main memory is a critical resource for several frequent itemset algorithms. The computation involves counting of occurrences of pairs when the algorithm processes the baskets. The counting of various parameters requires the usage of the main memory. Swapping the count values in/out between the main memory and the disk is not advisable.

The counting process does not eliminate useless items in later iterations, and hence wastes time without producing any useful result.

Consider the simple approach to finding frequent pairs (Similar approach can be extended for larger sets as well). It requires generating all the itemsets. Though the probability of being frequent decreases with size. It is important to count/keep track of itemsets that turn out to be frequent till the last.

The following example illustrates the method of estimating memory requirements.

EXAMPLE 7.8

Compute the memory required for finding frequent pairs in case of 1 million items.

SOLUTION

Assume an approach in which the algorithm reads the file once and counts the occurrences of each pair in the main memory. Considering n items in the basket, count process generates almost n. (n-1)/2 pairs using two nested loops. The number of calculations involve ~ $(\text{number of items})^2$. This may result into failure if square of number of items exceed the main memory.

Memory needs for number of pairs for 1 million items compute as:

=> Number of pairs of items = $10^6 \times (10^6 - 1)/2 = 5 \times 10^{11}$

Each count value is an integer that requires 4-byte memory.

Therefore, memory needed = $4 \times 5 \times 10^{11}$ bytes = 2×10^{12} = 2 TB.

Two popular approaches for counting pairs in memory: First is to count all pairs, using a triangular matrix. This approach requires only four bytes per pair (assume integers to use 4 bytes). The second approach maintains a table of triples [i, j, c] where c is the count of the pair of items {i, j}. This approach requires 12 bytes, but only for those pairs with count > 0. The second approach performs better than triangular matrix if less than one-third of possible pairs occur. This approach may also require extra space for retrieval of structure, such as a hash table.

Apriori Algorithm Section 6.5.3 discussed the algorithm. *Apriori* uses iterations (successive passes). Algorithm *Apriori* limits the need for the main memory. The first pass needs memory proportional to the number of items. The second pass needs memory proportional to the square of *frequent* items only (for counts).

Several proposed algorithms cut down on the size of candidate pairs. The following subsection describes Park, Chen and Yu (PCY), multistage and multihash algorithms [Anand Rajaraman *et al.*[2]]:

7.4.2.1 Algorithm of Park, Chen and Yu

Apriori Algorithm works efficiently when the counting of the candidate process is executing. During the first iteration, most of the memory is unused. Memory is required to store individual item counts only. Can one use the unused memory to reduce the memory required in the second iteration?

The PCY algorithm takes benefit of the fact that the first iteration of Apriori does not use lots of main memory for counting of single items. Iteration 1 of PCY algorithm saves item counts as well as maintains a hash table with sufficient buckets that fits in memory. It also maintains the counts for each bucket into which pairs of items are hashed.

An improved version of PCY exists. Between the iterations the buckets are replaced by a bit vector. Instead of four-byte integers, one bit is used to represent the presence and absence of a frequent bucket. Bit 1 means the bucket is frequent and bit 0 means it is not a frequent bucket. Thus, the memory requirement is reduced 32 times. Also, frequent items need to be selected and listed for the second iteration.

7.4.2.2 Multistage Algorithm

A refinement of the PCY algorithm is the *multistage algorithm*. This algorithm uses several successive hash tables to reduce the number of candidate pairs subsequently. The algorithm applies more than two iterations to find the frequent pairs. The idea is to rehash only those pairs that qualify for iteration 2 of PCY after iteration 1 of PCY. Since only a few pairs contribute to buckets in the middle iteration, fewer false positives may occur. Thus, it requires 3 iterations over the data. The two hash functions have to be independent.

7.4.2.3 Multihash Algorithm

A possibility exists for getting much of the benefit of the extra iterations of the multistage algorithm in a single iteration. Multihash algorithm is an improvement of PCY. The main idea is to use several independent hash tables during the first iteration. This can lead to benefits like multistage in only 2 iterations.

7.4.3 Limited Passes Algorithms

Multistage and multihash algorithms use more than two hash functions. There is a point of reducing returns in multistage algorithm since the bitmaps mostly consume all of the main memory. The bitmaps occupy exactly what one PCY bitmap does in multihash algorithm. But too many hash functions make all counts $\geq S_{th}$.

The algorithms for finding frequent itemsets discussed in the previous section process one iteration or pass for each size of itemset [One iteration means one pass through the sequence of instructions].

Therefore, finding itemsets of size k needs k passes. Many applications do not require finding every frequent itemset. For example, the online bookstore does not want to offer discount on all the books purchased together. Thus, they need to run an algorithm for limited number of iterations in order to find a good number of the frequent itemsets instead of all the frequent itemsets.

Simple random sampling algorithm There are certain algorithms that use two or fewer passes for all sizes. One of them is *simple random sampling algorithm.* The algorithm suggests selecting a random sample of the market baskets. Run Apriori algorithm or its improvements for sets of all sizes, not just pairs in the main memory. This does not put burden for disk I/O increase in the size of the itemsets. There should be enough space for counts while executing a simple algorithm. The algorithm reduces the support threshold proportionally to match the sample size. Thus, if the sample is 1/100 of the total number of baskets, s /100 will be the support threshold instead of s. The smaller threshold facilitates more truly frequent itemsets but requires more space.

An option to implement second pass as well can validate that the sample contains truly the frequent itemsets. This avoids false positives.

7.4.3.1 SON Algorithm

An algorithm called SON (Savasere, Omiecinski and Navathe) algorithm keeps away from both false negatives and false positives using two passes.

SON algorithm repetitively read small subsets of the baskets into the main memory, and run an in-memory algorithm to find all the frequent itemsets. Subsets are not samples. It is the processing of the entire file in memory-sized chunks. An itemset becomes a candidate if it is found to be frequent in any one or more subsets of the baskets.

Second pass counts all the candidate itemsets and determine those which are frequent in the entire set. The idea of *monotonicity* used here is that an itemset cannot be frequent in the entire set of baskets unless it is frequent in at least one subset.

Distributed Version of SON also implements in a parallel computing environment. The implementation distributes the baskets among many nodes. Frequent itemsets compute at multiple nodes. The candidates then distribute to all the nodes and finally, accumulate the counts of all the candidates.

7.4.3.2 *Toivonen's Algorithm*

Toivonen Algorithm is similar to the simple random sample algorithm but lowers the threshold slightly for sampling. For example, if the sample s is 1% of the baskets, use 0.008 s as the support threshold rather than 0.01s. The basic aim is not to miss any itemset that is frequent in the full set of baskets. As already stated, the smaller threshold results into more deserving frequent itemsets but requires more space.

After preparing the frequent itemsets for the sample, a negative border is prepared. An itemset is in the negative border when it is not considering that as frequent in the sample, but all its immediate subsets are frequent. For example, ABCD, which is not a frequent itemset, is in the negative border, if all of ABC, BCD, ACD and ABD are frequent itemsets.

Then count all the candidate frequent itemsets from the first pass and count their negative border in the second pass. If no itemset from the negative border turns out to be frequent in the second pass, then finally the candidates found to be frequent in the whole data, considered them as the frequent itemsets. The algorithm requires a restart if an itemset in the negative border is found to be actually frequent.

It suggests to choose the support threshold, which results into less probability of failure. Also, consider the number of itemsets computed on the second pass that fit in the main memory.

7.4.4 Counting Frequent Items in a Stream

The algorithms discussed in the previous subsections find frequent itemsets from a file of baskets. Now let us explore finding of frequent itemsets from a stream of baskets instead of a file of baskets.

Several large sources of data are modeled as data streams. For example, stream of network packets, sensor data, etc. It is impractical and undesirable to save and process all data exactly in such scenario. Instead, look for algorithms to find approximate answers with say one pass over data. When processing a stream, remember that only a small part of it can be kept in the memory.

Apriori algorithm cannot be used for mining frequent patterns over a data stream. Mining using Apriori is fundamentally a set of join operations. This cannot be performed over a data stream since at any instant, a program can only examine a very limited size window of a data stream. Computation for any itemset cannot complete without considering the past and future datasets. Here, consideration is only a limited size window. That is due to the massive amount of streaming data. It is difficult to mine and update the frequent patterns in the presence of a dynamic streaming data environment.

Finding Frequent Items in Place of Itemsets

A simple frequent item finding algorithm finds all items in a stream whose frequency exceeds a 1/k fraction of the total count. Given a stream S = (A, B, C, A, C, B, D, A), the frequency of an item a_i is f_i and total count n = 8. Thus $f_A = 3$, $f_B = 2$, $f_C = 2$, $f_D = 1$. For k-frequent items (if k = 0.2), the frequent items are the set $\{a_i \mid f_i > kn\}$.

Here, k × n=0.2 × 8 = 1.6, therefore, frequent items are A, B, C. Similarly, for k = 0.25, (k × n = 2.0), frequent item(s) is only A.

The frequent algorithm stores a designated number of pairs of items (say 20%) and counter for every pair of item (say a_i, c). The algorithm compares each new item against the stored items. A grouping argument is used to support the item, which occurs more than n/k times. The details are given in a research paper by Karp *et al*[5].

[5] Karp, R., Papadimitriou, C., Shenker, S. "A simple algorithm for finding frequent elements in sets and bags", ACM Transactions on Database Systems, Volume 28, Pp. 51–55, 2003

Literature suggests that the frequent item mining algorithm sometimes does not solve the frequency estimation problem accurately. Although the algorithm preserves the bound on the true frequency of the items, it may results in some errors. Observation suggests that executing the algorithm with $k = 1/\varepsilon$ implies that the count associated with each item on termination is at most $\varepsilon.n$ below the true value.

The other simplest approach is **randomized sampling based algorithm**. It suggests collecting some number of baskets and store them as a file. Run any one of the frequent itemset algorithms discussed in this chapter. The approach can have any two possibilities for future. Either the approach ignores the stream elements that arrive or stores them as another file, which it analyzes later. An estimate of the frequent item sets in the stream is obtained on the process completion of frequent itemsets algorithm.

Manku and Motwani[65] proposed **Lossy Counting algorithm** in 2002. The algorithm saves the tuples consisting of an item, a lower bound on its count and a "delta" (Δ) value, which records the difference between the upper bound and the lower bound. When i^{th} item in the stream processes, if information about the item is found then its lower bound is increased by one; else, create a new tuple for the item with the lower bound set to one, and Δ set to = $\lfloor i/k \rfloor$. Also, delete at times all tuples whose upper bound is less than $\lfloor i/k \rfloor$.

Accurate values of upper and lower bounds save on the count of each item. Thus, all items whose count exceeds n/k must save at the end of the stream. As like frequent items algorithm, setting $k = 1/\varepsilon$ ensures that the error in any approximate count is at most εn. A careful argument demonstrates that the worst-case memory space use by the algorithm is $O\left(\frac{1}{\varepsilon}\log \varepsilon n\right)$, and for certain time-invariant input distributions, it is $O\left(\frac{1}{\varepsilon}\right)$. The algorithm details are in research paper of Manku and Motwani[6].

7.4.4.1 Sampling Methods for Stream

Sampling is a statistical technique used for processing using a probabilistic choice of data item. The technique considers sampling in data stream and process selects a few data items from the incoming stream of data items for analysis. Section 7.3.2 explained these details.

7.4.4.2 Frequent Itemsets in Decaying Windows

Section 7.3.7 described the decaying window method for identifying the most common elements in a stream. The weight of ith previous item assigns as $(1 - C)^i \approx e^{-ci}$ where $0 < (1 - C)^i \leq 1$ where $i \geq 1$. Counting frequent items in a stream requires two modifications to the algorithm for decaying windows:

1. Stream elements are baskets, and not the individual items. Maintain a weighted count for itemsets. When a new itemset arrives,
   (i) Multiply all previous counts by 1 – C.
   (ii) Add a new itemset with an initial count of 1.
   (iii) Add 1 to an existing itemsets count.
2. Start counting an itemset only if all of its proper subsets are already being counted (Remember from the Apriori algorithm that if an itemset is frequent, then all of its subsets must also be frequent).

[6]G. Manku and R. Motwani, "Approximate frequency counts over data streams", International Conference on Very Large Data Bases, pages 346–357, 2002.

Self-Assessment Exercise linked to LO 7.3

1. How is frequent itemset analytics performed in market basket model? ○○●
2. How does the Apriori algorithm for frequent itemsets analyze? ○○●
3. How does the Park, Chen and Yu (PCY) algorithm for frequent itemsets analyze? How does PCY improve memory usages compared to the Apriori algorithm? . ○●●
4. Make a table comparing the PCY, multisate and multihash algorithms. ●●●
5. List the methods for finding frequent items in data stream and compare them. ○●●

7.5 REAL-TIME ANALYTICS PLATFORM (RTAP)—SparkStreaming

LO 7.4

Real-time analytics platform, SparkStreaming, and real-time analytics applications to real-time sentiments analytics and stock prices analytics

Real-time application relates to responsiveness. Data, when generated fast needs fast processing as well. An application sometimes requires updating the information at the same rate at which it receives data. Late decisions sometime cause loss of great opportunities. The term 'analytics' implies the identification of meaningful patterns from data. Thus, real-time analytics signifies finding meaningful patterns in data at the actual time of receiving it.

Real-Time Analytics Platform (RTAP) analyses the data, correlates, and predicts the outcomes in the real time. The platform manages and processes data and helps timely decision-making. The platform helps to develop dynamic analysis applications. The platform leads to evolution of business intelligence.

Following are the widely used RTAPs:

1. Apache SparkStreaming—a Big Data platform for data stream analytics in real time.
2. Cisco Connected Streaming Analytics (CSA)—a platform that delivers insights from high-velocity streams of live data from multiple sources and enables immediate action.
3. Oracle Stream Analytics (OSA)—a platform that provides a graphical interface to "Fast Data". Users can analyze streaming data as it arrives based on conditions and rules.
4. SAP HANA— a streaming analytics tool which also does real-time analytics. The SAP platform makes it easy for developers to incorporate smart stream capture and active event monitoring, alerting and event-driven response to applications.
5. SQL streamBlaze—an analytics platform, offering a real-time, easy-to-use and powerful visual development environment for developers and analysts.
6. TIBCO StreamBase—streaming analytics, which accelerates action in order to quickly build applications that analyze and act on real-time streaming data.
7. Informatica — a real-time data streaming tool which transforms a torrent of small messages and events into unprecedented business agility.
8. IBM Stream Computing—a data streaming tool that analyzes a broad range of streaming data—unstructured text, video, audio, geospatial, sensor—helping organizations spot the opportunities and risks and make decisions in real time.

7.5.1 Apache® Spark™ Streaming

Continuous arrival in multiple, rapid, time-varying, possibly unpredictable and unbounded streams have difficulties in processing, especially in Big Data with 3Vs characteristics. Streaming data processing needs computing in real time as the data arrives.

SparkStreaming is an extension of core Apache Spark API. Spark Streaming applications are in a variety of use cases and business applications. Some of the most interesting use cases of SparkStreaming include Uber (the ride sharing service), Pinterest, (the content sharing service), Netflix (a subscription service that provides access to movies and TV shows).

SparkStreaming brings Apache Spark's language integrated API to stream processing. It facilitates building of fault-tolerant processing of streaming data in real time. SparkStreaming is one of the most popular platforms to implement data processing and analytics software for real-time data received from IoT and sensors.

Figure 5.3 showed Spark stack main components, namely *Core, SQL, Streaming, R, GraphX, MLib* and *Arrow* in a five-layered architecture. The architecture presented the overall Apache Spark ecosystem. All software components are also available when using SparkStreaming.

Following are the features of data processing using SparkStreaming:

1. Combines batch processing and streaming processing in the same system
2. Applies Spark's machine learning and graph processing algorithms on data stream
3. Divides the stream of data into micro-batches of a pre-defined interval (N seconds) [The N is as per need of data stream processing]. A micro-batch is used in operations similar to Resilient Distributed Datasets (RDDs). A very low value of N means that the micro-batches may not have sufficient data for useful analysis.
4. Support Scala, Java, R and Python language in the form of suitable APIs
5. Results save at a data store for performing analytics later
6. Results also generate reports, display visuals on live dashboard and generate alerts on the events.

SparkStreaming library is used for processing a real-time data stream:

1. **DStream** (Discretized Stream)—an abstraction of a continuous data stream in SparkStreaming DStream creates either from basic sources or input data stream from sources, such as Kafka, Flume and Kinesis. Stream operators apply functions on DStreams. DStream represents streaming data from a TCP source.
2. **Type of Input Sources**—(i) Basic sources: Sources which are directly available in the *StreamingContext* API, such as a file system or a socket connection, and (ii) Advanced sources which are available from sources such as Kafka, Flume, Kinesis.
3. **Apache Kafka**— is a real-time, fault tolerant, scalable messaging system for moving data in real time. Kafka captures user activity on websites, logs, stock ticker data and instrumentation data. Kafka works like a distributed database and is based on a partitioned and replicated low latency commit log. Apache Kafka includes client API as well as a data transfer framework called Kafka Connect.
4. **ZooKeeper—**a centralized service providing reliable distributed coordination for distributed applications. Kafka, the messaging system for configuration details across the cluster.

Figure 7.7 shows various architecture components of SparkStreaming for Big Data applications, analytics, live data visualization, real-time online recommendations and instant fraud detection.

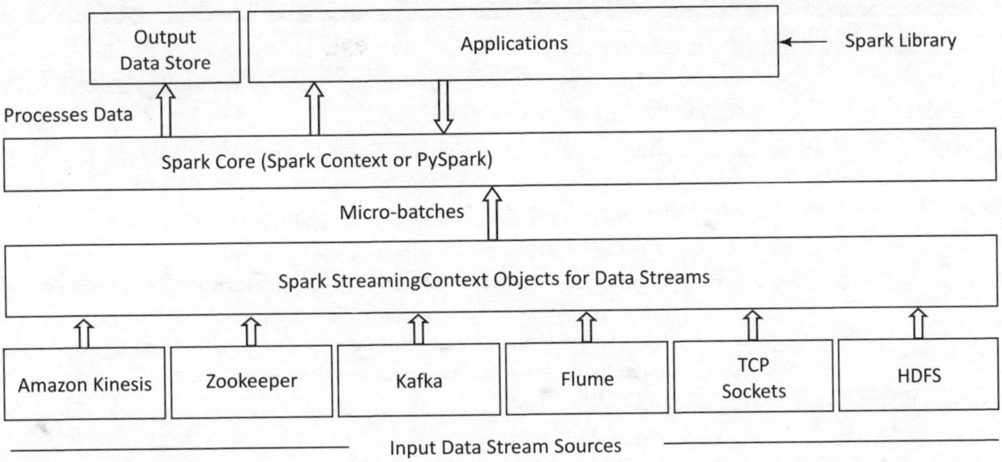

Figure 7.7 Various architecture components of SparkStreaming application

Table 7.2 gives the functionalities and operators of SparkStreaming

Table 7.2 Brief description of SparkStreaming functionalities and operators

Operator	Brief Description
Creating StreamingContext Object using SparkConf	
import org.apache.spark._ import org.apache.spark.streaming._ val conf = new SparkConf(). setAppName (appName). setMaster(master) val ssc = new StreamingContext(conf, Seconds(1))	Creates StreamingContext object named ssc configured with AppName; after the creation of ssc, subsequent steps define the (i) input sources by creating input DStreams, and (ii) the streaming computations by applying transformation and output operations to DStreams.
Operations on DStreams from input sources	
union (otherStream)	Return a new DStream that contains the union of the elements in the source DStream and otherDStream.
join(otherStream, [numTasks])	When called on two DStreams of (K, V) and (K, W) pairs, return a new DStream of (K, (V, W)) pairs with all pairs of elements for each key.
Cogroup (otherStream, [numTasks])	When called on a DStream of (K, V) and (K, W) pairs, return a new DStream of (K, Seq [V], Seq [W]) tuples.
Streaming transformation operations	
transform (func)	Return a new DStream by applying a RDD-to-RDD function to every RDD of the source DStream. This can be used to do arbitrary RDD operations on the DStream

(Contd.)

Operator	Brief Description
Stream APIs Processing RDD like Operations	
map(func):	Return a new DStream by passing each element of the source DStream through a function func.
flatMap(func);	Similar to map, but each input item can be mapped to 0 or more output items.
filter(func)	Return a new DStream after selecting the records of the source DStream on which func returns only true.
reduce(func)	Return a new DStream of single-element RDDs by aggregating the elements in each RDD of the source. DStream uses the function func (which takes two arguments and returns one). The function should be associative and commutative so that it can be computed in parallel.
repartition(numPartitions)	Changes the level of parallelism in this DStream by creating more or fewer partitions
count()	Count the number of elements in each RDD of the source DStream and return a new DStream of single-element RDDs.
countByValue()	When called on a DStream of elements of type K, return a new DStream of (K, Long) pairs where the value of each key is its frequency in each RDD of the source DStream.
reduceByKey(func, [numTasks])	Return a new DStream of (K, V) pairs when called on a DStream of (K, V) pairs. The values for each key are aggregated using the given reduce function.
updateStateByKey(func)	Return a new "state" DStream where the state for each key is updated by applying the given function on the previous state of the key and the new values for the key. This can be used to maintain arbitrary state of data for each key.
Streaming output operations	
foreach RDD(func)	'foreach' is the most generic output operator that applies a function, func, to each RDD generated from the stream. This function should push the data in each RDD to an external system, such as saving the RDD to files, or writing it over the network to a database.
saveAsTextFiles(prefix, [suffix]); saveAsObjectFiles(prefix, [suffix]) saveAsHadoopFiles(prefix, [suffix])	(i) Save the DStream contents as text files. The file name at each batch interval is generated based on prefix and suffix: "prefix-TIME_IN_MS [.suffix]". (ii) Save the DStream contents as SequenceFiles of serialized Java objects. The file name at each batch interval is generated based on prefix and suffix: "prefix-TIME_IN_MS [.suffix]". (iii) Save the DStream contents as Hadoop files. The file name at each batch interval is generated based on prefix and suffix: "prefix-TIME_IN_MS [.suffix]"
print() or pprint() in Python	Prints the first ten elements of every batch of data in a DStream on the driver node running the streaming application; This is useful for development and debugging.

(Contd.)

Operator	Brief Description
Stream APIs (time) Window Related Transformation Processing Operations	
Window(windowLength, slideInterval) countByWindow(windowLength, slideInterval) reduceByWindow(func, windowLength, slideInterval) reduceByKeyAndWindow(func, windowLength, slideInterval, [numTasks]) reduceByKeyAndWindow(func, invFunc, windowLength, slideInterval, [numTasks])	These transformation operations are performed for the stream of data during SlidingInterval for the time equal to windowLength. • WindowLength specifies the duration of the window. • Sliding interval specifies the interval at which the window operation is performed.
Starting data receiving and processing	
streamingContext.start()	Processing starts
Termination and stop operations	
streamingContext.awaitTermination()	Wait for the termination signal (CTRL+C or SIGTERM) from user to stop streaming process.
streamingContext.stop()	Stop streaming process immediately.

The following example shows use of SparkStreaming for count functions.

EXAMPLE 7.9

Create a program in Scala for counting the number of words from a socket in every 1 second, using window of length 60 seconds and sliding interval of 10 seconds, and save the result in windowed WordCounts. Use SparkStreaming context and API.

SOLUTION

(i) Refer Table 7.2. Import *SparkStreaming* using program statements as follows:

```
import org.apache.spark._
import org.apache.spark.streaming._
```

(ii) Configure *appName* and *StreamingContext* using program statements as follows:

```
val conf = new SparkConf().setAppName(StreamWordCount).setMaster(master)
val ssc = new StreamingContext(conf, seconds (1))
```

Here, ssc stands for SparkStreamingContext.

(iii) Create a *socketTextStream* at ip:port for count the words as follows:

```
// Replication necessary in distributed scenario for fault tolerance.
val lines = ssc.socketTextStream(args (0), args(1).toInt,
StorageLevel.MEMORY_AND_DISK_SER)
```

(iv) Compute streamWordCount using map( ) and reduce( ) as follows:

```
val streamWords = lines.flatMap(_.split(" "))
val windowedWordCounts = streamWords.map(x => (x, 1)).
reduceByKeyAndWindow(_ + _, Seconds(60), Seconds(10))
```

(v) Start the processing, and await termination using the program statement as follows:

```
ssc.start()
ssc.awaitTermination()
```

(vi) Print the results using the program statement as follows:

```
windowedWordCounts.print()
```

7.5.2 Real-Time Analytics Platform Applications

Some such applications are:

1. Fraud detection systems for online transactions
2. Log analysis for understanding usage pattern
3. Click analysis for online recommendations
4. Push notifications to the customers for location-based advertisements for retail
5. Action for emergency services such as fires and accidents in an industry
6. Any abnormal measurements require immediate reaction in healthcare monitoring
7. Social media.

7.5.3 Case Studies—Real-Time Sentiment Analysis, Positive Negative Sentiments Prediction and Stock Market Predictions

Real-time data feeds from social media (such as twitter) are easy to get. A use of this data is for sentiment analysis. The real-time data feeds of stock prices at stock trading exchange are available. A use of these feeds is in sentiment analysis and future price predictions.

The following subsections considers these examples for real-time analysis and predictions.

7.5.3.1 Real-Time Sentiment Analysis using Tweets

The case study provides the method of access of real-time social media information using Twitter. Tweets are received from the Twitter stream, pre-processed and then analyzed to extract the features. The method follows the steps as:

1. Collect a comprehensive training dataset that consists of data about potential users of a system.
2. Pull the specific tweets in real-time using Twitter API, then process and load this data into a persistent storage.
3. The cleaning of the data proceeds with punctuations, stop words, URLs, common emoticons and hash tags, references deletion. Multiple consecutive letters in a word are reduced to two (words like tooooooooo much… is replaced with too much). Spell checking is also performed to words that have been identified as misspelled in order to infer the correct word.

4. Classify various types of tweets and segment them after estimating the influence of each tweet using the predictive analysis library. Perform sentiment analysis by identifying whether people are tweeting positive or negative statements about some actions.
5. Use linguistic concepts, perform opinion mining, analyze data and bring out powerful insights. Use important feature of the analysis based on machine learning. Thus, applications learn by analyzing ever-increasing amounts of data.
6. The goal is to build the model for predicting the sentiments from tweets. Table 7.3 presents sentimental analysis features.

Table 7.3 Sentiment analysis features

Feature	Meaning
NEGATION	Presence of negating words
POSITIVE SMILEY	Presence of common positive emoticons
NEGATIVE SMILEY	Presence of common negative emoticons
DONT— YOU, OH, SO, AS FAR AS,	May indicate ironic or sarcastic text
LAUGH	Presence of popular laughter indications, such as haha, lol

Tweets sentiments prediction can face the following problem: The use of negatives and positives in the same sentence. For example, "I like red color but I hate blue color". A classification of such sentence is that it is a neutral sentence. The application handles that sentence by breaking the sentence into two subparts such that one is positive and the other is negative. The count value thus does not alter.

This classification model adapts to the evolution of tweets and employs the user (or domain expert) feedbacks.

The outcomes affect by:

1. Varying size of dataset
2. Different features
3. Rate with which tweets arrive
4. Changes in the textual content (for example, the changes in vocabulary, meaning of words, etc.)

Social media sentiment analysis also needs to identify various human emotions like sadness, anxiety, fear, confusion, depression and anger.

7.5.3.2 *Stock Market Predictions*

Stock market data is an example of a real-time data stream. Data stream algorithms compute the values over a time-window of stock trades. This window has fixed size and contains n stock trades. A sale–purchase is counted as one trade. The parameter studied is Volume-Weighted Average Price (VWAP).

The data stream model can be relational tuples-based model with tuples (sale_time, ticker_symbol, num_shares, price_per_share) for each stock sales in real time. Assume stock trade i has price Pi, with Si shares changing hands, then compute the volume-weighted average (VWAP) stock prices from stream of stock sales. P_{VWAP} (Price for VWAP) = ΣPiSi ÷ ΣSi.

The algorithm first transforms stock-sale data stream into a relation using a time-based sliding-window operator with sliding interval ΔT = 5 m (over last 5 minutes) of data. The window length is time from start of the day and thus increases as the day progresses.

The algorithm estimates value of P_{VWAP} continuously, and evaluates the relation factor r periodically during trading day.

Recapitulate equation (6.8a). The correlation coefficient *r* between two variables x and y is:

$$r = [\ 1 / (n-1)\ ] \times \Sigma\{[\ (x_i - \bar{x}) / s_x\ ] \times [\ (y_i - \bar{y}) / s_y\ ]\ \}, \qquad \text{... (7.3)}$$

where n is the number of observations in the sample. x_i *is the x value* (= time since start of trade in a day) for i^{th} observation. $\bar{x}$ *is the sample mean of x* values. y_i *is the y value* (= P_{VWAP}) for i^{th} observation. $\bar{y}$ *is the sample mean of y* values. s_x *is the sample standard deviation of x*. s_y *is the sample standard deviation of y.*

Compute a correlation factor (relation) containing aggregates using standard grouping/aggregation operations. The r is also sent as another stream (results stream).

Refer Sections 6.2.2 to 6.2.4. A prediction model can be building a relationship *r* with respect to time and then predict using machine learning tools. Value of $r > 0$ continuously over a window of time length, (for example, 4 hours) indicates a continued positive relationship (sentiment towards the stock price). Conversely, $r < 0$ indicates a negative relationship (sentiment) and $r = 0$ indicates no relationship (or that the variables are independent of each other and not related). A prediction for price increase or decrease can be based on positive or negative sentiments during the period of study from the start of the trade.

Self-Assessment Exercise linked to LO 7.4

1. List the applicaions of real-time analytics. ○○●
2. List the platforms available for real-time analytics. ○○●
3. How are the features in SparkStreaming used for data stream analysis? ○●●
4. Explain transformation functions in SparkStreaming. ○●●
5. How is real-time data stream used in making predictions? ●●●

KEY CONCEPTS

adapter
Apache Spark
Apriori algorithm
association rule
BDAS
Big Data
Bloom filter
correlation coefficient
COUGAR
counting distinct
counting ones
CQL
data stream
DBMS
decaying window
DSMS
DStream
filtering
frequent itemset
hash function
HDFS
Kafka
lambda architecture
moments
multihash algorithm
multistage algorithm
operator
predictive analytics
queries on data stream
real-time analytics
real-time data
relational tuple
representative sample
sample size
sampling
sentiments analysis
sliding window
StreamingContext
TelegraphCQ
tuple
window

Learning Outcomes

LO 7.1

1. A stream is a sequence of data elements or symbols made available over time. Transmitting or receiving (data) between computer systems or networks is streaming of data. Mostly, data stores process data using batched processing. Processing streaming data is different from processing the data saved at a store.
2. Stream processing uses graph-based data stream model, relation-oriented stream tuples model, object-based or windows-based model.
3. Data stream processing architecture is as follows: Queries are required to be processed on streaming data. Applications continuously handle queries from a query repository. Streaming data is processed after load sharding at the memory. The queries response saves at the output buffer before finally being retrieve in the application.
4. Data Stream Management System (DSMS) manages streaming data.
5. Issues in stream processing are large data stream from different domains, variation in frequency of data stream, zeros, unbounded sizes, need of scalable, near-real time or event-based processing and need of filtering undesirable data.

LO 7.2

1. Stream computing uses algorithms which analyze the data in real time at high speed and accuracy. Stream computing is the fastest and most efficient way to obtain useful knowledge from Big Data anaytics. Organizations react quickly on appearance of a problem and can predict new trends for the future.
2. Sampling in data stream means the selection of a few data items from incoming stream of data items for analysis. Choice of data items for processing is as per probabilistic sampling.
3. Several filtering techniques exist: Bloom Filter and its variant, Streaming Quotient Filter (SQF), Particle filter, Kalman filter, XML filters (XFilter, YFilter) are some of the popularly known stream filters. Bloom filter does conditional matching where a tuple matches with some desired value. The Bloom filter is simple to implement and space efficient.
4. The stream of data contains repeated elements. Counting distinct elements find the number of dissimilar elements in a data stream. This has applications in the area of networking and databases.
5. The sliding window model for data stream algorithms is the one in which data elements receive one by one and statistically compute over a sliding window of size N (not over the whole stream). The window covers the most recent data items arrived.
6. Decaying windows technique computes a smooth aggregation of all the 1s ever seen in the stream, with decaying weights. When it further appears in the stream, less weight is assigned.

LO 7.3

1. Finding frequent itemsets means finding associated items in sets which are found together sufficiently in number of baskets and to find dependencies among the items.
2. Apriori algorithm for frequent itemsets works efficiently when the counting of the candidate process is executing.

3. PCY algorithm takes benefit of the fact that in the first iteration of Apriori, the counting of single items does not require lots of main memory. Multistage algorithm uses several successive hash tables to reduce the number of candidate pairs subsequently. Multihash algorithm uses several independent hash tables on the first iteration. This can lead to benefit like multistage in only 2 iterations.
4. SON algorithm repetitively reads small subsets of the baskets into the main memory and runs an in-memory algorithm to find all the frequent itemsets.
5. Frequent algorithm helps in finding all the items in a stream. It finds the associated sets whose frequency exceeds a 1/k fraction of the total count. Lossy counting algorithm stores tuples consisting of an item, a lower bound on its count and Δ value which records the difference between the upper and lower bounds
6. Counting frequent items in a stream requires two modifications in the decaying window algorithm.

LO 7.4

1. Real-time application relates to responsiveness. When data is generated fast, it needs fast processing as well.
2. Apache SparkStreaming and several tools enable real-time analytics. SparkStreaming is an extension of core Apache Spark API. SparkStreaming brings Apache Spark's language-integrated API to stream processing.
3. SparkStreaming provides a number of transformation functions.
4. Real-time analytics with regression analysis, statistical functions and machine-learning tools can predict positive, negative or no correlations in real time from the stream of data for applications such as stock prices.

Objective Type Questions

Select one correct answer option for each of the following questions:

7.1 A stream processing engine may include (i) the core low-latency stream processing functionality with (ii) a rich set of stream-oriented operators, (iii) coordinator, (iv) loader, (v) manager, (vi) load shedder, (vii) fault tolerance module, (viii) graphical query editor, (ix) system visualizer, and (x) stream connection generator. ○○●

(a) all except viii to x (b) all
(c) all except iii, vi and viii (d) i, ii, ix and x

7.2 *DBMS* (i) stored sets of records with no pre-defined time concept, (ii) is suitable for applications that require persistent data storage and complex querying, (iii) sequence of data elements, (iv) one-time queries, and (v) bounded main memory. ●●●

Data Stream Management System (vi) provides online analysis of rapidly changing stream of data, (vii) is suitable for real-time, continuous, ordered (arrival time or timestamp) (viii) persistent relations (relatively static, stored), (ix) transient stream (on-line analysis), (x) implements sequential access, and (xi) unbounded disk storage.

(a) none (b) all except iii, v, viii and xi
(c) only ii (d) all

7.3 Data stream model for processing can be based on (i)windows, (ii) relation-oriented tuples, (iii) correlation, (iv) graph, and (v) queries. ○●●

(a) i, ii and iv (b) all
(c) i to iii (d) all except iv

7.4 Stream processing issues are (i) unfixed size stream, (ii) unbounded data, (iii) need of scalable processing, (iv) variation in frequency of data stream, (v) may need real-time processing, and (vi) large data streams from different domains. ○○●

(a) all except ii, iii, iv, xii and xiii (b) all
(c) all except ii to vi (d) all

7.5 Minimum sample size required for accuracy in estimating proportions, the following are taken into the consideration: (i) A precise estimate of key proportions P to be measured in the study. (ii) The degree of error D that is desired in the study, ~1%-5% or 0.01 and 0.05, (iii) the confidence level $Z = 95\%$ needed from the inference, and (iv) null hypothesis true. ○●●

(a) i, iii, iv (b) i to iv
(c) iii (d) All except iv

7.6 Process of deleting a particular element in the Bloom filter requires that (i) the corresponding positions computed by k hash functions in the bit vector be set to 1.In order to perform deletion of the element, the concept of the counting Bloom filters as a variant of Bloom filter functions as follows: (ii) The counting filter maintains a counter for each bit in the Bloom filter. (iii) The counters corresponding to the k hash values are incremented or (iv) decremented, whenever an element in the filter is deleted. (v) As soon as a counter changes from 0 to 1, the corresponding bit in the bit vector reset to 0. ●●●

(a) i, ii, iv (b) ii to v
(c) ii and iv (d) All except iv

7.7 The sliding window model for data stream algorithms is for (i) infinite, (ii) bounded data stream processing. The window refers to (iii) time interval (iv) number of data items during which stream raised the queries and processed. (v) The data elements are received one by one and the statistics are computed over a sliding window of size N (not over the whole stream). (vi) The window covers the last arrived data items. ○○●

(a) i, iii and v (b) all
(c) ii to iv (d) i, ii, iv, v

7.8 The goal of association rule mining is (i) to discover items that are found together in (ii) sufficient number of baskets and (iii) to find dependencies among these items. (iv) This simply implies finding the frequent itemsets. (v) Rule should define an itemset present in a certain percentage of baskets, then that set is a frequent itemset. (vi) It is not necessary that an itemset is present in a basket only once. (vii) Itemset presence is counted once though the itemset but it may be present 2, 3 or more times in a basket. ○●●

(a) all except ii, iii and v (b) all
(c) all except vi (d) i to iv

7.9 Multistage algorithm uses (i) several successive hash tables to reduce the number of candidate pairs subsequently. (ii) The algorithm applies more than two iterations to find the frequent pairs. (iii) The idea is to rehash only those pairs that qualify for iteration 3 of Park, Chen and Yu (PCY) algorithm after iteration 2 of PCY. (iv) Only a fewer pairs contribute to buckets in the middle iteration, (v) so fewer false positives may occur. (vi) It requires 3 iterations over the data. Iteration 3 does (vii) count only those pairs {i, j} that satisfy the certain candidate pair conditions and (viii) both i and j are frequent items. Conditions are (ix) the pair uses the first hash function to a bucket whose bit in the first bitmap is 1. (x) The pair uses the second hash function to a bucket whose bit in the second bitmap is 0. ●●●

(a) all except v and vii (b) all
(c) all except iii and x (d) i to vii

7.10 Consider frequent itemsets finding problem use (i) decaying window method for identifying the most common elements in a stream. (ii) The weight of ith previous item assigns as $(1 - C)^i \approx e^{-ci}$, ●●●

(iii) relation $0 < (1 + C)^i \leq 1$ exists, (iv) value of $i \geq 1$, and (v) start counting an itemset only if all its proper subsets already being counted.

(a) all (b) all except v
(c) all except ii to iv (d) all except iii and iv

7.11 A real-time application relates to responsiveness as soon as (i) a data source sends the data, (ii) the data stores in memory, (iii) the data generates and (iv) the data that is being generated fast must first be saved and then processed fast at any time. (v) An application sometimes requires updating information at the same rate as it receives data. (vi) Late decisions sometime lead to loss of great opportunities. ○○●

(a) all except ii and iv (b) all
(c) all except ii, iii and iv (d) ii to v

7.12 When making the real-time sentiments analysis for making predictions (i) a correlation coefficient (relation) r computes in real time, (ii) the coefficient r accounts for the aggregates using standard grouping/aggregation operations, (iii) The r is also sent as another stream (results stream). (iv) A prediction model can be first built using machine learning tools after building a relationship r with respect to number of frequent sets. (v) Value of $r < 0$ continuously over a window length indicates a continued positive relationship (sentiment towards the stock price). (vi) Conversely, $r > 0$ indicates a negative relationship (sentiment) and (vii) $r = 0$ indicates no relationship (or that the variables are independent of each other and not related). ●●●

(a) all except ii, iv and xii (b) all except iv, v and vi
(c) all except vii (d) all except ii and iv

Review Questions

7.1 Describe various data stream models for extracting knowledge structures from a continuous stream. Give reasons for using each of these models. **(LO 7.1)** ○○●

7.2 Describe Data Stream Management System. How does it differ from a DBMS? **(LO 7.1)** ○●●

7.3 Describe the difficulties in real-time data stream analytics. How are they solved? **(LO 7.1)** ○●●

7.4 List the approaches for calculating the sample size. What are the parameters considered for calculating the minimum sample size required for accuracy in estimating proportions? **(LO 7.2)** ●●●

7.5 How does a stream filter function? Describe Bloom filter. **(LO 7.2)** ○○●

7.6 Describe an algorithm to count the distinct number of dissimilar elements from data stream. **(LO 7.2)** ○○●

7.7 How do different algorithms find the associated items in sets, which are together in sufficient number of baskets? How do you find dependencies among these items? **(LO 7.3)** ●●●

7.8 How is the frequent items counting done in a stream? Describe the different methods used. **(LO 7.3)** ○●●

7.9 What are the types of applications in which Real-Time Analytics (RTA) enables timely decisions? What are the tools used by the RTA platform? **(LO 7.4)** ●●●

7.10 Make a diagram for SparkStreaming computing architecture components. **(LO 7.4)** ○○●

7.11 What are the features in Spark and SparkStreaming for stream computation on Big Data? **(LO 7.4)** ○●●

7.12 What are DStreams? What are the functions used for transformation and processing of a DStream? **(LO 7.4)** ○●●

Practice Exercises

7.1 A file has data of 1000 rows similar to table given below: ○●●

Table of Product categories, ProductId, and Product name

ProductCategory	ProductId	ProductName
Toy_Airplane	10725	Lost Temple
Toy_Airplane	31047	Propeller Plane
Toy_Airplane	31049	Twin Spin Helicopter
Toy_Train	31054	Blue Express
Toy_Train	10254	Winter Holiday Toy_Train

How will you use the relation-based data stream model? Assume no time-stamping of the data. **(LO 7.1)**

7.2 Summarize the commonalities and differences in data stream query languages, (i) Relation based—CQL (STREAM), StreaQuel (TelegraphCQ), (ii) Object-based: Tribeca or ADT model-based sources COUGAR and (iii) Procedural-based Aurora in which a user specifies the data flow. **(LO 7.1)** ○●●

7.3 Describe steps for developing the algorithm for various data stream filtering algorithms. **(LO 7.2)** ○●●

7.4 List the steps for developing the algorithm for various data stream counting of the distinct elements. **(LO 7.2)** ○○●

7.5 List the steps in algorithms Apriori, PCY, multistate and multihash methods of frequent itemsets analytics of data stream. **(LO 7.3)** ●●●

7.6 Write steps in computing the frequent itemsets in data stream using the decaying window method. **(LO 7.3)** ○○●

7.7 Create 80 exemplary tuples (sale_time, ticker_symbol, num_shares, price_per_share) on every five minutes from the start of stock trading at 9 am to 1 pm on the relation-oriented stream tuples model. Choose your own stock. (Can use http://www.moneycontrol.com charts for stock quotes during a day. Write the code in Python or Java, compute and plot correlation coefficient and stock prices as a function of time from the start of the stock trade. **(LO 7.4)** ●●●

Chapter 8

Graph Analytics for Big Data and Spark GraphX Platform

LEARNING OBJECTIVES

After studying this chapter, you will be able to:

- **LO 8.1** Model the database as graphs, and represent the graphs using triples
- **LO 8.2** Get knowledge of graphs, graph network-organization, choose the graphs for analytics, and know graph-analytics use cases
- **LO 8.3** Get conceptual understanding of graph parameters, methods, diagnostics and decisions, statistical model, StatsModel, probabilities-based graph-analytics, and understanding of technical complexities in analyzing the graphs
- **LO 8.4** Use the Apache Spark GraphX, a Big Data graph-analytics platform. Know the features, architecture and components. Apply them for graph-analytics

RECALL FROM EARLIER CHAPTERS

A Big Data store system is HDFS (Section 2.3). Big Data store uses NoSQL format datasets. NoSQL data do not model like relational tables. BigDdata analytics algorithms process the NoSQL format datasets.

Graph databases can model the NoSQL databases also. (Section 3.3.5). A graph database consists of edges which interconnect the data nodes (vertices). The interconnections represent the relationships, associations and properties.

Apache Spark includes GraphX. Graph analytics tasks execute with ease using Spark GraphX. GraphX extends the Spark and thus has RDD (Resilient Distributed Data) property. The API consists of a collection of graph algorithms for analytics. Computations in GraphX use fundamental operators (such as subgraphs, joinVertices and aggregateMessages). (Section 5.2)

This chapter focuses on graph databases, organization of graph networks and the graph analytics platform, GraphX.

8.1 INTRODUCTION

'Graph' is a set of vertices and edges. Graph theory is the theory of graphs and their properties. Examples of graphs are *hierarchy* graph, *monotone* graph, *connected* graph, *bipartite* graph, *planer* graph and *triangle free* graph.

Graphs have a number of characteristics. A graph:

1. *Represents a database* using graph parameters or properties assigned to each vertex, v and edge, e. An edge is a line joining two vertices. Graph nodes and edges connect each other through relations, associations and properties.
2. *Represents an abstract data type* for the relationships. A graph depicts relationships, such as, a relationship between two or more quantitative dependent variables with respect to an independent variable.
3. *Represents knowledge and reasoning* in a conceptual graph model
4. *Represents a network*, such as a social network
5. *Models the dataflows and programflows* using directed graphs: A Dataflow Graph (DFG) represents the flows of data and program. The DFG consists of sets of circles. A circle represents a node (vertex). Each node represents a set of computations or a set of operations which change the *initial state* to a *new state* (of entities or properties). State change occurs on receiving new inputs followed by computations at a node. The incoming directed edges represent the inputs received from the other nodes. The outgoing directed edges represent the output to the other nodes.
6. *Computes using path traversal*, which means going through a finite or infinite sequence of edges in a graph that connect a sequence of vertices between initial vertex v_0 and end vertex v_e. Traversing is along a path from v_0 to v_e along the connected edges.
7. *Analyzes data using graphic parameters*, relationships, associations and distribution of properties along the vertices in the path, and property variations on path traversal from a node to other nodes along the edges
8. *Analyzes data through the queries* on data using path traversal, which means from v_0 following the sequence of steps to v_e.

This chapter describes graph models, graph parameters, graph network organizations and graph analytics. It also describes statistical models for changes and distribution of properties on path traversal between the nodes. Section 8.2 describes modeling of databases as graphs and representations of graphs using triples. Section 8.3 describes graphs and graph networks. The section also describes choosing of a graph for analytics, and use cases of graph analytics. Section 8.4 describes graph parameters, methods of diagnostics and decisions, StatsModel, probabilities-based analytics, and technical complexities in analyzing the graphs. Section 8.5 describes the features of Apache Spark GraphX, its architecture, components, applications, and the considerations of using the dedicated appliances for the graphs.

8.2 GRAPH MODEL

LO 8.1

Modeling of databases as graphs and representations of graphs using triples

A graph represents *an abstract data type*. The edges of a graph represent relations, connections or associations. The vertices represent the entities. Each entity can have parameters assigned to that. Each node can have parameters and property assigned to that.

A set of vertices (nodes) $\mathcal{V}$ and edges (links) $\mathcal{E}$ define a graph $\mathcal{G}$. Relation in terms of set theory is $\mathcal{G} = (\mathcal{V}, \mathcal{E})$, which means that graph $\mathcal{G}$ is a set, which contains two sub-sets, vertices $\mathcal{V}$ and edges $\mathcal{E}$.

1. Elements of $\mathcal{V}$ represent the entities. A node or a vertex v in set $\mathcal{V}$ represents an entity, such as studentID [Example two nodes: 'studentID' and 'studentSem1SGPA'.
2. Elements of $\mathcal{E}$ represent the relations or associations. An edge connects the two nodes. An edge, e represents a relation or association between the two entities. An example of association is 'studies at'. Student of an ID *studies at* a UG course where the studentID and UG course are two entities at two interconnected nodes.

Order of a graph specifies by number of vertices N_v and number of edges N_e, where $N_v = |\mathcal{V}|$, and $N_e = |\mathcal{E}|$.

The degree of a node (node degree) specifies the number of edges linked to a node. The degree may vary from traversing from one node to the other. For example, three linkages v1 to v2, v1 to v3, v1 to v4 mean that v1 (node-degree) is 3. A distribution function represents the variation in degrees of the nodes on traversing (Section 6.2.5).

A graph model has the following features:

(i) A label near an edge can specify the context of relation or association. A label at an edge can also specify a value. For example, the grade point average in Semester 1, *studentSem1SGPA*.
(ii) A label near a vertex can specify identification for the entity. For example, *studentID*.
(iii) A weight near the edge can specify the weight of a relationship with respect to other edges of the same kind.
(iv) A property can associate with the vertex or edge. For example, *adding* property.
(v) Multiple relationships can associate a pair of vertices interconnected by multiple edges.
(vi) A direction can associate with the direction of flow of relationship or association.

A graph, called *property-graph*, consists of each vertex and edge assigned properties (Section 8.2.5).

A graph, called *directed graph*, consists of directed edges. A directed graph shows a sequence of edges (or arcs) which connect a sequence of vertices with a condition. All directed edges are in the same direction when a graph has edges directed inwards toward a node and outwards towards another node, such that inward edge(s) represent an input for computation or *state* change at the node and outward edge(s) represent the output(s) which is input to the next node in the graph.

The number of inward edges in a directed graph is a node parameter called *in-degree*. Directed graph node *out-degree* means the number of outgoing edges from the node. A directed graph represents the flow of the relationship using the directed edge. For example, assume Semester 1 and SGPA are vertices in a directed graph. The edge represents a relation between them, i.e., it represents that SGPA is the result of the examination of Semester 1.

A graph defines the entities and properties to each vertex and edge. A graph called *directed multigraph*, provisions for the multiple parallel edges and that enables multiple relationships between the entities. Multiple parallel edges share the common source and destination vertices. *Directed Acyclic Graphic* is a special kind of directed graph that contains no cycles.

Consider columnar data store in a tabular representation. Each row-group consists of a sequence of columns. Relationships between columns of the row groups are implicit (for search and queries for the values in columns) but not explicitly specified (Section 3.3.3).

Graph database explicitly stores the relationships at each edge. A hierarchy graph stores hierarchal relationships. Hierarchy relations between the tables do not store but implicit in the codes for a search or query.

The following example explains the usages of nodes, edges and properties in a graph model. The example gives a corresponding tabular Data Store.

EXAMPLE 8.1

Consider the students, that are studying Bachelor of Computer Science course and have appeared in Semester 1 examination in the department.

(i) How does a graph model show the relationships and semester grade point averages?

(ii) How does a table of grade point averages (GPAs) of a student in a departmental semester examination correspond to the graph model?

SOLUTION

(i) Figure 8.1 shows a graph model for a student grade-sheet database. The graph consists of nodes and edges for a first-semester UG computer-science student of ID = UGCS4268 . The figure shows the relationships using label and property at vertices and edges for a student.

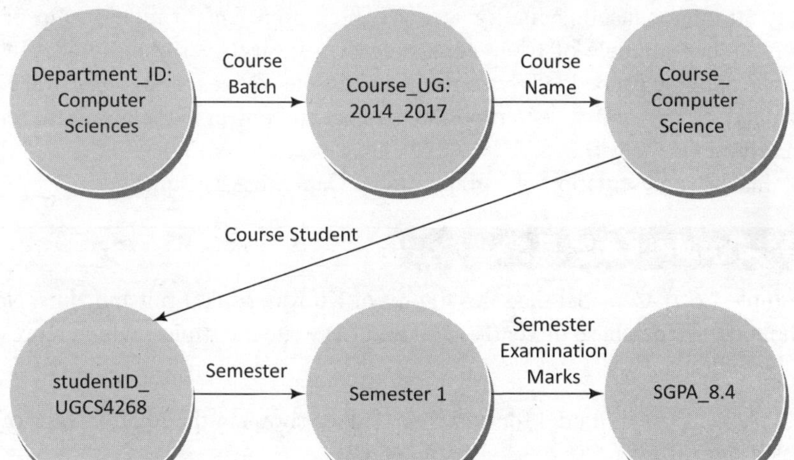

Figure 8.1 Graph model of a grade sheet

(ii) Tabular representation in an RDBMS mapped with the above graph model for the Semester Grade Point Averages (SGPAs) is as follows:

Department_ID	Course Batch	Course Name	Student ID	Semester	SGPA
Computer Sciences	UG 2014_2017	Bachelor in Computer Science	4268	1	8.4
...	...	...	...	...	...
...	...	...	...	...	...

8.2.1 Representing a Graph as Triples

Triple means a data entity consisting of three-components: subject, predicate and object. For example, consider a sentence, 'Spark includes GraphX'. Here, Spark is the subject, includes is the predicate and GraphX is the object.

Triples represent the Graph entities. Assume a directed graph. A triple is a sentence-like format. A sentence consists of three elements, 'subject' 'predicate' and 'object'. Similarly, a triple consists of three elements: *source node* (subject) connects to *destination node* (object) through an *edge* (predicate).

Triple has a subject-predicate-object format for representing three elements: source node, edge and destination node. Format is *instance identifier-property name-property value.* For example, StudentID: 42629 *obtained*:"GradePoint_Java "8.2". StudentID: 42629 is the instance identifier. Obtained is the property name. Value of Property GradePoint_Java is 8.2.Graph model represents instance identifier and property value at two nodes and property name as the edge connecting them.

A graph node defines by a vertex such that the two of them connect through a relationship or association. For example, consider a sentence, 'Raj Kamal wrote textbook on Internet of Things'. 'Raj Kamal' is a node and 'textbook on Internet of Things' is next node.

A graph edge is an interconnecting line or arrow, which represents a relationship or association in a sentence. Consider another example of triple consisting of a subject, verb, and object in a sentence, 'Raj Kamal wrote a classic book on Embedded Systems'. Verb 'wrote' relates the *subject* 'Raj Kamal' and *object* 'classic book on embedded system'. Two vertices are subject and object in the graphical representation. The edge joining them represents the *verb*.

Following explains the representation of a graph model Data Store as triples:

EXAMPLE 8.2

Recapitulate Example 1.6(i). Consider the sales figures of Kit Kat, Milk, Fruit and Nuts, Nougat and Oreo. (i) Show a graph model for database of yearly sales and (ii) write the triples, which represent the graph.

SOLUTION

(i) Figure 8.2 shows a graph model for nodes and edges showing the relationships of yearly sales of chocolates.

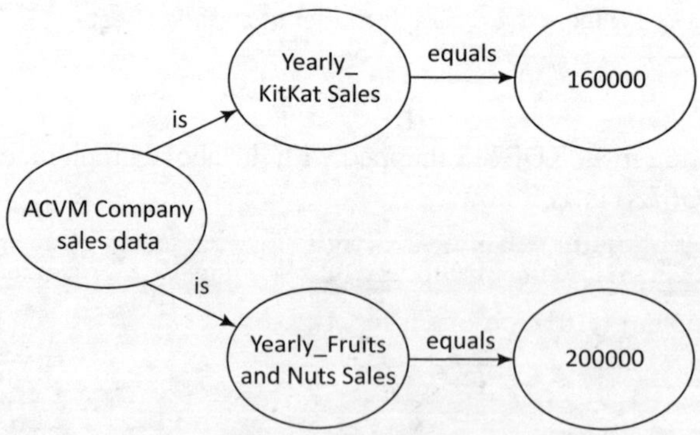

Figure 8.2 Example of a graph model of yearly total sales of an ACVM company

(ii) Graph *source node* (subject) connects to *destination node* (object) through an *edge* (predicate). The following set of triples represent a graph:

Yearly_Chocolate_Sales as triples

Subject	Predicate	Object
ACVM Company Sales Data	is	Yearly_KitKat_Sales
ACVM CompanySales Data	is	Yearly_FruitAndNuts_Sales
Yearly_KitKat_Sales	equals	160000
Yearly_FruitsandNuts _Sales	equals	200000
...	...	...
...	...	...
...	...	...

8.2.1.1 *Graph Database as Collection of Triples*

A collection of triples creates a semantic database, the two features of this database are as follows:

1. Can add additional properties, relationship, association or attribute with each triple.
2. Can include new entities and relationships, just as a tabular database adds additional rows, or a columnar-family database adds additional columns.

8.2.2 Resource Description Framework (RDF) for Graph Databases

A triple *instance identifier-property name-property value* uses a Universal Resource Indicator (URI) for instance identifier. Triples form a specialized graph database. A triple-store is also represented in RDF (Resource Definition Framework).

RDF is a simple, yet very effective language for representing information using triples. RDF is a W3C (World Wide Consortium) standard for storing a graph database. A graph database is thus a triplestore, which uses RDF. The features in RDF are as follows:

1. An RDF data file is similar to three columns of triples: subject-predicate-objects and are also similar to triplets of document-key-values in the MongoDB.
2. A standard RDF schema provides definitions of classes and relationships between the properties and classes; an RDF does not depend on a schema and is thus flexible.
3. Triples represent the nodes and edges; format of triple is 'instance-identifier', 'property-name' and 'property-value'; and format of identifier is URI. An instance identifier is like an entity in a SQL database, property name is like a *key*, and property value is like a *value* in a field.
4. RDF provides for inclusion of new entities and relationships, just as a tabular database provides for inclusion of additional rows, or a columnar-family database for additional columns.
5. RDF provides for inclusion of additional properties to the relationship, association and attribute in a triple.
6. Simple concatenation combines multiple datasets. The combined datasets are then used as a whole.
7. Splitting the triples into multiple lines does not change the collective meaning; therefore, sharding in data collections is easy.

The RDF software parses the lines in data file when processing the queries, analyzing, visualizing, reporting or any other operation. RDFLib is a Python library, which enables working with RDF. Number of contributors enriches the Python RDFLib continuously. The library contains (i) an RDF/XML parser/serialize and (ii) in-memory and persistent graph backend.

The following example explains the entries at a graph database:

EXAMPLE 8.3

Recapitulate Figure 8.2. It showed a snippet of graph database of ACVM Company daily and yearly sales. Write the triples in RDF.

SOLUTION

The following are steps in the RDF lines in a data file:

Step 1: Write two lines to specify the URIs for resource location.

```
@prefix acvmCompanyData: <http://acvmcompany.org/data/>
@prefix salesFigure: <http://acvmcompany.org/salesRecord/>
```

Step 2: Write triples for ACVM of ID, acvm8268. They are as follows:

```
acvmCompanyData:acvm8268 salesFigure: Yearly _ KitKat _ Sales "160000"
AcvmCompanyData: acvm8268 salesFigure: Yearly _ FruitAndNuts _ Sales
"200000"
```

8.2.3 SPARQL Querying Language for RDF Graph-Database

Spark Query Language (SPARQL) is a query language for RDF graph database. SPARQL is W3C accepted query language. Features of SPARQL are as follows:

1. Allows taking the data without definition for separate schema and considers a schema as part of the data itself (Schema information may be provided separately, which enable joining of datasets without any problem)
2. Provides query operators needed during graph analytics
3. Provides JOIN, SORT, AGGREGATE operators
4. Provides syntax for specific graph path traversals
5. Includes queries for conjunctions, disjunctions, triple patterns and optional patterns in triples
6. Provides for querying data using graph traversal along a path. Traversal may be single step, path expression, or full recursion. RDF (Resource Description Framework) is a specialized query language.

[Path means a finite or infinite sequence of edges in a graph that connect a sequence of vertices. Graph traversal uses a path along the connected edges. Path expression means an expression consisting of path names using ORs. The expression denotes a set of paths between two start and end nodes. (Sign Plus or OR is used between the terms in an expression to express a set of path traversals.)

For example, consider a path expression, V1V3 +V1V2V3 +V1V2V2V3+ ... First term V1V3 means path starting from V1, directs to V3. The term V1V2V2V3 means V1 to V2, then V2 output back to input of V2, and then V2 to V3.

Path recursion means repeated traversal of path till a certain condition satisfies. The following example explains how to write a SPARQL query and the output after query processing.

EXAMPLE 8.4

Recapitulate Example 8.3. (i) Write a SPARQL query for output of RDF triples. (ii) What will be the result from the query processor?

SOLUTION

(i) The following are the steps for query in SAPRQL:

Step 1: Specify the URIs for resource location.

```
PREFIX acvmComanyData: <http://acvmcomapny.org/data/>
PREFIX SalesFigure :< http://acvmcomapny.org/salesRecord/>
```

Step 2: Write query.

```
SELECT ? property ? value
WHERE {acvmComanyData: acvm8268salesFigure ? property ? value}
```

The ? mark is a wildcard as the query is for selecting all properties and their values for acvm8268 salesFigure. If instead of ? Yearly_KitKat_Sales is mentioned, then only sales figures for Kit Kat retrieve from the RDF data-file.

(ii) Following will be the output from the query:

```
Yearly _ KitKat _ Sales "160000"
Yearly _ FruitAndNuts _ Sales "200000"
```

8.2.4 NativeDB Graph Database

Relational DB distributes the relationships and stores as tables. Path traversal from a vertex to vertices retrieves the multi-step relationships. An efficient storage mechanism with ease in path traversals is thus needed, especially in a Big Data environment, which consists of distributed data-clusters and parallels computing data-nodes.

Neo4j developed Native Data Store for graph databases.[1] NativeDB focuses on efficient use of available computing resources. The design is architecture aware design. NativeDB graph stores nodes and relationships directly. Direct storage makes retrievals efficient. Figure 8.3 shows the relationships in use during path traversal and in use during operations in NativeDB.

Features of native data store are as follows:

1. Design provides for workload of memory management, query engine, and query language at storage
2. Design provides the safe storage, efficient querying consistently and without the aid of other components
3. Organizes the graph data and models both graph structure, vertex properties and edge properties
4. Represents the graphs in-memory and on-disk
5. Caches the graph data in-memory either in batch mode or on-demand from the on-disk
6. Enables timestamps
7. Persisting updates of graph along with the timestamps from in-memory graph to on-disk

[1] https://neo4j.com/product/

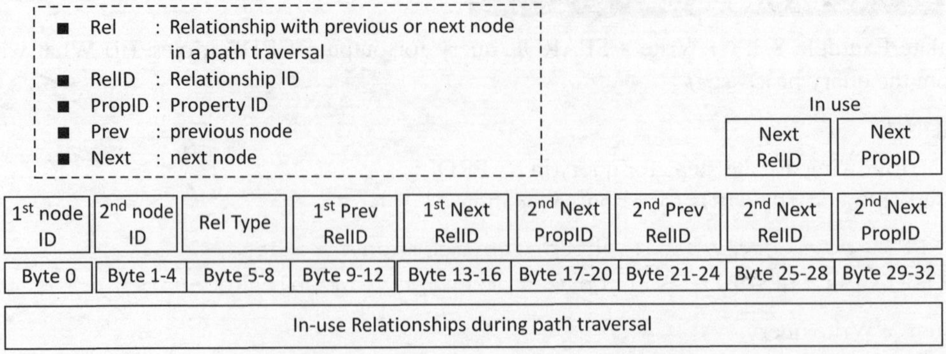

Figure 8.3 Native data graph relationships

8. Provides graph data streaming, graph data updates for modifying the graph structure and/or property data accordingly
9. Provides addition of the edges, removal of vertices and updates of properties
10. Performs querying of graph data by loading the graph structure and/or property data
11. Finds neighbours of a vertex, retrieves property of an edge bypath traversals.

Neo4j developed a query language called *Cypher* for the NativeDBs. Tests for execution times in the searches for 2nd, 3rd, 4th and remote neighbours show that the Neo4j Native Data Store is faster compared to other formats. IBM G system[2] for graph analytics, visualization and other graph applications also support NativeDBs.

8.2.5 Property Graph Model

A property graph assigns property to the nodes and edges. The following example explains a property graph:

EXAMPLE 8.5

(i) How do you draw a property graph for a student data? Student data contains student Id, semester, subject options, grades and teacher field.

(ii) How do property graphs model the RDBMS tables?

SOLUTION

(i) Figure 8.4 shows the property graph of student data with StudentId, semester, subject options, grades and teachers:

(ii) Figure 8.5 shows RDBMS tables to which the above property graph model corresponds.

[2] http://www.systemg.research.ibm.com/

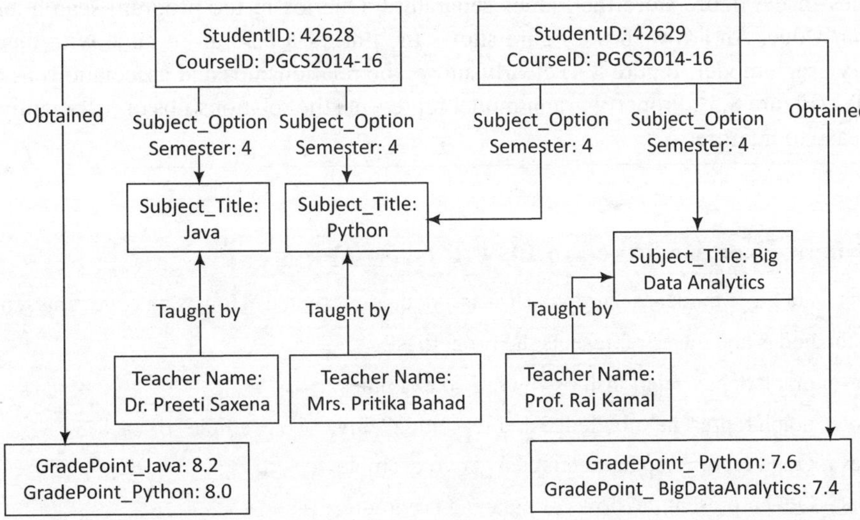

Figure 8.4 Property graph of students, semester, subject options, grades, and teachers

Student ID	Semester	Subject	Teacher	Grade Point
40628	4	Java	Dr. Preeti Saxena	8.2
40628	4	Python	Mrs. Pritika Bahad	8.0
40629	4	Python	Mrs. Pritika Bahad	7.6
40629	4	Big Data Analytics	Prof. Raj Kamal	7.4
…	…	…	…	…
…	…	…	…	…

StudentID	Course ID
40628	PGCS 2014-16
40629	PGCS 2014-16
…	…
4111	PGCS 2015-17
…	…
4212	PGCS 2016-18

StudentID	Semester	SubjectID	Grade Point
40628	4	CS-401	8.2
40629	4	CS-402	7.6
…	…	…	…
4111	2	CS-301	…
…	…	…	…
4212	5	CS-502	…

Course ID	Semester
PGCS 2014-16	1
PGCS 2014-16	2
PGCS 2014-16	3
PGCS 2014-16	4

SubjectID	Subject	Teacher
CS-401	Java	Dr. Preeti Saxena
CS-402	Python	Mrs. Pritika Bahad
CS-403	Big Data Analytics	Prof. Raj Kamal
CS-301	DBMS	…
CS-502	Cloud Computing	…

Figure 8.5 RDBMS tables for students, semester, subject options, grades and teachers

Three tables in the figure store the values separately. Queries in the program search and select the related column value. An arrow in the figure shows the link of a column in table with the next related table. Property graph model (Figure 8.4) clearly shows the relationships and associations as compared to RDBMS tables (Figure 8.5). Property graph model represents the relationships or associations pictorially and are thus easy to interpret.

Self-Assessment Exercise linked to LO 8.1

1. How does Data Store model as a graph? How is a node represented? How is an edge represented? ○○●
2. How do the nodes and edges represents the properties? ○●●
3. How does a graph depict relationships? Give two examples. ○○●
4. How does a graph represent knowledge and reasoning? Give two examples of each. ●●●
5. How does a graph represent parameters? Give two examples. ○○●
6. How does a DFG represent the flows of data and program. ○○●
7. List the meaning of the terms: (i) triple 'subject-predicate-object' format, (ii) triplestore, (iii) instance identifier-property name-property value RDFformat, and (iv) NativeDB. ○●●
8. List characteristic features of the Resource Description Framework. ○●●
9. How does a property graph represent RDBMS tables? ●●●

8.3 GRAPHS, NETWORK ORGANIZATION AND GRAPH ANALYTICS

LO 8.2

Graphs, graph network organization, choosing graph for analytics and graph analytics use cases

A network organization means where the persons or entities interconnect with others and have areas of common interest, business or study. A model of graph data store is a network organization. Graph network examples are weblinks network, social network, business network and students network. A network graph consists of vertices $\mathcal{V}$, interconnected by directed or undirected edges $\mathcal{E}$.

A network consists of items (entities, persons or web page links) and relationships or the associations between items. The graphs, such as trees, can store a relational DB. However, relational DBs have the following problems:

1. Mostly cumbersome to navigate
2. Difficult to scale up
3. Difficulties in adding new relationships or associations.

Graph Data Store nodes are easy to navigate through a traversal of paths. Path traversals can be optimized for faster traversing. Scaling up and adding new relationships or associations are easy in the Graph Data Stores.

Note: ○○● Level 1 & Level 2 category
○●● Level 3 & Level 4 category
●●● Level 5 & Level 6 category

8.3.1 Network Organization

Graph model of a network organization helps in followings tasks:

1. Detecting patterns
2. Finding organization inherent in the network
3. Finding communities and micro-communities. For example, finding the groups where new trends are emerging, and the groups of similar interests
4. Finding connections. For example, finding the student-specific connected groups showing preference for programming language subjects
5. Modeling communication. For example, finding the specific events which create active interest in the specific community-groups, such on launching a new luxury car model which creates interest in managers and chief executive officers, or starting a new course on Python which creates deep interest in postgraduate Computer-Science students
6. Modeling collaborations. For example, finding the collaborating and sharing communities which have similar interests, finding community sharing new techniques and algorithms that has interest in Big Data Analytics
7. Modeling influences. For example, finding the persons (nodes) with high degrees of interconnections to large number of entities compared to the others
8. Modeling distances between set of entities. For example, finding how much distance a path-traversal takes place on an average when searching a common-interest entity
9. Making discoveries and providing the previously unknown information after the search and analysis

Distance in a graph consisting ($\mathfrak{V}$ and $\mathfrak{E}$) refers to the number of edges connecting the two vertices v1 and v2 on the path traversal between them.

8.3.2 Probabilistic Graphical Network Organizations—Bayesian and Markov Networks

Probability means the chance of observing a dependent variable value with respect to some independent variable. Suppose a Grandmaster in chess won 22 out of 100 matches, 78 matches were a draw, and lost none of the matches. Then, the probability P of winning P_w is 0.22, P of drawn game P_D is 0.78 and P_L of losing, $P_L = 0$. The sum of the probabilities normalizes to 1, as only one of the three possibilities exist.

Probability states mean that states of P values as a function of all possible independent values, situations or variables. For example, if probabilities of winning, drawing and loosing for Chess-player supercomputer AlphaZero against a Grandmaster are P = (0.22, 0.78, 0), then the probability function has three states. Here, the probability state is a discrete function. Sum of P values is one.

Probability distribution means that distribution of P values as a function of all possible independent values, variables, situations, distances or variables. For example, P is given by a function P(x) and P varies as x changes. Variations in P(x) with x can be discrete or continuous. Here, again values are normalized such that sum of the P values is 1 (Section 6.2.5).

The probabilities distribute in the entities. The vertices represent the entities. The probability distribution function P(x) distributes at the neighbouring vertices of a parent. That means vertex x has a property with probability P(x), where x is the distance from the parent vertex. Neighbouring means associated, influence or effected vertices of the parent.

A *Bayesian Network Graph* (BNG) is a graph where each node represents a random variable in a DAG. The variable has s probabilistic distribution over the connected nodes. No cyclic path traversals occur in BNG during querying or computations.

Markov Network Graph (MNG) is a Graph where each node represents a random variable in an undirected graph. The variable has a probabilistic distribution over the connected nodes during path traversal. The cyclic path traversals may also take place in an MNG.

Propagation of a property in a network implements by a function, func (x) where x refers to neighbourhoods of the associated vertices (vertex1st, 2nd, 3rd, 4th and so on) with respect to a parent vertex. The func () is a propagation function which represents an inference, evidence, belief, expectation or influence as a function of distances. The distribution (propagation) over distance can be continuous or discrete (Section 3.2.1 for definition of distance between the vertices).

Func () can be a user defined function (UDF), vectorized UDF (VDUF) or group vectorized UDF (GVUDF) [Sections 5.3.2.2 to 5.3.2.4]. Func () can be a probability distribution (propagation) function P(x) or joint conditions probability function or potential function.

Probabilistic graphical models, such as Bayesian networks or Markov networks have number of applications. Probabilistic graphical models are used in machine learning. The models provide a compact representation. The model, for example Bayesian network, provides solutions for probabilistic inferences. Examples of applications are business strategies, risk assessments, medical diagnosis, speech recognition, assessment of loan risk default, etc.

Bayesian Network Graph (BNG)

A BNG network organization has the following features:

1. It is a directed graph model in which non-cyclic and no reverse path traversals take place for computations
2. Enables a compact representation which gives probabilistic relationships among a set of variables
3. Enables the computations of joint probability distributions over the probability state variables
4. Each node has a set of conditional probabilities which specifies quantitatively the influences (effects) of the parent
5. The property values at vertices have Conditional Probability-Distribution (CPD), table of graph nodes, node properties and probabilities, called Condition Probabilities Table (CPT)
6. An edge between two nodes means that these two nodes have conditional probabilistic dependency. A missing edge between two nodes means conditional independence of the node from the parent node.

The following example explains the concept of CPD and CPT.

EXAMPLE 8.6

Assume that a student chooses subjects in a semester examination and obtains GPAs and the probabilities of obtaining GPAs in the subjects are as follows:

Subject	Graph Node	Probability P_{8+} for GPA 8.0 or above	P_{8-} for GPA below 8.0
Subject 1	V1	0.85	0.15
Subject 2	V2	0.8	0.2
Subject 2 theory	V3	0.75	0.25
Subject 2 practical	V4	0.80	0.2
---	--	---	---
---	--	---	---

Number of rows in the table above depends on the subjects and their nature (theory, practical or general). V1 connects V2 by a directed edge e1 towards V2. V2 connects V3 by a directed edge e2 towards V3 and also connects to V4 by a directed edge e3 towards V4. Using this graph:

(i) Show diagrammatically Bayesian-Network Graph for obtained probabilities of GPAs with probability using distribution of probabilities P in different subjects, and

(ii) Explain the concept of conditional probability distribution (CPD) and conditional probability table (CPT).

SOLUTION

(i) Figure 8.6 shows Bayesian network graph for a student obtaining GPAs with probabilities distributions in the GPAs:

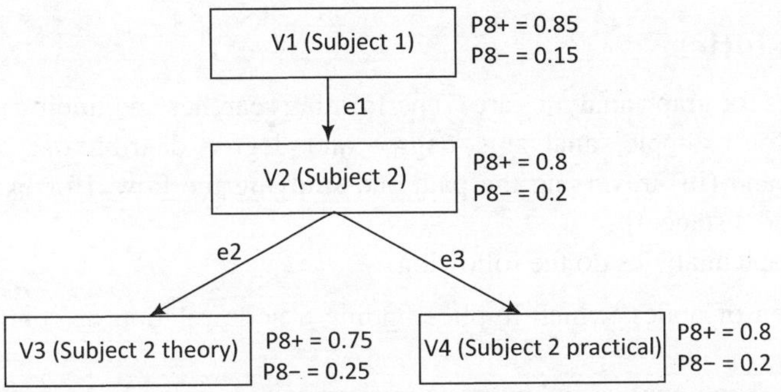

Figure 8.6 Bayesian network graph for a student obtaining GPAs with probabilistic distributions in the GPAs

(ii) Following are the probabilities distributions at the nodes:

V1	P (V1)
8–	$p_{10} = 0.85$
8+	$p_{11} = 0.15$

V2	P (V2)
8–	$p_{20} = 0.8$
8+	$p_{21} = 0.2$

V3	P (V3)
8–	$p_{30} = 0.85$
8+	$p_{31} = 0.15$

V4	P (V4)
8–	$p_{40} = 0.8$
8+	$p_{41} = 0.2$

The first column shows the property at V1, 8– means the student obtains below 8.0 and 8+ means above 8.0. The probability distribution values enable the computation of conditional probability, cp values and give the CPTs. The formats of CPTs are as follows:

V1	V2	P (V2|V1)
8–	8–	cp_{2100}
8–	8+	cp_{2101}
8+	8–	cp_{2110}
8+	8+	cp_{2111}

V2	V3	P (V3|V2)
8–	8–	cp_{3200}
8–	8+	cp_{3201}
8+	8–	cp_{3210}
8+	8+	cp_{3211}

V2	V4	P (V4|V2)
8–	8–	cp_{4200}
8–	8+	cp_{4201}
8+	8–	cp_{4210}
8+	8+	cp_{4211}

V3	V1	P (V3|V1)
8–	8–	cp_{3100}
8–	8+	cp_{3101}
8+	8–	cp_{3110}
8+	8+	cp_{3111}

cp_{2100} is probability when the conditions at nodes V1 and V2 correspond to GPs below 8.0 in both subjects. Similarly, other cp values are probabilities when conditions given at rows 1 and 2 are true. The CPTs enable computations of the probability of the conditions such as V1= 8+, V2 = 8+, V3 = 8+, V4 = 8+ being true. Four nodes have 2^4= 16 conditional probabilities in the Bayesian network. 16 conditions are possible for four nodes of the graph.

Markov Network Graph (MNG)

A Markov Network Graph (MNG) is a network organization which is undirected and can have cycles in path traversals.

Assume that all vertices are reachable from a starting vertex. Breadth first traversal (search) [BFS] is used when the graph has cycles. Therefore, the visited vertices are marked. The marks at each visited vertex can be stored in an array of bits (Booleans).

8.3.3 Graph Analytics

Three types of processes for graph analytics are (i) performing searches and finding matches, (ii) performing topological analysis (for example, analyzing degree and degree distribution, closeness, betweenness, centrality parameters), and (iii) traversing the path and studying the flow, [for example, probability flow (variation with respect to distance)].

APIs and tools of graph analytics do the following:

(i) Find association of nodes, which implies finding a node relation or connection with the next or previous node
(ii) Detect patterns, communities and micro-communities
(iii) Do a graph search and find graph matches for specific connected groups which show similar preferences
(iv) Find collaborations among entities having similar interests (for example, collaborations by sharing similar techniques and algorithms)
(v) Do shortest path analysis for communications
(vi) Analyze the distances between a set of common interest entities
(vii) Compute the centralities (degree centrality, closeness centrality, betweenness centrality, Eigen vector for centralities of the neighbours to a node of higher centrality than the neighbours)
(viii) Detect the anomaly and discover previously unknown information
(ix) Evaluate the influence distribution by comparing the nodes of high degrees of interconnections with large number of entities with respect to others,
(x) Find the ranking from PageRank, a term used in analogy with web PageRank.

Graph analytics use the methods of collaborative filtering (Section 6.4.3), stochastic gradient method (Section 6.7.3), triangle counting (Section 9.5.6), K-core analysis (Section 9.5.3), Web communities (Section 9.4.6), social communities (Section 9.5.8), and PageRank (Sections 9.4.1 and 9.4.3).

Node distance refers to the number of edges connecting a node from a node taken as origin. If two vertices v1 and v2 on path traversal are the nearest neighbour, then distance of v2 from v1 is 1; if the next nearest neighbour then 2; if next to next then 3, and so on.

A node distance is a measure of number of 1st, 2nd, 3rd, 4th and so on and corresponds to the neighbourhood associated with a vertex.

The parameters nn_1, nn_2, ... measure the node neighbourhoods, where nn_1, nn_2, … = number of 1st neighbour node, 2nd neighbour node, …, respectively, and so on to a querying node.

The *node centrality* of a node is defined in reference to other nodes using the metrics. Metrics for centrality are degree, closeness, betweenness or other characteristic of the node, such as rank, belief, expectation, evidence, reputation or status.

Nodes *closeness* to a vertex u is defined, as reference to other connected vertices in $\mathcal{V}_u$ with u. $\mathcal{V}_u$ is a subset of vertices in $\mathcal{V}$ that connect with u. The centrality (closeness index), c_C is function of distances of vertices.

$$c_C (v) = \sum_{u \in V} [d (u, v)]^{-1}, \quad \text{... (8.1)}$$

where d (u, v) is the distance between u and v when traversing the path, and u and v are elements of $\mathcal{V}_u$. Summation is overall connected vertices to u [Closeness is inverse of the node distance in terms of neighbourhood 1, 2, ... or N (Recall K-NN in Section 6.3.6).

Node *betweenness* defines the extent to which a vertex is located 'between' other pairs of vertices, measured by the number of times a node is present between the shortest paths. *Betweenness* c_B (v) relates to the number of pairing nodes.

Betweenness centrality of a vertex v requires calculating the lengths of shortest paths among all pairs (p, q) of vertices connected to u, and computations of summation for each pairing vertex in $\mathcal{V}_u$. The centrality (*betweenness* index), c_B (u) is function of shortest distances with the pair of vertices.

$$c_B (u) = \{ \sum_{p \neq q \neq u \in V} \alpha (p, q \mid u)] \times [\alpha (p, q)]^{-1} \}, \quad \text{... (8.2)}$$

α (p, q | v) is the shortest distance between u and pair (p, q). Divisor of the sum, α (p, q) is the shortest distance between p and q. α (p, q) is the normalization factor. Summation is overall the connected pairs of vertices to vertex u. Vertex u and vertex pairs (p, q) are elements associated with $\mathcal{V}_u$ subset of vertices.

EXAMPLE 8.7

Figure 8.7 shows a multi-directed graph with 12 vertices (p, q, r, s, t, u, p′, q′, r′, s′, t′ and u′).

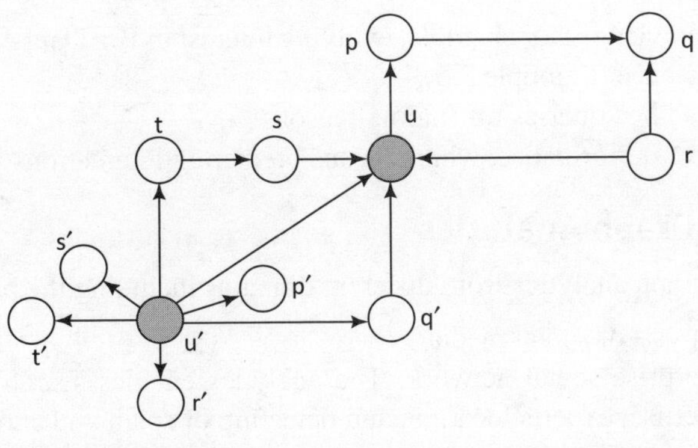

Figure 8.7 Graph with 12 vertices and 13 edges

(i) Compute order of the graph, in-degrees and out-degrees of u and u′, and 1st, 2nd, 3rd neighbourhoods of u.

(ii) Compute the centralities, closeness and betweenness using Eqs (8.1) and (8.2).

SOLUTION

(i) Order of the graph is given by number of vertices N_v = 12 and edges N_e = 13.
In-degrees of u = 4. Out-degrees of u = 1. In-degrees of u′ = 0. Out-degrees of u′ = 7
1st neighbourhood of u = 5 (p, q′, r, s, u′).
2nd neighbourhood of u = 7 (p', q, r′, s′, t, t′, u′). [u connects by path traversal through two edges.]
3rd neighbourhoods of u =8 (p, p′, r, r′, s′, t, t′, u′). [u connects by path traversal through three edges.]

(ii) Centrality closeness of u, CC (u) computes as follows:
Distances with the five nearest neighbours, p, q′, r, s and u′ = 1 each. Distances with the seven next to nearest neighbours p′, q, r′, s′, t, t′ and u′ = 2 each. Therefore, C_C (u) = (1/5 + 2/7) = 0.48 using equation (8.1).
Centrality betweenness index C_B of u computes as follows:
Connected Number of vertices pairs = 8 [(u′, t′), (u′, s′), (u′, r′), (q, r), (p, q), (s, t), (q′, u′), (u′, p′)]
Shortest distances with eight nearest pairs = 1 each. No other pairs connect u with distance = 2.
Therefore, C_B = 8.

8.3.4 Choosing Graph Analytics

When does graph analytics help? Loshin[3] in a study suggests that graph analytics can help in business or other problems where the following characteristics require analysis:

1. Connectivity from the number of relationships and association types
2. Undirected unidentified patterns, undirected graph path traversal, discovering new unidentified pattern (for example, finding students of new batches opting for Natural Language Processing subject, or finding emerging pattern for cycling near the sea beach)
3. Missing pattern (for example, finding none of computer science student interested in financial analysis in an organization)
4. Discovering new knowledge [for example, evolving interest in Big Data Analytics course in students of UG Computer Science (Example 8.5)]
5. Analysis using the ad hoc queries for finding reasons
6. Predicting interactive performance, which means predicting interactions among entities on events.

8.3.5 Use Cases of Graph Analytics

Following are use cases of graph analytics from different domains including the business domain:

1. Monitoring and analysis of social media
2. Analysis of an enterprise social network: The analytics enables search of expertise, knowledge, recommending expertise, experts location, and detecting of spam and anomaly

[3]David Loshin, Big Data Analytics from Strategic Planning to Enterprise Integration with Tools, Techniques, NOSQL and Graph, Morgan Kaufmann, 2013

3. Financial analysis for undertaking the financial decisions, new knowledge discovery, security analysis, anomaly and fraud detection, such as credit card frauds and fake bill payments, account manipulations
4. Commerce and trade analysis for customer behaviour prediction, planning and strategies for sales promotion, price discovery, detecting weak supply chain links and commerce frauds
5. Cellular network analytics in telecom companies for increasing their operations or helping police to track criminals
6. Disease diagnostics, patient and disease analytics in healthcare studies, health care quality analysis, medicine research and development in genomics
7. Analyzes breaches in cyber security, location of breaches, detects denial of service (DoS) attack, and finds the attack sources.

Self-Assessment Exercise linked to LO 8.2

1. How does a network organization model the communications, collaborations and correlations using the graph? ○●●
2. How do the centrality parameters specify the degree, closeness and betweenness? Demonstrate using examples. ○●●
3. How does propagation of probability distribution function over the vertices enable decisions? When does the Bayesian network graph model the distribution of influence? ●●●
4. When is graph analytics used? ○○●

8.4 GRAPH ANALYTICS ALGORITHMS AND APPROACHES

LO 8.3

Graph parameters, methods, diagnostics, decisions, statistical model, StatsModel, and probabilities-based analytics, and technical complexities in analyzing the graphs

A graph model for data store provides additional information about associations. Graph analytics thus enables analysis of additional properties, besides the ones using standard RDBMS or data warehouse framework.

Following are examples of algorithms for graph analytics which relate associations of entities:

8.4.1 StatsModel and Probability Based Analytics

Centralities Parameters in Graphs

Computations of the centralities of entities in terms of (i) in-degree in nodes of directed graphs and (ii) out-degrees, (iii) distribution of degrees among the nodes, (iv) closeness, (v) betweenness, (vi) other parameters such as effective closeness, reputation, status and link rank. Degree of a node is the number of edges linked to a node. Node closeness to other vertices depends on the sum of distances with other vertices. Node betweenness relates to the number of pairing nodes. Node relations or connections are associated with the next node and with the previous node.

Computation of financial worth of a company uses three parameters of centralities. Another application is monitoring the attacks on the network.

Path and Flow Analysis of Graphs

Path and flow analysis algorithms analyze the shapes (triangles, hexagons, trees and junction trees), shortest paths and top-K shortest paths. Algorithm for triangles counting finds the number of triangular relationships among the nodes. Top-K shortest paths means finding distances of the multiple paths which connect the vertices and which have the shortest paths among top K. Value of K is 2, 3, 4 and so on for top-2, top-3, top-4 and so on.

Matching and Search Analytics in Graphs

An algorithm matches the graphs and subgraphs after a graph search on path traversals. A filter algorithm uses the label, vertex-property, edge-property or geographical location for filtering the graph vertices. Collaborative filtering algorithm also does the searches. Collaborative filtering means finding matches in a bipartite weighted graph.

A subgraph is graph whose vertices and edges are subset of another graph. A graph $\mathcal{G}_1 = (\mathcal{V}', \mathcal{E}')$ is a subgraph of graph $\mathcal{G} = (\mathcal{V}, \mathcal{E})$ if $\mathcal{V}' \subseteq \mathcal{V}$, and $\mathcal{E}' \subseteq \mathcal{E} \wedge ((v1, v2) \in \mathbf{E}' \rightarrow v1, v2 \in \mathbf{V}')$ in set theory notations.

[Set theory uses symbols as follows: Symbol (i) ⊆ is for 'subset of', for example **V′** is subset of **V**. (ii) ∧ is logic symbol for 'and'. (iii) ∈ is for 'element of' (for example v1, v2 ∈**V′** means v1 and v2 are elements of **V′**).

Collaborative Filtering (CF)

Collaborative Filtering (CF) is a technique used by recommender systems (Section 6.4.3). The system collects references or test information from many collaborating users. The system makes predictions about the interests of a user and then recommends to new users.

Detection of Clusters

Clustering analysis identifies the groups of special cases. For example, in a study of effect of discount offered in versus sales, the identification of clusters enables the price discovery. Another example, a system identifies a cluster of students with deep interest in Big Data analytics. This enables a department to start additional new course in that area.

Detection and Analysis of Patterns

Pattern detection and pattern analysis are required in many applications. For example, identifying patterns of sales increase after an advertisement of a car model. That helps a car company for planning future advertisement strategies. Graphical detection of patterns identifies new patterns, which may lead to new opportunities (for example in education, business or health care)

Anomaly Detection

Anomaly detection and analysis find the abnormal behaviour, structure, feature, content or semantic features. Anomaly detection may also help in its usability and summarising anomaly attributes. It enables identification of spam source and can lead to detect frauds related to credit card, medical claim or detecting fictitious transactions.

Community and Network Analysis

The community and network analysis analyses the close-by entities, and fully mesh-like connected sets. The network graph analysis besides the centralities analysis, also find *page rank* of the links.

Community and network analyses use triangle count, clustering coefficient, K-neighbourhood, connected component and K-core analysis parameters.

K-neighbourhood analysis means finding the number of 1st neighbour nodes, 2nd neighbour nodes and so on. (K = 1, 2, 3, 4 and so on).

K-core analysis means number of cores within a marked area. A core may consist of a triangle of connected vertices. A core may consist of a rectangle with interconnected edges and diagonals. A core may also be a group of cores.

PageRank Based Analytics

PageRank is a metric for importance of each vertex in a graph. Assume an edge from *v1* to *v2* represents endorsement of importance of *v2* by *v1* by a connection. The importance of *v1* results from the interactions between them by creating a relationship between them, sharing a belief or some other mean (Term PageRank borrows from web PageRank).

StatsModel and Probability Based Analytics

Statistical model is a class of mathematical models. It considers a set of assumptions for the sample data representing a larger population. A statistical model represents, often in considerably idealized form, the data generating process.

StatsModel refers to a Python module that provides classes and functions for estimation of many different statistical models, as well as for conducting statistical-tests, and exploring the statistical data.

Analysis of Big Data need reasoning and prediction under uncertainties. Uncertainty requires usages of probabilities and StatsModel. Many critical Big-Data graph analytics uses the inter-relationships between the entities. Graph based representations need learning of graph structure, computations of conditional independence, and probabilistic inference.

Diagnosis and Decisions based on Probabilistic Graphical Models

Bayesian networks or Markov networks are used in various applications, such as assessment of loan default risk. Graph analytics algorithm first convert the network into junction trees and then, performs the graph traversal. This is due to use of distributed file system in Big Data graph database. A network probabilistic graph-model needs intensive numeric operations.

Advanced Concepts in Probabilistic Graphical Models

Use of Junction Trees Graph (JTG) formed for the Bayesian Consider four nodes BNG with 2 states per node (Example 8.6). That needs $2^4 = 16$ CPT entries for four probable conditions at all four vertices when jointly considered.

Assume a fifteen node BNG with five states per node. Consider five states at each node in Example 8.6. Assume that five states of GPA awarded probabilities are P8+, P8–, P6+, P6– and P4–. That needs 5^{15} CPT table entries. Therefore, 5^{15} CPT entries for five probable conditions at all 15 vertices when jointly considered. Therefore, an algorithm first reduces the Bayesian network graph to a JTG using a junction tree algorithm (JTAl).[4]

[4] https://ocw.mit.edu/courses/electrical-engineering-and-computer-science/6-438-algorithms-for-inference-fall-2014/lecture-notes/MIT6_438F14_Lec14.pdf

The number of incoming directed edges connect at each junction. A junction tree is a one that has a root node at a junction, which has number of directed edges to a set of junctions (daughter nodes). Each daughter is again a junction, which has number of directed edges to a next set of junctions. Thus, a tree-like structure exists starting from the root.

JTAl is a machine learning algorithm. JTAl is also called clique tree method. The method extracts *marginalization in* general graphs. It propagates *belief* (*evidence* collected at the junction from number of connected nodes in the junction tree, also called *inference* from that tree). JTAl does the belief computations for each junction tree. Usage of JTG eliminates the cycles in traversals also.

Probabilistic inferences at junction trees Probabilistic representation of the distributions in terms of the CPTs is replaced by *inference* computed for each junction tree of JTG.An algorithm computes Potential Tables (POTs) which replace the use of CPTs for analyses.

Knowledge Discovery

Algorithms for graph analytics along with machine learning algorithms lead to new facts. They discover new associations during the analyses. They lead to discovery of new knowledge.

8.4.2 Technical Complexity in Analyzing Graphs

Big Data analytics has challenges due to need of compact representation and parallelism of the computations when large datasets execute on the clusters. Following are the technical complexities in the Graph analytics:

Graph-Partitioning Complexity

Triangularly connected nodes or similar structures of high connectivity may be of specific interests. Big Data analytics depend on the distribution of data in HDFS-like files or distributed DBs. High connectivity structures pose the problem of partitioning and data sharding. When the data structures have such problems, the network access intervals increase significantly performance of the algorithm also reduces.

Graph-memory Accesses Unpredictability

Big Data analytics need parallelization of computations. Several path traversals thus initiate at the same instance. However, due to sequential node links through the edges, each path traversal follows a sequence of nodes.

Many traversals are necessary when finding new patterns. Poor locality and irregular memory accesses are the problems. The memory access times are unpredictable for each paralleled traversal. Much time is thus lost in accessing memory.

Analytics Problems and Topologies

Graph characteristics may inhibit the need of scalability due to performance issues. The large graphs and number of topological structures result in complexities.

Dynamic Interactions for Graphs

The dynamic computations enable update of cluster and subgraph. Graphs in a Big Data application need dynamic analysis of data with 3Vs characteristic. Therefore, rapid response issues are complex in case of dynamic interactions. Computations in dynamic graphs have poor locality and unpredictable access times from memory. The workload is also hybrid (sequential and parallel).

Self-Assessment Exercise linked to LO 8.3

1. How do the additional information about associations enable new parameters from analytics besides the one using standard RDBMS? ○○●
2. What are the graph parameters derived from graph analytics? Write equations for each of them. ○●●
3. Recapitulate Figure 6.9. How do the cluster results from the graph databases provide additional information compared to results shown in the figure? ●●●
4. How does graph-partitioning problem result in technical complexity during graph analytics? ○●●

8.5 Spark GraphX PLATFORM

LO 8.4

Apache Spark GraphX, its features, architecture and components, and their applications for graph-analytics

IBM System G offers a set of Big Data tools for graph computations. **G** (stands for graph, which may be a property graph, Bayesian network graph, or cognitive network graph. A graph may be static or dynamic, small or large, topological or semantic. G has library functions for graph analytics. G applications include creating and analyzing the database, visualization and middleware for graph.

Apache Spark GraphX is open source software that provisions a number of functions and operators for graph stored in HDFS environment. *Apache Spark* refers to a multi-component platform for Big Data computing that uses data store at a HDFS file system, HDFS compatible data sources, such as HBase, Cassandra, Ceph or S3. Spark enables the use of data frames in *Resilient Distributed Datasets (RDD)* (Section 5.4.2), and the creation of ETL pipelines (Section 5.5). An RDD is a collection of objects distributed on many computing nodes. Spark standard APIs enable creation of application APIs in Scala, Java, R and Python (Chapter 5).

Graph analytics need functions which compute degree centralities, degree distribution, separation of degrees, betweenness centralities, closeness centralities, neighbourhoods, strongly connected components, PageRank, shortest path, Breadth First Search (BFS), minimum spanning tree (forest), spectral clustering and cluster coefficient.

The following subsections describe Spark GraphX Architecture, fundamental operators, algorithms and their applications for graph analytics.

8.5.1 Features of a Graph Analytics Platform—Apache SparkGraphX

Apache Spark provides a software component known as GraphX. GraphX 2.2.1 released on December 01 2017 is a new version. GraphX is an open source tool for graphs and parallel computations for graphs. GraphX tool processes a Resilient Distributed Graph (RDG). GraphX tool is a stack component of BDAS (Section 1.6.4.3).

GraphX provides a set of fundamental operators such as `subgraph`, `joinVertices` and *aggregateMessages*. Apache GraphX provides for computations using the property graphs. Identifier in GraphX is 16-bit long unique-key. Edges have vertexIDs for corresponding source-destination paths.

GraphX programming features are:

1. Includes a growing collection of graph algorithms and graph creator operators (builders)[5]

[5] http://spark.apache.org/docs/latest/graphx-programming-guide.html#graph-builders

2. Extends the Spark for computing with Resilient Distributed Dataset (RDD) (Section 5.4.2). Graph builders do not repartition the edges by default, they are left in their default partitions (such as their original blocks in HDFS).
3. Introduces a new abstraction of graph called directed multigraph which has properties associated with each of the vertex and edge.
4. Provides several ways of building a graph; a graph builds from a collection of (**V**, **E**) [set of vertices and edges] in an RDD or on disk
5. Gives high performance and competes with the fastest graph systems
6. Retains features of Spark, ease in uses, flexibility, and fault tolerance
7. Unifies computations using iterative Graph, ETL, exploratory analysis within the GraphX because of association with Spark, PySpark, as well as StatsModel
8. View data, in the same manner as a graph and as a collection
9. Provides an optimized variant of the Pregel APIs
10. Enables writing of user defined iterative graph algorithms using the Pregel

Figure 8.8 shows GraphX architecture.

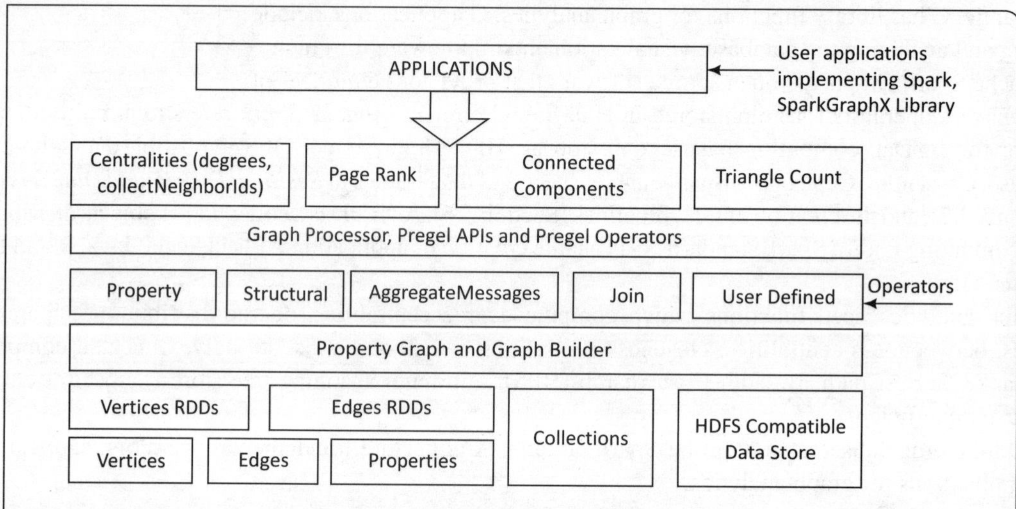

Figure 8.8 GraphX Architecture

GraphX operators

GraphX aggregation operator, page rank, connected components and triangle-counting algorithms do the following:

1. **Aggregation** operator—Several graph analysis tasks require aggregation of information about the neighbourhood of each vertex. Many iterative graph algorithms repeatedly aggregate properties of neighbouring vertices. Examples are computing the shortest path to a source, smallest reachable vertex id, connected components and PageRank. The operator applies a user defined sendMsg function to each *edge triplet* in the graph. Then, application uses the mergeMsg function, which aggregates those messages at their destination vertex.

2. **Pregel** operator—executes in a series of supersteps in which vertices receive the sum of their inbound messages from the previous superstep. (Superstep is a term used in Pregel vertex-centric processing in large distributed graphs. Supersteps do computations consisting of a sequence of iterations.) The operator computes fresh value for property at vertex. Then, that sends messages to the neighbouring vertices in the next superstep. GraphX Pregel-API provides computation of messages in parallel as a function of the edge triplet. A message for computation provide accesses to both attributes of source and destination vertices. When a vertex does not receive a message that is skipped within a superstep, the Pregel operator terminates the iteration and returns the final graph when no messages remain. Pregel operator in GraphX is a bulk-synchronous parallel-messaging abstraction that constrains to graph topology.
3. **PageRank** algorithm—Assume that an edge from v1 to v2 represents an endorsement of importance of v2 by v1. The function measures the importance of each vertex in a graph. For example, if many students opt for a teacher's course, then, teacher's rank is high. If many followers follow a twitter account then that account rank is high. Similarly, a web page is searched by many then that page rank is high. GraphX computes PageRank statically as well as dynamically. Term PageRank is from Google web PageRanking system for searches (Refer Section 9.4.3 also).
4. **ConnectedComponents** algorithm—labels each connected component of the graph with the ID. Each connected component ID is an identifier of the lowest-numbered vertex. For example, in a social network, connected component objects can approximate clusters. GraphX contains an implementation of the algorithm for the ConnectedComponentsObject.

The function `graph.connectedComponents().vertices` computes the connected components of the datasets (for example, student-teacher datasets, and social network datasets).

1. **Degree Computation Objects**: Functions `graph.inDegrees.reduce(max); graph.outDegrees.reduce(max); graph.degrees.reduce(max);` computes in-degree, out-degree and degrees in a graph. These functions analyze the degree distribution also at the vertices.
2. **Collection neighbour Ids and neighbours Operators**: The functions `collectNeighborIds(edgeDirection: EdgeDirection); collectNeighbors(edgeDirection: EdgeDirection)`
3. **Triangle Count** Algorithm—Determines the number of triangles passing through each vertex. The count is a measure of clustering. A vertex is part of a triangle when it has two adjacent vertices with an edge between them. TriangleCount **requires the edges to be in canonical orientation** (srcId < dstId) [Source vertex ID is `srcID` and Destination vertex ID is `dstID`.]. Graph is partitioned using `Graph.partitionBy` operator. The function `graph.triangleCount().vertices` counts the triangles formed by vertices.

Super step (*ss*) is a set of steps performed. The following steps may take place in the framework during a superstep:

(i) Receives and reads the messages that previous superstep *ss* – 1 had sent to v
(ii) Applies a user-defined function $f_{udf}()$ to each vertex in parallel, therefore, $f_{udf}()$ essentially specifies the behaviour of single vertex *v* at a single superstep *ss*
(iii) Can mutate the state of *v*
(iv) Can send the messages to other vertices (for example, along outgoing edges) that the vertices will receive in the next superstep *ss* + 1.

Pregel approach is that all communications [such a variable increment, aggregation, or applying $f_{udf}()$] takes place between *ss* and *ss* + 1. The same $f_{udf}()$ applies within each *ss* to all the vertices in parallel.

Property Operators in Class Graph [VD, ED] are `mapVertices [VD2](), mapEdges [ED2](), mapTriplets [ED2]()`}. These functions yield a new Graph.

Structural operators in Class Graph [VD, ED] use `subgraph()`, `mask()` and `groupEdges()`. Function `reverse()` returns a new graph with all directions reversed.

The function graph.apply() creates a graph from RDDs of vertices. Apply function arguments are `edges. vertices: RDD [(VertexId, VD)]; edges: RDD [Edge[ED]];` and `defaultVertexAttr: VD = null)`

Join Operator

Graph databases supports JOIN (Section 3.2). **Join Operator** joins the data from external collections (RDDs) with the graphs. Also, a function merges extra properties with an existing graph. Main join functions are `joinVertices` and `outerJoinVertices()`. The `joinVertices` joins the vertices with the input RDD and returns a new graph with the vertex properties obtained by applying the user.

Many examples are available at Github site[6], which demonstrate uses of GraphX functions. These examples guide the development of codes for Big Data graph analytics.

Page Rank Analytics

GraphX provides static and dynamic implementations of PageRank as methods of the PageRank object: `ranksByUsername =users.join(ranks).map {case (id, (username, rank)) => (username, rank)}`. A GraphX operation runs static PageRank for a fixed number of iterations.

The dynamic PageRank runs until the ranks converge. The run stops when the rank does not change by more than a specified tolerance. GraphOps enables calling these algorithms directly as methods on graph. The function `graph.pageRank(0.0001).vertices` does the following: When page ranking does not change during the run beyond the specified tolerance 0.0001 (1 in 10000) then the iterative process stops and the rank value converge.

The following explains the use of PageRank method on graph model for network organization of students modeled as a graph.

EXAMPLE 8.8

Consider a graph model for a network organization of students modeled as a graph. Some student's text-notes are widely exchanged with strongly connected ones compared to the others. Assume that set of students are in a file data/graphx/students.txt and a set of relationships between students is given in data/graphx/stronglyConnected.txt. What are the steps for PageRank computations for each student?

SOLUTION

(i) Import GraphLoader using the program statement given below:

```
importorg.apache.spark.graphx.GraphLoader
```

[6] https://github.com/apache/spark/blob/master/examples/src/main/scala/org/apache/spark/examples/graphx

(ii) Load the graph edges using program statement as follows:

```
val graph = GraphLoader.edgeListFile(sc,"data/graphx/stronglyConnected.
txt")
```

Here, sc stands for Spark Context.

(iii) Compute PageRank and get each student page rank from the text file using program statement as follows:

```
val ranks = graph.pageRank(0.0001).vertices
```

PageRank method runs using Pregel operator graph.pageRank( ).vertices and does bulk-synchronous parallel messaging over the vertices to compute the ranks of the vertices. (Message in present case is for computing the rank.)

The Pregel operator executes in a series of supersteps in which vertices receive the *sum* of their inbound messages from the previous superstep. Pregel computes using sequence of iterations till rank converges within specified tolerance.

(iv) Find students from the text file using program statement as follows:

```
val Students = sc.textFile("data/graphx/students.txt").map {line=>
val fields = line.split(",") (fields(0).toLong, fields(1))}
```

(v) Join the ranks of the students and map them with the username and rank. Use program statement as follows:

```
val ranksByUsername = students.join(ranks).map {case(id, (username, rank))
=> (username, rank)}
```

(vi) Print the results after making the strings separated by new lines using the program statement as follows:

```
println(ranksByUsername.collect().mkString("\n"))
```

8.5.2 Dedicated Appliances for Graph

Graph analytics can use the Berkeley Data Analytics Stack (BDAS) (Section 1.6.4.3), can use GraphX (Section 8.5.1), IBM System G[2], NativeDB[1], or the appliances dedicated for the graph-analytics.

A dedicated appliance is a computing platform for in-memory graph computing and native multi-threaded (MT) processing. In-memory graph computing means computing using data first taken into RAM memory from the data blocks which store the Big Data. Native MT processing means multiple program-threads processing at the platform in place processing at the cluster of data nodes. The appliance thus provides the faster IOs and results in very high performance in Big Data environment.

Dedicated appliances for graph are fully software based. They run graph analytics application on the existing server/cloud. They use triples based RDF format. They process using SPARQL query language.

Self-Assessment Exercise linked to LO 8.4

1. How do the Spark GraphX component enable Big Data analytics and high performance parallel computations? ○○●

2. How do property graph and directed multigraph provisioned in GraphX? ○●●
3. What are the uses of subgraph, joinVertices and aggregateMessages, PageRank, ConnectedComponents and Triangle Count algrorithms? ●●●
4. Describe usages of Pregel API and operator for iterative computing on the RDG datasets. ○○●
5. How does GraphX unify iterative Graph computation, ETL, exploratory analysis within GraphX? ○●●

KEY CONCEPTS

aggregation
anomaly
association
Bayesian network
BDAS
belief propagation
betweenness
centrality
closeness
clustering
collaboration
connected component
connectivity model
correlation
CPT
degree distribution
Directed Acrylic Graph
directed graph
directed graph in-degree
directed graph out-degree
directed multigraph
distance
edge
evidence propagation
flow analysis
graph
graph analytics
graph database
graph edge
graph model
graph node
graph partitioning
graph traversal
GraphX
GUDF
GVUDF
IBM system G
influence
instance identifier
interaction modeling
join
junction tree
knowledge discovery
Markov network
native data store
NativeDB
neighbourhood
node
node association
node centrality
node degree
node distance
node neighbourhood
nodes betweenness
nodes closeness
order of graph
PageRank
path
path analysis
path expression
path recursion
path traversal
pattern
potential table
predictive analytics
Pregel API
probabilistic graph
probability
probability distribution
probability states
propagation function
Property Graph
property h
rank
RDBMS
RDF
RDFLib
RDG
relationship
risk assessment
semantic database
Spark
SPARQL
StatsModel
subgraph
triangle count
triple
Triplestore
UDF
URI
vertex
vertexID
VUDF
W3C standard

Learning Outcomes

LO 8.1

1. Graph models the data stores and databases. A semantic database creates from a collection of triples. Triples format is similar to subject-predicate-object format in English sentences.
2. RDF is W3C standard triple format, *instance identifier-property name-property value.* A *URI* represents the identifier.
3. Two features of graph databases are as follows: A graph (i) can add additional properties with each triple relationship, association and attribute, and (ii) can include new entities and relationships, just as a tabular database adds additional rows, or columnar-family database adds more columns.
4. Nodes in graph are easy to navigate through traversing the paths using nodes (entities) or edges (relationships).
5. NativeDB provides fast execution as compared to other graphDBs.
6. Property graph model is used when relationships and properties also store in the database.

LO 8.2

1. A graph also models a network organization, such as social media and web links. A Graph models the connections, communications, collaborations, influences, correlations and distances between the entities.
2. Probabilistic graphical models, such as Bayesian networks or Markov networks have several applications. Graph models a Bayesian network organization, which uses directed graph, non-reversal paths and cycles. Graph models a Markov network organization that have undirected graph, can have reversal paths and cycles.
3. Three types of graph analytics are (i) finding matches and performing searches, (ii) topological analysis, for example analyzing the centralities, degree, closeness and betweenness, and (iii) paths between vertices and flow of properties, such as probabilities.

LO 8.3

1. Graph analytics algorithms enable the determination of centralities of entities in terms of the (i) directed graphs in-degree, (ii) out-degree at the nodes, (iii) degrees distribution of the nodes, (iv) closeness, (v) betweenness, (vi) parameters such as effective closeness, reputation, status and link rank.
2. Graph analytics algorithms enable path analysis, detection of clusters, find anomaly, detection of patterns, communities and perform network analysis. Graph analytics algorithms enable diagnostics and decisions making from computations of conditional probability tables, junction trees graph, inferences, evidences or beliefs and potential tables.
3. Big data store in distributed database environment presents technical difficulties due to sequential path traversals resulting in graph partitioning problems, and the slower responses from memory during parallel execution of the queries.

LO 8.4

1. Apache GraphX is (i) software of Spark for graphs, (ii) creates and computes Resilient Distributed Graphs (RDG), and (iii) does parallel computations, which give the high performance, thus competes with the

fastest graph analytics system. GraphX has features of Spark, such as ease of use, flexibility and fault tolerance.

2. Apache GraphX provides for creations and operations on property graphs. Identifier in GraphX is 16-bit long unique key. Edges have corresponding source and destination vertexIDs.
3. GraphX introduces new graph abstraction, directed multigraph, GraphX library of a set of fundamental operators, such as subgraph, joinVertices and aggregateMessages and inclusion of PageRank, ConnectedComponents, and TriangleCount algorithms.
4. GraphX unifies iterative graph computation, ETL and exploratory analysis using Pregel API and operator.

Objective Type Questions

Select one correct-answer option for each questions below:

8.1 A way of defining the centrality of a node in reference to other nodes, use (i) metrics. Metrics for centrality of a node are (ii) degree, (iii) closeness, (iv) betweenness, or other characteristics of the node such as (v) rank, (vi) belief, (vii) influence, (viii) expectation, (ix) evidence, (x) reputation, and (xi) status of a node. ○○●

(a) all except ii and vi (b) all vi and xi
(c) all except ii, iii, iv and vi to x (d) all

8.2 (i) Each DAG node represents a variable, traverses in one direction only along the edges with no cyclic traversals. (ii) When each node in a directed graph has no cyclic traversals then the directed graph is also called acyclic graph, (iii) directed multigraph provisions multiple parallel edges and that enables multiple relationships between two entities, (iv) Bayesian network graph in each node represents a random variable in an undirected graph. The variable has probabilistic distribution over the connected nodes. Cyclic path traversals takes place in a BNG, and (v) each Markov network graph node represents a random variable in a DAG and that variable has probabilistic distribution over the connected nodes, and no cyclic path traversal takes place. ●●●

(a) all except ii (b) i to iv
(c) i to iii (d) all

8.3 (i) Graph model can represent a hierarchy, which the sequence of columns does not specify. Graph (ii) triple format is subject-predicate-object, (iii) triple format can be instance *identifier-property name-property value,* (iv) identifier uses a Universal Resource Indicator (URI) in RDF, (v) SPARQL is query language for (vi) RDF, and (vii) RDD. (viii) Graph database can add additional properties of each triple relationship, association and attribute. ○●●

(a) all except vii (b) all except i and vii
(c) i to vi (d) all except iv

8.4 (i) Property graph model does not show relationships and associations. (ii) Tables in RDBMS represent the relationships or associations, (iii) An RDF data file is similar to three columns in triples: subject, predicate and object, and (iv) also similar to document-key-value pairs in MongoDB. (v) RDF schema standard declares the classes and relationships between properties and classes, and (vi) RDF does not depend on a schema and is thus flexible. ○○●

(a) all except i and ii (b) all except iii
(c) all except iii to v (d) all except iv and vi

8.5 Graph model of a network organization can help in the followings tasks: (i) detect patterns, (ii) finding inherent organization in the network, (iii) communities and micro-communities modeling, (iv) connectivity modeling, (v) collaboration modeling, (vi) influence modeling, ○●●

(vii) belief propagation, (viii) distance modeling, (ix) closeness computations, and (x) betweenness computations.
(a) all except vii and viii (b) all
(c) all except vii (d) All except vi to viii

8.6 Use cases of graph analytics are (i) enterprise-network analysis (ii) social network analytics (iii) expertise search, (iv) knowledge recommendation, (v) expertise location, (vi) anomaly detection, (vii) Spam detection, (viii) financial analysis for financial decisions, (ix) health care quality analysis, and (x) detection of cyber security breaches. ○○●
(a) all except vii (b) all except i
(c) all (d) i to viii

8.7 (i) K-neighbourhood analysis means the number of 1st neighbour nodes, 2nd neighbour nodes, and so on. (K = 1, 2, 3, 4 and so on), (ii) The community and network analysis analyzes the (iii) close-by entities, (iv) fully mesh-like unconnected sets, (v) network graph analysis beside centralities, (vi) also does computations of the *property* of the links, (vii) rectangle counts, and (viii) clustering coefficient. ●●●
(a) i to vi (b) all
(c) ii to iv (d) i to iii, v, viii

8.8 (i) Apache Spark new stack component is GraphX 2.2.1. GraphX (ii) is a Linux based open source tool for graphs, (iii) does the graph parallel computations, (iv) creates and computes Redundant Distributed Graph (RDG), and (v) provides a set of fundamental operators such as *subgraph*, *joinVertices,* and *aggregateMessages*. GraphX (vi) does not have functions for property graphs, (vii) uses 64-bit long unique key as identifier, (viii) is a part of BDAS architecture, and (ix) have Edges and corresponding source and destination vertexIDs. ○●●
(a) i, v to ix (b) all except ii, iv, vi, vii
(c) all except ii and ix (d) all

8.9 (i) The Pregel operator in GraphX is a bulk synchronous parallel messaging abstraction, (ii) with no constrains to the topology of the graph, (iii) the Pregel operator executes in a series of supersteps in which (iv) vertices receive the *sum* of their inbound messages from the (v) previous step. (vi) Superstep is a term used in Pregel edge-centric processing in large distributed graphs, and (vii) Pregel does computations consisting of a sequence of iterations. ●●●
(a) iii, vi and vii (b) all except ii
(c) all except ii and vi (d) all

8.10 ConnectedComponents algorithm in GraphX (i) labels each connected component of the graph with the ID, (ii) each connected component ID is ID of lowest numbered vertex. (iii) Connected component objects can approximate as clustersing a social network, and (iv) GraphX contains an implementation of (v) ConnectedComponentsObject in the algorithm. ○○●
(a) all (b) all except i
(c) all except ii (d) i to iv

Review Questions

8.1 How are the characteristics of a graph parameterized using the centrality parameters? **(LO 8.1)** ○○●

8.2 What are the benefits of modeling Data Store as a graph? What are the benefits of graph databases compared to RDBMS? **(LO 8.1)** ○●●

8.3 List the differences between the RDF and NativeDB for graph Data Stores. **(LO 8.1)** ○●●

8.4 How does a graph model a network organization? **(LO 8.2)** ○○●

8.5 When does a graph model a Bayesian network organization? **(LO 8.2)** ○●●

8.6 Explain the uses of graph analytics for (i) finding matches and performing searches and (ii) topological analysis, for example analyzing centralities, degree, closeness and betweenness and (iii) path and flow analysis. **(LO 8.2)** ●●●

8.7 How are path analysis, clustering detection, anomaly and patterns detection, communities and network analysis used in applications? **(LO 8.3)** ○●●

8.8 What are the technical complexities in Big Data graph analytics? **(LO 8.3)** ○○●

8.9 How are conditional probability tables in Bayesian network organization graph computed? What are the limitations of using CPTs? How do Potential tables differ from CPTs? **(LO 8.3)** ●●●

8.10 How do the probability and StatsModel based analytics of graphs enable diagnostics and decisions making from computations of conditional probability tables, junction trees graph, inferences, evidences or beliefs, and the potential tables? **(LO 8.3)** ●●●

8.11 What are the operators provided at Apache Spark GraphX architecture? What are their uses? **(LO 8.4)** ○●●

8.12 How does a property graph build using GraphX operators? **(LO 8.4)** ○○●

8.13 Describe functions of subgraph, joinVertices and aggregateMessages operators in GraphX. **(LO 8.4)** ○○●

8.14 What are the applications of GraphX PageRank, ConnectedComponents and Triangle Count Algorithms? **(LO 8.4)** ●●●

Practice Exercises

8.1 Recapitulate Practice Exercise 5.5. (i) Draw the property graph model for the product categories, names and IDs and (ii) Create GraphDB using the triples representing the graph in triple 'subject-predicate-object' format, and (iii) Create GraphDB in RDF; instance identifier-property name-property value format;

Table of Product categories, ProductId and Product name

ProductCategory	ProductId	ProductName
Toy_Airplane	10725	Lost Temple
Toy_Airplane	31047	Propeller Plane
Toy_Airplane	31049	Twin Spin Helicopter
Toy_Train	31054	Blue Express
Toy_Train	10254	Winter Holiday Toy_Train

(LO 8.1) ●●●

8.2 Make an RDF format database for nodes, edges and properties given in Example 8.3. **(LO 8.1)** ○○●

8.3 Recapitulate Example 8.5 for property graph of database of Students, semester, subject options, grades and teachers. Create an RDF data file using the graph shown in Figure 8.4. **(LO 8.1)** ○●●

8.4 Create RDF and Native Data Store for *Yearly_Car_Sales* given by following triples: ○●●

Subject	Predicate	Object
Jaguar Land Rover Sale (JLRDS)	is	8000
Hexa Sale (HDS)	is	12000
Zest Sales (ZDS)	equals	160000
Nexon Sale (NDS)	equals	200000
Safari Storme Sale (SSDS)	equals	24000

(LO 8.1)

8.5 Draw a property graph model for the RDF created in Practice Exercise 8.4 for *Yearly_Car_Sales*. **(LO 8.1)** ○○●

8.6 Draw network organization for property graph shown in Figure 8.4. **(LO 8.2)** ●●●

8.7 Consider 12 participants in a network, represented by vertices V1, V2, …, up to V11 and V12. Draw a figure for a network organization using graph model (i) where V2, V5, V8, V9 follows V1, (ii) where V8 to V12 follows V2, (iv) V1 to V3, V6 to V9 follows V4, (v) V3, V5 follows V8, and (vi) V10, V11, V12 follows only first neighbours. **(LO 8.2)** ○○●

8.8 Find the in-degrees and out-degrees of each vertex. Describe the steps to find centralities metrics of betweenness and closeness. Use figure drawn in Practice Exercise 8.7. **(LO 8.3)** ●●●

8.9 Describe steps to compute the triangles, junction trees, shortest paths, and top K-shortest paths in graph drawn in Practice Exercise 8.7 for V1, V2, …, V11 and V12. **(LO 8.3)** ○●●

8.10 List the steps for creating text file data/graphx/students.txt and a set of relationships between students is given in data/graphx/stronglyConnected.txt. Use Figure 8.4. **(LO 8.4)** ○●●

8.11 Write the program statements in GraphX for calculating in-degrees and out-degrees of each vertex. Describe the steps in GraphX to find centralities metrics of betweenness and closeness using text files created in Practice Exercise 8.10. **(LO 8.4)** ●●●

8.12 List the differences between SparkGraphX and IBM System G. **(LO 8.4)** ○●●

Chapter 9

Text, Web Content, Link, and Social Network Analytics

LEARNING OBJECTIVES

After studying this chapter, you will be able to:

- **LO 9.1** Use the methods of text mining and machine learning (ML)— Naïve-Bayes classifier, and support vector machines for text analytics
- **LO 9.2** Get knowledge and use the methods of mining the web-links, web-structure and web-contents, and analyzing the web graphs
- **LO 9.3** Get knowledge and use methods of PageRanking, analysis of web-structure, and discovering hubs, authorities and communities in web-structure
- **LO 9.4** Get concepts representing social networks as graphs, social network analysis methods, finding the clustering in social network graphs, evaluating the SimRank, counting triangles (cliques) and discovering the communities

RECALL FROM EARLIER CHAPTERS

Graph Data Stores consist of various interconnected data nodes (Section 3.3.5). Models of graph and graph network organization describe the entities and objects, along with their relationships, associations and properties (Sections 8.2 and 8.3). Web and social-network graphs are examples of Graph network organization.

Graph structure analytics discovers the degree of interactions, closeness, betweenness, ranks, influences, probabilities distribution, beliefs and potentials. Analysis of the community and network discovers the *close-by* entities and fully mesh like connected sets. Network graph analyzes centralities, and computes the PageRank of the links (Section 8.4 and 8.5).

9.1 INTRODUCTION

Text Analytics often termed as 'text mining' refers to analyzing and extracting the meanings, patterns, correlations and structure hidden in unstructured and semi-structured textual data. Text data stores consist of strong temporal dimensions, have modularity over time and sources, such as topics and sentiments.

Methods of machine-learning are prevalent in text analytics also. For example, when a user books an air-flight ticket using a tablet or desktop, the user receives an SMS on the mobile about details of the booking and flight timings. An ML algorithm, such as *Windows Crotona* at the mobile reads and learns by itself from the SMSs received at the phone. *Crotona* uses the ML for the SMS text analysis.. Learning results in SMS alerts to the user. An alert is reminder a day before the flight. Another alert is two hours before the flight, about the need to reach the airport. Those alerts are system-generated without prior request from the user.

The reader is required to know the meaning of the following select key terms:

Vector refers to an entity with number of interrelated elements. For example, a data point consists of n-elements in an n-dimensional space, and represents a vector to that point from the origin in the space. A word is a vector of characters as the elements. Consider a vector representation of word 'McGraw-Hill', then vector $\mathbf{V}_{MH}$ = [M, c, G, r, a, w, -, H, i, l, l]. V_{MH} is vector of 11 elements (characters) that refers to word McGraw-Hill.

Feature refers to a set of properties associated with an entity, object or category. For example, feature of properties, such as description of data analysis, data cleaning, data visualization and other topics in a book on data analytics.

Category refers to a classification on the basis of set of distinct features (for example, a category of text, document, cars, toys, students, news or fruits).

Label refers to a name assigned to a category, for example to sports-news, latest data analytics books.

Dimension refers to a number of associated values, features or states, along the distinct spaces (dimensions). For example, a sentence has a number of words, each word has a number of characters, each word may have a feature, and so the sentences are in a three-dimensional space. Two dimensions are in metric spaces, which mean values in quantifiable spaces, such as the number of words, probability of occurrences in sentences, etc. Third dimension is in feature space, measured by a feature such as noun, verb, adverb, preposition, punctuation marks and stop word.

Another example is *apples*. Metric space variables are values, such as variables n, *number of apples* of specific properties, and P the *probability of preferring* apples of specific properties. Assume, feature space variables are four properties, *colour*, *shape*, *type* and *freshness*. Metric parameters and properties of apples are said to be in six-dimensional space, two are metric space (n and P) and four are feature space.

Graph data model refers to the data modelled by a set of entities. The entities identify by vertices $\mathcal{V}$. A set of relations or associations identifies by edges $\mathcal{E}$. An edge ***e*** represents a relation or association between two entities. Nodes represent the entities in the graph. The model also represents a hierarchy between the parent and children nodes.

Graph data network organization refers to a structure created by organizing entities or objects in a network, such as social network, business network and student network. A network organization means where persons or entities interconnect with each other, and have areas of common interest, business or study. A graph enables ease in traversing from one entity, person or web page link to another in the network by following a path. Web graph and social network graph enable such analysis. A graph network organization models the web and social networks. Examples of social networks are SlideShare, LinkedIn, Facebook and Twitter. The analytics of social networks finds the link ranks, clusters and correlations. The analytics discovers hubs and communities.

Web content mining refers to the discovery of useful information from web documents and services. Search engines use web content mining. A search provides the links of the required information to the user.

Hyperlinks refer to links mentioned in the contents that enable the retrieval of contents at web, file, object or resources repository.

Link analytics means web structure mining of hyperlinks between web documents. The analytics of links and analyzing them for metrics such as page ranks, clusters, correlations, hubs and communities.

Count triangles Algorithm is an algorithm that finds a number of triangular relationships among the nodes. Triangular relationships mean interrelations between each other.

Graph node centrality metric means the centrality of a node in reference to other nodes using certain metrics. Metrics used for centrality of a node are degree, closeness, betweenness or other characteristics of the node, such as rank, belief, potential, expectation, evidence, reputation or status.

Degree centrality of a node refers to the number of direct connections. Having more number of direct connections is not always a better metric. Better measure is the fact that the connection directs to significant results and tell how the nodes connect to the isolated node.

Betweenness centrality is a measure that provides the extent to which a node lies on paths between other nodes. A node with high betweenness signifies high influence over what flows in the network indicating importance of link and single point of failure.

Closeness centrality is the degree to which a node is near all other nodes in a network (directly or indirectly). It reflects the ability to access information through the network.

The present Chapter focuses on text, web, contents, structure and social network graph analytics. Section 9.2 describes text mining and usage of ML techniques—Naïve-Bayes analysis and support vector machines (SVMs) for analyzing text. Section 9.3 describes web mining, methods to implement the system, and analyzing the web graphs.

Section 9.4 describes PageRank methods, web structure analytics and finding the hubs and communities. Section 9.5 describes social network analysis, representation of social networks as graphs and computational methods of finding the clustering in social network graphs, evaluating the SimRank, counting triangles (cliques) and discovering the communities.

This chapter follows a method of notations as mentioned earlier in Section 6.1 for fonts when absolute value, mean value, function value, vector element or set member, entity or variable when these denote by a character or character-set. This chapter follows the notations for the probabilities, earlier specified in Section 8.3.2. Condition probability P specifies as P $(x_i|c_k)$ which means probability of variable $x = x_i$ at condition $c = c_k$.

9.2 TEXT MINING

LO 9.1

Methods of text mining and machine learning (ML)—Naïve-Bayes classifier, and support vector machines for text analytics

Today, large amounts of textual data is generated in computing applications. Text stream arriving continuously over time generates text data. For example, news articles, news reports, online comments on news, online traffic reports, corporate reports, web searches, and contents at social media discussion-forums (such as LinkedIn, Twitter and Facebook), short messages on phones, chat messages, transcripts of phone conversations, blogs and e-mails.

The abundance of textual data leads to problems which relate to their collection, exploration and ways of leveraging data. Textual data presents challenges for computing and storage requirements, consists of a strong temporal dimension, has modularity over time and have sources such as topics and sentiments. Examples of text processing techniques are clustering analysis, classifications, evolution analysis and event detection. Following subsections describe text mining in details:

9.2.1 Text Mining

Three definitions are:

1. "The process of extracting the useful data from any standard language text is called text mining. Data, for example our text messages, files, this book, emails, etc, are all written in standard language text. Taking out the required data is text mining. It is also known as text data mining. "
2. "Text mining is the process of discovering and extracting knowledge from unstructured data." (National Center of Text Mining—The University of Manchester[1])
3. "Text mining is the process of analyzing collections of textual contents in order to capture key concepts themes, uncover hidden relationships, and discover the trends without requiring that you know the precise words or terms that authors have used to express those concepts." (IBM[2])

Applications of text mining in business domains are predicting stock movements from analysis of company results, decision making for product and innovations developed at the company and contextual advertising. Some other applications are (i) mail filtering (spam), (ii) drug action reports (iii) fraud detection (iv) knowledge management, and (iv) social media data analysis.

The applications provide innovative and insightful results. The results when combined with other data sources, find the answers to the following:

(i) Two terms which occur together
(ii) Information linkage with another information
(iii) Different categories that can be created from extracted information
(iv) Prediction of information or categories.

9.2.1.1 Text Mining Overview

Text mining includes extraction of high-quality information, discovering and extracting knowledge, and revealing patterns and relationships from unstructured data available in the form of text.

The term *text analytics* evolves from provisioning of strong integration with the already existing database technology, artificial intelligence, machine learning, data mining and text Data Store techniques. Information retrieval, natural language processing (NLP), classification, clustering and knowledge management are some of such useful techniques. Figure 9.1 shows process-pipeline in text-analytics.

9.2.1.2 Areas and Applications of Text Mining

Natural Language Processing (NLP) is a technique for analyzing, understanding and deriving meaning from human language. NLP involves the computer's understanding and manipulation of human language.

[1] http://www.nactem.ac.uk/brochure/NaCTeM_Brochure.pdf
[2] https://www.ibm.com/support/knowledgecenter/en/SS3RA7_18.1.1/ta_guide_ddita/textmining/shared_entities/tm_intro_tm_defined.html

NLP algorithms are typically based on ML algorithms. They automatically learn the rules. First, they analyze set of examples from a large collection of sentences in a book. Then, they make the statistical inferences.

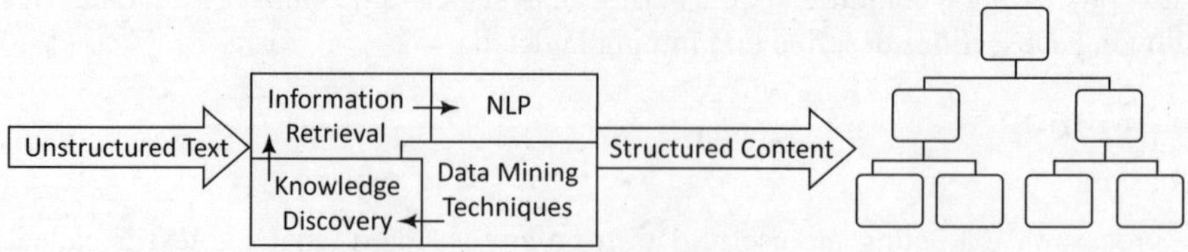

Figure 9.1 Text analytics process pipeline

NLP contributes to the field of human computer interaction by enabling several real-world applications such as automatic text summarization, sentiment analysis, topic extraction, named entity recognition, parts-of-speech tagging, relationship extraction and stemming. The common uses of NLP include text mining, machine translation and automated question answering.

Information Retrieval (IR) is a process of searching and retrieving a subset of documents from the abundant collection of documents. IR can also be defined as extraction of information required by a user. IR is an area derived fundamentally from database technology. One of the most popular applications of IR is searching the information on the web. Search engines provide IR using various advance techniques. For example, the crawler program is capable of retrieving information from a wide variety of data sources. Search methods use metadata or full-text indexing.

Information Extraction (IE) is a process in which the software extracts structured information from unstructured and/or semi-structured documents. IE finds the relationship within text or desired contents from text. IE ideally derives from machine learning, more specifically from the NLP domain. Content extraction from the images, audio or video is an example of information extraction.

IE requires a dictionary of extraction patterns (For example, "Citizen of <x>, or "Located in <x>") and a semantic lexicon (dictionary of words with semantic category labels).

Document Clustering is an application which groups text documents into clusters. Automating document organization, topic extraction and fast information retrieval or filtering use the document clustering method. For example, web document clustering facilitates easy search by users.

Document Classification is an application to classify text documents into classes or categories. The application is useful for publishers, news sites, blogs or areas where lot of contents are present.

Web Mining is an application of data mining techniques. They discover patterns from the web Data Store. The patterns facilitate understanding. They improve the services of web-based applications. Data mining of web usage provides the browsing behavior of a website.

Concept Extraction is an application that deals with the extraction of concept from textual data. Concept extraction is an area of text classification in which words and phrases are classified into a semantically similar group.

9.2.1.3 Text Mining Process

Text is most commonly used for information exchange. Unlike data stored in databases, text is unstructured, ambiguous and difficult to process. Text mining is the process that analyzes a text to extract information useful for a specific purpose.

Syntactically, a text document comprises characters that form words, which can be further combined to generate phrases or sentences. Text mining steps are (i) recognizing, extracting and using the information present in words. Along with searching of words, mining involves search for semantic patterns as well.

Text mining process consists of a process-pipeline. The pipeline processes execute in several phases. Mining uses the iterative and interactive processes. The processing in pipeline does text mining efficiently and mines the new information. Figure 9.2 shows five phases of the process pipeline.

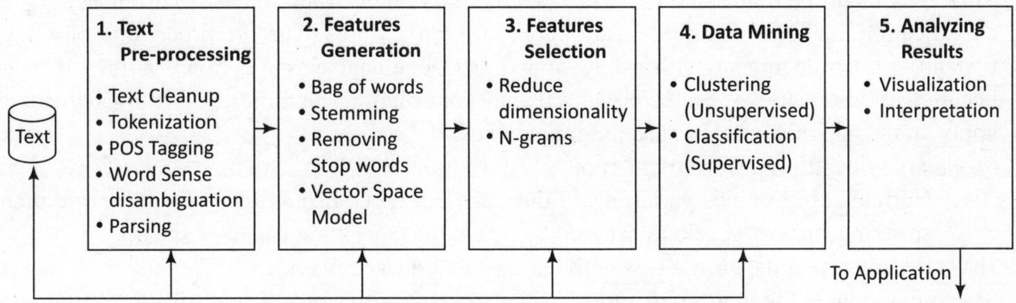

Figure 9.2 Five phases in a process pipeline

The following subsection describes these phases:

9.2.1.4 *Text Mining Process Phases*

The five phases for processing text are as follows:

Phase 1: Text pre-processing enables Syntactic/Semantic text-analysis and does the followings:

1. Text *cleanup* is a process of removing unnecessary or unwanted information. Text cleanup converts the raw data by filling up the missing values, identifies and removes outliers, and resolves the inconsistencies. For example, removing comments, removing or escaping "%20" from URL for the web pages or cleanup the typing error, such as teh (the), do n't (do not) [%20 specifies space in a URL].
2. *Tokenization* is a process of splitting the cleanup text into tokens (words) using white spaces and punctuation marks as delimiters.
3. *Part of Speech (POS) tagging* is a method that attempts labeling of each token (word) with an appropriate POS. Tagging helps in recognizing names of people, places, organizations and titles. English language set includes the noun, verb, adverb, adjective, prepositions and conjunctions. Part of Speech encoded in the annotation system of the Penn Treebank Project has 36 POS tags.[3]
4. *Word sense disambiguation* is a method, which identifies the sense of a word used in a sentence; that gives meaning in case the word has multiple meanings. The methods, which resolve the ambiguity

[3] https://www.ling.upenn.edu/courses/Fall_2003/ling001/penn_treebank_pos.html

of words can be context or proximity based. Some examples of such words are bear, bank, cell and bass.

5. *Parsing* is a method, which generates a parse-tree for each sentence. Parsing attempts and infers the precise grammatical relationships between different words in a given sentence.

Phase 2: Features Generation is a process which first defines features (variables, predictors). Some of the ways of feature generations are:

1. *Bag of words*—Order of words is not that important for certain applications.
   Text document is represented by the words it contains (and their occurrences). Document classification methods commonly use the bag-of-words model. The pre-processing of a document first provides a document with a bag of words. Document classification methods then use the occurrence (frequency) of each word as a feature for training a classifier. Algorithms do not directly apply on the bag of words, but use the frequencies.
2. *Stemming*—identifies a word by its root.
   (i) Normalizes or unifies variations of the same concept, such as *speak* for three variations, i.e., speaking, speaks, speakers denoted by [speaking, speaks, speaker → speak]
   (ii) Removes plurals, normalizes verb tenses and remove affixes.
   Stemming reduces the word to its most basic element. For example, impurification → pure.
3. *Removing stop words* from the feature space—they are the common words, unlikely to help text mining. The search program tries to ignore stop words. For example, ignores *a*, *at*, *for*, *it*, *in* and *are*.
4. *Vector Space Model* (VSM)—is an algebraic model for representing text documents as vector of identifiers, word frequencies or terms in the document index. VSM uses the method of term frequency-inverse document frequency (TF-IDF) and evaluates how important is a word in a document.
   When used in document classification, VSM also refers to the bag-of-words model. This bag of words is required to be converted into a term-vector in VSM. The term vector provides the numeric values corresponding to each term appearing in a document. The term vector is very helpful in feature generation and selection.

Term frequency and inverse document frequency (IDF) are important metrics in text analysis. TF-IDF weighting is most common—Instead of the simple TF, IDF is used to weight the importance of word in the document.

TF-IDF stands for the 'term frequency-inverse document frequency'. It is a numeric measure used to score the importance of a word in a document based on how often the word appears in that document and in a given collection of documents. It suggests that if a word appears frequently in a document, then it is an important word, and should therefore be high in score. But if a word appears in many more other documents, it is probably not a unique identifier, and therefore should be assigned a lower score. The TF-IDF is measured as:

$$\text{TF}-\text{IDF}(t) = \frac{\text{No. of times t appears in a document}}{\text{Total No. of terms in the document}} \times \log \frac{\text{No. of documents in the collection}}{\text{No. of documents that contain t}}, \tag{9.1}$$

where **t** denotes the term vector.

Following example suggests method of calculating TF-IDF (t):

EXAMPLE 9.1

Consider a document containing 1000 words wherein the word *toys* appears 16 times. How will the TF-IDF weight be calculated?

SOLUTION

The term frequency (TF) for *toys* is then (16/1000) = 0.016. Let, there are 10 million documents and the word *toys* appear in 1000 of them. Then, the inverse document frequency (IDF) is calculated as $\log_{10}$ (10,000,000/1,000) = 4.

$$\text{TF-IDF weight} = 0.016 \times 4 = 0.064$$

Additional weight is assigned to terms appearing as keywords or in titles. Documents are usually represented as a sparse vector of terms weights and extra weights are added to the terms appearing in title or keywords.

Pre-processing of web data succeeds the conversion of bag of words into vector space model (VSM) or simply by vector creation.

Common Information Retrieval Technique – Vector space model (VSM) is an algebraic model for representing textual information as vectors of identifiers, such as, index terms. Information retrieval methods use VSM.

Each document or HTML page represents by a sparse vector of term weights. The sparse matrices represent the term frequencies (TFs).

(Sparse vector and sparse-matrix have many elements as zero or null. An associated metadata enables data storing of them in a form which does not include zeros in case of large datasets. The metadata then includes indices map with the positions in the list of elements of the vector or matrix.)

The following example gives the conversion method for evaluating TFs and matrix in pre-processing phase.

EXAMPLE 9.2

Assume that the documents below define the document space with five documents d1, d2, d3, d4 and d5:

Train Document Set:

d1: Children like the toys.
d2: The toys are precious.

Test Document Set:

d3: There are many toys in the shop.
d4: Some toys are precious and some toys are costly as well.
d5: The toys shop is one of the famous shops.

How will be the documents term vector and matrix be calculated for features generation/selection?

SOLUTION

First, create an index vocabulary of the words of the train document set using the documents d1 and d2 from the document set. The index vocabulary E(t) where t is the term will be:

$$E(t) = \begin{cases} 1, \text{ when t = "children"} \\ 2, \text{ when t = "toys"} \\ 3, \text{ when t = "precious"} \\ 4, \text{ when t = "shop"} \\ 5, \text{ when t = "costly"} \\ 6, \text{ when t = "famous"} \end{cases}$$

Note that the stop words are already not considered during the pre-processing step. The term frequency (TF) is a measure of how many times the terms present in vocabulary E(t) are present in the documents d3, d4 and d5.

$$\text{TF}(t, d) = \sum_{x \in d} \text{count } (x, t) \tag{9.2}$$

where the count (x, t), is a simple function defined as:

$$\text{count}(x,t) = \begin{cases} 1, \text{ if } x = t \\ 0, \text{ otherwise} \end{cases} \tag{9.3}$$

For example, TF ("toys", d4) = 2.
Create the document vector as:

$$\overrightarrow{v_{dn}} = (TF(t1,dn), TF(t2,dn), \ldots.., TF(tn,dn)) \tag{9.4}$$

Thus, the documents d3, d4 and d5 are represented as vector as:

$$\overrightarrow{v_{d3}} = (TF(t1,d3), TF(t2,d3), \ldots.., TF(tn,d3))$$

$$\overrightarrow{v_{d4}} = (TF(t1,d4), TF(t2,d4), \ldots.., TF(tn,d4))$$

$$\overrightarrow{v_{d5}} = (TF(t1,d5), TF(t2,d5), \ldots.., TF(tn,d5)) \tag{9.5}$$

This gives:

$$\overrightarrow{v_{d3}} = (1,1,0,1,0,0)$$

$$\overrightarrow{v_{d4}} = (0,2,1,0,1,0)$$

$$\overrightarrow{v_{d5}} = (0,1,0,2,0,1) \tag{9.6}$$

The resulting vector $\overrightarrow{v_{d3}}$ shows 1 occurrence of the term "children", 1 occurrence of the term "toys" and so on. In the $\overrightarrow{v_{d4}}$, there is 0 occurrence of the term "children", 2 occurrences of the term "toys" and so on.

A collection of web documents requires representation as vectors. Another representation is a matrix with |D| × F shape, where |D| is the cardinality of the document space (total number of documents) and the F is the number of features. F represents the vocabulary size in the example. Matrix representation of the vectors described above is by 3 × 6 matrix as follows:

$$M_{|D| \times F} = \begin{bmatrix} 1 & 1 & 0 & 1 & 0 & 0 \\ 0 & 2 & 1 & 0 & 1 & 0 \\ 0 & 1 & 0 & 2 & 0 & 1 \end{bmatrix} \tag{9.7}$$

Example 9.2 shows that the matrices representing term frequencies tend to be very sparse (with majority of terms zeroed). A common representation of such matrix is thus the sparse matrices.

Phase 3: Features Selection is the process that selects a subset of features by rejecting irrelevant and/or redundant features (variables, predictors or dimension) according to defined criteria. Feature selection process does the following:

1. *Dimensionality reduction*—Feature selection is one of the methods of division and therefore, dimension reduction. The basic objective is to eliminate irrelevant and redundant data. Redundant features are those, which provide no extra information. Irrelevant features provide no useful or relevant information in any context.
   Principal Component Analysis (PCA) and Linear Discriminate Analysis (LDA) are dimension reduction methods. Discrimination ability of a feature measures relevancy of features. Correlation helps in finding the redundancy of the feature. Two features are redundant to each other if their values correlate with each other.
2. *N-gram evaluation*—finding the number of consecutive words of interest and extract them. For example, 2-gram is a two words sequence, ["tasty food", "Good one"]. 3-gram is a three words sequence, ["Crime Investigation Department"].
3. *Noise detection and evaluation of outliers* methods do the identification of unusual or suspicious items, events or observations from the data set. This step helps in cleaning the data.

The feature selection algorithm reduces dimensionality that not only improves the performance of learning algorithm but also reduces the storage requirement for a dataset. The process enhances data understanding and its visualization.

Phase 4: **Data mining techniques** enable insights about the structured database that resulted from the previous phases. Examples of techniques are:

1. Unsupervised learning (for example, clustering)
   (i) The class labels (categories) of training data are unknown
   (ii) Establish the existence of groups or clusters in the data
   Good clustering methods use high intra-cluster similarity and low inter-cluster similarity. Examples of uses – blogs, patterns and trends.
2. *Supervised learning (for example, classification*)
   (i) The training data is labeled indicating the class
   (ii) New data is classified based on the training set
   Classification is correct when the known label of test sample is identical with the resulting class computed from the classification model.
   Examples of uses are *news filtering application*, where it is required to automatically assign incoming documents to pre-defined categories; *email spam filtering*, where it is identified whether incoming email messages are spam or not.
   Example of text classification methods are *Naïve Bayes Classifier* and *SVMs*.
3. *Identifying evolutionary patterns* in temporal text streams—the method is useful in a wide range of applications, such as summarizing of events in news articles and extracting the research trends in the scientific literature.

Phase 5: Analysing results

(i) Evaluate the outcome of the complete process.
(ii) Interpretation of Result– If acceptable then results obtained can be used as an input for next set of sequences. Else, the result can be discarded, and try to understand what and why the process failed.
(iii) Visualization – Prepare visuals from data, and build a prototype.
(iv) Use the results for further improvement in activities at the enterprise, industry or institution.

Open source tools, such as *nltk* are available for text analytics. Online contents accompanying book describe how text analytics tasks can be performed using Python library *nltk* in the solution of Practice Exercise 9.2.

9.2.1.5 Text Mining Challenges

The challenges in the area of text mining can be classified on the basis of documents area-characteristics. Some of the classifications are as follows:

1. NLP issues:
   (i) POS Tagging
   (ii) Ambiguity
   (iii) Tokenization
   (iv) Parsing
   (v) Stemming
   (vi) Synonymy and polysemy
2. Mining techniques:
   (i) Identification of the suitable algorithm(s)
   (ii) Massive amount of data and annotated corpora
   (iii) Concepts and semantic relations extraction
   (iv) When no training data is available
3. Variety of data:
   (i) Different data sources require different approaches and different areas of expertise
   (ii) Unstructured and language independency
4. Information visualization
5. Efficiency when processing real-time text stream
6. Scalability

9.2.1.6 Supervised Text Classification

The categorization of text documents requires information retrieval, ML and NLP techniques. Some important approaches to automatic text categorization are based on ML techniques.

The *supervised text classification* requires labeled documents and additional knowledge from experts. The algorithms exploit the training data (where zero or more categories) to learn a classifier, which classifies new text documents and labels each document. A document is considered as a positive example for all categories with which it is labeled, and as a negative example to all others. The task of a training algorithm for a text classifier is to find a weight vector which best classifies new text documents.

The different approaches for supervised text classification are:

(i) K-Nearest Neighbour Method
(ii) Support Vector Machine

(iii) Naïve Bayes Method
(iv) Decision Tree
(v) Decision Rule

K-Nearest Neighbours (KNN) method makes use of training text document. The training documents are the previously categorized set of documents. They train the system to understand each category. The classifier uses the training 'model' to classify new incoming documents. KNN assumes that close-by objects are more probable in the same category. KNN finds k objects in the large number of text documents, which have most similar query responses. Thus, in KNN, predictions are based on a method that is used to predict new (not observed earlier) text data. The predictions are by (i) majority vote method (for classification tasks) and (ii) averaging (for regression) method over a set of K-nearest examples.

The decision trees or decision rules are built to predict the category for an input document. A decision tree or rule represents a set of nested logical if-then conditions on the observed values of the text features that enable the prediction of the target variable. The decision tree and decision rules are also used to classify (categorize) the document. Classification is done by recursively splitting the text features into a set of non-overlapping regions (Refer Section 6.8). (Section 6.7.4)

The following subsections describe Naïve Bayes Method and Support Vector Machines in detail.

9.2.2 Naïve Bayes Analysis

Naïve Bayes classifier is a simple, probabilistic and statistical classifier. It is one of the most basic text classification techniques, also known as multivariate Bernoulli method. Naïve Bayes classifies using Bayes theorem along with the Naïve independence assumptions (conditional independence). The classifier computes condition probabilities for the conditional independence (Refer Section 8.3.2).

Probability that a bag-of-words $\underline{\mathbf{x}}$ belong to k^{th} class equals the product of individual probabilities of those words. P $(\underline{\mathbf{x}}|c_k) = \Pi$ P $(x_i|c_k)$, where x_i is a discrete random variable (word), i = 1, 2, ..., n, where n is number of words in the bag. Π is sign for the product of n terms. [$P(\underline{\mathbf{x}}_i|c_k)$ means probability of condition that state the value = x_i and of c = c_k (Example 8.6)].

The P $(\underline{\mathbf{x}}|c_k)$ is normalized as all distributed probabilities equals 1. P $(\underline{\mathbf{x}}|c_k)$ is normalized by dividing the product on right hand side by Σ_i P $(x_i|c_k)$ P (c_k).

The following example gives the method of deciding the most likely class.

EXAMPLE 9.3

How is "maximum a posteriori (MAP)" used to obtain the most likely class and take a decision?

SOLUTION

Text classification problem uses the words (or tokens) of the document in order to classify it on the appropriate class. Bayes' rule is applied to documents and classes. For a document (d) and class (c), we get:

$$P(c|d) = \frac{P(d|c)P(c)}{P(d)} \tag{9.8}$$

The "maximum a posteriori (MAP)" (to obtain most likely class) decision rule is applied to documents and classes:

$$c_{MAP} = \text{argmax}_{c \in C}\ P(c|d) \tag{9.9}$$

(MAP is "maximum posteriori" = most likely class)

$$c_{MAP} = \text{argmax}_{c \in C} \left(\frac{P(d|c)P(c)}{P(d)} \right) \quad \text{(Bayes Rule)} \tag{9.10}$$

$$c_{MAP} = \text{argmax}_{c \in C} \left(P(d|c)P(c)\right) \quad \text{(Dropping the denominator)} \tag{9.11}$$

$$c_{MAP} = \text{argmax}_{c \in C} \left(P(t_1, t_2 \ldots, t_n | c)P(c)\right), \tag{9.12}$$

where t_1, t_2, ..., t_n are tokens of document.

Multinomial Naïve Bayes independence assumptions

$$P(t_1, t_2 \ldots, t_n | c) \tag{9.13}$$

Bag-of-words assumption: Assume the position of the word does not matter.

Conditional independence: Assume the feature probabilities $P(t_i | c_j)$ are independent given the class(c):

$$P(t_1, t_2 \ldots, t_n | c) = P(t_1 | c) \bullet P(t_2 | c) \bullet P(t_3 | c) \bullet \ldots \bullet P(t_n | c) \tag{9.14}$$

and thus, conditional independences are given by

$$c_{MAP} = \text{argmax}_{c \in C} \left(P(t_1, t_2 \ldots, t_n | c)P(c)\right) \tag{9.15a}$$

$$c_{NB} = \text{argmax}_{c \in C} \left(P(c_j) \prod_{t \in T} P(t | c) \right) \tag{9.15b}$$

Applying multinomial Naïve Bayes classifier to text classification where positions ← all word positions in the text document,

$$c_{NB} = \text{argmax}_{c_j \in C} \left(P(c_j) \prod_{i \in \text{Positions}} P(t_i | c_j) \right) \tag{9.16}$$

The equation estimates the product of the probability of each word of the document given a particular class (likelihood), multiplied by the probability of the particular class (prior) to find in which class one should classify a new document.

Select the one with the highest probability among all the classes of set C. Calculation of product of the probabilities leads to float point underflow when handling numbers with specific decimal point accuracy by computing devices. Such small numbers will be rounded to zero, implying the analysis is of no use at all. In order to avoid this, instead of maximizing the product of the probabilities, the maximization of the sum of their logarithms is done:

$$c_{NB} = \text{argmax}_{c_j \in C} \left(\log P(c_j) \prod_{i \in \text{Positions}} \log P(t_i | c_j) \right) \tag{9.17}$$

Here, choose the one with the highest log score rather than choosing the class with the highest probability. Given that the logarithm function is monotonic, the decision of MAP remains the same.

When compared with other techniques, such as Random Forest, Max Entropy and SVM, the Naïve Bayes classifier performs efficiently in terms of less CPU and memory consumption. Naïve Bayes classifier requires a small amount of training data to estimate the parameters. The classifier is not sensitive to irrelevant features as well. Furthermore, the training time is significantly smaller with Naïve Bayes as opposed to other techniques.

The classifier is popularly used in a variety of applications, such as email spam detection, personal email sorting, document categorization, language detection, authorship identification, age/gender identification and sentiment detection.

9.2.3 Support Vector Machines

Support vector machines (SVM) is a set of related *supervised learning methods* (the presence of training data) that analyze data, recognize patterns, classify text, recognize hand-written characters, classify images, as well as bioinformatics and bio sequence analysis.

A vector has in general n components, x2, x3, ..., xn. A datapoint represents by (X1, X2, ..., Xn) in n-dimensional space. Assume for the sake of simplicity, that a vector has two components, X1 and X2 (Two sets of words in text analysis).

Section 6.7.6 described the use of the concept of hyperplanes for classification. A *hyperplane* is a subspace of one dimension less than its ambient space in geometry (Figure 6.18). If a space is 3-dimensional then its hyperplanes are 2-dimensional planes, while if the space is 2-dimensional, its hyperplanes are 1-dimensional, which means lines.

The hyperplane which separates the two classes most appropriately has maximum distance from closest data points of the distinct classes. This distance is termed as margin. Figure 9.3 shows the concept of support vectors, separating hyperplane and margins when using B as a classifier. The margin for hyperplane B in Figure 9.3 is more as compared to two hyperplanes, A and C shown by dotted lines. The margin of the data points from B is maximum. Therefore, the hyperplane B is the **maximum margin classifier.**

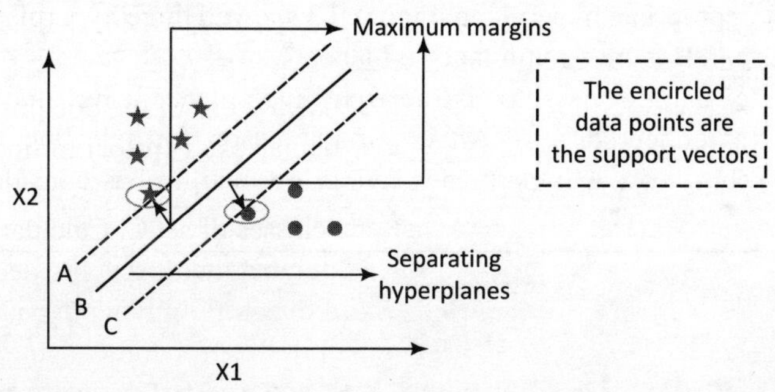

Figure 9. 3 Support vectors, separating hyperplane (B) and margins

A and C are closest (least margins) to the data points. These are called the ***support vectors***. They support the classifications of the star and dotted data points. [Remember that with n-dimensional datapoints space, a hyperplane has the vectors along (n – 1) axes.]

The support vectors are such that a set of data points lies closest to the decision (classification) surface (or hyperplane). Those points are most difficult to classify. They have direct bearing on the optimum location of the classification surface. Support vectors along maximum margin classification surface are thus gives the best results.

Thus, a SVM classifier is a ***discriminative classifier*** formally defined by a separating hyperplane. The concept applies extensively in number of application areas of ML. Applications of SVMs are as follows:

1. Classification based on the outputs taking discrete values in a set of possible categories, SVM can be used to separate or predict if something belongs to a particular class or category. SVM helps in finding a decision boundary between two categories.
2. Regression analysis, if learning problem has continuous real-valued output (continuous values of x, in place discrete n values, $(x_1, x_2, x_3, ..., x_n)$
3. Pattern recognition
4. Outliers detection.

The following example illustrates the discriminative classifier method, formally defined by a separating a hyperplane for taking the decision for effective elements (entities, set of words, itemsets) in a training set.

EXAMPLE 9.4

How is the discriminative classifier used?

SOLUTION

Consider a mapping function (f) used for linear separation in the feature space (H). An optimal separating hyperplane depends on the data through dot products in H $(f(x_i).f(x_j))$.

A kernel function k is required that acts as a measure of similarity. Let us use k where

$$k(x_i, x_j) = f(x_i)\cdot f(x_j) \quad (9.18)$$

The objective is to select the hyperplane which separates the two classes most appropriately. This helps in identifying the right or appropriate hyperplane. Figure 9.3 showed three hyperplanes. A, B and C. A and C are least margin planes and B is maximum margin plane.

A hyperplane,maximum margin classifier is the right hyperplane. It has maximum distances from the nearest data points (of either classes). An important reason for selecting the maximum margin classification surface is robustness. A hyperplane having low margin has considerably high chance of misclassifying.

Binary Classification

For a given training data $[x_i, y(x_i)]$ for i = 1 ...N, with $x_i \in \mathbb{R}^d$ and $y_i \in \{-1,1\}$, learn a classifier f(x) such that:

$$f(x_i)\begin{cases} \geq 0 & y_i = +1 \\ < 0 & y_i = -1 \end{cases} \quad (9.19)$$

The above equation implies that $y_i f(x_i) > 0$ for correct classification.

Figure 9.4 shows a two-class classification. The method is using one hyperplane B for separating two-class classification of data points.

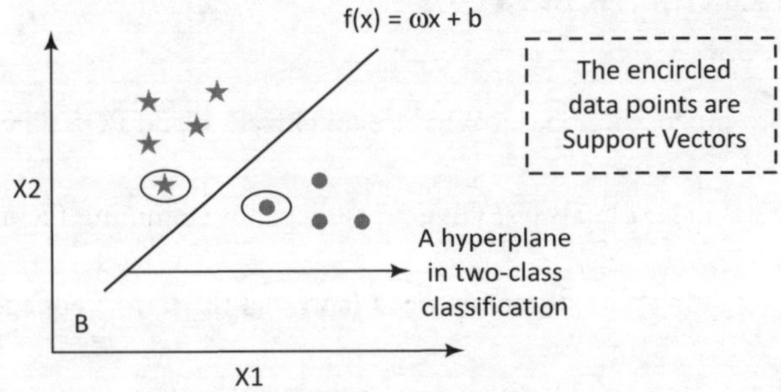

Figure 9. 4 Concept of training set data using support vectors

Let us take the simplest case of two-class classification. Suppose there are two features X1 and X2 and it is required to classify objects as shown in the Figure 9.4. Stars and dots represent the objects (itemsets, sets of words, entities) of two classes. The goal is to design a hyperplane (B) that classify all training vectors in two classes for linearly separable binary set.

The following example gives the method to design a hyperplane (B) that classify all training vectors:

EXAMPLE 9.5

How will you select an appropriate hyperplane that classifies all training vectors?

SOLUTION

Plane B is f(x) = ωx + b where ω is weight vector. Figure 9.5 shows the method of selecting the right hyperplane.

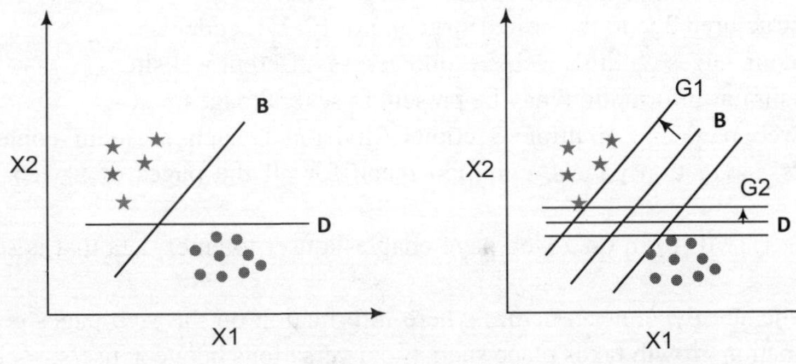

Figure 9.5 Method of selecting the right hyperplane

The best choice is the hyperplane that leaves the maximum margin from both the classes. Thus, B is the right choice, since G1 > G2.

Thus, for line segment B,

$$f(x) \geq 1 \ \forall \in \text{x} \rightarrow \text{class 1}$$

$$f(x) \geq -1 \ \forall \in \text{x} \rightarrow \text{class 2} \quad (9.20)$$

Self-Assessment Exercise linked to LO 9.1

1. Define text analytics. ○○●
2. List the steps in text pre-processing phase. Why are tokenization and POS tagging needed? Give an example of each step. ○●●
3. How is bag-of-word used in text analysis? Give 5 examples of stemming the affix wordforms to its root word. ○○●
4. How do the TF-IDF weighting and sparse matrices represent the term frequencies (TFs) for use in text analysis? ○○●
5. How does maximum a posteriori (MAP) in Naïve Bayes classifier enable the decision about classification? ●●●
6. How does support vectors in SVMs classify the data points in n-dimensional space. ○●●

9.3 WEB MINING, WEB CONTENT AND WEB USAGE ANALYTICS

LO 9.2

Mining the web-links, web-structure and web-contents, and analyzing the web graphs

Web is a collection of interrelated files at web servers. Web data refers to (i) web content—text, image and records, (ii) web structure—hyperlinks and tags, and (iii) web usage—http logs and application server logs.

Features of web data are:

1. Volume of information and its ready availability
2. Heterogeneity
3. Variety and diversity (Information on almost every topic is available using different forms, such as text, structured tables and lists, images, audio and video.)
4. Mostly semi-structured due to the nested structure of HTML code
5. Hyperlinks among pages within a website, and across different websites
6. Redundant or similar information may be present in several pages
7. Mostly, the web page has multiple sections (divisions), such as main contents of the page, advertisements, navigation panels, common menu for all the pages of a website and copyright notices
8. A web form or HTML form on a web page enables a user to enter data that is sent to a server for processing
9. Website contents are dynamic in nature where information on the web pages constantly changes, and fast information growth takes place such as conversations between users, social media, etc.

Note: ○○● Level 1 & Level 2 category
○●● Level 3 & Level 4 category
●●● Level 5 & Level 6 category

The following subsections describe web data mining and analysis methods:

9.3.1 Web Mining

Data Mining is a process of discovering patterns in large datasets to gain knowledge. The process can be shown as [Raw Data → Patterns → Knowledge]. Web data mining is the mining of web data. Web mining methods are in multidisciplinary domains: (i) data mining, ML, natural language, (ii) processing, statistics, databases, information retrieval, and (iii) multimedia and visualization.

Web consists of rich features and patterns. A challenging task is retrieving interesting content and discovering knowledge from web data. Web offers several opportunities and challenges to data mining.

Definition of Web Mining

Web mining refers to the use of techniques and algorithms that extract knowledge from the web data available in the form of web documents and services. Web mining applications are as follows:

(i) Extracting the fragment from a web document that represents the full web document
(ii) Identifying interesting graph patterns or pre-processing the whole web graph to come up with metrics, such as PageRank
(iii) User identification, session creation, malicious activity detection and filtering, and extracting usage path patterns

Web Mining Taxonomy

Web mining can broadly be classified into three categories, based on the types of web data to be mined. Three ways are web content mining, web structure mining and web usage mining. Figure 9.6 shows the taxonomy of web mining.

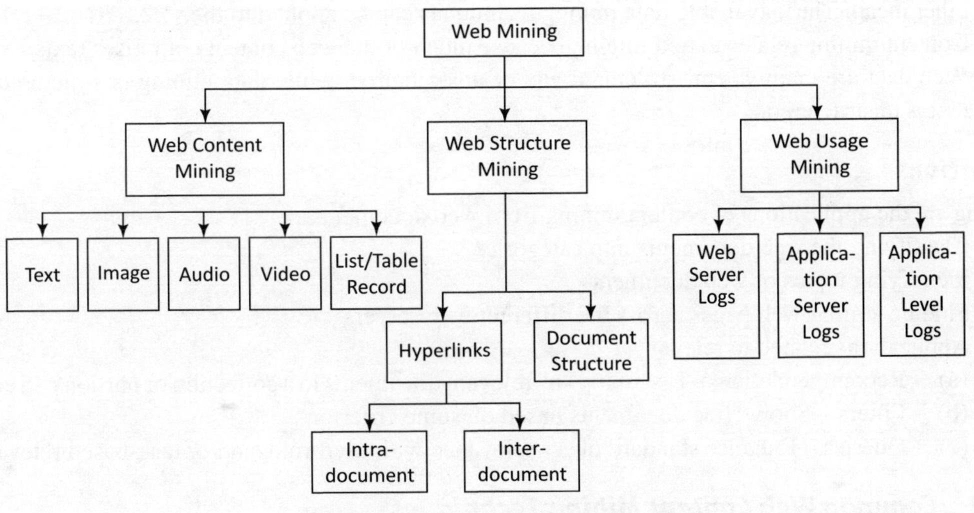

Figure 9.6 Web mining taxonomy

Web content mining is the process of extracting useful information from the contents of web documents. The content may consist of text, images, audio, video or structured records, such as lists and tables.

Web structure mining is the process of discovering structure information from the web. Based on the kind of structure-information present in the web resources, web structure mining can be divided into:

1. Hyperlinks: the structure that connects a location at a web page to a different location, either within the same web page (intra-document hyperlink) or on a different web page (inter-document hyperlink)
2. Document Structure: The structure of a typical web graph consists of web pages as nodes, and hyperlinks as edges connecting the related pages.

Web usage mining is the application of data mining techniques which discover interesting usage patterns from web usage data. The data contains the identity or origin of web users along with their browsing behavior at a web site. Web usage mining can be classified as:

(i) Web Server logs: Collected by the web server and typically include IP address, page reference and access time.
(ii) Application Server Logs: Application servers typically maintain their own logging and these logs can be helpful in troubleshooting problems with services.
(iii) Application Level Logs: Recording events usually by application software in a certain scope in order to provide an audit trail that can be used to understand the activity of the system and to diagnose problems.

9.3.2 Web Content Mining

Web Content Mining is the process of information or resource discovery from the content of web documents across the World Wide Web. Web content mining can be (i) direct mining of the contents of documents or (ii) mining through search engines. They search fast compared to direct method.

Web content mining relates to both, data mining as well as text mining. Following are the reasons:

(i) The content from web is similar to the contents obtained from database, file system or through any other mean. Thus, available data mining techniques can be applied to the web.
(ii) Content mining relates to text mining because much of the web content comprises texts.
(iii) Web data are mainly semi-structured and/or unstructured, while data mining is structured and the text is unstructured.

Applications

Following are the applications of content mining from web documents:

1. Classifying the web documents into categories
2. Identifying topics of web documents
3. Finding similar web pages across the different web servers
4. Applications related to relevance:
   (a) Recommendations – List of top "n" relevant documents in a collection or portion of a collection
   (b) Filters – Show/Hide documents based on some criterion
   (c) Queries – Enhance standard query relevance with user, role, and/or task-based relevance.

9.3.2.1 Common Web Content Mining Techniques

Pre-processing of contents The pre-processing steps are quite similar to the pre-processing for text mining. The content preparation involves:

1. Extraction of text from HTML

2. Data cleaning by filling up the missing values and smoothing the noisy data
3. *Tokenizing*: Generates the tokens of words from the cleaned up text
4. *Stemming*: Reduce the words to their roots. The different grammatical forms or declinations of verbs identify and index (count) as the same word. For example, stemming will ensure that both "closed" and "closing" are derived from the same word "close". Stemming algorithm, *Porter*, can be used here. The java code for *Porter* stemming algorithm can be obtained from *https://tartarus.org/martin/PorterStemmer/java.txt,*
5. *Removing the stop words*: The common words unlikely to help in the mining process such as articles (a, an, the), or prepositions (such as, to, in, for) are removed.
6. *Calculate collection wide-word frequencies*: The distinct-word stem obtained after stemming process and removing the stop words results into a list of significant words (or terms). Calculating the occurrence of a significant term (t) in a collection is called collection frequency (CF_t). CF counts the multiple occurrences.)
   Now, find the number of documents in the collection that contains the specific term (t). This numeric measure is the document frequency (DF_t).
7. *Calculate per Document Term Frequencies* (TF). TF is a numeric measure that is used to score the importance of a word in a document based on how often it appeared in that document (Refer Example 9.1).
8. *Bag of words*: Web document is represented by the words it contains (and their occurrences.

The following example explains the concept of CF and DF using the data of toy sales collection.

EXAMPLE 9.6

Using the table below on collection and document frequencies, which is prepared from the toys sales collection, analyze the numeric values of CFs and DFs.

Collection frequency (CF) and document frequency (DF)

Word	CF	DF
discount	15565	550
sale	15567	1230

SOLUTION

The table suggests that the collection frequency (CF) and document frequency (DF) can behave differently. The CF values for both *discount* and *sale* are nearly equal, but their DF values differ significantly. The reason is that the word sale is present in a large number of documents and the word discount in a less number of documents. Thus, when a query related to *discount* is generated, it must be searched in the concerned documents only.

Mining Tasks for Web Content Analytics

Following are the tasks for web content analytics:

1. Classification – A supervised technique which:
   (i) Identifies the class or category a new web documents belongs to from the set of predefined classes or categories
   (ii) Categories in the form of a term vector that are produced during a "training" phase

   (iii) Employs algorithms using term vector to categorize the new data according to the observations at the training set.
2. *Clustering* – An unsupervised technique:
   (i) Groups the web documents (clustered) with similar features using some similarity measure
   (ii) Uses no pre-defined perception of what the groups should be
   (iii) Measures most common similarity using the dot product between two web document vectors.
3. *Identifying the association* between web documents – Association rules help to identify correlation between web pages that occur mostly together.

The other significant mining tasks are:

1. *Topic identification, tracking and drift analysis* – A way of organizing the large amount of information retrieved from the web is categorizing the web pages into distinct topics. The categorization can be based on a similarity metric, which includes textual information and co-citation relations. Clustering or classification techniques can automatically and effectively identify relevant topics and add them in a topic-wise collection library.
   Adding a new document to a collection library includes:
   (i) Assigning each document to an existing topic (category)
   (ii) Re-checking of collection for the emergence of new topics
   (iii) Tracking the number of views to a collection
   (iv) Identifying the drift in a topic(s)
2. *Concept hierarchy creation* – Concept hierarchy is an important tool for capturing the general relationship among web documents. Creation of concept hierarchies is important to understand a category and sub-categories to which a document belongs. The clustering algorithms leverage more than two clusters, which merge into a cluster. That is merging the sub-clusters into a cluster.
   Important factors for creation of concept hierarchy include:
   (i) Identifying the organization of categories, such as flat, tree or network
   (ii) Planning the maximum number of categories per document
   (iii) Building category dimensions, such as domain, location, time, application and privileges.
3. *Relevance of content* – Relevance or the applicability of web content can be measured with respect to any of the following basis:
   (i) Document relevance describes the usefulness of a given document in a specified situation.
   (ii) Query-based relevance is the most useful method to assess the relevance of web pages. Query-based relevance is used in information retrieval tools such as search engines. The method calculates the similarity between query (search) keywords and document. Similarity, results can be refined through additional information such as popularity metric as seen in Google or the term positions in AltaVista.
   (iii) User-based relevance is useful in personal aspects. User profiles are maintained, and similarity between the user profile and document is calculated. The relevance is often used in push notification services.
   (iv) Role/task-based relevance is quite similar to user-based relevance. Instead of a user, here the profile is based on a particular role or task. Multiple users can provide input to profile.

9.3.3 Web Usage Mining

Web usage mining discovers and analyses the patterns in click streams. Web usage mining also includes associated data generated and collected as a consequence of user interactions with web resources.

Figure 9.7 shows three phases for web usage mining.

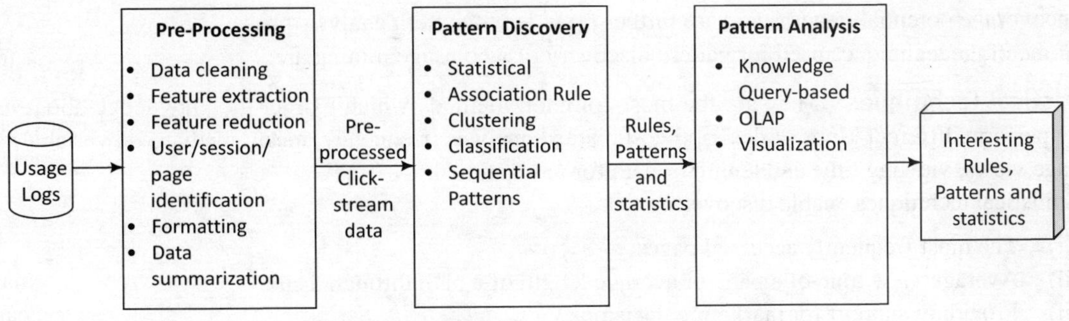

Figure 9.7 Process of web usage mining

The phases are:

1. Pre-processing – Converts the usage information collected from the various data sources into the data abstractions necessary for pattern discovery.
2. Pattern discovery – Exploits methods and algorithms developed from fields, such as statistics, data mining, ML and pattern recognition.
3. Pattern analysis – Filter outs uninteresting rules or patterns from the set found during the pattern discovery phase.

Usage data are collected at server, client and proxy levels. The usage data collected at the different sources represent the navigation patterns of the overall web traffic. This includes single-user, multi-user, single-site access and multi-site access patterns.

9.3.3.1 Pre-processing

The common data mining techniques apply on the results of pre-processing using vector space model (Refer Example 9.2).

Pre-processing is the data preparation task, which is required to identify:

(i) User through cookies, logins or URL information
(ii) Session of a single user using all the web pages of an application
(iii) Content from server logs to obtain state variables for each active session
(iv) Page references.

The subsequent phases of web usage mining are closely related to the smooth execution of data preparation task in pre-processing phase. The process deals with (i) extracting of the data, (ii) finding the accuracy of data, (iii) putting the data together from different sources, (iv) transforming the data into the required format and (iv) structure the data as per the input requirements of pattern discovery algorithm.

Pre-processing involves several steps, such as data cleaning, feature extraction, feature reduction, user identification, session identification, page identification, formatting and finally data summarization.

9.3.3.2 Pattern Discovery

The pre-processed data enable the application of knowledge extraction algorithms based on statistics, ML and data mining algorithms. Mining algorithms, such as path analysis, association rules, sequential patterns, clustering and classification enable effective processing of web usages. The choice of mining techniques depends on the requirement of the analyst. Pre-processed data of the web access logs transform into knowledge to uncover the potential patterns and are further provided to pattern analysis phase.

Some of the techniques used for pattern discovery of web usage mining are:

Statistical techniques They are the most common methods which extract the knowledge about users. They perform different kinds of descriptive statistical analysis (frequency, mean, median) on variables such as page views, viewing time and length of path for navigational.

Statistical techniques enable discovering:

(i) The most frequently accessed pages
(ii) Average view time of a page or average length of a path through a site
(iii) Providing support for marketing decisions

Association rule The rules enable relating the pages, which are most often referenced together in a single server session. These pages may not be directly connected to one another using the hyperlinks.

Other uses of association rule mining are:

(i) Reveal a correlation between users who visited a page containing similar information. For example, a user visited a web page related to admission in an undergraduate course to those who search an eBook related to any subject.
(ii) Provide recommendations to purchase other products. For example, recommend to user who visited a web page related to a book on data analytics, the books on ML and Big Data analytics also.
(iii) Provide help to web designers to restructure their websites.
(iv) Retrieve the documents in prior in order to reduce the access time when loading a page from a remote site.

Clustering is the technique that groups together a set of items having similar features. Clustering can be used to:

(i) Establish groups of users showing similar browsing behaviors
(ii) Acquire customer sub-groups in e-commerce applications
(iii) Provide personalized web content to users
(iv) Discover groups of pages having related content. This information is valuable for search engines and web assistance providers.

Thus, user clusters and web-page clusters are two cases in the context of web usage mining. Web page clustering is obtained by grouping pages having similar content. User clustering is obtained by grouping users by their similarity in browsing behavior.

Model-based or distance-based clustering can be applied on web usage logs. The model type is often specified theoretically with model-based clustering. The model selection techniques and parameters estimate using maximum likelihood algorithms, such as Expectation Maximization (EM) determines the structure of model. Distance-based clustering measures the distance between pairs of web pages or users, and then groups the similar ones together into clusters. The most popular distance-based clustering techniques include partitional clustering and hierarchical clustering (Section 6.6.3).

Classification The method classifies data items into predefined classes. Classification is useful for:

(i) Developing a profile of users belonging to a particular class or category
(ii) Discovery of interesting rules from server logs. For example, 3750 users watched a certain movie, out of which 2000 are between age 18 to 23 and 1500 out of these lives in metro cities.

Classification can be done by using supervised inductive learning algorithms, such as decision tree classifiers, Naïve Bayesian classifiers, k-nearest neighbour classifiers, support vector machines.

Sequential pattern discovery User navigation patterns in web usage data gather web page trails that are often visited by users in the order in which pages are visited. Markov Model can be used to model navigational activities in the website. Every page view in this model can be represented as a state. Transition probability between two states can represent the probability that a user will navigate from one state to the other. This representation allows for the computation of a number of significant user or site metrics that can lead to useful rules, pattern, or statistics.

9.3.3.3 Pattern Analysis

The objective of pattern analysis is to filter out uninteresting rules or patterns from the rules, patterns or statistics obtained in the pattern discovery phase.

The most common form of pattern analysis consists of:

(i) A knowledge query mechanism such as SQL
(ii) Another method is to load usage data into a data cube in order to perform Online Analytical Processing (OLAP) operations
(iii) Visualization techniques, such as graphing patterns or assigning the colors to different values, can often highlight overall patterns or trends in the data
(iv) Content and structure information can filter out patterns containing pages of a certain usage type, content type or pages that match a certain hyperlink structure.

Data cube enables visualizing data from different angles. For example, *toys* data visualization using category, colour and children preferences. Another example, news from category, such as sports, success stories, films or targeted readers (children, college students, etc).

Self-Assessment Exercise linked to LO 9.2

1. Define web mining. Discuss the broad classifications of web mining and their applications. ○○●
2. List the tasks in pre-processing of web contents. ○○●
3. How are web-content mining tasks performed using machine learning algorithms? ○●●
4. How are topic identification, tracking and drift analysis done? ●●●
5. List and explain three phases of web-usage mining. ○●●
6. Highlight the techniques used for pattern discovery in web-usage mining giving an example of each. ●●●

9.4 PAGE RANK, STRUCTURE OF WEB AND ANALYZING A WEB GRAPH

LO 9.3

PageRanking, analysis of web- structure, and discovering hubs, authorities and communities in web-structure

Sections 9.2 and 9.3 described text data and web contents analysis. Hyperlinks links exist between the web contents. Link analysis finds the answers to the following:

1. Can a linked (web) page rank them higher or lower?

2. Can the links be modeled as edges of graphs, structure of web as graph network, and applied the tools same as for graph analytics?
3. Can web graph mining method analyze and find a link sending spams?
4. Does a set of links correspond to a hub? Do the links correspond to an authority?
5. Does a linked page has higher authority compared to others?

Links analysis applies to domains of social networks and e-mail. The following sub-sections describe the applications of link analysis:

9.4.1 Page Rank Definition

The in-degree (visibility) of a link is the measure of number of in-links from other links. The out-degree (luminosity) of a link is number of other links to which that link points.

PageRank definition according to earlier approaches

Assume a web structure of hyperlinks. Each hyperlink in-links to a number of hyperlinks and out-links to a number of pages. A page commanding higher authority (rank) has greater number of in-degrees than out-degrees. Therefore, one measure of a page authority can be in-degrees with respect to out-degrees.

PageRank refers to the authority of the page measured in terms of number of times a link is sought after.

PageRank definition according to the new approach

Earlier approach of page ranking based on in-links and out-links does not capture the relative authority (importance) of the parents. Page and co-authors (1998) defined a page ranking method,[4] which considers the entire web in place of local neighbourhood of the pages and considers the relative authority of the parent links (over children).

9.4.2 Web Structure

Web structure models as directed-graphs network-organization. Vertex of the directed graph models an anchor. Let n = number of hyperlinks at the page **U**. Assume **u** is a vector with elements u_1, u_2, ... u_n. Each page Pg (**u**) has anchors, called hyperlinks. Page Pg (**v**) consists of text document with m number of hyperlinks. **v** is a vector with elements v_1, v_2, ... v_m. The m is number of hyperlinks at Pg (**v**). A vertex u directs to another Page **V**. A page Pg (**v**) may have number of hyperlinks directed by out-edges to other page Pg (**w**). Consider the following hypotheses:

1. Text at the hyperlink represents the property of a vertex u that describes the destination **V** of the out-going edge.
2. A hyperlink in-between the pages represents the conferring of the authority.

Pages **U** and **U′** hyperlinks u and u′ out-linking to Page **V**. Let Page U has three hyperlinks parenting three Pages, V one, W two, X two, U' one, and Y two, respectively. Figure 9.8 shows a web structure consisting of pages and hyperlinks.

[4] http://papers.cumincad.org/data/works/att/2873.content.pdf "The Anatomy of a Large-Scale Hypertextual Web Search Engine" Sergey Brin Lawrence Page, 1998

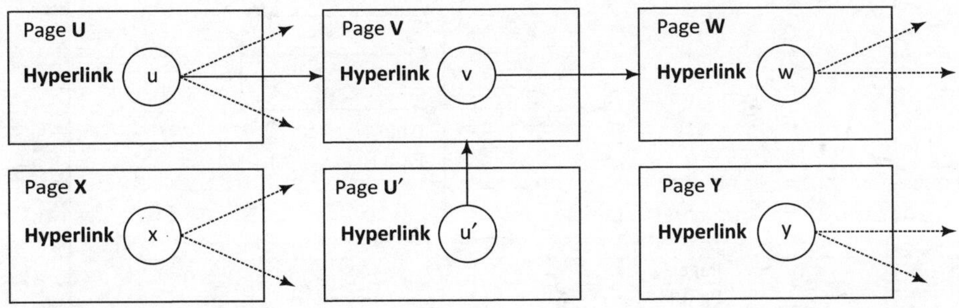

Figure 9.8 Web structure with hyperlinks from a parent to one or more pages

9.4.2.1 *Dead Ends*

Dead-end web pages refer to pages with no out-links. When a web page links to such pages, its page rank gets reduced. Dead ends are on a website having poor linking structure.

The web structure of service pages may have pages with a dead end. The end causes no further flows for further action and no internal links. Good website structures have the pages designed such that they specifically gently guide the visitors toward actions and towards next step. For example, if one searches for a book title on Amazon, then visitor gets links of other books also on a similar topic.

9.4.2.2 *Analyzing and Implementing a System with Web Graph Mining*

Number of metrics analyze a system using web graph mining. Following are the examples:

1. In-degrees and out-degrees
2. Closeness is centrality metric. Closeness, $Cc(v) = 1/\sum_{u \in V} gdist(v,u)$, where gdist is the geodesic distance between vertex v with u and sum is over all **u** linked with **V**. Geodesic distance means the number of edges in a shortest path connecting two vertices. Assume v has an edge with w, and w has an edge with u. Assume u does not have direct edge from v. Then, geodesic distance = 2 (two edges between v and u in shortest path).
3. Betweenness
4. PageRank and LineRank
5. Hubs and authorities
6. Communities parameters, triangle count, clustering coefficient, K-neighbourhood
7. Top K-shortest paths

9.4.3 Computation of PageRank and PageRank Iteration

Assume that a web graph models the web pages. Page hyperlinks are the property of the graph node (vertex). Assume a Page, Pg (**v**) in-links from Pg (**u**), and Pg (**u**) out-linking similar to Pg (**v**), to total N_{out} [(Pg (**u**)] pages. Figure 9.9 shows Pg (**v**) in-links from Pg (**u**) and other pages.

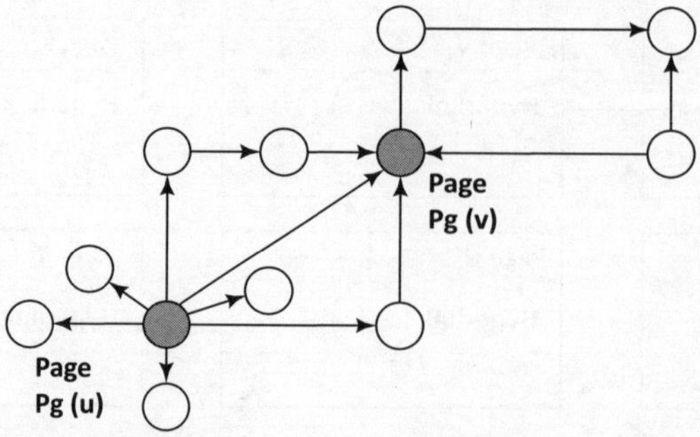

Figure 9.9 Page Pg (**v**) in-links from Pg (**u**) and other pages

N_{out} for page U is 7 and for V is 1 in the figure. Number of in-linking N_{in} for page V is 4. Two algorithms to compute page rank are as follows:

1. PageRank algorithm using the in-degrees as conferring authority

Assume that the page **U**, when out-linking to Page **V** "considers" an equal fraction of its authority to all the pages it points to, such as Pgv. The following equation gives the initially suggested page rank, PR (based on in-degrees) of a page Pgv:

$$PR(Pgv) = nc \cdot \sum_{Pgu:Pgu \rightarrow Pgv} \left[PR(Pgu)/N(Pgu)\right] \tag{9.21}$$

where N(Pgu) is the total number of out-links from **U**. Sum is over all Pgv in-links. Normalization constant denotes by nc, such that PR of all pages sums equal to 1.

However, just measuring the in-degree does not account for the authority of the source of a link. Rank is flowing among the multiple sets of the links. When Pgv in-links to a page Pgu, its rank increases and when page Pgu out-links to other new links, it means that N (Pgu) increases, then rank PR(Pgv) sinks (decreases). Eventually, the PR (Pgv) converges to a value.

Therefore, rank computation algorithm iterates the rank flowing computations as shown below:

EXAMPLE 9.7

Assume $\mathbb{S}$ corresponds to a set of pages. Initialize ∀ Pg ∈ $\mathbb{S}$. Symbols mean that initialize all pages Pg contained in the S and initialize Page Rank (Pgv) for each page as follows:

$$PRinit\ (Pgv) = 1/|S| \tag{9.22}$$

How are the page ranks of the pages in a given set of pages iterated and computed till the ranks do not change (within specified margin, that means untill converge)?

SOLUTION

Iterate and compute PR (Pgv) for each page as follows:

Until ranks do not change (within specified margin) (that means converge)

{

for each Pgv ∈ S compute,

$$\text{PR(Pgv)} = \sum_{\text{Pgu:Pgu}\rightarrow\text{Pgv}} [\text{PR(Pgu)} / \text{N(Pgu)}] \tag{9.22}$$

and normalization constant,

$$\text{nc} = \sum_{\text{Pgv}\in\text{S}} [\text{PRnew(Pgv)}] \tag{9.23a}$$

for each Pgv ∈ **S**: PR(Pgv) = nc PR(Pgv) (9.23b)

}

2. PageRank algorithm using the relative authority of the parents over linked children

A method of PageRank considers the entire web in place of local neighbourhood of the pages and considers the relative authority of the parents (children). The algorithm uses the relative authority of the parents (children) and adds a rank for each page from a rank source.

The PageRank method considers assigning weight according to the rank of the parents. Page rank is proportional to the weight of the parent and inversely proportional to the out-links of the parent.

Assume that (i) Page v (Pgv) has in-links with parent Page u (Pgu) and other pages in set PA (v) of parent pages to v that means ∈ PA(v), (ii) R(v) is PageRank of Pgv, (iii) R (u) is weight (importance/rank) of Pgu, and (iv) ch (u) is weight of child (out-links) of Pgu. Then the following equation gives PageRank R (v) of link v:

$$\text{R(v)} = \sum_{u\in \text{PA(v)}} \left[\text{R}(u)/|\text{ch}(u)|\right] \tag{9.25}$$

where PA(v) is a set of links who are parents (in-links) of link v. Sum is over all parents of v. nc is normalization constant whose sum of weights is 1.

Assume that a rank source E exists that is addition to the rank of each page R (v) by a fixed rank value E(v) for Pgv. E(v) is fraction α of [1/|PA(v)|].

An alternative equation is as follows:

$$\text{R(v)} = \text{nc}\cdot\left\{(1-\alpha)\sum_{u\in \text{PA(v)}}\left[\frac{\text{R}(u)}{|\text{ch}(u)|}\right] + \alpha\cdot\text{E(v)}\right\}, \tag{9.26}$$

where nc = [1/R(v)]. R(v) is iterated and computed for each parent in the set PA(v) till new value of R(v) does not change within the defined margin, say 0.001 in the succeeding iterations.

Significance of α PageRank can be seen as modeling a "random surfer" that starts on a random page and then at each point: E(v) models the probability that a random link jumps (surfs) and connect with out-link to Pgv. R(v) models the probability that the random link connects (surf) to Pgv at any given time. The addition of E(v) solves the problem of Pgv by chance out-linking to a link with dead end (no outgoing links).

Therefore, rank computation algorithm iterates the rank flowing computations as shown in Example 9.8.

EXAMPLE 9.8

Assume PA corresponds to a set of parent pages to a page v. Initialize ∀ Pg ∈ PA (v). Symbols mean that initialize all pages **u** contained in the set of parent pages of PA (v) and initialize Page Rank R(v) for each page as follows:

$$R(v) = [1/|PA(v)|]$$

How are the page ranks of the pages in a given set of pages iterated and computed till the ranks do not change (within specified margin, that means untill converges)?

SOLUTION

Iterate and compute R (v) for each page as follows:

Until ranks do not change that means converges (within specified margin, say 0.001)

{

for each v ∈ PA (v) compute,

$$R(v) = nc \cdot \left\{(1-\alpha) \sum_{u \in PA(v)} \left[\frac{R(u)}{|ch(u)|}\right] + \alpha \cdot E(v)\right\} \tag{9.27}$$

and normalization constant,

$$nc = \sum_{u \in PA(v)} [R(v)] \tag{9.28a}$$

for each v ∈ PA(v): R(v) = nc.R(v) (9.28b)

}

PageRank Iteration using MapReduce functions in Spark Graph

The computation of PageRank using SparkGraph method (Section 8.5),

```
graph.pageRank(0.0001).vertices
ranksByUsername = users.join(ranks).map{case id, (username, rank)) =>
(username, rank).
```

The method includes conversions to MapReduce functions and using HDFS compatible files. Functions PageRank (), ranksByUsername () do the computations using the PageRankObject. GraphX consists of these functions (GraphOps). GraphX Operators includes the functions (Section 8.5).

Static PageRank algorithm runs for a fixed number of iterations, while dynamic PageRank runs until the computed rank converges. Convergence means that after certain iterations, the rank does not change significantly and any change remains within a pre-specified tolerance. Thereafter the iterations stop.

Assume specified tolerance at the start of iterations is 0.0001 (1 in 10000). When the rank does not change beyond that tolerance, it means rank value will converge and then the iterative process will stop.

9.4.4 Topic Sensitive PageRank and Link Spam

Number of methods have been suggested for computations of topic-sensitive page ranking, R_{TS}. The R_{TS} (v) of a page P (v) may be higher for a specific topic compared to other topics. A topic associates with a distinct bag of words for which the page has higher probability of surfing than other bags for that topic.

Topic-sensitive PageRank method uses surfing weights (probabilities) for the pages containing the topic or bag of words corresponding to a topic. Method for creating topic-sensitive PageRank is to compute the bias to rank R(v) and thus increase the effect of certain pages containing that topic or bag of words.

Refer equation (9.25) for computations of R (v), and equation (9.26) for computations after introducing additional influence to the page. A method of introducing biasing is simple. It assumes that a rank source E exists that is additional having in-links from other pages, and thus adds to the rank of each page R (v) by a fixed (uniform) or non-uniform weight factor α. The factor α is a multiplication factor to actual in-links without the bias.

Recapitulate equation (9.26). Probability of random jump to page v is E(v). An alternative equation for topic sensitive PageRank, R(v) computation for page P (v) is as follows:

$$R(v) = nc \cdot \left\{ (1-\alpha_t) \cdot P(v) \sum_{u \in PA(v)} \left[\frac{R(u),}{|ch(u)|} \right] + \alpha_t \cdot E(v) \right\}, \tag{9.29}$$

Probability of random jump to page v is $E(v)$. $\alpha_t = 0$ for page unrelated to a topic α is not 0 for page related to a topic. α_t = surfing probability for in-links for a topic t. Further, coefficient $(1-\alpha)$ is considered as biasing factor depending on the web page P (v) selected for a queried topic t.

The page is having in-links from other pages. Assume N_t is number of topics to which a page is sensitive to surfing those topics. Effect of topics on PageRanks increases by using a non-uniform $N_t \times 1$ personalization vector for surfing probability p. Higher α means higher p.

Assume that the topics are t1, t2, ..., tn. Fix the number N_t. R_{TS} is to be computed for each of them. Therefore, compute for each topic t_j, the PageRank scores of page v as a function of t_j, which means compute R (v, j), where j = 1, 2, ..., n. That also means compute the n elements of a non-uniform $N_t \times 1$ personalization vector $\mathbf{R}_{TS}$ **(v)** for t1, t2, ..., tn.

Link Spam

Effects of a *link spam* can be nullified using the topic-sensitive PageRank algorithm. Link Spam tries to mislead the PageRank algorithm. A link spam attempts to make PageRank algorithm ineffective. The spam assisting pages connects to the page repeatedly and increases the in-degree of a page, thereby enhancing the rank to a large value.

A link spam creator website *ws* also has a page l_s for whom w_s attempts to enhance the PageRank. The w_s has a large number of assisting pages al_s which out-links to *ls* only. The al_s pages also prevent the PageRank of l_s from being lost. A spam mass consists of w_s, l_s and its al_s pages.

Methods nullify the effect by introducing a trust rank for a page u used in equation (9.29) and tracing spam mass of in-link pages to the page v.

Following are the steps for finding spam mass:

1. A distant topic sensitive page has unusually high in-degrees compared to the other pages of the same topic. A plot known as power-law plot is drawn between the log of number of web pages on the y-axis out-linking to the page v and logs of them in-degrees of v on the x-axis.
2. Plot is nearly linear as the number exponential decays is within degrees. N is proportional to exp (-d), where d is decay constant.
3. An unusual pattern with marked deviation from near linearity identifies the distant link spam mass.

9.4.5 Hubs and Authorities

A hub is an index page that out-links to a number of content pages. A content page is topic authority. An authority is a page that has recognition due to its useful, reliable and significant information.

Figure 9.10(a) shows hubs (shaded circles) with the number of out-links associated with each hub. Figure 9.10(b) shows authorities (dotted circles) with the number of in-links and out-links associated with each link.

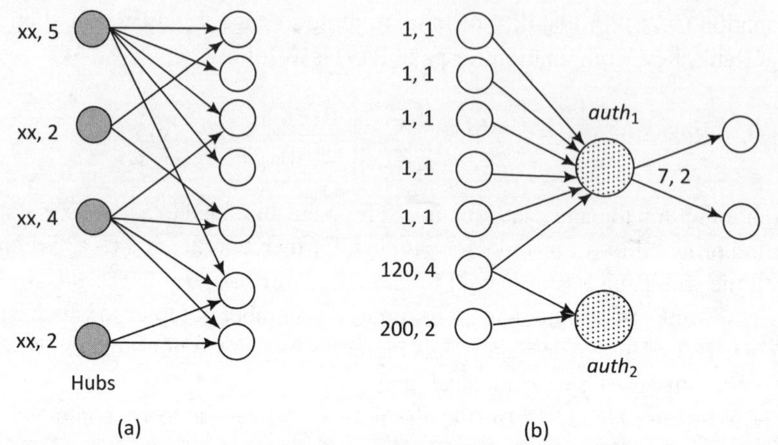

Figure 9.10 (a) Hubs (shaded circles) and (b) Authorities (dotted circles)

In-degrees (number of in-edges from other vertices) can be one of the measures for the authority. However, in-degrees do not distinguish between an in-link from a greater authority or lesser authority.

Authority, $auth_1$ in Figure 9.10(b) has in-links from 6 vertices (in-degrees = 6) and $auth_2$ has in-links to just 2 (in-degree = 2). However, $auth_1$ has link with six vertices with in-degrees = 1, 1, 1, 1, 1 and 120 (total = 125). Authority, $auth_2$ has links with two vertices with in-degrees = 120 and 200 (total = 220). $Auth_2$ has association with greater authorities. Therefore, in-degrees may not be a good measure as compared to authority.

Kleinberg (1998) developed the Hypertext-Induced Topic Selection (HITS) algorithm.[5] The algorithm computes the hubs and authorities on a specific topic t. The HITS analyses a sub-graph of web, which is relevant to t. Basis of computation is (i) hubs are the ones, which out-link to number of authorities, and (ii) authorities are the ones, which in-link to number of hubs. A bipartite graph exists for the hubs and authorities.

Consider a specifically queried topic t. Following are the steps:

1. Let a set of pages discover a root set R using standard search engine. Root pages may limit to top 200 for *t*.

[5] J. Kleinberg (1998), Authoritative sources in a hyperlinked environment, Proceedings of the 9th ACM-SIAM Symposium on Discrete Algorithms. A longer version appears in the Journal of the ACM 46, 1999.Available from http://www.cis.hut.fi/Opinnot/T-61.6020/2008/pagerank_hits.pdf

2. Find a sub-graph of pages S, using a query that provides relevant pages for t and pointed by pages at **R**. Sub-graph S pages form Set for computations as it includes the children of parent R and limit to a random set of maximum 50 pages returned by a "reverse link" query.
3. Eliminate purely navigational links and links between two pages on the same host.
4. Consider only **u** (||*u*|| ≅4-8) pages from a given hyperlink as pointer to any individual page. (Section 9.4.2)

Sub-graph for HITS consisting of root set **R** of pages and children of parents in the sub-graph **S**. Figure 9.11 shows subgraph **S** for HITS consisting of root set R of pages and all the pages pointed to by any page of R.

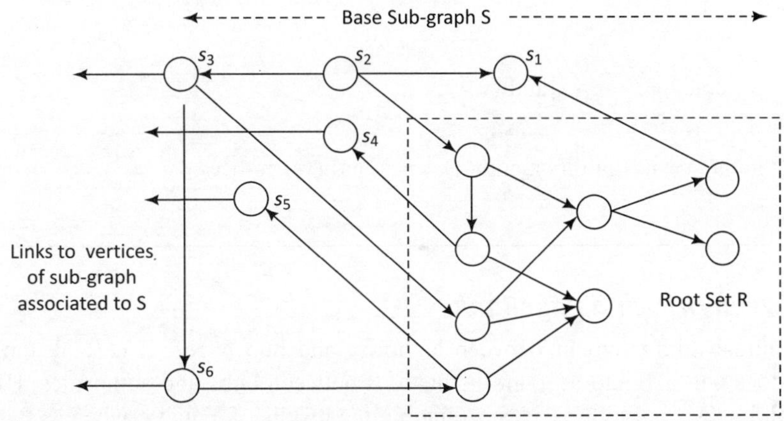

Figure 9.11 Sub-graph for HITS consisting of root set R of pages and base sub-graph **S** including all the pages pointed to by any page of R.

The left directed leftmost arrows from s3, s4 , s5 and s6 are pointing to nodes in sub-graph(s) associated to S. The following example explains the algorithm steps to compute hub score and authority score.

EXAMPLE 9.9

Assume that v has number of in-links and v has number of out-links. Assume $\mathbb{S}$ corresponds to base set of pages and $\mathfrak{R}$ corresponds to root set. (i) Initialize $\mathbb{S}$ to R. (ii) Initialize ∀ u ∈ $\mathbb{S}$. Symbols mean that initialize all pages **u**, contained in the $\mathbb{S}$. (iii) Normalization constant is nc. The (i) hub (v) hub score and (ii) auth authority score of page v for each page is as follows:

$$\text{For each } v \in S, \text{auth}(v) = 1; \text{hub}(v) = 1; nc = 1; \tag{9.30}$$

How are the hub and authority of pages in a given set of pages iterated and computed till the ranks do not change (within specified margin, that means untill converges)? Usually 20 iterations converge the result within margin, usually set to 0.001.

SOLUTION

Iterate and compute auth (v) and hub (v) for each page as follows:

Until ranks do not change (within specified margin) (that means converges)
{
for each v ∈ $\mathbb{S}$ compute,

$$\text{auth(v)} = \text{nc} \cdot \sum_{\mathbf{u}:\mathbf{u}\to \text{v}} [\text{hub}(\mathbf{u})], \tag{9.31a}$$

$$\text{hub(v)} = \text{nc2} \cdot \sum_{\mathbf{u}:\text{v}\to \mathbf{u}} [\text{auth}(\mathbf{u})], \tag{9.31b}$$

and normalization constant,

$$\text{nc1} = \sum_{\text{Pgv}\in \text{S}} 1/[\text{auth(v)}]^2, \tag{9.32a}$$

$$\text{nc2} = \sum_{\text{Pgv}\in \text{S}} 1/[\text{auth(v)}]^2, \tag{9.32b}$$

for each v ∈ $\mathbb{S}$: auth(v) = nc1.auth(v); auth(v) = nc1.auth(v); auth(v); (9.32c)

}

Difference between HITS and PageRank

HITS considers mutual reinforcement between authority and hub pages. PageRank ranks the pages just by authority and does not take into account distinctions between hubs and authorities. HITS considers the local neighbourhood between 4 to 8 pages surrounding the results of a query, whereas PageRank is applied to the entire web. HITS depends on topic t, while PageRank is topic-independent. PageRank effects by dead-ends.

9.4.6 Web Communities

Web communities are web sites or collections of websites, which limit the contents view and links to members. Examples of web communities are social networks, such as LinkedIn, SlideShare, Twitter and Facebook.

The communities consist of sites for do-it-yourself sites, social networks, blogs or bulletin boards. The issues are privacy and reliability of information.

Metric for analysis of web-community sites are web graph parameters, such as triangle count, clustering coefficient and K-neighbourhood.

K-neighbourhood analysis means the number of 1st neighbour nodes, 2nd neighbour nodes, and so on (K = 1, 2, 3, 4 and so on).

K-core analysis means the number of cores within a marked area. A core may consist of a triangle of connected vertices. A core may consist of a rectangle with interconnected edges and diagonals. A core may also be a group of cores.

Spark GraphX (Section 8.5) described functions for degree centralities, degree distribution, separation of degree, betweenness centralities, closeness centralities, neighbourhoods, strongly connected components, triangle counts, PageRank, shortest path, Breadth First Search (BFS), minimum spanning tree (forest), spectral clustering and cluster coefficient.

9.4.7 Limitations of Link, Rank and Web Graph Analysis

Following are the limitations of link and web graph analysis:

1. Search engines rely on metatags or metadata of the documents. That enhances the rank if metadata has biased information.
2. Search engines themselves may introduce bias while ranking the pages of clients higher as the pages of advertising companies may provide higher searches and hence lead to biased ranks.
3. A top authority may be a hub of pages on a different topic resulting in increased rank of the authority page.
4. Topic drift and content evolution can affect the rank. Off-topic pages may return the authorities.
5. Mutually reinforcing affiliates or affiliated pages/sites can enhance each other's rank and authorities.
6. The ranks may be unstable as adding additional nodes may have greater influence in rank changes.

Self-Assessment Exercise linked to LO 9.3

1. Write and explain the equations for computing PageRank using relative authority of parent nodes. ●●●
2. Show diagramatically network organization model of directed graphs for the structure of the web. How are the page hub and page authority computed? ○●●
3. What are the metrics which Spark GraphX compute? ○○●
4. How does the equation for computing the hub of a page differ from the computing authority of a page? ○●●
5. How does link spam function? How is the link spam discovered from the plot between the number of web pages and in-degrees? ○○●

9.5 SOCIAL NETWORKS AS GRAPHS AND SOCIAL NETWORK ANALYTICS

LO 9.4

Representation of social networks as graphs, methods of social network analysis, finding the clustering in social network graphs, evaluating the SimRank, counting triangles (cliques) and discovering the communities

A **social network** is a social structure made of individuals (or organizations) called "nodes," which are tied (connected) by one or more specific types of inter-dependency, such as friendship, kinship, financial exchange, dislike or relationships of beliefs, knowledge or prestige. (*Wikipedia*)

Social networking is the grouping of individuals into specific groups, like small rural communities or some other neighbourhoods based on a requirement. The following subsections describe social networks as graph, uses, characteristics and metrics.

9.5.1 Social Network as Graphs

Social network as graphs provide a number of metrics for analysis. The metrics enable the application of the graphs in a number of fields. Network topological analysis tools compute the degree, closeness, betweenness, egonet, K-neighbourhood, top-K shortest paths, PageRank, clustering, SimRank, connected components, K-cores, triangle count, graph matches and clustering coefficient. Bipartite weighted graph matching does collaborative filtering.

Apache Spark GraphX and IBM System G Graph Analytics tools are the tools for social network analysis.

Centralities, Ranking and Anomaly Detection

Important metrics are degree (centrality), closeness (centrality), betweenness (centrality) and eigen vector (centrality). Eigen vector consists of elements such as status, rank and other properties. Social graph-network analytics discovers the degree of interactions, closeness, betweenness, ranks, probabilities, beliefs and potentials.

Social network analysis of closeness and sparseness enables detection of abnormality in persons. Abnormality is found from properties of vertices and edges in network graph. Analysis enables summarization and find attributes for *anomaly*.

Social network characteristics from observations in the organizations are as follows:

1. Three-step neighbourhoods show positive correlation between a person and high performance. Betweenness between vertices and bridges between numbers of structures are not helpful to the organization. Too many strong links of a person may have a negative correlation with the performance.
2. Social network of a person shows high performance outcome when the network exhibits structural diversity. Person with a social network with an abundant number of structural holes exhibits higher performance. This is because having diverse relations help an organization.

Social network analysis enables detection of an anomaly. An example is detection of one dominant edge which other sub-graphs are follow (succeed). *Ego network* is another example. The network structure is such that a given vertex corresponds to a sub-graph where only its adjacent neighbours and their mutual links are included.

The analysis enables spam detection. Spam is discovered by observation of a near star structure. Figure 9.12 shows discovering anomaly, ego-net and spam from the analysis.

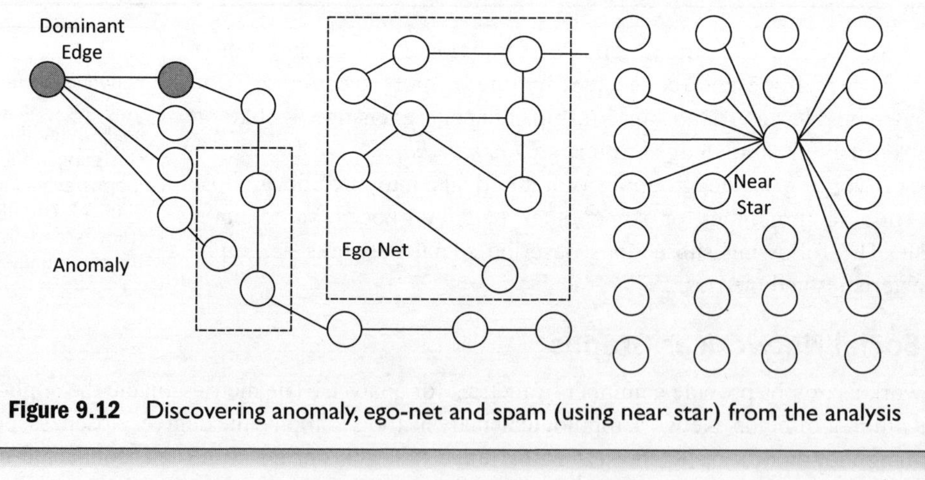

Figure 9.12 Discovering anomaly, ego-net and spam (using near star) from the analysis

Social network has concerns of privacy, security and falsehood dissimentation. Security issues are phsishing attacks and malwares.

9.5.2 Social Graph Network Topological Analysis using Centralities and PageRank

Social graph network can be topologically analyzed. The centralities (degree, closeness, effective closeness and betweenness) and PageRank (vertexRank similar to PageRank in web graph network) are the parameters analyzed.

Degree

Degree of a graph vertex means the total number of edges linked to that. *In-degree of a vertex* means the number of in-edges from the other vertices. *Out-degree of a vertex* means the number of out-edges to other vertices to which that vertex directs. *Degree distribution function* means the distribution function for the degrees of vertices (Section 6.2.5 described the common distribution functions).

Closeness

Graph vertex closeness $c_C(v)$ is a way of defining the centrality of a vertex in reference to other vertices. Sum is the overall vertices connected to other vertices **u**. The **u** is a subset of vertices in set **V**.

The centrality (closeness index), c is function of distances of vertices.

$$c_C(v) = [\sum_{u \in V} d(u, v)]^{-1},$$

where d (u, v) is distance between u and v for path traversal.

Effective Closeness

Effective closeness $C_{ec}(v)$can also be analyzed. Use approximate average distance from v to all other vertices in place of the shortest paths. C_{ec} reduces run time for cases with a large number of edges and near linear scalability in computations.

Betweenness

Graph vertices betweenness means the number of times a vertex exists between the shortest path and the extent to which a vertex is located 'between' other pairs of vertices. Betweenness $c_B(v)$ of a vertex v requires calculating the lengths of shortest paths among all pairs of vertices and computations of the summation for each pairing vertex in V.

PageRank

PageRank is a metric for the importance of each vertex in a graph, assuming an edge from *v1* to *v2* represents endorsement of importance of *v2* by *v1* by connecting, following, interacting, opting for relationship, sharing belief or some other means.

Contacts Size

Contacts size means a vertex connection to many vertices. The size of each vertex does not convey any meaningful information. A big social graph network will also require high maintenance cost.

Indirect Contacts

Indirect contacts metric means betweenness, which is the sum of the shortest paths within geodesic distances from all other pairing vertices. Three-step contact metric means a number of edges to other vertices plus the number of edges from other vertices within geodesic distances = < 3.

Both metrics convey meaningful information. The indirect contacts metric has meaning in terms of magnitude of betweenness centrality.

Structure Diversity

Structure diversity metric means that social graph has access to diverse sub-graphs (knowledge).

9.5.3 Social Graph Network Analysis using K-core and Neighbourhood Metrics

K-core is a sub-graph in a graph network structure. *Graph Vertex* K^{th} neighbourhood is number of 1st neighbour vertices, 2nd neighbour vertices and so on to a querying vertex that are correlated, linked, and have weighted correlations or the associations.

K-nearest neighbourhood (KNN) finds K-similar objects, items, or entities, which are nearest neighbours after computing the similarities. For example, KNN is K-documents (or books) in the large number of text documents (books) that are most similar to the queried document.

Collaborative filtering for frequent itemsets uses weighted bipartite graph matching.

Figure 9.13 shows the K-cores and K-neighbourhood metrics for a social network graph. The figure also shows frequent itemsets obtained from collaborative filtering algorithm (Sections 6.4 and 6.8.1).

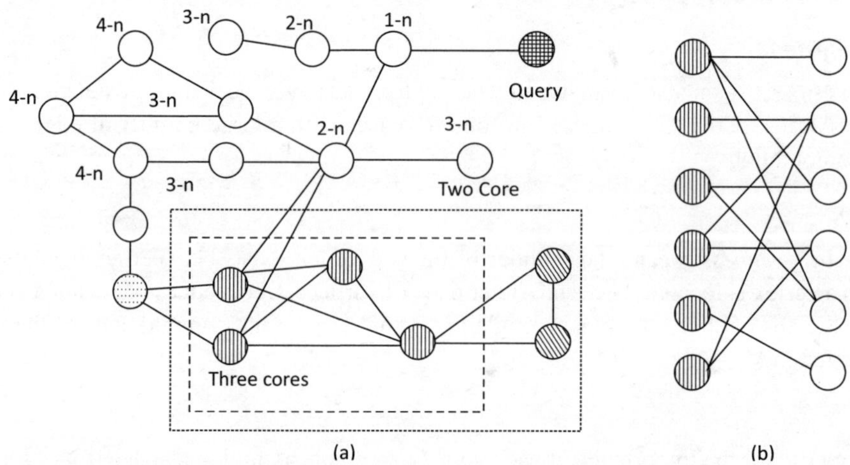

Figure 9.13 (a) K-cores and K-neighbourhoods with K = 1, 2, 3 and 4 and (b) Frequent itemsets from collaborative filtering algorithm (weighted bipartite graph matching)

Figure 9.13(a) shows three cores of two triangles, one quadrilateral, two cores of one pentagon and one traingle) in K-neighbourhoods. K = 1, 2, 3 and 4. Figure 9.13(b) shows frequent itemsets from collaborative filtering algorithm (weighted bipartite graph matching).

9.5.4 Clustering in Social Network Graphs

One of the methods of detecting communities from social graph analysis is finding clustering and cluster coefficients. A clustering coefficient is a metric for the likelihood that two associated vertices of a vertex are also associated with other vertices. A higher clustering coefficient indicates a greater association and cohesiveness.

Connected components mean components of the datasets (represented by properties of vertices) connected together. For example, finding student–teacher datasets, social network datasets, etc.

9.5.5 SimRank

Similarity can be defined by properties of graph vertices. For example course, subject, student, scientist, Java programmer, status, values, or any other salient characteristic. Social network analysis of graphs computes *SimRank*.

SimRank is the metric for measuring similarity between vertices of the same type. The computation starts from a vertex possessing specific property and path traversals through the edges search the similarities. The vertices having similar properties are counted to the SimRank. The counting continues till counts per unit traversals converge within a prefixed margin, say .001. SimRank converges to a value which is applicable for path traversals within, say geodesic distance, say up to 200. The computations are analogous to ones for PageRank as in Example 9.7

9.5.6 Counting Triangles and Graph Matches

One of the methods of detecting communities is counting of triangles. A triangle means three vertices forming a triangle with edges interconnecting them.

Triangle count refers to the number of triangles passing through each vertex. The count is a measure of clustering. A vertex is part of a triangle when it has two adjacent vertices with an edge between them.

Graph matches are computed using filtering or search algorithm, which uses the properties, labels of vertices, edges or the geographic locations.

Figure 9.14 shows triangles and triangles between similar graph properties found from graph matches. Edge labels show the GPAs of students socially connected.

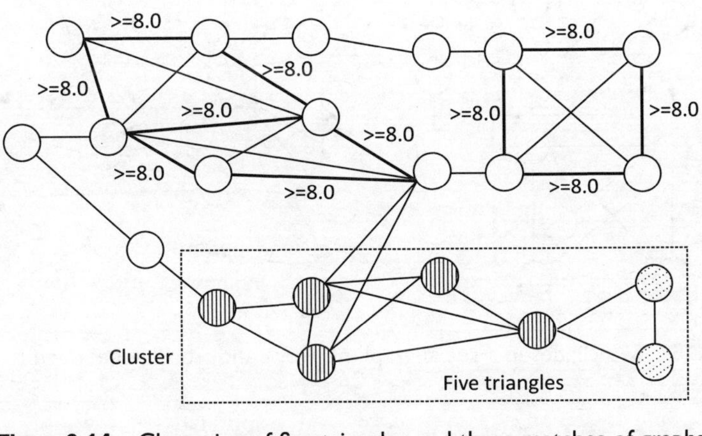

Figure 9.14 Clustering of five triangles and three matches of graphs

9.5.7 Using SparkGraph (Map-Reduce) for Network Graphs

Section 8.5 describes Spark GraphX algorithms for analyzing graphs. Connected components compute by `graph.connectedComponents().vertices` method in SparkGraph. Connected Components Algorithm labels each connected component of the graph with an ID. Each connected component ID is ID of the lowest-numbered vertex. For example, in a social network, connected component objects can approximate clusters. GraphX contains an implementation of the algorithm in the ConnectedComponentsObject. The clusters are found by discovering close-by connected components using closeness centrality metric.

SparkGraphX triangle-count algorithm computes the number of triangles passing through each vertex. The count is a measure of clustering. TriangleCount requires the edges to be in canonical orientation (srcId < dstId). Source vertex ID is srcId and Destination vertex ID is dstID. Graph is partitioned using *Graph. partitionBy* operator.

9.5.8 Direct Discovery of Communities

Three metrics identify groups and communities from a social graph:

1. Cliques – A clique forms by a set of vertices when each of the vertices directly connects to every other individual vertex through the edges. Detecting the cliques leads to direct discovery of communities.
2. Structurally cohesive blocks.
3. Social circles from connections and neighbourhoods

A bridge enables the link between two groups. Application of analyzing communities, SimRanks and bridges are finding a set of experts, specific areas of expertise, and ranking the expertise in an organization.

Experience in social science fields shows that the social network of a person is the key indicator of the stature of the person and his/her success potential. Social graph analysis enables finding key bridges and persons with most connections.

Figure 9.15 shows a social graph with two cliques and a bridge.

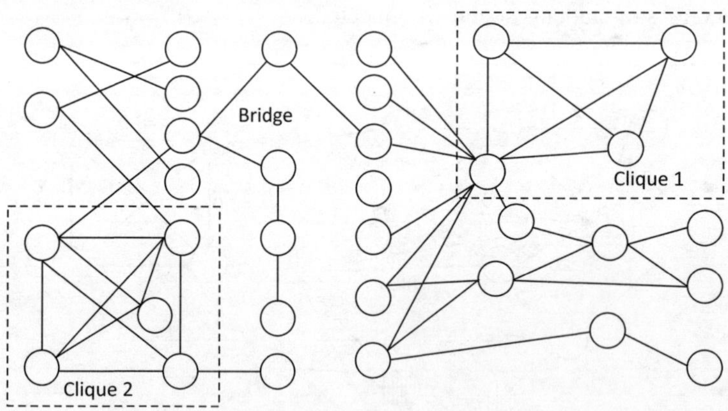

Figure 9.15 Two cliques in a social graph network and a bridge between the cliques

Clique 1 has set of four vertices, each connected with three edges to three others. Clique 2 has five vertices, each connected by edges to other four. Two edges in the figure provide the bridge between two sub graphs, on left and right sides.

Self-Assessment Exercise linked to LO 9.4

1. How do the metrics analyze a social network graph of persons in an organization? How do they relate to inter-dependency, performance, groups, expertises, beliefs, knowledge or prestige? ●●●
2. Define the terms degree, closeness, betweenness, egonet, K-neighbourhood, top-K shortest paths, PageRank, clustering, SimRank, connected components, K-cores, triangle count, graph matches and clustering coefficient. ○●●
3. How the cliques discover communities from social network analysis? ○○●
4. What are the uses of Apache GraphX ConnectedComponents and triangles count methods in social graph anaysis? ○●●

KEY CONCEPTS

anomaly detection	hub	structured text
authority	hyperplane	SVM classifier
bag of words	in-degrees	term frequency
betweenness	KNN	text analytics process pipeline
centralities	link analysis	text cleanup
clique	marginalization	text features generation
closeness	Naïve Bayes classifier	text mining
collaborative filtering	out-degrees	text pre-processing
collection wide-word frequency	outliers	TF-IDF
concept extraction	PageRank	Top K shortest paths
content relevance	part-of-speech tagging	triangles count
document frequency	pattern analysis	unstructured text
documents classification	pattern discovery	vector space model
documents clustering	sequential patterns	web community
effective closeness	SimRank	web content analytics
ego net	social network	web graph
feature selection	social network graph	web structure
HITS algorithm	spam detection	web usage mining

Learning Outcomes

LO 9.1

1. Text mining techniques help revealing the patterns and relationships in large volumes of textual content that are not directly visible. The mining leads to new business opportunities and improvements in processes.
2. Five phases in text mining are (i) text pre-processing, (ii) feature generation, (iii) feature selection, (iv) text data mining, and (v) analysing the results. Text analytics involves provisions of strong integration with the already existing database, artificial intelligence, machine learning, and text mining techniques such as, information retrieval, natural language processing, classification, clustering and knowledge management, respectively.
3. Machine learning based text classification methods are (i) K nearest neighbour classifier, (ii) Naïve Bayes method, (iii) decision trees, (iv) decision rules classification, and (v) support vector machines.
4. Naïve Bayes classifier is a simple, probabilistic and statistical classifier. The classifier computes the conditional probability tables.
5. SVMs based classifier is a discriminative classifier formally defined by a separating hyperplane. SVM seeks a decision surface to separate the training data points into two classes and makes decisions based on the support vectors that select the only effective elements in the training set.

LO 9.2

1. Web data mining is a process of discovering patterns in large datasets to gain knowledge. The process can be shown as Raw Data → Patterns → Knowledge. Web data refers to (i) web content – text, image, records, (ii) web structure – hyperlinks and tags, and (iii) web usage – http logs and application server logs.
2. Steps for pre-processing of web-data are quite similar to pre-processing for text mining. The steps include collection of wide-word frequencies and document frequencies. Machine learning techniques for web content analytics are clustering, classification and association rule mining.
3. Web usage mining discovers and analyses the patterns in click stream and associated data generation and collection as a consequence of user interactions with web resources on the World Wide Web.
4. A link spam creator website *ws* also has a page *ls*. *ws* attempts to enhance the PageRank of *ls*.
5. A hub is an index page that out-links to number of content pages. A content page is topic authority. Authority is a page that has recognition due to provisioning useful, reliable and significant information. HITS algorithm computes the hubs and authorities on a specific topic t.
6. Web community is website or collection of the websites that limits the view of contents, and that links the members (for example, LinkedIn). Metric for analysis of web community sites are web graph parameters, such as triangle count, clustering coefficient and K-neighbourhood.

LO 9.3

1. Link analysis enables finding the PageRank, centralities, hubs, and authorities. Page ranking method considers the entire web in place of local neighbourhoods of the pages. PageRank of a page refers to relative authority of the parents out-linking to the page.

2. Web structure models as directed-graphs network-organization. A page may have a number of hyperlinks directed by out-edges to other pages. Text at the hyperlink represents the property of vertex that describes the destination of the out-going edge. A hyperlink in-between the pages represents the conferring of the authority.
3. SparkGraph includes conversions to MapReduce functions and use HDFS compatible files. Page rank() and ranksByUsername() are static and dynamic methods compute on the PageRankObject

LO 9.4

1. A social network is a social structure made of individuals (or organizations) called "nodes", which are tied (connected) by one or more specific types of interdependency, such as friendship, kinship, financial exchange, dislike or relationships of beliefs, knowledge or prestige
2. Social network topological analysis tools compute the degree, closeness, betweenness, egonet, K-neighbourhood, Top-K shortest paths, PageRank, clustering, SimRank, connected components, K-cores, triangle count, graph matches and clustering coefficient. Bipartite weighted graph matching does collaborative filtering.
3. Analysis enables summarization and find attributes for anomaly.
4. Apache Spark GraphX includes PageRank, ConnectedComponents and TrianglesCount algorithms, and fundamental operations for social graph analytics.
5. Analysis of cliques discovers groups and communities. Analysis also finds the bridge between the cliques.

Objective Type Questions

Select one correct-answer option for each questions below:

9.1 The term *text analytics* evolves from (i) provisioning of strong integration with the already existing (ii) database, (iii) artificial intelligence, (iv) machine learning, and (v) text Data Store techniques such as (vi) information retrieval, (vii) natural language processing, (viii) classification, (ix) clustering, and (x) knowledge management, respectively. ○○●

(a) all except ii and iv (b) ii to ix
(c) all except ii, iii, iv and vii (d) all

9.2 SVMs main uses are (i) classification based on the outputs taking discrete values in a set of possible categories, (ii) separation or prediction, if something belongs to a particular class or category. Other uses are (iii) finding a decision boundary between two categories, (iv) clustering, (v) regression analysis, and regression, if continuous real-valued output (continuous values of x, in place discrete n values, x2, x3, ..., xn), and (vi) discriminative classifier. ○●●

(a) all except iii (b) i, ii and iv
(c) all except iv (d) i to v

9.3 Applications of (i) web content mining, and (ii) web-structure mining of web documents are: (iii) Classifying the web documents into categories, (iv) identifying the topics of the web documents, (v) creation of tables and databases, (vi) finding similar web pages across different web servers, and (vii) relevance or the applicability of web content measured with respect to a basis, such as making recommendations, filtering or querying ○●●

(a) all except vii (b) all except ii
(c) all except iv (d) i to v

9.4 The HITS analyses a (i) subgraph of web, which is relevant to (ii) topic t, (iii) query q. The assumptions are (iv) authorities are the ones, which out-link to number of hubs, and (v) hubs ●●●

are the ones, which in-link to number of authorities. (vi) A bipartite graph exists for the hubs and authorities. (vii) First *set* of pages discovers a root set R using standard search engine, then (viii) finds a sub-graph of pages S, using a query that provides relevant pages for t and pointed by pages at R.

(a) all except iii to v (b) all except iii and vi
(c) all except vi (d) all except iv and vi

9.5 Web contents mining tasks are: (i) finding clustering, (ii) classifying, (iii) mining association rules, and (iii) topic identification, tracking and drift analysis for adding new documents to a collection library. Other tasks are: (iv) assigning by rechecking for the emergence of new topics, (v) creation of concept hierarchy, building of category dimensions, such as domain, location, time, application, privileges, and (vi) measuring the relevance or the applicability of web content on basis of documents, queries, roles or tasks or user profiling. ○●●

(a) all except vii and viii (b) all
(c) all except vii (d) All except vi to viii

9.6 The most common form of pattern analysis consists of (i) a knowledge query mechanism such as SQL, (ii) loading usage data into a data cube in order to perform OLAP operations, (iii) visualization techniques, such as graphing patterns or assigning colors to different values. The analysis also finds (iv) content and structure information which can filter out patterns containing pages of a certain usage type, content type, or pages that match a certain hyperlink structure. ○○●

(a) all except iii (b) all
(c) all except i and ii (d) i to ii

9.7 PageRank method considers (i) the entire web in place of a local neighbourhood of the pages, (ii) queries top 10 pages, and (iii) considers the relative authority of the children pages with respect to parent page. *PageRank method* considers assigning weight (iv) as 1, and (v) according to the rank of the parents. (vi) PageRank is inversely proportional to the weight of the parent and proportional to out-links of the parent. ○●●

(a) i, iii, and v (b) i and v
(c) all except ii and vi (d) all

9.8 Social network graph analysis tools do the (i) clustering analysis which means the number of 1st neighbour nodes, 2nd neighbour nodes, and so on. (K = 1, 2, 3, 4 and so on), (ii) social network community and network analysis. The graph analysis finds the (iii) close-by entities, (iv) fully mesh-like connected sets, (v) network graph analysis beside centralities, (vi) also does computations of the *property* of the links, (vii) rectangle counts, and (viii) clustering coefficient. ●●●

(a) i to vi (b) all except i, vi and vii
(c) ii to iv (d) i to iii, v, viii

Review Questions

9.1 How are the features evaluated in the text documents? **(LO 9.1)** ○○●

9.2 Explain five phases and steps in the phases during text analytics. **(LO 9.1)** ○●●

9.3 When is the Naïve Bayes conditional probabilities based classifier used? When is the support vectors based discriminative-classifier used? Write details of each. **(LO 9.1)** ●●●

9.4 What are the tasks in web data analytics? Describe the pre-processing steps and mining tasks in web contents analytics. **(LO 9.2)** ○○●

9.5 How is the emergence of new topics discovered? How do concept hierarchy create and build from category dimensions, such as domain, location, time, application and privileges? **(LO 9.2)** ●●●

9.6 How does the web usage mining discover and analyze patterns in click stream, and generate and and collect associated data? **(LO 9.2)** ○●●

9.7 Describe various link analysis metrics used for analytics. How is PageRank iterated and computed using relative authority of in-linking pages? How does ranking algorithm compute topic-sensitive PageRank? **(LO 9.3)** ●●●

9.8 How does structure of web model as graph network? Draw a diagram for web graph nodes and edges. What are the metrics computed for a web graph? **(LO 9.3)** ○●●

9.9 Describe HITS algorithm to iterate and compute the hubs and authorities? **(LO 9.3)** ○○●

9.10 How does social graph analysis relate to positivity and negativity analysis about the persons? How does social graph network anomaly detection help an organization? **(LO 9.4)** ○●●

9.11 How are social graph analytics metrics, degree, closeness, betweenness, egonet, K-neighbourhood, Top-K shortest paths and SimRank computed by path traversals? **(LO 9.4)** ●●●

9.12 What are the operators provisioned in Apache Spark GraphX for social network graphs analysis? **(LO 9.4)** ○○●

Practice Exercises

9.1 List the steps in the methods used for grouping the text documents into clusters, automating the document organization, topic extraction. Take the example of HTML pages or your University or Company website. **(LO 9.1)** ○○●

9.2 Explain how text analytics tasks performs using Python library *nltk*. **(LO 9.1)** ●●●

9.3 List the steps in document clustering method. How do you use the clusters for the fast information retrieval or filtering? Take the example of student grade cards or Company annual reports. **(LO 9.1)** ○●●

9.4 List the steps in classifying web documents into categories, identifying similar pages across different web documents to classify them as web pages of a university or company. **(LO 9.2)** ○●●

9.5 List the steps in recommendations for top N relevant documents in a collection or portion of a collection. List the steps in filtering – show/hide documents based on most/least relevancy. **(LO 9.2)** ○○●

9.6 Using Example 9.7, write algorithms for PopularityRank, SimRank and best student search. **(LO 9.3)** ●●●

9.7 Rewrite PageRank and HITS algorithms using vectors and matrices. **(LO 9.3)** ○●●

9.8 Write the steps in performing bipartite weighted graph matching in social network graph analysis. **(LO 9.4)** ○●●

9.9 Describe steps to compute the triangles, junction trees, shortest paths and top K-shortest paths and discover the communities in social network graphs of students. **(LO 9.4)** ●●●

Chapter 10

Programming Examples in Analytics and Machine Learning using Hadoop, Spark and Python

LEARNING OBJECTIVES

After studying this chapter, you will be able to:

- **LO 10.1** Learn steps for installation of Hadoop and Spark, and storage and processing of Big Data and large datasets
- **LO 10.2** Get acquainted with steps of programming for deploying and exploring the open source Lego datasets and its schema, processing and storage of datasets, counting of dataset items using MapReduce, creating HBase tables from the CSV format datasets and creating DataFrames from the RDDs
- **LO 10.3** Get knowledge of programming steps in Hive and PySpark for operations of Merge and Join on DataFrames, usages of SQL-equivalent functions for join and processing queries, and using the UDFs
- **LO 10.4** Get introduced to data visualization using Python Plotting (graphing) library, Programming for pi graph, bar charts and scatter plots
- **LO 10.5** Learn steps in the programs and machine learning algorithms for the clustering, classification, regression analysis and predictive analytics

Readers shall also be able to learn the following from the ***Practice Exercises*** given at the end of the chapter:

1. Big Data analytics applications in business
2. Uses of datasets for analyzing and predicting future
3. Develop codes to solve problems in analytics, predict and visualize using Sklearn, PySpark and Mahout

RECALL FROM EARLIER CHAPTERS

Previous chapters 1 to 9 described the followings:

- Hadoop, MapReduce, map tasks using key-value pairs, Hadoop ecosystem tools, Hbase, Hive, HiveQL (DDL, DML, Querying data, Aggregation and Join), Pig (Pig Latin data model, commands, relational operations, Eval functions and user defined functions), Apache Spark
- Spark for distributed and faster in-memory analytics, cluster computing and APIs in Java, Scala, Python and R
- Spark architectural features, software stack components, their functions, steps in data analysis with Spark, ETL processes using built-in functions and operators, ETL pipelines, analytics, data/information reporting, visualizing methods, using Spark with Python advanced features, and UDFs, vectorized UDFs, grouped vectorized UDFs
- Developing and testing Spark codes, programming with RDDs, applications of MLib, and Machine Learning (ML) methods for analysis of datasets
- Apache Mahout architecture, components, their applications for clustering analysis, classification, Naïve Bayes analysis, SVMs for analytics, collaborative filtering, recommender system, and regression analysis for predictions
- Stream computing and SparkStreaming
- Graph databases, graph analytics, Apache SparkGraphX, its Architecture, components, and their applications for graph analytics
- Text mining, web content and web usage analytics, link analysis and web structure analytics

This chapter focuses on Hadoop/Spark/PySpark programming examples. Programs explore datasets, perform analytics and demonstrate machine learning algorithms and data visualization.

10.1 INTRODUCTION

Hadoop provides Big Data storage and computing using clusters. Hadoop manages both large-sized structured and unstructured data in different formats efficiently and effectively. The formats, such as XML, CSV, JSON, text files. Hadoop ecosystem provides running of applications on Big Data. Hadoop deploys MapReduce, HBase distributed databases and other application programming models. Hadoop ecosystem includes Hive and Pig. Hadoop applications support layer and application layer components include Hive, Pig Spark, Spark and Mahout.

Apache® Spark™ is an advanced Big Data analytics tool. Spark is fast and general compute engine. Spark provides in-memory, distributed and faster cluster computing. Spark supports data stored at HDFS, Hadoop compatible data source, such as HBase, Cassandra, Ceph and Amazon S3.

Spark SQL includes SQLContext and JDBC datasource that can read from (and write to) SQL databases. Spark SQL provides DataFrames(SchemaRDDs) to allow processing of a large amount of structured data. Spark SQL does the following: runs SQL-like scripts for query processing, using catalyst optimizer and tungsten *execution engine,* processes structured data, and provides flexible APIs for support for many types of data sources.

SparkSQL has built-in functions and operators for creating ETL pipelines and analytics. Spark SQL does ETL operations by creating ETL pipeline on the data from different file-formats, such as JSON, Parquet, Hive, Cassandra and then running ad hoc queries.

Spark enables programming with the RDDs, and machine learning applications with MLib. Apache Mahout and components have applications for the development of clustering, classification, collaborative filtering and recommender system algorithms.

Spark provides APIs in Java, Scala, Python and R. Spark architecture has many features, and software stack components for data analysis. Apache Spark contains interactive shell for Python programming known as PySpark. PySpark embibes the advanced features of Python, such as UDFs, vectorized UDFs and grouped vectorized UDFs. Python has strong libraries for analytics, machine learning and natural language processing.

Spark Streaming is a stream-processing platform for data mining and real-time analytics. Stream processing requires samples of streaming data, and does the filtering, counting of distinct elements, analysis of frequent itemsets, and mining of association rules. The analysis gives the count of the instances of frequent itemsets present in the stream. Spark streaming facilitates real-time sentiment analytics and stock prices analytics.

Spark is thus one of the most important components for Big Data Analytics Stack. This chapter focuses on Hadoop/Spark/PySpark program examples. The programs explore datasets, perform analytics, visulaizes data, and run machine learning algorithms using famous toy company, Lego Inc. open source datasets.

Section 10.2 describes installation methods for Hadoop, Hive, Pig and Spark on Ubuntu platform.

Section 10.3 describes datasets used in the examples in subsequent sections of this chapter. The section describes deploying and exploring Lego datasets, schema, processing and storage, MapReduce implementation for counting items in the dataset, creating Hive data tables from CSV format dataset and creating DataFrame from the RDDs.

Section 10.4 describes Hive and PySpark programs using functions, Merge and Join of DataFrames, SQL equivalent join functions and UDFs for customized query processing.

Section 10.5 describes programs for data visualization using pi, bar and scatter plots.

Section 10.6 describes machine learning programs using sklearn for SVM, Naïve Bayes classifiers, linear and polynomial regression analysis and predictive analytics.

Practice exercises at the end of the chapter describe the csv files of open source datasets of an automobile company. Datasets for new car sales can be used for analyzing and predicting future sales. The datasets contain monthly car sales for 2007–2017 by the *make* and the data for the most popular car models. The exercises for the analytics shall make a reader through in understanding of algorithms described in the Chapters 5 and 6, and the usage of PySpark and Mahout. Online solution-guide associated with the book explains the methods and codes for them.

10.2 INSTALLATION STEPS FOR HADOOP AND SPARK

LO 10.1

Steps for installation of Hadoop and Spark, and enabling the storage and processing of Big Data and large datasets

The following subsections describe the steps for installation of Hadoop and Spark processes, and configuration of platform used for computing.

10.2.1 Installation Steps for Hadoop, Hive and Pig

Following are the steps for Hadoop Installation for setting up of a single-node cluster of Hadoop 2.9.0 on Ubuntu 16.04 Operating System.[1] Latest version is Hadoop 3.0[2] which is in alpha phase. Apache community has incorporated many changes and is still working on some of them.

[1] https://hadoop.apache.org/ Hadoop
[2] https://www.edureka.co/blog/hadoop-3/

1. Updates all repositories

   ```
   sudo apt-get update
   ```

2. Install Java and ssh
   Hadoop Java Versions
   Version 2.7 and later of Apache Hadoop requires Java 7. Earlier versions (2.6 and earlier) support Java 6.

   ```
   sudo apt-get install openjdk-7-jdk
   sudo apt-get install ssh
   ```

3. Download Hadoop-2.9.0.tar.gz, hive-1.2.2.tar.gz, pig-0.17.0 files.
   The Apache™ Hadoop® project and other Hadoop-related projects at Apache are available at: http://hadoop.apache.org
4. Create a dedicated user hduser. This creates a directory in "home" name as "hduser".
5. Copy the given `hadoop-2.9.0.tar.gz`, `hive-1.2.2.tar.gz`, `pig-0.17.0` files into the "hduser" directory
6. Extract all files in the "hduser" directory:

   ```
   tar -xvzf hadoop-2.9.0.tar.gz
   ```

7. Go to hadoop-2.9.0/conf/
   Following XML files are present:

   ```
   1) core-site.xml
   2) hdfs-site.xml
   3) mapred-site.xml
   4) yarn-site.xml
   ```

   7.1 Open core-site.xml with text editor. Copy the following lines in to core-site.xml:

   ```
   <configuration>
           <property>
                   <name>fs.default.name</name>
                   <value>hdfs://localhost:8020</value>
           </property>
   </configuration>
   ```

   7.2 Open `hdfs-site.xml` with text editor. Copy the following lines in to hdfs-site.xml:

   ```
   <configuration>
           <property>
                   <name>dfs.replication</name>
                   <value>1</value>
           </property>
           <property>
                   <name>dfs.namenode.name.dir</name>
                   <value>/home/hduser/hadoopdata/hdfs/namenode</value>
           </property>
   ```

```
        <property>
                <name>dfs.datanode.data.dir</name>
                <value>/home/hduser/hadoopdata/hdfs/datanode</value>
        </property>
</configuration>
```

7.3 Open yarn-site.xml with text editor. Copy the following lines in to yarn-site.xml:

```
<configuration>
<property>
                <name>yarn.nodemanager.aux-services</name>
                <value>MapReduce shuffle</value>
</property>
<property>
        <name>yarn.nodemanager.aux-services.mapreduce.shuffle.class</
        name>
                <value>org.apache.hadoop.mapred.ShuffleHandler</value>
</property>
</configuration>
```

7.4 Open mapred-site.xml with text editor. Copy the following lines in to mapred-site.xml:

```
<property>
        <name>mapreduce.framework.name</name>
        <value>yarn</value>
</property>
```

7.5 Open hadoop-env.sh with text editor
Copy the following line where the JAVA_HOME path is given in to hadoop-env.sh or below this line "# export JAVA_HOME=/usr/lib/*********" :

```
export JAVA _ HOME=/usr/lib/jvm/java-7-openjdk
```

8. Update $HOME/.bashrc
open bashrc file with command:

```
sudo gedit ~/.bashrc
```

copy following lines to the End of File:

```
export JAVA _ HOME=/usr/lib/jvm/java-7-openjdk
export HADOOP _ HOME=/home/hduser/hadoop-2.9.0
export HIVE _ HOME=/home/hduser/hive-1.2.2
export PIG _ HOME=/home/hduser/pig-0.17.1
export PATH=$PATH: $JAVA _ HOME/bin: $HADOOP _ HOME/bin: $HIVE _ HOME/bin:
$PIG _ HOME/bin
export HADOOP _ MAPRED _ HOME=$HADOOP _ HOME
export HADOOP _ COMMON _ HOME=$HADOOP _ HOME
export HADOOP _ HDFS _ HOME=$HADOOP _ HOME
```

```
export YARN_HOME=$HADOOP_HOME
export HADOOP_COMMON_LIB_NATIVE_DIR=$HADOOP_HOME/lib/native
export HADOOP_OPTS="-Djava.library.path=$HADOOP_HOME/lib"
```

9. Refresh the bashrc file

```
source ~/.bashrc
```

10. Disable the SSH

```
ssh localhost(enter the password)
ssh-keygen -t dsa -P '' -f ~/.ssh/id_dsa
cat ~/.ssh/id_dsa.pub >> ~/.ssh/authorized_keys
```

11. Format the namenode

```
hadoop namenode -format
```

or

```
hadoop namenode -format -force
```

12. Start hadoop

```
start-all.sh
```

13. Check all services of Hadoop are running or not using JPS (Java Virtual Machine Process Status Tool) command.

```
jps
```

Check whether the following processes are running:

```
7770 RunJar
8704 JobTracker
8929 Jps
6495 RunJar
8316 NameNode
8610 SecondaryNameNode
8460 DataNode
8866 TaskTracker
```

The installation is successful if all the above processes are displayed on console.

10.2.2 Installation Steps for the Spark on Ubuntu

Section 5.4 introduced steps for downloading Apache Spark, getting started, Spark shell, developing and testing Spark codes, programming with the RDDs and applications to MLib. The steps for installation of Spark on Ubuntu are as follows:

Step 1: Installing Java
Check whether Java is already installed.

```
java -version
```

Step 2: Install Scala

```
sudo apt-get install scala
```

Check whether Scala installed.

```
scala
```

Test scala.

```
println("Hello World")
```

Quit Scala

```
: q
```

Step 3: Install Spark

Download a pre-built for Hadoop 2.7 version of Spark (preferably, Spark 2.0 or later) from

```
https://spark.apache.org/downloads.html
```

Save `.tgz` file on computer.

Go to terminal and change directory to where `.tgz file` saved (or just move the file to r home folder), then use

```
tar xvf spark-2.2.1-bin-hadoop2.7.tgz
```

Extract the Spark folder and use.

```
cd spark-2.0.2-bin-hadoop2.7.tgz
mv spark-2.0.2-bin-hadoop2.7 spark
```

Make an entry for spark in .bashrc file

Edit the Hadoop user profile /home/hadoop/.profile and add the following lines:

```
export SPARK_HOME=/home/hadoop/spark
export PATH=$SPARK_HOME/bin: $PATH
```

Source the changed .bashrc file by the command

```
source ~/.bashrc
```

Then use

```
cd bin
```

and then

```
./spark-shell
```

Spark shell will pop up. Here, one can load

```
.scala scripts
```

Test the environment.

```
print(sc.version)
```

The output should read:

```
2.2.1
```

The `sc` is SparkContext that is automatically created for you when `PySpark` starts. Initializing a `PySpark` session creates `sqlContext` as well. To exit the PySpark session:

```
quit()
```

10.2.3 Computing Platform Configuration

The examples presented in this chapter are executed on a system with the following configuration:

- Operating System Ubuntu 16.04 LTS 64-bit
- Processor: Intel® Core™ i7-4790 CPU @ 3.60GHz x 8
- RAM: 16 GB
- Hard Disk: 116.5 GB
- Graphics: GeForce GT 710/PCIe/SSE2

10.3 DATASETS USED IN THE EXAMPLES, DATA DEPLOYMENT AND EXPLORATION

LO 10.2

Steps of programming for deploying and exploring the open source Lego datasets, specifying the schema, the processing and storage of datasets, counting of dataset items using MapReduce, creating HBase tables from the CSV format datasets and creating DataFrames from the RDDs

Analytics requires data. A collection of data is called a Dataset. A dataset must be strongly-typed, immutable collection of objects that map to a relational schema. A rich dataset is needed to provide high-quality analytics results. A dataset needs to be rich, which means must offer vast opportunity for exploration and offer an immense range of data patterns.

Here, we have chosen datasets from Lego database. Lego is a renowned brand of construction-toys. The different varieties of toys are sold in sets which build a specific object. A set contains colourful interlocking plastic bricks and other parts. The number, sizes and shapes of the parts vary with sets. The parts can be assembled and connected in many ways, to construct objects, vehicles, buildings and working robots. The parts can be taken apart to make other objects as well.

The Lego database contains information about the parts in different Lego sets. This dataset was compiled by *Rebrickable*[3] for kaggle.com as a public dataset [LDB[4]], with the objective of using these files for any purpose.

This dataset contains Lego sets from year 1950 to July, 2017. The dataset is arranged in 8 CSV files.

The dataset comprises various toy themes. There are in all 614 themes defined in `themes.csv` for various Lego toys, such as Robot, Airport, Building and Train. Almost 11,673 sets are manufactured in year starting from 1950 to July, 2017 (`sets.csv`). Sets have different number of parts (field: `num _ parts in sets.csv`).

Table 10.1 shows a sample row of `sets.csv` that represents a Tractor set with set number 378-1 developed in 1972. It belongs to Theme Id 397 and has 36 parts in total:

[3] https://rebrickable.com/about/

4 LDB⊠ The LEGO Parts/Sets/Colors and inventories of every official LEGO set, available at: https://www.kaggle.com/rtatman/lego-database

Table 10.1 A sample row of sets.csv file

set_num	Name	Year	theme_id	num_parts
378-1	Tractor	1972	397	36

The inventories of parts and sets are also provided in the dataset. Inventory Ids of 11,681 parts and their set numbers are available in `inventories.csv`. Overall there are 25,993 parts (`parts.csv`) belonging to 57 different part categories (`Part_categories.csv`), whereas inventory of parts contains 5,80,251 parts (`inventory_parts.csv`). Inventory of parts also stores the colour information of the part (field: `color_id` in `inventory_parts.csv`). Similarly, the inventory of sets contains 2,846 sets (`inventory_sets.csv`).

The colours are defined in `colors.csv` where the RGB values of 133 colors and two values for `unknown color` and `No color` are specified. The colors are also featured as transparent and non-transparent using Boolean value `is_trans`. Sample of `colors.csv` is presented in Table 10.2.

Table 10.2 Sample of colors.csv file

id	Name	rgb	is_trans
-1	Unknown	0033B2	f
4	Red	C91A09	f
36	Trans-Red	C91A09	t

f stands for false and t for true.

Figure 10.1 shows the dataset schema of the Lego database that helps in figuring out how the files are related.

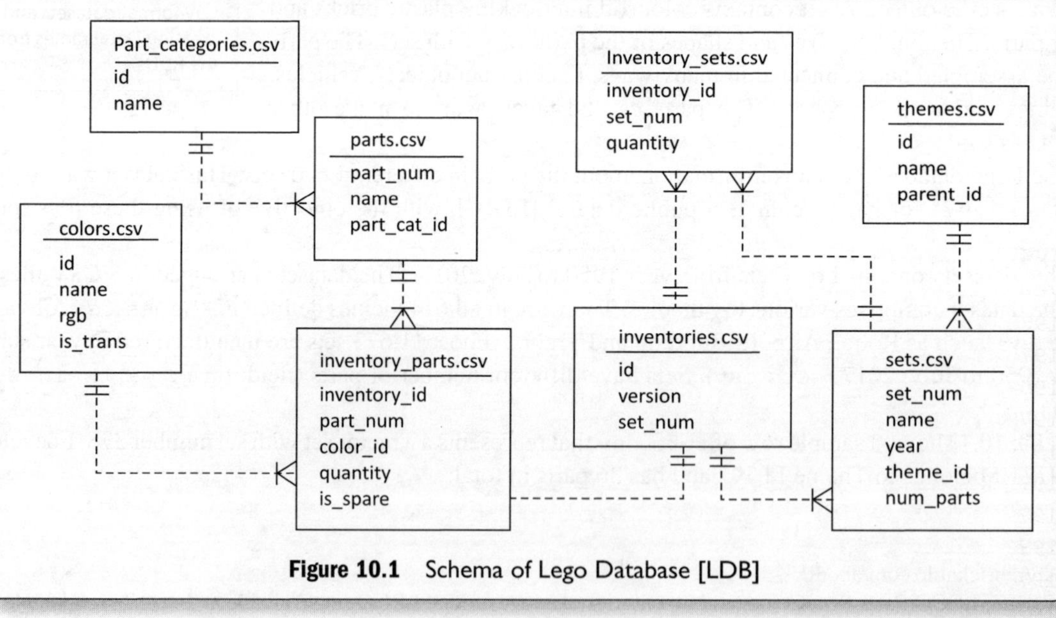

Figure 10.1 Schema of Lego Database [LDB]

10.3.1 Counting and Sorting of Items in Datasets using MapReduce

Objective of Program MapReduce program presented in the section counts sets of toys in the given dataset on the basis of year of introduction and sorts them from the highest count to the lowest.

Mapper loads the input csv file (`sets.csv`), prepares dataframe with two columns (year and number of parts) and passes the prepared dataframe to the reducer.

Reducer loads the dataframe obtained from the Mapper, performs an aggregate function, `count`, to count the year wise sets, and sorts the sets in descending order of `count`.

Mapper and Reducer programs use the dataframe to store the data extracted from files. Section 5.3.1 describes the concept of Dataframe and Section 10.3.3 describes the method of creating DataFrame From CSV file and the RDD.

Input file(s): `sets.csv`

Code of Mapper

```
#file: mapper.py

import pandas as pd      #import pandas python package
#Define mapper Function
def mapper():
    #Extract records of CSV file into Dataframe df1
    df1 = pd.read_csv('/home/.../sets.csv')

    #Prepare dataframe with two columns(year and number of parts)only
    df2 = df1[["year","num_parts"]].copy()

    # Now print out the data that will be passed to the reducer
    print(df2.to_string(index=False))

#Execute mapper function
mapper()
```

Run the Mapper Code using command on the prompt

```
$: python mapper.py
```

Output of Mapper (Note: Shown only 10 records, Total there are 11,673 records):

```
year      num_parts
1970            471
1978             12
1987              2
1979             12
1979             12
1979             12
1979             18
1978             15
1976            147
1976            149
```

Note: The output of mapper.py transfers to reducer.py in MapReduce.

Code of Reducer

```
#file: reducer.py
  import pandas as pd    #import pandas python package
  import sys             #import System-specific parameters
                         #and function module
  import re              #import regular expressions module
                         #for splitting the console input data
def reducer():
    #obtain the list of lines from stdin
    data = sys.stdin.read().splitlines()
    #split each line into 2 items: 'year' and 'num_parts'
    data = [re.split(r'\s+(?=\d+$)', l) for l in data]

    #construct the dataframe
    df = pd.DataFrame(data, columns=['year','num_parts'])
    #Count the rows Group by year and arrange them in ascending order
    sd=df.groupby('year')['year'].count().sort_values(ascending=False)
    print(sd)      #Display desired output

#Execute reducer function
reducer()
```

Note: Regular expressions \s matches Unicode whitespace characters and `\d` matches any Unicode decimal digit. `? =...` is *lookahead* assertion. The pattern character '`$`' matches at the end of the string.

Run the Reducer Code using command on the prompt

```
$:  python mapper.py | python reducer.py
```

The above command executes the `mapper.py` file and the output of `mapper.py` is provided to `reducer.py`

(**Note:** The symbol "|" denotes a pipe. The Pipe is a command in Linux that allows to use two or more commands such that output of one command serves as input to the next.)

Output of Reducer (Counts sets on the basis of year of introduction and sorts them from the highest count to the lowest):

```
year
2014      713
2015      665
2012      615
2016      596
2013      593
```

```
2011        503
2002        447
2010        444
2003        415
2009        402
2004        371
2008        349
2001        339
2005        330
```

10.3.2 Storing CSV Dataset into Hive Database

Create a Table in Hive

```
hive> create table sets(set _ num string, name string, year int, theme _
id int, num _ parts int, category string) row format delimited fields
terminated by ',';
```

Output of Create Table Query

OK

Time taken: 0.107 seconds

Load the Data

```
hive> Load data local inpath '/home/... /sets.csv' overwrite into table sets;
```

Output of Load Data Query

Loading data to table default.sets

Table default.sets stats: [numFiles =1, numRows =0, totalSize = 507514, rawDataSize = 0]

OK

Time taken: 1.124 seconds

Initial step in this exploration process is to read in the data and print a quick summary statistics.

10.3.3 Storing CSV Dataset into the Spark DataFrame

A Spark DataFrame is a two-dimensional data structure with rows and columns. It is similar to a matrix of data rows or a table in relational database or an Excel sheet with column headers. Columns may contain data of different types.

A sample of one of the data file is as follows:

```
set _ num, name, year, theme _ id, num _ parts
00-1, Weetabix Castle, 1970, 414, 471
0011-2, Town Mini-Figures, 1978, 84, 12
0011-3, Castle 2 for 1 Bonus Offer, 1987, 199, 2
```

The file format is csv (comma separated values). Each row of the data is a different record of set (toy set), and different data fields within each row are separated by commas. The first row is the header row and illustrates each data field. Remaining rows contains the data values for data fields correspondingly. The entire set of one data field (say set_num) of all the rows, is a column. The dataset can be visualized in matrix format as:

set _ num	name	year	theme _ id	num _ parts
00-1	Weetabix Castle	1970	414	471
0011-2	Town Mini-Figures	1978	84	12
0011-3	Castle 2 for 1 Bonus Offer	1987	199	2

Reading the data Reading the data requires creation of a dataframe first. This can be done in multiple ways:

- Using different data formats. For example, loading the data from JSON, CSV.
- Loading data from Existing RDD (Resilient Distributed Dataset).
- Programmatically specifying schema

Create a DataFrame from CSV file Pandas is a high level data processing and analysis library of Python, which provides easy-to-use data structures. Pandas is built on functionality provided by the Numpy package and its key data structure is the DataFrame.

Import pandas for data processing functions with `import pandas as pd`. The data from a CSV file is used to create DataFrame, using the read_csv method.

Following code creates a dataframe, `toy _ sets`, from csv file, `sets.csv` and print the column name of dataframe:

```
# Import the pandas library.
  import pandas as pd
# Read in the data.
  toy _ sets = pd.read _ csv("sets.csv")
# Print the names of the columns in toy _ sets.
  print(toy _ sets.columns)
```

Output The code above reads the data in, and shows all the column names:

```
Index(['set _ num', 'name', 'year', 'theme _ id', 'num _ parts'], dtype ='object')
```

The shape of the data displays the number of rows and columns in the data file.

```
print(toy _ sets.shape)
```

Output The toy_sets has 11673 rows, or sets, and 5 columns or data points describing each set:

```
(11673, 5)
```

10.3.4 Creating DataFrame from the RDD

First create a `SparkContext` to connect with Apache Cluster. when operations are required to be executed in a cluster `SparkContext` is needed. `SparkContext` specifies to Spark how and where to access a cluster. The `SparkContext` already exists when Spark shell is used. Otherwise, it can be created by importing, initializing and providing the configuration settings:

```
from pyspark import SparkContext
sc = SparkContext()
```

Two ways to prepare a DataFrame from RDD are as follows:

1. Wrap the elements that belong to the same row in Dataframe by a parenthesis at the time of creation of RDD by parallelize function. Name the columns by `toDF` function where all the columns' names are wrapped by a square bracket.

```
rdd = sc.parallelize([(10, 20, 30),(11, 21, 31), (12, 22, 32)])
dataFrame = rdd.toDF(["p","q","r"])
```

2. Use `pyspark.sql` and assign a name to each element in every row. Now convert the RDD into a dataframe by `toDF` function in which there are no other names.

```
from pyspark.sql import Row
rdd = sc.parallelize([Row(p=10, q=20, r=30), Row(p=11, q=21, r=31),
Row(p=12, q=22, r=32)])
df = rdd.toDF()
```

10.4 PROGRAMMING STEPS USING HIVE AND PYSPARK

LO 10.3

Steps for Programming steps in Hive and PySpark for the operations of Merge and Join on DataFrames, usages of SQL-equivalent functions for join and processing the queries, and using the UDFs

The following subsections describe Merge and Join functions for DataFrame objects, analysis using UDFs for query-processing in Hive and Pyspark.

10.4.1 Merge and Join Functions for DataFrame Objects

Pandas provides a `merge` function as the entry point for all standard database join operations between DataFrame objects.

Syntax of merge function:

```
pd.merge(left, right, how='inner', on=None, left_on =None, right_on = None,
left_index = False, right_index = False, sort = True)
```

Following are the meanings of the terms used:

1. *left* – First Dataframe object.
2. *right* – Second Dataframe object.
3. *how* – Similar to SQL join types ('left', 'right', 'outer' and 'inner'). *inner* is default value. (Table 10.3).
4. *on* – Columns (names) to join on. The column name should be present in both the left and right DataFrame objects. If value of *on* is None, the intersection of the columns in both DataFrames are selected to join by default.

5. *left_on* – Columns from the left Dataframe to use as keys.
6. *right_on* – Columns from the right Dataframe to use as keys.
7. *left_index* – Join keys from left Dataframe is set as the index, when set as true. In case of a Dataframe with a multiIndex (hierarchical), the number of levels must match the number of join keys from the right DataFrame.
8 *right_index* – Similar to left_index for the right Dataframe.
9 *sort* – Sort the result DataFrame by the join keys in lexicographical order. True is default value.

Table 10.3 Merge types and their SQL equivalent names

Merge options	SQL Equivalent	Description
left	LEFT OUTER JOIN	Use keys from left object
right	RIGHT OUTER JOIN	Use keys from right object
outer	FULL OUTER JOIN	Use union of keys
inner	INNER JOIN	Use intersection of keys

The Join operations on DataFrames are also available in Pandas. The operations are like SQL JOIN in RDBMS. They are high performance in-memory join with full features. This implies Join columns with other DataFrame either on index or on a key column.

Syntax of join function

```
Dataframe.join(other, on = None, how='left', lsuffix = '', rsuffix = '', sort = False)
```

Following are the meanings of the terms used:

1. Dataframe: First Dataframe object.
2. other – Second Dataframe object
3. on – Columns (column name, tuple/list of column names, or array-like) to join on. The column name should be present in both the left and right DataFrame objects.
4. how – Similar to SQL join types. Values are 'left', 'right', 'outer', 'inner'. left is the default value (Table 10.3).
5. lsuffix – Suffix to use from left frame's overlapping columns. Its data type is string.
6. rsuffix – Suffix to use from right frame's overlapping columns. Its data type is string.
7. sort – Order result DataFrame lexicographically by the join key. If false, preserves the index order of the calling (left) DataFrame. False is the default value.

10.4.2 Analysis and Query-Processing Using UDFs in Hive and Pyspark

UDF is a customized function for which user specifies the code, input datasets and output datasets. A UDF helps in query processing for total inventories for user defined input itemsets and user defined outputs. Examples of inputs and outputs in the UDF are as follows:

1. Input Datasets (Color), (Year), (Color and Year), (Theme and Color), (Theme, Color and Year)
2. Output Datasets (Inventory), (Color), (Theme)

Python scripts for Customized UDF in Hive Hive provides for writing codes for the UDFs, similar to other programming languages. A UDF enables the code to introduce any new functions to the cluster for computations, as needed. Hive has limited built-in Hive functions (Section 4.4.7). Each dataset specifies a schema and has several features. The analytics require additional 'user defined functions' (UDFs) over and above built-in functions.

UDF are implemented for actions, such as transformations and even for aggregations. User-Defined Aggregation Functions (UDAFs) transform a group of rows into one or more rows, meaning that one can reduce the number of input rows to a single output row by some customized aggregation function. An example of coding in HiveQL, that feeds the data to the Python script is given below. The code uses standard input and reads the result from its standard out.

Custom UDF in Python Objective: Return the toys category in text format, whether *new* or *intermediate* or *old* on the basis of year.

NumPy is the fundamental package for scientific computing with Python. Following code uses Python library numpy:

```
#myUdf.py
import sys
import numpy as np
import datetime
#Define udf (User defined function)
#Function returns category in text format on the basis of year
def year_to_rank(year):
    if year >= 2015: return 'New'
    elif year >= 2010: return 'Intermediate'
    elif year >= 1970: return 'Old'
    else: return 'Not known'
#input
for line in sys.stdin:
    line =line.strip()
    set_num,name,year,theme_id,num_parts,category=line.split('\t')
    name=name.lower()
    category=year_to_rank("year")
    print('\t'.join([str(set_num),str(name), year,theme_id,num_
    parts,str(category)]))
```

The above code is saved in a file named myUdf.py

Add Python script into Hive

It is essential to add the Python file as resource to the Hive cluster. The following command add file myUdf.py to the Hive cluster:

```
hive> add file /home/ … /Lego/myUdf.py;
```

Output of add file command

```
Added resources: [/home/…/Lego/myUdf.py]
```

Run a Python UDF in Hive

```
hive>  select  transform(set _ num,name,year,theme _ id,num _ parts,category)
using 'python myUdf.py' as set _ num,name,year,theme _ id,num _ parts,category
from sets limit 10;
```

Output of transform Query

```
Query ID = hduser1_20180301115757_fa8bd58a-6e70-43ff-b8c3-f24f1d7e444c
Total jobs = 1
Launching Job 1 out of 1
Number of reduce tasks is set to 0 since there's no reduce operator
Job running in-process (local Hadoop)
2018-03-01 11:57:59,164 Stage-1 map = 100%, reduce = 0%
Ended Job = job_local1723749830_0002
MapReduce Jobs Launched:
Stage-Stage-1:  HDFS Read: 642682 HDFS Write: 507514 SUCCESS
Total MapReduce CPU Time Spent: 0 msec
OK
set_num   name                            NULL   NULL   NULL   New
00-1      weetabix castle                 1970   414    471    Old
0011-2    town mini-figures               1978   84     12     Old
0011-3    castle 2 for 1 bonus offer      1987   199    2      Old
0012-1    space mini-figures              1979   143    12     Old
0013-1    space mini-figures              1979   143    12     Old
0014-1    space mini-figures              1979   143    12     Old
0015-1    space mini-figures              1979   143    18     Old
0016-1    castle mini figures             1978   186    15     Old
00-2      weetabix promotional house 1    1976   413    147    Old
Time taken: 1.256 seconds, Fetched: 10 row(s)
```

10.5 DATA VISUALIZATION USING PYTHON PLOTTING LIBRARY

LO 10.4

Data visualization using Python Plotting (graphing) library and Programming for pi and bar charts and scatter plots

`Matplotlib` is Python plotting library. `Matplotlib` is used to generate the output for the visualization. It could be interesting to plot a chart. The library imports using:

`import pandas` for data processing functions, and
`import Matplotlib` for visualizing the output.

Plotting functions in `Matplotlib` are included using `import matplotlib.pyplot as plt statement`. The functions in pyplot package facilitates drawing and showing the plots.

Pie Chart Plot Example

Objective Let's plot a pie chart of color transparency that can visualize the distribution of non-transparent and transparent colors.

`Input file(s): colors.csv`

Following is the code of plotting a pie chart:

```
import pandas as pd #Import pandas for processing the CSV file I/O
import matplotlib.pyplot as plt  #Import matplotlib plotting library

#Read CSV file and Extract data into dataframe df
df = pd.read_csv('/home/.../colors.csv')

# Apply aggregation function count and store the result in a new
# dataframe sd
sd = df.groupby('is_trans')['is_trans'].count

y= sd.values        # Extract count values in array a

# Define an array, expl, which specifies the fraction of the
# radius with which to offset each wedge.
expl =(0.1, 0)

labels = 'Non-Transparent', 'Transparent'    # Define Data Labels
colors = ['while', 'grey']                   # Define wedge colors

# Plot the pie chart
plt.pie(y, labels=labels, explode=expl, colors=colors, autopct='%1.1f%%',
shadow=True, startangle=90)
plt.axis('equal')
plt.show()
```

The parameters of `pie` function are as follows:

1. *x*: Array of the wedge sizes.
2. *explode*: Array that specifies the fraction of the radius with which to offset each wedge.
3. *labels*: An optional list parameter with default value None. It is a sequence of strings providing the labels for each wedge.
4. *colors*: An optional array parameter with default value None. It is a sequence of matplotlib color arguments through which the pie chart will cycle. If None, will use the colors in the currently active cycle.
5. *autopct*: An optional parameter with default value None. It is a string or function that is a label of wedges with their numeric value. The label will be placed inside the wedge.

6. *shadow*: An optional Boolean parameter with default value False. It draws a shadow beneath the pie.
7. *startangle*: An optional float parameter with default value = None. If startangle not None, then rotates the start of the pie chart by an angle mentioned in degrees. The rotation is counterclockwise from the x-axis.
8. *radius*: An optional float parameter with default value None. It defines the radius of the pie. If radius is None it will be set to 1.

Figure 10.2 shows a pie chart output.

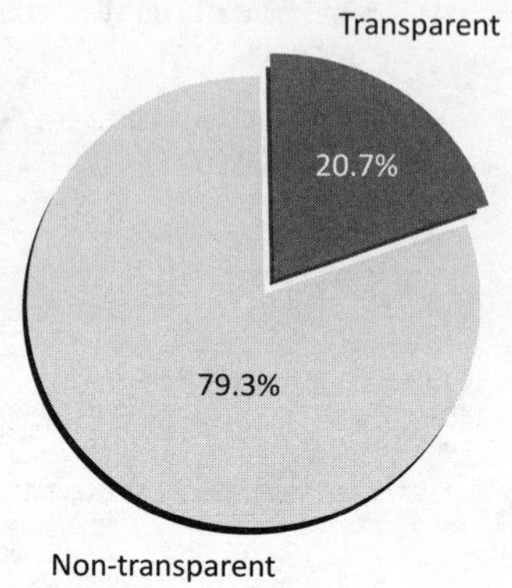

Figure 10.2 Pie chart depicting the color transparency

Example of Bar Chart Plot

Bar chart is another visualization tool. The chart presents the data of different groups that are being compared with each other. The plotting of bar chart requires data at x- and y-axes.

Objective Let's plot bar chart for number of parts in each category of toys.

Aggregation function `count` is used on `part_cat_id` field. The `part_cat_id` field is arranged in descending order before performing the aggregation.

Code for the bar chart is as follows:

```
import pandas as pd                #Import pandas data processing,
                                   #CSV file I/O functions
import matplotlib.pyplot as plt   #Import matplotlib plotting library

#Read CSV file and Extract data into dataframe df
df = pd.read _ csv('/home/.../parts.csv')

# Apply aggregation function count then sort function on df
# and store the result in a new dataframe sd
```

```
sd = df.groupby('part _ cat _ id') ['part _ cat _ id'].count().sort _
values(ascending=False)
y= sd.values        # Extract count values
x =sd.index# Extract index
# Display the bar chart
plt.title('Bar Chart')  #Define Title of the chart
plt.xlabel('Part Category Id')  #Define Label of X-axis
plt.ylabel('Category Count')#Define Label of Y-axis
plt.bar(x, y,color = 'gray')# Plot the bar chart for x and y
plt.show()# Display the bar chart
```

Input file(s) `parts.csv`

Figure 10.3 shows the bar chart depicting category-wise counts for parts.

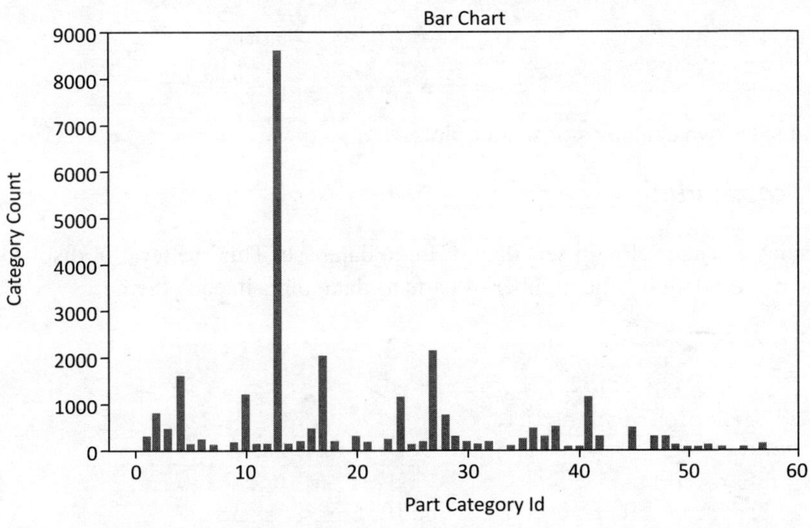

Figure 10.3 Bar chart depicting category-wise parts counts

The result in Figure 10.3 suggests that Category 13 has the highest number of parts (8,556), while Category 56 has the lowest number of parts (8).

Scatter Function Syntax

Scatter charts or scatter plots are used to plot data points on the horizontal and vertical axes. Scatter functions are used to draw scatter plot. Before an example of scatter plot, let us understand the various parameters of scatter function.

Syntax of scatter function is `(x, y, marker = "x", s = 150, linewidths = 5, zorder = 10)`

Following are the meanings of the terms used above:

1. *x*, *y*: Label or position, optional – Coordinates for each point.

2. *s*: Scalar or array_like, optional – Size of each point.
3. *color*: Label or position, optional, default: ‘*b*’ – Color of each point.
4. *marker*: MarkerStyle, optional, default: ‘o’ – Marker Symbol
5. *alpha*: Scalar, optional, *default*: None – The alpha blending value, between 0 (transparent) and 1 (opaque).
6. *linewidths*: Scalar or array_like, optional, default: None – The linewidth of the marker edges.
7. *Zorder*: Top-to-bottom order of the layers; Used when objects are overlapping in two-dimensional view

Table 10.4 shows eight common markers in plots.

Table 10.4 Eight common Markers

Marker	Symbol	Marker	Symbol
“.”	point	“v”	triangle_down
“,”	pixel	“^”	triangle_up
“+”	plus	“<”	triangle_left
“x”	cross	“>”	triangle_right

Now, let us consider two examples of scatter plots.

Example 1 of Scatter Plot

Objective Display a scatter plot on sets data of Lego database. This scatter plot displays the `theme Id` and `number of parts` defining the number of parts as datapoints in each theme.

Input file(s) `sets.csv`

```
#Import matplotlib plotting library
import matplotlib.pyplot as plt
# Import pandas for processing the CSV file I/O
import pandas as pd
#Read CSV file and Extract data into dataframe df
df = pd.read _ csv('/home/ ... /sets.csv')
# Extract features from df and store them in arrays x and y
# respectively.
x = df['theme _ id'].values        #Extract theme _ id values in array x
y = df['num _ parts'].values       #Extract num _ parts values in array y
# Create Scatter plot of data points(x,y)
plt.scatter(x, y, color='gray', s=10) #s is size of scatter plot point
plt.xlabel('Theme Id')#Define Label of X-axis
plt.ylabel('Number of Parts')    #Define Label of Y-axis
#plot the x & y axis# Define the min & max value of x axis and y axis
# as(x _ min, x _ max, y _ min, y _ max)
x _ min = 0
```

```
x_max = 40
y_min = -1
y_max = 50
plt.axis([x_min, x_max, y_min, y_max])
plt.title('Scatter Plot') #Define title of the scatter plot
plt.show()                #Display the scatter plot
```

Figure 10.4 shows a scatter plot which represents relationships between themes (represented by themeId) and number of parts.

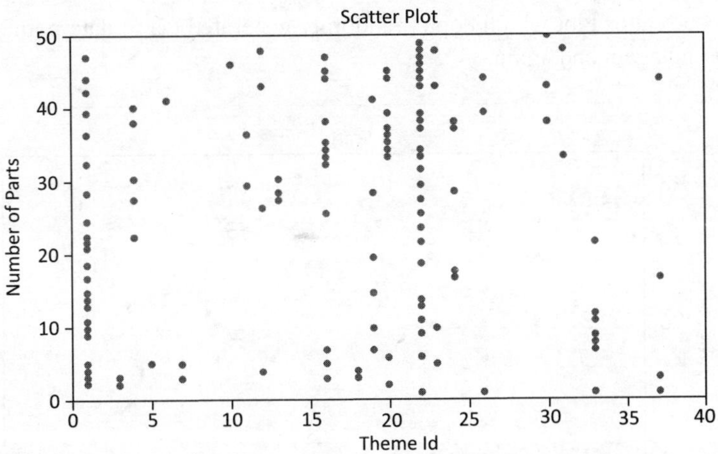

Figure 10.4 Scatter Plot which represents relationships between themes and number of parts

Example 2 of Scatter Plot

This example is for displaying a scatter plot for some random datapoints. numpy library is required for creating random number. `randint( )` function present in this library returns random integers from the "discrete uniform" distribution in the "half-open" interval (low, high). If high is None (the default), then results are from (0, low). Size parameter of `randint` function defines the number of integers to be generated.

Objective Display a scatter plot on say, 50 random datapoints generated between (1,1) and (10,10).

Following is the code:

```
#Import matplotlib plotting library
import matplotlib.pyplot as plt
#Import NumPy for random number generation function
```

```
import numpy as np
#Generate 50 Random numbers(x, y) between (1,1) to (10,10)
x = np.random.randint(low=1, high=10, size=50)
y = np.random.randint(low=1, high=10, size=50)
#Create Scatter plot of data points (x,y)
plt.scatter(x, y,color='black',s=10) #s is size of point
plt.xlabel('X axis')
plt.ylabel('Y axis')
plt.axis([-1,11,-1,11])
plt.title('Scatter Plot')
plt.show()
```

Figure 10.5 shows a scatter Plot which depict randomly generated (x, y) data points. Output may vary if you execute the program again and again.

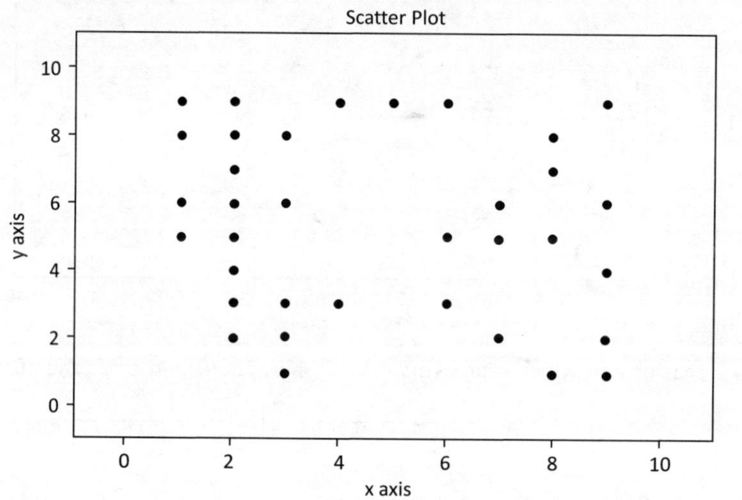

Figure 10.5 Scatter plot depicting randomly generated (x, y) data points

10.6 MACHINE-LEARNING ALGORITHMS IMPLEMENTATION

LO 10.5

Machine-learning programs using PySpark for the clusters identification, SVM and Naïve Bayes Classifiers and linear, and linear and polynomial regression analysis for enabling predictions

Machine learning (ML) is a domain which focuses on the development of algorithms to exploit the data and learn from the data to make predictions. This has an immense range of applications, from effective web search to stock price prediction.

Python libraries `Scikit-learn` and `Pandas` are used to implement the ML algorithms. The library contains implementations of most common algorithms, including k-means, random forests, SVMs, and logistic regression. Scikit-learn has a consistent API for accessing these algorithms.

The following subsections provide insight into machine learning algorithms for clustering, classification and regression in Python.

10.6.1 Clustering Algorithm

Let us discuss a way to figure out more features about the datasets of Lego database. Clustering finds patterns within the data easily by grouping similar rows together.

Brief description of the K-means algorithm code is as follows:

1. Perform basic imports first. Import NumPy which is a scientific computing module (used here for returning a matrix from an array of year and color_id values, then matplotlib for graphing, and then K-means from sklearn).
2. Next, read the input csv files into individual dataframes and merge or join (use inner join) those to get a final dataframe with multiple attributes.
3. Initialize k-means with the required parameters to the K-means algorithm—(i) number of clusters (n_clusters) as 2. Change the n_clusters value to get output for n (say, 3 or 4) numbers of clusters. (ii) Another parameter is random_state which is an integer or None, used for initializing the internal random number generator, which decides initialization (of centroids). Remember, K-means is stochastic method (the results may vary even for the same input values). Hence, in order to make the results reproducible, one can specify a value for the random_state parameter.
4. Next, use fit () function to fit the data (learning)
5. Next, take the values found for the centroids, based on the fitment, as well as the labels for each centroid.
6. The "labels" here are labels that the machine assigns on its own. Similarly, the centroids also.
7. Finally, plot and visualize the machine's findings based on the data, and the fitment according to the number of clusters defined in the code.
8. x and y axes take the min_x, max_x, min_y and, max_y values. Here, theme Id is plotted on x-axis that has values 0 (minimum) to 614 (maximum). Color Id has values between 1 to 9999.
   Restrict unknown (Color Id=–1), No Color (Color Id=9999) and New colors (Color Id from 1000 to 1007) for clearer visualization. User can implement the program for all colours to see the difference.
9. colors = ["g.","r.","c.","y."] statement defines green, red, cyan and yellow colors for cluster no. 1, 2, 3 and 4, respectively.

Objective of the Program The cluster example prepares 2, 3 and 4 clusters of features theme_id and color_id. The program plots the resultant clusters using scatter plot. The clusters are represented in various colors with centroid drawn with X marker within each cluster. The values of centroids are also displayed.

Input file(s): sets.csv, inventories.csv, inventory_parts.csv and colors.csv

Following example implements K-means clustering algorithm and give full code:

```
#import the numpy, pandas, matplotlib and sklearn libraries
import numpy as np
import pandas as pd
from matplotlib import pyplot as plt
from sklearn.cluster import KMeans #KMeans Clustering Algorithm

#Read csv files and extract data in dataframes df1, df2, df3 and df4
df1 = pd.read_csv('/home/.../sets.csv')
```

```
df2 = pd.read_csv('/home/.../inventories.csv')
df3 = pd.read_csv('/home/.../inventory_parts.csv')
df4 = pd.read_csv('/home/.../colors.csv')
#Restrict(unknown, No Color and New colors here for better visualization.
df4 = df4[((df4['id'] <1000) & (df4['id'] >= 0))]

#Join/Merge all the dataframes into a new dataframe say, df1 ##
df1 = pd.merge(df1, df2, left_on="set_num", right_on = "set_num")
df1 = pd.merge(df1, df3, left_on="id", right_on = "inventory_id")
df1 = pd.merge(df1, df4, left_on="color_id", right_on = "id")

#Extract the theme_id and color_id features from merged dataframe df1
#and Store in dataframe df
df = pd.DataFrame(df1, columns= ['theme_id', 'color_id'])

#Store feature data from df in the `f1` and `f2` arrays.
f1 = df['theme_id'].values          #Extract theme id column values
f2 = df['color_id'].values          #Extract color_id column values

X=np.column_stack((f1, f2))


#Obtain minimum & maximum of X and y values for drawing axes
min_x= f1.min()
max_x= f1.max()
min_y= f2.min()
max_y= f2.max()
#combine them into a feature matrix `X` before entering it into the algorithm
#Execute KMeans algorithm
K=2  #Define number of clusters 2,3,4 here
kmeans = KMeans(n_clusters=K,random_state=1)
#fit the data
kmeans.fit(X)
#Obtain the values found for the Centroids & labels for each centroid
labels = kmeans.labels_
centroids = kmeans.cluster_centers_
#Display the centroids and labels values before plotting them
print("Centroids for ", K, "clusters are : ")
print(centroids)
print("Labels are : ")
print(labels)
#Define colours of the clusters. plot each cluster with a
#different colour. For example, 1 with green, 2 with red, 3 with Cyan,
```

```
#4 with yellow --- Add more colours for drawing more than 4 clusters
colors = ["g.","r.","c.","y."]
# plot the scatter graph for clusters
for i in range(len(X)):
    plt.plot(X[i][0], X[i][1], colors[labels[i]], markersize=10)
plt.scatter(f1, f2, colors="k")
plt.scatter(centroids[:, 0], centroids[:, 1], marker="x", s=150, linewidths=5,
zorder=10)
plt.axis([min _ x, max _ x, min _ y, max _ y])
plt.xlabel('Theme Id')
plt.ylabel('Color Id')
plt.show()
```

Output of the K-means algorithm Figure 10.6 shows K-means Output for 2, 3 and 4 clusters.

10.6.2 Classification Algorithm Example 1: SVM Classifier

SVM can be implemented with the help of scikit-learn library. Following is a simple demonstration which helps in building understanding of working with Linear Support Vector Classifier (SVC). The objective of a Linear SVC is to fit to the data provided and returning a "best fit" hyperplane that divides or categorizes the data.

Brief description of the SVM classifier algorithm code:

1. Perform basic imports first. Import NumPy is a scientific computing module (used here for returning a matrix from an array of year and theme_id features, then matplotlib for graphing, and then SVC from sklearn.
2. Next, Load the data from csv files into individual dataframes and join (use inner join) them to get a final dataframe of multiple attributes.
3. A function specifies `Build _ Data _ Set` using two parameters `year` and `theme _ id`.
4. Next, fill the X parameter with the NumPy array containing rows of the above mentioned two features using `np.array` function. Then populate the y variable with the "targets" (or labels) converted to numerical data. Here, Boolean f is converted to 0 and t is converted to 1. The targets are basically binary or multivalued in a classification model.
5. The SVM calls the `Build _ Data _ Set` function, builds the linear SVC. Specify the kernel type to be used in the algorithm. Kernel type must be one of 'linear', 'poly', 'rbf' (Default), 'sigmoid', 'precomputed' or a callable.
6. Next, use fit () function to fit the predictor and target variables.
7. Calculate the feature weights and plot the scatter graph as well as classifier.
8. After being fitted, the model can also be used to predict new values using `clfr.predict(X)`.For example, `clfr.predict([2020])` to predict values in year 2020.

Objective of the Program The SVM classifier example which classifies the input dataset on the basis of transparency of the colors. Features selected are year and theme_id. The program plots the resultant classes using the scatter plot. The classes are represented *using different colors*. The dataset size is restricted for demonstration purpose only. User can execute the entire code on complete dataset. Here in the following example, we also restricted unknown (Color Id=–1), No Color (Color Id=9999) and New colors (Color Id from 1000 to 1007) for clearer visualization. User can implement the program for all colors to see the difference.

Input file(s) sets.csv, inventories.csv, inventory_parts.csv and colors.csv

Following is the complete code of SVM Classifier :

```
#import the numpy, pandas, matplotlib and sklearn libraries
import numpy as np
import pandas as pd
from matplotlib import pyplot as plt
from sklearn.svm import SVC    #Support Vector Classifier

#Read csv file and extract data in dataframes df1, df2, df3 and df4
df1 = pd.read_csv("/home/.../sets.csv")
df2 = pd.read_csv("/home/.../inventories.csv")
df3 = pd.read_csv("/home/.../inventory_parts.csv")
df4 = pd.read_csv("/home/.../colors.csv")

#Join/Merge all the dataframes into a new dataframe say, df##
df1 = pd.merge(df1, df2, left_on="set_num", right_on = "set_num")
df1 = pd.merge(df1, df3, left_on="id", right_on = "inventory_id")
df1 = pd.merge(df1, df4, left_on="color_id", right_on = "id")
df1 = pd.DataFrame(df1, columns= ['year','theme_id', 'color_id','is_trans'])

#Define a function to build data set with two features
#The function returns the X(predictor) and Y(target)
def Build_Data_Set(features = ["year","theme_id"]):
    df = df1

    #Color Id=0, 9999  and 1000 to 1007 are ignored
    #for better visualization
    df = df[((df['id'] <1000) & (df['id'] >= 0))]

    X = np.array(df[features].values)
    y = (df["is_trans"].replace("f",0).replace("t",1).values.tolist())
    return X,y

#SVM Analysis Code begins from here
X, y = Build_Data_Set()
clfr = SVC(kernel="linear", C= 1.0)
clfr.fit(X,y)
```

(a) Number of clusters = 2

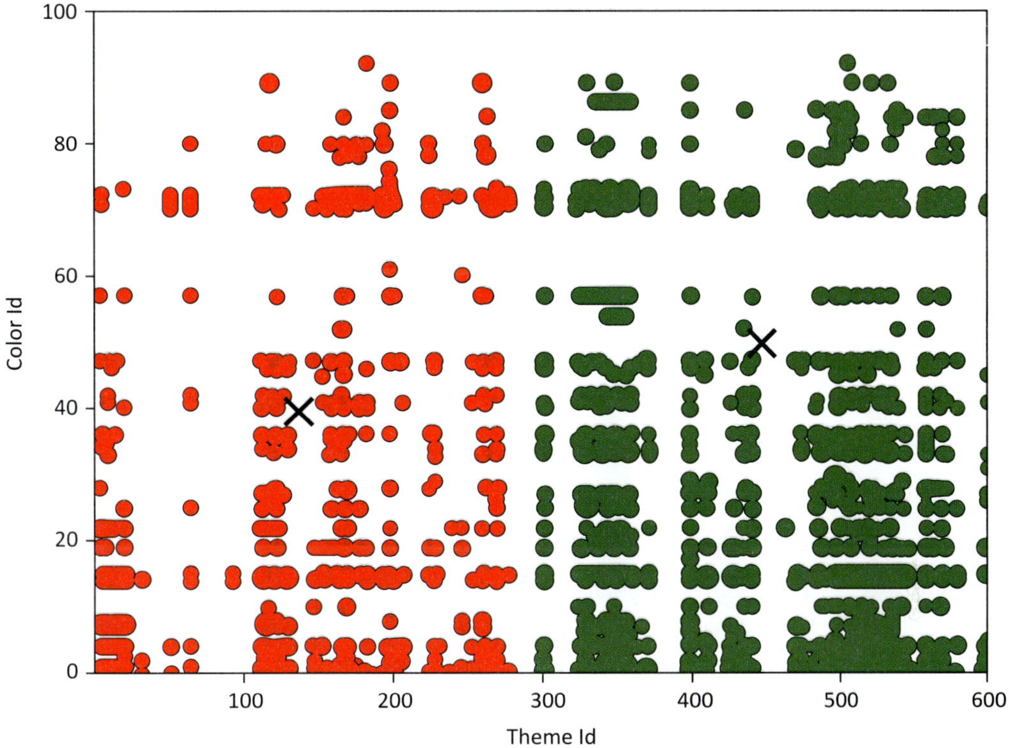

Centroids for 2 clusters are:
[[446.56017471 48.83862413]
 [136.22700043 39.61788618]]
Labels are:
[1 1 1 ... 0 0 0]

Green Colour Cluster – *Centroid at (446.56,48.84)*
Red Colour Cluster – *Centroid at (136.28, 39.62)*

Figure 10.6 (a)

(b) Number of clusters = 3

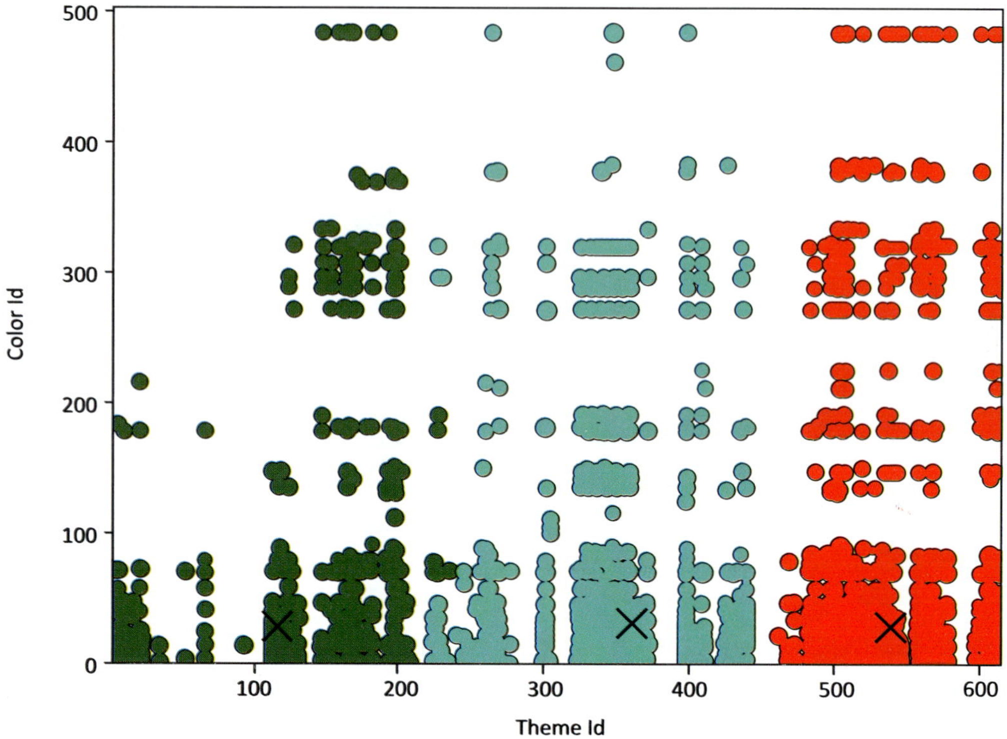

Centroids for 3 clusters are:
[118.88014572 39.92094718]
[538.40949679 43.14846032]
[358.34057677 52.59077985]]

Labels are:
[1 1 1 ... 0 0 0]

Green Colour Cluster – *Centroid at (118.88, 39.92)*
Red Colour Cluster – *Centroid at (538.40, 43.14)*
Cyan Colour Cluster – *Centroid at (358.34, 52.59)*

Figure 10.6 (b)

(c) Number of clusters = 4

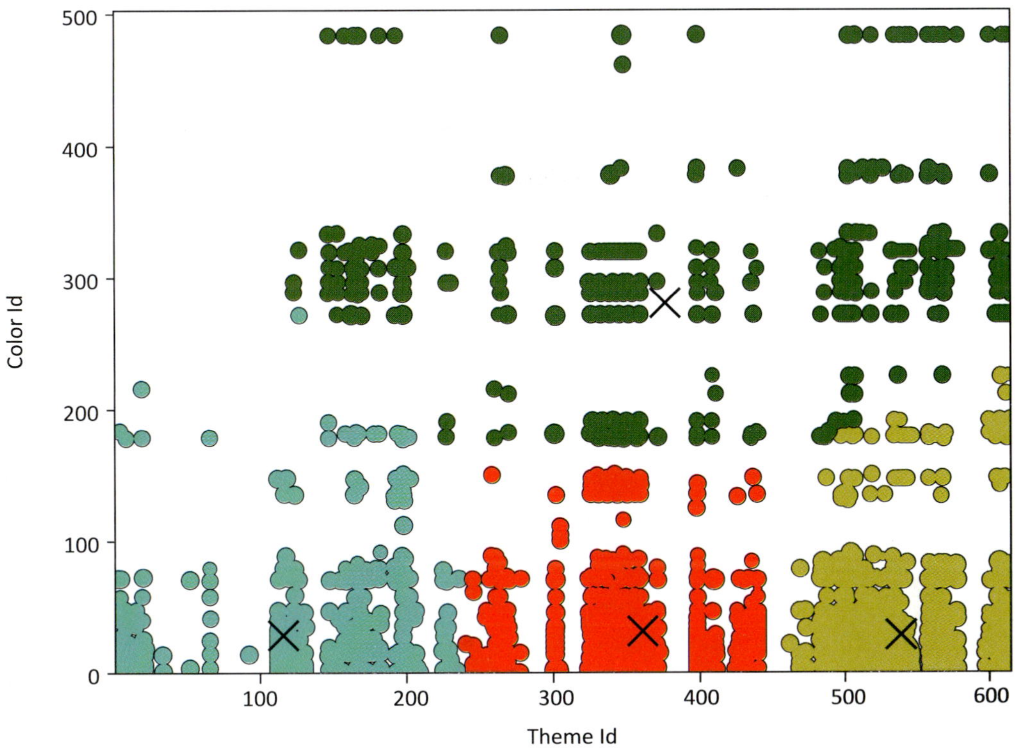

Centroids for 4 clusters are:
[[376.06290957 280.93709043]
 [359.61648532 31.85713221]
 [116.65735944 28.69564119]
 [537.88362069 28.59060521]]
Labels are:
[1 1 1 ... 0 0 0]
Green Colour Cluster – *Centroid at (376.06, 280.93)*
Red Colour Cluster – *Centroid at (359.61, 31.86)*
Cyan Colour Cluster – *Centroid at (116.65, 28.69)*
Yellow Colour Cluster – *Centroid at (537.88, 28.59)*

Figure 10.6 (c)

Figure 10.6: K-means output for 2, 3 and 4 clusters

(a) OUTPUT for rows 1000 to 2077 of the merged dataframe df

```
df = df [1000:2077]
```

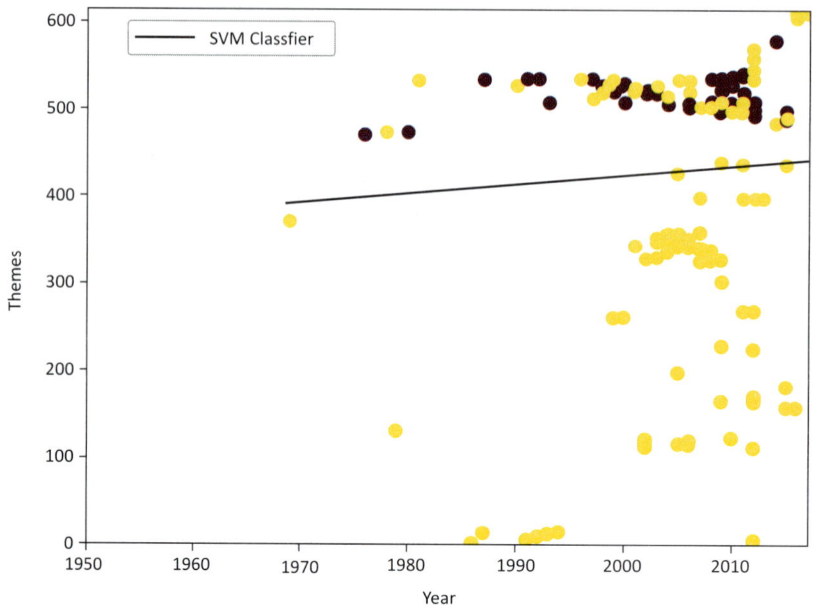

(b) OUTPUT for first 5000 rows of the merged dataframe df

```
df = df [1:5000]
```

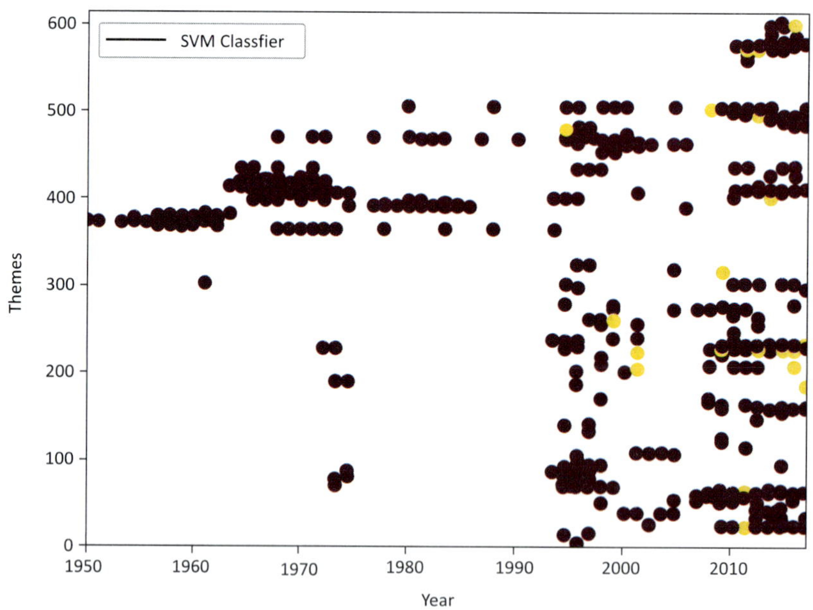

Figure 10.7: SVM outputs for two different data subsets

```
#Calculate the feature weights
w = clfr.coef _ [0]
m = -w [0] / w[1]
xx = np.linspace(min(X[:, 0]), max(X[:, 0]))
yy = m * xx - clfr.intercept _ [0] / w[1]

#Plot the classifier
h0 = plt.plot(xx,yy, "k-", label="SVM Classifier")

#plot the scatter graph for classification
plt.scatter(X[:, 0], X[:, 1],c=y)
plt.axis([1950,2017,0,614])
plt.xlabel("Year")
plt.ylabel("Themes")
plt.legend()
plt.show()
```

Output of SVM classifier Figure 10.7 shows SVM outputs for two different data subsets

Salient Observations from SVM Outputs SVM does not directly provide probability estimates. The outputs illustrated in Figures 10.7(a) and (b) are not significant. When tried with the complete dataset (which has more than 5 lakh 70 thousand rows), the output is not revealing any significant interpretation. Taking the time in order of 1-2 hours for classifying complete dataset since single cluster machine is used here. The datasets have limited number of dimensions and the sample size is very large. It is identified that SVM does not perform well due to two reasons.

Reason 1: When the dataset is large, it requires high training-time thus, training becomes extremely slow.
Reason 2: When dataset has more noise, the target classes are overlapping.

Thus, from the practical experience, SVMs are proven to be better for small to medium datasets and datasets with low noise. SVMs are better for datasets with larger feature dimensions.[5,6]

This also indicates that the suitability of the classifier depends upon the characteristics of datasets.

10.6.3 Classification Algorithm Example 2: Naïve Bayes Classifier

Naïve Bayes classification uses Bayes theorem to determine class of new data points. Consider an example where we want to know whether various themes and the colors used are more than 800 or not. The Naïve Bayes classification algorithm is presented in this section to classify the similar problem as in Section 10.6.2.

Brief Description of the Naïve Bayes Classifier:

1. Load the data from CSV files, merge them and store them in a dataset.
2. Optional Step: Re-index the dataframe if you are interested in partial dataset so that the data obtained becomes randomized using following syntax: `df = df1.reindex(np.random.permutation (df1.index))`

[5] https://www.analyticsvidhya.com/blog/2017/09/understaing-support-vector-machine-example-code/
[6] https://sadanand-singh.github.io/posts/svmpython/

3. Extract Theme _ id and Color _ id features from dataset and store them in X.
4. Convert year field to binary feature. The year having 'num_parts' more than 800 as '1' and year having 'num_parts' less than or equal to 800 as '0'.
5 Split dataset in training set and test set so that machine can be trained using X_train and Y_train.
6. test_size in float represents the proportion of the dataset to include in the test split, here taken as 0.33(33%). random _ state, is an integer or None, used for initializing the internal random number generator, which decides the splitting of data into train and test sets. Default is None. If random_state is None, then a randomly-initialized RandomState object is returned. If random_state is an integer, then it is used to seed a new RandomState object.
7. Use feature scaling for X _ train.
8. Import GaussianNB from sklearn.naive _ bayes
9. Create a classifier and fit training set to it.
10. Make a Prediction—Estimate the accuracy of the model by making predictions for each data instance in the test dataset.
11. Estimate Accuracy—Evaluate the accuracy of the model's predicted values by comparing the two arrays (test _ labels vs. preds).
12. Use the sklearn function accuracy _ score() to determine the accuracy of your machine learning classifier. (optional)
13. Visualize the training and test result sets. Here we have drawn a curve and created two sections: One section for those themes and colors that are using more than 800 and other section for those themes and colors that are not having more than 800 number of parts.

Objective of the Program The Naïve Bayes classifier example presented in the section classifies input dataset on the basis of number of parts (more than 800 and less than-equal to 800) in a set. Features selected are theme_id and color_id. The program plots the resultant classes using scatter plot and contours. The classes are represented using different colors. The entire dataset is considered. User can experience the followings: handling data, summarizing data to present training and test datasets, making a prediction, evaluating accuracy and visualization of classes in the given example. Use the complete code for standalone implementation of the Naïve Bayes algorithm.

Input file(s) sets.csv, inventories.csv, inventory_parts.csv and colors.csv

Following is the complete code of complete code of Naïve Bayes classifier

```
#import the numpy, pandas, matplotlib and sklearn library
import numpy as np
import pandas as pd
from matplotlib import pyplot as plt
from sklearn.naive _ bayes import GaussianNB

#Read csv files and extract data in dataframes df1, df2, df3 and df4
df1 = pd.read _ csv('/home/.../sets.csv')
df2 = pd.read _ csv('/home/.../inventories.csv')
df3 = pd.read _ csv('/home/.../inventory _ parts.csv')
df4 = pd.read _ csv('/home/.../colors.csv')

#Join/Merge all the dataframes into a new dataframe say, df
```

```
df1 = pd.merge(df1, df2, left_on="set_num", right_on="set_num")
df1 = pd.merge(df1, df3, left_on="id", right_on="inventory_id")
df1 = pd.merge(df1, df4, left_on="color_id", right_on="id")
df1 = pd.DataFrame(df1, columns=['year', 'theme_id', 'color_id', 'is_trans'
, 'num_parts'])

def Build_Data_Set(features= ["theme_id", "color_id"]):
    df = df1
    X = df.iloc[:, [1, 2]].values
    df['year'] = np.where(df['num_parts']>800, '1', '0')
    y = df['year'].values
    return X, y

# Naïve Bayes Classification Code begins from here
X, y = Build_Data_Set()

# Splitting the dataset into the Training set and Test set
from sklearn.model_selection import train_test_split
X_train, X_test, y_train, y_test = train_test_split(X, y,
      test_size=0.33, random_state=0)

# Feature Scaling
from sklearn.preprocessing import StandardScaler
sc = StandardScaler()
X_train = sc.fit_transform(X_train)
X_test = sc.transform(X_test)

#Define Gaussian Naïve Bayes Classifier
classifier = GaussianNB()
classifier.fit(X_train, y_train)

# Predicting the Test set results
y_pred = classifier.predict(X_test)
# Making the Confusion Matrix
from sklearn.metrics import confusion_matrix
cm = confusion_matrix(y_test, y_pred)

# Plot the Training set results
from matplotlib.colors import ListedColormap
X_set, y_set = X_train, y_train
X1, X2 = np.meshgrid(np.arange(start = X_set[:, 0].min() - 1, stop =    X_
set[:, 0].max() + 1, step = 0.01),
np.arange(start = X_set[:, 1].min() - 1, stop = X_set[:, 1].max() + 1, step = 0.01))
```

```
plt.contourf(X1, X2, classifier.predict(np.array([X1.ravel(),   X2.ravel()]).T).
reshape(X1.shape),
alpha = 0.5, cmap = ListedColormap(('grey', 'blue')))
plt.xlim(X1.min(), X1.max())
plt.ylim(X2.min(), X2.max())
for i, j in enumerate(np.unique(y _ set)):
    plt.scatter(X _ set[y _ set == j, 0], X _ set[y _ set == j, 1],
    c = ListedColormap(('red', 'green'))(i), label = j, s = 7)
plt.title('Classifier(Training set)')
plt.xlabel('Theme Id')
plt.ylabel('Color Id')
plt.legend()
plt.show()

#Estimate Accuracy
from sklearn.metrics import accuracy _ score
print("Prediction = ", y _ pred)
print("Accuracy = ", accuracy _ score(y _ test, y _ pred))

# Visualizing the Test set results
from matplotlib.colors import ListedColormap
X _ set, y _ set = X _ test, y _ test
X1, X2 = np.meshgrid(np.arange(start = X _ set[:, 0].min() - 1, stop = X _ set[:, 0].
max() + 1, step = 0.01),
 np.arange(start = X _ set[:, 1].min() - 1, stop = X _ set[:, 1].max() + 1, step = 0.01))
plt.contourf(X1, X2, classifier.predict(np.array([X1.ravel(),    X2.ravel()]).T).
reshape(X1.shape),
  alpha = 0.5, cmap = ListedColormap(('cyan', 'yellow')))
plt.xlim(X1.min(), X1.max())
plt.ylim(X2.min(), X2.max())
for i, j in enumerate(np.unique(y _ set)):
plt.scatter(X _ set [y _ set == j, 0], X _ set [y _ set == j, 1], c =
ListedColormap(('red', 'green')) (i), label = j, s = 7)
plt.title('Naive Bayes(Test set)')
plt.xlabel('Theme Id')
plt.ylabel('Color Id')
plt.legend()
plt.show()
```

Output of Naïve Bayes classifier

Figure 10.8 shows output of Naïve Bayes classifier. The rows of df dataframe are shuffled and selected first 50,000 rows only (df = df[1:50000]). The Green data points are themes and colors with more than 800 number of parts and Red for less than equal to 800 parts.

(a) Training Set Output

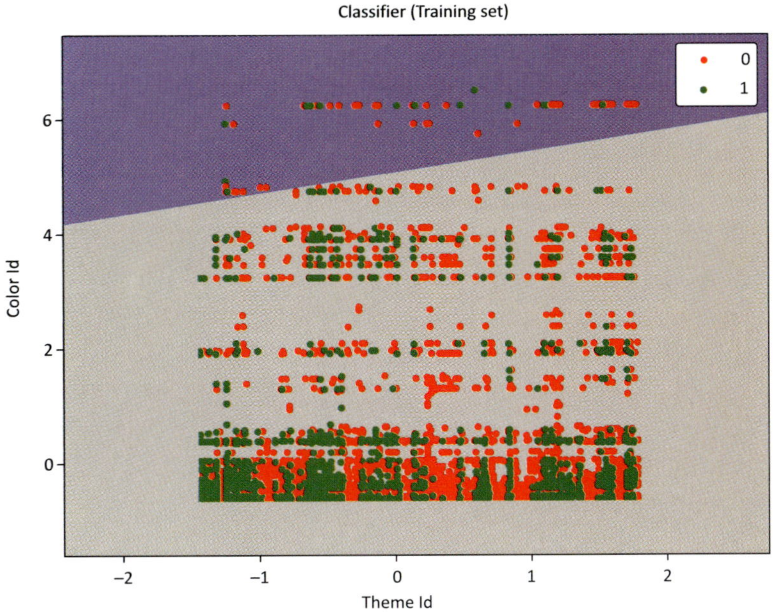

(b) Test Set Output

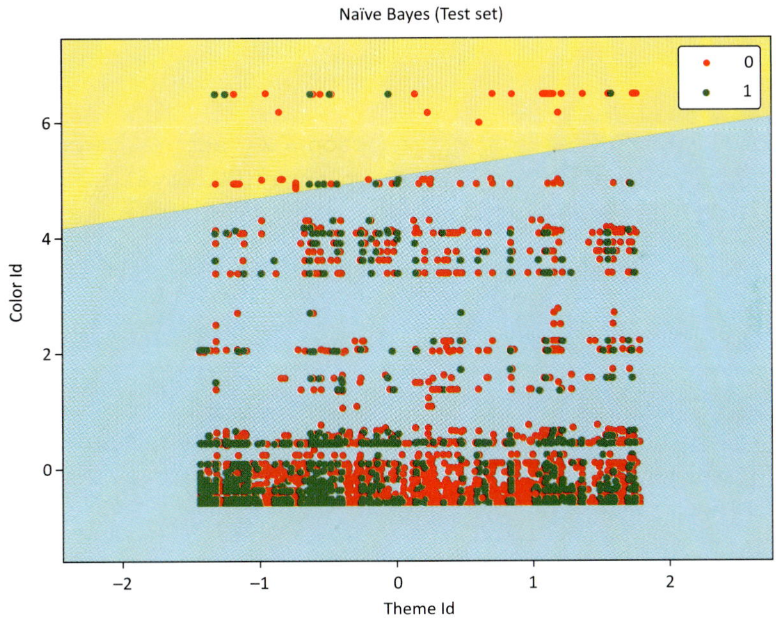

('Prediction = ', array(['0', '0', '0', ..., '0', '0', '0'], dtype='|S1'))
('Accuracy = ', 0.818060606060606)

Figure 10.8: Output of Naïve Bayes classifier

10.6.4 Regression Analysis Algorithms

The following subsections consider data fitting using Linear Regression and Polynomial Regression Functions:[7,8,9]

10.6.4.1 Fitting a Linear Regression Function

Linear regression model predicts a direct proportional (linear) relationship between the dependent variable (plotted on the vertical or y-axis) and the predictor variables (plotted on the x-axis). Figure 10.9 shows linear regression example. The figure shows that the model produces a straight line.

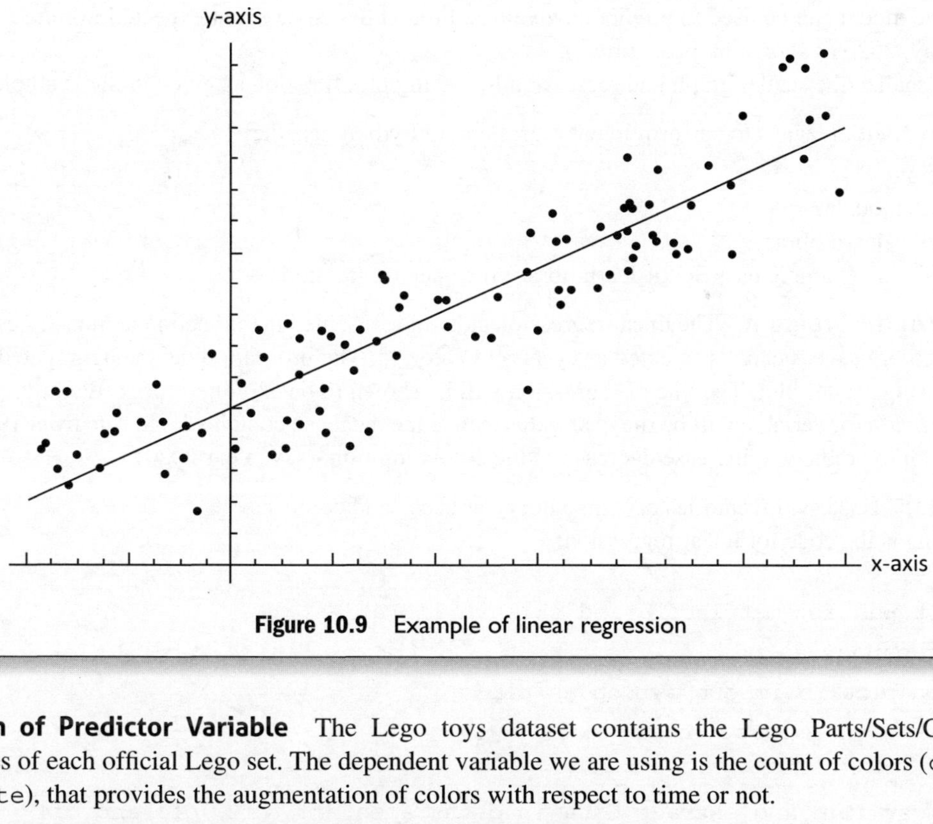

Figure 10.9 Example of linear regression

Selection of Predictor Variable The Lego toys dataset contains the Lego Parts/Sets/Colors and Inventories of each official Lego set. The dependent variable we are using is the count of colors (`color_id aggregate`), that provides the augmentation of colors with respect to time or not.

Brief Description of the Linear Regression Algorithm Code

1. Perform basic imports first. Import Pandas for reading the data from csv files and creating pandas dataframes for doing data analysis, then matplotlib for graphing, and `linear _ model` from sklearn.
2. Next, read the input csv files into individual dataframes and merge them to get a final dataframe `df` of year and `color _ id` attributes.

[7] http://www.learndatasci.com/predicting-housing-prices-linear-regression-using-python-pandas-statsmodels/
[8] https://codefying.com/2016/08/18/two-ways-to-perform-linear-regression-in-python-with-numpy-ans-sk-learn/
[9] http://statisticsbyjim.com/regression/difference-between-linear-nonlinear-regression-models/

3. Filter the undesired data, if required. Here year 2017 is not being included since it has data up to July only. The incomplete data (not the full year data) may result into wrong prediction.
4. Calculate the color usage in each year from 1950 to 2016 and store the year and count value in a new dataframe called yearwise_colour_count.
5. Next, extract the independent variable or predictor (X) and dependent variable or target (Y) values from data. For example, here the color usage depends upon the year value. Thus, year is independent variable while color count is dependent.
6. Apply the linear regression function from linear_model library to obtain regression line with slope, intercept values and Next, use fit () function to fit the predictor and target variables and to obtain a model.
7. The model can be used to predict new values. Predict the color count expected in future year value (say, 2020 as shown in the example).
8. Visualize the scatter graph and regression line using plot function as given in the example.

There are multiple ways to perform linear regression in Python, use the:

1. Scipy
2. Statsmodels
3. Scikit-learn library.

The following example uses Scikit-learn library for linear regression.

Objective of the Program The linear regression example presented in the section demonstrates year wise growth of color usage. Features selected are year and color_id. The program plots the aggregated counts of year field using scatter plot. The line of regression will be shown to be exploited for predicting future count value. The predictor variable will be the year value. Since the database contains Lego sets from 1950 to July 2017, we aim to predict the increase/decrease of the colors in future (say, Year 2020)

Input file(s) sets.csv, inventories.csv, inventory_parts.csv and colors.csv

Following is the code for linear regression:

```
#import pandas, matplotlib and sklearn libraries
import pandas as pd
from matplotlib import pyplot as plt
from sklearn import linear_model

#Read csv file and extract data in dataframes df1, df2, df3 and df4
df1 = pd.read_csv("/home/.../sets.csv")
df2 = pd.read_csv("/home/.../inventories.csv")
df3 = pd.read_csv("/home/.../inventory_parts.csv")
df4 = pd.read_csv("/home/.../colors.csv")

#Join/Merge all the dataframes into a new dataframe say, df1##
df1 = pd.merge(df1, df2, left_on="set_num", right_on = "set_num")
df1 = pd.merge(df1, df3, left_on="id", right_on = "inventory_id")
```

```
df1 = pd.merge(df1, df4, left_on="color_id", right_on = "id")
#Extract the year and color_id features from merged dataframe df1
#and Store in dataframe df
df = pd.DataFrame(df1, columns=['year','color_id'])
#Year 2017 may be ignored since it has data up to July
#(which is not the full year data)
df = df[(df['year'] <2017)]
# Count the colour usage in each year from & store as
# in  yearwise_colour_count
yearwise_colour_count = pd.DataFrame({'count' : df.groupby('year')[ "year"].
count()}).reset_index()
#Extract X(predictor) and Y(target)values from yearwise_colour_count
X = yearwise_colour_count.iloc[:, :-1].values
y = yearwise_colour_count.iloc[:,1].values

#Obtain Line of regression with slope, intercept and other values
regression =linear_model.LinearRegression()
# feed the linear regression with the train data to obtain a model.
regression.fit(X,y)
#Calculate slope and intercept
slope= regression.coef_[0]
intercept= regression.intercept_
#Display slope and intercept
print("Slope = ", round(slope,2), ", Intercept = ", round(intercept,2))

# Obtain prediction for the year 2020
newX = 2020
newy = newX*slope + intercept #Using Line Equation
                                        #Y=X*SLOPE+INTERCEPT

#output of Colour Count Predicted in year 2020
print("Colour Count predicted in ", newX, " = ", round(newy,0))
# plot the scatter graph and regression line
plt.plot(X, y, '.', color='gray')
plt.xlabel("YEAR")
plt.ylabel("COLOUR COUNT")
#Display Year on X axis that varies from Year 1950 to 2016
```

```
#Display Colour Count on Y axis that varies from 0 to 50,000
plt.axis([1950,2020,0,50000])
#Display line of Regression
plt.plot(X, X*slope+intercept, 'k')
plt.show()
```

Output of the Linear Regression Figure 10.10 shows linear regression output

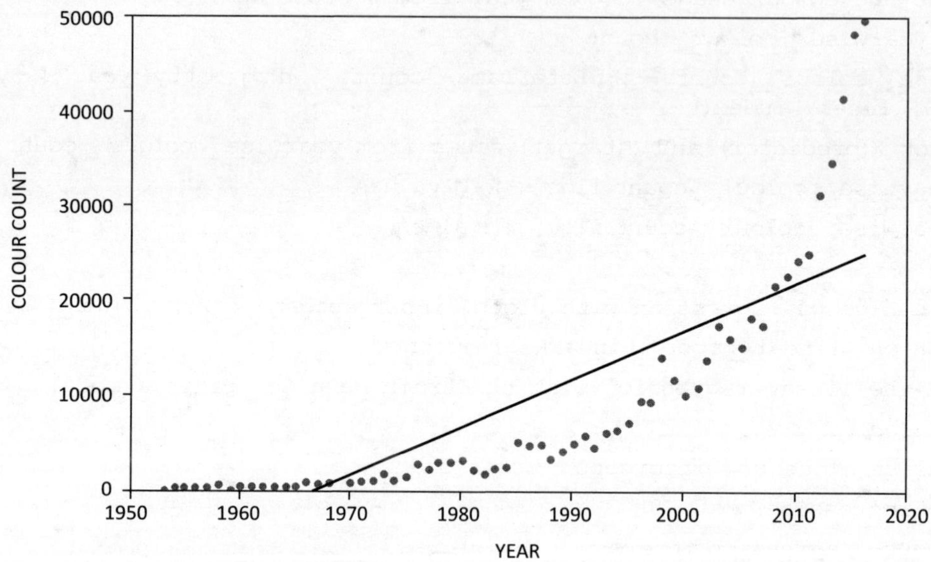

Slope = 508.66 , Intercept = -1000662.09
Colour Count predicted in 2020 = 26835

Figure 10.10 Linear regression output

Function for regression line in Scikit-learn library used in above example is as follows:

```
from sklearn import linear_model
regression =linear_model.LinearRegression()
regression.fit(X, y)
slope= regression.coef_[0]
intercept= regression.intercept_
```

Scipy Library also provides a function for linear regression analysis. This library provides the `linregress` function. Replace the above written statements with the following statements in the complete code of linear regression while you are using scipy library:

```
from scipy import stats
slope, intercept, r_values, p_values, std_err = stats.linregress(X, y)
```

The output will be the same as Figure 10.10.

Salient Observation The output illustrated in Figure 10.10 is inappropriate. When the color count value is 49,904 in 2016, the predicted value of 2020 being 26,834.690 is misleading. We can observe that the data points are following a curve and the regression line in the figure is not fitting the curve.

The solution to this is a polynomial regression (also termed as quadratic regression) that has quality to fit a non-linear model to the data. Curve fitting is the process of constructing a curve, or mathematical function that has the best fit to a series of data points.

Linear regression equation is:

Dependent variable = Constant + Parameter * Independent variable1 + … + Parameter * Independent variable n

$$y = b_0 + b_1x_1 + \cdots + b_nx_n \tag{10.1}$$

The regression equation (10.1) is linear in the parameters. However, it is possible to model curvature using this equation. The function parameters are linear but one can raise independent variable by an exponent to fit a curve. For example, by squaring the independent variable (Equation 10.2), the model can follow a U-shaped curve.

$$y = b_0 + b_1x_1 + \cdots + b_nx_n^2 \tag{10.2}$$

While the independent variable is squared, the model is still linear in the parameters. Linear models can also contain log terms and inverse terms to follow different kinds of curves and yet continue to be linear in the parameters.

10.6.4.2 Fitting a Polynomial Regression Function

Brief description of the polynomial regression algorithm code is as follows:

1. Perform basic imports first. Import Pandas for reading the data from csv files and creating pandas dataframes for doing data analysis, then matplotlib for visualization through graphs.
2. Next, read the input csv files into individual dataframes and merge them to get a final dataframe df of year and color_id attributes.
3. Filter the undesired data, if required. Here, year 2017 is not being included since it has data up to July only. The incomplete data (not the full year data) may result into wrong prediction.
4. Calculate year wise number of colors usage and store it in a new dataframe called data here.
5. Next, extract the independent variable or predictor (X) and dependent variable or target (Y) values from data. For example, here the color usage depends upon the year value. Thus, year is independent variable while color count is dependent.
6. Define the degree of polynomial, say 2, 3, 4 and 5
7. Apply the polyfit function from numpy library with defined degree of polynomial. The function outputs the regression coefficients.[10,11]
8. Use the coefficients to obtain a polynomial. The polynomial models the regression curve that fits the independent variables.

[10] https://autarkaw.org/2008/07/05/finding-the-optimum-polynomial-order-to-use-for-regression/

[11] https://in.mathworks.com/help/matlab/ref/polyfit.html?requestedDomain=true

9. The model can be used to predict new values. Predict the color count expected in future year value (say, 2020 as shown in the example)
10. Visualize the scatter graph and regression line using plot function as given in this example.

Objective of the Program The polynomial regression example presented in the section demonstrates year-wise growth of color usage. Features selected are year and color_id. The program plots the aggregated counts of year field using scatter plot. The growth actually forms a curve when drawn against year. The regression polynomial fits the curve and predicts the future count value (Proven to be more accurate then linear regression for this particular example).

Input file(s) sets.csv, inventories.csv, inventory_parts.csv and colors.csv

The complete source code for polynomial Regression using Scipy Library is as follows:

```
#import numpy, pandas, matplotlib and sklearn libraries
import numpy as np
import pandas as pd
from matplotlib import pyplot as plt
import math # For trunc() to truncate the decimal values

#Read csv file and extract data in dataframes df1, df2, df3 and df4
df1 = pd.read_csv("/home/.../sets.csv")
df2 = pd.read_csv("/home/.../inventories.csv")
df3 = pd.read_csv("/home/.../inventory_parts.csv")
df4 = pd.read_csv("/home/.../colors.csv")

#Join/Merge all the dataframes into a new dataframe say, df1##
df1 = pd.merge(df1, df2, left_on="set_num", right_on = "set_num")
df1 = pd.merge(df1, df3, left_on="id", right_on = "inventory_id")
df1 = pd.merge(df1, df4, left_on="color_id", right_on = "id")
df = pd.DataFrame(df1, columns=['year','color_id'])
#Year 2017 may be ignored since it has data up to July
#: Not the full year data
df = df[(df['year'] <2017)]

# Count the colour usage in each year and store as yearwise_colour_count
yearwise_colour_count = pd.DataFrame({'count' : df.groupby('year')[ "year"].
count()}).reset_index()

#Extract X(predictor) and Y(target)values from yearwise_colour_count
X = yearwise_colour_count ['year'].values
```

```
y = yearwise _ colour _ count ['count'].values
#Obtain minimum & maximum of X and y values for drawing axes
min _ x= X.min()
max _ x= X.max()
min _ y= y.min()
max _ y= y.max()

#Initialize degree of polynomial, say 2,3,4,5
degree _ of _ polynomial = 2
#Fit the polynomial regression and Obtain the coefficients values
coefs = np.polyfit(X, y, degree _ of _ polynomial)
#Create a polynomial from the obtained coefficients
p = np.poly1d(coefs)

# prediction # Obtain prediction for the year 2020
newx = 2020
newy = p(newx)

#output of Colour Count Predicted in year 2020
print("Colour Count predicted in ",newX, "= ", math.trunc(round(newy,0)))

# plot the scatter graph and regression curve
plt.plot(X, y, "bo", markersize= 2)
plt.plot(X, p(X), "r-", color='k') #p(X) evaluates the polynomial at X
plt.plot(X, y, '.', color='gray')
plt.xlabel("YEAR")
plt.ylabel("COLOUR COUNT")
#Display Year on X axis that varies from min _ x(1950) to max _ x(2016)
#Display Colour Count on Y axis that varies from min _ y(0) to max _ y
plt.axis([min _ x,max _ x,min _ y,max _ y])
plt.show()
```

Output of the Polynomial Regression with Different Degrees of Polynomial

Figure 10.11 shows polynomial regression outputs for 2 and 3 degree polynomials. Figure 10.12 shows polynomial regression outputs for 4 and 5 degrees. Figure 10.13 shows polynomial regression output for 6 degree.

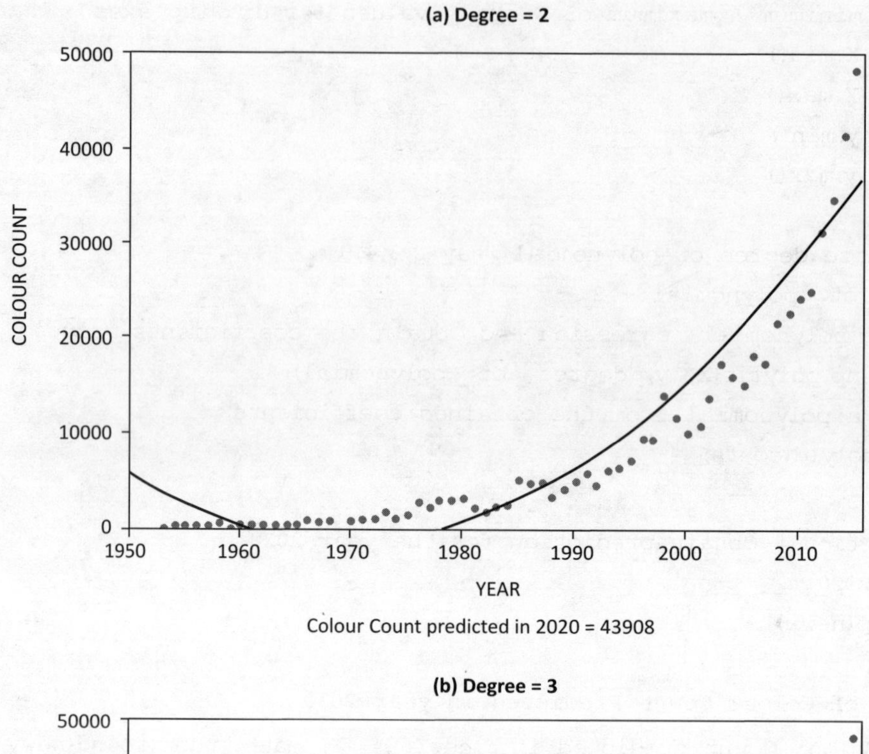

Figure 10.11 Polynomial regression outputs for 2 and 3 degrees

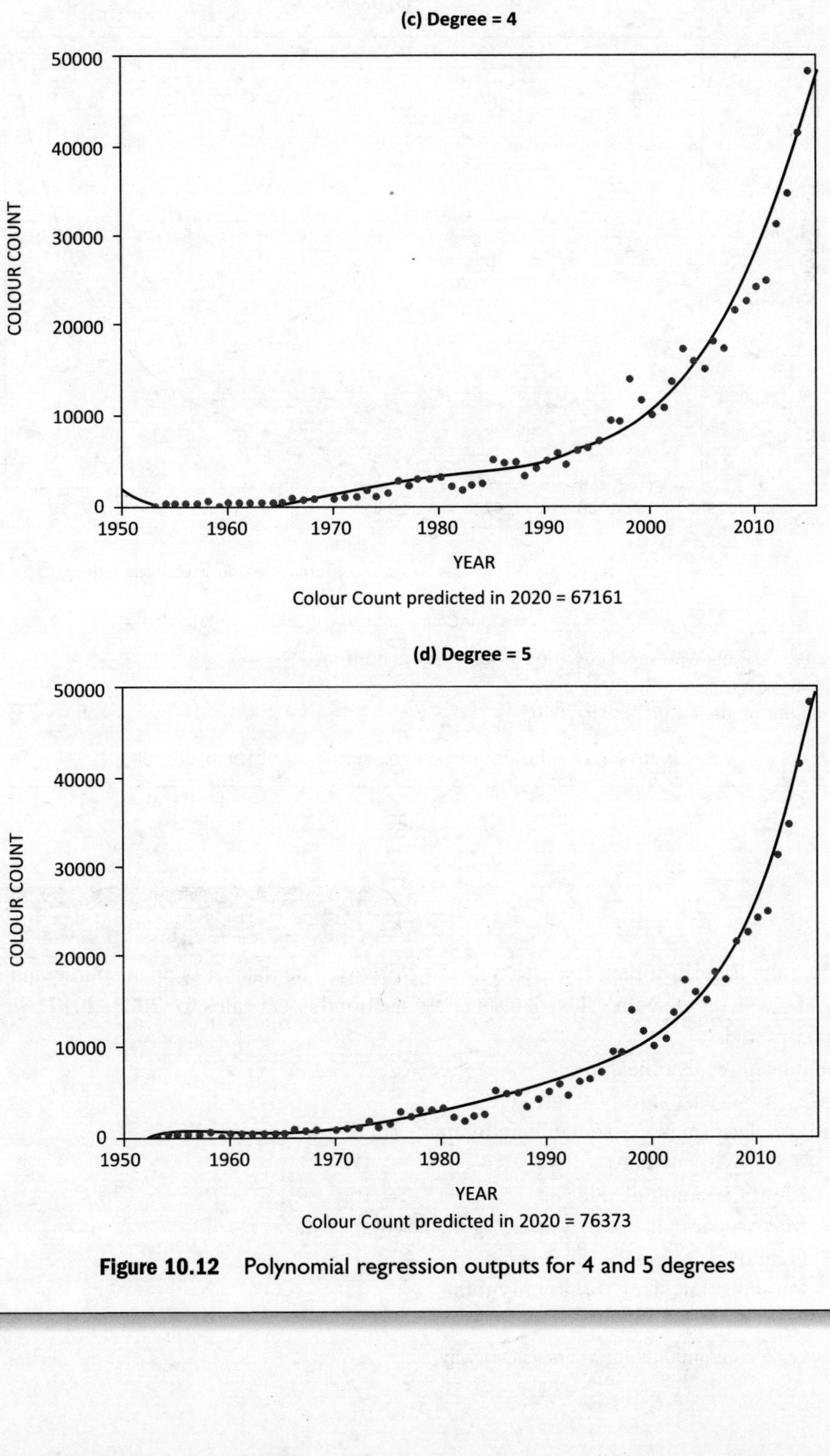

Figure 10.12 Polynomial regression outputs for 4 and 5 degrees

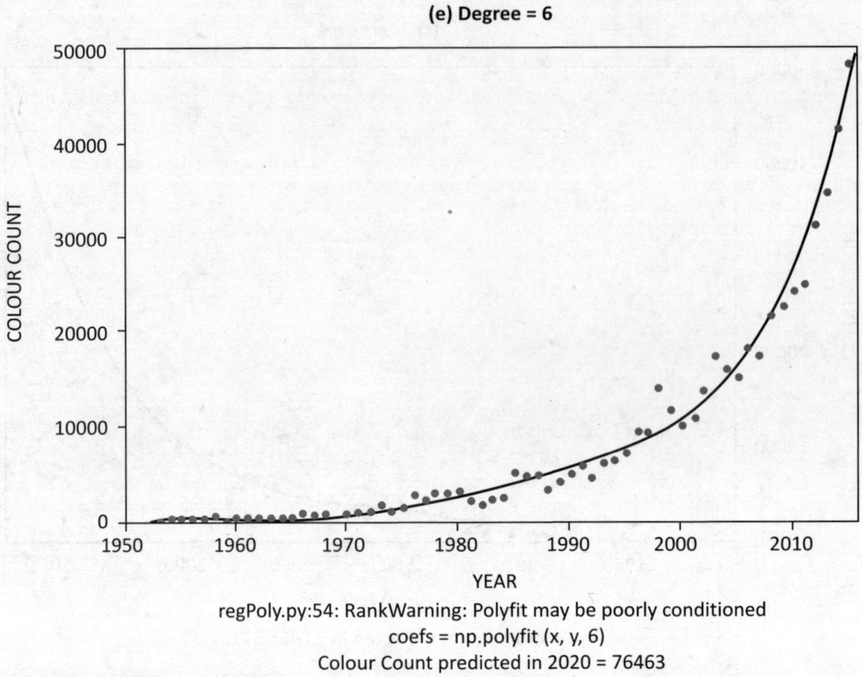

regPoly.py:54: RankWarning: Polyfit may be poorly conditioned
  coefs = np.polyfit (x, y, 6)
Colour Count predicted in 2020 = 76463

Figure 10.13 Polynomial regression output for 6 degree

Practice Exercises

10.1 Explore the dataset of the New Car Sales in Norway. The dataset is open source and downloadable from at www.kaggle.com[12] The dataset contains monthly car sales for 2007–2017 by make and most popular models.

Dataset includes three csv files:

1. **Norway_new_car_sales_by_make.csv:**
   Monthly sales of new passenger cars by make (manufacturer brand)
   1. Year – year of sales
   2. Month – month of sales
   3. Make – car make (e.g. Volkswagen, Toyota, Tesla)
   4. Quantity – number of units sold
   5. Pct – percent share in monthly total

[12] https://www.kaggle.com/dmi3kno/newcarsalesNorway

2. **Norway_new_car_sales_by_model.csv:**
   Monthly summary of top-20 most popular models (by make and model)
   1. Year – year of sales
   2. Month – month of sales
   3. Make – car make (e.g. Volkswagen, Toyota, Tesla)
   4. Model – car model (e.g. BMW-i3, Volkswagen Golf, Tesla S75)
   5. Quantity – number of units sold
   6. Pct – percent share in monthly total
3. **Norway_new_car_sales_by_month.csv:**
   Summary statistics for car sales in Norway by month
   1. Year – year of sales
   2. Month – month of sales
   3. Quantity – total number of units sold
   4. Quantity_YoY – change YoY in units
   5. Import – total number of units imported (used cars)
   6. Import_YoY – change YoY in units
   7. Used – total number of units owner changes inside the country (data available from 2012)
   8. Used_YoY – change YoY in units
   9. Avg_CO2 – average CO2 emission of all cars sold in a given month (in g/km)
   10. Bensin_CO2 – average CO2 emission of bensin-fueled cars sold in a given month (in g/km)
   11. Diesel_CO2 – average CO2 emission of diesel-fueled cars sold in a given month (in g/km)
   12. Quantity_Diesel – number of diesel-fueled cars sold in the country in a given month
   13. Diesel_Share – share of diesel cars in total sales (Quantity_Diesel / Quantity)
   14. Diesel_Share_LY – share of diesel cars in total sales a year ago
   15. Quantity_Hybrid – number of new hybrid cars sold in the country (both PHEV and BV)
   16. Quantity_Electric – number of new electric cars sold in the country (zero emission vehicles)
   17. Import_Electric – number of used electric cars imported to the country (zero emission vehicles)

Norway new car sales dataset can be used for analyzing and predicting future car sales. Explore the dataset to solve the following problems for analysis, prediction and visualization using Sklearn and PySpark:

1. Print year-wise total car sales and visualize the output (Hint: use bar chart for Year vs. total car sales).
2. Print monthly total car sales and visualize for a specified year.
3. Print monthly total car sales from 2007 to 2017 and visualize them to represent the month numbers (1 for Jan 2 for Feb) and total car sales value. (Hint: Use bar chart). Also find the month for number of highest and lowest car sales.
4. Calculate the total amount of the sales for each manufacturer from 2007 to 2017. Find the top 10 manufacturers based on the total sale and visualize the output. (Hint: Sort make-wise total car sales and visualize them using bar chart).
5. Draw pie chart for the sales of all the models of "Toyota" in year 2012.
6. Find which model of each manufacturer has the highest sales in year 2015.
7. Find which model of each manufacturer has the highest sales during 2007 to 2017.
8. Find which model of each manufacturer has the lowest sales during 2007 to 2017.

9. Compare car models with percentage shares.
10. Predict (forecast) the car sales for all the months of 2020 using the month-wise car sales quantity from the Jan 2007 to Jan 2017.
11. Plot the sales of new cars and sales of the diesel cars to see the comparison. Similarly, plot the sales of new car and electric cars. (Hint: Use line chart).
12. Calculate year-wise share of diesel car sales in total sales.
13. Compare year-wise average consumption of CO_2 emission of all cars sold with year-wise average consumption of CO_2 emission in benzene-fueled cars sold and diesel-fueled cars sold.
14. Calculate and visualize year-wise new and used (import) car sales to compare the statistics.
15. Calculate and visualize year-wise sales of all used (import) car and sales of electric-used cars (import_electric) to make a comparison.
16. Predict the rise of green vehicles in 2018. (Hint: Green Vehicle = Import_Electric + Quantity_Hybrid + Quantity_Electric).
17. Forecast and visualize the diesel market share. State whether it represents growth or reduction in the sales.
18. Rank top 10 car brands. Visualize the year-wise result using line graph.

Bibliography

A. Printed and E-Books

[1] Anand Rajaraman and Jeffrey David Ullman, *Mining of Massive Datasets*, Cambridge University Press, 2012

[2] Andrew Gelman, Jennifer Hill, *Data Analysis Using Regression and Multilevel/Hierarchical Models*, Cambridge University Press, 2007

[3] Andrew Gelman, John B. Carlin, Hal S. Stern, David B. Dunson, Aki Vehtari, Donald B. Rubin, *Bayesian Data Analysis*, 3rd Ed., CRC Press, 2013

[4] Aurèlien Gèron, *Hands-On Machine Learning with Scikit-Learn and Tensor Flow: Concepts, Tools, and Techniques to Build Intelligent System*, O'Reilly Media, 2017

[5] Bernard Marr, *Big Data in Practice: How 45 Successful Companies Used Big Data Analytics to Deliver Extraordinary Results*, Wiley, UK, 2016

[6] Carl Shan, William Chen, Henry Wang, Max Song, *The Data Science Handbook: Advice and Insights from 25 Amazing Data Scientists*, Paperback, The Data Science Bookshelf, 2015

[7] Christopher M. Bishop, *Pattern Recognition and Machine Learning*, Springer, 2006

[8] David Dietrich, Barry Heller, Beibei Yang, *Data Science & Big Data Analytics: Discovering, Analyzing, Visualizing and Presenting Data*, EMC Education Services, Wiley, Indianapolis, 2015

[9] David A. Freedman, *Statistical Models: Theory and Practice*, Paperback, 2nd Ed., Cambridge University Press, 2009

[10] David J.C. MacKay, *Information Theory, Inference and Learning Algorithms*, Cambridge University Press, 2003

[11] David Loshin, *Big Data Analytics: From Strategic Planning to Enterprise Integration with Tools, Techniques, NoSQL, and Graph*, Morgan Kaufmann (Elsevier), MA 02451, 2013

[12] E. T. Jaynes, *Probability Theory, The Logic of Science*, Cambridge University Press, 2003

[13] Edward Capriolo, *Cassandra High Performance Cookbook*, Packt, 2011

[14] Edward R. Tufte, *Visual Explanations: Images and Quantities, Evidence and Narrative*, Google Books, 1997

[15] Erik Brynjolfsson, Andrew McAfee, *The Second Machine Age: Work, Progress, and Prosperity in a Time of Brilliant Technologies,* W. W. Nortan, 2014 (Also available at ACM Digital Library)

[16] Erwin Kreyszig, *Advanced Engineering Mathematics,* 12th Ed., Wiley, 2016 (Paperback Edition, Wiley, 2014)

[17] Francois Chollet, *Deep Learning with Python*, Manning, 2018

[18] Garry Kasparov, Mig Greengard, *Deep Thinking— Where Artificial Intelligence Ends and Human Creativity Begins*, Google Books, 2017

[19] Garry Turkington, *Hadoop: Beginner's Guide*, Packt, 2013

[20] George Casella, Roger L. Berger, *Statistical Inference*, 2nd Ed., Cengage Learning, 2006

[21] Giancarlo Zaccone, Md. Rezaul Karim, *Deep Learning with Tensor Flow*, 2nd Ed., Packt, 2018

[22] Hadley Wickham, *ggplot2: Elegant Graphics for Data Analysis*, 2nd Ed., Springer, 2016

[23] I. Craig, Allen Thornton, *Mathematical Statistics*, 5th Ed., Macmillan, NY, 1989 [1st E. 1958]

[24] Ian Goodfellow, Yoshua Bengio, Aaron Courville, *Deep Learning* (eBook), MIT Press, 2017

[25] Ian Robinson, *Graph Databases,* Paperback, O'Reilly Media, 2nd Ed., 2015

[26] Jeff Hawkins, Sandra Blakeslee, *On Intelligence, How a New Understanding of the Brain will Lead to the Creation of Truly Intelligent Machines*, Paperback, St. Martin Griffin, 2005 [Prentice Hall, New Jersey, 2004]

[27] John A. Rice, *Mathematical Statistics and Data Analysis,* 3rd Ed., Thomson Learning, Is Indian Reprint, 2007

[28] John H. Mathews, Kurtis D. Fink, *Numerical Methods Using Matlab*, Paperback, Pearson, 2015

[29] John W. Foreman, *Data Smart: Using Data Science to Transform Information into Insight*, Paperback, Wiley, Indianapolis, 2014

[30] Joshan D. Suereth, *Scala in Depth*, Manning, 2012

[31] Kevin P. Murphy, *Machine Learning: A Probabilistic Perspective*, MIT Press, Cambridge, 2012

[32] M. Gopal, *Applied Machine Learning*, McGraw Hill, India, 2018

[33] Malcom Gladwell, *Outliers: The Story of Success*, Penguin, London, 2013

[34] Max Kuhn, Kjell Johnson, *Applied Productive Modeling*, Springer, 2013

[35] Maxim Lapan, Deep Reinforcement Learning Hands-On, Packt, 2018

[36] Michael Frampton, *Complete Guide to Open Source Big Data Stack*, Apress, 2018

[37] Michael G. Milton, *Head First Data Analysis: A Learner's Guide to Big Numbers, Statistics, and Good Decisions*, O'Reilly Media, 2010

[38] Mike Barlow, *Realtime Big Data Analytics: Emerging Architecture*, O'Reilly Media, 2014

[39] Mike Driscoll, *Python Interviews*, Packt, 2018

[40] Mike Frampton, *Mastering Apache Spark*, Packt, 2017

[41] Mohammed Guller, *Big Data Analytics with Spark: A Practitioner's Guide to Using Spark for Large Scale Data Analysis*, Apress, 2015

[42] Nathan Marz, *Big Data: Principles and Best Practices of Scalable Realtime Data Systems,* Paperback, Manning, 2015

[43] Niranjan Raychaudhuri, *Scala in Action*, Manning, 2012

[44] Paul C. Zikopoulos, Chris Eaton, Dirk deRoos, Tom Deutsch, George Lapis, *Understanding Big Data: Analytics for Enterprise Class Hadoop and Streaming Data*, McGraw Hill, NY 2012 (India ed., 2015)

[45] Peter Norvig, *Paradigms of Artificial Intelligence Programming, Case Studies in Common LISP*, Paperback, Morgan Kaufmann, California, 1992

[46] Philip E. Tetlock, *Superforecasting: The Art and Science of Prediction*, Broadways Books, N.Y. (Penguin), 2015

[47] Prateek Joshi, *Python Machine Learning Cookbook*, Packt, 2016

[48] Richard W. Hamming, *Numerical Methods for Scientists and Engineers*, McGraw-Hill, New York, 1973 (2nd Ed. 1987, Dover. Available at the ACM Digital Library)

[49] Robert J. Kabacoff, *R in Action— Data Analysis and Graphics with R*, Manning, 2011

[50] Robert V. Hogg, I. Craig, Allen T. Craig, *Introduction to Mathematical Statistics*, 4th Ed., McMillan N.Y., 1978

[51] Romeo Kienzler, *Mastering Apache Spark 2.x*, 2nd Ed., Packt, 2017

[52] Satnam Alag, *Collective Intelligence in Action*, Manning, 2008

[53] Sean Owen, Robin Anil, Ted Dunning, Ellen Friedman, *Mahout in Action*, Manning, 2012

[54] Sean T. Allen, Matthew Jankowski, Peter Pathirana, *Storm Applied*, Manning, 2015 (Also available at ACM Digital Library)

[55] Sebastian Raschka, Vahod Mirjalili, *Python Machine Learning*, 2nd Ed., Packt, 2017

[56] Seema Acharya, Subhasini Chellappan, *Big Data and Analytics*, Wiley, 2015

[57] Seema Acharya, *Data Analysis using R*, McGraw Hill, India, 2018

[58] Steven C. Chapra, Raymond Canale, *Numerical Methods for Engineers*, Google Books, 1985

[59] Stuart J. Russell, Peter Norvig, *Artificial Intelligence: A Modern Approach*, Springer, New York, 1995

[60] Tanmay Deshpandey, *Hadoop Real World Solutions*, 2nd Ed., Packt, 2016

[61] Trevor Hastie, Robert Tibshirani, Jerome Friedman, *The Elements of Statistical Learning: Data Mining, Inference, and Prediction*, 2nd Ed., Springer, 2001

[62] Tomasz Draba, Denny Lee, Learning PySpark, Packt, Manning, 2017

[63] Trevor Hastie, *The Elements of Statistical Learning: Data Mining, Inference, and Prediction*, 2001

[64] William H. Press, Saul A. Teukolsky, William T. Velterling, Brian P. Lannery, *Numerical Recipes in C++: The Art of Scientific Computing,* 3rd Ed., Cambridge Press, 2002 (South Asian Ed. Foundation Books, India, 2002; Originally Published in FORTRAN, Available as pdf open source)

[65] Yifeng Jiang, *HBase Administration Cookbook*, Packt, 2012

B. Website References

[1] https://aws.amazon.com/machine-learning/amis/ AWS Deep Learning AMIs, *Pre-configured Environments to Quickly Build Deep Learning, Applications*

[2] https://arxiv.org/abs/1709.02840 (Cornell University Library), Osvaldo Simeone, *A Brief Introduction to Machine Learning for Engineers*, 2018

[3] https://web.stanford.edu/~hastie/Papers/ESLII.pdf, Trevor Hastie, Robert Tibshirani, Jerome Friedman, *The Elements of Statistical Learning: Data Mining, Inference, and Prediction, 2nd Ed., 2001*

[4] https://vuquangnguyen2016.files.wordpress.com/2018/03/applied-predictive-modeling-max-kuhn-kjell-johnson_1518.pdf, Max Kuhn, Kjell Johnson, *Applied Productive Modeling,* Springer, 2013

[5] http://www.freetechbooks.com/the-elements-of-data-analytic-style-t1257.html, Jeff Leek, *The Elements of Data Analytic Style*, 2016

[6] https://www.cin.ufpe.br/~tfl2/artificial-intelligence-modern-approach.9780131038059.25368.pdf, Stuart J. Russell, Peter Norvig, *Artificial Intelligence: A Modern Approach*, 2005

[7] https://www.thedatasciencehandbook.com, Carl Shan, William Chen, Henry Wang, Max Song, *The Data Science Handbook: Advice and Insights from 25 Amazing Data Scientists*, Paperback, 2015

[8] https://tecnoclub4u.files.wordpress.com/2015/05/hadoop_-beginners-guide.pdf, *Hadoop Beginners Guide*, Packt

[9] http://barbie.uta.edu/~jli/Resources/MapReduce&Hadoop/Hadoop%20MapReduce%20Cookbook.pdf, Srinath Perera Thllina Gunarathne, *Hadoop MapReduce CookBook*, Packt

[10] http://www.ieee.org.ar/downloads/Srivastava-tut-pres.pdf, Jaideep Srivastava, *University of Minnesota USA, Web Mining: Accomplishments & Future Directions*:

[11] https://www.isical.ac.in/~acmsc/WBDA2015/slides/hg/Oreilly.Hadoop.The.Definitive.Guide.3rd.Edition.Jan.2012.pdf

[12] https://www.isical.ac.in/~acmsc/WBDA2015/slides/hg/Oreilly, Tom White, *Hadoop: The.Definitive.Guide.* 3rd. Edition, Jan. 2012 pdf

[13] https://websites.pmc.ucsc.edu/~fnimmo/eart290c_17/NumericalRecipesinF77.pdf, William H. Press, Saul A. Teukolsky, William T. Velterling, Brian P. Lannery, *Numerical Recipes in FORTRAN 77: The Art of Scientific Computing,* Cambridge Press, 2nd Ed., Reprinted with Corrections/New Software version 2.08, 1997

C. Chapter-wise Website References

Chapter 1

[1] http:// www.gartner.com/it-glossary/big-data

[2] https://statswiki.unece.org/display/bigdata/Classification+of+Types+of+Big+Data

[3] https://www.ibm.com/developerworks/library/bd-archpatterns1/

[4] https://docs.microsoft.com/en-us/sql/odbc/reference/data-sources

[5] https://docs.oracle.com/cd/E17984_01/doc.898/e14695/undrstnd_datasources.htm

[6] https://www.ibm.com/support/knowledgecenter/en/SSMPHH_9.5.0/com.ibm.guardium95.doc/ common_tools/topics/datasources.html
[7] http://docs.aws.amazon.com/datapipeline/latest/DeveloperGuide/dp-object-copyactivity.html
[8] http://docs.aws.amazon.com/datapipeline/latest/DeveloperGuide/dp-object-snsalarm.html
[9] https://support.rackspace.com/how-to/cloud-database-instance-parameters/
[10] https://cloud.google.com/bigquery/docs/loading-data

Chapter 2

NIL

Chapter 3

[1] https://cwiki.apache.org/confluence/display/Hive/LanguageManual+ORC#LanguageManual ORC-ORCFileFormat
[2] http://www.semantikoz.com/blog/orc-intelligent-big-data-file-format-hadoop-hive/

Chapter 4

NIL

Chapter 5

[1] https://cwiki.apache.org/confluence/display/Hive/LanguageManual+ORC# LanguageManualORC-ORCFileFormat
[2] https://www.tecmint.com/install-java-jdk-jre-in-linux/
[3] https://www.vultr.com/docs/how-to-manually-install-java-8-on-ubuntu-16-04
[5] https://data-flair.training/blogs/create-rdds-in-apache-spark/
[6] http://data-flair.training/forums/topic/how-to-create-rdd

Chapter 6

[1] https://en.wikipedia.org/wiki/Kernel(statistics)
[3] https://en.wikipedia.org/wiki/Levenshtein_distance

Chapter 7

[4] http://algo.inria.fr/flajolet/Publications/FlMa85.pdf

Chapter 8

[1] https://neo4j.com/product/
[2] http://www.systemg.research.ibm.com/

Chapter 9

[1] http://www.nactem.ac.uk/brochure/NaCTeM_Brochure.pdf
[2] https://www.ibm.com/support/knowledgecenter/en/SS3RA7_18.1.1/ta_guide_ddita/ textmining/shared_entities/tm_intro_tm_defined.html
[3] https://blogs.aws.amazon.com/bigdata/post/Tx22THFQ9MI86F9/Applying-Machine-Learning-to-Text-Mining-with-Amazon-S3-and-RapidMiner
[4] https://www.ling.upenn.edu/courses/Fall_2003/ling001/penn_treebank_pos.html
[5] http://papers.cumincad.org/data/works/att/2873.content.pdf "*The Anatomy of a Large-Scale Hypertextual Web Search Engine*" Sergey Brin Lawrence Page, 1998

Chapter 10

[1] https://hadoop.apache.org/ Hadoop
[2] https://www.edureka.co/blog/hadoop-3/
[3] https://rebrickable.com/about/
[4] LDB— The LEGO Parts/Sets/Colors and inventories of every official LEGO set, available at: *https://www.kaggle.com/rtatman/lego-database*
[5] https://www.analyticsvidhya.com/blog/2017/09/understaing-support-vector-machine-example-code/
[6] https://sadanand-singh.github.io/posts/svmpython/
[7] http://www.learndatasci.com/predicting-housing-prices-linear-regression-using-python-pandas-statsmodels/
[8] https://codefying.com/2016/08/18/two-ways-to-perform-linear-regression-in-python-with-numpy-ans-sk-learn/
[9] http://statisticsbyjim.com/regression/difference-between-linear-nonlinear-regression-models/
[10] https://autarkaw.org/2008/07/05/finding-the-optimum-polynomial-order-to-use-for-regression/
[11] https://in.mathworks.com/help/matlab/ref/polyfit.html?requestedDomain=true
[12] https://www.kaggle.com/dmi3kno/newcarsalesNorway

D. Printed/e-Journal Paper References

[1] IEEE Transactions on Big Data, Quarterly, Since 2015
[2] Elsevier Big Data Research Journal, Latest Issue Volume 13, Sept 2018, Quarterly Since 2016, (First Issue 2011)
[3] Springer, Journal of Big Data, Open Access, Since 2014
[4] BMC Series Springer Nature, Big Data Analytics

Answers to Multiple Choice Questions

Chapter 1

1.	2.	3.	4.	5.	6.	7.	8.	9.	10.
(d)	**(c)**	**(b)**	**(a)**	**(c)**	**(d)**	**(b)**	**(d)**	**(a)**	**(b)**
11.	12.	13.	14.	15.	16.				
(c)	**(d)**	**(c)**	**(c)**	**(d)**	**(a)**				

Chapter 2

1	2	3	4	5	6	7	8	9	10
(d)	**(b)**	**(c)**	**(a)**	**(c)**	**(b)**	**(a)**	**(c)**	**(b)**	**(a)**
11	12								
(d)	**(d)**								

Chapter 3

1	2	3	4	5	6	7	8	9	10
(a)	**(a)**	**(c)**	**(b)**	**(d)**	**(b)**	**(a)**	**(d)**	**(b)**	**(b)**
11	12	13	14	15.					
(a)	**(c)**	**(d)**	**(c)**	**(b)**					

Chapter 4

1	2	3	4	5	6	7	8	9	10
(c)	(a)	(d)	(b)	(d)	(d)	(b)	(c)	(a)	(b)
11	12								
(c)	(a)								

Chapter 5

1	2	3	4	5	6	7	8	9	10
(b)	(a)	(d)	(c)	(c)	(a)	(a)	(d)	(b)	(b)
11	12	13	14						
(d)	(c)	(b)	(a)						

Chapter 6

1	2	3	4	5	6	7	8	9	10
(a)	(c)	(d)	(b)	(d)	(a)	(d)	(c)	(c)	(a)
11	12	13	14						
(b)	(d)	(b)	(c)						

Chapter 7

1	2	3	4	5	6	7	8	9	10
(b)	(b)	(a)	(d)	(c)	(c)	(a)	(b)	(c)	(d)
11	12								
(a)	(b)								

Chapter 8

1	2	3	4	5	6	7	8	9	10
(d)	(c)	(a)	(a)	(b)	(c)	(d)	(b)	(c)	(a)

Chapter 9

1	2	3	4	5	6	7	8
(d)	(c)	(b)	(a)	(b)	(b)	(b)	(b)

Index

C

D

S

T

U

V

W

X

Y

Z